Booklist's 1000 Best Young Adult Books since 2000

BOOKLIST'S 1000 BEST YOUNG ADULT BOOKS SINCE 2000

Edited by *Gillian Engberg and Ian Chipman*

Foreword by *Michael Cart*

CHICAGO 2014

Printed in the United States of America
18 17 16 15 14   5 4 3 2 1

ISBNs: 978-0-8389-1150-1 (paper); 978-0-8389-1950-7 (PDF); 978-0-8389-1951-4 (ePub); 978-0-8389-1952-1 (Kindle). For more information on digital formats, visit the ALA Store at alastore.ala.org and select eEditions.

Library of Congress Cataloging-in-Publication Data

Booklist's 1000 best young adult books since 2000 / edited by Gillian Engberg
and Ian Chipman ; foreword by Michael Cart.
pages cm
Includes bibliographical references and indexes.
ISBN 978-0-8389-1150-1 (alk. paper)
1. Young adult literature—21st century—Bibliography. 2. Teenagers—Books and reading—United States. 3. Young adults' libraries—Book lists. 4. Best books—United States. I. Engberg, Gillian. II. Chipman, Ian. III. Booklist (Chicago, Ill. : 1969)
Z1037.B72195 2014
015.73062′5—dc23   2013044904

Cover design by Casey Bayer.
Text design by Adrianna Sutton in the Arno Pro and DIN Pro typefaces.

♾ This paper meets the requirements of ANSI/NISO Z39.48-1992 (Permanence of Paper).

Contents

Foreword

Michael Cart

The start of the twenty-first century has been a new golden age of young adult, or YA, literature. If you doubt that, take a hard look at the titles reviewed in this important and useful book. In their literary quality, their variety, and their innovative nature, these books are not only the best of a splendid new millennium, they are—compared with other decades—the best of the best.

This remarkable rebirth of YA literature has its roots in the 1990s, which is ironic because—at the beginning of that decade—the genre was being pronounced near death. Fortunately, the diagnosis was premature, and thanks to a surge in the teenage population, an explosion of youth culture, and—more important—the dedication of YA librarians, the field began to recover and the story of the 1990s became one of increasingly robust health.

The first evidence of the renaissance to come was the rise in the mid-'90s of a new, hard-edged realism that reflected both the tenor of the times and an increasingly sophisticated young adult population. Though dismissed by some as "bleak," this newly gritty literature of realism attracted the kind of older YA audience that had abandoned the genre by the end of the '80s, when it had largely turned into a middle-school literature featuring protagonists aged 12 to 14. By the end of the '90s, however, the typical protagonists were 17, and the books featuring them had a newly sophisticated, adult appearance.

Unlike the problem novels of the late 1970s, these novels were literary in their style and content, so much so that they spurred the creation in 1999 of the Michael L. Printz Award, which is now presented annually to the author of the best YA book of the year—*best* being defined solely in terms of literary merit. Not only did the Printz recognize the newly literary form YA literature was manifesting, but it also encouraged further experiments in style and narrative structure, epitomized by the award's first winner, in the year 2000: Walter Dean Myers' memorable novel *Monster*. In its first decade, the Printz Award put to bed—permanently, one hopes—the claim that *young adult literature* is an oxymoron, like *new classic* or *congressional cooperation*.

The rise of literary fiction is only one of the many trends that have informed and enriched YA literature in the twenty-first century. One need go no further than the list of Printz winners to find some of these trends. Consider that the Printz may be awarded not only to a novel but also to a work of nonfiction, a work of poetry, a graphic novel, an anthology, or a book first published in another country. More about these and other trends in a moment, but first we need to acknowledge additional evidence of the nearly exponential growth of YA literature between 2000 and 2013: the creation of separate YA imprints at North America's publishing houses. Historically, YA books were issued by the publishers' children's divisions, but that began to change in 1999 with the establishment of the first two separate YA imprints: Harper's Tempest and Simon &

Schuster's Pulse. Scarcely a year has gone by in the time since without the establishment of at least one new YA imprint. In addition to Pulse and Tempest, they include Scholastic's PUSH; Tor's Starscape; Penguin's Speak, Firebird, and Razorbill imprints; Houghton Mifflin's Graphia; Abrams' Amulet; Llewellyn's Flux; Aladdin M!X; Harlequin's Kimani TRU; Sourcebooks Fire; Sterling's Splinter; Albert Whitman Teen; and the YA titles from St. Martin's Press.

The growth of these imprints resulted in a corollary growth in the number of YA titles being published each year. Since publishers report children's and young adult book statistics together, it's virtually impossible to determine precisely how many YA books are published each year. A common estimate is 2,500, in which case the annual number has increased tenfold since the early '90s, when it was estimated that only 250 YA titles were published each year.

Further spurring the expanding YA market was a shift from the shrinking institutional market (i.e., libraries and schools) to the growing retail one. This began in the early years of the twenty-first century and has continued apace thanks to several factors. One is that publishing companies now consist of vast international conglomerates that are putting increased pressure on their subsidiary publishers to generate more and more revenue. One means of doing this is simply to publish more and more books. Another more salutary reason is that young adults themselves have become a major market. As early as 2001, the *Los Angeles Times* was reporting that YAs constituted a $1.5 billion industry for publishers, while *USA Today* noted that teens aged 14 to 17 had purchased 35.6 million books that year, 6 million more than the previous year.

As the YA field has become more expansive and dynamic, it has begun attracting adult authors. In the past decade such stellar names as Joyce Carol Oates, Francine Prose, James Patterson, Carl Hiaasen, Michael Chabon, and too many others to list here have written books targeted at young adults. Publishers have encouraged this not only for the marquee value of the authors' names but also because these authors attract their established adult audiences to YA lit. This crossover phenomenon—adults reading young adult books—works the other way, too, as publishers are issuing more and more adult titles with intrinsic appeal to older YAs, such as Mark Haddon's *The Curious Incident of the Dog in the Night-Time* (2003) and Curtis Sittenfeld's *Prep* (2004).

While all of these factors served to expand the YA field, another eclipsed them all, and that, of course, was the Harry Potter series. Published between 1998 and 2007, J. K. Rowling's books about the boy wizard have sold more than 450 million copies to date, according to the *New York Times*, and the individual volumes have been translated into 70 languages.

The Potter phenomenon has had a profound impact on publishing. It stimulated, for example, the internationalization of YA literature, as more and more books first published in England, Australia, New Zealand, and Canada began appearing here in the United States. It also promoted what is called event publishing. As was the case with the Potter books, many titles now are embargoed until their publication date; no advance reading or review copies are released prior to publication, and bookstores put them on sale at one minute after midnight on the official publication date.

The success of the Potter books also stimulated a vast wave of fantasy titles, which are well represented in this book. For good or for ill, virtually every new fantasy title is now the first volume in a planned series, and each title is also—or so it seems—500 or more pages in length (the last two Potter books were, respectively, 759 and 870 pages long).

As the Potter phenomenon was approaching its end, publishers began frantically searching for the next Harry Potter. They didn't have far to look: Stephenie Meyer's 498-page novel *Twilight* was published in 2005. The Twilight Saga books have now sold 116 million copies worldwide and offer another spectacular success story, which in turn guaranteed that the next trend in YA publishing would be the paranormal romance. This trend featured not only vampires and werewolves à la *Twilight* but also zombies, demons, and fallen angels.

Meanwhile, a more traditional kind of romance—human boy meets human girl, but with a twist—had also become a hot area of publishing. This is the phenomenon known as chick lit. Often told in the form of a diary, chick lit typically consists of a humorous story of a young girl in pursuit—with mixed success—of love. The first YA example of this type of romance was Louise Rennison's antic *Angus, Thongs, and Full-Frontal Snogging,* which was published in 2000 and copped a Printz Honor Book citation. Countless chick-lit romances have followed, even as a new and related trend appeared in 2002 with the publication of Cecily von Ziegesar's *Gossip Girl,* which soon sparked a series about "poor little rich girls, throbbing to shop," as the *New York Times* memorably put it. These girls were less interested in loving boys than in loving designer labels. The Gossip Girl series spawned numerous others, such as the A-List, the Carlyles, the Au Pairs, Privilege, and more. Most—though not all—of these series have been created not by publishers but, instead, by book packagers who develop projects, hire authors, design the books, and present a ready-to-publish package to publishers. This is hardly a new phenomenon—it dates back to the turn of the twentieth century and the Stratemeyer Syndicate (think Nancy Drew and the Hardy Boys)—but it has become one of the major success stories of the first decade of the 2000s.

Another major success story is the rise of the dystopian novel—the story of a future world ruined, often, by present or threatened societal ills such as global warming, wars and rumors of wars, nuclear weaponry, and unbridled consumerism, all of which haunt M. T. Anderson's *Feed* (2002). The novel that truly jump-started this genre, however, is Suzanne Collins' hugely successful *The Hunger Games* (2008), which has rivaled *Twilight* and even the Harry Potter books in popularity and influence. That the titles in this particular genre are often well written is evidenced by Paolo Bacigalupi's *Ship Breaker* receiving the 2011 Printz Award.

Another genre, historical fiction, is at the leading edge of one more trend informing the first years of the 2000s: what is called genre bending (or blending), in which two or more genres are mixed, as in the case of paranormal romance or science fiction and fantasy. As *Booklist* columnist Joyce Saricks recently observed, "Blending with other genres is the most conspicuous trend in historical fiction." Thus there are historical romances, historical mysteries, historical adventures, and even, in the case of alternative histories, historical fantasies. Another interesting phenomenon is the book that combines historical elements with a contemporary story—for example, Aidan Chambers' Printz Award–winning *Postcards from No Man's Land* (2002), which is set both in the present and the past, during WWII.

Clearly, genre fiction has ruled the roost of YA fiction in the twenty-first century. Not that there haven't been other success stories. One of these is often mistakenly called a genre, but it is, instead, a literary form. I refer, of course, to the graphic novel. Once sniffily dismissed as mere comic books, the form began to come of age artistically in the mid-1980s with the publication of Art Spiegelman's *Maus,* Frank Miller's *The Dark Knight Returns,* and Alan Moore and Dave Gibbons' *Watchmen.* The graphic novel (the term was popularized by legendary comics artist Will Eisner) continued to evolve through the 1990s, but it wasn't until the Young Adult Library Services Association (YALSA) devoted an ALA preconference to the form in 2002 that libraries began to acquire graphic novels in significant numbers. That same year, YALSA launched its Great Graphic Novels for Teens list and chose "Get Graphic @ your library" as the theme for Teen Read Week. More recognition of the artistry of the graphic novel came in 2007, when Gene Luen Yang received the Printz Award for his groundbreaking graphic novel *American Born Chinese,* which was also the first graphic novel to be short-listed for the National Book Award.

Another form of the graphic novel, Japanese comics called *manga,* started appearing in significant numbers in the mid-1990s and became a major phenomenon in the first decade of the 2000s. Many of these manga are part of seemingly endless series (evoking, it might be suggested, television soap operas). In his 2007 book *Manga: The Complete Guide,* Jason Thompson identifies 900 such series! More recently, graphic novels from Korea—called *manhwa*—have also become popular.

The leading YA publisher of graphic novels is Macmillan's First Second imprint, though virtually every publisher of series nonfiction—Rosen, Capstone, World Almanac, ABDO, and others—has been releasing titles in the graphic-novel format. It should be noted here that though the form is called graphic *novel,* it also clearly includes nonfiction.

Speaking of nonfiction, this is another form that came of age starting in the 1990s and remains popular in the 2000s. The new type of informational book is often called narrative nonfiction because it borrows some of the tools of fiction to generate something that reads like a novel but respects the integrity of the factual content. Another hallmark of this new nonfiction is its illustrative content. Much like Dorling Kindersley's Eyewitness books, these titles often have the appearance of photo essays. An example of this is Elizabeth Partridge's *John Lennon: All I Want Is the Truth* (2005), which received a Printz Honor Book citation in 2006. Further recognizing the artistry of the new nonfiction, YALSA created in 2009 the Award for Excellence in Nonfiction for Young Adults. In the past several years, the number of nonfiction books for older teens has waned a bit; however, nonfiction for middle-school readers continues to grow apace.

Another type of nonfiction—poetry—has had mixed success. Though it receives universal respect, it seldom commands a large readership. An exception is the novel in verse, a form pioneered by Mel Glenn with titles such as *Who Killed Mr. Chippendale?* (1996) and which came of age in 1999 with the publication of Sonya Sones' *Stop Pretending.* In the years since, such distinguished poets as Ron Koertge, Nikki Grimes, Helen Frost, and Marilyn Nelson have also contributed to the genre. Both Frost's and Nelson's titles were named Printz Honor Books, as was Stephanie Hemphill's *Your Own, Sylvia* (2007), a biography in verse.

The first years of the 2000s have also been a period of growth in novels for and about gay, lesbian, bisexual, and transgender teens. Though there have been YA novels with gay content since John Donovan's *I'll Get There, It Better Be Worth the Trip* was published in 1969, the numbers of such books were meager (only 8 appeared in the entire decade of the 1970s and 40 in the 1980s) until the 1990s, when 75 were published. The numbers have continued to increase in the first decade of the 2000s, with 34 such titles published in 2009 alone. Even more important is the literary quality of these works, never more clearly manifested than in 2003, when Aidan Chambers received the Printz Award for *Postcards from No Man's Land*, a novel with gay content, and Nancy Garden received the Margaret A. Edwards Award for her body of work, including her pioneering lesbian novel *Annie on My Mind* (1982).

It was not until 2004, however, that the first YA novel to feature a transgender character—Julie Anne Peters' *Luna*—appeared. In the years since, only a scant handful of others have been published, including Ellen Wittlinger's *Parrotfish* (2007) and Brian Katcher's *Almost Perfect* (2009). The few others that have appeared as of this writing are sufficient at least to suggest that this once invisible minority will finally begin to find faces in YA literature.

On a less positive note, the years between 2000 and 2013 have in common with the decades preceding them a paucity of titles featuring minorities more generally. The Cooperative Children's Book Center at the University of Wisconsin–Madison has been tracking the publication of multicultural titles since 1985. The staff there reports that though they have seen the numbers ebb and flow since then, they have yet to see multicultural literature make up more than 10 percent of the children's and YA books published in a given year. When the titles are limited to books written and illustrated by persons from within the culture being portrayed, that number drops to 5 percent. This is clearly one area of YA publishing that urgently requires remedial action. One hopes that—as America's minority populations continue to gain visibility and prominence—YA literature will reflect their stories in even greater numbers.

In the meantime, the start of the 2000s has witnessed abundant and salutary growth in YA literature, as the books reviewed in this volume amply demonstrate. May you enjoy confirming this assertion for yourself.

Preface

Gillian Engberg and Ian Chipman

The years 2000 to 2013 saw an unprecedented growth in young adult publishing, as author and *Booklist* contributor Michael Cart has demonstrated in his foreword to this retrospective volume. In fact, YA publishing has exploded in the twenty-first century, bringing a thrilling expansion of genres, subjects, and narrative forms, as well as a reputation as one of the most robust sectors in the volatile world of contemporary publishing.

Throughout it all, *Booklist* magazine has tracked this exciting growth, page by page, book by book. In this volume we offer a compendium of reviews that represent the most noteworthy fiction and nonfiction titles reviewed in *Booklist* between January 2000 and August 2013. Stars appearing next to individual titles indicate our choices of the top 50 books published for young adults during this time period (see the appendix for the full list).

As with any such project, our compilation is a subjective one, and we've relied on the expertise of our staff editors—Ilene Cooper, Daniel Kraus, and Ann Kelley—and freelancers, with close attention paid to the winners of the Michael L. Printz Award, which is sponsored by Booklist Publications, as well as the Young Adult Library Services Association's additional book award winners and best-of lists. Our intention is that this volume will serve as both a useful tool for readers' advisory with teens (and adult fans of teen literature) and a comprehensive overview of the influential trends and milestones that continue to shape the extraordinary growth of YA literature as we continue into our second decade of this new century.

We hope that these pages offer valuable support to librarians, teachers, curriculum specialists, professors, authors, publishers, and all others who, in their daily work, share our mission: to help teens develop a lifelong love of reading by connecting them with the best books written just for them.

YOUNG ADULT FICTION 2000–2013

Going Batty Over *Going Bovine*

Ian Chipman

It was a pretty massive task to select the best YA books published between 2000 and the first half of 2013, but it turns out that was only half the battle. We had a zoo with no cages. What we needed now was a way to divvy up all these reviews in an accurate, meaningful, and, most of all, helpful way.

Our first thought was to fall back on the established categories of romance, fantasy, general fiction, science fiction, mystery, historical fiction, westerns, horror, and so forth. This seemed to be a meaningful, straightforward approach. But a single thought pretty much crushed this plan: where do you put Stephenie Meyer's *Twilight* (2005)? Does it fall under romance or fantasy? Then there was Scott Westerfeld's *Leviathan* (2009). Should we slip it into historical fiction or science fiction? And, for that matter, are there really that many YA novels that *aren't* romances at some level? Does one consider John Green a writer of romances because his books deal with matters of the heart as much as matters of the brain, funny bone, and soul? You'd need an impossibly calibrated meter to figure out just when a work of general fiction tips into outright romance, or when a Victorian whodunit falls under either historical fiction or mystery.

Genres are obviously meant to be bent, and books—especially the best of them—resist attempts at easy categorization. One of the greatest features of our online counterpart, *Booklist Online*, is the ability to assign multiple taxonomies to any one book. But here on the printed page, we're allowed no such luxurious dynamism. We floated the idea of repeating reviews in each applicable genre grouping, but that would have given this volume shelf-long proportions. Even setting up an elaborate cross-referencing scheme seemed problematic, and not particularly helpful in any case.

So we rethought the genre approach. There were two directions we could have gone: simplicity or specificity. In the case of the latter, introducing more narrowly defined classifications seemed appealing. You can solve the *Twilight* problem by introducing the category of paranormal romance. You solve the *Leviathan* problem by tossing it into steampunk.

But in the end, this wound up creating more problems than it solved and threatened to turn the book into something of a chaotic mess of increasingly drilled-down and still-subjective subgenres.

So we pivoted and went with the simple approach. And it was good.

We set up a broad parameter that answered the question, where does this book take place? The *where* doesn't refer to any setting, but rather the established reality in which it occurs. We came up with three big groups. Books that happen in our world today would be contemporary fiction. Books that happen in our world in the past would be historical fiction. Books that happen in pretty much anything else (our world as it may be in the future, our world as it might have been in the past, our world today as it isn't, or an entirely imagined world) would be speculative fiction.

This idea clicked. *Twilight* takes place in what is ostensibly our present world, except with vampires, and *Leviathan* takes place in WWI–era Europe, except with flying whales, so they both belong in speculative fiction. And we didn't have to worry about how much romance was in John Green's *Looking for Alaska* (2005) because it sat right where it should in contemporary fiction.

A bit of tinkering was necessary. We added the mystery and suspense category to place books in which the mystery or suspense is clearly paramount to what kind of a world they take place in. And we pulled graphic novels into their own home as a format distinct from prose novels. But the general plan seemed right, and it looked like figuring out where everything else would go would be a snap.

Alas, the best laid plans . . .

Take, for example, Terry Pratchett's *Nation*, a 2009 Printz Honor Book. At first blush, it seems to be technically a work of historical fiction that takes place on a remote island sometime in the nineteenth century. But the ocean is called the Pelagic, not the Pacific; heroine Ermintrude is from somewhere very much like Britain but perhaps not exactly Britain; and Pratchett himself explains in an endnote that the story "is in fact set in a parallel universe. . . . Different things happened, some people lived at different times, some bits of history have been changed, some things are made up out of real pieces." Isn't that pretty much exactly what historical fiction is? If there wasn't a little bit of make-believe, it would be nonfiction. The question remains, where, exactly, does alternative history cross the line from historical fiction into speculative fiction? Do a certain percentage of details need to be historically true (assuming there's any way to actually know such a thing)? In the end, we decided that *Nation* is a work of speculative fiction according to our rules, even if we couldn't defend the position in a court of law.

And what do you do with books based on Arthurian lore? Depends on the book, it turns out. We sent Jane Yolen's *Sword of the Rightful King* (2003) to speculative fiction because there's outright magic in the book, whereas Philip Reeve's *Here Lies Arthur* (2008) goes to historical fiction because Merlin's so-called "magic" is in fact nothing more than cheap parlor tricks used to dupe the oafish masses, and is thus not "real." Even so, Yolen's novel, for the most part, follows the traditional legend as we accept it, and therefore is part of our "real" world, whereas Reeve reimagines the whole thing from the foundation up, and therefore dreams up an entirely new "reality" for the Arthurian story that is, in fact, plausibly historical. Confused yet?

It all started to make sense after we gave it some dedicated thought, and we were still pretty happy with our strategy. But then, with a shudder, we wondered about Libba Bray's 2010 Printz Award winner, *Going Bovine*. We invite you to try to figure out whether it's a realistic story of a kid going crazy with mad cow disease or a fantastical, kaleidoscopic look, through the mind of that same kid, at a world that has itself gone crazy. We don't know. We just know it's an extraordinary novel that explodes any attempts at classification.

So, organizing this volume has been a difficult, quixotic endeavor riddled with fascinating problems. And it has reminded us all that books, especially the best of them, cannot with certainty and clarity be penned into rickety cages of categorization. It's kind of what makes them great.

Contemporary Fiction

Abdel-Fattah, Randa. *Does My Head Look Big in This?* 2007. 342p. Scholastic/Orchard (9780439919470). Gr. 7–10.

Like the author of this breakthrough debut novel, Amal is an Australian-born, Muslim Palestinian "whacked with some seriously confusing identity hyphens." At 16, she loves shopping, watches *Sex and the City*, and IMs her friends about her crush on a classmate. She also wants to wear the hijab, to be strong enough to show a badge of her deeply held faith, even if she confronts insults from some at her snotty prep school, and she is refused a part-time job in the food court (she is "not hygienic"). Her open-minded, observant physician parents support her and so do her friends, Muslim, Jewish, Christian, secular. Her favorite teacher finds her a private space to pray. The first-person present-tense narrative is hilarious about the diversity, and sometimes heartbreaking. For her uncle who wants to assimilate, "foreign" is the *f*-word, and his overdone Aussie slang and flag-waving is a total embarrassment. On the other hand, her friend Leila nearly breaks down when her ignorant Turkish mom wants only to marry her daughter off ("Why study?") and does not know that it is Leila's Islamic duty "to seek knowledge, to gain an education." Without heavy preaching, the issues of faith and culture are part of the story, from fasting at Ramadan to refusing sex before marriage. More than the usual story of the immigrant teen's conflict with her traditional parents, the funny, touching contemporary narrative will grab teens everywhere. —Hazel Rochman

★ **Alexie, Sherman.** *The Absolutely True Diary of a Part-Time Indian.* 2007. 256p. Little, Brown (9780316013680). Gr. 7–10.

Arnold Spirit, a goofy-looking dork with a decent jump shot, spends his time lamenting life on the "poor-ass" Spokane Indian reservation, drawing cartoons (which accompany, and often provide more insight than, the narrative), and, along with his aptly named pal Rowdy, laughing those laughs over anything and nothing that affix best friends so intricately together. When a teacher pleads with Arnold to want more, to escape the hopelessness of the rez, Arnold switches to a rich white school and immediately becomes as much an outcast in his own community as he is a curiosity in his new one. He weathers the typical teenage indignations and triumphs like a champ but soon faces far more trying ordeals as his home life begins to crumble and decay amidst the suffocating mire of alcoholism on the reservation. Alexie's humor and prose are easygoing and well suited to his young audience, and he doesn't pull many punches as he levels his eye at stereotypes both warranted and inapt. A few of the plotlines fade to gray by the end, but this ultimately affirms the incredible power of best friends to hurt and heal in equal measure. Younger teens looking for the strength to lift themselves out of rough situations would do well to start here. —Ian Chipman

Almond, David. *Raven Summer.* 2009. 240p. Delacorte (9780385738064). Gr. 7–12.

Big issues are front and center in Almond's gripping new novel, told in the present-tense voice of teenage Liam and set in contemporary northern England. War rages in Iraq and elsewhere, and army jets fly low over where he lives. "All of us are beasts at heart. . . . We have to help the angel in us to overcome the beast." Yes, the messages are spelled out, but readers will want to talk and argue about them, sparked by the authentic characters and the searing drama of their lives. In spare, stirring words, Liam tells of his tenderness for a foundling baby that his family takes in; his fear and rage about his bullying classmate, Nattrass; and his friendship with a young Liberian asylum seeker, Oliver, who saw soldiers slaughter his family, soldiers who said that God was on their side. Nattrass calls Oliver a terrorist and thinks he should be sent back, as do the immigration officials. Always there is the pull of violence, felt by both children and adults, including tourists who visit ancient castles and other remnants of past wars. Is God a war criminal? The tension builds to a shocking and totally believable ending. Readers will recognize that "the murderer in all of us is just below the skin," but the kindness in every chapter is heartbreaking too. A haunting story, perfect for group discussion. —Hazel Rochman

Anderson, Laurie Halse. *Prom*. 2005. 224p. Viking (9780670059744). Gr. 9–12.

Ashley understands that the senior prom at her Philadelphia school is a big deal to her close friends even though she thinks it's "stupid." So imagine her shock at finding herself the most likely candidate to save the prom after a troubled math teacher makes off with the funds. Many of Anderson's previous novels have been heart-wrenching accounts of teen survivors, such as the date-rape victim in *Speak* (1999) and the yellow fever survivor in *Fever 1793* (2000). Here, though, Anderson's bright, witty narrator is a self-professed "ordinary kid," whose problems, while intensely felt, are as common as a burger and fries. Ashley's as ambivalent about her gorgeous but undependable boyfriend as she is about her college prospects; her part-time job serving pizza in a rat costume is far from fulfilling; and her family, which she calls "no-extra-money-for-nuthin'-poor," mortifies her (her pregnant mother's belly "screams to the world" that her parents have sex), even as they offer love and support. In clipped chapters (some just a sentence long), Ashley tells her story in an authentic, sympathetic voice that combines gum-snapping, tell-it-like-it-is humor with honest questions about her future. The dramatic ending may be a bit over the top, but teens will love Ashley's clear view of high-school hypocrisies, dating, and the fierce bonds of friendship. —Gillian Engberg

Anderson, Laurie Halse. *Twisted*. 2007. 256p. Viking (9780670061013). Gr. 9–12.

Tyler Miller was a socially invisible nerd ("Your average piece of drywall who spent too much time playing computer games") before he sprayed some attention-getting graffiti and became a legend. Sentenced to a summer of physical labor, he enters his senior year with new muscles that attract popular Bethany Millbury, whose father is Tyler's dad's boss. On probation for his graffiti stunt, Tyler struggles to balance his consuming crush with pressure that comes from schoolwork and his explosive father, and after Tyler is implicated in a drunken crime, his balancing act falls apart. The dialogue occasionally has the clichéd feel of a teen movie ("Party's over." "We're just getting started. And I don't remember inviting you"). What works well here is the frank, on-target humor ("I was a zit on the butt of the student body"), the taut pacing, and the small moments, recounted in Tyler's first-person voice, that illuminate his emotional anguish. Writing for the first time from a male perspective, Anderson skillfully explores identity and power struggles that all young people will recognize. —Gillian Engberg

Anderson, Laurie Halse. *Wintergirls*. 2009. 288p. Viking (9780670011100). Gr. 9–12.

Problem-novel fodder becomes a devastating portrait of the extremes of self-deception in this brutal and poetic deconstruction of how one girl stealthily vanishes into the depths of anorexia. Lia has been down this road before: her competitive relationship with her best friend, Cassie, once landed them both in the hospital, but now not even Cassie's death can eradicate Lia's disgust of the "fat cows" who scrutinize her body all day long. Her father (no, "Professor Overbrook") and her mother (no, "Dr. Marrigan") are frighteningly easy to dupe—tinkering and sabotage inflate her scale readings as her weight secretly plunges: 101.30, 97.00, 89.00. Anderson illuminates a dark but utterly realistic world where every piece of food is just a caloric number, inner voices scream "NO!" with each swallow, and self-worth is too easily gauged: "I am the space between my thighs, daylight shining through." Struck-through sentences, incessant repetition, and even blank pages make Lia's inner turmoil tactile, and gruesome details of her decomposition will test sensitive readers. But this is necessary reading for anyone caught in a feedback loop of weight loss as well as any parent unfamiliar with the scripts teens recite so easily to escape from such deadly situations. —Daniel Kraus

Andrews, Jesse. *Me and Earl and the Dying Girl*. 2012. 304p. Abrams/Amulet (9781419701764). Gr. 8–11.

Greg Gaines, 17, would be the first to tell you that his constant "dickhead behavior" makes him the least likely person to befriend a classmate dying of leukemia. But he is pushed into it by his mother and, well, the result is this "horrifyingly inane," "unstoppable barf-fest" of a book. Greg prefers to keep a low profile at school, instead collaborating with his almost-gangsta pal, Earl, on terrible remakes of classic films: *Apocalypse Later* with Super Soakers, *The Manchurian Cat-idate* with cats. But his knack for cracking jokes keeps the dying girl, Rachel, smiling, and pretty soon the whole school thinks he is some kind of hero. He is even pushed into making a final opus: *Rachel the Film*, aka "the worst film ever made." One need only look at the chapter titles ("Let's Just Get This Embarrassing Chapter Out of the Way") to know that this is one funny book, highlighted by screenplay excerpts and Earl's pissy wisdom. What's crazy is how moving it becomes in spite of itself. The characters are neither smart nor precocious. Greg is not suitably moved by Rachel's struggle. His film sucks. He thinks *bereavement* means "being attacked by beavers." But it's this honest lack of profundity, and the struggle to overcome it, that makes Andrews' debut actually kinda profound. —Daniel Kraus

Asher, Jay. *Thirteen Reasons Why*. 2007. 256p. Penguin/Razorbill (9781595141712). Gr. 8–11.

When Clay Jenson plays the cassette tapes he received in a mysterious package, he's surprised to hear the voice of dead classmate Hannah Baker. He's one of 13 people who receive Hannah's story, which details the circumstances that led to her suicide. Clay spends the rest of the day and long into the night listening to Hannah's voice and going to the locations she wants him to visit. The text alternates, sometimes quickly, between Hannah's voice (italicized) and Clay's thoughts as he listens to her words, which illuminate betrayals and secrets that demonstrate the consequences of even small actions. Hannah, herself, is not free from guilt, her own inaction having played a part in an accidental auto death and a rape. The message about how we treat one another, although sometimes heavy, makes for compelling reading. Give this to fans of Gail Giles' psychological thrillers. —Cindy Dobrez

Barnes, John. *Tales of the Madman Underground*. 2009. 544p. Viking (9780670060818). Gr. 9–12.

After a long career in science fiction, Barnes has taken a heroic stab at the Great American Novel. Set over the span of just six days in 1973—but weighing in at more than 500 pages—Barnes' coming-of-age epic is overlong, tangled with tangents, and takes a kitchen-sink approach when it comes to teenage trauma. Yet rarely will you read something so lovingly vulgar, so fiercely warmhearted, and so exuberantly expansive that even its long-windedness becomes part of its rogue charm. It's the story of Karl Shoemaker, a senior starting the first week of classes in his blue-collar Ohio town. This year he's determined to execute Operation Be Fucking Normal, but that isn't easy when he is working five jobs to pay the bills of his drunkard, star-child mother; wakes up early to clean up the poop from their zillions of cats (and bury the dead ones in their backyard Cat Arlington); and is deeply connected to the other kids forced to take school therapy—aka the Madman Underground. The plot is slight, but Karl's fellow madmen revel in their wild tales of survival and revenge, and the culmination comes off like a high-school *One Flew over the Cuckoo's Nest*. Always ambitious, often caustic, and frequently moving. —Daniel Kraus

Bauer, Joan. *Hope Was Here*. 2000. 192p. Putnam (9780399231421). Gr. 7–9.

Ever since her mother left, Hope has, with her comfort-food-cooking aunt Addie, been serving up the best in diner food from Pensacola to New York City. Moving has been tough, so it comes as a surprise to 16-year-old Hope that rural Wisconsin, where she and her aunt have now settled, offers more excitement, friendship, and even romance (for both Hope and Addie) than the big city. In this story, Bauer has recycled some charming devices from her popular *Rules of the Road* (1998): Jenna's road rules have become the Best-of-Mom tips for waitressing; the disappearing parent is Hope's irresponsible mom; and the villains are politicians, not corporate

America. Like Bauer's other heroines, Hope is a typical teenage girl who works hard, excels at her part-time job, and plans for her future. The adults around her, though mostly one-dimensional, together create a microcosm of society—the best and the worst of a teenager's support system. It's Bauer's humor that supplies, in Addie's cooking vernacular, the yeast that makes the story rise above the rest, reinforcing the substantive issues of honesty, humanity, and the importance of political activism. Serve this up to teens—with a dash of hope. —Frances Bradburn

Bauman, Beth Ann. *Rosie and Skate*. 2009. 224p. Random/Wendy Lamb (9780385737357). Gr. 9–12.

High-school sophomore Rosie and her year-older sister Skate have one unshakable reality in their lives: their father is a drunk, whom Skate calls Old Crow after the booze he drinks. After their father is thrown in jail for petty theft, an older cousin comes to stay in the family's decrepit ocean-front Victorian on the Jersey shore. Skate, though, prefers to live with the mother of her college-freshman boyfriend, Perry. If there's one other reality Skate holds firmly to, it's that she and Perry are in love and will successfully negotiate a long-distance relationship. So you know how that's going to go. Told in alternating chapters by sisters who are very different from one another yet bound by their hardships and their laughter, this is a novel as brisk and refreshing as an ocean breeze. The descriptions are always vivid, whether first-time author Bauman is describing the boardwalk or the ways sex can be used to pacify or agitate a situation. Both sisters write in first person, and their narratives have a scratchy uniqueness, miles apart from the ubiquitous voice so often heard in YA novels. Rosie is dear and hopeful, and Skate, nicknamed for her skateboarding abilities, is knowing and crisp. Bauman's subtle melding of their personalities as life shapes them shows surprising skill from a debut author. —Ilene Cooper

Booth, Coe. *Kendra*. 2008. 292p. Scholastic/Push (9780439925365). Gr. 10–12.

Fans of *Tyrell* (2006) will welcome another tale about a Bronx teen facing big challenges. Fifteen-year-old Kendra has been raised by her grandmother, Nana, while her 29-year-old mother has been away earning university degrees. Now that her mother's PhD is complete, Kendra is hoping that the family will finally reunite, but her mom chooses to get a studio apartment without her daughter. Kendra's longing for love leads her too quickly into a physical relationship with hot Nashawn. Kendra doesn't want sex, in part because Nana threatens to have her physically "checked" to confirm her virginity, but Nashawn suggests oral and anal sex as alternatives to traditional intercourse. Kendra agrees, and she is guilt ridden over the acts (which are frankly discussed) as well as confused by the passion she feels. Her father, who is in a dead-end job as a snack-food truck driver, rounds out the strong secondary characters. Kendra's talent at architectural drawing and set design will attract artistic teens, while her realistic daily problems with friends, family, and boys will appeal to a wide audience. —Cindy Dobrez

Booth, Coe. *Tyrell*. 2006. 320p. Scholastic (9780439838795). Gr. 9–12.

"You don't hardly get to have no kinda childhood in the hood." At 15, Tyrell is trying to keep his little brother in school and safe in their roach-infested shelter in the Bronx. He has dropped out of school, and Moms wants him to sell drugs to make money. But Tyrell is too smart. He doesn't want to end up in prison like his dad, so he tries to organize a neighborhood party to raise money. His girlfriend, Novisha, isn't happy that Tyrell has dropped out. She loves him, and they make out, but he respects her wish to remain a virgin. Booth, who was born and raised in the Bronx, is now a social worker there, and her first novel is heartbreakingly realistic. There are some plot contrivances—including Tyrell's stumbling upon Novisha's diary—but the immediate first-person narrative is pitch perfect: fast, funny, and anguished (there's also lots of use of the *n*-word, though the term is employed in the colloquial sense, not as an insult). Unlike many books reflecting the contemporary street scene, this one is more than just a pat situation with a glib resolution; it's filled with surprising twists and turns that continue to the end. —Hazel Rochman

Brashares, Ann. *Girls in Pants: The Third Summer of the Sisterhood*. 2005. 352p. Delacorte (9780385729352). Gr. 8–12.

It's the summer before the Septembers go to college, a summer in which old and new boyfriends appear, families grow and change, crises occur and are resolved, and the pants continue their designated rounds. Despite their diverse schedules, the four friends who appeared in the previous Traveling Pants books reunite one final weekend before they go off to four different colleges. Readers of the other books won't be disappointed with these new adventures: Carmen's mother is pregnant; Bee is back at soccer camp with her old crush, Eric; Tibby's sister falls from her second-story window; and Lena's parents refuse to pay for art school. Beneath these crisis-ridden plotlines lies an artist at work—an author who encourages her readers to look, feel, trust, and empathize with her characters. It's a strong ending to a series about four fully developed, strikingly different, equally fascinating teenage girls. —Frances Bradburn

Brashares, Ann. *The Sisterhood of the Traveling Pants*. 2001. 294p. Delacorte (9780385729338). Gr. 6–9.

The pants were magic—worn, thrift-shop jeans that made each of the four best friends look absolutely fabulous. Obviously they were life-changing pants. Thus the plan: route them to each of the four at their various summer destinations, with appropriate rules attached, of course, and watch wonderful things happen. Only they don't. Carmen's dad still remarries; Lena's trip to Greece to visit her grandparents is still marred by a terrible misunderstanding with a gorgeous Greek teen; Bridget still does dumb things at a Baja California soccer camp; and Tibby must work at Wallman's. The pants are just pants, and life is just life, full of joys, sorrows, living, and dying. This is the charm of *The Sisterhood of the Traveling Pants*. Carmen, Lena, Bridget, and Tibby are growing to adulthood, and Brashares accurately portrays one glorious, painful summer in their evolution. Young teens will identify with one, or even all four, of these interesting, funny young women, and they'll be on the lookout for their own pair of traveling pants. —Frances Bradburn

Brooks, Bruce. *All That Remains*. 2001. 168p. Atheneum (9780689833519). Gr. 7–12.

In this trio of novellas, Brooks' trademark razor-sharp wit illuminates tales of death and earthly remains. Despite the topic, there is nothing ghoulish or creepy here. Clever wordplay and gallows humor bring a new dimension to death and how we deal with it. In one story, cousins conspire to cremate their beloved aunt (who has just died of AIDS) in a potter's kiln to circumvent laws that would put her in a pauper's grave. The most conventional story follows a slick, hip teen who takes his decidedly uncool cousin under his wing to keep a promise made to a dying uncle. The final story is a gem: a lone girl, laden with backpack, insists on joining a trio of young male golfers and blows them away with her talent. The contents of her backpack, however, are even more surprising than her sudden presence. Touching on AIDS, homophobia, popularity, hockey, and golf, these surprising, clever, and poignant stories show Brooks at his best. —Debbie Carton

Brooks, Martha. *Mistik Lake*. 2007. 224p. Farrar/Melanie Kroupa (9780374349851). Gr. 9–12.

Throughout her childhood, 17-year-old Odella has watched her mother, Sally, "sink deeper into whatever it is that keeps her from us." As a teen, Sally was the only survivor of a car accident on frozen Mistik Lake, and she seems forever haunted by the trauma, turning to alcohol and, finally, leaving her husband and three daughters for Iceland and another man. Then the news arrives that Sally has died, and Odella tries to hold the family together while swimming in her own complicated grief: "It's hard to be angry at a ghost." Set in Odella's Winnipeg home and the tiny town of Mistik Lake, where Odella's Icelandic Canadian family has deep roots, Brooks' affecting novel explores the weighty legacy of family secrets and cultural heritage. Many characters believe in the significance of dreams, and the perspectives, which move among Odella, her new boyfriend, and her great-aunt, create a dreamlike collapse of past and present, emphasizing the common themes shared through generations. The many characters' stories threaten to overcrowd the plot, but Brooks skillfully keeps the focus on Odella, whose chapters are the only ones narrated in a first-person voice. Readers will connect strongly with the teenager's astonished, powerful feelings of first love and her shocked realization that painful family burdens can also be life-changing gifts. —Gillian Engberg

Brooks, Martha. *True Confessions of a Heartless Girl*. 2003. 192p. Farrar/Melanie Kroupa (9780374378066). Gr. 9–12.

Pembina Lake is a tiny town with more than its share of the world weary. After escaping an abusive marriage, Lynda runs a cafe and is raising a young son; middle-aged Del carries the guilt of his brother's drowning; and Dolores is coping with her daughter's death. Then 17-year-old Noreen rides into town in a stolen truck—screwed up, knocked up, and so beaten by life that her scarred psyche wakes even the sleep-walking souls in the Molly Thorvaldson Café. Noreen, who has ruined her relationship with her baby's father, is a sad spirit, who can't catch a break or do the right thing, even on the rare occasions when she wants to. In 10 short days, she nearly kills Lynda's dog, wrecks Del's house, and ruins the restaurant. The writing is plain, with a flatness about it that mirrors the Canadian prairie where the story is set. The style also suits the novel's bleak mood; even the most horrific events seem somehow expected. The characterizations are bare-to-the-bones as well, but the people are so expertly revealed that their pain is palpable. This is particularly true of Noreen, who has not experienced a major tragedy—just the steady erosion of her soul. The baby sparks something in her, but she miscarries. Then, through the alchemy of shared heartache, she begins to reclaim herself. Heartless once; hopeless no more. —Ilene Cooper

Brothers, Meagan. *Debbie Harry Sings in French*. 2008. 240p. Holt (9780805080803). Gr. 8–12.

Debut author Brothers tackles the topic of teenage transvestism in this ode to '80s music. After a stint in rehab where the music of Blondie becomes his recovery touchstone, 16-year-old former alcoholic Johnny is sent to live with his uncle to start anew. School bullies call him "faggot," but eyeliner-wearing Johnny knows he's not gay because he's smitten with Maria, a Goth chick who shares his love of '80s punk. Maria helps him explore his need to cross-dress by encouraging him to enter a drag contest as Debbie Harry, while Johnny's unconditional love helps her come to terms with past suicidal impulses. With Maria's support and his family's gradual acceptance, Johnny learns to proudly embrace his inner Debbie. Though the story takes time to build momentum and the prose occasionally slides into cliché, this compelling and ultimately uplifting novel fills a niche in the growing body of GLBTQ literature for teens. Offer this to groupies of James St. James' *Freak Show* (2007), Cecil Castellucci's *Beige* (2007), and Ellen Wittlinger's *Parrotfish* (2007). —Jennifer Hubert

Brown, Jennifer. *Hate List*. 2009. 416p. Little, Brown (9780316041447). Gr. 9–12.

It is September, and senior Valerie Leftman is heading back to school. Five months earlier, her boyfriend, Nick, opened fire in the school cafeteria, killing six and wounding others before committing suicide. Despite being wounded herself while trying to stop Nick and save classmates, Val has been the focus of police investigations and rumors due to the Hate List, composed of classmates' names, which she created to vent her frustration about bullies. Struggling with guilt and grief, Val begins school as the ultimate outcast, but she finds one unexpected ally. Most books about school shootings focus on the horrifying event itself, but this debut novel breaks ground by examining the aftermath. Brown uses a creative structure of alternating narratives that incorporate excerpts from newspapers. The characters, including the many adults, are well drawn and become more nuanced as Val heals and gains perspective. Filled with unanswered questions, this compelling novel will leave teens pondering the slippery nature of perception and guilt. —Lynn Rutan

Budhos, Marina. *Ask Me No Questions*. 2006. 176p. (9781416903512). Gr. 8–11.

What is it like to be an illegal alien in New York now? In a moving first-person, present-tense narrative, Nadira, 14, relates how her family left Bangladesh, came to the U.S. on a tourist visa, and stayed long after the visa expired ("Everyone does it. You buy a fake social security number for a few hundred dollars and then you can work."). Their illegal status is discovered, however, following 9/11, when immigration regulations are tightened. When the family hurriedly seeks asylum in Canada, they are turned back, and Nadira's father, Abba, is detained because his passport is no longer valid. The secrets are dramatic ("Go to school. Never let anyone know. Never."), and so are the family dynamics, especially Nadira's furious envy of her gifted older sister, Aisha. But Aisha breaks down, and Nadira must take over the struggle to get Abba out of detention and prevent the family's deportation. The teen voice is wonderfully immediate, revealing Nadira's mixed-up feelings as well as the diversity in her family and in the Muslim community. There's also a real drama that builds to a tense climax: Did Abba give funds to a political organization? Where has the money gone? Will Immigration hear his appeal? The answer is a surprise that grows organically from the family's story. Readers will feel the heartbreak, prejudice, kindness, and fear. —Hazel Rochman

Burd, Nick. *The Vast Fields of Ordinary*. 2009. 320p. Dial (9780803733404). Gr. 9–12.

It's Dade's last summer at home before college and things are looking bleak: his parents' marriage is disintegrating; his father has a girlfriend; his mother is self-medicating with pills and booze; his sorta boyfriend, Pablo, refuses to acknowledge the nature of their "friendship"; the local media are obsessed with the mysterious disappearance of an autistic little girl; and Dade himself is feeling pretty lost and invisible, too. But then he meets the dangerous yet fascinating (and unapologetically gay) Alex, and things take a turn for the better . . . for a while. Burd's first novel has some of the trappings of the traditional coming-out-while-coming-of-age story, and his ending seems more willful than artful. Also, some readers may find the subplot about a missing girl more distracting than symbolically resonant. That said, Burd is a terrific writer with a special gift for creating teenage characters who are vital, plausible, and always engaging (even when they're being mean and menacing). His take on the complications in Dade's life is sophisticated and thoughtful, especially on the ambiguities of that "relationship" with Pablo, while his limning of the growing friendship with Alex is deeply satisfying, never striking a discordant emotional note. Clearly, Burd is a new talent to watch. —Michael Cart

Burgess, Melvin. *Doing It*. 2004. 336p. Holt (9780805075656). Gr. 10–12.

Burgess' third novel follows three best mates as they shag, attempt to shag, try to get out of shagging, masturbate while contemplating shagging, and then shag some more. Ben is sleeping with his obsessive drama teacher; Jon finds himself irresistibly attracted to Deborah, who would be perfect if her pudginess didn't make him subject to ridicule; and Dino, as handsome as he is horny, just wants to shag the gorgeous Jackie—or, failing that, anyone else. From snogging to shagging to buggering, *Doing It* discusses *it* in a dizzying array of contexts, and it is relentlessly and refreshingly honest: this is certainly the first YA novel to feature two boys who lose their erections while trying to lose their virginity. Scenes like that make the book less erotic than comforting: boys will be pleased to learn they are not alone in their sexual anxieties; and girls will learn that boys want sex, but are also confused and fearful about it. But while the content will raise eyebrows, it's the writing that's problematic. Though periodically very funny and excellently plotted, the alternating-voices narration falls flat because the characters sound nearly identical, and the writing is surprisingly undescriptive, a disappointing departure from Burgess' previous novels (*Smack and Lady*, e.g.). Still, there's a lot to like here, and to say that *Doing It* will generate interest among readers would be to understate the matter dramatically. —John Green

Cabot, Meg. *The Princess Diaries*. 2000. 224p. HarperCollins (9780380978489). Gr. 7–10.

Teens like novels written in diary format, and you can bet they'll be lining up for this hilarious story about a gawky 14-year-old New Yorker who learns she's a princess. Mia spends every available moment pouring her feelings into the journal her mother gave her:

she writes during algebra class, in the ladies' room at the Plaza (much nicer than the one in Tavern on the Green), in her grandmother's limousine. She writes down her thoughts on everything—from algebra and her mother's love life to her jet-setting father's announcement that she's the heir to the throne of the principality of Genovia. Then, of course, she records Grandmother's efforts to turn her into a princess, her dealings with classmates, the press, and a bodyguard, and also her attraction to the most gorgeous guy in school and her attempts to be assertive and happy with her new life. She whines; she gloats; she cheers, worries, rants, and raves. Reading her journal is like reading a note from your best friend. Cabot has a fine grasp of teen dialect (and punctuation), an off-the-wall sense of humor that will have readers laughing out loud, and a knack for creating fully realized teen and adult characters that readers will miss when the story ends. —Chris Sherman

Cameron, Peter. *Someday This Pain Will Be Useful to You*. 2007. 240p. Farrar/Frances Foster (9780374309893). Gr. 9–12.

Though he's been accepted by Brown University, 18-year-old James isn't sure he wants to go to college. What he really wants is to buy a nice house in a small town somewhere in the Midwest—Indiana, perhaps. In the meantime, however, he has a dull, make-work job at his thrice-married mother's Manhattan art gallery, where he finds himself attracted to her assistant, an older man named John. In a clumsy attempt to capture John's attention, James winds up accused of sexual harassment! A critically acclaimed author of adult fiction, Cameron makes a singularly auspicious entry into the world of YA with this beautifully conceived and written coming-of-age novel that is, at turns, funny, sad, tender, and sophisticated. James makes a memorable protagonist, touching in his inability to connect with the world but always entertaining in his first-person account of his New York environment, his fractured family, his disastrous trip to the nation's capital, and his ongoing bouts with psychoanalysis. In the process he dramatizes the ambivalences and uncertainties of adolescence in ways that both teen and adult readers will savor and remember. —Michael Cart

Canales, Viola. *The Tequila Worm*. 2005. 176p. Random/Wendy Lamb (9780385746748). Gr. 6–9.

From an early age, Sofia has watched the *comadres* in her close-knit barrio community, in a small Texas town, and she dreams of becoming "someone who makes people into a family," as the *comadres* do. The secret, her young self observes, seems to lie in telling stories and "being brave enough to eat a whole tequila worm." In this warm, entertaining debut novel, Canales follows Sofia from early childhood through her teen years, when she receives a scholarship to attend an exclusive boarding school. Each chapter centers on the vivid particulars of Mexican American traditions—celebrating the Day of the Dead, preparing for a cousin's *quinceanera*. The explanations of cultural traditions never feel too purposeful; they are always rooted in immediate, authentic family emotions, and in Canales' exuberant storytelling, which, like a good anecdote shared between friends, finds both humor and absurdity in sharply observed, painful situations—from weathering slurs and other blatant harassment to learning what it means to leave her community for a privileged, predominately white school. Readers of all backgrounds will easily connect with Sofia as she grows up, becomes a *comadre*, and helps rebuild the powerful, affectionate community that raised her. —Gillian Engberg

Caletti, Deb. *The Fortunes of Indigo Skye*. 2008. 304p. Simon & Schuster (9781416910077). Gr. 10–12.

What would you do if you were to come into two and a half million dollars unexpectedly? That's the question facing Indigo Skye, a high-school senior whose life has consisted primarily of spending time with her boyfriend, navigating her family (Dad has left the family to sell surfboards in Hawaii), and working mornings at Carrera's restaurant in Seattle. Indigo can tell what people are like by what they eat for breakfast, especially the regulars. But when a well-dressed stranger on an orange Vespa comes in and orders only a cup of coffee, Indigo finds him hard to figure out—even after he becomes a semiregular. After the stranger gives her a fortune, Indigo's search for answers takes her to Hawaii to confront her benefactor and also to ritzy Hollywood suburbs, where she learns that being rich is not all it is cracked up to be. Caletti's coming-of-age story with an infinitely likeable heroine and richly limned supporting characters makes a fine counterpoint to the ubiquitous rich-girl series books. —Bina Williams

Castellucci, Cecil. *Beige*. 2007. 320p. Candlewick (9780763630669). Gr. 7–10.

While her mother is off on an archaeological dig, Katy is forced to leave Montreal and go to Los Angeles to visit her long-lost father. Her father, "The Rat," is a drummer for the punk band Suck, and his apartment is a mess—even the soap is dirty. When he asks what Katy might like to do in L.A., she thinks, "There is nothing I want to do in L.A. Not one thing. Except leave." Castellucci gives a fresh spin to the familiar exiled-teen plot by mixing details of the L.A. punk scene with memorable characters and witty dialogue. Nicknamed "Beige" for her bland personality by Lake (a girl bribed to befriend her), Katy becomes the "merch girl," selling T-shirts for Lake's band, even though she hates its music. But by the end of the story, Katy has lost some of her Beige ways, and the lessons she has learned will help her deal with a sudden change in her mother's plans. Chapter titles of punk songs and band names will give readers a starting point for learning more about the music. Consider this pure Nirvana. —Cindy Dobrez

Castellucci, Cecil. *Boy Proof*. 2005. 208p. Candlewick (9780763623333). Gr. 7–10.

With her shaved head, ring-covered ears, and a swirling cloak, brilliant Victoria insists her name is Egg, after the hero in her favorite sf movie, *Terminal Earth*, which she has seen 42 times. Who cares that she has no friends in her high-school senior class in Hollywood? She will never be normal. She is "post-apocalyptic." What she loves is working with her dad in movie special effects, tinkering with "eyeballs or aliens or ears." But when brilliant, gorgeous Max arrives, she cannot help loving him, especially because he is also in tune with the sf/fantasy world, and he shows her that she can be her own person, and fight real apocalyptic conservation issues right on earth. Of course, Max is too perfect, and the turnaround message is heavy. But this first novel's clipped, funny, first-person, present-tense narrative will grab teens (and not just sf fans) with its romance and the screwball special effects, and with the story of an outsider's struggle both to belong and to be true to herself. —Hazel Rochman

Chambers, Aidan. *This Is All: The Pillow Book of Cordelia Kenn*. 2006. 808p. Abrams (9780810970601). Gr. 9–12.

With the publication of *This Is All*, Chambers completes his ambitious, six-novel Dance sequence, which began with *Breaktime* in 1978 and also includes *Dance on My Grave* (1982), *Now I Know* (1988), *The Toll Bridge* (1995), and—most recently—the Carnegie and Printz Award winner *Postcards from No Man's Land* (2002). Each title is intended by the author to explore aspects of contemporary adolescent life, and this title is Chambers' most ambitious effort. Its premise, at least, is fairly straightforward. Nineteen-year-old Cordelia Kenn records the story of her life for the daughter with whom she is pregnant, planning to present it to the girl on her sixteenth birthday. The form Cordelia chooses for her tale is unusual: she is writing—or constructing—a pillow book (à la the tenth-century Japanese *Pillow Book of Sei Shōnagon*), in which she not only records a narrative but also jots down poetry, ideas, observations, lists (she's a compulsive list-maker), musings, and more. Cordelia is such an acute observer and has such a lively, inquiring mind that, ultimately, her pillow book becomes six books. Each one has its own structure and narrative strategy, and readers must choose the order in which to read them. Some will complain about this; others will complain about the novel's great length. But the curious, the patient, and the adventurous will treasure the novel's challenges and savor its great rewards, which will grow richer and larger with each reading. —Michael Cart

Christopher, Lucy. *Stolen*. 2010. 304p. Scholastic/Chicken House (9780545170932). Gr. 9–12.

Drugged and kidnapped from her parents at the Bangkok airport, English teen Gemma wakes to find herself in the weirdly beautiful but desolate Australian outback. Her only company is her captor, a handsome young Australian named Ty, who is obsessed with her. Indeed, he tells her that he has been watching her since she was a child and now plans to keep her with him forever. Told in the form of a letter Gemma is writing to Ty, Christopher's first novel is a complex psychological study that is also a tribute to the hypnotic beauty of the outback, which Ty passionately loves and feels has been "stolen" by those who would exploit it for gain. Though Gemma at first hates both her kidnapper and the landscape, she gradually begins to warm toward both. Some readers may feel the novel is weighted down by too much symbolism (if the outback is Edenic, watch out for a serpent!) and find Ty to be too sympathetic a character, but at the same time these potential drawbacks offer ample opportunity for thought and discussion. —Michael Cart

Clarke, Judith. *One Whole and Perfect Day*. 2007. 250p. Front Street (9781932425956). Gr. 8–10.

Lily feels both love for and embarrassment about her eccentric family: a grandmother with an imaginary friend, an ax-brandishing grandfather, a mother who brings home patients from the elder-care facility where she works, and an estranged older brother, Lonnie, who still can't seem to get his life together. In a series of implausibly coincidental events (Lonnie's girlfriend's mother also happens to be the random stranger who teaches his grandfather a lesson about racism, for example), all of the family members, and many with whom they come into contact, reach new understanding about themselves and their lives, and all make both small and large changes for the better. In the end, Lily realizes her dream: one "whole and perfect day," in which her entire family comes together and finds happiness. The third-person narration alternates among the many characters' experiences, offering the reader an omniscient view of interconnecting lives in a down-to-earth, Australian setting. —Heather Booth

Coburn, Jake. *Prep*. 2003. 176p. Dutton (9780525471356). Gr. 9–12.

The staccato rhythm of Coburn's prose is the best part of this tale of Manhattan prep-school gangsters. Coburn, himself a prep-school graduate, sheds light on a fascinating subculture of privileged teens who lack for nothing save their parents' attention. Nick is in love with Kris, whose younger brother, Danny, is being threatened by a gang. To save Danny, Nick calls on friends from his tagging (graffiti) days and, in doing so, faces difficult memories of his own cowardice. There is a fair amount of action, but what pulls readers along is the language. Realistic, slang-filled dialogue and short, crisp narrative passages create a minimalist world of frenetic gang warfare, substance abuse, and wild parties that become nightmares. —Debbie Carton

Cohen, Joshua C. *Leverage*. 2011. 352p. Dutton (9780525423065). Gr. 10–12.

Sports novels don't hit much harder than this. Sophomore Danny may be a rising star on the gymnastics team, but that figures little in his daily life, where his small size makes him a target for the school's ruling class—the hormone-pumped, college-scouted stars of the football team. A minor grudge escalates until horrific revenge is taken upon one of Danny's teammates. Coming to the rescue, however, is Kurt, a behemoth new fullback whose scarred face and stuttering speech hint at a past that puts him at odds with his teammates. Told from the well-drawn alternating perspectives of Danny and Kurt, this is not a book about steroids; they exist, and they exacerbate the strife, but even Kurt admits that they have some short-term benefits. Rather, this is a novel about being trapped inside a web of expectations, where one's family, community, team, and future rest on the assumed perpetuation of the established social order. Sports fans will love Cohen's style: direct, goal oriented, and filled with sensory detail. Characters and subplots are overly abundant yet add a deepness rarely found in comparable books. Drugs, rape, language, and violence make this book serious business, but those with experience will tell you that sports is serious business, too. —Daniel Kraus

Cohn, Rachel. *Gingerbread*. 2002. 176p. Simon & Schuster (9780689843372). Gr. 9–12.

Sixteen-year-old Cyd Charisse's parents call her "Little Hellion." When she's kicked out of an exclusive boarding school, she returns to her privileged home in San Francisco, where she fights constantly with her mother and stepfather, who don't know about her recent abortion. She finds her place with new friends: a boyfriend Shrimp, a sexy surfer, and Honey Pie, an elderly woman who understands her secrets. After a broken curfew escalates into bitterness, Cyd is sent to her biological father in New York City. "Frank real-dad" isn't what Cyd had imagined: nor are his two grown kids. Cyd's New York experience helps her confront her most painful questions. Written in Cyd's hilarious, contemporary voice, Cohn's first novel is a fast, uncomfortable read. Bratty, spoiled, and prone to tantrums, Cyd is often unlikable and is all the more realistic for it. Some characters, particularly Cyd's parents, and details about the world of wealth occasionally collapse into stereotype, and Cyd spikes her honest, revealing speech with such aggressively hip words as *crazysexy*, which may date quickly. But teens will recognize themselves in Cyd's complex, believable mix of the arch and the vulnerable, the self-aware and the self-destructive, and also in her struggle between freedom and the protective safety of family. —Gillian Engberg

Cohn, Rachel, and David Levithan. *Nick & Norah's Infinite Playlist*. 2006. 192p. Knopf (9780375835315). Gr. 10–12.

Cohn and Levithan contribute alternating chapters in this high-energy romance that follows two high-school seniors through a single, music-fueled night in Manhattan. Nick, the "nonqueer bassist in a queercore band," is playing with The Fuck Offs, when he spots his ex-girlfriend, Tris. Once offstage, he propositions a girl he has never met, hoping to make Tris jealous: "Would you mind being my girlfriend for five minutes?" Norah, also heartbroken (and hoping Nick will drive her home), agrees. What begins as a spontaneous ploy turns into something surprising and real in the course of one night as Nick and Norah roam Manhattan, listen to bands, confront past hurts, and hurtle toward romance. The real-time pacing may slow some readers, and a few Manhattan in-jokes ("Hunter from Hunter") may exclude teens in the wider world. Still, many readers will respond to the tough, clever, amped-up narratives, which include mosh-pit coarse language (Nick sound-checks the microphones with the words "Fuck. Shit. Cock," for example) and the characters' wild yearning for love, and music, which feels powerful and true. —Gillian Engberg

Coman, Carolyn. *Many Stones*. 2000. 160p. Front Street (9781886910553). Gr. 7–12.

In plain words, as hard as stones, this small, riveting book connects the anguish in one family with the struggle of a country to come to terms with its savage past. Teenager Berry doesn't want to leave her boyfriend and her mother in Washington, D.C., and go to South Africa on a 10-day tourist trip with her take-charge, divorced dad. They see Johannesburg and the wild game reserve, Robben Island (where Mandela was imprisoned) and the Cape; but theirs is more than a sightseeing tour. Berry's beloved older sister, Laura, was murdered a year before near the church school where she was volunteering, and Dad wants Berry with him for the unveiling of a memorial to Laura. The idea is that being together will help them cope with their loss and reconcile them (Dad left home for another woman, other women). The hearings of South Africa's Truth and Reconciliation Commission (TRC) are going on, where apartheid perpetrators come forward to confess their crimes, including murder and torture, in return for amnesty. Coman makes no slick parallels between the political reconciliation and Berry's personal struggle with her father, except, perhaps, to show that both are difficult, incomplete. She gets exactly right the continuing racism and "apartness" that exists between white wealth and black poverty. Far from the glossy tourist-in-primitive-Africa panoramas, this story says what is. There are many parallels with the true case of Amy Biehl, the California Fulbright scholar murdered near Cape Town. Readers moved by this book might want to view the searing video *Long Night's Journey into Day* about the TRC. —Hazel Rochman

Connelly, Neil. *The Miracle Stealer*. 2010. 240p. Scholastic/Arthur A. Levine (9780545131957). Gr. 9–12.

The power and danger of religion receives a realistic, gutsy—and yet movingly spiritual—examination in this ambitious and graceful drama. "You ain't special" is what 19-year-old Andi tells her 6-year-old brother, Daniel, over and over. It's for his own protection: ever since he was rescued from a well on national TV as a baby, he has been known as "Miracle Boy," and his prayers and touches have purportedly remedied everything from stillborns to arthritis. Despite Andi's objections, her devout mother feels it is their duty to help others—especially during the Paradise Days festival that, it is hoped, will bring tourists back to their struggling town. Andi is a remarkable protagonist, a no-bullshit atheist convinced that this "superstitious crap" will damage her brother. Secondary characters breathe just as deeply: a horribly scarred but gentle reverend; Andi's ex-boyfriend, dragged into her dangerous Anti-Miracle Plan; and a creepy lurker known as Scarecrow who wants to "test" Daniel. Rarely has the dilemma of miracles been articulated so succinctly; if people start changing for the better, is it a miracle regardless of the impetus? Connelly writes with such calm assurance—never too much, never too little—that what could have been an overwhelming epic is instead a slim book that reads with miraculous speed. —Daniel Kraus

Conway, Celeste. ***The Melting Season*****. 2006. 288p. Delacorte (9780385733397). Gr. 9–12.**

Sixteen-year-old Giselle lives in a household where little has changed in the 10 years since the death of her father, a legendary dancer and choreographer. She attends a New York City school for students gifted in the arts; studies ballet under the watchful eye of her mother, an eminent former ballerina; and snatches what little free time she has with her best friend, Magda. After meeting Will, though, everything begins to change. Smart, ironic, constrained, and vulnerable, Giselle tells of the spring when her life suddenly shifts, allowing her to see the past differently and move forward in the direction of her choosing. From the opening descriptions of the school's Medieval Pageant to the difficulties of a teen communicating with her mother to the catch-your-breath evocation of first love, this novel will capture readers with vivid imagery, emotional subtlety, and fine dialogue. Often droll, the writing features apt turns of phrase and laugh-out-loud moments as well as a convincing backstory and sensitive portrayals of characters' interactions. Readers will find themselves rereading this for the sheer pleasure of spending more time with these idiosyncratic, engaging characters. —Carolyn Phelan

Cooney, Caroline B. ***A Friend at Midnight*****. 2006. 160p. Delacorte (9780385733267). Gr. 6–9.**

Readers who seek out Cooney's novels for their clever, suspenseful scenarios—as in *The Face on the Milk Carton* (1990) and its sequels—may be surprised to find that, in her latest, the expected thrills move into an exploration of Christian forgiveness. The book's first section plunges readers into the action: an 8-year-old is abandoned at an airport by his self-absorbed, negligent father, and his 15-year-old sister, Lily, makes a secret airplane journey to retrieve him. The toll that her father's cruelty takes on Lily unfolds in the book's two remaining sections, in which Cooney writes movingly about the dynamics of divorce, the hate that "occupied [Lily] like an army," and the sense of cosmic resentment that shakes her relationship with God. Though the psychological and spiritual themes may lose some readers, the promise of a resolution to Lily's anguish will pull at readers (non-Christians included) to the end, where meaty questions about God's obligation to believers, and vice versa, make the book a natural choice for youth ministers to share with teens. —Jennifer Mattson

Cooney, Caroline B. ***Hit the Road*****. 2006. 176p. Delacorte (9780385729444). Gr. 6–9.**

Brit is a brand-new driver when her parents send her to stay with grandmother Nannie while they're off on a cruise. She quickly learns she's going to have to put her driving to the test because Nannie and her college roommates, Florence and Aurelia, are determined to go to their sixty-fifth college reunion. Thus begins an on-the-road buddy story that precisely captures the impatience—and the warmth—of teenagers, as well as the fragility and stubborn audacity that comes with age. Bullied by Nannie, whose car keys have been taken from her, Brit finds herself driving through the greater Northeast to fulfill her grandmother's plans, which include hiding the trip from Brit's parents, finding Flo's house, and kidnapping Aurelia from the nursing home where her son, Aston, has stashed her. There are plenty of over-the-top moments, and Aston is a villain of the Snidely Whiplash variety. But Cooney masterfully combines nonstop, cleverly plotted action with heartfelt emotion; Brit realistically becomes frustrated with impediments that come with age, even as she valiantly protects her charges. Perhaps it takes an adult to empathize with the aging process, but Brit comes as close as possible to understanding, and she'll make teen readers realize that what really separates them from the elderly is the fact that they are experiencing doors opening, while older people are watching them close. For another on-the-road, cross-generational tale, suggest Joan Bauer's *Rules of the Road* (1998). —Ilene Cooper

Corrigan, Eireann. *Ordinary Ghosts*. 2007. Scholastic (9780439832434). Gr. 9–12.

Sixteen-year-old Emil lives alone with his militaristic father after his mother dies and his charismatic older brother, Ethan, disappears. While searching Ethan's room for drugs and clues to his whereabouts, Emil discovers that Ethan had the master key to their elite boys' school. According to school tradition, one senior holds the key, pulls off a tremendous prank, and anonymously passes the key to another student, who is expected to carry on the tradition the next year. Determined to fulfill Ethan's role, Emil sneaks into his school at night, looking for inspiration for a key-worthy prank. Instead, he finds a girl, Jade, working in the art studio. He and Jade begin talking, tiptoe around each other with their secrets, and finally develop a relationship. When Emil comes to shocking revelations about his mother's death and Ethan's sudden departure, Jade helps Emil cope with the earth-shattering news. Following two books in verse, Corrigan's first prose novel shines with language that authentically echoes teen speech patterns and slang (including some swearing). The tone and complex male protagonist will remind readers of Markus Zusack's Printz Honor Book, *I Am the Messenger* (2005). This similarly memorable novel will capture older teens with its realistic, fully developed characters who come of age on the page. —Heather Booth

Corrigan, Eireann. *Splintering*. 2004. 192p. Scholastic (9780439535977). Gr. 9–12.

A stranger high on PCP crashes a family gathering, brandishing a machete. Dad's heart gives out while fending off the intruder, who then hacks his way into the bedroom where 15-year-old Paulie is hiding. A scene from a lurid horror novel? Nope. No one dies, for one thing. Corrigan is interested in what happens after such a traumatic experience, how "the knots of people someone decided to unravel" knit themselves together again. In the same potent, naturally cadenced poetry that she applied to her own anorexia in *You Remind Me of You* (2002), Corrigan alternates between the viewpoints of fierce 15-year-old Paulie and her reclusive older brother, Jeremy, also present during the attack. Corrigan's poetry captures every nuance of the siblings' relationship, although it proves a somewhat clumsy tool for explaining the family issues that hover in the background, including some hazily described physical abuse. But teens will be drawn to the terrifying premise and the characters' searing intensity. —Ilene Cooper

Craig, Colleen. *Afrika*. 2008. 192p. Tundra (9780887768071). Gr. 7–12.

The riveting revelations of South Africa's Truth and Reconciliation Commission (TRC) are at the heart of this powerful novel, in which, like Carolyn Coman's award-winning *Many Stones* (2000), political history is fused with one girl's discovery of family secrets. Growing up in Canada, Kim, 13, has never known her father. Her mom, journalist Riana van der Merwe, refuses to talk about him or about her South African home. But when Kim goes with Riana to cover the TRC hearings for three months, she learns about her Afrikaner family roots in the heart of the rural Karroo. Then tension quietly builds, until she finally meets her father and discovers why Riana, pregnant with Kim, ran away and never returned. There is some plot contrivance, and Kim's black friend and mentor, Themba, son of a family servant in the backyard shack, is much too wise and understanding. But the author, who lived in South Africa in the 1980s (before the TRC hearings), gets the way things were for ordinary people, especially in the farm areas, exactly right. The teen outsider's viewpoint reveals the shocking apartheid cruelty, which includes what happened to Themba's father. Readers will be stirred by the connections with other history they know ("I was only carrying out orders") and by the ultimate message about forgiveness. —Hazel Rochman

Crutcher, Chris. *Whale Talk*. 2001. 224p. Greenwillow (9780688180195). Gr. 8–12.

Crutcher's fans will recognize the author's signature style and subject matter in his new novel, his first in six years. Adopted, biracial high-school senior The Tao Jones (his birth mother seems to "have been a little too 'spiritual'") is well-adjusted on the surface. A smart, likable kid with a great sense of humor and athletic ability, he glides through academia with everything an adolescent boy needs—decent grades and female companionship. What T. J. doesn't need is competitive sports, which Cutter High School jocks and coaches see as a personal snub. T. J.'s resolve weakens, however, when English teacher–coach Mr. Simet makes an unconventional offer: Be the anchor of the swim team and pick your fellow fish. Perfect, especially since racist football bully Mike Barbour has taken up letter jackets as a cause. It seems developmentally disabled Chris Coughlin has been wearing his dead brother's jacket, and Mike is annoyed. If Chris, naturally comfortable in the water, is on the swim team, T. J. reasons, Chris will earn a jacket of his own, and Mike will be put in his place. The veteran author once again uses well-constructed characters and quick pacing to examine how the sometimes cruel and abusive circumstances of life affect every link in the human chain. A heart-wrenching series of plot twists leads to an end in which goodness at least partially prevails. Through it all, as expected, shines Crutcher's sympathy for teens and their problems. —Kelly Halls

Curtis, Christopher Paul. *Bucking the Sarge*. 2004. 240p. Random/Wendy Lamb (9780385323079). Gr. 5–9.

Curtis moves from the historical fiction of *The Watsons Go to Birmingham—1963* (1995) and his Newbery Medal winner *Bud, Not Buddy* (1999) to the contemporary scene in this hilarious, anguished novel set in his hometown of Flint, Michigan. The narrator is smart, desperate 15-year-old Luther (not Loser, as some call him) Farrell, who speaks with wit, wisdom, and heartbreaking realism about family, work, school, friends, and enemies. He hates his vicious mom (the "Sarge"), who has made herself rich by milking the system, including evicting poor families from slum housing. Luther's job is to care for four men in Sarge's Adult Rehab Center, another scam. At school he wants to win the science fair medal again, even if his rival is the girl he has loved since kindergarten. Bits of philosophy from Luther's various mentors, who range from Socrates to Judge Judy, blend with the comedy and sorrow. There are some real surprises in plot and character, including a substitute parent Luther finds in an unexpected place and a science project that does change the world. His schemes of revenge and escape are barely credible, but the farce and the failure tell the truth in this gripping story. —Hazel Rochman

Danforth, Emily M. *The Miseducation of Cameron Post*. 2012. 480p. HarperCollins/Balzer and Bray (9780062020567). Gr. 9–12.

It begins with a preadolescent kiss between protagonist Cameron and her friend, Irene. The very next day Cameron's parents die in an automobile accident, and the young girl is left riddled with guilt, feeling her forbidden kiss was somehow responsible for the accident. This is an old convention of GLBT literature, but freshly handled here and given sophisticated thematic weight. As Cameron grows into her teenage years, she recognizes that she is a lesbian. After several emotional misadventures, she meets and falls in love with the beautiful Coley, who appears to be bisexual. Both girls attend the same fundamentalist church, and when Cameron's conservative Aunt Ruth discovers the affair, she remands Cameron to God's Promise, a church camp that promises to "cure" young people of their homosexuality. Such "religious conversion therapy" is rooted in reality, and Cam's experiences at the camp are at the heart of this ambitious literary novel, a multidimensional coming-of-age reminiscent of Aidan Chambers' equally ambitious *This Is All* (2006). There is nothing superficial or simplistic here, and Danforth carefully and deliberately fleshes out Cam's character and those of her family and friends. Even the eastern Montana setting is vividly realized and provides a wonderfully apposite background for the story of Cam's miseducation and the challenges her stint in the church camp pose to her development as a mature teenager finding friendship and a plausible future. —Michael Cart

De Goldi, Kate. *The 10 P.M. Question*. 2010. 256p. Candlewick (9780763649395). Gr. 7–12.

Twelve-year-old Frankie dreams of having his best friend Gigs' worry-free disposition. But in his family, Frankie feels like he is the only one who "bother[s] doing the thinking" about everything from grocery lists to smoke-alarm batteries, and nothing seems to quiet his internal "rodent voice . . . the perpetual bearer of unpalatable facts," once it gets rolling. Then irrepressible tomboy Sydney arrives at school and befriends Frankie almost against his will. Prompted by her brash charm, Frankie begins to follow Sydney's "book of wacko etiquette and, for once, talk straight and tough" about family mysteries, beginning with the most obvious and avoided question: Why does Ma never leave the house? An award-winning best-seller in New Zealand, where it was published in 2008, De Goldi's novel is an achingly poignant, wryly comic story of early adolescence that invites comparisons to works by authors as varied as Lynne Rae Perkins, Nick Hornby, and J. D. Salinger. Nearly every character, from Frankie's cheerfully sardonic teacher to the trio of pillowy, cigar-smoking aunties who give him sanctuary, is a loving, talented, unforgettable eccentric whose dialogue, much like De Goldi's richly phrased narration, combines heart-stopping tenderness with perfectly timed, deliciously zany humor. Readers from early teens through adults will be drawn to this beautifully nuanced, unsentimental view of family life, friendship, the heroic requirements of growing up, and the rewards of speaking the unspeakable out loud. —Gillian Engberg

de la Peña, Matt. *Ball Don't Lie*. 2005. 288p. Delacorte (9780385732321. Gr. 9–12.

"I think God put me here to play ball," says 17-year-old Sticky. Shuffled between foster homes since childhood, the skinny, white teen devotes himself to playing basketball at Lincoln Rec, a gritty Los Angeles gym, where he has found a family among the serious players, mostly black men. In colloquial language filled with the words and rhythms of hip-hop and the street, de la Peña's debut tells a riveting story about Sticky's struggle to secure a college basketball scholarship and deepen his relationship with his girlfriend. The disjointed narrative, which loops between past and present, may slow a few readers. Others, though, will see the nonlinear story as a reflection of Sticky's own internal journey as he faces violent childhood tragedies, his numbed emotions, and his sometimes-compulsive behavior (he repeats actions such as shoe-tying until they feel right). Teens will be strongly affected by the unforgettable, distinctly male voice; the thrilling, unusually detailed basketball action; and the questions about race, love, self-worth, and what it means to build a life without advantages. —Gillian Engberg

de la Peña, Matt. *Mexican White Boy*. 2008. 256p. Delacorte (9780385733106). Gr. 9–12.

Biracial Danny Lopez doesn't think he fits anywhere. He feels like an outsider with his Mexican father's family, with whom he is staying for the summer, and at his mostly white school, and he wonders if his confusion drove his father away. He also struggles with his obsession for baseball; a gifted player with a blazing fastball, he lacks control of his game. With the support of a new friend and his caring cousins, Danny begins to deal with the multitude of problems in his life, which includes his tendency to cut himself, an unusual characteristic in a male YA protagonist. The author juggles his many plotlines well, and the portrayal of Danny's friends and neighborhood is rich and lively. Where the story really lights up is in the baseball scenes, which sizzle like Danny's fastball. A violent scene, left somewhat unresolved, is the catalyst for him to confront the truth about his father. Danny's struggle to find his place will speak strongly to all teens but especially to those of mixed race. —Lynn Rutan

de la Peña, Matt. *We Were Here*. 2009. 368p. Delacorte (9780385736671). Gr. 7–12.

After being sentenced to a year in a California group home, Miguel Casteñeda, 16, breaks out with two other teens, Mong and Rondell. Together, they try to cross the border to Mexico, and Miguel writes in his journal about their journey. His colloquial narrative, laced with insults (but not obscenities), is fast, funny, smart, and heartbreaking as he describes how the three homeless runaways steal, hide, work, fight, bond, and care for each other. Unlike his mates, Miguel is an avid reader, and with the account of their daily struggle, he weaves in references to classics. There may be too much detail for some, but the contemporary survival adventure will keep readers hooked, as will the tension that builds from the story's secrets. What did Miguel do that landed him in the group home? Why won't his mother talk to him? The riveting climax shows, without a heavy message, that the hero's journey is a search for himself. —Hazel Rochman

Dessen, Sarah. *Along for the Ride*. 2009. 384p. Viking (9780670011940). Gr. 9–12.

Dessen has built a well-deserved reputation for delicately depicting teen girls in turmoil. This novel showcases a socially awkward young woman who seeks solace in the comforting rigidity of academic success. Auden is about to start college in the fall, and decides to escape her control-freak professor mom to spend the summer with her novelist father, his new young wife, and their brand-new baby daughter, Thisbe. Over the course of the summer, Auden tackles many new projects: learning to ride a bike, making real connections with peers, facing the emotional fallout of her parents' divorce, distancing herself from her mother, and falling in love with Eli, a fellow insomniac bicyclist recovering from his own traumas. The cover may mislead readers, as despite the body language of the girl in pink and the hunky blue-jeaned boy balanced on a bike, this is no slight romance: there's real substance here. Dessen's many fans will not be deterred by the length or that cover; they expect nuanced, subtle writing, and they won't be disappointed. —Debbie Carton

Dessen, Sarah. *Just Listen*. 2006. 384p. Viking (9780670061051). Gr. 8–11.

After being caught with her best friend's Sophie's boyfriend at a summer party, Annabel Greene is starting her junior year alone and ostracized. But what appeared to be infidelity was really attempted rape. Fans of Laurie Halse Anderson's *Speak* (1999) will find obvious parallels here, including the play on the title, but Dessen spins her own quality tale of a young girl finding her voice, and finding an audience. Annabel's troubles are exacerbated by her family's refusal to acknowledge its problems: middle sister Whitney's severe anorexia or the three sisters' waning interest in modeling. A budding friendship with classmate Owen, a DJ at the community radio station who is never without music to drown out the silence, helps Annabel listen to her own heart and risk speaking out honestly. Characterization and dialogue are expertly done, and Owen's anger-management advice and efforts to broaden Annabel's music tastes ("Don't think, or judge. Just listen") strengthen the theme of the story: honesty. Teen girls who meet Dessen for the first time here will be looking for her backlist. —Cindy Dobrez

Dessen, Sarah. *This Lullaby*. 2002. 352p. Viking (9780670035304). Gr. 8–12.

Remy never knew her father, but everyone knows the song he wrote for her, "This Lullaby," a schmaltzy tune with the line, "I will let you down." Well, he did, and Remy expects every boy to do the same thing, so she stays in control of her relationships. When Remy meets Dexter the summer after she graduates from high school, she breaks her cardinal rule: never get involved with a musician. And oh, the horror: irrepressible Dexter makes her care too much. This is a very full book. Remy's fear of commitment juxtaposed against her mother's embracement of life is the main theme, but subplots about a wandering stepdad, a smitten brother, and the affairs of assorted friends also take space. Moreover, the story evolves over a summer—and sometimes reads like every day of it. What's wonderful, however, is that this nuanced book is also a real romance; Dessen, who can turn out terrific prose, gets every feeling, every touch just right. Remy and Dexter (especially Dexter) jump off the pages into the hearts of readers, who will wish for a romance like this of their own. —Ilene Cooper

Dole, Mayra Lazara. ***Down to the Bone*****. 2008. 384p. HarperTeen (9780060843106). Gr. 9–12.**

After being expelled from her Catholic school for being lesbian, Lauri, 17, is thrown out by her Cuban mom for being "abnormal." Worst of all, Lauri's beloved partner, Marlena, leaves and does her family's bidding by marrying a man. Lauri gets a job and finds a home with her straight, black friend, Soli, and she begins to wonder if she can fall in love with a guy and regain her family and acceptance. At the same time she has her own prejudices to overcome. The dialogue is fast and funny in this debut novel, which is set in Miami's Cuban American community. Laura's first-person, present-tense narrative shows and tells the farce and the sorrow at home, and teens will recognize some of the traditional prejudices, as well as the joy of friendship and the happiness of real love ("my smile barely fits in my face"). Supportive precisely because it is laugh-out-loud irreverent (in one hilarious scene Laura and Soli mock their tacky quinces with their pink-ruffled gowns), this breakthrough novel is sure to be welcomed. —Hazel Rochman

Ehrenberg, Pamela. ***Ethan, Suspended*****. 2007. 265p. Eerdmans (9780802853240). Gr. 7–10.**

After Ethan is suspended from his suburban Philadelphia junior high, his soon-to-be-divorced mother sends him to the grandparents he barely knows in an inner-city neighborhood in Washington, D.C. Suddenly the white, privileged kid finds that he is the "cracker" freak in an almost entirely black and Latino school. He feels as if he is in a time warp—no IM, cable, or malls. And he feels alone, often eating lunch by himself at school. But as he makes some friends, falls in love with smart, beautiful Kameka, learns to play oboe in the jazz band, and works on a school project on civil rights, he comes to redefine his meaning of home. In her first novel, Ehrenberg focuses on themes of race and class without sounding preachy, and the politics are right at the surface in an unforgettable scene, in which Ethan's friend, Diego, connects segregation and poverty: "You don't need no laws to keep people out if people can't afford to go there." Ethan's first-person narrative about his family conflicts drive the story and reveal the issues. Best of all are the portraits of his scrappy Jewish grandparents. Along with the hilarious details of how they obsess about weird stuff, eat healthy food, and irritate each other and Ethan, there is also Ethan's growing respect for their decision not to leave their neighborhood. —Hazel Rochman

Ellis, Ann Dee. ***This Is What I Did*****. 2007. 176p. Little, Brown (9780316013635). Gr. 6–9.**

Eighth-grader Logan is struggling to deal with a violent situation he witnessed a year ago between his best friend, Zyler, and Zyler's abusive father but insists to everyone around him that he is fine. Just fine. Reluctant readers will be drawn into this story, which also includes bullying classmates and a dismal winter camping trip. Frequent line breaks, screenplay-style dialogue, and e-mails and notes illustrated with black icons break up the scenes. Logan gets to play one of the Lost Boys in the school play, and finds that the theater crowd offers a respite from bullies. A friendship with a girl named Laurel (a palindrome collector who is thinking of changing her name to Laral) and a relationship with a counselor help Logan to begin the healing process and convince him to reconnect with Zyler. This psychological drama effectively explores our failure to protect youth from abuse inflicted by peers or adults. Caution: there's a slang term for *scrotum* on page 1. —Cindy Dobrez

Farish, Terry. ***The Good Braider*****. 2012. 224p. Amazon Children's (9780761462675). Gr. 8–12.**

Like Mark Bixler's adult book *The Lost Boys of Sudan* (2005), this powerful novel tells today's refugee story from a young viewpoint, but here the Sudanese teen is a girl. In free-verse poems, Viola, 16, remembers being driven from home in the brutal civil war, then the long, barefoot trek to Khartoum and Cairo, escaping land mines and suffering hunger along the way, until at last she and her mother get refugee status, board a plane, and join her uncle in Portland, Maine's Sudanese community. Never exploitative, Viola's narrative will grip readers with its harsh truths: the shame of her rape in Sudan and the loss of her "bride wealth"; the heartbreak when her little brother dies during their escape; her wrenching separation from her grandmother. The contemporary drama in Maine is also moving and immediate. At 17, Viola is thrilled to go to school, and she makes friends, even a boyfriend who teaches her to drive: but can he get over her rape? Always there is her mother, enraged by the new ways. An essential addition to the growing list of strong immigrant stories for youth. —Hazel Rochman

Ferris, Jean. *Eight Seconds*. 2000. 192p. Harcourt (9780152023676). Gr. 6–12.

Despite a childhood heart operation that has left him feeling different from others, 18-year-old cowboy John Ritchie goes to rodeo camp with high aspirations for success. Although he and his buddies do well, their skills pale in comparison to those of handsome, mature Kit. But after becoming friends with Kit, John discovers his new rodeo friend is gay, and his old perceptions are challenged in a way that changes him forever. Ferris burrows her story firmly, and very authentically, in the heart of her characters. Through John's thoughts, Kit's dialogue, and a wealth of raging emotions that pack dramatic punch, she compassionately shares the challenges of gay teens, both those comfortable with who they are, and those just discovering their true feelings. In this context, she explores quite eloquently what it means to really accept oneself and one's friends. This is one of the best novels on this theme; older teens looking for others may want to read William Taylor's *The Blue Lawn* (1999). —Roger Leslie

Ferris, Jean. *Of Sound Mind*. 2001. 224p. Farrar (9780374355807). Gr. 6–9.

Change with a capital C comes crashing down on a high-school senior, the only hearing member of his family. Forced since childhood into the twin roles of interpreter and, sometimes, caretaker, Theo finds himself doing a bit of wing stretching after meeting Ivy. Ivy can both hear and sign, but she also makes friends easily and is such a self-starter that she's already running a small catering business. Then Theo's loving, affectionate father suffers a stroke, leaving him suddenly in charge of a dependent younger brother, a semi-invalid parent, and, hardest of all, a demanding, high-strung, seriously unstable mother. Although Ferris warns at the outset that this is "not a factual discussion of the complexities of deafness," those complexities twine about every relationship and situation here. But she does more than "inform"; along with a sensitive portrayal of the dynamics within Theo's family, she creates a cast of characters who are shaped by much more than their ability or inability to hear. This is, then, both a thought-provoking study of just when being deaf matters and when it does not, and an unusually rich coming-of-age story that explores universal issues of family responsibility, emotional maturation, love, and loss. —John Peters

Flake, Sharon G. *Begging for Change*. 2003. 240p. Hyperion (9780786806010). Gr. 7–12.

"Would *you* be all right if your mother got hit in the head with a pipe and your father was high as a kite?" In this sequel to *Money Hungry* (2001) Raspberry Hill's mother is in the hospital after being attacked by a neighborhood teenage girl, and Raspberry's father, homeless and addicted to drugs, resurfaces. Terrified that she and her mother may land back on the streets, Raspberry steals money from a friend. Is she turning into her father? Flake's charged, infectious dialogue will sweep readers through the first-person story as Raspberry describes her fears and moral quandaries; her new romance; her fierce love for her mother; and her powerful, conflicted feelings about her dad. Although vivid images of urban poverty, violence, and drug addiction clearly illustrate why Raspberry is so afraid, Flake never sensationalizes. The identity struggles of some of Raspberry's biracial friends threaten, at times, to distract from the main story, but Flake manages ultimately to balance her many plots and blend them into a hopeful novel that encourages readers to share Raspberry's questions: Can money buy security? How do you forgive those who have hurt you? Does violence ever stop rippling through a community once it begins? —Gillian Engberg

Flake, Sharon G. *Money Hungry*. 2001. 208p. Disney/Jump at the Sun (9780786805488). Gr. 7–10.

"If you got money, people can't take stuff from you—not your house, or your ride, not your family. They can't do nothing much to you, if you got a bankroll backing you up." Thirteen-year-old Raspberry Hill knows what it's like not to have security. After leaving her drug-addicted father, Raspberry and her mother lived on friends' couches and on the street before they landed in the projects. Now, while Raspberry's mom works two jobs and goes to school, Raspberry obsessively does anything she can to grow that bankroll to back her up; she sells pencils and old candy; cleans houses for the elderly; and washes cars at stoplights. Her three close friends both support her and mock her. There's Mia, who fights against her Korean and African American parents, wanting to identify herself only as black; Ja'nae, who lives with loving grandparents but yearns for her flaky, estranged mother; and Zora, whose divorced physician father, Dr. Mitchell, seems to be romancing Raspberry's mother, which upsets both girls. The razor-sharp dialogue and unerring details evoke characters, rooms, and neighborhoods with economy and precision, creating a story that's immediate, vivid, and unsensationalized. Without synthetic drama or stereotypes, Flake shows poverty and how it touches everyone, whether it's the actual absence of money or the fear of losing it. A few of the characters are less developed; Dr. Mitchell in particular is vague and a little too perfect. But Flake creates scenes of heart-stopping tenderness and tension between Raspberry and her friends and especially with her mother, as they struggle to leave the projects, suffering breakdowns and break-ins along the way, finally moving into a house of their own. Whatever teens' own familial insecurities may be, they will read something of their own lives in this title from the author of *The Skin I'm In* (1998). —Gillian Engberg

Flake, Sharon G. *Who Am I Without Him?* 2004. 160p. Disney/Jump at the Sun (9780786806935). Gr. 6–12.

Hilarious and anguished, these 10 short stories about growing up black today speak with rare truth about family, friends, school, and especially about finding a boyfriend. Erika is a "ghetto girl" who likes white boys; she can't help it, and the other black kids in school can't stand her, because they know. Class is a big issue for Erin, who steals clothes so he can take a suburban girl to the homecoming dance. The church girls are forbidden to date, and they get hurt when they go hunting for boys. But their well-meaning parents don't have it right, and the girls won't stop looking. As with Janet MacDonald's fiction, the talk here is wild, angry, and outrageous, but there's no overt sex or obscenity. Yes, there are messages, but the narrative is never preachy or uplifting; it's honest about the pain. When one girl's boyfriend hits her, she apologizes "just like my momma does when daddy slaps her." The best advice comes from a dad who abandoned his family, who now tells his teenage daughter how to avoid getting stuck with someone like him ("you is so much more than a pretty face and a tight pair of jeans, some boy's girlfriend or some man's wife"). Not everyone makes it. The stories work because Flake never denies the truths of poverty, prejudice, and failure. —Hazel Rochman

Fleischman, Paul. *Breakout*. 2003. 128p. Cricket/Marcato (9780812626964). Gr. 9–12.

Seventeen-year-old Del, a perpetual foster child, is breaking out. A rusting Datsun is taking her out of town, but it's the traffic jam on the freeway that gives her the time to frame a new life. Amplifying this structure are two concurrent narratives: Del's interior monologue as she worries, rages, and waits for the logjam to break, and a narrative taking place eight years in the future, as Del, a playwright now calling herself Elena, performs her one-woman show about being caught in freeway traffic. Del is a sharp observer, and the jam-up allows her to notice the people around her: a father trying to sell insurance and care for a baby at the same time; a guy tutoring a younger man in the art of picking up women, who mistakenly tries his tactics on a lesbian. Elena's narrative, less specific and more wide-ranging, reveals some of the decisions that she made to get to where she is. This artful, insightful work makes demands on its readers, but teenagers will find the rewards very much worth the effort. —Ilene Cooper

Fleischman, Paul. *Seek*. 2001. 176p. Cricket/Marcato (9780812649000). Gr. 7–12.

Like *Joyful Noise* (2004), which works best when performed aloud, this scriptlike story, "a collage of voices," begs to be used as readers' theater. But even teens who read the story silently will be struck by the unfolding sound bites, which will remind them of what they hear when someone continuously hits the "seek" button on a radio. Seventeen-year-old Rob has to write an autobiography for his senior thesis. Realizing that he "grew up in a house built of voices" and that he keeps "listening back" rather than looking back, he decides to write a sound self-portrait. As Rob recounts his past and the influences of his polyglot mother, storytelling grandmother, and history professor grandfather, he also describes his search over the airwaves for his musician-DJ father, who left after Rob was born. Readers will be drawn in quickly: Rob is an appealing narrator, and the story of how he gradually comes to terms with his father's absence (and unexpected reentry into his life) is alternately quirky, comic, and poignant. —Chris Sherman

Flinn, Alex. *Breathing Underwater*. 2001. 272p. HarperCollins (9780060291983). Gr. 9–12.

A diary format, an enticing locale, and the hot issue of abusive teen relationships combine in a quick and absorbing read. Key Biscayne High School sophomore Nick is rich, handsome, and a good athlete and scholar. He has finally found the girl of his dreams in Caitlin. Unfortunately, his father's physical and verbal abuse has shaped Nick's ideas of how to behave in a relationship: he bullies, tortures, and finally hits Caitlin. A restraining order and an anger-management course result in the diary entries we read, with flashbacks that show how Nick got to this point. Noteworthy in this first novel is Nick's believable relationship with best friend Tom, full of awkward silences and shameful secrets. The situations and dialogue ring frighteningly true, perhaps due to the author's background as a lawyer who has tried domestic violence cases. No graphic sex, but realistic violence makes this more appropriate for high-school readers. —Debbie Carton

Forman, Gayle. *If I Stay*. 2009. 208p. Dutton (9780525421030). Gr. 10–12.

Forman (*Sisters in Sanity*, 2007) provides a compelling and highly textured account of the brutal 24 hours that may be 17-year-old Mia's last. Her day starts with a drive, with her loving and moderately punk parents and her effervescent little brother, to a bookstore. A collision with another vehicle leaves Mia's parents dead. The narrative is told in a robust first-person voice, with flashbacks, flash-forwards, and out-of-body reports on her immediate surroundings as Mia is transported, in grave condition, to the hospital. The story then follows the medical efforts to save her life, extended family and friends' efforts to provide emotional care, and Mia's coming to terms with what has happened and what might still await her. Mia, a gifted cellist, finds support from her alt-rock boyfriend and a best friend whose own mother is a hysteric. Mia's recounting of this critical day is laced with insight, good humor, and wonder, allowing the reader to enter the scene as fully as Mia herself seems to have, at least for now, left her broken body. More developed and satisfying than a Lurlene McDaniel drama, Mia's story will engage readers willing to suspend their disbelief that the future can be seen in the present. —Francisca Goldsmith

Frank, E. R. *America*. 2002. 256p. Atheneum/Richard Jackson (9780689847295). Gr. 10–12.

"This is what I think. You can know who you're mad at but still know you're bad and ought to be dead." America is a survivor of sexual abuse. A mixed-race teenager born to a crack-addicted mother, he was rejected as a baby by adoptive white parents "after he started turning his color." His childhood swings between years lost within an incompetent system and a home that's at first loving and then abusive. America tells his own story in chapters that alternate between the "then" of his past and the "now" of the hospital where he has landed after years of institutionalized care and, finally, a suicide attempt. Raging and honest, America's voice is straight off the street: a favorite response is "that's pussy"; his confused, surreal nightmares swirl with "tits and dicks." Frank, the author of the much-acclaimed *Life Is Funny* (2000), exposes with compassion, clarity, and deeply unsettling detail the profound shame and horror of abuse as well as the erratic nature of a medical system that tries to reclaim the victims. She also creates an extraordinary character in America who, with the help of his doctor, confronts the deepest betrayals and, finally, lets himself be found. A piercing, unforgettable novel. —Gillian Engberg

Frank, E. R. *Friction*. 2003. 208p. Atheneum (9780689853845). Gr. 9–12.

Twelve-year-old Alex loves Forest Alternative school: she plays soccer with the guys; her best friend, Tim, is in her class; and her all-day teacher is Simon, who's young, energetic, and adored by the students. But a new student, Stacy, changes things with her outrageous stories, her family secrets, and her way of seeing sex in everything, including the way that Simon interacts with Alex. Alex doesn't believe Stacy, but as her classmates begin to second-guess Simon, she wonders, too, and her confusion and anxiety become overwhelming, and she's unsure how to talk about her feelings to her loving but overextended parents. Frank tells a riveting story of abuse and peer pressure in Alex's pitch-perfect voice that's just on the cusp of adolescence. Never too self-aware, Alex describes her anguish in palpable terms—"it crushes my stomach." Frank has a keen awareness of the subtle power and politics of middle-school groups, and she weaves messages about good and bad touching seamlessly into the text. Like *America* (2002), but for a younger audience, this gripping, unsettling novel is filled with fully realized characters who are faced with unspeakable abuse and adult betrayals. —Gillian Engberg

Frank, E. R. *Life Is Funny*. 2000. 272p. DK Ink/Richard Jackson (9780789426345). Gr. 7–12.

First novelist Frank breaks new ground with a realistic, lyrical novel about 11 teens in Brooklyn now. Without drowning in particulars that will date overnight, their contemporary voices ring true. Their talk is painful, rough, sexy, funny, fearful, furious, gentle. Each chapter, each vignette within a chapter, builds to its own climax, and the stories weave together to surprise you. The first time Eric appears, he is seen through the eyes of Ebony and her friends: he's the glaring special ed. kid with a "hatchet murder face," every sentence a curse. Later he speaks in his own voice, and he's a tender, fiercely protective "father" to his little brother, Mickey, who asks, "Why Mama putting a needle in her?" There's Grace, a beautiful white girl, who defies her racist mother and leans on Ebony and her friends. And there's hyperactive Gingerbread, on "riddle-in," born to a crack addict, adopted as a baby by a caring, middle-class interracial couple. He's smart and strong and lucky, and he tells you so in a galloping, rhythmic narrative. He loves Keisha, who loves him. It's sometimes hard to keep track of the huge cast, but the voices are distinct, heartfelt. This would be a great book for readers' theater and for group discussion. Teens will open up to the yearning and the poetry in their own daily lives. —Hazel Rochman

Frank, Hilary. *Better Than Running at Night*. 2002. 240p. Houghton (9780618104390). Gr. 10–12.

With honesty, wit, and a wild first-person narrative, this first novel breaks boundaries in YA fiction with a story about college freshman Ellie Yelinsky and her search for art, love, sex, and meaning. On the night Ellie loses her virginity with fellow art student Nate, she enjoys the touching, but when he pushes inside her, she can't wait for it to be over. She thinks she could love Nate—but not while he has all those other girlfriends. He is too much like her ex-hippie mom, who slept around so much that Ellie, to her deep sorrow, will never know the identity of her biological father. Frank makes Ellie's intellectual quest just as exciting as her love life. She learns a lot from her wildly eccentric, gifted art teacher, who yells about discipline, work, and subtlety. The laughter and the truth here are in the details, especially when Frank skewers the pretentiousness of the art scene ("I place headphones on a tomato and play Bach," one student declaims). Great monologue material for readers' theater, this is clearly for older high-schoolers and college students, who will recognize the wry self-parody and the insider's raw wicked take on coming-of-age. —Hazel Rochman

Frank, Hilary. ***The View from the Top.*** **2010. 240p. Dutton (9780525422419). Gr. 8–12.**

Everything begins and ends with Anabelle in Frank's richly layered, interconnected short stories about a group of small-town high-school students in their last summer before college. Anabelle's egocentric boyfriend, Matt, calculates how the quality and quantity of his art will increase as a result of their inevitable breakup. Jonah, Matt's buddy and resident Lothario, considers hooking up with Anabelle to distance himself from a messy dalliance with an older woman. Lexi, Matt's sister, is trying to work up the courage to tell Anabelle that she wants to be more than friends, while rich, depressed Mary-Tyler has a chance meeting with Anabelle that raises both of their spirits. Quiet, intense Tobin, who loves Anabelle from afar, contemplates telling her how he feels when they find themselves together at the top of a Ferris wheel at summer's end. And Anabelle? She is just struggling to understand who she is, let alone who she is in a relationship. These elegantly written character-driven episodes, each from a different point of view, intimately examine issues of unrequited love, social class, and identity seeking through pitch-perfect interactions that teens will find achingly familiar. Like Natalie Standiford's *How to Say Goodbye in Robot* (2009), this quirky love story about falling for yourself first will appeal to teens' hearts and heads. —Jennifer Hubert

Fredericks, Mariah. ***The True Meaning of Cleavage.*** **2003. 224p. Simon & Schuster/Richard Jackson (9780689850929). Gr. 7–10.**

Sari is "madly, psychotically" in love with David, a senior at Manhattan's Eldridge Alternative School. Jess, a freshman like Sari, and the story's narrator, has not crossed the psychological divide that makes boyfriends more important than girlfriends and is frustrated, even frightened, as Sari begins drifting away when David shows some interest. But rather than a girlfriend (he already has one of those, a cool kid like himself), Sari is his backstreet girl, dutifully visiting David to service him on Thursday afternoons and telling herself they have a secret romance. At first, Jess tries to be a supportive friend, but in a fit of pique, she discloses the relationship to a blabbermouth, and the law of unintended consequences immediately kicks in. Fredericks, a first-time novelist, writes with amazing truth and perception. These characters are kids whom readers see every day, and the emotions so clearly on display are ones that they've experienced in their guts. Some readers will recognize Jess' wrenching feelings of being left behind and the desperate gyrations to turn the world right again. But others will identify with Sari, whose first hormonal surges lead her to places like behind a bathroom door at a party, when she first catches David's eye. The book's ending is both honest and hopeful. Things happen, corrections are made, and then—with luck—everyone moves on. —Ilene Cooper

Freitas, Donna. ***The Possibilities of Sainthood.*** **2008. 288p. Farrar/Frances Foster (9780374360870). Gr. 8–10.**

Fifteen-year-old Antonia Labella is a busy girl. She goes to Catholic school, helps her widowed mother in the family grocery, and dreams about kissing Andy Rotellini. However, updating her saint diaries is the most pleasurable way to fill her time. Each year Antonia starts a new diary, filling it with pictures and cards of saints to venerate and pasting in copies of her letters to the Vatican as well as the infrequent replies. Antonia writes regularly, noting oversights in patron-saint specializations and recommending the logical candidate to fill the position—that would always be Antonia. First-time novelist Freitas hops into the romance genre and brightens and heightens it by providing characters who are anything but run-of-the-mill (though Mom's a little stereotypical) and expanding the tale to include a religious fervor not usually seen in today's teens, not so amusingly anyway. Yes, it's kind of silly that Antonia thinks she has a shot at being the Patron Saint of the Kiss, but her first-person narrative is so smile inducing, it's easy to go along with the premise. As Antonia sorts out her feelings for longtime crush Andy, as well as Michael, the boy who makes her blush, readers will be hard-pressed to decide what interests them most—make-out sessions or martyrs. —Ilene Cooper

Freymann-Weyr, Garret. *After the Moment*. 2009. 336p. Houghton (9780618605729). Gr. 10–12.

As in the Printz Honor Book *My Heartbeat* (2002) and other novels, Freymann-Weyr offers another rare, sophisticated exploration of love at the end of adolescence. After Leigh moves from New York City to Maryland to live with his father, stepmother, and adoring stepsister, he meets and falls deeply for Maia, a "huge head case," who battles anorexia, along with a list of other challenges. Tracking back from a portentous first scene, set four years later when Leigh and Maia meet by chance at a Manhattan party, the story focuses on the teens' emotionally wrenching senior year, which begins in love before a possible date rape sets off escalating tragedy. Leigh's mother worries that he "works too hard at being good," and Freymann-Weyr writes with extraordinary perception and depth about his yearning to act with integrity and care for everyone around him. Leigh's struggle to come to terms with the recent U.S. invasion of Iraq sometimes feel purposeful, but his response touches on broader themes of violence and how it permeates public and private worlds. Within this story's raw, honest, psychologically attuned scenes, older teens will find their own aching questions about how best to love, shape a future, and "do the right thing." —Gillian Engberg

★ Freymann-Weyr, Garret. *My Heartbeat*. 2002. 160p. Houghton (9780618141814). Gr. 8–12.

This beautiful novel tells a frank, upbeat story of teen bisexual love in all its uncertainty, pain, and joy. Ellen, 14, has always been very close with her brilliant older brother, Link, and since seventh grade she's been "totally madly in love" with Link's gorgeous best friend, James. She hangs out with the boys as they watch classic foreign movies and talk and argue about books and art and everything. Unlike the teen characters in many recent YA novels, Ellen isn't shocked to discover that the boy she loves is gay. She's always known that James loves her brother. When the rumors start at school that Link and James are a "couple," Link breaks away, won't talk about it, starts a relationship with a girl, and deliberately scuttles his college-entrance exams. Finally Ellen has James to herself. He has had sex with men and he loves Link, but he also loves her. There's some contrived interweaving of the classics Ellen is reading—*Pride and Prejudice* ("boring!"), *Jane Eyre* ("the best ever")—but readers will appreciate the connections. The fast, clipped dialogue will sweep teens into the story, as will Ellen's immediate first-person, present-tense narrative, "curious, careful, kind, and intense." The family dynamics are just as compelling as the love and friendship drama, especially Ellen's bewilderment about the unwritten laws that can make people strangers even within the family they love. —Hazel Rochman

Freymann-Weyr, Garret. *Stay with Me*. 2006. 320p. Houghton (9780618605712). Gr. 10–12.

Leila Abranel's dyslexia makes both books and situations difficult to read, and her life is full of opaque relationships. At 16, she is the youngest daughter of a father who has two daughters from a previous marriage, both 20-some years older than Leila. Along with their mother, these other Abranels, Clare and Rebecca, are mysterious and intriguing to Leila, pieces of a family with an interesting history that doesn't seem to be hers. Then Rebecca commits suicide, and Leila is determined to find out why. She goes to live with Clare, and begins a search to learn what happened to Rebecca—and what will happen to her. Freyman-Weyr's beautiful *My Heartbeat* (2002) also dealt with the complications of family dynamics, but where that book had an immediate energy, this first-person narrative is leisurely, even as Leila pushes hard against the waves of memory and loss. Elegant and sophisticated, this is a young adult novel only because of Leila's age; almost everyone else in the book is an adult—even Leila's lover, a 31-year-old television writer. Like Leila, readers often feel awkwardness coupled with anticipation in the adult world, and capturing this duality is one of the book's many strengths. Like Andreas Steinhofel's *Center of the World* (2005), this novel pushes the markers of YA fiction onward and upward. —Ilene Cooper

Frost, Helen. ***Keesha's House*. 2003. 128p. Farrar/ Frances Foster (9780374340643). Gr. 6–10.**

Like Virginia Euwer Wolff's *True Believer* (2001) and much contemporary YA fiction, this moving first novel tells the story in a series of dramatic monologues that are personal, poetic, and immediate, with lots of line breaks that make for easy reading, alone or in readers' theater. Keesha finds shelter in a house in her inner-city neighborhood and helps other troubled teens find home and family there ("like finding a sister when I'm old / enough to pick a good one"). Stephie is pregnant, and she's heartbroken that her boyfriend doesn't want the baby. Harris is gay; his dad has thrown him out. Carmen is fighting addiction. Dontay's parents are in jail, and he doesn't feel comfortable in his latest foster home. Interwoven with the angry, desperate teen voices are those of the adults in their lives: caring, helpless, abusive, indifferent. In a long note, Frost talks about the poetic forms she has used, the sestina and the sonnet. But most readers will be less interested in that framework than in the characters, drawn with aching realism, who speak poetry in ordinary words and make connections. —Hazel Rochman

Fusco, Kimberly Newton. ***Tending to Grace*. 2004. 176p. Knopf (9780375828621). Gr. 7–10.**

Like Katherine Paterson's classic *The Great Gilly Hopkins* (1978) and many other stories of the rejected kid who finds a family with a rough solitary older adult, this quiet, beautiful first novel makes the search for home a searing drama. Cornelia, 14, is dumped by her mother and stuck with elderly Great-aunt Agatha in a backwoods cottage thick with dust, cobwebs, and dirty dishes. There's not even a toilet. An unusual twist on the theme is that Cornelia arrives with a crate of books, including *Oliver Twist* and *Tom Sawyer*. She knows she's "a bookworm, a bibliophile," and, yes, she finds metaphor in ordinary things. But no one knows how smart she is, because she's ashamed of her stammering and barely speaks. With poetic simplicity, her desperate first-person, present-tense narrative, rooted in the physical facts of her life, reveals how she feels "caught in that lonely place between what I want to say and what I can't." She and Agatha slam doors and scream; they discover secrets and hurt each other deeply. But Cornelia's speech improves, and she no longer looks away when she talks. Readers may guess the secrets, and the ending is predictable, but there's wonderful drama in the relationship, and mixed with all the sorrow is helpless laughter. —Hazel Rochman

Gallo, Donald R., ed. ***Destination Unexpected*. 2003. 221p. Candlewick (9780763617646). Gr. 7–12.**

This outstanding collection of 10 short stories features teen protagonists experiencing a transforming experience while on some kind of journey. In Joyce Sweeney's "Something Old, Something New," Darius is apprehensive about leaving his poor neighborhood to go to a rich part of town to receive an award for a writing contest, but his fears are put to rest when he is warmly welcomed as a writer among equals instead of a poor black kid. Margaret Haddix's "My People" features a high-school girl from rural Appalachia who attends a summer college program and discovers that living in the city or suburbs and having money does not necessarily make one smarter or more sophisticated. Graham Salisbury, Alex Flinn, Kimberly Willis Holt, Ron Koertge, David Lubar, Richard Peck, Will Weaver, and Ellen Wittlinger contribute stories, as well. Whether humorous or serious, the stories are consistently well written and engaging. They will be great for booktalking as they will appeal to a wide range of teen readers. A solid roundup from an experienced anthologist. —Ed Sullivan

Gallo, Donald R., ed. ***On The Fringe*. 2001. 240p. Dial (9780803726567). Gr. 7–10.**

There's no question it's tough to put together a good written-to-order anthology, but once again Gallo has managed very well. This time, the subject is outsiders, and to be sure, the stories come complete with moral underpinnings. They are, however, sufficiently different to keep interest high, and, as usual, they have been written by a talented bunch of YA authors already familiar to many teen readers. Ron Koertge's biting story is laced with his typical humor; Jack Gantos' dark, cynical tale is built around the main character in his YA novel *Desire Lines* (1997); and Chris Crutcher's story, the most graphic and, arguably, the most philosophical in the mix, recalls headline events at Columbine High School. Joan Bauer, Angela Johnson, and Graham Salisbury are among the other contributors. Teens will find plenty of stereotypic geeks and nerds, but they'll also find outsiders who are unexpected. The discovery may make them think about who's "in" and who's "out," and why. Information about each of the 11 authors, often with an e-mail address, follows each selection. —Stephanie Zvirin

Garsee, Jeannine. *Say the Word*. 2009. 368p. Bloomsbury (9781599903330). Gr. 9–12.

Ten years ago, Shawna's mom, Penny, came out, moved out, and never looked back. For 10 years Shawna aspired to be everything her protective, perfectionist father, Jack, wanted her to be, distancing herself as much as possible from the shame that Penny's abandonment caused her. But at 17, Shawna is pulled by her mother's death into contact with Penny's partner, Fran, and their sons, Arye, 17, and Schmule, 10. Jack, who legally remains Penny's next of kin, financially ruins Fran's family and then goes after Schmule, who is revealed to be Penny and Jack's biological child. Shawna finds herself questioning her allegiances, but she is powerless in the shadow of her domineering father. The more Shawna tries to connect with Schmule and to make amends with Fran and Arye, the more vicious Jack becomes, leaving Shawna alone to deal with the dawning realization that Schmule is a great danger to himself. There are many issues at play in this powerful and compelling novel—gay rights, acceptance, shame, first love, domestic violence, harassment, depression—all swirling around Shawna, whose thoughts and emotions are not always politically correct, but are always genuine. This sensitive and heart-wrenching story slowly unfolds into a gripping read featuring realistically flawed characters who undergo genuine growth. —Heather Booth

★ Going, K. L. *Fat Kid Rules the World*. 2003. 177p. Putnam (9780803729483). Gr. 8–12.

His name is Troy, but to the world—and in his internal dialogues—he is the Fat Kid. Really Fat. Almost 300 pounds of sweating, unhappy insecurity. Then out of a moment of despair comes magic. As Troy considers whether to splatter himself on a subway track, Curt MacCrae, a charismatic punk rocker/homeless kid/dropout, comes along and stops him. For the price of a meal, Curt befriends Troy, and he sees something under all those layers: a potential musician, a friend, and someone with the ability to see through life's bull. First-time novelist Going has put together an amazing assortment of characters. Troy is the ultimate fat kid, the kind whose every move, every thought is predicated on what it is like to wear a coat of blubber. Curt, as thin as Troy is fat, is a combination of Kurt Cobain, Ratso Rizzo, and a fairy godfather. He sprinkles Troy with the dirt and grime of punk rock and brings out the prince hiding inside the weight (to the book's credit, Troy doesn't get any thinner). Equally well drawn are the lesser characters, including Troy's father, a former Marine with an innate sense of what kids need. The narrative could have been tighter in places, but this is an impressive debut that offers hope for all kids—dross transmuted into gold. —Ilene Cooper

Going, K. L. *Saint Iggy*. 2006. 272p. Harcourt (9780152057954). Gr. 8–11.

When he is suspended from high school for an altercation with a teacher, Iggy feels completely misunderstood. As he waits for the hearing that will decide whether he will be expelled, he vows to change everyone's perception of him by following his principal's advice: "Do something that contributes to the world." Expecting no support from his drug-addicted mother and "stoned off his ass" father, Iggy turns to a former tutor and friend, Mo, a college dropout interested in pot and Eastern religions. Then Mo's own drug habit escalates. With Iggy tagging along, Mo heads to his wealthy parents' apartment for money, and in Mo's mother, Iggy finds the parental care he craves. Readers will want to talk about the shocking ending and its religious imagery, which raises questions about martyrdom, class politics, and the many ways that children can slip away from help. Going, the author of the Printz Honor Book *Fat Kid Rules the World* (2003), grounds her story in grim, realistic urban details, and she creates a memorable character in Iggy, whose first-person voice is earnest, angry, and sarcastic, and filled with small insights that reveal how people care for and mistreat each other. Teens will connect with Iggy's powerful sense that although he notices everything, he is not truly seen and accepted himself. —Gillian Engberg

Goode, Laura. *Sister Mischief*. 2011. 352p. Candlewick (9780763646400). Gr. 10–12.

Goode's debut is a provocative, authentic coming-of-age story that explores the power of language in shaping identity, structured around the subversive, expressive nature of hip-hop music. "Word nerd" Esme is a 16-year-old Jewish lesbian in the "sterile minivan parade" of Holyhill, Minnesota. She and her friends—butch Marcy, religious Tess, and Indian Rowie—are the members of hip-hop crew Sister Mischief, who write rhymes to confront issues of race, gender, class, and sexuality. When the principal outlaws "violence-inducing culture," including hip-hop, the girls plan a guerilla performance to bring awareness to the masses, while Esme and Rowie's burgeoning relationship sends them spinning in new directions. Esme's flowing, slangy narrative is expressive and idiosyncratic, and her relationship with Rowie is sweet and seductive. All of the girls realistically defy stereotypes, and their strong relationships with each other and their families (particularly Esme and Marcy's amazing dads and Rowie's mom) are the linchpin of the story. Goode sometimes tries too hard to deconstruct hip-hop culture, and the slang may trip up some readers, but, overall, this debut is full of big ideas, big heart, and big poetry, with a positive, activist message. Sex, language, and alcohol and drug use limit this to older teens. —Krista Hutley

Goodman, Shawn. *Something Like Hope*. 2010. 208p. Delacorte (9780385739399). Gr. 9–12.

Smart, angry, and desperate, Shavonne, 17, is in juvenile detention again, and in her present-tense, first-person narrative, she describes the heartbreaking brutality that she suffered before she was locked up, as well as the harsh treatment, and sometimes the kindness, she encounters in juvie. With a mother who is a crack-addicted prostitute, and a father she never knew who died in prison, she was sent into the foster-care system as a young child. One foster mother needed money for drugs, so she forced Shavonne, 11 at the time, to go with a man who raped her. While she was locked up, Shavonne gave birth, and she is glad that her daughter is now in a kind foster home. As the title suggests, the story leaves room for "something like hope"; with all the pain and sorrow Shavonne endures, she is never broken. Not only does the African American teen survive, but she also nurtures needy fellow inmates, and she bonds with her counselor even as she tries to escape a vicious, racist supervisor. More than a situation, the story builds to a tense climax: What is the secret Shavonne cannot even think about? Shavonne's voice—witty, tender, explicit, and tough—will grab readers. In the tradition of Walter Dean Myers' and Jacqueline Woodson's novels, this winner of Delacorte's 2009 prize for best YA debut gets behind the statistics to tell it like it is. —Hazel Rochman

Green, John. *An Abundance of Katherines*. 2006. 256p. Dutton (9780525476887). Gr. 9–12.

Green follows his Printz-winning *Looking for Alaska* (2005) with another sharp, intelligent story, this one full of mathematical problems, historical references, word puzzles, and footnotes. Colin Singleton believes he is a washed-up child prodigy. A graduating valedictorian with a talent for creating anagrams, he fears he'll never do anything to classify him as a genius. To make matters worse, he has just been dumped by his most recent girlfriend (all of them have been named Katherine), and he's inconsolable. What better time for a road trip! He and his buddy Hassan load up the gray Olds (Satan's Hearse) and leave Chicago. They make it as far as Gutshot, Tennessee, where they stop to tour the gravesite of Archduke Franz Ferdinand, and meet a girl who isn't named Katherine. It's this girl, Lindsey, who helps Colin work on a mathematical theorem to predict the duration of romantic relationships. The laugh-out-loud humor ranges from delightfully sophomoric to subtly intellectual, and the boys' sarcastic repartee will help readers navigate the slower parts of the story, which involve local history interviews. The idea behind the book is that everyone's story counts, and what Colin's contributes to the world, no matter how small it may seem to him, will, indeed, matter. An appendix explaining the complex math is "fantastic," or as the anagrammatically inclined Green might have it, it's enough to make "cats faint." —Cindy Dobrez

★ Green, John. *The Fault in Our Stars*. 2012. 336p. Dutton (9780525478812). Gr. 9–12.

At 16, Hazel Grace Lancaster, a three-year stage IV–cancer survivor, is clinically depressed. To help her deal with this, her doctor sends her to a weekly support group where she meets Augustus Waters, a fellow cancer survivor, and the two fall in love. Both kids are preternaturally intelligent, and Hazel is fascinated with a novel about cancer called *An Imperial Affliction*. Most particularly, she longs to know what happened to its characters after an ambiguous ending. To find out, the enterprising Augustus makes it possible for them to travel to Amsterdam, where *Imperial*'s author, an expatriate American, lives. What happens when they meet him must be left to readers to discover. Suffice it to say, it is significant. Writing about kids with cancer is an invitation to sentimentality and pathos—or worse, in unskilled hands, bathos. Happily, Green is able to transcend such pitfalls in his best and most ambitious novel to date. Beautifully conceived and executed, this story artfully examines the largest possible considerations—life, love, and death—with sensitivity, intelligence, honesty, and integrity. In the process, Green shows his readers what it is like to live with cancer, sometimes no more than a breath or a heartbeat away from death. But it is life that Green spiritedly celebrates here, even while acknowledging its pain. In its every aspect, this novel is a triumph. —Michael Cart

★ Green, John. *Looking for Alaska*. 2005. 240p. Dutton (9780525475064). Gr. 9–12.

Sixteen-year-old Miles Halter comes to his boarding school in Alabama looking for what the dying Rabelais called "the Great Perhaps." What he finds is smoking, pranks, friendship, and love when he meets reckless Alaska Young, who is witty, pretty, and generous (though not to herself). Told in Miles' self-deprecating voice, this is the story of a young man's awakening and search for meaning in things both large and small—he even hopes to find a bit of understanding in the famous last words he so earnestly catalogues. Readers will see parts of themselves in all of the characters: best friend Chip's pugnaciousness, Alaska's bravado and self-loathing, and Miles' willingness to dream. Teens often must substitute articulation with longing. Green, whose writing both stirs and slays, leads them through the labyrinth and gives them hope that they can find their way. —Ilene Cooper

Green, John. *Paper Towns*. 2008. 352p. Dutton (9780525478188). Gr. 9–12.

Quentin—or "Q," as everyone calls him—has known his neighbor, the fabulous Margo Roth Spiegelman, since they were two. Or has he? Q. can't help but wonder, when, a month before high-school graduation, she vanishes. At first he worries that she might have committed suicide, but then he begins discovering clues that seem to have been left for him, which might reveal Margo's whereabouts. Yet the more he and his pals learn, the more Q. realizes he doesn't know and the more he comes to understand that the real mystery is not Margo's fate but Margo herself—enigmatic, mysterious, and so very alluring. Yes, there are echoes of Green's award-winning *Looking for Alaska* (2005): a lovely, eccentric girl; a mystery that begs to be solved by clever, quirky teens; and telling quotations (from *Leaves of Grass*, this time) beautifully integrated into the plot. Yet, if anything, the thematic stakes are higher here, as Green ponders the interconnectedness of imagination and perception, of mirrors and windows, of illusion and reality. That he brings it off is testimony to the fact that he is not only clever and wonderfully witty but also deeply thoughtful and insightful. In addition, he's a superb stylist, with a voice perfectly matched to his amusing, illuminating material. —Michael Cart

Green, John, and David Levithan. *Will Grayson, Will Grayson*. 2010. 320p. Dutton (9780525421580). Gr. 9–12.

Two superstar authors pair up and really deliver the goods, dishing up a terrific high-energy tale of teen love, lust, intrigue, anger, pain, and friendship threaded with generous measures of comedy and savvy counsel. Though the ensemble cast revolves around Tiny Cooper, "the world's largest person who is really, really gay, and also the world's gayest person who is really, really large," the central characters are the two titular narrators, who share a name (but don't meet until partway through) and trade off alternate chapters. One Will has been Tiny's satellite for years but is starting to chafe at the role—especially after Tiny forcibly sets him up with Jane, an infuriatingly perfect match. The other, whose clinical depression is brilliantly signaled by an all-lowercase narrative and so intensely conveyed that his early entries are hard to read, sees at least a glimmer of light fall on his self-image after a chance meeting with Tiny sparks a wild mutual infatuation. The performance of an autobiographical high-school musical that Tiny writes, directs, and stars in makes a rousing and suitably theatrical finale for a tale populated with young people engaged in figuring out what's important and shot through with strong feelings, smart-mouthed dialogue, and uncommon insight. —John Peters

Griffin, Adele. *Amandine*. 2001. 220p. Hyperion (9780786806188). Gr. 6–9.

Delia Blaine is the new girl at DeWolf High School, and though she'd like to be in with the popular crowd, she is willing to be drawn into a friendship with the enigmatic Amandine: artist, dancer, dangerous. From the first, Delia knows she is out of her depth. Amandine's grotesque drawings, her way of making up secret stories for the two of them to improvise, even the rapport Amandine shares with Delia's parents, intrigue and repulse Delia. It scares her to realize how much she enjoys belonging to Amandine. Yet when Amandine's cruelty becomes too much, Delia finds the courage to dump her—and that's when the trouble starts. Griffin is at the top of her game here. She takes well-worn stereotypes—the fat, friendless girl and the malevolent temptress—and through wholly realized characterizations and some unexpected twists, makes them seem much more: more real, more vulnerable, more scary. Delia is not quite the innocent that she seems. And what Amandine is willing to do for revenge may startle readers. Here's a story that is well-crafted and will resonate with readers, many of whom will feel they know this story, some from real life, some from their nightmares. —Ilene Cooper

Griffin, Adele. *Where I Want to Be*. 2005. 160p. Putnam (9780399237836). Gr. 7–10.

Griffin returns to a topic she has tackled before, the loss of a sibling, but she frames the story in the alternating narratives of two sisters—one of whom is dead. The story begins with Jane visiting her grandparents and nursing her grudges about her younger, more popular sister, Lily. Told in the third person, Jane's restless recounting is followed by Lily's first-person narrative, which chronicles her romance with Caleb, a relationship that nourishes her and keeps her grounded as she tries to deal with Jane's death. Readers will find themselves off balance at first as they switch between the narratives and try to understand Jane's reality. But they'll eventually learn that although Jane is dead, she is real enough to Lily, who can't move past the hole in her family. Griffin artfully dabs details on her canvas, then overlays her story with a supernatural patina that will immediately draw in the audience. More impressive is the way she shapes the sisters—each one with her own fears, wishes, and grievances that overlap to push the story forward. The conclusion, in which both Jane and Lily seek freedom, seems hurried, but the buildup is superbly accomplished, as each girl struggles with her ghosts. —Ilene Cooper

Griffin, Paul. *The Orange Houses*. 2009. 160p. Dial (9780803733466). Gr. 10–12.

Much like Rita Williams-Garcia's *Jumped* (2009), this story follows three kids through the pressure cooker of inner-city teenage life as it moves toward its crushing conclusion. Whereas that book mined the minor humiliations and overblown dramas that swirl during a single school day, this has a much more diffuse scope. The three characters couldn't be any more different: Tamika Sykes is a partially deaf student agonizing over whether she really wants to hear all the noise surrounding her; Fatima Espérer is a 16-year-old refugee who fled the violence and poverty of her unspecified

African country to live in the shadow of the Statue of Liberty; and depending on who you ask, Jimmy Sixes, already a disturbed veteran at age 18, is either a street poet or a junkie. The three form an unusual friendship, connecting both artistically and emotionally. All this is set in a city that has become a powder keg of anti-immigration sentiment (thanks to a recently passed law that rewards citizens for reporting illegals) and is perilously close to the ever-present spark of gang violence. Griffin clearly knows teens, especially the way they speak. In another writer's hands, this story of three outcasts might have turned into a sentimental mess, but he keeps the depth of emotion honest as his characters battle alienation and find strength in sacrifice. Although readers will be prepared for an unnerving journey from the opening scene, they will nevertheless be floored by some of the turns in this swift, tense, and powerful book. —Ian Chipman

Grimes, Nikki. *Bronx Masquerade*. 2002. 176p. Dial (9780803725690). Gr. 7–12.

Tyrone Bittings doesn't believe in a future: "Life is cold . . . What I've got is right here, right now, with my homeys." But an English-class open mike changes everything. Grimes' first novel since *Jazmin's Notebook* (1998) comprises brief monologues in the voices of students and their poems. Funny and painful, awkward and abstract, the poems talk about race, abuse, parental love, neglect, death, and body image ("Don't any of these girls like the way they look?" asks Tyrone). Most of all, they try to reveal the individuals beyond the stereotypes. With such short vignettes, the characters are never fully realized, and the message about poetry's ability to move beyond color and cultural boundaries is anything but subtle. Even so, readers will enjoy the lively, smart voices that talk bravely about real issues and secret fears. A fantastic choice for readers' theater. —Gillian Engberg

Halpin, Brendan. *Shutout*. 2010. 192p. Farrar (9780374368999). Gr. 8–10.

A heel condition (as well as being a freshman in a seniority-dominated system) keeps Amanda from making the varsity soccer team. That wouldn't be so bad except her best friend, Lena, makes the cut, plays like a star, and becomes popular to boot. Amanda, stuck playing goalie for the first time (though turns out she's pretty good), has to deal with the mortifying crucible of entering high school without the crutch of her best bud, yet eventually she finds some friendly faces and learns a bit about what the choices you make say about you. Lena's preference for parties and cute boys over a lifelong friend is an all-too-common high-school situation. Halpin (*Forever Changes*, 2008) has a knack for fleshing out a wide cast of characters and a keen ear for realistic dialogue. While he keeps the soccer-action details subdued, this is still a very sports-oriented read, and he instills a solid sense of what team sports are so good at (building confidence, creating bonds) without sounding like a tired gym teacher repeating maxims about teamwork and sportsmanship. In addition, Amanda makes her share of mistakes involving (others') drinking and lying but responds to them in a believably smart fashion. A quick, good-natured, and perceptive read about best friends growing apart, no doubt one of the hardest parts of growing up. —Ian Chipman

Han, Jenny. *The Summer I Turned Pretty*. 2009. 288p. Simon & Schuster (9781416968238). Gr. 7–10.

Belly spends every summer at the beach house owned by her mom's best friend, Susannah. While all the usual occupants—Belly's brother, her mom, Susannah, and Susannah's sons, Jeremiah and Conrad—are present, this year things are different. A note of finality hangs in the air, as Conrad will start college in the fall. He's always been closed off, but now he's taken up drinking and smoking, and gets moody whenever other boys pay attention to Belly. In addition to Conrad, there's Cam, Belly's summer fling, and Jeremiah also seems to have a crush on her. Who will she end up with? Some chapters return to summers past, revealing Susannah's cancer and Belly's first kiss with one brother, Jeremiah, and her unwavering love for the other, Conrad. Han plants enough seeds throughout the book for readers to ascertain what's really going on with Susannah, while keeping Belly—who is appropriately self-centered, alternating between typical teenage vanity and vulnerable insecurity—clueless. This is a quick, satisfying read, with a poignant conclusion good for budding romance fans. —Courtney Jones

Handler, Daniel. *Why We Broke Up*. 2011. 368p. Little, Brown (9780316127257). Gr. 9–12.

This novel may sound like another tale of boy meets girl, but, folks, it's all in the delivery. In faltering pitter-patter dialogue and thick, gushy, grasping-for-words paragraphs, Handler takes a tired old saw, the romance between senior basketball cocaptain Ed Slaterton and junior cinephile Min Green, and injects us into the halting, breathless, disbelieving, horny, and nervous minds of two teens who feel "different" only in how they define themselves in contrast to each other—that dumbstruck, anthropological joy of introducing foreign films to a dude schooled only in layups, and vice versa. The story is told from Min's perspective, a bittersweet diatribe of their breakup arranged around objects (a matchbox, a bottle cap, a dish towel, an—ahem—condom wrapper) of varying importance that she intends on returning to him. (Kalman's full-color drawings of these objects were not available for review.) It is fitting that the chapters center upon these items; the story itself feels like blurry photos, snippets of stray recordings—all the more powerful because of how they evoke truth more than any mere relaying of facts. Yes, the relationship breaks apart like a predictable song, but Handler's genius is to make us hear those minor-key notes as if they were playing on our first—and last—dates, too. In the mood to break additional hearts? Pair this with Pete Hautman's *The Big Crunch* (2011). —Daniel Kraus

Hartnett, Sonya. *Stripes of the Sidestep Wolf*. 2005. 208p. Candlewick (9780763626440). Gr. 10–12.

Satchel's world seems defined by suffering: his construction job is ending; his father's religious delusions preclude his earning a living; his mother's work aggravates her painful skin condition; and their town is withering economically. After Satchel's best friend, Leroy, moves away, his only companions are his dog and Leroy's sister, 21-year-old Chelsea. An emotionally crushed misfit, Chelsea believes that the wolflike animal Satchel has seen on a nearby mountain is a thylacine, an extinct Tasmanian marsupial. Tempted to exploit the thylacine's presence to help his town, his friend, and himself, Satchel finds the animal again and makes his decision. Given Satchel's emotionally grinding situation, the pivotal scene, involving an injury to his dog, seems almost too much to bear. Hartnett, an award-winning Australian novelist, keeps Satchel at the forefront of the story, but in the background lurks a parallel sort of miracle: the animal that was hunted to extinction somehow survives. The story is uncompromisingly stark, but readers will find Satchel a sympathetic figure who willingly remains in a situation that limits his prospects even as he grows beyond its confines. —Carolyn Phelan

★ Hartnett, Sonya. *Surrender*. 2006. 256p. Candlewick (9780763627683). Gr. 9–12.

In the small, desolate town of Mulyan, a well-behaved young boy plays with a toy car atop the fence rail surrounding his front yard. A very different sort of boy—sunbaked, unkempt, and vaguely dangerous—appears on the street side of the fence to scratch his name in the wood and taunt the young boy to move beyond his boundaries. So begins the eerie relationship between Gabriel and Finnegan: the first, an isolated and disturbed child in a profoundly dysfunctional family with an ugly history; the second, a cruel and destructive yet wildly freeing force. The two determine to be each other's reflection: one all good, the other all bad. Together they share dark secrets, make plans, and experience a pure love for Surrender, Gabriel's adopted hound. Told retrospectively from the deathbed of 20-year-old Gabriel, this is a potent and disquieting psychological tale. Given its complex vocabulary, troubling characters, and grim content, this is a book for older teens willing to experience some of humanity's bleaker aspects. —Holly Koelling

Hassan, Michael. *Crash and Burn*. 2013. 544p. HarperCollins/Balzer and Bray (9780062112903). Gr. 9–12.

Sprawling, messy, vulgar, sexy, irreverent, violent, bighearted, harrowing. These are just a few of the many adjectives about to be hurled in the direction of this roaring freight train of a debut. In telling the tale of a tumultuous decade-long antagonism between two boys destined to fulfill their yin/yang fate, Hassan constructs three of the most vividly alive characters in recent YA fiction: Steven "Crash" Crashinsky, the oversexed, good-natured, dope-smoking C student; David "Burn" Burnett, the bipolar, tragedy-plagued genius given to openly weeping and obsessed with revenge; and Burn's older sister, Roxanne, a world-weary goth whose headlong fight against her demons has both boys enthralled. Hassan begins at the end: Crash is a media darling for saving his entire high school from Burn's siege of guns and explosives. National attention scores Crash a book deal, and between horny interludes, he begins to work. Both of them, he writes, have been connected since grade school when Burn tried to blow up the building, promising Crash upon his failure, "One day, I am going to kill you." A travelogue of the subsequent 10 years of parties, drugs, sex, and secrets may sound exhausting, but Hassan writes with such fire and drills down so deep that it's difficult to believe these characters are fictional—this would read quickly even at twice the length. Gutsily conceived, written, and edited, this is, quite simply, a great American novel. —Daniel Kraus

Hautman, Pete. *The Big Crunch*. 2011. 288p. Scholastic (9780545240758). Gr. 8–11.

When June starts her junior year of high school in Minneapolis, she isn't looking for love. Thanks to her management-consultant dad's constantly shifting positions, this is June's sixth new school in four years, and she's learned to guard against getting attached. Then she literally crashes into classmate Wes at a convenience store, and what begins with a black eye for June and a head bump for Wes turns into a true, deep romance that the teens try to sustain after June's dad moves the family once again. As in Lynne Rae Perkins' novels, this story's delight lies in the details. National Book Award–winning Hautman writes with wry humor and a comic's sense of juxtaposed phrases and timing. From guys' lunchroom conversations ("How come you didn't just go online for your porn," says Wes to a friend who excavates an old *Penthouse* from his neighbor's recycling bin) to June's father's corporate mantras of self-control and forward thinking, the dialogue is refreshingly honest, particularly in the bewilderingly urgent, awkward exchanges that fuel the attraction between June and Wes. Hautman skillfully subverts clichés in this subtle, authentic, heart-tugging exploration of first love, but his sharp-eyed view of high-school social dynamics and the loving friction between parents and teens on the edge of independence is just as memorable. —Gillian Engberg

Hautman, Pete. *Godless*. 2004. 208p. Simon & Schuster (9780689862786). Gr. 7–10.

Hautman knows how to project a voice. In *Sweetblood* (2003), the voice was that of a diabetic who felt a kinship with vampires. Here, the voice belongs to a disaffected 16-year-old, Jason Block, who decides to invent a new religion with a new god—the town's water tower. Finding converts is surprisingly easy. His small group includes his twitchy friend Shin, a self-styled scribe who is writing the new testament (snippets enticingly appear at the beginning of each chapter), and Henry, a bully who undergoes changes when he is named high priest of the "Chutengodians." In a smartly structured narrative that is by turns funny, worried, and questioning, Jason watches as his once-cohesive little congregation starts wanting to "worship" in its own ways, some of them deadly. Not everything works here. Shin's meltdown doesn't seem real, even though it has been thoroughly foreshadowed. But most scenes are honest and true to the bone, such as the one in which Jason and Harry agree that their dangerous stunts are worth their weight in memories. Anyone who has questioned his or her religion, especially as a teenager, will respond to Jason's struggles with belief. Many individuals, upon reading this, will consider their own questions once more. —Ilene Cooper

Hautman, Pete. *Invisible*. 2005. 160p. Simon & Schuster (9780689868009). Gr. 7–10.

It's hard to tell if Hautman meant this to be a mystery, but it's clear from the start that there's something not right about the relationship between narrator Doug Hanson and his best friend, Andy Morrow. Doug, a self-proclaimed nerd, is primarily interested in building a matchstick replica of the Golden Gate Bridge for his model railway town. Andy is popular, a football player and actor. But the boys live next door to each other and talk from their bedroom windows at night. In an almost robotic voice that still manages to be intensely insightful, Doug takes readers to his school, where he is mocked and eventually beaten, and to his neighborhood, where he turns into a Peeping Tom, watching school star Melanie Haver undress. Hautman does a superb job of crafting the odd sanctuary that is Doug's mind. But Doug's defenses are crumbling, and the secret he's been keeping about Andy is oozing through the cracks. The truth about Andy won't come as a surprise, but there are some unexpected plot turns here, and the chilling but ambiguous denouement is definitely unsettling. —Ilene Cooper

Hautman, Pete. *Sweetblood*. 2003. 192p. Simon & Schuster (9780689850486). Gr. 8–12.

Sixteen-year-old Lucy Szabo, who dresses in black and is a frequent visitor to a vampire chat room where she calls herself Sweetblood, is a diabetic whose condition dictates her life. She constantly monitors her glucose level, watches her calorie intake, and keeps an eye on her physical activity. After she submits a creative, but grim, composition theorizing that vampire legends are based on the appearance and behavior of untreated diabetics, her teacher becomes alarmed, her parents are called, and she's packed off to a therapist. Meanwhile, Lucy has become acquainted with an older man who runs a salon for young goths, fancies himself a vampire, and has his eye on her. Hautman does an outstanding job of making Lucy's theory and her struggle to accept herself credible. The diabetes/vampire idea, based on information Hautman discovered while investigating vampire stories, eventually gives way to a cautionary motif about teen safety in chat rooms, but that's not enough to undermine some really good writing: Lucy's clever, self-deprecating voice is endlessly original. This imaginative, intriguing "what if" novel will attract fans of vampire stories, as well as teens who feel different from the norm—in short, all of them. —Debbie Carton

Headley, Justina Chen. *North of Beautiful*. 2009. 384p. Little, Brown (9780316025058). Gr. 9–12.

Sixteen-year-old Terra seems to be a typical high-achieving high-school student. Under her heavy makeup, though, she hides a port-wine colored birthmark on her cheek that makes her feel like an outsider. During yet another attempt to remove the birthmark, Terra runs into Jacob, a gorgeous goth with a cleft-palate scar. That encounter initiates a transformation in both Terra and her subservient mother. Headley has written an exquisite book that explores the difference between physical and true beauty as Terra and her mother travel from Washington state to China, and from the home of a shame-faced, cruel cartographer into the presence of an adventurous, strong woman and her insightful teenage son. Headley uses map metaphors throughout, even in the activity, geocaching, which helps bond Terra and Jacob in both Washington and China. She also uses Terra's artistic medium, collage, as a literary device to create layer upon layer of experiences and insights into a artfully written journey of self-discovery, self-actualization, and love. With every carefully chosen word, well-crafted sentence, and fully developed character, Headley maps out a wholly satisfying reading experience that takes readers from terra nullis to terra firma. —Frances Bradburn

Hidier, Tanuja Desai. *Born Confused*. 2002. 432p. Scholastic (9780439357623). Gr. 9–12.

Dimple Lala is an ABCD, American Born Confused Desi, a charming, articulate Indian teen who spends her seventeenth summer trying to find herself with both her American friends and her loving immigrant parents who are still steeped in India's traditions and language. Growing up in Springfield, New York, down the street from her blonde, blue-eyed "supertwin," Gwyn, Dimple feels American, and she's rebellious when her parents start talking about finding her "a suitable boy." The arranged meeting with Karsh, an NYU student and son of Indian friends, is predictably strained and frustrating. "It's like *Titanic*. Without the romance," she confides to Gwyn, a comment she will rue all summer as her best friend gradually takes "the suitable boy." As Gwyn and Karsh move on, Dimple loses herself in her family and her background, only to find her many-cultured self, as well as a stronger, different friendship and "a suitable boy." Dimple is a photographer. Her "third eye" is always with her, and her narrative is a feast for the senses, creating a reading experience that is unusual in YA literature today. Yet this will not be an easy read. While it is the story of every teen, the writing is dense and detailed, with a vocabulary and references that will challenge readers. It's the careful choice of every word that marks this reading experience. —Frances Bradburn

Holt, Kimberly Willis. *Keeper of the Night*. 2003. 320p. Holt (9780805063615). Gr. 6–10.

On the first page 13-year-old Isabel finds her mother dead. She committed suicide. What follows is the story of the family's grief, anger, and guilt, told in Isabel's voice in short, sharp vignettes (most a page or less) that capture moments in her life on the island of Guam. There are sudden sharp memories of Mom; compulsive lists Isabel makes to try to get control; fun and rivalry with her friends at school; anger at her cold, distant Tata (he asks her about school but doesn't stop to hear her answer); and always, her anguished feeling of responsibility for her younger siblings. As a child Holt spent several "magical" years on Guam with her father, who was in the military, and the place and culture are an integral part of the story. Occasionally, the local color overwhelms the plot, and the family survivor therapy is purposive. But Holt, who won the National Book Award for *When Zachary Beaver Came to Town* (1999), is never reverential. Her exquisite, plain, concrete prose never plays down the loss ("At dinner her chair is empty") or the dark, painful struggle to heal. —Hazel Rochman

Hornby, Nick. *Slam*. 2007. 304p. Putnam (9780399250484). Gr. 9–12.

For Hornby, author of *About a Boy* (1988) and *High Fidelity* (1995), the move from adult to young adult fiction represents more of a natural progression than a change in course. So it should come as no surprise that he has written an accomplished teen novel featuring a character whose voice hits its groove at the downbeat and sustains it through the final chord. Sam is a disarmingly ordinary 15-year-old kid who loves to skate (that's skateboarding, to you and me). But then he is blindsided: his girlfriend gets pregnant, and he lands in the middle of his mum's nightmare (she had Sam when she was 16). This may sound like an old-fashioned realistic YA problem novel, but it's a whole lot more. Sam, you see, has a sort-of-imaginary friend: the world's greatest skater, Tony Hawk, whose poster Sam talks to when he has problems. And the poster talks back, maybe, or maybe Sam is just reciting quotes from Tony's autobiography. And is it really Tony who is "whizzing" Sam into the future for glimpses of what is to come? With or without Tony's help, Sam gives us the facts about his very eventful couple of years, but as he reminds us, "there comes a point where the facts don't matter anymore . . . because you don't know what anything felt like." Which is where Hornby comes in. We know exactly how Sam feels—even when he feels differently from the beginning of a sentence to the end—and it feels just right: a vertiginous mix of anger, confusion, insight, humor, and love. —Bill Ott

Horvath, Polly. *The Canning Season*. 2003. 208p. Farrar (9780374399566). Gr. 6–9.

Horvath's 2002 Newbery Honor Book had a sprightly title, *Everything on a Waffle*. This title is more mundane, but both books follow the pattern Horvath set in *The Trolls* (1999): a young person is in some sense orphaned and put in the care of an older relative with stories to spin. Here the girl is 13-year-old Ratchet, who is sent by her boorish mother to the wilds of Maine, where Ratchet's twin great-aunts, Tilly and Penpen, live in splendid isolation, gardening, fending off bears, and reminiscing about the old days, like the time Penpen tripped over her mother's head (the depressed woman had managed to chop it off). But this is more the aunts' story than Ratchet's; the girl is primarily a "talk-to" character until another unwanted teen, Harper, arrives. The girls are the filler in a sandwich that is both dark and wry, with most of the pages taken up by the problems of various adults. Will the intended audience appreciate the truths and idiosyncrasies contained in the tales of the two sisters? Horvath is a winning writer, luxurious in her descriptions, so perhaps she can overcome the problem of audience appeal. A caveat: the term "little fucks" is used at one point; otherwise, the language is sometimes salty but not vulgar. —Ilene Cooper

Howe, James, ed. ***The Color of Absence: 12 Stories about Loss and Hope*****. 2001. 256p. Atheneum (9780689828621). Gr. 6–10.**

The uneasy intersection of loss and hope provides the thematic setting for this collection of 11 original stories and one excerpt, "The Rialto," from a novel-in-progress coauthored by Jacqueline Woodson and Chris Lynch. Other contributors include such leading young adult authors as Walter Dean Myers, Annette Curtis Klause, Norma Fox Mazer, and Virginia Euwer Wolff. All of the stories are professionally executed, but—perhaps because loss is inherently sad—too many strike the same note of melancholy and deal with the theme in ways that are often predictable. Happily there are notable exceptions. Klause reintroduces Simon the vampire in a story invested with emotional resonance; Naomi Shihab Nye feeds loss with metaphoric food; and Wolff demonstrates the spare power of understatement in her story-in-dialogue, "The Chair." What these and several other good stories in the book demonstrate is that loss can be redeemed not only by hope but also by art. —Michael Cart

Hubbard, Jenny. ***Paper Covers Rock*****. 2011. 192p. Delacorte (9780385740555). Gr. 9–12.**

At the beginning of his junior year of high school, Alex loses a good friend to an accidental—and drunken—death, and by the end of that first semester, he has lost his moral innocence as well. After Alex's friend dies, he retreats emotionally while also allowing his new, young, and pretty English teacher to coax out his poetic abilities. Meanwhile, Glenn, another student and former friend, tortures Alex with doubts about Alex's own motives related to both the dead boy and the English teacher, encouraging Alex to question his very self. Although Alex knows that his admiration for the teacher is fanciful and not connected to the fact that she may have witnessed certain events related to the death, he recognizes that he is socially outclassed by the powerful Glenn. Can Alex muster the will to counter Glenn's manipulations to oust the teacher? Both plotting and characters are thoroughly crafted in this stellar first novel. The poetry that Hubbard produces from Alex's pen is brilliant, and the prose throughout is elegant in its simplicity. Although the novel takes place in the early 1980s, it could indeed unfold at almost any time, and its boarding-school setting is specific yet accessible to readers in any school setting. Reminiscent of John Knowles' classic coming-of-age story, *A Separate Peace* (1959), this novel introduces Hubbard as a bright light to watch on the YA literary scene. —Francisca Goldsmith

Hughes, Pat. ***Open Ice*****. 2005. 288p. Random/Wendy Lamb (9780385746755). Gr. 9–12.**

"In the dream, there's always open ice," but in real life, high-school hockey player Nick Taglio has a knack for getting blindsided, and he has the concussions to prove it. His latest bell-ringer has left him with a bad case of post-concussion syndrome, prompting his doctor to forbid him from playing hockey, possibly forever. It only gets worse, as Nick lapses into emotional free-fall, blowing off school, fighting with his parents, getting dumped by his girlfriend (who is only interested in healthy hockey stars), and even endangering his baby brother. Yes, this sounds like readers of Hughes' first YA novel are in danger themselves—of getting their bells rung by coming-of-age overload—but every time we think we see an oppressive author's message on the horizon, Hughes feints left and skates right, confounding our expectations with a subtle twist of character that draws us deeper into the story. Nick does plenty of soul-searching, but it happens around the edges of his bitter, knifing wit. His relationships with his friends and family, too, are always multidimensional, and while there is plenty of sex in the story, it proves as confusing for Nick and his peers as it does exhilarating. Best of all, though, is the hockey: sure, the open ice thing is a metaphor—the virus of sports novels—but thankfully, it never overwhelms the taut physicality of the game itself. By being true to the sport, Hughes unlocks the truth in her characters. —Bill Ott

Jenkins, A. M. *Damage*. 2001. 224p. HarperCollins (9780060290993). Gr. 11–12.

Austin Reid is depressed as he enters his senior year of high school. He's glad to start another season of football, likes his few buddies, and even begins an intense relationship with Heather, one of the most unattainable young women on campus. But none of that really helps. He drifts through his days so detached from himself that even during intense sexual passion he doesn't really feel alive. The possibility of suicide intrigues him to the point that it dominates his every thought: having everything—good looks, athletic ability, a beautiful girlfriend, a great mom—simply doesn't seem enough to live for. Jenkins uses an intriguing second-person point of view to depict Austin's detachment, and lets the story drift, echoing Austin's own aimlessness. Graphic though well-handled scenes of oral sex will likely limit the audience, as will the somber subject matter (including a twisted relationship between Austin and his girlfriend). But it's rare to find such an unflinching, powerful depiction of depression in a YA novel, and Jenkins evokes the lumbering, overwhelming emotional burden with vivid accuracy. —Roger Leslie

Jenkins, A. M. *Out of Order*. 2003. 256p. HarperCollins (9780066239682). Gr. 8–10.

Colt Trammel, popular baseball player and sophomore-class wise guy, knows in his gut that he's a dumb jock, much dumber than most of his classmates and his sexy girlfriend, Grace. But he is determined to cover up his inadequacies with his good looks, athleticism, and clever comments and stunts. His carefully crafted persona begins to crumble when Grace jilts him and his failing grades could mean that he won't be eligible to play ball. Then comes intelligent, green-haired Corrine, who becomes Colt's tutor and saddleburr. Colt's fast-talking first-person narrative paints a humorous, poignant portrait of a young man with learning disabilities who is savvy yet self-destructive. The well-drawn young characters will hook both male and female teen readers, who will recognize the high-school insider-outsider culture: its lies and cruelties, and its ultimate preparation for the real world. —Frances Bradburn

Jocelyn, Marthe. *Would You*. 2008. 176p. Random/Wendy Lamb (9780375837036). Gr. 8–10.

Would you rather lose all your hair or all your teeth? Those are the kinds of questions Natalie and her friends ask each other when they sit around their hangout, the Ding-Dong. Would you rather die or have everyone else die? That becomes more than a question when Natalie's beloved sister, Claire, is hit by a car. In short chapters that are wrenching, honest, even funny at times, Jocelyn takes readers on Natalie's journey from Before to After. Natalie is coming home from a night out with friends when she gets the phone call. As she learns later, Claire was breaking up with her boyfriend, and when the exchange became emotional, she ran into the street without looking. Now, she lies in her hospital room, tethered to machines, body swollen, head shaved, in a coma. In the few days that pass from book's beginning to end, Natalie and her family go through the familiar stages of grief. Friends rally, tempers flare, there are even the painfully realistic moments as when a secret crush kisses Natalie, and she is guiltily glad she is alive. The book's brevity makes the sadness bearable, but this will stay with readers for a long time. —Ilene Cooper

Johnson, Angela. *Bird*. 2004. 144p. Dial (9780803728479). Gr. 6–10.

"I thought it was enough that I had to lose two fathers before I'm even a teenager." At 13, Bird runs south from Ohio, searching for the stepfather that left her family. Ethan, a boy with a fragile heart, knows Bird is hiding on his family farm, but he doesn't know why. Ethan's neighbor Jay is still in shock over the recent death of his beloved younger brother. Alternating between these three young voices, Johnson tells a poignant, lyrical story about children struggling to overcome nearly irreparable heartbreak. Some of the connections between characters seem stretched, particularly the links made through the extraordinary kindness of aging Mrs. Pritchard, who knows just what to ask and when. But Johnson writes with a poet's knowledge of rhythm and knows how to use the space between words; the disconnect between what the boys think and what they say is especially well done.

Johnson also creates a visceral sense of each character's search for love and connection, particularly Bird's deep loneliness and her longing for parents who aren't there. —Gillian Engberg

★ Johnson, Angela. *The First Part Last*. 2003. 144p. Simon & Schuster (9780689849220). Gr. 6–12.

Bobby, the teenage artist and single-parent dad in Johnson's Coretta Scott King Award winner, *Heaven* (1998), tells his story here. At 16, he's scared to be raising his baby, Feather, but he's totally devoted to caring for her, even as she keeps him up all night, and he knows that his college plans are on hold. In short chapters alternating between "now" and "then," he talks about the baby that now fills his life, and he remembers the pregnancy of his beloved girlfriend, Nia. Yes, the teens' parents were right. The couple should have used birth control; adoption could have meant freedom. But when Nia suffers irreversible postpartum brain damage, Bobby takes their newborn baby home. There's no romanticizing. The exhaustion is real, and Bobby gets in trouble with the police and nearly messes up everything. But from the first page, readers feel the physical reality of Bobby's new world: what it's like to hold Feather on his stomach, smell her skin, touch her clenched fists, feel her shiver, and kiss the top of her curly head. Johnson makes poetry with the simplest words in short, spare sentences that teens will read again and again. The great cover photo shows the strong African American teen holding his tiny baby in his arms. —Hazel Rochman

Johnson, LouAnne. *Muchacho*. 2009. 208p. Knopf (9780375861178). Gr. 8–12.

In a voice that feels authentic from the first line, Johnson (played by Michelle Pfeiffer in *Dangerous Minds*) has crafted a memorable portrait of a young man doing his best to get back on the right track in the face of serious societal pressures. Eddie is a "secret reader" beneath his tough-guy attitude and bad behavior. A final infraction pushes Eddie's strict father to exile him to his *tio*'s rural home, where Eddie makes a fresh start as Eduardo, a studious and confident guy who just might be a great poet. The caring adults in Eddie's life provide just enough support for Eddie to find his way on his own, and peers who choose different paths provide a counterpoint to his good decision making. The vibrant voice, the episodic nature of the story, and Eddie's almost-there hopeful conclusion will likely draw parallels to Sherman Alexie's *The Absolutely True Diary of a Part-Time Indian* (2007). Display this prominently so other "secret readers" will find a kindred spirit in Eduardo and numerous other reading suggestions cleverly woven into the text. —Heather Booth

Johnson, Maureen. *13 Little Blue Envelopes*. 2005. 336p. HarperCollins (9780060541415). Gr. 8–11.

Seventeen-year-old Ginny had always admired her aunt Peg, a free-spirited artist who often disappeared for months, most recently to Europe. Now Aunt Peg has died of brain cancer, and in a characteristically cryptic gesture made before her death, she arranged for her niece to receive a plane ticket to London, where Ginny will begin a series of adventures. Guided by Peg's friends and the instructions in each of 13 letters her aunt wrote, Ginny sets off across Europe. Staying with Peg's contacts or in hostels, Ginny begins to peel away some of the mythic layers surrounding her aunt, even as she falls into thrilling escapades and a blossoming romance. Johnson's plot stretches plausibility. Would Ginny's practical mother really have agreed to such a solo, undefined journey? But readers will probably overlook any improbabilities and willingly accompany Ginny through her sensitive, authentically portrayed experiences—uncomfortable, lonely, giddy, and life changing—as she pieces together family mysteries and discovers herself. —Gillian Engberg

Johnson, Maureen. *Devilish*. 2006. 272p. Penguin/Razorbill (9781595140609). Gr. 8–11.

Fast paced and very funny, this is the story of high-school senior Jane Jarvis, who gets in over her head—which isn't difficult because she's very short. She's also very smart, and when her best friend, Allison, starts acting oddly, it doesn't take Jane long to figure out that there's some unholy connection between Ally and mysterious Lanalee, a new girl at their Catholic school. Connection, indeed. As it turns out, Ally has sold her soul to junior devil Lanalee in exchange for popularity; however, Jane doesn't buy Ally's tearful confession. Boldly, she informs Lanalee that she will take Ally's place (she really thinks the whole thing is bunk). Bunk it is not, and soon enough Jane finds herself in the fight of (and for) her life. Johnson does a very clever thing here. She takes a typical high-school story about popularity (amusing enough in Jane's snarky voice) and turns it on its head when evil comes on the scene. Decorated in fine detail and well served by a terrific supporting cast, this page-turner will have high appeal and get great word-of-mouth. —Ilene Cooper

Johnson, Maureen. *Suite Scarlett*. 2008. 368p. Scholastic/Point (9780439899277). Gr. 7–12.

The Hopewell Hotel, 75 years ago a stylish Upper East Side haunt, has fallen on hard times. Its proprietors, the Martin family, have let the last remaining employee go, and now it's up to the four children, Spencer, Lola, Scarlett, and Marlene, to keep things afloat. Enter one Mrs. Amy Amberson, a flamboyant, mysterious guest, back in New York after a long absence, with some clandestine motives. Mrs. Amberson is to occupy the Empire Suite, just today entrusted to Scarlett as a "present" on her fifteenth birthday (a family tradition), for the entire summer, and keeping her happy will test Scarlett's ingenious mettle. What follows is some utterly winning, madcap Manhattan farce, crafted with a winking, urbane narrative and tight, wry dialogue. Beneath the silvered surface, Johnson delivers a complex sibling relationship. Like the Hilary McKay's Casson quartet, first introduced in *Saffy's Angel* (2002), these siblings are bound by tender, poignant connections, all the more real for the absurdity of their circumstances. We can only hope that they, too, return for more intrepid adventures. —Thom Barthelmess

Johnson, Peter. *What Happened*. 2007. 133p. Front Street (9781932425673). Gr. 7–12.

"Believe, believe," the unnamed young narrator of this extraordinary first novel tells himself. But in what? His mother is dead, his father has abandoned both him and his older brother, Kyle, and now the two have been involved, as passengers, in a hit-and-run accident. Should they go to the police? Or should they obey the wealthy father of the boy who was driving and remain silent? Peter Johnson, an award-winning poet, writes with unusual grace and tenderness about kids who are troubled—and occasionally baffled—by the necessity of moral choice when their lives seem to be nothing but a "combination of catastrophes and dumb decisions." No wonder the narrator is afraid, despite the meds he must take, and frustrated by his search for meaning and something to believe in. The voice that Johnson has given this boy—also a poet—is breathtakingly good, each word conspiring with every other word to create an irresistibly seductive tone that is a haunting combination of sadness and fragile hope. Fans of Robert Cormier will welcome this similarly satisfying invitation to reflect on religion, reality, and reasons for getting out of bed in the morning. —Michael Cart

Juby, Susan. *Alice, I Think*. 2003. 304p. HarperTempest (9780060515430). Gr. 8–12.

Poor Alice. She went to kindergarten dressed as a hobbit, and life has gone downhill ever since. Now, at 15, she is about to enter alternative high school after being homeschooled by her aging hippie mother and a father who attempts to write "bodice rippers." Naturally, all the angst is recorded in her diary. Juby has some very funny scenes here as Alice tries to make friends, meet boys, get a good haircut, and make her counselor feel like he's accomplishing something. But the plot tends to go over the top (Alice gets skin poisoning! Alice is beaten up!), and the first-person voice pushes up the ante to make events seem too wacky by half. Juby, a first-time writer, needs to accept that "less is more" and abandon the overused diary format, but her potential is clear. The scene in which the family gets a computer and finds porn sites (Butt Pages!) will strike kids as hysterical. Adults may not be quite as amused. —Ilene Cooper

Juby, Susan. *Another Kind of Cowboy*. 2007. 352p. HarperTeen (9780060765170). Gr. 8–11.

The author of *Alice, I Think* (2003) offers a change of pace in this charming story. Alex Ford fell in love with horses at age six, and then with the sport of dressage. But Alex knows that Turnip, the sturdy horse his dad won in a poker game, will never manage dressage, and resigns himself to becoming a cowboy. When a new horse enters his life, Alex, by now 16 and struggling with his sexuality, finds himself in a dressage class. The only other member of the class is Cleo, a spoiled American who was sent to the Vancouver riding school after getting in trouble at home. The two lonely teens develop a friendship that eventually helps them realize their identities and strengths. Wry humor infuses this quiet story with a gentle warmth, and the secondary characters are well developed. Juby clearly knows horses and dressage, and her portrait of this world adds to the book's appeal. Readers don't have to be horse lovers to find this a winning read. —Lynn Rutan

Kass, Pnina Moed. *Real Time*. 2004. 192p. Clarion (9780618442034). Gr. 9–12.

A suicide bomb attack on a crowded Jerusalem bus is the focus of Kass' tense, terrifying debut, told from the viewpoints of the passengers and their families, friends, and lovers. Among the narrators are a German boy wanting to find out if his grandfather was a Nazi; a young woman who has reclaimed her Jewish heritage, which her father denied; and an elderly Holocaust survivor. Their stories draw readers in. Then the bomb explodes, and the second half of the book focuses on the wounded and those who care for them in a Jerusalem hospital. The Israelis and the victims, if somewhat idealized, are drawn with complexity. In contrast, the brief, first-person Palestinian perspectives are flat and distant, with little sense of the Palestinian experience: the Arab doctor is perfect, and the teenage suicide bomber and his mentor are ignorant and poor, filled with hate, and trying to be martyrs. What's unforgettable is the grief and the chaos of the bombing and its aftermath—the stories behind the news headlines. —Hazel Rochman

Katcher, Brian. *Almost Perfect*. 2009. 368p. Delacorte (9780385736640). Gr. 9–12.

Transsexuality is the issue in this candid novel told from the viewpoint of Logan, a high-school senior in a small Missouri town. The story quickly moves from Logan's attraction to Sage, a cute, strange new girl at school, to his shock at the discovery that Sage was born male and is in transition to become a female. More than anything, Logan worries that once Sage's identity is revealed, people will think that he is gay for being attracted to a boy. Then Sage attempts suicide, and Logan feels guilty about failing her. Unlike Sage's brutal father, though, Logan never denies that Sage is a "she." The story is long and repetitive, and the messages are overt, but many teens—both those familiar with transgender issues and those who are not—will welcome the honest take on a rarely explored subject. The biological facts about hormones and Sage's changing body are woven in, and Katcher clearly dramatizes the characters' secrets, lies, shame, and denial, as well as the cruel prejudice they experience with family and friends. —Hazel Rochman

Katcher, Brian. *Playing with Matches*. 2008. 304p. Delacorte (9780385735445). Gr. 8–11.

"Three billion women in the world, and the universe couldn't spare one for Leon Sanders." Leon is a D & D–playing, Monty Python–watching, lame joke–telling, high-school junior. An act of kindness with loner Melody, a burn victim with severe scars and facial disfigurement, leads to friendship and then romance. Leon enjoys her company but worries about what others think, while Melody revels in feeling beautiful for the first time. Following a familiar plot trajectory, Leon pushes Melody aside after the class hottie, Amy, makes her move on him. First-time author Katcher pulls out a nice twist at the end, revealing Melody to be a girl who has been through fire both literally and figuratively and has emerged with uncommon strength. This is a successful blend of laugh-out-loud humor and a serious look at relationships. The secondary characters are delightful, including ADHD friends Jimmy and Johnny, Parking Lot Pete, and even Dan, the junior Hannibal Lector, who has more heart than he lets on. Recommend this to fans of John Green's books; Katcher is an author to watch. —Cindy Dobrez

Keller, Julia. *Back Home*. 2009. 208p. Egmont (9781606840054). Gr. 6–9.

Thirteen-year-old Rachel believes that "parents aren't supposed to change." But the truth is they do, as she discovers to her sorrow when her father's National Guard unit is sent to Iraq and he comes home a different man, horribly wounded by a bombing. The traumatic brain injury he suffers will not only change him, it will also change Rachel. In fact, it will change everything. A Pulitzer Prize–winning journalist, Keller wrote a series about traumatic brain injury for the *Chicago Tribune*, and she clearly knows her subject both intellectually and viscerally, particularly the emotional impact visited on the loved ones of the injured. While her first novel isn't perfect—Rachel's voice is too old and her sensibility too mature, and in the interest of verisimilitude there is perhaps too much information that is didactic instead of aesthetic in its presentation—no one who reads this heartbreaking book will ever forget it. With integrity, authenticity, and immediacy, Keller has captured the extraordinary complexity and challenge of unexpected change and, to her everlasting credit, unsparingly shares the whole truth of it with her readers. —Michael Cart

Kephart, Beth. *The Heart Is Not a Size*. 2010. 240p. HarperTeen (9780061470486). Gr. 8–11.

Drawn by a flyer promising "two weeks that will change your life," Pennsylvania high-school student Georgia convinces her best friend, Riley, to join her on a trip to Juarez, Mexico, where chaperoned teens will build community projects. Georgia is hoping that the newness of the experience will help her shed both the secret panic attacks she has been experiencing as well as her sense of herself as a "freakishly well-behaved" and predictable decision-maker. As expected, the trip does widen the teens' cultural awareness ("Privilege doesn't make you smarter. It doesn't gift you decency"), but it also forces Georgia and Riley to confront previously unspoken personal troubles. Kephart is an award-winning poet as well as a novelist, and her prose, filled with memorable, original imagery, has the subtlety and spare, rhythmic feel of verse, a sense that is extended by the characters' own enthusiasm for poetry. There is a sameness in the voices, but Kephart writes with great respect for her characters, and thoughtful teens will recognize their own intelligence, capability, talents, confusion, and big hearts in these young people. —Gillian Engberg

Kephart, Beth. *Undercover*. 2007. 288p. HarperCollins/Laura Geringer (9780061238932). Gr. 7–10.

"Dad likes to say, about both of us, that we're undercover operatives who see the world better than the world sees us." Like her father, a traveling consultant, Elisa has leveraged her talent for looking closely and seeing what others don't. A loner and a talented writer, she operates an undercover business ghostwriting love messages for boys who struggle to express their feelings. Elisa finds her inspiration in nature, particularly on trips to a secluded pond, where, in winter, she teaches herself how to skate. As her parents' marriage strains dangerously during her father's long absences, Elisa escapes to the pond, where one of her clients, fellow student Theo, begins to follow her. In her first novel for young adults, Kephart tells a moving story of a young teen whose first powerful crush is tempered by the aching sense that her family is pulling apart. Although it's too convenient that Elisa's English class is studying Edmund Rostand's *Cyrano de Bergerac*, readers will fall easily into the compelling premise and Elisa's memorable, graceful voice, and have no trouble recognizing the teen's quiet courage as she leaves her comfortable isolation, claims her own talents, and embraces the people who matter most. —Gillian Engberg

Kerr, M. E. *Someone Like Summer*. 2007. 272p. HarperTempest (9780061141003). Gr. 7–12.

In Kerr's stirring teen romance, there are many parallels with Phyllis Reynolds Naylor's popular Alice series, including *Dangerously Alice*: in both, the narrator is a smart high-school junior with a sweet older brother and a widowed father who is dating a nice woman. But the big difference here is that issues of race, class, and politics (including the war in Iraq) are a part of the contemporary Romeo-and-Juliet drama. Tall, blonde, blue-eyed Annabel, 17, is in love with Esteban, a Latino immigrant, who turns out to be part of an undocumented group of workers in her town in the Hamptons. The love is intense. They can't keep their hands off each other; in fact, he is the one who stops them from going too far. Prejudice is rough from all sides, including the town's powerful benefactor, who targets the illegals, and values, will be caught up in the contemporary drama of strength, shame, and heartbreak. —Hazel Rochman

Koertge, Ron. *The Brimstone Journals*. 2001. 128p. Candlewick (9780763613020). Gr. 7–12.

"He wants to be stopped." The teenage voices in this story sound like those interviewed on the nightly news about the latest high-school shootings. Fifteen students in a suburban high school speak in short poetic monologues, which are very easy to read. They are all troubled; some have a suppressed rage that could explode. Tran feels boxed in by his immigrant father's dreams; Kelli is trying to break with her macho boyfriend, Damon; Allison, who is being sexually abused by her stepdad, is "ready to kill"; David retreats and watches violent videos; Joseph is sick of his parents' passivity; Lester is always the bully's victim. At the center is Boyd, violent, racist, desperate, encouraged by an adult to join the "Brotherhood" and build an arsenal of guns and chemicals. Boyd makes a list of "everybody who ever blew me off, flipped me off, or pissed me off." The students hear about the list. The power is in the feeling of violence brewing. Who will be drawn in? Boyd even warns his favorite people to stay home first period on Tuesday. That's when someone realizes that "Boyd wants you to stop him." Will someone tell the authorities before it's too late? The ending is too hopeful; too many problems are solved. But Koertge avoids simplistic therapy, and the dramatic monologues are spare, poetic, and immediate, great for readers' theater and for opening group discussion. —Hazel Rochman

Koertge, Ron. *Margaux with an X*. 2004. 176p. Candlewick (9780763624019). Gr. 9–12.

Like Ben and Colleen in Koertge's *Stoner and Spaz* (2002), the author's latest dissimilar teen protagonists find refuge in their unlikely friendship. Gorgeous Margaux has grown weary of her usual social scene: cynical repartee with her best friend, Sara; shopping; and dates with vacuous jocks. Home with her remote parents—a "dazed," channel-surfing mother and a professional gambler father—is even more bleak. Desperate to find a meaningful connection with someone who can match her sharp wit and astonishing vocabulary, Margaux finds herself drawn to Danny, a skinny, bookish junior. As the surprising pair forms an intense bond, each confronts deep childhood sorrows. Margaux's "specialty" is "conversation meant to baffle," and Koertge's own narrative, like Margaux's speech, is laden with self-consciously challenging vocabulary and opaque, overreaching metaphors, resulting in a confused blurring between narrative and character voices. Still, the dramatic situations and sympathetic characters' painful secrets will intrigue teens, particularly language lovers who, like Margaux and Danny, have opened a thesaurus for fun. —Gillian Engberg

Koertge, Ron. *Shakespeare Bats Cleanup*. 2003. 128p. Candlewick (9780763621162). Gr. 7–10.

Koertge has written a standout among the growing number of young adult novels told through verse. Faced with months at home because of a bout of mono, 14-year-old Kevin Boland begins to write poems, using a book from his father's collection to guide him. He writes about such things as the recent death of his mother, his love of baseball, and his make-out sessions with girls. When he recovers, he continues his writing habit and finds a new girlfriend, experimenting with different forms of poetry along the way, including free verse, haiku, sonnets, ballads, and even a sestina. Koertge does an excellent job of creating the authentic voice of a teenage boy exclusively through poems. The poems are funny, touching, and always energetic, and they show both Kevin's growing love for poetry and his struggles as a writer. Several of his attempts at difficult forms break apart in the middle, and some poems have rough edges, giving an extra dose of realism to the somewhat artificial concept of the book. Readers will find themselves identifying with Kevin and perhaps come to understand his attraction to poetry. —Todd Morning

★ Koertge, Ron. *Stoner and Spaz*. 2002. 176p. Candlewick (9780763616083). Gr. 8–12.

Benjamin Bancroft, a 16-year-old with cerebral palsy, strikes up a startling friendship with Colleen values, will be caught up in the contemporary drama of strength, shame, and heartbreak. —Hazel Rochman

Koertge, Ron. *The Brimstone Journals*. 2001. 128p. Candlewick (9780763613020). Gr. 7–12.

"He wants to be stopped." The teenage voices in this story sound like those interviewed on the nightly news about the latest high-school shootings. Fifteen students in a suburban high school speak in short poetic monologues, which are very easy to read. They are all troubled; some have a suppressed rage that could explode. Tran feels boxed in by his immigrant father's dreams; Kelli is trying to break with her macho boyfriend, Damon; Allison, who is being sexually abused by her stepdad, is "ready to kill"; David retreats and watches violent videos; Joseph is sick of his parents' passivity; Lester is always the bully's victim. At the center is Boyd, violent, racist, desperate, encouraged by an adult to join the "Brotherhood" and build an arsenal of guns and chemicals. Boyd makes a list of "everybody who ever blew me off, flipped me off, or pissed me off." The students hear about the list. The power is in the feeling of violence brewing. Who will be drawn in? Boyd even warns his favorite people to stay home first period on Tuesday. That's when someone realizes that "Boyd wants you to stop him." Will someone tell the authorities before it's too late? The ending is too hopeful; too many problems are solved. But Koertge avoids simplistic therapy, and the dramatic monologues are spare, poetic, and immediate, great for readers' theater and for opening group discussion. —Hazel Rochman

Koertge, Ron. *Margaux with an X*. 2004. 176p. Candlewick (9780763624019). Gr. 9–12.

Like Ben and Colleen in Koertge's *Stoner and Spaz* (2002), the author's latest dissimilar teen protagonists find refuge in their unlikely friendship. Gorgeous Margaux has grown weary of her usual social scene: cynical repartee with her best friend, Sara; shopping; and dates with vacuous jocks. Home with her remote parents—a "dazed," channel-surfing mother and a professional gambler father—is even more bleak. Desperate to find a meaningful connection with someone who can match her sharp wit and astonishing vocabulary, Margaux finds herself drawn to Danny, a skinny, bookish junior. As the surprising pair forms an intense bond, each confronts deep childhood sorrows. Margaux's "specialty" is "conversation meant to baffle," and Koertge's own narrative, like Margaux's speech, is laden with self-consciously challenging vocabulary and opaque, overreaching metaphors, resulting in a confused blurring between narrative and character voices. Still, the dramatic situations and sympathetic characters' painful secrets will intrigue teens, particularly language lovers who, like Margaux and Danny, have opened a thesaurus for fun. —Gillian Engberg

Koertge, Ron. *Shakespeare Bats Cleanup*. 2003. 128p. Candlewick (9780763621162). Gr. 7–10.

Koertge has written a standout among the growing number of young adult novels told through verse. Faced with months at home because of a bout of mono, 14-year-old Kevin Boland begins to write poems, using a book from his father's collection to guide him. He writes about such things as the recent death of his mother, his love of baseball, and his make-out sessions with girls. When he recovers, he continues his writing habit and finds a new girlfriend, experimenting with different forms of poetry along the way, including free verse, haiku, sonnets, ballads, and even a sestina. Koertge does an excellent job of creating the authentic voice of a teenage boy exclusively through poems. The poems are funny, touching, and always energetic, and they show both Kevin's growing love for poetry and his struggles as a writer. Several of his attempts at difficult forms break apart in the middle, and some poems have rough edges, giving an extra dose of realism to the somewhat artificial concept of the book. Readers will find themselves identifying with Kevin and perhaps come to understand his attraction to poetry. —Todd Morning

★ Koertge, Ron. *Stoner and Spaz*. 2002. 176p. Candlewick (9780763616083). Gr. 8–12.

Benjamin Bancroft, a 16-year-old with cerebral palsy, strikes up a startling friendship with Colleen with deft magical realist conventions that recall *Everybody Sees the Ants* (2011). Astrid's consciousness is exemplified by Socrates, an agent of truth and logic who silently judges her for not owning up to her personal truths. King also incorporates the first-person narrations of the passengers in the planes, whose stories unknowingly parallel and carry Astrid's affections and desire for escape. Another thoughtful, and often breathtaking, achievement for King, whose star is ascending as quickly as one of Astrid's planes. —Courtney Jones

King, A. S. *Everybody Sees the Ants*. 2011. 282p. Little, Brown (9780316129282). Gr. 9–12.

Fifteen-year-old Lucky Linderman doesn't feel lucky. After creating an ill-conceived school survey on suicide, he is besieged by well-meaning but ineffective adults who want to "make sure he's okay." But though he is honest about how "not okay" Nader McMillion's bullying is, no one intervenes, not even his parents, who are too caught up with their own inadequacies. Better to pretend everything's fine, even when Nader's bullying escalates, and Lucky begins seeing the ants, a tiny Greek chorus that voices what he cannot. The only place Lucky has agency is in his dreams, where he runs rescue missions to save his POW-MIA grandfather from Vietnam. But are they only dreams? Blending magic and realism, this is a subtly written, profoundly honest novel about a kid falling through the cracks and pulling himself back up. Lucky narrates with bewildered anger and bitter humor, his worrisome moments of emotional detachment going unnoticed by the adults around him. Though heartbreaking, the story is ultimately uplifting, as Lucky accepts responsibility for himself, his family, and the other bullying victims he knows are out there, waiting for someone to speak up. Another winner from King, author of the Printz Honor Book *Please Ignore Vera Dietz* (2010). —Krista Hutley

King, A. S. *Please Ignore Vera Dietz*. 2010. 336p. Knopf (9780375865862). Gr. 10–12.

High-school senior Vera never expects her ex–best friend, Charlie, to haunt her after he dies and beg her to clear his name of a horrible accusation surrounding his death. But does Vera want to help him after what he did to her? Charlie's risky, compulsive behavior and brand-new bad-news pals proved to be his undoing, while Vera's mantra was always "Please Ignore Vera Dietz," as she strives, with Charlie's help, to maintain a low profile and keep her family life private. But after Charlie betrayed her, it became impossible to fend off her classmates' cruel attacks or isolate herself any longer. Vera's struggle to put Charlie and his besmirched name behind her are at the crux of this witty, thought-provoking novel, but most memorable is the gorgeous unfurling of Vera's relationship with her father. Chapters titled "A Brief Word from Ken Dietz (Vera's Dad)" are surprising, heartfelt, and tragic; it's through Ken that readers see how quickly alcohol and compromised decision making are destroying Vera's carefully constructed existence. Father and daughter wade gingerly through long-concealed emotions about Vera's mother's leaving the family, creating a powerful redemption story. Although King's characters turn into the people they've long fought to avoid becoming, they ultimately rise above their challenges, reflect, and move on. A worthy, well-crafted addition to any YA collection. —Courtney Jones

Knowles, Jo. *Jumping Off Swings*. 2009. 240p. Candlewick (9780763639495). Gr. 9–12.

When Josh, 16, has sex with Ellie, it is his first time, and he is thrilled to boast to his mates that he is now elevated from "virgin geek to ultrastud." But after Josh's condom falls off, Ellie finds herself pregnant. At first she plans to have an abortion. Then she changes her mind, goes through the pregnancy and painful childbirth, and gives the baby up for adoption. At school the word *slut* is scratched on her locker, but she does get support from her best friend, Corinne, who calls herself Miss Horny Forever Virgin, even as she has a fun romance with Caleb. Told in the alternating first-person narratives of four high-schoolers over nine months, Knowles' novel unveils surprises to the very end about family, friends, love, and sex. The simple words are eloquent about being "together and alone at the same time," and because there is no easy resolution, readers, whatever their personal choices and

Esteban's older sister, who calls Annabel "flour face" and thinks all white girls are loose. The main characters disturb all the stereotypes. Annabel's loving, gruff dad employs illegals because he can pay them less, and he treats them well even as he badmouths them—but no way will he allow Esteban to hook up with his daughter. As things build to a searing climax, Annabel realizes she has asked little about Esteban's dad, who was assassinated back "home" in Colombia. And Kerr crosses other romantic boundaries. Esteban is short—he stands on his toes to kiss—and hot. —Hazel Rochman

Kessler, Cristina. ***No Condition Is Permanent.*** **2000. 192p. Philomel (9780399234866). Gr. 8–12.**

Ambitious and likely to be controversial, this first novel tackles cross-cultural boundaries and the difficult subject of female circumcision. As in Joan Abelove's acclaimed *Go and Come Back* (1998), the story involves a foreign anthropologist in a developing country, but this time the narrator is American rather than indigenous. Fourteen-year-old Jodie moves from California to a coastal village in Sierra Leone with her mother, who is conducting research. Although she is initially overwhelmed by the new culture, Jodie quickly befriends Khadi, a village girl of the same age, who introduces her to the local language and daily routines. The plot takes a dramatic turn when Jodie learns that Khadi will undergo secret female initiation rites that include circumcision. Defying strict taboos against foreign interference, Jodie attempts to "save" her friend, which ultimately forces her to flee the village with her mother and return to the States. The novel's pacing and character development are uneven: Jodie's passage from culture shock to assimilation is quickly glossed over, and many of the characters come off as devices rather than fully defined personalities. In addition, the frequent use of dialect may be an obstacle for some readers, despite the appended glossary. But the author, a longtime resident of Africa, brings the landscape vividly to life with sensory details, and Jodie's strident, flawed attempts at heroic behavior raise crucial questions about cultural perspectives and human rights. —Gillian Engberg

Kessler, Cristina. ***Our Secret, Siri Aang.*** **2004. 208p. Philomel (9780399239854). Gr. 7–12.**

Told from the viewpoint of a Masai girl in Kenya today, this novel brings close the painful conflict between the traditional and modern in a changing world. In the exciting opening scene Namelok, 12, witnesses the birth of a baby rhinoceros in the bush and vows to keep it secret to protect the animals from dangerous poachers. Her other secret is getting her period, which she keeps to herself to delay the painful traditional initiation ceremony and arranged marriage. (There's no clear explanation of what that initiation is except in the glossary; presumably it's female circumcision, which has long been practiced by the Masai and is now being challenged.) Namelok wants to go to school, but her beloved father, the tribal leader, heartbroken that his people have been displaced and angered by tourists who pay for posed photos, insists she follow the old ways. Neither exotic nor sentimental, Namelok's personal story is part survival and part coming-of-age. She spends days alone in the bush as she tracks the poacher who killed the mother rhino, and she takes her first step toward independence when she learns the poacher's shocking identity. Kessler has spent many years in Kenya, and she writes with authority about both the wildlife and the cultural struggle. Always there are the questions: Is tradition sentimental? Are all new ideas bad? —Hazel Rochman

King, A. S. ***Ask the Passengers.*** **2012. 296p. Little, Brown (9780316194686). Gr. 9–12.**

Astrid has a lot of love to give, and she gives it freely to schoolmates, friends, and even her dysfunctional family. But most of all, she sends her love to the passengers in the planes whizzing high above her small, gossipy, intolerant town: "Because if I give it all away, no one can control it." But she does love her coworker Dee and her best friend Kristina, whose biggest secret she keeps. Printz Honor Book author King (*Please Ignore Vera Dietz*, 2010) continues to expertly plumb the lovely numbness of a young person struck by emotional paralysis. Afraid to come out, afraid to be boxed in, and afraid to fall under the scrutiny of her town, Astrid lives a rich inner life, which King depicts discovers to her sorrow when her father's National Guard unit is sent to Iraq and he comes home a different man, horribly wounded by a bombing. The traumatic brain injury he suffers will not only change him, it will also change Rachel. In fact, it will change everything. A Pulitzer Prize–winning journalist, Keller wrote a series about traumatic brain injury for the *Chicago Tribune*, and she clearly knows her subject both intellectually and viscerally, particularly the emotional impact visited on the loved ones of the injured. While her first novel isn't perfect—Rachel's voice is too old and her sensibility too mature, and in the interest of verisimilitude there is perhaps too much information that is didactic instead of aesthetic in its presentation—no one who reads this heartbreaking book will ever forget it. With integrity, authenticity, and immediacy, Keller has captured the extraordinary complexity and challenge of unexpected change and, to her everlasting credit, unsparingly shares the whole truth of it with her readers. —Michael Cart

Kephart, Beth. *The Heart Is Not a Size*. 2010. 240p. HarperTeen (9780061470486). Gr. 8–11.

Drawn by a flyer promising "two weeks that will change your life," Pennsylvania high-school student Georgia convinces her best friend, Riley, to join her on a trip to Juarez, Mexico, where chaperoned teens will build community projects. Georgia is hoping that the newness of the experience will help her shed both the secret panic attacks she has been experiencing as well as her sense of herself as a "freakishly well-behaved" and predictable decision-maker. As expected, the trip does widen the teens' cultural awareness ("Privilege doesn't make you smarter. It doesn't gift you decency"), but it also forces Georgia and Riley to confront previously unspoken personal troubles. Kephart is an award-winning poet as well as a novelist, and her prose, filled with memorable, original imagery, has the subtlety and spare, rhythmic feel of verse, a sense that is extended by the characters' own enthusiasm for poetry. There is a sameness in the voices, but Kephart writes with great respect for her characters, and thoughtful teens will recognize their own intelligence, capability, talents, confusion, and big hearts in these young people. —Gillian Engberg

Kephart, Beth. *Undercover*. 2007. 288p. HarperCollins/Laura Geringer (9780061238932). Gr. 7–10.

"Dad likes to say, about both of us, that we're undercover operatives who see the world better than the world sees us." Like her father, a traveling consultant, Elisa has leveraged her talent for looking closely and seeing what others don't. A loner and a talented writer, she operates an undercover business ghostwriting love messages for boys who struggle to express their feelings. Elisa finds her inspiration in nature, particularly on trips to a secluded pond, where, in winter, she teaches herself how to skate. As her parents' marriage strains dangerously during her father's long absences, Elisa escapes to the pond, where one of her clients, fellow student Theo, begins to follow her. In her first novel for young adults, Kephart tells a moving story of a young teen whose first powerful crush is tempered by the aching sense that her family is pulling apart. Although it's too convenient that Elisa's English class is studying Edmund Rostand's *Cyrano de Bergerac*, readers will fall easily into the compelling premise and Elisa's memorable, graceful voice, and have no trouble recognizing the teen's quiet courage as she leaves her comfortable isolation, claims her own talents, and embraces the people who matter most. —Gillian Engberg

Kerr, M. E. *Someone Like Summer*. 2007. 272p. HarperTempest (9780061141003). Gr. 7–12.

In Kerr's stirring teen romance, there are many parallels with Phyllis Reynolds Naylor's popular Alice series, including *Dangerously Alice*: in both, the narrator is a smart high-school junior with a sweet older brother and a widowed father who is dating a nice woman. But the big difference here is that issues of race, class, and politics (including the war in Iraq) are a part of the contemporary Romeo-and-Juliet drama. Tall, blonde, blue-eyed Annabel, 17, is in love with Esteban, a Latino immigrant, who turns out to be part of an undocumented group of workers in her town in the Hamptons. The love is intense. They can't keep their hands off each other; in fact, he is the one who stops them from going too far. Prejudice is rough from all sides, including the town's powerful benefactor, who targets the illegals, and

Minou, the school's infamous druggie, much to his prim grandmother's horror. Colleen is an unlikely self-esteem booster and aphrodisiac, talking, teasing, then touching, kissing, and seducing Ben. And he has a surprising effect on her: she becomes less abrasive and even occasionally sober. Stoner and Spaz are good for each other. This is vintage Koertge. Funny, touching, and surprising, it is a hopeful yet realistic view of things as they are and as they could be. Few authors write better dialogue than Koertge, and he is at his best in this short, fast-moving novel, using Ben and Colleen's repartee to reveal both their longings and insecurities. The temptation will be to compare this with Terry Trueman's *Stuck in Neutral* (2000), yet that would be unfair to both books. This is a realistic story, and Ben is high-functioning, a teenager we often see at school, the movies, in the workplace. The first-person narrative is Ben's, but the human face, the fully developed personality of Ben Bancroft, is revealed through Colleen's drug-enhanced innocence and acceptance. Didactic? No. Revealing and consciousness raising? Absolutely. Buy several copies. —Frances Bradburn

Koertge, Ron. ***Strays.*** **2007. 176p. Candlewick (9780763627058). Gr. 7–10.**

Sixteen-year-old Ted prefers animals to humans; animals "never lie," and unlike the kids at school, he understands them. When Ted loses his parents in a car accident, he particularly identifies with strays—after all, as a foster kid, that's what he is. Ted lands in a new home, where his basic needs are met by fair but semi-dysfunctional foster parents and where he coexists with Astin, his older roommate, and C. W., who has had 19 placements in six years. Ted also starts a new school, and with Astin and C. W. at his back, he learns to express himself and to rely upon people as well as animals. Ted's two-way conversations with animals may initially surprise readers, but this magic realism effectively emphasizes his emotional withdrawal, and his outsider's observations of human nature are by turns insightful, devastatingly funny, and suffused with loneliness. Though Koertge never soft pedals the horrors experienced by some foster children, this thoughtful novel about the lost and abandoned is a hopeful one, in which some strays find a place to belong. —Krista Hutley

Koja, Kathe. ***The Blue Mirror.*** **2004. 128p. Farrar/Frances Foster (9780374308490). Gr. 9–12.**

Koja's writing talent, hinted at in *Straydog* (2001), reaches remarkable fruition in this cautionary tale of infatuation. Maggy, a talented, 17-year-old artist who spends long hours sketching at a local cafe, notices a beautiful boy of extraordinary grace (and dark blue lipstick) through the window. Eventually she and Cole meet, and she falls head over heels in love. Despite the well-meaning advice of a friend, Maggy is unable to see Cole's considerable flaws, and the relationship spirals downward until a tragedy finally forces her to see what is really going on. The familiar plot of first love gone awry is not particularly special. It's Koja's writing that is noteworthy. Long stream-of-consciousness sentences with creative (but recognizable) spelling and clever use of italics will enchant readers, while the atmospheric cover art will draw teens seeking stories about extraordinary experiences. —Debbie Carton

Koja, Kathe. ***Buddha Boy.*** **2003. 128p. Farrar/Frances Foster (9780374309985). Gr. 6–10.**

No one in the rich, suburban high school likes the weird new kid who looks like a Buddhist monk and begs at lunch. But Justin is drawn to the stranger and defends him against vicious school bullies. Koja's short novel is openly preachy, and the packed plot is absurdly contrived: the saintly outsider turns out to be an amazingly gifted artist who was once a delinquent as violent as the school bullies—until his parents died and he went catatonic and a Buddhist art teacher showed him how to find truth and beauty in art and religion . . . It's the simple writing, along with Justin's informal first-person narrative, that will draw readers to the crucial ethical issues, especially "the social-status in-out thing" among the kids, and the way school authorities accept it. Then there's the elemental question of how hard it is to do the right thing, and to keep on doing it. "We're all gods inside, right? Karma, right?" Teens will find much to talk about here. —Hazel Rochman

Koja, Kathe. *Kissing the Bee*. 2007. 128p. Farrar/Frances Foster (9780374399382). Gr. 9–12.

In the spring before high-school graduation, Dana helps her best friend, Avra, and Avra's boyfriend, Emil, prepare costumes for the masquerade-themed prom. As the dance approaches, though, Dana begins to question the depth of her friendship with demanding, self-absorbed Avra, even as she realizes the urgency of her sweet, secret feelings for Emil: "I wanted him from the very beginning, before Avra even saw him." Dana, a scholarship-winning science student, is preparing a senior project on bees, and passages from her research are woven into her authentic first-person narrative. Some of the metaphors of bees and honey feel purposeful, but their effect is still powerful, and readers will recognize their own lives in the descriptions of queen bees and a hive's workings. Particularly poignant are the connections that Dana draws between the bees' unchanging roles of worker, drone, and queen and her own capacity for choice and transformation as she approaches adulthood: "Like metamorphosis. Once you start changing, you've already changed." Poetic, realistic, and filled with memorable characters, this spare novel captures first love's exquisite, earth-shattering joy and the struggle and thrill that come with claiming one's own life. —Gillian Engberg

Konigsberg, Bill. *Openly Straight*. 2013. 336p. Scholastic/Arthur A. Levine (9780545509893) Gr. 9–12.

Now a junior in high school, Rafe, who has been out since he was 14, is thoroughly sick of being labeled "the gay kid." So he does something bold: he leaves his Colorado school to enroll in a private boys' academy in New England, where no one knows he's gay and he can be a label-free, "openly straight" part of a group of guys. Does this mean he goes back into the closet? No, he tells himself, not exactly: "It was more like I was in the doorway." But is he fooling himself? Can you put a major part of yourself on hold, and what happens when you then find yourself falling in love with your new (straight) best friend? Lambda Literary Award winner Konigsberg (*Out of the Pocket*, 2008) has written an exceptionally intelligent, thought-provoking coming-of-age novel about the labels people apply to us and that we, perversely, apply to ourselves. A sometimes painful story of self-discovery, it is also a beautifully written, absolutely captivating romance between two boys, Rafe and Ben, who are both wonderfully sympathetic characters. With its capacity to invite both thought and deeply felt emotion, *Openly Straight* is altogether one of the best gay-themed novels of the last 10 years. —Michael Cart

Konigsburg, E. L. *Silent to the Bone*. 2000. 272p. Atheneum (9780689836015). Gr. 5–9.

Did the British nanny do it? She says it was 13-year-old Branwell who dropped his baby sister, Nikki, and he's the prime suspect. Why has he been struck dumb? What does he know? Is his silence a weapon? Is it survivor guilt? Shame? Konigsburg gets behind today's tabloid headlines with a compelling mystery that is also a moving story of family, friendship, and seduction. The story is told by Branwell's best friend, Connor, who visits the Juvenile Detention Center and tries to get Branwell to communicate by blinking his eyes at letters and flash cards. Like Branwell, Connor is also part of a tense stepfamily, where he feels abandoned by a parent's remarriage. And Connor has another link with the accused: he understands his friend's attraction to the sexy babysitter, Vivian, especially when he learns that she has a habit of leaving the bathroom door open when she takes a bath. Everything makes you want to go back and reread the story, not only to think about the clues and suspects you missed the first time around (What exactly does the tape of the 911 call reveal?) but also for the wit and insight, the farce, and the gentleness of the telling. As in Laurie Halse Anderson's Printz Honor Book, *Speak* (1999), the mutism is an eloquent part of the narrative. Like his silent friend, Connor comes to know the power of keeping quiet, that "the cruelest lies are often told in silence."—Hazel Rochman

Korman, Gordon. *The Juvie Three*. 2008. 256p. Hyperion (9781423101581). Gr. 7–10.

What are the odds a teenage gangbanger, a 15-year-old murderer, and a 14-year-old who crashed a stolen car can keep it together when the saintly social worker who has given them a second chance at redemption ends up comatose in the hospital? Terence, Arjay, and Gecko become unlikely co-conspirators at keeping Doug Healy's absence hidden from teachers, their psychologist, and especially from their nasty case worker. Arjay and Gecko, determined not to do anything that will land them back in jail, become model students and strong-arm Terence into extremely reluctant compliance. It seems to be working until Doug awakens with amnesia, Terence annoys a gang leader, and a high-ranking cop tells Gecko to stop seeing the daughter of a wealthy businessman. Korman keeps lots of balls in the air as he handles each boy's distinct voice and character—as well as the increasingly absurd situation—with humor and flashes of sadness. His use of present tense is occasionally jarring, but it effectively heightens the tension and the sense that these kids are living minute to minute, where one false step may haunt them forever. Readers will love the feel-good, almost too-good-to-be-true ending, so be prepared for high demand. —Chris Sherman

Korman, Gordon. *Schooled*. 2007. 224p. Hyperion (9780786856923). Gr. 6–9.

Homeschooled on an isolated "alternate farm commune" that has dwindled since the 1960s to two members, 13-year-old Cap has always lived with his grandmother, Rain. When she is hospitalized, Cap is taken in by a social worker and sent—like a lamb to slaughter—to middle school. Smart and capable, innocent and inexperienced (he learned to drive on the farm, but he has never watched television), long-haired Cap soon becomes the butt of pranks. He reacts in unexpected ways and, in the end, elevates those around him to higher ground. From chapter to chapter, the first-person narrative shifts among certain characters: Cap, a social worker (who takes him into her home), her daughter (who resents his presence there), an A-list bully, a Z-list victim, a popular girl, the school principal, and a football player (who unintentionally decks Cap twice in one day). Korman capably manages the shifting points of view of characters who begin by scorning or resenting Cap and end up on his side. From the eye-catching jacket art to the scene in which Cap says good-bye to his 1,100 fellow students, individually and by name, this rewarding novel features an engaging main character and some memorable moments of comedy, tenderness, and reflection. Pair this with Jerry Spinelli's 2000 *Stargirl* (and its sequel, *Love, Stargirl*, 2007) for a discussion of the stifling effects of conformity within school culture or just read it for the fun of it. —Carolyn Phelan

Koss, Amy Goldman. *Side Effects*. 2006. 144p. Roaring Brook (9781596432949). Gr. 8–11.

Fourteen-year-old Isabella is a typical teenager. She is concerned with friends, school, and gaining weight until the fateful morning that she discovers the enlarged glands in her neck. With the subsequent diagnosis of stage-four Hodgkin's lymphoma, she enters the netherworld of cancer: IVs, PICC lines (which she refuses), chemotherapy, hair loss, nausea and more nausea, and even medical marijuana. It's a harsh, realistic story of teen cancer, one that author Koss describes in her introduction as Issy's "descent into hell, with a safe return." Chronicling the appearance, disappearance, and rearrangement of friends (which will remind readers of Cynthia Voigt's 1986 *Izzy Willy-Nilly*), as well as the overwhelming side effects as the chemo takes its toll, Koss refuses to glamorize Issy's illness or treatment. Instead, she settles for an honesty and frankness that will both challenge and enlighten readers. —Frances Bradburn

Kraus, Daniel. *Rotters*. 2011. 464p. Delacorte (9780385738576). Gr. 9–12.

After his mother is killed in a bus accident, teenager Joey moves from Chicago to a small Iowa town, where he will live with Harnett, the father he has never met. After no one greets him at the train station, Joey finds his way to his father's home: a remote shack saturated in a foul, mysterious odor. The source of that odor becomes clear after Joey learns that his father, known as "the Garbage Man" around town, is, in fact, a grave robber who relies on deeply rooted traditions and a network that stretches across the country. As Joey forms a wary relationship with his father, he finds himself increasingly drawn into Harnett's shocking underworld, even as he becomes an untouchable pariah at the local high school. Weaving in humor, tenderness, and fascinating lore about the biology and history of burial, Kraus' ambitious novel explores archetypal tensions between fathers and sons, outsiders and insiders, faith and science, and beauty and horror. —Gillian Engberg

Krovatin, Christopher. *Heavy Metal and You*. 2005. 186p. Scholastic/Push (9780439736480). Gr. 10–12.

It was Slayer that first turned Sam Markus into a metalhead. "Slayer was like Rob Zombie, only without the camp value and with better musicianship. They scared the hell out of me at first, and I loved it. Pure fucking evil." Sam and his buddies hang out drinking, smoking, and exchanging vulgar insults when not attending their NYC prep school. But after Sam starts to date Melissa, things change. He makes her a disc of tunes to draw her into his world (the songs are listed so readers can re-create the mix), and goes "straightedge" for her, giving up his favorite vices. Ultimately, though, he realizes that he's becoming one of the phonies that his idol, Holden Caulfield, detests. Infusing the story with music, humor, and anger, Krovatin records a perfect take on relationships and how they change. From the terrific cover and portrait of selfish love to the clever CD player icons indicating narrative switches (PLAY, PAUSE, SKIP AHEAD, BACK, and on the final page, STOP), this is an authentic portrayal of an obsession with music. Teens don't have to like heavy metal to appreciate this novel, which is guaranteed to attract readers looking for a book to reach their death-metal souls. —Cindy Dobrez

LaCour, Nina. *The Disenchantments*. 2012. 304p. Dutton (9780525422198). Gr. 9–12.

LaCour's sophomore novel, following her Morris Award finalist *Hold Still* (2009), features coming-of-age themes—truth, uncertainty, pain, passion—which are as common as high-school graduates in June. Yet the novel also possesses an on-the-cusp-of-something soul as unique and memorable as new experiences are to every individual teen. The story tells of a group of creative friends who road trip from San Francisco to Portland so that the titular band, comprising three hot girls, can play gigs (poorly), and the one guy can pine (unrequitedly) before going away to college . . . or not. The tattoo artists, bartenders, secrets, and lies the teens experience along the way are life changing, as they are destined to be; the feelings of betrayal, confusion, and wonder, and the words used to express them, such as *love* and *f*-bombs, are so authentic that introspective readers will feel that the characters understand them exactly. LaCour's skill and compassion make proclamations such as "We all want to feel something, we want to be someone to one another" seem more sincere than sappy and will entice readers to download the girl-band music. This is about the inside and outside of characters, the past and future of their lives—and it is astonishing. —Andrew Medlar

LaCour, Nina. *Hold Still*. 2009. 240p. Dutton (9780525421559). Gr. 9–12.

After teen Ingrid commits suicide, Caitlin, 16, is overcome with grief and guilt: "My best friend is dead, and I could have saved her." Why didn't she see it coming? Then she finds Ingrid's diary, and the journal entries (including a secret of sexual trauma) are woven into the story along with Caitlin's memories as she goes through stages of sorrow, depression, anger, and recovery, with the support of her loving parents. She also becomes close to a gorgeous, understanding classmate, Taylor ("his lip grazes my earlobe, and my body fills with light"); makes friends with her lesbian classmate, Dylan; works on her photography; and bonds with her art teacher. Set in the suburbs of San Francisco, this first novel may try to cover too much. But the immediate, present-tense, first-person narrative stays true to a teen's daily experience, and whether Caitlin is building a tree house or watching the demolition of a theater, the metaphors of loss and recovery are rooted in the surprising dramas of daily life. —Hazel Rochman

Lake, Nick. *Hostage Three*. Oct. 2013. 320p. Bloomsbury (9781619631816). Gr. 9–12.

Lake's follow-up to *In Darkness* (2012) shares two distinct traits with that Printz Award–winning novel: a Cormac McCarthy style of nonattributed dialogue and a canny ability to generate sympathy for those who are ostensibly villains. Still smarting from the suicide of her mother, Amy, 17, is unenthused to be spending months aboard her wealthy father's yacht, along with "the stepmother" and a small crew. Their edgy boredom is torn apart when the ship is overwhelmed by Somali pirates—or "coast guard" as they prefer to be known—who have nothing personal against Amy's family and wish them no harm. What they want is simple: a few million dollars in ransom. But until they get it, there are rules, guns, secrets, and nerve-shredding negotiations with the navy. Right away, Amy feels a connection with 25-year-old Somali translator Farouz, who soon returns her attentions. Lake doesn't play this as Stockholm syndrome, so readers' mileage will vary on their ability to believe in such a sudden and intense emotional affair: "It was like our skins spoke to each other," moons Amy after an accidental touch. With a verisimilitude that recalls Mal Peet, Lake illustrates how pirating is the best hope Farouz has to get his brother out of prison and forge a real life for himself. Like Amy, readers will be torn. Intelligent, empathetic, and eye-opening. —Daniel Kraus

Lake, Nick. *In Darkness*. 2012. 352p. Bloomsbury (9781599907437). Gr. 10–12.

Shorty, 15, is in a Haitian hospital with a bullet in his arm when the walls fall down during an earthquake. As he waits for help, drinking blood to try to quench his thirst, he remembers how he got to the hospital and the haunting gang violence he witnessed in the slums: his beloved twin sister was taken; his father was chopped to pieces. His mother loved freedom-fighter Aristide, but his father did not. Shorty's present-day narrative switches back and forth with a historical plotline set in the eighteenth century, when Touissant l'Ouverture, a former slave, led Haiti in the fight for freedom, calling for justice, not vengeance, in the struggle to emancipate the slaves. The constantly shifting narratives, large cast of characters, and cultural detail may overwhelm some readers, and the unspeakable brutality is not for the fainthearted. But older readers, especially those who have seen the devastating footage of Haiti's recent earthquake, will want to read about the grim, contemporary drama and the inspiring history. —Hazel Rochman

Larochelle, David. *Absolutely, Positively Not*. 2005. 224p. Scholastic/Arthur A. Levine (9780439591096). Gr. 7–10.

In a touching, sometime hilarious coming-out story, Steven DeNarski, 16, tries to deny he is gay. He covers his Superman posters with pictures of women in skimpy bikinis and lacy lingerie, and he follows the aversion therapy prescribed in a parents' handbook for getting over his "deviant" desires and awakening his sluggish interest in girls. He hangs out with the hockey players and tries to start dating (even kissing), to the delight of his fussy mom and macho dad. It doesn't work. When he reluctantly tells his friend Rachel that he is gay, he has to restrain her from celebrating it to the world and "empowering" him at school. The wry, first-person narrative is wonderful as it moves from personal angst to outright farce (Steven takes a pet golden retriever to the school dance). The characters are drawn with surprising depth, and Steven finds quiet support, as well as betrayal, in unexpected places. Many readers, gay and straight, will recognize Steven's need to talk to someone. —Hazel Rochman

Lawrence, Iain. *The Lightkeeper's Daughter*. 2002. 256p. Delacorte (9780385729253). Gr. 10–12.

Like the secluded British Columbian setting, Lawrence's latest novel is lush and deceptively quiet. After a three-year absence, 17-year-old Squid McRae returns with her toddler daughter to her childhood home on a small island, where her father, the lighthouse keeper, and her mother still live as the only residents. Squid's brilliant brother, Alastair, drowned four years earlier, and Squid's return prompts the family members to reflect on the past and try to uncover their complicated sorrows—the profound power struggles between children and parents and even an intimation of incest between Squid and Alastair. Teens who demand swift plots may tire of the introspective, meandering story and the thick detail in Lawrence's lyrical, sophisticated telling, but those who make it through won't easily forget this novel. Though Lawrence raises interesting questions about freedom, responsibility, and happiness, the strongest moments are subtle, piercing scenes that uncover the unspoken emotions layered between family members—the guilt, shame, joy, anger, and almost unbearable love. A beautiful, unsettling story. —Gillian Engberg

Leavitt, Martine. *My Book of Life by Angel*. 2012. 256p. Farrar/Margaret Ferguson (9780374351236). Gr. 9–12.

Sixteen-year-old Angel's life on the street begins when Call, the man she thinks is her boyfriend, gets her hooked on "candy," and before she knows it, she is forced to sell herself to support him—and her habit. But when Call brings home an 11-year-old girl, Melli, and demands that Angel train her for the street, Angel realizes that things must change. However, change may require a miracle. This novel is itself something of a miracle: a spot-on, compassionate—and passionate—account of a heartbreakingly horrible life. Perhaps there are angels looking after Angel, though; her efforts to save Melli and herself are heroic and, ultimately, inspired. In this novel in verse, Leavitt has created in Angel's voice a perfect mix of innocence and experience, a blend that is underscored by seamlessly introducing passages from Milton's *Paradise Lost* into her narrative. Death, too, is present in Angel's life as women she knows begin vanishing from the street—victims, perhaps, of a serial killer. The story is loosely based on the epidemic of murders that began in Vancouver in 1983 and continued through 2002. But Angel's story is uniquely her own, and Leavitt has done a brilliant job of imagining and recording it. —Michael Cart

Les Becquets, Diane. *Love, Cajun Style*. 2005. 300p. Bloomsbury (9781582346748). Gr. 8–11.

Like a spicy Cajun stew, this mixes together lots of ingredients, and the result is delicious. The height of excitement for Lucy Beauregard and her friends Evie and Mary in their Louisiana town is going skinny-dipping and finding their clothes have been stolen. Then some strangers come to town. Mr. Savoi, an artist, opens a gallery, and suddenly Lucy's mom becomes interested in posing for him—nude. Mr. Savoi's son, Dewey is causing some heat in Lucy, but what about the attention she is receiving from Mr. Banks, the new teacher who has cast Lucy as the lead in a community play? Les Becquets creates a wonderful world that captures not only the emotions and dreams of youth but also the longings and regrets of adults. Populating the small town are richly drawn characters who waltz in and out of scenes with grace and humor. Religion and talk of God and morality also slide easily through the narrative. This is romantic, real, and lots of fun. —Ilene Cooper

Levchuk, Lisa. *Everything Beautiful in the World*. 2008. 208p. Farrar (9780374322380). Gr. 9–12.

Seventeen-year-old Edna is in the midst of having a fight with her mother when a telephone call forces her mother to say, "All fights postponed." She has been told she has cancer. So begins an interesting experiment in writing that gives this book a quite different sound from so many YA novels with their ubiquitous first-person voice. In a flat tone that's much more reportage than confessional, Edna relates how an affair begins with her art teacher, Mr. Howland, while her mother is in the hospital. Making it clear she will not visit her mother, and ignoring a father who ignores her, Edna is given a "free pass" to do what she wants. And what she wants is to live in the cocoon that surrounds her and Mr. Howland, eating lunches in seclusion, going to their secret spot for sex. Although this story has been done before, it is the way Levchuk writes it that is both startling and affecting. Reminiscent of Brock Cole's remote style in *The Facts Speak for Themselves* (1997), this technique allows readers to get farther inside Edna's head than she is herself. We see, more clearly than she does, how Mr. Howland can annoy her and how his neediness scares her. Her questions about a long-dead brother reveal more about her than she would be comfortable with anyone knowing. There are some flaws. Although the book is set in the 1980s, Edna's mother's long hospital stay seems necessary to accommodate the plot rather than her illness, and the end seems rushed. But, overall, Levchuk does a remarkable job of writing a novel that offers the facts on the pages; all the emotion is underneath. —Ilene Cooper

Levithan, David. ***Are We There Yet?*** **2005. 224p. Knopf (9780375828461). Gr. 10–12.**

Elijah and Danny are brothers who have grown apart. Elijah is a mellow, kind, live-in-the-moment, pot-smoking teen who likes to wonder about things and to wander without a plan. Danny, six years Elijah's senior, is a young up-and-comer with a prestigious New York law firm, who dresses meticulously and exerts a rigid control both on his own life and on the lives of those around him. In an attempt to draw their sons back together, the boys' parents arrange a vacation to Italy. But the appearance of a girl who may have the power to separate the two brothers even further means the trip may not reach its intended goal. Levithan's latest is a stylized, pensive, almost mournful piece that outwardly travels through three of Italy's most famed cities but is focused almost exclusively on the interior landscapes of two uniquely sympathetic young men. At times overly self-aware, the book's literary complexity and minimal action make this a title for older readers attracted to mature psychological and philosophical perspectives. —Holly Koelling

★ **Levithan, David.** ***Boy Meets Boy.*** **2003. 208p. Knopf (9780375824005). Gr. 9–12.**

Paul, a high-school sophomore, is gay. Big deal! He's known he was gay since he was in kindergarten. Remarkably, everybody else knows it, too, and nobody cares. Clearly, the world Paul inhabits in this breakthrough book (the first upbeat gay novel for teens) differs from the real world: two boys walk through town holding hands; the cross-dressing quarterback, named Infinite Darlene, is not only captain of the football team but also homecoming queen; the school has a biker cheerleading team. Even in this whimsical world, however, the course of true love doesn't always run smoothly: Paul meets—and gets—the boy, Noah, a new kid in town, but loses him. Then, in perfect balance with this extraordinarily large-hearted, cheerful book, something unpredictable but deeply satisfying happens. Though at times arch and even precious, this wacky, charming, original story is never outrageous, and its characters are fresh, real, and deeply engaging. In its blithe acceptance and celebration of human differences, this is arguably the most important gay novel since Nancy Garden's *Annie on My Mind* (1982); it certainly seems to represent a revolution in the publishing of gay-themed books for adolescents. —Michael Cart

Levithan, David. ***The Realm of Possibility.*** **2004. 224p. Knopf (9780375828454). Gr. 9–12.**

In this hugely ambitious novel in verse, Levithan (*Boy Meets Boy*, 2003) again writes of both gay and straight young love with integrity and insight. But this time, Levithan asks a lot of patience from his readers. The novel is separated into five parts; at the start of each, a title page lists four names. Although nothing in the book design makes it clear, readers will eventually figure out that Daniel is the author of the first poem, and he and the others all attend the same school. At first, the poems seem largely unconnected (Daniel writes of approaching his one-year anniversary with his boyfriend, Jed, for instance; Clara of buying pot for her cancer-stricken mother), but readers who pay close attention (and don't mind frequently flipping back to see who's writing what and who wrote what about whom four poems ago) will be rewarded; a kind of narrative emerges around Jed, who is a charming and well-liked kid. Many readers, even good ones, will be put off by the challenging, often confusing structure. But the distinct voices and plethora of poetic styles make for interesting reading, and some teens will return to this again and again, seeking to uncover the subtle connections between the characters within the poems. —John Green

Levithan, David. ***Wide Awake.*** **2006. 240p. Knopf (9780375834660). Gr. 8–11.**

In *Boy Meets Boy* (2003), Levithan created a town where being gay is no big thing. In his latest, he imagines a future America—after the Reign of Fear, after the Greater Depression, the War to End All Wars, the Jesus Revolution, and the Prada Riots. Living in this not quite but almost believable America are Duncan and his boyfriend, Jimmy, who start out the book rejoicing that Abe Stein, both gay and Jewish, has been elected president. Unsurprisingly, however, the governor of Kansas demands a recount, causing both Stein supporters and Stein haters to travel en masse to Kansas. Into this politically charged atmosphere go Duncan and Jimmy, who experience what proves to be a life-changing journey for them and their country. Levithan is best when he's focused on the two nuanced teenagers. Duncan's first-person narration—vulnerable, insecure, caring—absolutely sings, and his relationship with the outspoken Jimmy has all the awkwardness and intensity of first love. Clearly responding to current politics, Levithan's vision of the future occasionally dips into heavy-handed moralizing, but the politics are so well integrated and thought-provoking that those moments are forgivable. As much about love as about politics, Levithan's latest reaches out to shake readers awake, showing them how each person's life touches another, and another, until ultimately history is made. —Krista Hutley

Levitin, Sonia. *Strange Relations*. 2007. 304p. Knopf (9780375837517). Gr. 8–11.

After her mother receives a work assignment in Paris, 15-year-old Marne is eager to spend the summer in Hawaii with relatives. She yearns to escape the unspoken grief and tension that remains at home following her younger sister's disappearance years earlier. Imagining languid afternoons at the beach, Marne is confronted with a much different scene on arrival in Hawaii. Aunt Chaya and her husband, Yitz, a Hasidic rabbi, oversee a chaotic household filled with children and visiting members of their Jewish community. Marne, raised by secular Jewish parents, finds the cultural differences startling. "Are they from Mars?" she writes in an e-mail to her best friend, Kim, and she feels resentful when her conservatively dressed cousins question her shorts and tank tops. Gradually, though, she realizes that she loves the feeling of Shabbat—"the sudden quiet, the comfort"—and when Kim comes to visit and wants to hook up with some local guys, Marne feels on a "different wavelength." Too few novels give such a revealing, believable view of contemporary Jewish American kids wrestling with tradition and faith. The debates and cultural details sometimes feel like documentary, but Marne's authentic, first-person voice wraps purposefully inserted passages into an honest, sensitively told story that's filled with spot-on teen talk and inner monologues. Marne's active, earnest search for who she is and who she wants to become will touch readers of all backgrounds. —Gillian Engberg

★ Lockhart, E. *The Disreputable History of Frankie Landau-Banks*. 2008. 352p. Hyperion (9780786838189). Gr. 7–12.

In the summer between her freshman and sophomore years, Frankie Landau-Banks transforms from "a scrawny, awkward child" with frizzy hair to a curvy beauty, "all while sitting quietly in a suburban hammock, reading the short stories of Dorothy Parker and drinking lemonade." On her return to Alabaster Prep, her elite boarding school, she attracts the attention of gorgeous Matthew, who draws her into his circle of popular seniors. Then Frankie learns that Matthew is a member of the Loyal Order of the Basset Hounds, an all-male Alabaster secret society to which Frankie's dad had once belonged. Excluded from belonging to or even discussing the Bassets, Frankie engineers her own guerilla membership by assuming a false online identity. Frankie is a fan of P. G. Wodehouse's books, and Lockhart's wholly engaging narrative, filled with wordplay, often reads like a clever satire about the capers of the entitled, interwoven with elements of a mystery. But the story's expertly timed comedy also has deep undercurrents. Lockhart creates a unique, indelible character in Frankie, whose oddities only make her more realistic, and teens will be galvanized by her brazen action and her passionate, immediate questions about gender and power, individuals and institutions, and how to fall in love without losing herself. —Gillian Engberg

Lockhart, E. *Dramarama*. 2007. 311p. Hyperion (9780786838158). Gr. 8–12.

She was just big-boned, big-nose Sarah living in Brenton, Ohio, where, as she puts it, "committing suicide would be redundant." Then she meets Demi, who is trying hard to be invisible—surprisingly easy considering he's black and gay. Alone they are, well . . . alone, but brought together by their love of musical theater, they light up. All this might sound like a stereotypical take on gay men and the women who love them, and there is some of that, but there's also so much more. The renamed Sayde and Demi make their way to a summer theater camp, and that's where things change. Encouraged to become part of the ensemble, Sayde finds she is too opinionated to do that, even as it turns out that she is less talented than she believed. At the same time, Demi is discovering that he's a star who can hang out with actual boyfriends rather than Sayde. Lockhart mixes this all up neatly. Most of the story is told in a bright, bitchy voice that, while familiar, is very smart and very funny; transcripts of tapes made for "posterity" add delicious detail. Although it's hard to say what kids who aren't into musical comedy will make of the myriad detail offered here (*Birdie*! *Cabaret*! *Cats*!), theater lovers will applaud, and everyone else will appreciate the twists and the ending you don't see coming. —Ilene Cooper

Lowry, Brigid. *Follow the Blue*. 2004. 205p. Holiday (9780823418275). Gr. 8–12.

Imagine a more functional Georgia Nicolson (of Louise Rennison's *Angus, Thongs and Full-Frontal Snogging*, 2000) in Perth, Australia, and you'll have the main character in this exhilarating novel. When 15-year-old Bec's parents leave for a month-long business trip (following her father's mental breakdown and subsequent recovery), Bec and her two younger siblings are left in the care of a dowdy housekeeper. Bec is tired of being the good, sensible girl who keeps everything together, and she takes advantage of this parent-free time to indulge in a little rebellion, such as coloring her hair and discovering the opposite sex. A lot goes on in this very funny romp, some of it quite profound, and Lowry manages to remain mercifully nonpreachy throughout. As in her previous title, *Guitar Highway Rose* (2004), Lowry uses many different stylistic devices (lists, postcards, poems, how-to instructions, and cleverly titled vignettes) to terrific effect. The text is filled with Aussie and British phrases and sayings (and there's no glossary), but that won't stop readers from thoroughly enjoying this delightful trip down under. —Debbie Carton

Lupica, Mike. *Heat*. 2006. 324p. Philomel (9780399243011). Gr. 6–9.

Michael Arroyo is a 13-year-old Cuban American who lives in the shadow of Yankee Stadium. Yes, he is a Little League ballplayer, and, yes, he has a dream: to pitch in the Little League World Series. To do so, his South Bronx All-Stars will need to beat the best the greater New York area has to offer in the regional championship, to be played in—you guessed it—Yankee Stadium. This setup sounds like yet another *Rocky* meets *Bad News Bears* tearjerker: the immigrants from the Bronx take on the white-bread rich kids from the suburbs. It is that (with some notable twists), but it's much more, too. Michael and his brother, 17-year-old Carlos, have a problem: their beloved father is dead, and the boys are hoping to avoid a foster home by pretending Papi is visiting a sick relative in Miami. Lupica wrings plenty of genuine emotion from the melodramatic frame story, but he sidesteps the slough of social significance by building characters who speak for themselves, not the author, and by enlivening the story with a teen version of street humor. The dialogue crackles, and the rich cast of supporting characters—especially Michael's battery mate, catcher and raconteur Manny—nearly steals the show. Top-notch entertainment in the Carl Hiaasen mold. —Bill Ott

Lyga, Barry. *The Astonishing Adventures of Fanboy and Goth Girl*. 2006. 320p. Houghton (9780618723928). Gr. 8–11.

"I'm a computer geek, a comic book geek, a study geek. Even in the Fast-Track classes, I'm apart." Fifteen-year-old Fanboy is miserable at school, where he is bullied, and at home, with his pregnant mother and her husband, the "step-fascist." His only relief is the late hours spent creating his own comic book. Then he receives an instant message from Kyra, an enigmatic goth who seems to be the only witness to the violence he endures, and the two form a cagey, charged friendship. Unlike Daniel Ehrenhaft's *Drawing a Blank* (2006), in which a young comics fan embarks on a wild, fantastical adventure, Lyga's debut novel is a darkly comic, realistic, contemporary story of bullying and a teen's private escape in artistic pursuits. Fanboy entertains plenty of violent thoughts. He carries a bullet, keeps a tally of his abusers ("The List"), and lashes out with sometimes-cruel remarks, which feel sharply authentic. The insider comics details will slow some readers, and the open-ended questions about Kyra's personal story will frustrate others. Yet Fanboy's whip-smart, often hilariously sarcastic voice skillfully captures a teenager's growing self-awareness, and adds a fresh, urgent perspective to age-old questions about how young people cope with bullying and their own feelings of helplessness, rage, and being misunderstood as they try to discover themselves. —Gillian Engberg

Lynch, Chris. *Inexcusable*. 2005. 176p. Atheneum/ Ginee Seo (9780689847899). Gr. 10–12.

Many YA novels about rape, such as Laurie Halse Anderson's *Speak* (1999), have shown the horror and pain from the victim's perspective, but Lynch's bone-chilling novel is told in the defensive voice of the accused rapist, Keir, whose terrifying denial ("I am a good guy . . . and so I could not have done this") sets the book's tone. Attempting to defend his character with anecdotes from his senior year of high school, Keir relates a string of disturbing, morally ambiguous stories in an energetic voice that's alternately playful, earnest, rational, and, as almost all readers will recognize, deluded. Through expertly drawn, subtle details, Lynch creates a nuanced, wholly believable character that will leave many readers shaking with recognition: They know this guy, a strong athlete who fleetingly struggles with his self image, loves (and is disappointed by) his family, wants to have fun with his friends, and has a deep crush on a girl. His very familiarity, combined with his slippery morality, violent actions, and shocking self-denial, will prompt many readers to question themselves, and their own decisions and accepted ways of talking and behaving with each other. Teens may doubt Keir's reliability as a narrator, but his self-recognition, in a final, searing scene, rings true. Here, and throughout this unforgettable novel, Lynch raises fierce, painful questions about athletic culture, family denial, violence, and rape, and readers will want to think and talk about them all. Where does personal responsibility begin? What defines a "good guy"? Are we all capable of monstrous things? —Gillian Engberg

MacCullough, Carolyn. *Stealing Henry*. 2005. 208p. Roaring Brook (9781596430457). Gr. 9–12.

"Don't look back. It's bad luck. Never look back." Savannah hears her mother's refrain in her head the night she hits her abusive stepfather, Jake, with a sizzling frying pan and leaves town with her eight-year-old half-brother, Henry. Sav is no stranger to the road, having lived a nomadic childhood with her mother, who never looked back as she floated from one state and boyfriend to another in her white Chevrolet. The day the car breaks down on the New Jersey turnpike, they meet Jake, and the roaming stops. The story of Savannah and Henry's journey to New York City and, eventually, to Maine, is interspersed with Sav's memories of childhood. Intermittent chapters titled "Alice 1986" chronicle events from Mom's teen years that dovetail with the current flight and the choices that Savannah makes. Tiny strokes of details paint whole backstories for the characters, revealing the tenuous love between mother and daughter and shining a light on the poverty and heartache that lead to their estrangement. MacCullough's dialogue is flawless; without a didactic note she leaves teens to ponder some heavy issues: interracial relationships, teen pregnancy, runaways, and responsible parenting. The journey is fascinating. —Cindy Dobrez

Mack, Tacy. *Birdland*. 2003. 208p. Scholastic (9780439535908). Gr. 7–10.

"True healing," Jed's English teacher declaims, "begins with imagination." But Jed, displaying that bedrock realism teens use to see through the idealistic preenings of adults, isn't quite buying it: "So what if you imagine something to be healed. It's still the same broken thing, isn't it?" The beauty of this rigorously unsentimental novel about a family in crisis is the way that Mack, even as she lets her characters' imaginations soar, keeps her story grounded in the pain of broken things. Jed is the middle child in a family torn asunder by the death of Zeke, Jed's jazz-loving older brother. To fulfill an assignment for English class, Jed, with his friend, Flyer, sets out to videotape the sights and sounds of Lower East Side Manhattan, as recorded in Zeke's journals and poems. Along the way, Jed encounters a mysterious homeless girl who may hold the key to why Zeke died, if Jed can somehow unlock her secrets. This is hardly the first novel to use a teen's adventures with video as a metaphor for coming-of-age, but Mack, author of the acclaimed *Drawing Lessons* (2000), never lets the technology take over. Jed's family has shut down almost completely in the wake of Zeke's death—symbolized by Jed's psychosomatic speech impediment—but the camera lets the tongue-tied auteur see without speaking. Even when the talking starts, though, the words remain powerfully ambiguous, the healing poignantly attenuated. —Bill Ott

Mackler, Carolyn. *The Earth, My Butt, and Other Big Round Things*. 2003. 256p. Candlewick (9780763619589). Gr. 7–10.

Fifteen-year-old Viriginia Shreves is the blond, round, average daughter in a family of dark-haired, thin superstars. Her best friend has moved away, and she's on the fringes at her private Manhattan school. She wants a boyfriend, but she settles for Froggy Welsh, who comes over on Mondays to grope her. The story follows Virginia as she tries to lose weight, struggles with her "imperfections," and deals with the knowledge that her idealized older brother has committed date rape. There's a lot going on here, and some important elements, such as Virginia's flirtation with self-mutilation, are passed over too quickly. But Mackler writes with such insight and humor (sometimes using strong language to make her point) that many readers will immediately identify with Virginia's longings as well as her fear and loathing. Her gradually evolving ability to stand up to her family is hard won and not always believable, but it provides a hopeful ending for those trying stand on their own two feet. —Ilene Cooper

Madigan, L. K. *Flash Burnout*. 2009. 336p. Houghton (9780547194899). Gr. 9–12.

Fifteen-year-old Blake believes he has the perfect setup—a gorgeous girlfriend (Shannon) and a friend who shares his love for photography who just happens to be a girl (Marissa). But a chance photo op of a street person begins the unraveling of his happy situation when Marissa realizes that the passed-out woman in the picture is her meth-addict mother. It's impossible for Blake to be the friend Marissa needs while being the boyfriend Shannon wants. Many of the story lines are traditional—sibling rivalry, boy-girl love, lust, and drama (and a high-school setting replete with cafeteria and parking lot scenes)—but Madigan also introduces the unexpected. Blake's parents are strong, loving, and likable (his dad is a medical examiner who occasionally brings his work home, his mom is a hospital chaplain); his teachers are engaged, empathetic, and human; his girlfriend works at not being jealous while his friend-who-is-a-girl respects that relationship, but it all ends badly. With just enough humor to diffuse the tension, and with the art and science of photography as a backdrop, this rich romance explores the complexities of friendship and love, and the all-too-human limitations of both. It's a sobering, compelling, and satisfying read for teens and a promising debut for a new young adult author. —Frances Bradburn

Maia, Love. *DJ Rising*. 2012. 304p. Little, Brown (9780316121873). Gr. 8–12.

Born in a first-aid tent at a Bob Marley concert, 16-year-old half-black/half–Puerto Rican Marley Johnnywas Diego-Dylan entered the world surrounded by music. In this fresh debut, music continues to course through Marley's veins as he dreams of becoming a professional DJ and spinning records at Fever, the hottest nightclub. If not for this dream, he might not survive his daily reality: a dead father, busing tables six nights a week at a fancy restaurant to support his heroin-addict mother, being shunned for being a "transplant" (scholarship student) at an elitist prep school, and suffering an unrequited crush on popular Lea. When Marley scores an audition at a top Fever competitor, assumes the name DJ Ice, and realizes a date with Lea may be imminent, his future looks brighter than ever. But interrupted by tragedy, Marley finds himself torn between obligation and fame. This gritty, pulsating peek into a lesser-known world reverberates with the energy of a thumping dance club. Clashes with Marley's mentor, a spinning purist who uses only vinyl, bring out the subtleties of the art form and the ongoing debate between vinyl and DJ software. Blending both forms to crowd-pleasing results, Marley fights for what he wants, and it is a fight well worth reading. —Angela Leeper

Mankell, Henning. ***Shadow of the Leopard.*** **2009. 240p. Annick (9781554512003). Gr. 10–12.**

Mankell, the acclaimed mystery writer for both youth and adults, once again draws on true events in Mozambique in this haunting, contemporary story of violence and courage. In *Secrets in the Fire* (2003), Sofia, 9, lost both of her legs in a land-mine explosion that killed her sister. Now, 10 years later, she has three children with her husband, Armando, who works in a nearby town and can only visit Sofia in their village on the weekends. After Sofia discovers that Armando is involved with another woman, she throws him out, and he breaks down, leaves his job, and, in desperation, becomes a thief, a choice that leads to a horrifying, violent climax. Mankell writes without sentimentality in a clear, matter-of-fact style, and it is the frank, vivid details of Sofia's struggle that will stay with readers: how she dreams of having electricity in her home; walks miles on her crutches; cares for her children, including the baby on her back; takes off her legs every night before bed; and confronts her husband about his infidelity. Is she responsible for what happens to him? This isn't a detective story, like many of the author's best-known works, but the drama of betrayal is riveting and will draw many of Mankell's high-school and adult fans. —Hazel Rochman

Marchetta, Melina. ***Jellicoe Road.*** **2008. 432p. HarperTeen (9780061431838). Gr. 9–12.**

Taylor Markham isn't just one of the new student leaders of her boarding school, she's also the heir to the Underground Community, one of three battling school factions in her small Australian community (the others being the Cadets and the Townies). For a generation, these three camps have fought "the territory wars," a deadly serious negotiation of land and property rife with surprise attacks, diplomatic immunities, and physical violence. Only this year, it's complicated: Taylor might just have a thing for Cadet leader Jonah, and Jonah might just be the key to unlocking the secret identity of Taylor's mother, who abandoned her when she was 11. In fact, nearly every relationship in Taylor's life has unexpected ties to her past, and the continual series of revelations is both the book's strength and weakness; the melodrama can be trying, but when Marchetta isn't forcing epiphanies, she has a knack for nuanced characterizations and punchy dialogue. The complexity of the backstory will be offputting to younger readers, but those who stick it out will find rewards in the heartbreaking twists of Marchetta's saga. —Daniel Kraus

Martin, C. K. Kelly. ***The Lighter Side of Life and Death.*** **2010. 240p. Random (9780375845888). Gr. 9–12.**

When best friends Mason and Kat lose their virginity to each other, they react quite differently. Mason is obsessed with Kat; Kat responds by ignoring him completely. Partly from a desire for revenge, partly from fascination, Mason begins an intense physical relationship with 23-year-old Colette, a dalliance that soon becomes just as obsessive as his relationship with Kat was. This is not your ordinary teen romance. It's heavy on the sex but carefully nuanced. Although the lust is palpable, so is the affection and intrigue. Yes, Mason is in love with the act itself, but he cares deeply for both young women. The layers of emotion, so rarely evoked by young men in YA novels, give a depth and authenticity to Mason's personality that expose his naivete and occasional bewilderment. The book's other characters are equally complex. Kat and Colette have strong, genuine feelings for Mason, each battling her own distinct emotions. Even Mason's relationships with his new stepfamily are painfully true to life. Counteracting its apparently happy ending, this taut novel propels readers from one corroding relationship to another. A more genuine representation of teen life would be hard to find. —Frances Bradburn

Matson, Morgan. ***Second Chance Summer.*** **2012. 480p. Simon & Schuster (9781416990673). Gr. 7–12.**

Ever since Taylor's disastrous seventeenth birthday, when her father received his diagnosis of untreatable pancreatic cancer, the family has scrambled to make up for lost time. Now all they have is one final summer with him at their old Poconos lake house. For Taylor there are opportunities to revisit idyllic childhood summers and to share a final, special few months with her father. But there's also the challenge of witnessing his unbearably swift decline with no option of escaping the deep sorrow. Author Matson gets the dynamic of family death just right—the highs and lows, the dailiness of life as an antidote to the pull of sadness, the attempt at normalcy through the lens of a thousand "last" times. She artfully allows the reader to become another family member as Taylor and her brother and sister move through their personal summer firsts—first love, first jobs, first best friends. Teens will share in the exciting milestones of the characters' youth and empathize as they cope with their inevitable guilt of indulging in pleasure as their father deteriorates. This is a bittersweet, powerful tale of family devotion, the sustainability of true friendship, and the silent courage of loving someone enough to stay and watch them die. —Frances Bradburn

McCormick, Patricia. *Cut*. 2000. 168p. Front Street (9781886910614). Gr. 7–10.

Callie ("ST" for Silent Treatment) is part of Group, teenage girls (make that "guests") hospitalized at Sea Pines (or "Sick Minds") for a variety of psychological "issues"—food, drugs, behavior problems, etc. Callie has begun to cut herself, a fact she reveals only to the reader, for she has stopped talking. Self-mutilation has become her cry for help from a terrifyingly delicate, asthmatic brother; a nonfunctioning mother; and an escaping father. She is so depressed and overwhelmed by her burden of caretaking that she requires the rush of pain and the high of watching her own blood seep to the surface. Like E. L. Konigsburg's *Silent to the Bone* (2000) and Laurie Halse Anderson's *Speak* (1999), *Cut* is another authentic-sounding novel in which elective mutism plays a part, this time with humor making the pain of adolescence gone awry more bearable. A too-tidy ending notwithstanding, this is an exceptional character study of a young woman and her hospital mates who struggle with demons so severe that only their bodies can confess. —Frances Bradburn

McCormick, Patricia. *Purple Heart*. 2009. 208p. HarperCollins/Balzer and Bray (9780061730900). Gr. 9–12.

McCormick, never one to shy away from heavy issues (self-mutilation in *Cut*, 2000; sexual slavery in *Sold*, 2006), now takes readers into the dark heart of wartime Iraq. Private Matt Duffy awakes in a hospital bed, suffering from a severe brain injury sustained during a confrontation with insurgents. His memory of the encounter is foggy, but the pieces that slowly settle in contradict the story told by his squadmate and friend, Justin. An Iraqi kid was killed, though no one seems to know why or by whom, and Matt gets the distinct feeling that the army doesn't want to know. McCormick clearly evokes Matt's longing to return to his unit and his buddies and sets that against the psychological trauma of reentering the fray and coming to terms with a death for which he holds himself accountable. Gripping details of existence in a war zone bring this to life, and penetrating questions about duty and guilt drive it home. Pair this novel with Ryan Smithson's *Ghosts of War* (2009), a teen soldier's account of his time in Iraq. —Ian Chipman

McCormick, Patricia. *Sold*. 2006. 288p. Hyperion (9780786851713). Gr. 9–12.

Lakshmi, 13, knows nothing about the world beyond her village shack in the Himalayas of Nepal, and when her family loses the little it has in a monsoon, she grabs a chance to work as a maid in the city so she can send money back home. What she doesn't know is that her stepfather has sold her into prostitution. She ends up in a brothel far across the border in the slums of Calcutta, locked up, beaten, starved, drugged, raped, "torn and bleeding," until she submits. In beautiful clear prose and free verse that remains true to the child's viewpoint, first-person, present-tense vignettes fill in Lakshmi's story. The brutality and cruelty are ever present ("I have been beaten here, / locked away, / violated a hundred times / and a hundred times more"), but not sensationalized. An unexpected act of kindness is heartbreaking ("I do not know a word / big enough to hold my sadness"). One haunting chapter brings home the truth of "Two Worlds": the workers love watching *The Bold and the Beautiful* on TV though in the real world, the world they know, a desperate prostitute may be approached to sell her own child. An unforgettable account of sexual slavery as it exists now. —Hazel Rochman

McDonald, Janet. *Spellbound*. 2001. 144p. Farrar (9780374371401). Gr. 7–12.

One of the best of the many recent stories about teens in the city projects, this first novel is read-aloud funny, even as it tells the harsh truth about how hard it is to break free. Raven Jefferson, 16, a bookish student, was sure she was on her way to college like her older sister, Dell—perfect childless Dell, with her big salary and her small hips. But Raven got pregnant after her first sexual experience, and now she's stuck at home, bored and cooped up with a baby all day. Raven's girlfriend Aisha is also a single parent, and their talk—from hair to music to boys—manages to be hilarious, wild, insulting, and irreverent without using curse words. Unlike Aisha, Raven will eventually get to college, but not before she's had to confront issues of race and class prejudice. Many teens, especially fans of the movie *Ghost World*, will recognize Raven's cruel encounters with the job scene. McDonald wrote the acclaimed adult memoir *Project Girl* (1999), and what's great in this novel is the depiction of the grim reality of the neighborhood and the slick clichés of success. Best of all, she humanizes the individual people behind the stereotype of poor people who are "project trash." —Hazel Rochman

McDonald, Janet. *Twists and Turns*. 2003. 144p. Farrar/Frances Foster (9780374399559). Gr. 7–12.

Raucous and tender, harsh and hopeful, McDonald's latest fast-talking story about teen project girls in Brooklyn Heights focuses on the sisters, Keeba and Teesha. They have both finished high school, and avoided the traps of pregnancy, drugs, gangs, and crime. With the support of friends and the community, they start a small neighborhood hair salon. But business is slow, very slow; and, worse, there's a movement afoot to privatize the housing projects and move out the poor residents. As in *Chill Wind* (2002) and *Spellbound* (2001), the poetry and wit are in the daily details: the gossip on the benches, the homegirls when they feel "premenstrual and mean." The salon is destroyed by vandals from the neighborhood where the sisters live and also by the landlords and politicians. Yet the story is inspiring—not because of a slick resolution or a heavy message, but because McDonald shows how hard things are, even as she tells a story of teens who find the strength in themselves and in those around them to rebuild and carry on. —Hazel Rochman

McGowan, Anthony. *The Knife That Killed Me*. 2010. 224p. Delacorte (9780385738224). Gr. 10–12.

After introducing a boy and his mouthy brain tumor in *Jack Tumor* (2009), McGowan returns with a razor-sharp tale set in a school in a lower-class area of Leeds. Paul Varderman is mostly a nobody, pretty much ignored by the jocks, geeks, punks, straights, freaks, and other microcliques, and only sometimes picked on by the brutal bully Roth and his cronies. He gets ensnared in Roth's web when he is coerced into delivering a package to a rival gang leader (in an echo of the famous *Godfather* horse scene); at the same time, he is tentatively drawn into the fold of the freaks, captained by the charismatic Shane. Paul is repulsed by Roth's easy capacity for tremendous violence, and he begins to warm up to his new friends. But his morality is tested by his role in an upcoming gang fight and the power he feels carrying around the wicked blade given to him by Roth. McGowan's intense portrayal of a teen struggling to fit in is especially precise in depicting the conflicting desire to win approval and acceptance from someone you hate, and how easy it is to fall under that person's sway when he wields power with ruthless efficiency. The title and a clever bit of narrative structuring all but ensure a headlong dash through this book to find out what's going to happen with that fateful blade dripping blood on the cover. —Ian Chipman

Monninger, Joseph. *Wish*. 2010. 208p. Delacorte (9780385739412). Gr. 8–11.

Fifteen-year-old Bee's younger brother, Tommy, an avid shark buff, has cystic fibrosis. A wish-granting charity fulfills Tommy's dream to see great whites up close, so Bee, 11-year-old Tommy, and their mother fly from New Hampshire to San Francisco. But after the outing proves disappointing, and their single mother seems more focused on a new man than on family, Bee and Tommy travel down the coast to meet Tommy's pen pal and hero, Ty, a surfer and shark-attack survivor. There, Bee finds friendship, including a potential romance with Ty's 16-year-old younger brother, while Tommy gets his longed-for sea adventure, which ends up being difficult and inspiring. Bee's intimate, first-person narrative is wholly compelling and emotionally resonant. Monninger creates diverse, well-drawn characters, and Tommy's illness is portrayed without sentimentality in straightforward detail. Interspersed among the breathtaking, vivid descriptions of events and settings are shark facts (further discussed in an author's note) that illuminate nature's brutality and beauty. What shines most, though, are the relationships among characters, particularly between conscientious, school-achiever Bee and courageous, touching Tommy. With mutual admiration, support, and love, they draw strength and perspective from one another and together gain further appreciation for human frailties and resilience. An absorbing, beautifully written novel that will affect readers on many levels. —Shelle Rosenfeld

Moriarty, Jaclyn. ***The Year of Secret Assignments.*** **2004. 352p. Scholastic/Arthur A. Levine (9780439498814). Gr. 8–12.**

In her debut for youth, Moriarty follows her adult title, *Feeling Sorry for Celia* (2000), with another winning novel. Written entirely in letters, diary entries, lists, quizzes, transcripts, and mock subpoenas (there are a disproportionate number of lawyerly parents here), the novel focuses on three Australian girls who have each been assigned to write to a student at a rival school. The girls' pen friends turn out to be three boys, and the entertaining correspondence between the couples reveals the characters' quirky ingenuity, pranks, burgeoning romances, and fierce friendships as well as deeper family stories, including one about a parent's death. When one of the boys turns out to be an abusive fraud, the others craft a delicious retribution scheme that propels the story to a satisfying conclusion. Moriarty's characters speak in voices as playful and inventive as the novel's format. There are a few coarse moments—a reference to a blow job and some caustic outbursts ("eat shit and die" and "bitch face")—and the story's myriad devices wear thin in places. But this is an unusual novel with an exhilarating pace, irrepressible characters, and a screwball humor that will easily attract teens, many of whom will yearn for madcap adventures and unshakably devoted friends like these. —Gillian Engberg

Mosher, Richard. ***Zazoo.*** **2001. 224p. Clarion (9780618135349). Gr. 6–9.**

Zazoo is a young French girl of Vietnamese descent who lives beside a canal in Burgundy with an old man named Grand-Pierre. At first she knows little about her own or Grand-Pierre's past, but a chance meeting with a 16-year-old Parisian boy starts her on a journey of discovery. The novel's multiple stories unfold gradually, at a slow yet appropriate pace. Zazoo learns of Grand-Pierre's morally ambiguous role in the French Resistance and as a soldier in Vietnam and why he has not spoken to the town's pharmacist for many years. Ultimately, the characters come to understand more fully the toll that war has taken on each of them, but this finely crafted novel, told in Zazoo's authentic first-person narrative, speaks to more than one message; it also evokes the quiet passage of the seasons and the joys of friendship. A novel with a big message well told through the smallest details. —Todd Morning

Murdock, Catherine Gilbert. ***Dairy Queen.*** **2006. 288p. Houghton (9780618683079). Gr. 6–9.**

D. J.'s family members don't talk much, especially about the fact that 15-year-old D. J. does all the heavy work on their Wisconsin dairy farm since her father broke his hip and her two older brothers left for college. Nor do they talk about why D. J.'s mom, a teacher, is so busy filling in for the middle-school principal that she's never home. And they never, ever discuss the reason why her brothers haven't called home for more than six months. So when D. J. decides to try out for the Red Bend football team, even though she's been secretly training with (and falling for) Brian Nelson, the cute quarterback from Hawley, Red Bend's rival, she becomes the talk of the town. Suddenly, her family has quite a bit to say. This humorous, romantic romp excels at revealing a situation seldom explored in YA novels, and it will quickly find its place alongside equally well-written stories set in rural areas, such as Weaver's *Full Service* (2005), Richard Peck's *The Teacher's Funeral* (2004), and Kimberly Fusco's *Tending to Grace* (2004). —Jennifer Hubert

Murdock, Catherine Gilbert. *The Off Season*. 2007. 288p. Houghton (9780618686957). Gr. 7–10.

This funny, touching follow-up to *Dairy Queen* (2006), a 2007 Best Book for Young Adults, succeeds whether read on its own or as a sequel. D. J.'s junior year starts off promisingly: she has finally been accepted as a valuable player on the football team, and Brian Nelson, quarterback for a rival school, is still coming around to see her. Storm clouds gather, though, as her close friend is bullied for being gay, money problems on the farm increase, and an injury forces D. J. to choose between football and basketball, which could net her a college scholarship. She also begins to wonder why Brian makes out with her but never wants to take her anywhere. Then brother Winn is seriously injured on the football field, forcing her to gain some much-needed perspective. D. J. is an easygoing, likable narrator, full of self-deprecating humor and insight, and her struggles, whether they are everyday or life altering, will resonate with teen audiences. —Krista Hutley

Myers, Walter Dean. *Darius & Twig*. 2013. 208p. Amistad (9780061728235). Gr. 9–12.

Darius and Twig have been best friends since they were 9. Now 16, the two dream of finding a world beyond the confines of their daily lives on 145th Street in Harlem. Certainly, their talents are on their side: Darius is a highly intelligent writer, and Twig is a gifted runner. But are the two free to use their gifts? A story Darius has written has been accepted by a college journal contingent on his making editorial changes. Must he give up his singular voice to conform to an editor? As for Twig, are his gifts as a runner being exploited by an unscrupulous adult for personal gain? In his imagination, Darius is his alter ego—a falcon flying to impossible heights. But in real life, he and Twig are the targets of mindless bullies who seek to drag them down to their miserable level. Will the friends ultimately be able to soar, or will they remain earthbound victims of their circumstances? Myers has written another gritty, suspenseful, street-smart novel with a viscerally real setting in which young men must struggle to overcome obstacles by finding the best within themselves. In the process, they become the heroes of their own lives and surely will inspire their readers to seek to do the same. —Michael Cart

Myers, Walter Dean. *Shooter*. 2004. 224p. HarperCollins (9780060295196). Gr. 7–12.

Like Myers' Printz Award Book, *Monster* (1999), this story is told from multiple viewpoints, and questions of guilt and innocence drive the plot and stay with the reader. This time there's a shooting in a high school. Len, a senior, commits suicide after he shoots a star football player and injures several others in the schoolyard. The actual facts of that carnage emerge slowly, as Len's best friend, Cameron, is interviewed at length by a therapist, a sheriff, and a threat-prevention specialist. Adding more perspective are newspaper and police reports, and Len's personal journal, which reveals his fury and hurt about his macho father and school bullies. The multiple narratives move the story far beyond case history, the chatty interview format is highly readable, and Cameron's voice is pitch perfect. One of the few black students in the school, he's an outsider like Len, but he's quiet about it, "an ordinary guy." He doesn't want to stand out; he does nothing about the racism implicit in an image of Martin Luther King on a shooting-range practice target, and he's ashamed. It's this bystander role readers will want to talk about, as well as who is to blame. Why does Cameron just go along with things? What about the parents, the principal, the counselors who knew about the bullying and tell Len to "grow up"? —Hazel Rochman

Myers, Walter Dean. *Street Love*. 2006. 144p. HarperCollins/Amistad (9780060280796). Gr. 9–12.

In short lines of free verse, teens in Harlem tell a story of anger, loss, and love across social-class lines. Damien, 17, is a basketball champion and academic star, accepted into a top college. His parents want him to date middle-class Roxanne, but he falls in love with gorgeous Junice, 16, who is desperate to protect her little sister after their single-parent mom is sentenced to 25 years for dealing drugs. Written with rap beat and rhyme but no invective or obscenity, the switching viewpoints make this great for readers' theater—from Damien's furious "manhood jam" when he confronts his rival, and Junice's anguished visit to her raging mama in prison ("a wolf caught in a trap"), to the lyrical simplicity of the teens' love ("Flying through an endlessly / Expanding universe / Away from the me that was / Toward a me that is beyond / understanding"). The young people also invoke their history in the tradition of Langston Hughes and other great writers ("these hands have scrubbed mats on the banks of / the Congo"). The realistic drama on the street and at home tells a gripping story. Readers will want to reread the lines they loved. —Hazel Rochman

Meyers, Walter Dean. *What They Found: Love on 145th Street*. 2007. 256p. Random/Wendy Lamb (9780385321389). Gr. 7–11.

A neighborhood beauty salon is the setting for lots of the fast, funny talk in these stirring contemporary stories, which nonetheless give a grim view of being "poor and black," whether on the streets of Harlem, in prison, or on the war front in Afghanistan. Rooted in the harsh realism of widespread unemployment, drug use, and trouble ("more brothers going to jail than going to college"), the teens' tender connections are heartbreaking. A single teenage mother loves her baby, and so does the young dad, who wishes he could support them. Some teens are college-bound, but a boy with a high-school diploma can't find work: will he get a gun? Tough gangster Burn is gentle with handicapped kids, but he cannot connect with the girl he loves. In "Mama," a kid who cares for her mom, a recovering addict, and tries to get her brother to preschool turns out to be only eight years old. There are lighter moments, too; in "Poets and Plumbers," Noee feels uncomfortable in Kyle's apartment until she shows him how to unplug his kitchen drain. Each story stands alone, but some are connected, and readers familiar with Myers' *145th Street* (2000) will welcome back some characters. Hope lies in what the book title says, finding love and community. —Hazel Rochman

Myracle, Lauren. *Kissing Kate*. 2003. 176p. Dutton (9780525469179). Gr. 7–10.

"It was one thing for someone else to be gay. It was something else entirely if it was me." Lissa, 16, has been best friends with beautiful Kate for four years, but everything changes when Kate gets drunk at a party, and she and Lissa passionately kiss. Lissa is desperate to talk about it, but Kate wants to pretend that nothing happened. This first novel does a great job of showing the girls' surprise at the situation and the way their emotions swing from attraction to denial. Funny and anguished, Lissa's first-person narrative expresses her hurt, anger, and confusion as she tries to date a guy; searches for an adult to talk to (and for a bra that fits); and downloads depressing statistics from the Net about the high suicide rate among gay teens. There's some contrivance about "lucid dreaming," with heavy metaphors and connections, but most readers will skim that for the lively realistic story about friends and lovers. For another, very different take on the subject, see David Levithan's *Boy Meets Boy* (2003). —Hazel Rochman

★ Na, An. *A Step from Heaven*. 2001. 156p. Front Street (9781886910584). Gr. 9–12.

Young Ju's parents don't want her to become too American, and Young Ju is ashamed of them. It's the classic immigrant child conflict, told here in the present tense with the immediacy of the girl's voice, from the time she's a toddler in a small Korean village wondering why the adults talk about America as "heaven." Then there's her bewilderment as a first-grader in the U.S. trying to learn the rules and understand the words and the accents. Each chapter is a story in itself, with dramatic surprise or quiet reversal. The tales blend together into a beautiful first novel that takes Ju through her teenage years until she's an A student ready to leave for college. The focus is on family and what happens at home. Her father, furious at having to work two laboring jobs and grief-stricken at his mother's death in Korea, becomes an increasingly violent alcoholic. He forbids Young Ju from seeing her best friend. She disobeys him, but she's careful never to bring her friends to her shabby home. Most moving is the chapter about her visit with her father to the Immigration Office. He's distrustful, enraged that he's so helpless and that she's in control; she's embarrassed by his behavior even as she feels his anguish. Young Ju's mother is a strong figure in the background until the girl suddenly sees her as a person, who tells her, "In America, women have choices." This isn't a quick read, especially at the beginning when the child is trying to decipher American words and customs, but the coming-of-age drama will grab teens and make them think of their own conflicts between home and outside. As in the best writing, the particulars make the story universal. Steer teens who like this on to Amy Tan's adult book *The Joy Luck Club* (1989). —Hazel Rochman

Na, An. *Wait for Me*. 2006. 176p. Putnam (9780399242755). Gr. 8–11.

The author of the Printz Award Book *A Step from Heaven* (2001) tells another contemporary Korean American story of leaving home. This time, though, love is as powerful as the intense family drama. The focus is on high-school senior Mina, trapped in the web of lies invented to satisfy her overbearing mom, Uhmma, who expects Mina to attend Harvard and escape the drudgery of their small-town dry-cleaning store. Mina's brilliant friend, Jonathan Kim, helps her cheat and steal. She uses him, but he thinks he loves her—and he eventually rapes her. Then Mexican immigrant Ysrael, a gifted musician on his way to San Francisco, comes to work in the store, and he and Mina fall passionately in love. Will she go with him and make a new life free of lies? Ysrael is too perfect, just as Uhmma is demonized, but both are shown from Mina's viewpoint, and it is her struggle with her secrets that is spellbinding. Alternating with Mina's first-person narrative are short vignettes from the perspective of Mina's deaf younger sister, who Mina protects. The conflicts of love, loyalty, and betrayal are the heart of the story—and they eventually show Mina her way. —Hazel Rochman

Nilsson, Per. *Heart's Delight*. 2003. 160p. Front Street (9781886910928). Gr. 9–12.

"This is no gushy, sentimental, happy teenage love story," warns the nameless 16-year-old narrator of this moving, truthful novel, originally published a decade ago in Sweden. After returning from a visit to America, the teenager discovers that a dizzying romance begun before his departure has abruptly ended. He forces himself to relive the relationship as he creatively disposes of his keepsakes ("It took him four minutes to eat the Swedish folk song 'Uti Var Hage'"). Finally, only two items remain: a razor and a bottle of pills. Nilsson tells the tautly structured story in alternating chapters that toggle between past and present, and his precise, measured prose (jealousy is a "sharp-toothed rat gnawing at your heart") builds suspense. Adding dimension is an honest treatment of teen sexuality: the couple consider the rhythm method as an appropriate level of sexual caution, even though "kids learn in junior high how good condoms are." A conclusion touched with magic realism provides a measure of closure that avoids both bleak fatalism and preachy earnestness. If its European honors are any indication, this searing portrait of a teen caught unawares by the transience of love may well become the *Forever* of a new generation. —Jennifer Mattson

Nolan, Han. *Crazy*. 2010. 352p. Harcourt (9780152051099). Gr. 7–10.

Jason, 15, lives a precarious life with his mentally ill father, who thinks he is an Argonaut and wears tinfoil ear guards as he prepares for imminent attack from the Furies. When Jason was 6, his father tried to bury him alive, and his nightmares of suffocation continue to haunt him. Now that his mother has died from a stroke, Jason struggles to care for his needy father alone and with few resources. To help him cope, he creates an imaginary audience that includes Crazy Glue, Sexy Lady, and sympathetic, nurturing Aunt Bee, of Mayberry fame. There's a laugh track, too, and Jason directly addresses the reader. In less-capable hands, these narrative experiments could have fallen flat, but Nolan skillfully uses the story's intriguing structure to maneuver the minefield that is Jason's life. As Jason finds support in group therapy, social services intervention, and a foster family, the voices in his head recede, and he becomes less fearful that he, too, is going crazy. Nolan leavens this haunting but hopeful story with spot-on humor and a well-developed cast of characters, and she shows with moving clarity the emotional costs of mental illness, especially on teens forced to parent their own parents. —Cindy Dobrez

Oaks, Adams. ***Why I Fight.*** **2009. 240p. Atheneum (9781416911777). Gr. 8–12.**

Ever since he turned 12-and-a-half, Wyatt has been on the road with his cool uncle Spade, who lives by his wits and has a different "ladyfriend" in every new town they visit. For six years his uncle's Chevy "was my house," Wyatt tells the reader, and "all his ladyfriends was my mom." It's Spade's idea that Wyatt, who is unusually tall and strong, should start bare-knuckle fighting for money, and the boy, heartbreakingly eager to please, complies, winning fight after fight . . . until the last one. Oaks' first novel is a breathtaking debut with an unforgettable protagonist, a boy who may claim he hates the word *love* but is nonetheless desperately in search of it and of himself. The voice Oaks has created for Wyatt to tell his painful and poignant story is a wonderful combination of the unlettered and the eloquent. One example, his description of Spade: "I looked at him real good: his skin like a greasy diner, his black eyes like spiders in holes, his body like a starved bird." Will Wyatt ever find himself? Readers who meet him will care desperately about the answer. —Michael Cart

Oates, Joyce Carol. ***Big Mouth & Ugly Girl.*** **2002. 272p. HarperCollins (9780066237565). Gr. 8–12.**

Matt Donaghy's big mouth gets him a three-day suspension when "unnamed witnesses" allege that the Rocky River High School junior has threatened to bomb the school if his play isn't accepted for the Spring Arts Festival. Fortunately, his classmate Ursula Rigg, who calls herself "Ugly Girl," heard what he really said, and despite her parents' reservations, demonstrates the courage to come to his defense. An awkward friendship between the two self-styled misfits begins to develop but is threatened when Matt's parents sue the school system for slander. Distinguished novelist Oates' first young adult novel is a thought-provoking, character-driven drama about the climate of hysteria created by school violence in America, and how two teenagers find the courage to fight it and to find themselves in the process. Ursula, who tells her part of the story in an edgy, often angry first-person voice, appears at first to be the more interesting character, but Matt, whose story unfolds in the third person, gradually emerges as a sweetly engaging, multidimensional character in his own right. His aching loneliness will break readers' hearts. This title is also being published simultaneously in audio and e-book versions. —Michael Cart

Orenstein, Denise Gosliner. ***The Secret Twin.*** **2007. 400p. HarperCollins (9780060785642). Gr. 7–10.**

As enigmatic as the tarot cards that grace the book, this spellbinding story will entangle readers at the first sentence: "They say the newborn doesn't see, but I remember this. . . ." The story is told in two voices. One belongs to Noah, the prissy 13-year-old who has lived with his grandmother Mademoiselle since his parents were killed in a car crash. The other belongs to Grace, a determined health-care worker who has come to stay with Noah after Mademoiselle's facelift. Wraithlike Noah is used to eating the salad Mademoiselle favors. Grace is outsize, and her feelings about food and Noah are as ample as her figure. Yet despite outward differences, an invisible cord binds Noah and Grace: Grace's brother died in a hit-and-run accident, and Noah was born a twin, sharing a heart with his weaker brother, who was sacrificed so Noah could live. He sees fleeting images of his brother everywhere. Orenstein's writing is magic—every word and phrase precisely chosen. Coupled with creative language are a nail-biting plot and intense characterizations. Throughout, readers are kept off balance with questions both concrete and abstract: What's really wrong with Mademoiselle? Who is shooting people in the neighborhood? Can Grace help Noah survive? Will he let her? —Ilene Cooper

Orenstein, Denise Gosliner. ***Unseen Companion.*** **2003. 368p. HarperCollins (9780060520564). Gr. 10–12.**

In this kaleidoscopic first-person novel, set in 1968 and 1969, the point of view shifts from one Alaskan teenager to another. Each contributes something to the shadowy portrayal of the novel's central, tragic figure, Dove Alexie, a 16-year-old "mixed-breed" who was imprisoned for striking a white teacher, beaten by his racist jailer, and lost in the system until the story's end. The narrators are two Gussak (Caucasian) girls who live with their single-parent families in Bethel, Alaska, and a Yup'ik (native Alaskan) girl and boy sent away from their communities to live in a boarding school. Though their tales revolve around pivotal questions concerning Dove's history and his fate, it is their own lives that are more sharply in focus and fully developed here. In distinctive voices, the four narrators tell their own involving stories, separate from each other at the beginning, but increasingly interconnected. Hope, love, and occasional humor provide welcome relief from the sadness and despair that pulse through the characters' lives as they deal with separation, anger, alienation, blackmail, rape, and death. Slowly the pieces of narrative fall into place to form an intricately patterned mosaic. The appended glossary defines Alaskan terms. A sensitive observer and a compelling storyteller, Orenstein offers a novel that is both touching and harsh. —Carolyn Phelan

Osa, Nancy. *Cuba 15*. 2003. 256p. Delacorte (9780385730211). Gr. 6–10.

Violet Paz, growing up in suburban Chicago, barely knows Spanish, and her dad refuses to talk about his Cuban roots, so it's a real surprise when Abuela insists that Violet have a grand *quinceanero*, the traditional Latina fifteenth-year coming-of-age ceremony. But Violet insists that she is an American. After all, she looks a lot like her Polish American mother. What's more, she wouldn't be caught dead in any onstage ceremony wearing a ruffled pink dress and a tiara. As wonderfully specific as this first novel is to one immigrant family, many teens will recognize the cross-generational conflict between assimilation and the search for roots. Violet's hilarious, cool first-person narrative veers between slapstick and tenderness, denial and truth, as she shops for her party dress, attends a Cuban peace rally, despairs of her dad's values and his taste in clothes, sees that her American friends are also locked in crazy families, and finds the subject for her school comedy monologue in her own wild home, where she is "sentenced to life." There's no message, unless it's in the acceptance that resolution doesn't happen and that Dad is still worth loving—even if he comes to the elegant *quinceanero* in his favorite sunshine-yellow shirt with multicolored monkeys printed on it. —Hazel Rochman

Ostow, Micol. *So Punk Rock (and Other Ways to Disappoint Your Mother)*. Illus. by David Ostow. 2009. 255p. Flux (9780738714714). Gr. 8–12.

Fact: most dudes start bands to get girls, and Ari is no exception. Another fact: Ari is a Jewish-day-school junior, and not exactly a likely candidate for indie-rock stardom. But with aid from Jonas (the alpha to his beta on bass), Yossi (the very observant klezmer drummer), and Reena (Yossi's sister, backup vocals), they form The Tribe and earn modest fame after their first performance. But with great popularity comes great ego. Jonas becomes insufferable, Yossi increasingly withdrawn, and Ari resents Jonas stealing both the spotlight and the girl. Sister-and-brother team Micol and David Ostow hilariously deliver insight into the small world of teen Jewish punk-rock bands in tones dripping with sarcasm and music snobbery. David's comic-strip-style illustrations are true show-stoppers: amusing, ironic, and helpful, whether expanding on Ari's school schedule or defining Jewish, musical, or "otherwise esoteric terms" in the glossary. Teens involved in faith-based communities will recognize Ari's mild resentment toward his faith, and breathe a sigh of relief when he reconciles his musical ambitions with his beliefs. A rollicking, witty, and ultra-contemporary book that drums on the funny bone and reverberates through the heart. —Courtney Jones

Paulsen, Gary. *The Beet Fields: Memories of a Sixteenth Summer*. 2000. 192p. Delacorte (9780385326476). Gr. 9–12.

He's known only as "the boy." Readers meet him twisting away from his drunken mother as she crawls into his bed and follow until he enlists in the army. In between is the ultimate coming-of-age story, told in language that is as clean as bleached bones. But beneath the quiet, direct telling there is every earthy emotion—hunger, exhaustion, fear, passion. After his mother's drunken attempt, the boy runs away and finds work in a beet field, hard, backbreaking work. Mexican migrant workers share their food and teach him about responsibility to the group: he climbs to the rafters and wrings the necks of pigeons so he can add to the cooking pot. He leaves the beet fields when he spies a girl named Lynette, but he never sees her again. He's picked up as a runaway by a deputy who steals his money, then hitchhikes with a man who is killed when a bird flies into the car's windshield. A woman who has lost her son befriends him, but he leaves her to join the carnival—where he sets up and breaks down, shills for the geek who bites the heads off chickens, and has his first sexual experience with Ruby, the carnival's exotic dancer, who helps him learn what it's like to please a woman. Paulsen has visited some of this personal material before, but showed it in a softer light. This time the story is gritty and unblinking. If this were just an uncompromising look at a boy's sixteenth summer, it would be involving. It's Paulsen's ability to put readers behind the boy's eyes—so they can feel what's going on as well as see it—that makes this novel exceptional and so heartbreakingly real. —Ilene Cooper

Paulsen, Gary. ***How Angel Peterson Got His Name: And Other Outrageous Tales about Extreme Sports.*** **2003. 160p. Random/Wendy Lamb (9780385729499). Gr. 6–9.**

Every boy who is 13 or about to be 13 or who remembers being 13 should read this short story collection based on people and events from Paulsen's own life. Even though the action takes place 50 or so years ago, they will recognize themselves. And every girl who has ever liked a 13-year-old-boy, or been related to one, or wondered about one, should read this, too, because although the book doesn't explain why boys like to do things like pee on electric fences, it does give an insight into how their funny little minds work. Writing with humor and sensitivity, Paulsen shows boys moving into adolescence believing they can do anything: wrestle with bears; shoot waterfalls in a barrel; fly eight-by-twelve-foot Army surplus kites—and hang on, even as they land in the chicken coop. None of them dies (amazingly), and even if Paulsen exaggerates the teensiest bit, his tales are side-splittingly funny and more than a little frightening. —GraceAnne A. DeCandido

Pearson, Mary E. ***The Miles Between.*** **2009. 288p. Holt (9780805088281). Gr. 9–12.**

Destiny Faraday is a loner who has a long pattern of moving from one prestigious private school to another. Preoccupied with numbers, patterns, and chance, she keeps her distance from her classmates even as she obsessively observes them. That all changes on October 19, when she finds herself in possession of a car that contains a glove compartment filled with cash. Accompanied unexpectedly by three of her classmates, she sets out to live a single day in which everything feels "right." While coincidence, luck, and fate are all recurring themes, Pearson's story is actually driven by very real secrets and events. Destiny's journey is convincing and moving, despite the stunning circumstances under which it is taken. Observant readers who think they have worked out the plot's direction will find themselves questioning connections until the very last moment. Pearson skillfully separates truth from illusion and offers an uplifting book, in which grace and redemption are never left to chance. —Kara Dean

Pearson, Mary E. ***A Room on Lorelei Street.*** **2005. 272p. Holt (9780805076677). Gr. 9–12.**

Seventeen-year-old Zoe feels alone and neglected by her family; she has become the caretaker for her alcoholic mother. Since she feels alone, she wants to be alone, abdicating all responsibility for anyone other than herself. She rents a room in an old house on Lorelei Street, a neighborhood as charming as her landlady, Opal. Her waitress job at Murray's and Opal's generosity hold promise for her survival on her own, but Zoe can't seem to overcome her penchant for bad academic and economic decisions, choosing inappropriate comments to a teacher over stoicism, and cigarettes over food and gas for the car. Ultimately, survival wins, but not without incredible pain inflicted on Zoe, her family, and her friends. Pearson paints a compelling portrait of a teen, easily recognizable to most YAs, who is simultaneously intent on survival and self-sabotage. —Frances Bradburn

Perera, Anna. ***Guantanamo Boy.*** **2011. 352p. Albert Whitman (9780807530771). Gr. 7–12.**

Is torture ever justified? Can a confession given under torture be considered the truth? What if the suspect is only 15? There are adult books about abuse at Guantanamo Bay. But what about the many kids held without trial? Set six months after 9/11, this unforgettable novel raises crucial headline issues through the story of teenage Khalid, born near Manchester, England, into a secular Muslim family. Close with his mates on the soccer field and excited about a girl in his class, Khalid grabs every spare minute at home to play war games online with his Pakistani cousin, Tariq, whom Khalid has never met. Then, on his first family trip to Pakistan, Khalid is suddenly arrested in the street, named an "enemy combatant," beaten, and questioned, first in Pakistan, then Afghanistan, and then Guantanamo Bay, where he is deprived of sleep, shackled, and water-boarded until he "confesses" to everything in order to stop the pain and get back home. Tariq is also a prisoner. Did he "confess" and betray Khalid? Were they victims of bounty hunters? Finally, after almost two years and with the help of his family's lawyer, Khalid does return home to a heartfelt welcome, but many young suspects remain in prison. The extensive back matter by the author and human-rights activists includes detailed discussion questions and more facts. Teens, and adults, too, will want to talk about the terrifying stories like Khalid's, which are happening now to young people. —Hazel Rochman

Perkins, Lynne Rae. ***As Easy as Falling Off the Face of the Earth.*** **2010. 352p. Greenwillow (9780061870903). Gr. 8–11.**

Sixteen-year-old Ry opens a letter en route to a summer program informing him that camp has been canceled because "a statistically improbable number of things have gone wrong." He hops off the train in Montana to figure out what to do, and his own series of improbable misfortunes begins—the train moves on without him (but with all his stuff), leaving him alone with a dying cell phone in the precise middle of nowhere. Oh, and one of his shoes just floated off down a river. He befriends a man named Del, who figures there's nothing he can't fix (when it comes to other people's problems, anyway). They set off on a cross-country road trip to get Ry back home and then, due to any number of minor and major catastrophes, to an island in the Caribbean. Ever-placid Del and milquetoast Ry make for affable traveling companions, but the real pleasure is Perkins' relentlessly entertaining writing. She dabbles just on the clever side of intruding on the narrative, and she infuses her prose with more personality than many could squeeze out of an entire cast. The knock against her Newbery-winning *Criss Cross* (2005) was a lack of plot, and although a lot of things happen here, it would be a stretch to call this leisurely novel plot-driven. The point is that it doesn't matter, and wallowing in the wry humor, small but potent truths, and cheerful implausibility is an absolute delight. —Ian Chipman

Perkins, Lynne Rae. ***Criss Cross.*** **2005. 368p. Greenwillow (9780060092726). Gr. 6–9.**

This lyrical sequel to *All Alone in the Universe* (1999), a *Booklist* Editors' Choice, begins with one of many black-and-white drawings and a caption that reads, "People move back and forth in this area like molecules in steam." As the title and caption imply, this story reads like a series of intersecting vignettes—all focused on 14-year-old Debbie and her friends as they leave childhood behind. Perkins writes with subtle, wry humor about perceptive moments that will speak directly to readers: universe-expanding crushes, which fill the world with "signs and wonder"; scornful reappraisals of childhood things (Debbie's disdain for Nancy Drew is particularly funny); urgent concerns about outfits, snappy retorts, and self-image. Perkins adds many experimental passages to her straightforward narrative, and she finds poetry in the common exchanges between teens. One section of dialogue, written entirely in haiku, reads, "Jeff White is handsome, / but his hair is so greasy. / If he would wash it—." A few cultural references set the book in the 1970s, but most readers will find their contemporaries in these characters. Best of all are the understated moments, often private and piercing in their authenticity, that capture intelligent, likable teens searching for signs of who they are, and who they'll become. —Gillian Engberg

Peters, Julie Anne. ***Luna*****. 2004. 256p. Little, Brown (9780316733694). Gr. 8–12.**

Peters tells two stories in this groundbreaking novel—one about Regan, and the other about Liam, Regan's transgender brother, who is the son his father expects by day but a young woman, Luna, by night. Fiercely protective of Liam/Luna, Regan has put her life on hold; she worries about her brother's female self being discovered and the family's reaction, and she fears that her brother may someday give in to despair. While Regan wonders if she will ever be able to have a life separate from the needs of her sibling, Liam seriously begins to consider a permanent change. Peters isn't putting forward a political agenda here. Rather, she's bringing the circumstances surrounding a difficult situation to light, and her sensitively drawn characters realistically encompass a wide range of reactions—from tentative acceptance by a best friend to Mom's feigned ignorance and Dad's total disbelief. The subject matter and occasional rough language will undoubtedly raise some eyebrows, but this book belongs in most YA collections. —Cindy Welch

Pitcher, Annabel. ***My Sister Lives on the Mantelpiece*****. 2012. 211p. Little, Brown (9780316176903). Gr. 7–10.**

Readers of Pitcher's debut should brace themselves: this book pulls no emotional punches. Jamie Matthews was five years old when his sister Rose was killed in a terrorist attack in London. While her urn on the mantelpiece dominates his family's life, he can barely remember her, much less love her; all he knows is the wreck that her death has left behind. When his parents split, Jamie moves with his father and sister Jas—Rose's surviving twin—and starts a new life and a new school in the Lake District. Jamie becomes friends with the clever and effervescent Sunya. But Sunya is a Muslim, and, as Jamie's dad constantly reminds him, "Muslims killed your sister." Jamie's mother has abandoned him, his father is sinking into alcoholism, and he's bullied at school—when it seems things can't get worse, Jamie endures a personal tragedy that puts the previous five years in perspective while finally offering some solace. Just as the macabre title straddles that fine line between funny and tragic, so does this book. As a study of grief's collateral damage, it deals with the topic realistically without losing sight of hope. Jamie is a frank narrator whose naivete is tempered by the wisdom he acquires. He relies on his relationship with Jas for stability and eventually sets his own moral compass. An outstanding first novel. —Kara Dean

Portman, Frank. ***Andromeda Klein*****. 2009. 416p. Delacorte (9780385735254). Gr. 9–12.**

Portman's follow-up to *King Dork* (2006) will leave some readers turning to less demanding fare, like, say, advanced calculus. Yet it's a must-read simply because of how rare it is to see any topic tackled with such manic specificity. Andromeda is a high-school junior obsessed with magic. (How many teens do you know who have a favorite occultist?) With the help of a well-worn Tarot deck, copious rituals, and a vast array of tomes with titles like *Babylonian Liver Omens*, Andromeda scrutinizes her world in search of "synchs" that will help elucidate why she is flat-chested, how to navigate a mean-girl environment, and what to make of the leukemia death of Daisy, her former partner-in-astral-journeys. Though clearly Andromeda hides behind her rituals, Portman's handling of the subject is nonjudgmental and lots of fun. Laughs are guaranteed, particularly as Andromeda's poor hearing leads to constant misinterpretations, which she dutifully incorporates into her "lexicon" (example: *bagel worm agony* stands for *naked girl magazine*). With impish prose and ridiculously researched detail, Portman fully fleshes a one-of-a-kind character whose idea of the perfect pick-up line is "Want to see my Necronomicon?" —Daniel Kraus

Portman, Frank. ***King Dork*****. 2006. 352p. Delacorte (9780385732918). Gr. 9–12.**

From its subtle cover, featuring the title superimposed over the yellow lettering on a vintage red copy of *Catcher in the Rye*, to its intelligent, self-deprecating, opinionated narrator, Portman's novel is a humorous, scathing indictment of the current public education system. Sophomore Tom Henderson is bored with AP classes in which creating international foods and a "collage and *Catcher*" curriculum pass for academic instruction. What does he do to engage his mind? Along with his best friend, he invents a new band every few hours—a band name, cover art, song titles—no matter that neither boy owns a guitar. The guys aren't popular; they're picked on by the alpha sadists in gym class and nicknamed in humiliating ways, but they still survive. A mystery about the death of Tom's father and the caricatured assistant principal's illicit activities are weakly executed, but Tom's voice carries the story. Mature situations, casual sexual experiences, and allusions to Salinger suggest an older teen audience, who will also best appreciate the appended bandography and the very funny glossary. —Cindy Dobrez

Rabb, Margo. ***Cures for Heartbreak*****. 2007. 224p. Delacorte (9780385734028). Gr. 10–12.**

"I was ashamed of my family for having such bad luck." In the same year, teenage Mia's mother dies of cancer and her father has a heart attack. In stand-alone chapters (versions of some have been published in magazines), Raab gives Mia a distinctive voice, leavening her heartbreak with surprising humor and dark absurdity. Rabb is an exceptionally gifted writer who draws subtle connections between abstract history and intimate lives, particularly in scenes contrasting the dry school coverage of the Holocaust with Mia's Jewish family's personal history—"the kind of history that seeps in slowly and colors everything, like a quiet, daily kind of war." In Mia, Rabb creates a remarkable character whose ordinary teen experiences—crushes, friendships, sexual fumblings, mortification over her family's behavior—seem all the more authentic set within the larger tragedies. With almost unbearable poignancy, Mia talks about how to grow up, survive loss and family history, and heal her heart: "If grief had a permanence, then didn't also love?" Readers will cherish this powerful debut. —Gillian Engberg

Rapp, Adam. ***The Children and the Wolves*****. 2012. 160p. Candlewick (9780763653378). Gr. 9–12.**

In the wake of such modern masterpieces as *33 Snowfish* (2003) and the Printz Honor–winning *Punkzilla* (2009), readers should know the kind of grueling, soulful, gut-punching work to expect from Rapp. Still, be warned: this is his most hellish—and hellishly readable—vision yet. Bounce, a rich 14-year-old genius (and one of the most frightening characters you'll find in YA lit), has two 13-year-old lowlife friends, Orange and Wiggins (her "two lost wildebeests"), in her thrall, thanks to her towering IQ, brash sex appeal, and endless supply of OxyContin. For two months they've been keeping a three-year-old girl locked in Orange's basement, feeding her a selection of cold cereal and stolen pharmaceuticals, and meanwhile canvassing the neighborhood to solicit donations, ostensibly to help find the girl but really so that they can buy a gun to shoot a local poet who annoyed Bounce during a school visit. The point of view jumps between the four characters, though it is Wiggins, who suffers sporadic drug-addled attacks of consciousness, who becomes the novel's closest thing to a moral center. Naysayers could gripe that Rapp keeps plumbing the same territory. But he's also creating, book by book, a vital library of the furies and hopes of a forgotten underclass, and always in their own confused, desperate, and endlessly resourceful voices. —Daniel Kraus

★ Rapp, Adam. ***Punkzilla*****. 2009. 256p. Candlewick (9780763630317). Gr. 10–12.**

The 61-word run-on sentence on the first page sets the stream-of-consciousness tone, and then two pages later there's hand jobs and meth—yep, it's a Rapp novel, all right. And the quality hits the high standards of *33 Snowfish* (2003) and *Under the Wolf, Under the Dog* (2004). Fourteen-year-old Jamie (aka "Punkzilla") has gone AWOL from his military school, is off his meds, and is making his way from Oregon to Memphis, where his older brother, Peter, is dying of cancer. Though he is thankful to leave behind his career as an iPod thief, life on the road doesn't seem much better: his fellow Greyhound riders are frightening, he gets jumped in a roadside restroom, and his androgynous features land him in increasingly disturbing situations. You expect such bleakness from Rapp, but it's the flashes of humor and optimism that exhilarate. Beneath a surface of disease, despair, and disfigurements, Rapp's road trip is populated with good souls who, despite their circumstances, make significant sacrifices to help Punkzilla. Rapp constructs the book as a series of unsent letters to Peter and punctuates them with correspondence, some old enough to be heartbreakingly out of date, that Punkzilla has received from friends and family. This is devastating stuff, but breathtaking, too. —Daniel Kraus

Rapp, Adam. ***Under the Wolf, Under the Dog.*** **2004. 320p. Candlewick (9780763618186). Gr. 10–12.**

Steve Nugent is a character as distinctive and disturbing as Salinger's Holden Caulfield was 50 years ago. Steve, who is writing from a Michigan facility for troubled teens, chronicles both the events leading up to his hospitalization and his interactions with fellow patients, the Blue Groupers (suicidal teens) and the Red Groupers (addicts), as a part of his counseling. Rapp effectively uses canine references (and some scatology) to illustrate Steve's loss of control as he struggles to find a place in the pack after his mother's death and his brother's suicide. Opening pages paint a horrific picture of Steve's older brother's death, but as the novel cycles through to a final coda of this same scene, shock turns to deep regret for all that Steve has lost, and readers will come away with a fervent hope that Steve's opening journal entry will come true: "By the time anyone reads this, hopefully I'll be out of this place and on to better things." Like *33 Snowfish* (2003), this is not for timid readers or those easily offended or shocked by rough language or graphic descriptions, but teens will root from their hearts and even laugh a little as Steve struggles to fight his way out from under the dog of depression that has him pinned down. —Cindy Dobrez

Reinhardt, Dana. ***A Brief Chapter in My Impossible Life.*** **2006. 224p. Random (9780385746984). Gr. 9–12.**

Olive skinned and dark eyed, Simone looks nothing like her fair-haired family. She is, nonetheless, the beloved daughter of her adoptive parents and enjoys a close and supportive relationship with her younger brother. It therefore comes as a terrible intrusion in Simone's comfortable life when, after 16 years, her birth mother asks to meet her. After some resistance, Simone makes contact with Rivka, a 33-year-old self-exiled Hasidic Jew who is dying of ovarian cancer. Despite a fairly transparent setup, once Simone and Rivka are brought together, their shared story is developed with skill, attention to detail, and poignancy. Both Simone and Rivka are strong, complicated characters who benefit greatly from each other: Simone is gifted with her heritage and history and thus a richer identity, and Rivka is able to leave the world having known her daughter. Some sexual content and strong language in Simone's friendships and school life may make this an inappropriate selection for younger teens, and with a poorly representative cover, the book may require hand selling. —Holly Koelling

Reinhardt, Dana. ***How to Build a House.*** **2008. 240p. Random/Wendy Lamb (9780375844539). Gr. 8–12.**

"When you live in California and have relatives in New York, everything in between feels like a big inconvenience," says 17-year-old Harper. But even the middle of the country sounds better to Harper than her own home, which feels empty since her stepmother and stepsiblings moved out. Harper is also eager to leave Gabriel, her "sort-of boyfriend" behind, so she signs up as a summer volunteer to build houses for tornado victims in Bailey, Tennessee. In chapters that alternate between recollections of her past year and her Tennessee summer, Harper slowly reveals the events in L.A. that led to heartbreak and then the healing work, friendships, and romance she finds in Bailey. Reinhardt adds great depth to the familiar story of a teen changed by a summer escape with strong characters and perceptive, subtle explorations of love, family, sex, and friendship—all narrated in Harper's believable voice. Teens, especially young women on the verge of independence, will see themselves in Harper, her questions, and her resilient heart. —Gillian Engberg

Reinhardt, Dana. ***The Things a Brother Knows.*** **2010. 256p. Random/Wendy Lamb (9780375844553). Gr. 9–12.**

In a Boston suburb, Levi's older brother, Boaz, has just returned from fighting in "some desert country half a world away." The U.S. Marines say Boaz is "healthy," but Levi thinks otherwise; Boaz doesn't want to ride in a car, sleep in a bed, or even come out of his room, and he dives for cover at unpredictable moments. Levi misses Boaz as he remembers him, before he left two years earlier: a high-school hero; a happy, well-adjusted son and grandson; and a difficult but still-wonderful older brother. Reinhardt's poignant story of a soldier coping with survivor's guilt and trauma, and his Israeli American family's struggle to understand and help, is timely and honest. The clever, authentic dialogue beautifully captures the disparate dynamics of the family, friends, and marines in the brothers' lives. Indeed, the characters seem so real that they may live in readers' minds long after the final page is turned. Unlike Walter Dean Myers' *Fallen Angels* (1998), about Vietnam, or *Sunrise over Fallujah* (2008), set in Iraq, this novel is not anchored in a specific war, but Reinhardt sensitively explores universal traumas that usurp the lives of many soldiers and their loved ones. Readers won't soon forget Boaz and Levi's search for understanding and the healing power of love. —Frances Bradburn

Rennison, Louise. *Angus, Thongs, and Full-Frontal Snogging: Confessions of Georgia Nicolson*. 2000. 256p. HarperCollins (9780756904593). Gr. 6–9.

American readers wondering what on earth "full-frontal snogging" is will find the answer in the helpful (and hilarious) glossary appended to this antic diary of a year in the life of an English girl named Georgia Nicolson. Snogging is, simply, "kissing with all the trimmings," and it's much on 14-year-old Georgia's mind these days. For even though she's still reeling from her devastatingly bad decision to go to a party dressed as a stuffed olive, she has fallen in love with an older man (he's 17), a Sex God named Robbie. The trouble is, S. G. is dating a girl named Lindsay who—brace yourself—wears a thong. Honestly, how wet (idiotic) can you get! In the meantime, life on the homefront is spinning out of control. Dad has gone to New Zealand in search of a better job, and pet cat Angus, who can usually be spotted stalking the neighbor's poodle, has gone missing. Although performer and comedy writer Rennison clearly owes a large debt to Helen Fielding's *Bridget Jones's Diary* (1998), her Georgia is a wonderful character whose misadventures are not only hysterically funny but universally recognizable. This "fabbity fab fab" novel will leave readers cheering, "Long live the teen!" and anxiously awaiting the promised sequel. —Michael Cart

Rennison, Louise. *On the Bright Side, I'm Now the Girlfriend of a Sex God: Further Confessions of Georgia Nicholson*. 2001. 256p. HarperCollins (9780060288136). Gr. 7–10.

She's back! Georgia Nicholson, the ultimate self-involved teenager, returns in a sequel that is as "fabbity fab fab" as its predecessor, *Angus, Thongs, and Full-Frontal Snogging*, a 2001 Printz Honor Book. Georgia's latest crisis is the family's anticipated move to New Zealand ("Kiwi-a-gogo"), where her father has found work. The news comes just when she's finally snogging Robbie the Sex God. But wait! Her father decides to leave Kiwi and return to England, so the move is off—and more snogging with the Sex God is on. But wait! S. G. decides Georgia is too young for him, so she must trap Dave the Laugh into being a red herring to lure S. G. back. As Georgia records these events in her politically incorrect diary, she continues to bemoan the more mundane details of her life: her huge conk (nose), which means she will forever have to live in Ugly Home, Ugly Kingdom, Ugly Universe; her sister, Libby, who hides "pooey" knickers in Georgia's bed; and her miserable classmates, the Bummer twins, who use Georgia as an armchair. As the last line of the laugh-out-loud diary reads, "Good grief! What in the name of pantyhose is going to happen next?!?" Look for more immediate laughs in the glossary. —Ilene Cooper

Resau, Laura. *Red Glass*. 2007. 288p. Delacorte (9780385734660). Gr. 7–10.

Sixteen-year-old Sophie finds plenty of room in her heart for Pablo, a five-year-old Mexican orphan whose parents died during their illegal border crossing. Silent since his parents' death, he finally speaks and tells Sophie's family the name of his Mexican village. Though fearful of everything from kitchen-sponge bacteria to leprosy, not to mention relationships with boys, Sophie makes the momentous decision to take Pablo back to see his relatives. Then, she hopes that he will return with her to Tucson. Pablo, Sophie, and her great-aunt Dika will drive to southern Mexico with Dika's Guatemalan gentleman friend, Mr. Lorenzo, and his handsome, enigmatic son, Ángel. With these companions, Sophie undertakes an epic journey of chance, change, and discovery. The author of *What the Moon Saw* (2006), Resau works her magic again in this compelling first-person narrative. Full of longing and trepidation, Sophie is limited at the beginning of the story. But as she travels and comes to understand people better; life-altering perspectives awaken a newfound courage. Late in the novel, magical elements and coincidence demand suspension of disbelief; but many readers will be willing to follow Sophie's story wherever it leads. The vivid characters, the fine imagery, and the satisfying story arc make this a rewarding novel. —Carolyn Phelan

Resau, Laura. *What the Moon Saw*. 2006. 272p. Delacorte (9780385733434). Gr. 6–9.

"In all my fourteen years, I hadn't thought much about Mexico," says Clara, who lives in suburban Maryland with her American mother and Mexican father, who crossed the border illegally long ago. Then Clara's Mexican grandparents invite her to spend the summer with them in Oaxaca, and she finds herself on a plane, traveling to see a part of her father's life she has barely considered. Resau's deeply felt, lyrical debut follows Clara through her summer with her grandparents, who live in small huts in the remote Oaxacan mountains. After her grandfather tells Clara that her grandmother "can see a whole world that the rest of us cannot," Clara learns that Abuelita is a healer, and in alternating first-person narratives, Resau juxtaposes Abuelita's stories of her coming-of-age with Clara's own awakening. Pedro, a young neighbor, stirs some of Clara's first romantic desires and forces questions about cultural misperceptions. The metaphors of personal discovery are sometimes heavy and esoteric, and the transitions between narrators are occasionally contrived. But in poetic, memorable language, Resau offers a rare glimpse into an indigenous culture, grounding her story in the universal questions and conflicts of a young teen. Readers who enjoyed Ann Cameron's *Colibrí* (2003) will find themselves equally swept up in this powerful, magical story, and they'll feel, along with Clara, "the spiderweb's threads, connecting me to people miles and years away." —Gillian Engberg

Ritter, John H. *Under the Baseball Moon*. 2006. 304p. Philomel (9780399236235). Gr. 7–10.

In *The Boy Who Saved Baseball* (2003), Ritter seasoned the familiar *Bad News Bears* formula with a splash of myth and a touch of otherworldliness. Here he uses the same spicing in a story that mixes softball and jazz—and the results are equally tasty. Andy Ramos is a San Diego teen with dreams of making it big in the music business, but even his head-turning trumpet playing won't be enough without a few breaks. Enter a mysterious street person who claims to be able to launch Andy's career—think Robert Johnson at the crossroads, making a deal with the devil—and suddenly those elusive breaks fall Andy's way. Then a childhood friend, Glory Martinez, a talented softball pitcher with Olympian dreams, returns to Andy's Ocean Beach (OB) neighborhood, and romantic sparks fly—until it appears that Andy's strange benefactor sees Gloria as a threat, not a soul mate. Ritter pulls out all the stops in his myth-heavy plot, but what really makes the book soar is his sense of place: the laid-back, hippie-influenced, communal spirit of the OB permeates every scene, offering stark contrast to the coldly commercial world toward which Andy aspires. As in his earlier work, Ritter melds style to content beautifully, telling his story in a hip, street-smart argot that perfectly matches Andy's trumpet improvisations. Teen friendly, lots of fun, never preachy, but with plenty of thematic pizzazz. —Bill Ott

Rosen, Renee. *Every Crooked Pot*. 2007. 240p. St. Martin's/Griffin (9780312365431). Gr. 10–12.

In a debut novel that could easily have been published as an adult memoir, Rosen looks back at the life of Nina Goldman, whose growing up is tied to two pillars: a port-wine stain around her eye and her inimitable father, Artie. The birthmark, she hates; her father, she loves. Both shape her in ways that merit Rosen's minute investigation, which begins with an incident both funny and shocking. Stopped for speeding, her father tells the officer he is rushing young Nina to the hospital and shows him her eye, which looks as though it's hemorrhaging. When the cop leaves, father and daughter take off for the beach. The story highlights how Nina's eye is both liability and excuse, and it reveals the high-wire act that is her father—an emotional man who shapes reality and the people around him. As Nina grows older, readers feel the pain she endures by being physically marked (boys bark at "the dog"). Difficult in different ways is having a father whose love feels like sunshine; withheld, all is dark. There's real power in the writing, as well as a subtle message when a grown Nina finds a cache of notes showing how she clung to her disability, even after treatment. Rosen writes honestly about sex, and there are some raw words, but this story offers hope for teenagers who, as ever, are trying to separate from their perceived flaws, and from their parents. —Ilene Cooper

Rosoff, Meg. *Just in Case*. 2006. 256p. Random/Wendy Lamb (9780385746786). Gr. 9–12.

After rescuing his baby brother from an open window's ledge, 15-year-old David Case concludes "just two seconds were all that stood between normal everyday life, and utter, total catastrophe." Convinced that Fate is toying with him, David tries to elude detection by creating a new identity, starting with his name and his wardrobe. Eventually, he refuses to return home and plunges into an affair with an older girl. In frequently inserted passages, Fate actually speaks, and it's clear that David's fears are warranted. Rosoff's second novel, following the Printz Award winner *How I Live Now* (2004), is an explosive, challenging story that sometimes reads more like metaphysical meditation than coming-of-age narrative. Starting with the wordplay of David's new name (Justin Case), the author's experimentation with story elements to further philosophical questions is sometimes distracting, and readers may feel distanced by characters who occasionally seem more like archetypes and intellectual vehicles than flesh and blood. Even so, many teens will relish Rosoff's wild, unsettling, often poetic plunge into subjects of cosmic proportion, such as faith, time, free will, illusions, and the boundaries of love and sex: "Could sexual feeling be totally one-sided? While he ached with lust, was she thinking about shoelaces?" Balancing ruminations on the connections between everything are the solid friendships: "The answer isn't in your head, it's out here, with us," David's young friend tells him angrily. Readers will want to ponder the provocative questions that wrap around their own hopes and terrors. —Gillian Engberg

Rowell, Rainbow. *Eleanor and Park*. 2013. 320p. St. Martin's/Griffin (9781250012579). Gr. 9–12.

Right from the start of this tender debut, readers can almost hear the clock winding down on Eleanor and Park. After a less than auspicious start, the pair quietly builds a relationship while riding the bus to school every day, wordlessly sharing comics and eventually music on the commute. Their worlds couldn't be more different. Park's family is idyllic: his Vietnam vet father and Korean immigrant mother are genuinely loving. Meanwhile, Eleanor and her younger siblings live in poverty under the constant threat of Richie, their abusive and controlling stepfather, while their mother inexplicably caters to his whims. The couple's personal battles are also dark mirror images. Park struggles with the realities of falling for the school outcast; in one of the more subtle explorations of race and "the other" in recent YA fiction, he clashes with his father over the definition of manhood. Eleanor's fight is much more external, learning to trust her feelings about Park and navigating the sexual threat in Richie's watchful gaze. In rapidly alternating narrative voices, Eleanor and Park try to express their all-consuming love. "You make me feel like a cannibal," Eleanor says. The pure, fear-laced, yet steadily maturing relationship they develop is urgent, moving, and, of course, heartbreaking, too. —Courtney Jones

Roy, Jennifer. *Mindblind*. 2010. 256p. Marshall Cavendish (9780761457169). Gr. 6–9.

Formulas are 14-year-old Nathaniel's friends because they relax him, an important consideration for someone given to panic attacks when he has to interact with people. Nathaniel is a high-functioning "Aspie," a term that those—like him—with Asperger's syndrome employ to describe themselves. Fortunately, formulas aren't Nathaniel's only friends. His neighbor Cooper is one; pretty, vivacious Jessa, upon whom Nathaniel has a serious but unarticulated crush, is another; and Molly—an Aspie like him—is a third. The multitalented Nathaniel plays keyboards in a band, teaches himself Mandarin Chinese, and is an absolute whiz at mathematics. And why not? He has an IQ of 182. A genius, you say? Well, yes, but don't tell Nathaniel that, for he has read that to be a bona fide genius, you have to make a contribution to the world, something he is determined to do (just as he is determined to kiss Jessa). Roy (*Yellow Star*, 2006) has written an extraordinary novel with highly developed, good-hearted, and appealing characters (except for Nathaniel's father, who is a real stinker); a beautifully realized first-person voice that offers us an often humorous and intimate look into the mind and daily life of an Aspie; and a compelling story filled with surprises and drama. To read it is to want to read it again and again. —Michael Cart

Ryan, P. E. *Saints of Augustine*. 2007. 320p. HarperTempest (9780060858100). Gr. 8–11.

Teens Charlie and Sam were best friends, until Sam stopped speaking to Charlie. In his first book for young people, Ryan (*Send Me*, 2006) slowly reveals the cause of the rift in chapters that alternate between the two boys' viewpoints. Over a Florida summer, each boy wrestles alone with problems. Following his mother's death, Charlie worries about his shut-in dad, who drinks too much. He escapes by smoking pot, a habit that's put him into deep debt to a threatening dealer. Sam's dad lives with his male lover, and Sam, who has been hiding his own male attractions, worries if he is gay, too. When each boy reaches a crisis point, he finally turns to the other. In a less-gifted author's hands, this novel could have felt crowded. But Ryan offers complex views of family lives, realistic language (including some anti-gay slurs), and convincing characters in Sam and Charlie. Sam's new romance with another guy is a buoyant subplot; just as welcome is the sensitive story of two teen boys forging a close, honest friendship. —Gillian Engberg

Ryan, Sara. *Empress of the World*. 2001. 192p. Penguin (9780670896882). Gr. 9–12.

Fifteen-year-old Nicola is spending the summer at an institute for gifted youth, where she's studying archaeology. To her surprise, she falls in love with another girl, Battle, a lovely dancer with long hair, and Battle with her. Nic's intense feelings for Battle cause a breakup that sends Battle off with a guy, but unlike many stories of young love, this has a happy ending. Interestingly, Ryan writes this just like most teen romances; as far as the events go, Battle could easily have been a boy. A few muttered "dykes" is the extent of reaction from the other students, and though Nic, who has liked boys in the past, wonders about her sexuality, this seems to be a side issue; the main one is how Battle feels about her. There are subplots about parents and archaeology, but as in real life, the girls are submerged in the relationship. The dialogue may be a bit like *Dawson's Creek*'s at times, but first-novelist Ryan has a good handle on her characters and on her story, which is romantic without being explicit and feels very much like today. —Ilene Cooper

Sachar, Louis. *The Cardturner*. 2010. 352p. Delacorte (9780385736626). Gr. 9–12.

With his latest novel, the Newbery-winning author of *Holes* (1998) fulfills a need the world probably didn't even know it had: the great teen bridge novel. Alton Richard's great-uncle Lester Trapp is rich and ailing, a combo that leads Alton's parents to hatch a plan for the teen to cozy up to the old man and carve out a chunk of inheritance. Though blind, Trapp is a brilliant, world-class bridge player and needs someone to read him his cards and make his plays. Enter Alton, who wouldn't begin to know how to decipher questions like "One banana, pass, pass, two no-trump. Is that unusual?" But he withstands the constant barbs from his irascible uncle and grows more intrigued by the game (in no small part due to the cute, kind-of-crazy girl who also plays). Sachar liberally doles out detailed commentary on the basics and then nuances of the game, and in a nod to the famously dull *Moby-Dick* chapter on the minutiae of whaling, a little whale image appears when the bridge talk is about to get deep so readers can skip right ahead to a pithy wrap-up. But don't be fooled: it is astonishing how Sachar can make blow-by-blow accounts of bridge not only interesting but exciting, treating each play like a clue to unravel the riddle of each hand. An obvious windfall for smart and puzzle-minded teens, this is a great story to boot, with genuine characters (save the scheming parents) and real relationships, balanced by casual, confident storytelling. —Ian Chipman

Sáenz, Benjamin Alire. *Aristotle and Dante Discover the Secrets of the Universe*. 2012. 368p. Simon & Schuster (9781442408920). Gr. 9–12.

When Aristotle and Dante meet, in the summer of 1987, they are 15-year-olds existing in "the universe between boys and men." The two are opposites in most ways: Dante is sure of his place in the world, while Ari feels he may never know who he is or what he wants. But both are thoughtful about their feelings and interactions with others, and this title is primarily focused on the back-and-forth in their relationship over the course of a year. Family issues take center stage, as well as issues of Mexican identity, but the heart of the novel is Dante's openness about his homosexuality and Ari's suppression of his. Sáenz (*Sammy and Juliana in Hollywood*, 2004) writes toward the end of the novel that "to be careful with people and words was a rare and beautiful thing." And that's exactly what Sáenz does—he treats his characters carefully, giving them space and time to find their place in the world, and to find each other. This moves at a slower pace than many YA novels, but patient readers, and those struggling with their own sexuality, may find it to be a thought-provoking read. —Ann Kelley

Sáenz, Benjamin Alire. *Sammy and Juliana in Hollywood*. 2004. 294p. Cinco Puntos (9780938317814). Gr. 9–12.

"Someone's gonna hurt you. And you're gonna wish you never had a heart." The warning quickly becomes reality as Sammy struggles with his girlfriend Juliana's violent death. Sammy and Juliana's Hollywood is a New Mexico barrio, where Sammy loses more than his virginity and his girlfriend during his difficult 1969 senior year. A good student and an avid reader (his classmates nickname him "The Librarian"), he works hard for his dream of college. One friend is drafted for Vietnam, another dies of a drug overdose. Two gay friends leave town in exile, and Sammy's father is injured in an automobile accident, altering Sammy's plans. But Dad suggests that they shouldn't feel so bad about loss: "I mean—it's the only thing we're good at." The barrio setting is as palpable as the wings that beat against Sammy's insides when danger lurks. The tough but caring family, neighbors, and friends speak in authentic dialogue liberally laced with Spanish that adds texture to the story, and an empathetic teacher and a stand against the school dress code provide a small victory to help Sammy weather the racism and poverty that fuel his emotions and his losses. —Cindy Dobrez

Saldaña, Rene. *The Whole Sky Full of Stars*. 2007. 144p. Random/Wendy Lamb (9780385730532). Gr. 8–12.

Saldaña (*The Jumping Tree*, 2001) delivers another moving coming-of-age novel about the perils of friendship and the burdens of parental expectations. Barry Esquivel is a high-school senior dealing with the responsibility he feels as the new man of the family in the wake of his father's death. Barry's best friend, Alby, has problems of his own: in trying to live up to his father's credo that "we're winners not losers," he has amassed gambling debts to an unsavory type who wants his money now. Playing on their friendship, Alby convinces Barry, long schooled by his father as a boxer, to enter a shady competition called the Man o' Mite. Knowing this kind of exploitive venture would be condemned by his father, Barry still agrees to fight—anything to keep the family from selling Pop's treasured 1964 Ford Galaxy to make ends meet. The premise screams *Rocky*, but Saldaña skillfully dodges that punch, focusing less on the fights and more on the boys' imperiled friendship. Comparisons to Markus Zusak's *Fighting Ruben Wolfe* (2001) are inevitable, but Saldaña avoids the overwriting that marred Zusak's first novel. —Bill Ott

Sanchez, Alex. *Getting It.* **2006. 224p. Simon & Schuster (9781416908968). Gr. 9–12.**

In this nod to TV's *Queer Eye for the Straight Guy*, 15-year-old Carlos is the only one of his buds who is still a virgin. He wants more than anything to have sexy Roxie as his girlfriend—"and hopefully get laid." When she ignores him, he secretly hires smart Sal, who is gay, to give him a makeover. In return, Sal wants him to help form a Gay-Straight Alliance (GSA) in their Texas high school. A too-perfect mentor-therapist, Sal doesn't seem real, but the wry, self-help makeover details about grooming, shopping, and good manners are fun, and when Carlos hooks up with Roxie, their sexy fumbling is drawn with wry realism. Carlos and Roxie talk online, and they make out on the couch, but then she snubs him in public and dumps him—leaving him to discover the difference between a hookup and a girlfriend. At the core of the story is Carlos' growing friendship with Sal, the questions and answers about being gay or straight, and their fight against homophobia, at school and in Carlos himself. The message of tolerance is strong, but it is dramatized with humor and truth. —Hazel Rochman

Scheidt, Erica Lorraine. *Uses for Boys.* **2013. 240p. St. Martin's/Griffin (9781250007117). Gr. 9–12.**

Many girls will relate to the fact that "there are no fathers in this story." Anna Bloom and her mother are everything to each other, for a time anyway. Then her mother starts falling for one man after the next, leaving young Anna alone for extended periods of time and marrying and divorcing in a vicious cycle. It's no wonder Anna starts to look to boys in order to define her own self-worth, and she mistakenly equates sex with love. Her first sexual experience comes at 14, and by 16, she has moved in with Joey ("I want to take care of him") and dropped out of school. There's desperation in Anna's need for sex—in her need to mold boyfriends into the family she never had—and her loneliness is palpable. By novel's end, readers will find themselves emotionally exhausted but hopeful. Scheidt's spare and poetic debut offers up pretty images for some decidedly unpretty situations ("the unmade bed is peaked and stormy"); at times, her prose feels as tightly wrought as a novel in verse. This is a story about where we come from and how, sometimes, we have to break free from the past in order to shape our own future. Scheidt could have easily spiraled into preachy territory here, but she never does. Lots of teens will see themselves in the pages of this beautiful, honest novel. —Ann Kelley

Schindler, Holly. *A Blue So Dark.* **2010. 288p. Flux (9780738719269). Gr. 8–11.**

As her beautiful mother, Grace, an artist, sinks into schizophrenia and refuses medication, 15-year-old Aura feels terrified and isolated. Aura also worries that she may have inherited her mother's genetic disposition for the disease, and because she associates it with creativity, she stops exploring her own painting and writing. Soon, both the caretaking and the secrecy her mother's illness engenders become impossible for Aura to sustain, and as she increasingly misses days of school, her mother's erratic behavior spills over into public scenes. Debut novelist Schindler paints a graphic picture of mental illness and the toll it takes on its victims and their families. Schindler's astute, powerful descriptions of the creative process and its ability to mirror the anguish and terror of schizophrenia, as well as its potential to alleviate pain and suffering, elevate this story beyond problem-novel stereotypes or a clinical recounting of symptoms. Grace's relentless descent into madness is breathtakingly, gut-wrenchingly authentic, and while Schindler does not sugarcoat the grim possibilities for either Aura or her mother, she leaves readers with some hope for the characters' futures. A haunting, realistic view of the melding of art, creativity, and mental illness and their collective impact on a young person's life.
—Frances Bradburn

Scott, Elizabeth. *Living Dead Girl.* **2008. 176p. Simon & Schuster/Simon Pulse (9781416960591). Gr. 10–12.**

Scott gives the phrase *emotionally wrenching* a whole new meaning in this searing book. When Alice was

10, Ray abducted her from a class trip and taught her how to be a "good girl." After five years of horrifying sexual and emotional abuse, Alice believes no one will help her. Despite near starvation, wax treatments to remove her pubic hair, and pills to suppress her periods, Alice's body is becoming too mature—and she knows Ray will kill her soon. After opening with chapters that intriguingly utilize first-, second-, and third-person points of view, the narrative settles into first person with a matter-of-fact tone that magnifies the horror. The description of the violence and sexual abuse, though vivid, is not explicit, but Alice's hopeless acceptance at times makes the book almost too painful to read. Skillfully crafted vignettes, particularly some disturbing scenes depicting Alice's sexual interactions with a teen boy, allow readers to draw their own conclusions about the impact of long-term abuse. Events leading to the conclusion are too convenient, but the ending itself will leave readers gasping. "You can get used to anything," Alice says, though some readers will not be able to get used to the sheer emotional power of this raw voice. —Lynn Rutan

Shulman, Polly. *Enthusiasm*. 2006. 208p. Putnam (9780399243899). Gr. 7–10.

"There is little more likely to exasperate a person of sense than finding herself tied by affection and habit to an Enthusiast. I speak from bitter experience." So begins the wry, engaging narrative in which Julie relates the trials and rewards of her firm friendship with Ashleigh, an enthusiast. Since elementary school, Ashleigh has taken up one craze after another, from military strategy to ballet, from Harriet the Spy to King Arthur, and dragged her best friend along for companionship. But when Ashleigh begins sophomore year speaking Jane Austen's prose and crashing an exclusive prep school's cotillion to dance the Founder's Quadrille, she commits a double fault: she takes ownership of Julie's favorite book, *Pride and Prejudice*, and she sets her determined sights on the boy Julie secretly adores. Shulman captures the agony and the irony of Julie's struggles to find her own way as she navigates the conventions of a culture that, for all its twenty-first-century trappings, still leaves young women hoping that the young men of their dreams will recognize and return their unspoken affections. While familiarity with Austen's world through her books or, more likely, the movie renditions will deepen readers' appreciation for Shulman's impressive first novel, it is by no means a prerequisite to enjoying this involving and often amusing narrative of friendship, courtship, and (of course) true love. —Carolyn Phelan

Shusterman, Neal. *Antsy Does Time*. 2008. 256p. Dutton (9780525478256). Gr. 6–9.

The wisecracking teenage Brooklynite introduced in Shusterman's award-winning *The Schwa Was Here* (2004) takes a second ride on the emotional roller coaster in this equally screwball sequel. When classmate Gunnar Ümlaut announces that he is going to die in six months from a rare disease, Antsy Bonnano prints up a formal contract that signs over a month of his own life to his gloomy buddy. This impulsive gesture of comfort unexpectedly nets Antsy a series of dates with Gunnar's hot older sister Kjersten—but also takes on a life of its own when everyone who finds out about the good deed wants to get into the act. Meanwhile, Antsy and his closest friend (and ex-girlfriend), blind Lexie, plot to kidnap Lexie's irascible grandpa "Creepy" Crawley (again), and Antsy's father works his way toward heart-attack country struggling to get the Bonnano family's new restaurant on its feet. Featuring a terrific supporting cast led by Antsy's wise, acerbic mother, an expert blend of comedy and near tragedy, and the wry observations of a narrator whose glib tongue and big heart are as apt to get him into trouble as out of it, this will keep tween readers hooked from start to finish.
—John Peters

Shusterman, Neal. *The Schwa Was Here*. 2004. 276p. Dutton (9781435266995). Gr. 6–9.

When Anthony "Antsy" Bonano and his friends meet Calvin Schwa, they are impressed and puzzled by his ability to appear and disappear before their very eyes. Antsy concocts a moneymaking scheme based on the Schwa's invisibility that seems promising until he and his friends overreach and are caught by the town's legendary mean millionaire, Mr. Crawley. Their resulting community service project—walking the 7 virtues and 7 vices (Crawley's 14 afghan hounds) and going out with Crawley's granddaughter Lexie—cements and ultimately challenges friendships. The humor is just right for boys, but the complexity of plot, the depth and richness of the characters, and the underlying seriousness of the issues belies the easy-to-read comedy. Schwa is an average kid who hangs on the periphery of the crowd and longs to be noticed and included, not simply ignored. His character is extreme, but far too many adolescents—and the adults who work with them—will sadly and guiltily recognize him. —Frances Bradburn

Simmons, Michael. *Vandal*. 2006. 176p. Roaring Brook (9781596430709). Gr. 7–10.

"Just in case you've been thinking that I'm a funny, lighthearted guy, and that this is going to be a funny story, let me say one more thing: this is a sad story. Really." No disagreement here, but it's also a deftly structured, refreshingly unsentimental, and witty analysis of the resilient, complicated bonds that connect siblings. Sixteen-year-old Will has conflicted emotions about his delinquent older brother; he fears Jason's wild, frightening behavior but continues to yearn for a closer relationship. When Jason returns from a stint in juvenile hall, he accepts a job with Will's up-and-coming KISS tribute band, triggering events with consequences devastating to the entire family. Evolving alongside the tense drama is the equally fascinating story of Will's guitar-playing career, well stocked with behind-the-scenes glimpses of gigs and as articulate about the joys of music as Christopher Krovatin's *Heavy Metal & You* (2005). The boys' "unblemished, totally enchanting" younger sister is too angelic, but other off notes are difficult to find: the character study of a bully who "was more than just a brute" is nuanced, the pacing is skillfully modulated, and the conclusion, free of nostrums about catharsis and rehabilitation, feels touching and true. For another novel about a teen grappling with a sibling's misdeeds, look to David Klass' *Dark Angel* (2004). Steer teens looking for more books with a music theme to Mike Tanner's *Resurrection Blues* (2005) or Blake Nelson's *Rock Star Superstar* (2004). —Jennifer Mattson

Smith, Andrew. *Winger*. 2013. 448p. Simon & Schuster (9781442444928). Gr. 9–12.

After he opened a vein in YA lit with *The Marbury Lens* (2010) and then went completely nutso in *Passenger* (2012), about the only thing that Smith could do to surprise would be a hornball boarding-school romantic romp. Surprise! Well, sort of. At 14, Ryan Dean West is a couple years younger (and scrawnier) than the rest of the juniors at Pine Mountain. He is a plucky kid—despite a tendency to punctuate his every thought with "I am such a loser"—who stars in the rugby team due to his speed and tenacity. The rail ties of his single-track mind, though, are his exploits (or lack thereof) with the opposite sex, particularly his best friend Annie, who thinks he is "adorable." In short, Ryan Dean is a slightly pervy but likable teen. He rates the hotness of every female in sight but also drops surprising bombs of personal depth on a friend's homosexuality, the poisonous rivalries that can ruin friendships, and his own highly unstable mix of insecurity and evolving self-confidence. Much of the story seems preoccupied with the base-level joys and torments of being a teenager, content to float along with occasional bursts of levity from some nonessential but fun minicomics by Bosma. But at its heart, it is more in line with *Dead Poets Society*, and by the end this deceptively lightweight novel packs an unexpectedly ferocious punch. —Ian Chipman

Sones, Sonya. *One of Those Hideous Books Where the Mother Dies*. 2004. 272p. Simon & Schuster (9780689858208). Gr. 7–12.

After the death of her mother, high-schooler Ruby is sent from Boston to L.A. to live with the father she has never met: "He's such a scumbag / that he divorced my mother / before I was even born." The "scumbag" is Whip Logan, a famous movie actor, but Ruby is too angry to be impressed; at the airport she wonders whether to "ask him for his autograph, / or kick him in the balls." Sones' latest free-verse novel follows Ruby through her first few months in her new home, a mansion where her every desire is granted—except what she longs for most: her best friend, her boyfriend, and of course, her mother. Sones' novel is an unusual combination of over-the-top Hollywood fairy tale and sharp, honest story about overcoming grief. Teens may predict the novel's surprises long before Ruby discovers them, including a revelation about Whip's sexuality, and, as in every fairy tale, many things are too good to be true—especially Whip's eager devotion and celebrity. It's Ruby's first-person voice—acrimonious, raw, and very funny—that pulls everything together, whether she is writing e-mails to her deceased mother, attending Dream Analysis class at a private L.A. high school, or finally learning to accept her father and embrace a new life. A satisfying, moving novel that will be a winner for both eager and reluctant readers. —Gillian Engberg

Sones, Sonya. *What My Girlfriend Doesn't Know*. 2007. 304p. Simon & Schuster (9780689876028). Gr. 7–10.

In *What My Mother Doesn't Know* (2001), 14-year-old Sophie, a Cambridge, Massachusetts, teen, describes her surprise when she is drawn to Robin, the school-appointed loser who makes her laugh. In this sequel, Robin picks up the narrative in rapid-fire, first-person free verse as he describes their school's reaction to the relationship: "They're gawking at us / like Sophie's Beauty and I'm the Beast." Sophie compares the two to outlaws: "It's just you and me against the world." But after Sophie's friends dump her, Robin feels guilty for the "random acts of unkindness" she endures: "Sophie may feel like an outlaw, / but thanks to yours truly, / what she really is / is an outcast." A talented artist, Robin finds escape in a Harvard drawing class, where a new friendship threatens his closeness with Sophie. The story of a thrilling and faltering first love may be familiar, but Robin's believable voice is distinctive, and Sones uses her spare words (and a few drawings) to expert effect. From bad puns to breathless accounts of locking lips to anguished worries about losing Sophie, Robin reinforces the picture of an awkward, likable, intelligent, and realistically flawed young man. Many teens will see themselves, and they'll cheer when Sophie and Robin thwart the bullies and reclaim their social standing. Like Sones' other titles, this is a great choice for reluctant and avid readers alike. —Gillian Engberg

Sones, Sonya. *What My Mother Doesn't Know*. 2001. 272p. Simon & Schuster (9780689841149). Gr. 6–10.

In a fast, funny, touching book, Sones uses the same simple, first-person poetic narrative she used in *Stop Pretending: What Happened When My Big Sister Went Crazy* (1999), but this story isn't about family anguish; it's about the joy and surprise of falling in love. Sophie, 14, thinks she has a crush on handsome Dylan, but she discovers that her most passionate feelings are for someone totally unexpected, a boy who makes her laugh and shows her how to look at the world. And when they kiss, every cell in her body is on fire. Meanwhile, she fights with her mom—who fights with Sophie's dad—and she refuses to wear a pink flowered dress to the school dance, secretly changing into a slinky black outfit with the help of her girlfriends. Their girl talk is hilarious and irreverent in the style of Naylor's Alice books. The poetry is never pretentious or difficult; on the contrary, the very short, sometimes rhythmic lines make each page fly. Sophie's voice is colloquial and intimate, and the discoveries she makes are beyond formula, even while they are as sweetly romantic as popular song. A natural for reluctant readers, this will also attract young people who love to read. —Hazel Rochman

Sonnenblick, Jordan. *Curveball: The Year I Lost My Grip*. 2012. 304p. Scholastic (9780545320696). Gr. 8–10.

Ignoring the shooting elbow pains that have plagued him all summer, star pitcher Pete Friedman throws everything he's got into one final fastball to close out the league championship in the summer before freshman year. He doesn't get the out, and worse, he has wrecked his arm and whatever identity he had to look forward to as a high-school athlete. But in true closed-door–opened-window fashion, Pete's camera skills (inherited from his grandpa) offer the chance to stay close to sports as a sideline photographer and to get close to the cute girl in his photography class. But the real tension in his life comes from the fact that the tack-sharp grandfather he has always looked up to is slipping from mildly forgetful into dangerous bouts of dementia that Pete's parents seem to want to ignore.

Sonnenblick (*After Ever After*, 2010) again shows an adept ability to tackle big-deal life issues, treat them seriously and believably, and filter them into a high-spirited, even fun story. He also sprinkles in technical photography details that kids handy with F-stops and lens specs will dig, but won't leave others out in the cold. A bittersweet look at freezing moments in time, and how Alzheimer's can scour even the younger generations in a family. —Ian Chipman

Sonnenblick, Jordan. *Notes from the Midnight Driver*. 2006. 264p. Scholastic (9780439757799). Gr. 8–11.

While his mother is out on a first date, 16-year-old Alex decides to get drunk, steal her car, and drive to his father's home, hoping to catch him romancing one of Alex's former teachers. His goal? Revenge. Reality? A damaged car, a decapitated gnome, a drunk driving charge, and community service. He is ordered to serve his 100 hours visiting Solomon Lewis, the meanest, crankiest resident at Egbert P. Johnson Memorial Home for the Aged. Alex discovers that Solomon is also witty, intelligent, and a fighter—an old man who has lived all the joys, sorrows, and regrets of a long life. Sonnenblick has created a memorable cast of characters: acerbic Sol, a former famous jazz guitarist who is now dying of emphysema; narrator Alex, a budding guitarist with a tendency to make excuses rather than assume responsibility; and Alex's best friend Laurie, a tiny, pixielike karate master whom Sol refers to as Alex's "wife." Even minor characters, such as Alex's parents and the judge, take on a heft and weight uncommon in YA literature, and teens will easily connect with Alex's epiphanies: "You can't just throw someone out of your life when they displease you," and, "We're all free to choose some people to love, and then do it." It all adds up to a funny, bittersweet tour de force.
—Frances Bradburn

Spinelli, Jerry. *Stargirl*. 2000. 192p. Knopf (9780679886372). Gr. 6–9.

Sixteen-year-old Leo recounts Stargirl's sojourn at Mica High in an allegorical story that is engagingly written but overreaches. Everyone notices Stargirl when she comes to school. She wears a granny gown, strums a ukulele, and sings "Happy Birthday" to kids in the cafeteria. She also carries around a pet rat. Her classmates veer between ignoring her and being discreetly fascinated by her weirdness—dancing when there's no music, speaking in class of trolls and stars. Slowly, Stargirl attracts a following, especially after she gives a spellbinding speech in an oratorical contest and singlehandly stirs up school spirit. But her intense popularity is short-lived as, predictably, the teens turn on her. Leo is attracted by Stargirl and her penchant for good works. But just about the time they get together, the rest of the school is shunning her, and to his confusion and despair, Leo eventually turns his back on Stargirl, too. Spinelli firmly captures the high-school milieu, here heightened by the physical and spiritual barrenness of an Arizona location, a new town where people come to work for technology companies and the school team is called the Electrons. Dialogue, plot, and supporting cast are strong: the problem here is Stargirl herself. She may have been homeschooled, may not have seen much TV, but despite her name, she has lived on planet earth for 15 years, and her naivete is overplayed and annoying. When Leo tells her that not everyone likes having somebody with a ukulele sing "Happy Birthday" to them, she is shocked. That she has not noticed she is being shunned is unbelievable, and, at times, readers may feel more sympathy for the bourgeois teens than the earnest, kind, magical Stargirl. That's too bad, because Spinelli's point about the lure and trap of normalcy is a good one. But to make it real, Stargirl needed to have at least one foot on the ground. —Ilene Cooper

Standiford, Natalie. *How to Say Goodbye in Robot*. 2009. 288p. Scholastic (9780545107082). Gr. 9–12.

The hot pink cover featuring a telephone dangling by the cord fairly screams "teen romance!" but might give the wrong impression of this quirky novel. Bea, the new girl in a school where most of the kids have known each other since kindergarten, befriends Jonah, an outcast deemed "Ghost Boy" after a cruel middle-school prank. She finds herself torn between normal high-school activities and spending time with Jonah, listening to the bizarre but engaging "Night Light," a radio show haunted by some of Baltimore's loneliest weirdos. Theirs is not a budding romance, but a tumultuous, hot-and-cold friendship; they love each other, but should never even think about a relationship. Credit is due to Standiford for the delicate portrayal of Jonah's home life, which could have veered into soap-opera territory, especially with the reappearance of his long-thought-dead, mentally disabled twin brother. The heart of this novel is neither cold and metallic nor full of romance and delusion. Instead, it's very human. —Courtney Jones

Staples, Suzanne Fisher. *Under the Persimmon Tree*. 2005. 288p. Farrar/Frances Foster (9780374380250). Gr. 7–10.

In the mountains of northern Afghanistan after 9/11, Najmah watches in horror as the brutal Taliban kidnap her father and older brother. Will they ever return home? When her mother and baby brother die in an American air raid, she stops speaking, and, disguised as a boy, makes a perilous journey to a refugee camp in Pakistan. In a parallel narrative, Nusrat (her American name was Elaine), who converted to Islam when she met Faiz in New York, has set up a rough school for the refugees. She has had no news of Faiz, her husband, since he left to establish a clinic in the north. The two stories come together when Najmah and Nusrat meet in the camp, where they wait in anguish for news of the people they love. Staples weaves a lot of history and politics into her story (including information about the Taliban's suppression of women), and she includes a map, a glossary, and brief background notes to give even more context. But as with her Newbery Honor Book, *Shabanu* (1989), it's the personal story, not the history, that compels as it takes readers beyond the modern stereotypes of Muslims as fundamentalist fanatics. There are no sweet reunions, but there's hope in heartbreaking scenes of kindness and courage. For another book about post-9/11 Afghanistan, suggest Catherine Stine's *Refugees* (2004). —Hazel Rochman

Stein, Tammar. *Light Years*. 2005. 240p. Knopf (9780375830235). Gr. 8–12.

Maya, 20, blames herself for the death of her boyfriend, who is killed by a suicide bomber in a Tel Aviv restaurant. Haunted by grief and guilt, she leaves Israel for college in the U.S., but although she makes friends, studies, and even begins to fall in love and have sex again, she can't forget. The first-person narrative moves eloquently back and forth between Maya's American present and her Israeli past: growing up in Israel, serving in the army, working in a Tel Aviv office, falling in love, and finally, losing someone in a shocking bombing. Most characters in this novel, one of the first about a contemporary Israeli young woman in a high-tech, secular world, are drawn with some complexity. Maya's "healing" seems a little preachy, but there's depth to her character: she's needy and angry, sarcastic and warm. She also loves her country, yet she doesn't talk politics. Though she considers the Palestinians as "those" people over the border ("They hated us"), she doesn't always focus on herself as living in a war-torn place. Of course, one book isn't enough to tell the whole story of the Middle East, so recommend this with other books that speak from the diverse viewpoints of young Arabs and Jews caught up in the violence. —Hazel Rochman

Steinhofel, Andreas. *The Center of the World*. 2005. 480p. Delacorte (9780385729437). Gr. 10–12.

Growing up on the edge of a small provincial German town, Phil, 17, knows he is gay, and that his free-spirited mother totally accepts him. All his life he has dreamed of finding the American father who walked out on Mom. Phil loves the gorgeous athlete Nicholas, and they have great sex, but Nicholas is afraid to come out in their conservative community, which regards Phil's mother as a whore and Phil and his twin sister as the "witch's children." Then Phil makes a shocking discovery that helps him grow up and confront truth and lies about family, friends, and lovers. Weaving together Phil's past and present, this long novel, a prizewinner in Germany, is not a quick read. But Jaffa's translation is clear and immediate, and the funny, aching first-person narrative will keep many teens enthralled with the story about secrets and betrayal. As in the best writing, the surprises that seem shocking are revealed as natural parts of character and story, and they raise questions about passion, sex, and intimacy. What does Phil deny about his best friend? Why can't his twin sister speak to Mom? Always leaving space for what is not said, tension builds to the very last page. —Hazel Rochman

Stork, Francisco X. *The Last Summer of the Death Warriors*. 2010. 352p. Scholastic/Arthur A. Levine (9780545151337). Gr. 8–12.

Though the police say that his sister, Rosa, died of natural causes, 17-year-old Pancho Sanchez is convinced she was murdered, and he is looking to exact revenge. With no surviving family (his mother died when he was five, and his father only three months before Rosa), Pancho is placed in an orphanage in Las Cruces, where he meets D. Q., a boy who is dying from a rare form of brain cancer. D. Q. is not just determined to find a cure, he's also equally set on training Pancho to become what he calls a "Death Warrior." Together, the unlikely companions embark on a quest to Albuquerque (Stork acknowledges echoes of *Don Quixote* here), and though they travel for their own reasons, once arrived, each will have to come to terms with what it might actually mean to be a Death Warrior. Stork (*Marcelo in the Real World*, 2009) has written another ambitious portrait of a complex teen, one that investigates the large considerations of life and death, love and hate, and faith and doubt. Though the writing occasionally tends toward the didactic, this novel, in the way of the best literary fiction, is an invitation to careful reading that rewards serious analysis and discussion. Thoughtful readers will be delighted by both the challenge and Stork's respect for their abilities. —Michael Cart

★ Stork, Francisco X. *Marcelo in the Real World*. 2009. 320p. Scholastic/Arthur A. Levine (9780545054744). Gr. 9–12.

Seventeen-year-old Marcelo is on the very high-functioning end of the autism spectrum. He prefers an ordered existence, which includes taking care of the ponies at Paterson, his special school; reading religious books; and listening to the music in his head. Then his father, a high-powered attorney, insists that Marcelo spend the summer working in his law firm. If he does his best, Marcelo will be given the choice of returning to Paterson or being mainstreamed. After finding a photo of a disfigured girl injured by the negligence of his father's biggest client, Marcelo must decide whether to follow his conscience and try to right the wrong, even as he realizes that decision will bring irrevocable changes to his life and to his relationship with his father. That story alone would be thought-provoking, but Stork offers much, much more. Readers are invited inside Marcelo's head, where thoughts are so differently processed, one can almost feel them stretch and twist as the summer progresses and Marcelo changes. Much of the impetus for change comes from his relationship with his mailroom boss, Jasmine. In a chapter near the end, Jasmine takes Marcelo to the family farm in Vermont, where he meets her raunchy father. It's a scene many writers wouldn't have bothered with, but the layers it adds mark Stork as a true storyteller. Shot with spirtualism, laced with love, and fraught with conundrums, this book, like Marcelo himself, surprises. —Ilene Cooper

Strasser, Todd. *Can't Get There from Here*. 2004. 208p. Simon & Schuster (9780689841699). Gr. 7–12.

She calls herself Maybe. Thrown out by her abusive mom, she struggles to survive on the streets of New York with homeless teens who become a family in the asphalt jungle. They try to care for one another, but it doesn't help much. They beg and forage for food. Maybe knows some of them work as prostitutes and deal drugs. One or two do find loving homes, but most will die—from AIDS, violence, exposure, suicide. Without sentimentality or exploitation, Maybe's disturbing first-person narrative lets readers know exactly what it's like to live without shelter, huddling in nests of rags, newspapers, and plastic bags. In one vivid chapter, Maybe and her friend enjoy hot-water luxury in the library bathroom, until a brutal security guard makes the nude girls clean the place before throwing them out. Some adults are kind, including a librarian, and with his help, Maybe might make it in a youth home. Maybe. A story about people that we pretend don't exist; Strasser makes us know them. —Hazel Rochman

Stratton, Allan. *Chanda's Secrets*. 2004. 200p. Firefly/Annick (9781550378351). Gr. 9–12.

The statistics of the millions infected with HIV/AIDS in southern Africa find a human face in this gripping story of one teenager, Chanda Kabele, who sees the disease threaten her family and community. Far from case history, Chanda's immediate, first-person, present-tense narrative is neither sentimental nor graphic as it brings close the personal struggle with all its pain and loss, shame and guilt. Chanda's stepfather and baby stepbrother died of the disease. Now Mama may have it. No one will talk about the cause. Is Chandra infected? Her best friend, driven to prostitution, does get AIDS, which is dormant. Should Chanda take her in? Stratton, who has lived and worked in southern Africa, creates an authentic sense of the community in town and in the bush, including the poverty, overburdened hospitals, struggling schools, and packed cemeteries. The message about overcoming ignorance and shame and confronting the facts is ever present, but the tense story and the realistic characters—caring, mean, funny, angry, kind, and cruel—will keep kids reading and break the silence about the tragedy. Proceeds from sales go to fighting AIDS.
—Hazel Rochman

Tashjian, Janet. *The Gospel According to Larry*. 2001. 240p. Holt (9780805063783). Gr. 7–10.

The frame story is intriguing: a teenager encounters Tashjian in a grocery store. He knows she's a writer and hands her a bundle of typed pages. At first she demurs, but then she agrees to help facilitate its publication. The story begins as the boy, the undeniably bright Josh, decides he wants to change the world. Using the pseudonym Larry, he posts sermons against consumerism online, hoping to get some hits from kindred spirits. His message takes off with frightening speed. Josh is determined to keep his identity a secret, even as Larry clubs are springing up around the country. But trouble lurks in the form of "betagold," the e-mail moniker of a woman who is determined to discover Larry's identity. Soon Josh's hellish visions about consumerism and celebrity become his personal nightmare. Killing himself seems to be his only way out, but after he fakes his death, the nightmare grows even darker. Tashjian does something very fresh here. She takes the natural idealism young people feel, personalizes it in the character of Josh/Larry, and shows that idealism transformed by unintended consequences. The book's frank discussion about topics paramount to kids—celebrity worship, consumerism, and the way multinational corporations shape our lives—is immediate, insightful, and made even more vivid because it's wrapped in the mystery of Larry.
—Ilene Cooper

★ Teller, Janne. *Nothing*. Tr. by Martin Aitken. 2010. 240p. Atheneum (9781416985792). Gr. 7–12.

Indelible, elusive, and timeless, this uncompromising novel has all the marks of a classic. A group of Danish seventh-graders have their insulated suburban world jolted when classmate Pierre Anthon stands up and announces, "Nothing matters." He promptly takes up residence in a plum tree and creates an existential crisis among the group with his daily reports on the pointlessness of life. Feeling a need to refute the alarming notion, the kids decide to assemble a pile of objects that will prove Pierre Anthon wrong. It starts simply: Agnes gives up her favorite shoes; Dennis, his beloved books. But as each sacrifice grows in intensity, each kid enacts revenge by demanding an ever-greater sacrifice from the next. With chilling rapidity, the "heap of meaning," which they keep stored in an abandoned sawmill, is towering with gut-wrenching artifacts of their loss of innocence—if innocence is something that ever existed. Teller offers just enough character detail to make the suffering and cruelty palpable. The terse purposefulness of her prose may put off some readers, but that singularity is also what will endure the test of time. Already a multiple award winner overseas, this is an unforgettable treatise on the fleeting and mutable nature of meaning. —Daniel Kraus

Tharp, Tim. *Knights of the Hill Country*. 2006. 240p. Knopf (9780375836534). Gr. 8–11.

In the hill country of Oklahoma, where high-school football ranks "next to God and country, and truth be known, sometimes came in first," Hampton Green is a star linebacker of the Kennisaw Knights, and he feels the weight of carrying on his team's fifth undefeated season like "one hell of a big sack of rocks." Things are heavy at home, too, where he often finds his single mother with a new guy. Blaine is Hamp's teammate and best friend, but he doesn't understand Hamp's interest in Sara, whose wild hair and baggy clothes separate her from the football players' girlfriends. Tharp's debut novel is a sensitive portrait of small-town life and a young athlete's growing awareness that he is more than just the sport he plays so well. Taut scenes on the football field and the dilemmas about choosing what feels right over what's expected are all made memorable by Hamp's unforgettable, colloquial voice, which speaks about feelings and football with the same unwavering, fully realized personality. A moving, sensitive debut from a writer to watch. —Gillian Engberg

Tharp, Tim. *The Spectacular Now*. 2008. 304p. Knopf (9780375851797). Gr. 8–12.

All the seniors in Sutter Keely's high school are planning for the future, except for him. The Sutterman is the original party boy, with a perpetual 7-Up and whiskey in his hand and a story to entertain all who will listen. He is a ladies' man, but he loses interest when the ladies demand that he pay attention to them, instead of himself, or make other unreasonable requests, such as remember dates or call when he promises. But it is Aimee, a social outsider, who gets under his skin and loves him in spite of his flaws. Tharp offers a poignant, funny book about a teen who sees his life as livable only when his senses are dulled by drink and only as fodder for the next joke or story. Lulled into believing he is happy in spite of his father's abandonment and his mother's emotional neglect, Sutter is an authentic character, and his unsteady sense of himself, as well as his relationships with his friends, will strike a chord with teen readers. —*Frances Bradburn*

Tolan, Stephanie S. *Surviving the Applewhites*. 2002. 192p. HarperCollins (9780066236025). Gr. 6–9.

Clever, clever. Tolan has pulled off something special here. She takes a rather predictable plot (tough kid is tamed by exposure to a good family) and twists it into a screwball comedy that pushes the story to a whole new place. The delicious cover sets the scene: E. D., the normal daughter in the Applewhite family, is glaring at pierced, spiky-haired Jake. Juvenile delinquent Jake, who has literally burned his bridges, gets a last chance at the Creative Academy, where the Applewhite children are "home schooled"; actually, the kids do what they please, and only E. D. is organized enough to plan a curriculum. Jake is pushed into life on the Applewhite farm Wit's End, full of creative types, goats, and manic energy. He does his best to resist, but before long he is sucked into Mr. Applewhite's little theater production of *The Sound of Music*. Told in alternating chapters narrated by E. D and Jake, the story is reminiscent of the movie and play *You Can't Take It with You*, also about a manic household. In fact, Tolan employs several old movie conventions: the family even winds up putting on the show in a barn. Though in some ways an homage, this always feels fresh, and Jake's road to self-discovery is the strong linchpin holding the story together. —Ilene Cooper

Torres, Laura. *Crossing Montana*. 2002. 144p. Holiday (9780823416431). Gr. 7–10.

Stark and beautiful, this first novel takes the classic YA identity quest story to new places. When 15-year-old Callie's beloved grandfather goes missing again, she leaves her hopeless mom, steals the car and credit card, and drives across Montana searching for him at the fishing places she knows he loves. She thinks she's alone, but her desperate little stepbrother has smuggled himself in the trunk. As there's no one else to care for him, he pleads to stay with her, and though she yells at him, she knows he's right. She finds Grandpa and sobers him up, and they all go home. But her real discovery on the journey is the truth about her dead dad—and about herself. Her father didn't die in an accident. He killed himself, something she has not allowed herself to know, and as she remembers his depression, the days he couldn't get out of bed, she confronts the darkness in herself. Could she be like him? Does she have the strength to carve her own path? The only real flaw in the story is the picture of Callie's impossibly perfect boyfriend and his impossibly perfect family, though every lost kid will recognize

Callie's longing for an idyllic home. Torres' characters are drawn with spare realism, and Callie's scenes with her brother, hurt and angry, are heartbreaking. Callie's brave, desperate, present-tense narrative tells the truth and doesn't let you go. —Hazel Rochman

Triana, Gaby. *Cubanita*. 2005. 208p. HarperCollins (9780060560201). Gr. 9–12.

One great advantage in writing about one's own culture is the freedom to be irreverent. Triana, born in Miami to Cuban immigrants, takes advantage of the opportunity in a fast, hilarious, first-person narrative that focuses on Cuban American Isabel Diaz's coming-of-age. As with all good writing, the particulars of the story, the search for roots, and the conflicts in leaving home will speak to teens everywhere—not just those in immigrant families. At 17, Isabel struggles with hovering, overanxious Mami, who knows how to push the guilt buttons and won't learn proper English ("You'd think in twenty-six years, she could learn how to speak correctly"). Mami is sure that sexy, funny Andrew is nothing but trouble, but Isabel denies all the signs. The love interest and the truth about family help build a strong story, but the sentimental twists that allow Isabel to find and then leave home are not nearly as satisfying and fun as the insider's view of the community. Triana doesn't include a glossary; the Spanish is clear from the context, and as Isabel points out, the best idioms are not translatable anyway. Pair this with Nancy Osa's *Cuba 15* (2003). —Hazel Rochman

Trueman, Terry. *Inside Out*. 2003. 128p. HarperCollins (9780066239620). Gr. 7–10.

Sixteen-year-old Zach isn't frightened when two armed teenagers hold up the coffee shop where he's waiting for his mother. "The thing is," Zach says, "I'm used to seeing and hearing really weird stuff." In his second novel, the author of *Stuck in Neutral* (2000) takes readers inside the mind of a schizophrenic teenager. Excerpts from Zach's psychiatric records interweave with his first-person account of the dramatic robbery, offering readers the medical facts as well as Zach's personal story, especially the terror and confusion he feels when he can't distinguish between the real and the imagined. The narrative blend isn't entirely successful. The facts often feel clumsily inserted, and Zach's unreliable voice doesn't allow his story to develop fully. The shocking ending also feels tacked on. But Trueman sometimes captures moments of heartbreaking truth, and his swift, suspenseful plot will have particular appeal to reluctant readers. Suggest Angela Johnson's *Humming Whispers* (1995) and Lisa Rowe Fraustino's *Ash* (1995) for more nuanced stories about a young person living with the illness. —Gillian Engberg

Tullson, Diane. *Red Sea*. 2005. 176p. Orca (9781551433318). Gr. 8–11.

Libby, the book's sullen, cranky 14-year-old heroine, fights her stepfather, Duncan, at every turn and finds ways to cross her mother. But she is on a year's sailing voyage with them, whining all the way. They miss departing with their flotilla on the Red Sea because Libby is deliberately late. So intending to catch up, the family sails alone; then, modern-day pirates attack them, and, almost simultaneously, a storm comes up. Duncan is murdered, the boat trashed, and Libby's mother seriously injured, leaving Libby to figure out their location, sail the boat, whose engine was wrapped in nets by the pirates, and to try and keep her mother and herself alive. Libby's first-person voice is by turns cocky and terrified, and there's lots of fascinating sailing lore and the joy of watching Libby figure out what to do next, and how to do it. An absolute page-turner. —GraceAnne A. DeCandido

Vaught, Susan. *Trigger*. 2006. 304p. Bloomsbury (9781582349206). Gr. 9–12.

Seventeen-year-old Jersey Hatch returns home after a year in a brain-injury treatment center. Having no memory of the event, Jersey has been informed that he shot himself in the head. With no internal points of reference, he is compelled to confirm through those around him that he really pulled the trigger, and more important, to discover why. Plagued by numerous physical challenges, and struggling to think sequentially and to avoid inappropriate vocalization, this proves difficult.

Worse yet, Jersey has returned to parents broken by his actions and to peers who despise him. Armed with a binder to record his easily scattered thoughts, and with two champions—the magnificently depicted Mama Rush and her granddaughter Leza—Jersey sets out to solve his own mystery. The interior landscape revealed through Jersey's unreliable yet sympathetic narration is dense, repetitious, and fragmented, granting readers entrée into a damaged mind. Despite its somber character, the story, both engrossing and excruciating, never descends into heavy-handed messages and has nicely placed touches of humor. An original and meaningful work that provokes thought about action, consequence, redemption, and renewal. —Holly Koelling

Venkatraman, Padma. *Island's End*. 2011. 240p. Putnam (9780399250996). Gr. 7–10.

As a short introduction tells readers, tribal people continue to preserve their ancient culture on the Andaman Islands, located east of India in the Bay of Bengal. Without that note, readers may well think they are reading a historical novel as this story opens. In her family's hut, Uido, 15, wakes from a dream in which she has wandered in the Otherworld. Later that day, though, a boat with hairy strangers arrives on her island, bringing the modern world to Uido's community. Venkatraman, author of the well-received *Climbing the Stairs* (2008), goes in a different direction here and succeeds spectacularly as she tells the story of a young woman destined to be her tribe's spiritual leader. In this difficult time, her people are threatened with extinction not just because of the outsiders' influence but also because the tribe itself is undergoing change. Juxtaposed against these challenges is Uido's harrowing vision quest, directed by the group's elderly shaman, which will ready her for her new role. Uido is a remarkable heroine—a girl who is involved with her family and hoping for love, yet also a strong presence, aware of her powers, and unwilling to compromise about where they might lead her. As infused with spirituality as this novel is, there is also heart-stopping action and, of course, the larger issues of modernity versus tradition. An intricate yet wholly accessible story. —Ilene Cooper

Vivian, Siobhan. *Same Difference*. 2009. 304p. Scholastic/Push (9780545004077). Gr. 8–11.

On her first day of summer art school in the big city, Emily makes a shocking discovery: "I don't see anyone here who looks like me, and that feels strange." Though she never felt entirely herself at home, she is clearly an outsider here. Emily leaves her bland strip-mall and Starbucks existence behind, boards the commuter train every day, and dives into the artist's life. Fiona, a bold and inventive student who draws shadows, takes Emily on as a pet project and new best friend. As the semester unfolds and Emily's skills improve, she begins to see that the glamorous and gritty art life has its own share of petty cliques and drama—just like home. She navigates a sweet but forbidden relationship with Yates, her TA, and slowly comes to redefine herself in a way that is genuine and fulfilling. As in Laurie Halse Anderson's *Speak* (1999), the art is a crucial element and vividly described, helping develop the characters and plot. Emily's artistic and personal journeys will resonate with teens longing to break free from predefined roles. —Heather Booth

Vizzini, Ned. *It's Kind of a Funny Story*. 2006. 448p. Hyperion (9780786851966). Gr. 9–12.

When Craig Gilner gets into Manhattan's exclusive Executive Pre-Professional High School, it's the culmination of a year of intense focus and grinding hard work. Now he has to actually attend the school with other equally high-performing students. Oops. And so the unraveling begins, with a depressed Craig spending more time smoking dope and throwing up than studying. Although medication helps his depression, he decides to stop taking it. Soon after, he makes another decision: to commit suicide. A call to a suicide hotline gets him into a psychiatric hospital, where he is finally able to face his demons. Readers must suspend their disbelief big time for this to work. Because the teen psych ward is undergoing renovations, Craig is put in with adults, which provides the narrative with an eccentric cast of characters rather than just similarly screwed-up teens. And in his five days in the hospital, Craig manages to cure his eating disorder, find a girlfriend, realize he wants to be an artist, and solve many of his co-residents' problems, including locating Egyptian music for his roommate, who won't get out of bed. What could he do if he wasn't depressed! But what's terrific about the book is Craig's voice—intimate, real, funny, ironic, and one kids will come closer to hear. Many readers will be familiar with the drugs, the sexual experimentation, the language, and, yes, the depression—or they'll know someone who is. This book offers hope in a package that readers will find enticing, and that's the gift it offers. —Ilene Cooper

Volponi, Paul. *Black and White*. 2005. 160p. Viking (9780670060061). Gr. 9–12.

"Kids who are different colors don't get to be all that tight in my neighborhood. But we get past all that racial crap," says Marcus, an African American senior whose best friend, Eddie, is white. Together, the boys are known at school as Black and White. Both are basketball stars entertaining scholarship offers from local New York City colleges, but they risk everything for more spending money. Considering fast-food jobs too demeaning, they turn to armed stickups, and during their third robbery, they shoot and wound their victim. In alternating chapters, Marcus and Eddie recount the terrifying days after the event as they wait for the police to find and arrest them. The disparate treatment each receives highlights their racial divide, which is occasionally echoed on the streets in harsh language full of hate: a man on the subway tells a white girl that "niggers are going to fuck you, too." Using authentic voices that will draw in both strong and reluctant readers, Volponi writes a taut novel that avoids didacticism and deftly balances drama and passion on the basketball court with each boy's private terror and anguish. Teens will want to discuss the story's layered moral ambiguities, heartbreaking choices, and, as Marcus says, "the line that separates black and white." —Gillian Engberg

Volponi, Paul. *The Final Four*. 2012. 256p. Viking (9780670012640). Gr. 9–12.

There's a strange alchemy in the sporting world, where a single game can take on mythic proportions, thanks to orbiting clusters of minidramas in perfect alignment around it. Volponi's novel creates such a game in an NCAA tournament Final Four match between the heavily favored Michigan State Spartans and the über-underdog Trojans, of Troy University. The Spartans are loaded with NBA-caliber talent, including "one-and-done" freshman superstar and trash-talker extraordinaire Malcolm McBride, while the Trojans fuel their Cinderella-story winning streak with team play led by an underrated Croatian point guard, Roko Bacic. But there's also a Spartan benchwarmer who's flailing under the weight of his name, Michael Jordan, and a Trojan center struggling to keep his mind on the court and off his maybe-cheating fiancée and cheerleader, Hope, nicknamed "Hope of Troy" by the media, angling for a feel-good human-interest story. Volponi dribbles out the players' backstories as the game goes into single, double, and then triple overtime, and in so doing finds room to comment on the divide between raw talent and focused dedication, individualism and teamwork, and confidence and arrogance. Most fascinating and timely is the discussion of the uncomfortable truth that although college athletics has become a multibillion-dollar business, the players who make it all possible aren't allowed a dime of the earnings. As with all clutch performances, Volponi nails it when it counts in this dynamic story. —Ian Chipman

Volponi, Paul. *Rooftop*. 2006. 208p. Viking (9780670060696). Gr. 8–11.

After Clay makes some poor choices, his parents enroll him in a drug program and day school for teens, and now he is clean and studying for the GED. Then his first cousin, Addison, is admitted to the same program, where the childhood buddies reconnect. Drug-dealer Addison may have been "into shit on the streets," but Clay finds much to admire in his cousin, who is confident, funny, and caring. Their reunion is cut short when Addison is killed by a cop on a project rooftop, with Clay as a witness. Here Volponi's intimate, detailed story of the challenges facing poor, urban youth swells to encompass broader racial and political realities: Addison was a black teen killed by a white officer, and the ensuing investigation becomes a focus for activists protesting the arguably corrupt justice system. Under pressure, Clay lies about Addison's role in the shooting. He cannot undo the lie, but he begins to seek redemption in smaller ways. Despite some overdone symbolism, this thoughtfully crafted, deceptively simple story knits together a high-interest plot, a readable narrative crackling with street slang, and complex personal and societal issues that will engage teen readers. —Holly Koelling

Vrettos, Adrienne Maria. *Skin*. 2006. 240p. Simon & Schuster/Margaret K. McElderry (9781416906551). Gr. 8–11.

Like Sonya Sones' *Stop Pretending* (1999), this devastating novel plumbs the anguish of a teen facing a sibling's illness. First-time novelist Vrettos' gloves-off approach is apparent from the opening page, in which 14-year-old Donnie fruitlessly gives CPR to his elder sister, who has starved herself to death. The first-person narrative then recounts the year leading to the tragedy, hinting at how parental strife may have triggered or magnified Karen's anorexia and dissecting how Donnie's emotional withdrawal parallels his sister's wasting. Memorable language ("My sister looks like she could fold inside a paper cup") sharply etches the particulars of Donnie's experience, though at times Vrettos' allusive writing style clouds the significance of certain plot elements, such as Donnie's chronic ear infections and his bond with a rebellious cousin. But the overwhelming alienation Donnie endures will speak to many teens, while his honest perspective will be welcomed by boys—so often the terrified bystanders in anorexia battles—as an alternative to the girl-focused, patient-centered titles typical of fiction about eating disorders. —Jennifer Mattson

Wallace, Rich. *Playing Without the Ball*. 2000. 224p. Knopf (9780679886723). Gr. 7–11.

Senior Jay McLeod eats and sleeps basketball in spite of being cut from the high-school team. His daily schedule revolves around pick-up ball, school, work, and church-league ball. A short-order cook in the bar below his apartment, he copes with a lonely life that is occasionally brightened by basketball and fleeting relationships with the opposite sex. There are plenty of rough themes here—sex (not graphic), drugs (though Jay is clean), irresponsible parents (Jay's mother left when Jay was nine; his father recently took off to "find himself" in Los Angeles), and the bar scene. But Wallace's picture is authentic: the compromise of community basketball when the high-school dream fizzles; the uneasy fascination with girls and sex as young men struggle toward adulthood; the attempt to juggle school, work, and relationships; the reality of planning for the future; and the loneliness—always the loneliness. Like Wallace's other books, the game action—so well-written that even church league takes on the tension of an NBA playoff—will carry the most reluctant reader into a deeper story of the struggle for identity and self acceptance. Wallace scores with this one! —Frances Bradburn

Warman, Jessica. *Breathless*. 2009. 320p. Walker (9780802798497). Gr. 9–12.

Says 15-year-old Katie, "The only thing I really love is swimming. Sometimes I feel like I don't really exist outside of the water." When her parents send her to boarding school after her schizophrenic brother, Will, attempts suicide, Katie loves the escape that Woodsdale offers from her family: institutionalized and increasingly violent Will, her emotionally distant dad, and her alcoholic mom. She also loves the intensity of the school's swim team, with its motto that "practice isn't over until someone pukes," and she begins a tender relationship with a gorgeous fellow swimmer, Drew, a devout Christian who, unlike most of their classmates, is still a virgin. After a misunderstanding leads to a lie, Katie tells her new friends that Will is dead. Only Katie's roommate, Mazzie, knows the truth, and that shared secret begins the deep friendship at the core of this heartbreaking debut. Stretched over three years, the episodic novel, narrated in Katie's raw voice, meanders occasionally in its focus. But Warman's achingly realistic scenes and characters transcend cliché, and with rare, refreshing honesty and flashes of wry humor, she writes about the intimacy of boarding school, the anguish of family illness, finding a sense of self in sports and in life, and the small, mysterious, imperfect moments that add up to love in all its forms. —Gillian Engberg

Whaley, John Corey. *Where Things Come Back*. 2011. 240p. Atheneum (9781442413337). Gr. 9–12.

An answer to complaints about simplistic YA problem fiction, this debut novel, set in Lily, Arkansas, takes on the whole small town with alternating viewpoints, beginning with the first-person narrative of Cullen, 17, and moving on to a huge cast of friends, enemies, family members, lovers, and neighbors. In a parallel plotline, Benton, 18, fails as a missionary in Ethiopia ("passing out food, water, and Christ") and, after returning to college in the U.S., commits suicide, setting off a chain of interconnected, unexpected events. What will hold readers most is the moving story of Cullen's beloved younger brother, who suddenly goes missing, leading to mystery, heartbreak, and an astonishing resolution on the very last page. Whaley's numerous themes range from religion to Internet technology to the environment, and a wry subplot about the so-called sighting of a long-extinct Lazarus woodpecker brings levity, as Lily's residents try to capitalize on the new tourist trade with creations such as the "Lazarus burger." An intriguing, memorable offering teens will want to discuss. —Hazel Rochman

Whelan, Gloria. *Homeless Bird*. 2000. 128p. HarperCollins (9780060284541). Gr. 6–9.

Thirteen-year-old Koly is getting married, not uncommon for girls her age in India. Although apprehensive, she knows this will lessen the financial burden on her family, and hopes for the best. Unfortunately, her husband is younger than promised, and sickly. Soon she is a homeless widow, deprived of her pension and abandoned by her selfish mother-in-law. She finds unexpected support in a widow's home, self-sufficiency in her gift of embroidery, and, ultimately, love and a new, rewarding life. This beautifully told, inspiring story takes readers on a fascinating journey through modern India and the universal intricacies of a young woman's heart. Whelan's lyrical, poetic prose, interwoven with Hindi words and terms, eloquently conveys Koly's tragedies and triumphs, while providing a descriptive, well-researched introduction to India's customs, peoples, and daily life. Koly is an appealing, admirable character, portrayed with sympathy and depth, who learns that art, heart, dreams, and perseverance can bring unexpected joy. Hindi terms are defined in an extensive glossary at book's end. An insightful, beautifully written, culturally illuminating tale of universal feelings in which riches are measured not in monetary wealth but in happiness and personal fulfillment. —Shelle Rosenfeld

Wiess, Laura. *Such a Pretty Girl*. 2007. 212p. Pocket/MTV (9781416521839). Gr. 9–12.

With her father imprisoned, 15-year-old Meredith thinks she could live out her high-school days safely, but when he is released early for good behavior, her security is shattered. A popular youth baseball coach, her father has abused Mer as well as other boys and girls. With strict orders that he not be left alone with his daughter, he is returned to the condo complex where she and her mother live. In contrast to Mer's terror, her mother is giddy with delight at his return, and together the reunited couple plans to conceive another child. Yet in the shadows and stillness, Mer's nightmare begins anew. This is a gritty, terrifying novel about a father's abuse of power and trust, and the way two different teens, Meredith and her paraplegic friend, Andy, deal with that reality. Although not explicit, the novel is honest in its telling. Admittedly sensational, Wiess' story is a page-turner that ultimately sends a startling message of empowerment that, while improbable, is extremely satisfying. —Frances Bradburn

Wild, Margaret. *Jinx*. 2002. 228p. Walker (9780802788306). Gr. 9–12.

In a series of short poems, Wild tells the story of Jinx, self-named because her boyfriends have died in rapid succession—one by his own hand and one who slips and hits his head after being called a name by another teen. Verse-form novels are becoming so familiar that they are beginning to sound alike, but Wild has ultimately made a wise choice by choosing the form here. The plot (angry girl torments the name-caller she deems responsible for her friend's death and then falls in love with him) is predictable. The surprise is in the intricate, vivid language Wild uses ("hearts don't just

break— / that's too easy, / too quick, / like dropping a plate"), and in the way she gives each member of the large cast of characters his or her own poetry. Among the supporting players are Jinx's mother and her story of her unrequited love, and Jinx's sister, Grace, who has Down syndrome, and is the reason their father, the "Rat," left the family. Jinx's friends, both the girls and the boys, are also revealingly introduced. But perhaps most noteworthy of all is Wild's talent for weaving ribbons of want, need, and love through her characters' stories, entwining them together beautifully.
—Ilene Cooper

Williams, Carol Lynch. *The Chosen One*. 2009. 224p. St. Martin's/Griffin (9780312555115). Gr. 7–10.

Taking a story "ripped from the headlines," Williams looks inside a polygamist cult and the dangers it poses for one girl. Kyra and her father, three mothers, and 20 siblings live in an isolated community under the thumb of a prophet, who controls every aspect of his apostles' lives. The most shocking intrusion of all comes when the prophet decrees that Kyra is to become the wife of her 60-year-old uncle. A secret patron of a local mobile library, Kyra knows there's a world away from the compound she might escape to, but first she pins her hopes on her father's ability to change the prophet's mind. Instead, her family is threatened, and the stakes for her refusal to marry are raised. The clandestine relationship Kyra is having with one of the compound's teenage boys is a romance more convenient than convincing (everyone is carefully watched except this duo, it seems). Contrivances notwithstanding, this is a heart pounder, and readers will be held, especially as the danger escalates. Williams' portrayals of the family are sharp, but what's most interesting about this book is how the yearnings and fears of a character so far from what most YAs know will still seem familiar and close.
—Ilene Cooper

Williams, Gabrielle. *Beatle Meets Destiny*. 2010. 336p. Marshall Cavendish (9780761457237). Gr. 8–12.

He is Beatle because his name is John Lennon. She is Destiny McCartney. Their meeting is unexpected and intense and perfect and romantic. It's not until several chapters later that readers learn there's an impediment in the form of a girlfriend, Cilla, who happens to be best friends with Beatle's twin, Winsome. Oh, and even though they're twins, he was born 45 days early, so their sun signs are different. And BTW, Destiny writes a horoscope column. Williams, a Melbourne native (where this book is set), crosses continents with ease in a book that's deliciously plotted, crossing story lines as delicate as the chair embroidered by Wallis Simpson, which Destiny steals from her neighbor, albeit unintentionally. Although it does lead to the woman's death. In the hands of a less-talented writer, this might seem crammed. (Have I mentioned Beatle's stroke? The movie about twins?) Here, it's just the sort of jumble that can happen in the course of a year. Filled with superstitions and portents, and lots of fun. —Ilene Cooper

Williams-Garcia, Rita. *Every Time a Rainbow Dies*. 2001. 176p. HarperCollins (9780688162450). Gr. 9–12.

Thulani, 16, is on the roof of his Brooklyn apartment with his beloved pigeons when he witnesses a brutal rape in the alley below. He helps the naked, injured teenager, Ysa, and afterward tries to get to know her. He looks for her at school and follows her on the street; he can't stop thinking of her. This is the first time he's been freed from the grief that has immobilized him, since his mother went home to Jamaica to die three years ago. For a long time Ysa furiously turns him away, but gradually she lets him closer. She tells him her story, including the horror of her boat journey from Haiti, and finally they become friends and lovers. Once again, Williams-Garcia creates characters that are both fierce and gentle. Without graphic language, she portrays violence and anger in contemporary troubled teens who find courage and connection. Ysa's meanness and Thulani's obsession get tiresome, but the scenes between them are electric, almost all in dialogue: her hurt and fury, his stubborn tenderness and passion. There's a strong sense of their Brooklyn neighborhood, a home to immigrants from many places who have left family behind. Ysa gets a college scholarship; Thulani is dropping out. But their intimacy helps him break free. —Hazel Rochman

Williams-Garcia, Rita. ***Jumped*****. 2009. 176p. HarperTeen (9780060760915). Gr. 9–12.**

Leticia, a gossipy high-school student, knows that "Girl fights are ugly. Girl fights are personal." She says this after overhearing that Dominique, the tough-as-nails basketball player, is planning to beat up pink-clad fashion-plate Trina at 2:45. The infraction was minor—the oblivious Trina cut off Dominique in the hallway—but for Dominique it was the last of a series of insults, the worst of which was being benched by Coach for failing to improve her grades. Bouncing between the three first-person accounts within the span of a single school day, Williams-Garcia makes the drama feel not only immediate but suffocatingly tense, as each tick of the clock speeds the three girls toward collision. Dominique's anger and frustration are tangible; Leticia's hemming over whether or not to get involved feels frighteningly authentic; and only Trina's relentless snobbery seems a bit simplified. Most impressive is how the use of voice allows readers to fully experience the complicated politics of high school; you can sense the thousand mini-dramas percolating within each crowded classroom. Along the way, the characters' disregard of such high-school stalwarts as *A Separate Peace* and *Of Mice and Men* subtly prepares the reader for the messy and gut-wrenching conclusion. —Daniel Kraus

Winston, Sherri. ***The Kayla Chronicles*****. 2008. 188p. Little, Brown (9780316114301). Gr. 5–9.**

A refreshing departure from YA books' tendency to emphasize underprivileged teens of color, this novel, set among well-heeled African Americans, rolls together gender politics and a friendship rift into a buoyant, thoughtful comedy. When Kayla is steam-rolled by stridently feminist Rosalie into auditioning for their elite high school's hip-hop team, intending to expose discriminatory standards of beauty, something unforeseen occurs: Kayla actually makes the cut. To her surprise, the almost-15-year-old finds a sense of empowerment in dance, but Rosalie remains contemptuous of both the "hoochie-mama" dancers and of Kayla's decision to join them. The widening gap between the girls touchingly illustrates the shifts that can rock adolescent friendships, while memorable scenes, such as one in which a dancer matches Rosalie line for line in a Nikki Giovanni–recitation smack down, will win exuberant supporters for Winston's inclusive message: "Why settle for being just one type of girl?" Kayla's family tensions are underdeveloped, and some readers will feel shortchanged by the lack of dance specifics. Still, few recent novels for younger YAs mesh levity and substance this successfully, and while some of Kayla's concerns are specifically African American (such as whether using hair-relaxing treatments constitute buying into oppression), her smart, gently self-mocking voice will transcend racial lines to hit home with a large number of young women.
—Jennifer Mattson

Wittlinger, Ellen. ***Razzle*****. 2001. 256p. Simon & Schuster (9780689835650). Gr. 7–12.**

Rail-thin Razzle, with her buzz cut, strange conversation, and penchant for discarded junk, is not the friend Kenyon Baker imagined for himself when he moved to Cape Cod from Boston the summer before his junior year. But when he's not helping his self-absorbed parents rehab their crumbling, newly purchased resort, he and Razzle develop a tenuous friendship, which blows apart when Kenyon betrays Razzle's trust to please Harley, a manipulative "glamour puss." At the same time, Razzle learns devastating secrets about her own family. Wittlinger doesn't let Kenyon off easily; only a glimmer of reconciliation closes the book. There are more loose ends here than in Wittlinger's *Hard Love,* a *Booklist* Editors' Choice selection and a 1999 Michael L. Printz Honor Book. Undeveloped themes, such as a recurring angel motif, may frustrate some readers, and a few of the peripheral characters, especially Harley, veer into stereotypes. But smart, vibrant Kenyon and Razzle are startling originals, and it's the details that Wittlinger gets right—the banter, Kenyon's inner dialogues, and small moments (the sudden awkwardness of bare feet, for example)—that create a profound sense of the characters' physical and emotional vulnerability that readers won't forget. —Gillian Engberg

Wittlinger, Ellen. *What's in a Name*. 2000. 160p. Simon & Schuster (9780689825514). Gr. 7–10.

Like Wittlinger's novels *Lombardo's Law* (1993) and *Hard Love*, a *Booklist* 1999 Editors' Choice, these 10 connected short stories dramatize serious identity issues in a sharp, funny, touching contemporary narrative. Each short story is told by a different teenager at suburban Scrub Harbor High School, and the voices personalize complex issues of class, family, race, and sexual orientation. There's sophomore O'Neill, who stops lying to himself and publicly admits he's gay; yes, it helps, but it's also difficult ("Are you sure?" his older brother, a football star, asks). And there's Nelson, the popular black senior who tries unsuccessfully to connect with Shaquanda, a black girl bused to the school from the city. It's revealing to read Shaquanda's point of view about class, which follows Nelson's ("Skin color is not the only thing"). What Wittlinger does is show you the stereotypes from the outside—prom queen, football star, computer nerd, immigrant kid, etc.—and then take you up close as the characters tell their own stories and reveal their yearning and difficulties. —Hazel Rochman

Wittlinger, Ellen. *Zigzag*. 2003. 192p. Simon & Schuster (9780689849961). Gr. 8–12.

High-school junior Robin is devastated when her college-bound boyfriend Chris chooses a study program in Rome instead of a summer in Iowa with her. Then Aunt Dory, a new widow with two children, asks Robin to join her on a cross-country car vacation. Wittlinger follows Robin through the difficult summer on the road as she grows close to Dory's grieving, troubled kids ("Superbitch" and "the next school shooter," Robin thinks as they set off); reconnects with her long-absent father; and finds new ideas for a future that doesn't revolve around Chris. Narrated in Robin's wry, likeable voice, the story pivots around a familiar formula (a teen's summer of discontent becomes a turning point of growth and discovery), but Wittlinger elevates the familiar into a moving, realistic exploration of first love, class issues, girls' self-confidence, and the process of healing. Teens will easily hear themselves in Robin's hilarious, sharp observations and feel her excitement as she travels through new country and discovers her own strength. —Gillian Engberg

Wizner, Jake. *Spanking Shakespeare*. Illus. by Richard Ewing. 2007. 304p. Random (9780375840852). Gr. 9–12.

Now in his final year at Hemingway High School, Shakespeare Shapiro decides to write his memoir, a project he hopes will justify his strange name and its obvious role in the more embarrassing aspects of his childhood and adolescence: "a series of catastrophes, one after another." Shakespeare sees the humor in any painful situation, from romantic rejection to embarrassing episodes with his parents. The chapters, which flip between Shakespeare's first-person account of his senior year and excerpts from his memoir, are written in language that's often irreverent and off-color as he wonders about sex, family, friends, pets, and even Internet porn. Despite their over-the-top portrayals, the characters, especially Shakespeare, ring true, and the mix of formats, including some yearbook messages, enhance the authentic voices and humor. This debut novel is a delightful, thought-provoking look at the lives of middle-class, adolescent males in America. —Frances Bradburn

★ Wolff, Virginia Euwer. *True Believer*. 2001. 272p. Atheneum (9780689828270). Gr. 7–12.

"My heart was so stretching, like a room wanting company," LaVaughn says at the end of *Make Lemonade* (*Booklist*'s 1993 Top of the List winner for Youth Fiction). In this equally powerful sequel, LaVaughn, now 15, challenges her heart's resilience again when she develops her first deep crush. Other things are going on as well. She drifts apart from her best friends Myrtle and Annie, who join a "Cross Your Legs for Jesus" club; her mother dates for the first time since LaVaughn's father died; and always there is the poverty and violence of the neighborhood, the pressure of school, and her unwavering goal to get to college. Her deepening intellectual excitement is an anchor, but LaVaughn struggles under the confusing new weight of her emotions, particularly when she sees her crush kiss another boy. As in *Lemonade*, LaVaughn tells her own story in heart-stopping stream-of-consciousness that reveals her convincing naivete and her blazing determination, intelligence, and growth. Yet the writing style still allows the supporting characters to shine. Transcendent, raw, and fiercely optimistic, the novel answers some of its own questions about overcoming adversity when, in the end, LaVaughn's strength and capacity to love surprise even herself. A natural for readers' theater, this will capture even reluctant readers. —Gillian Engberg

Woodson, Jacqueline. *After Tupac and D Foster*. 2008. 160p. Putnam (9780399246548). Gr. 6–9.

"The summer before D Foster's real mama came and took her away, Tupac wasn't dead yet." From this first line in her quiet, powerful novel, Woodson cycles backward through the events that lead to dual tragedies: a friend's departure and a hero's death. In a close-knit African American neighborhood in Queens, New York, the unnamed narrator lives across from her best friend, Neeka. Then D Foster wanders onto the block, and the three 11-year-old girls quickly become inseparable. Because readers know from the start where the plot is headed, the characters and the community form the focus here. A subplot about Neeka's older brother, a gay man serving prison time after being framed for a hate crime, sometimes threatens to overwhelm the girls' story. But Woodson balances the plotlines with subtle details, authentic language, and rich development. Beautifully capturing the girls' passage from childhood to adolescence, this is a memorable, affecting novel about the sustaining power of love and friendship and each girl's developing faith in her own "Big Purpose." —Gillian Engberg

Woodson, Jacqueline. *Hush*. 2002. 192p. Putnam (9780399231445). Gr. 5–9.

At 12, Toswiah must suddenly leave her happy life in Denver, Colorado. Her policeman father saw two of his white cop friends shoot an unarmed black teenager dead, and because Daddy couldn't keep quiet about it, his friends are in jail, and he and his family must re-create themselves in the witness protection program. Toswiah is now Evie, a stranger with a secret, alone in a new school; her mother joins the Jehovah's Witnesses; her beloved father slips into a deep depression and attempts suicide. Woodson writes with beautiful simplicity, confronting the elemental moral issues through the eyes of a young girl who suddenly loses the protection of home and must make herself over. The only false note is the idyllic life Evie led before the upheaval, when everything was "absolutely perfect." Evie's narrative draws the reader so close to the family's difficulties and the results of Daddy's action that it comes as a shock when she remembers the boy. Should Daddy have kept quiet? Woodson shows that while Evie's situation is extreme, everyone has to leave home and come to terms with many shifting identities. —Hazel Rochman

Woodson, Jacqueline. *Miracle's Boys*. 2000. 192p. Putnam (9780399231131). Gr. 6–10.

Lafayette, 12, tells his family story in a voice that's funny, smart, and troubled. It's a story of poverty and grief, of family secrets and brotherly love. Lafayette's oldest brother, Ty'ree, has given up hope of college so that he can work and raise Lafayette and their middle brother, Charlie, who robbed a local candy store two years ago and has returned home from the correctional facility an angry stranger. Charlie is now in trouble again; this time it's a gang fight. With the boys always is the absence of their beloved mother and the guilt, blame, and sorrow they all feel and incite in one another. Mama is too saintly a figure, at least in her three sons' soft-glowing sorrowful memories, but the fast-paced narrative is physically immediate, and the dialogue is alive with anger and heartbreak, "brother to brother to brother." As in Walter Dean Myers' novel *145th Street*, the city block in the story is hard and dangerous—and it is home. —Hazel Rochman

Wyatt, Melissa. *Funny How Things Change*. 2009. 208p. Farrar (9780374302337). Gr. 9–12.

Remy's life in the West Virginian mountain town of Dwyer has always been the same: hard, quiet, and monotonous, and that's just how he likes it. But with graduation behind him, Remy agrees to go with his girlfriend, Lisa, to Pennsylvania as she begins college. It seems like a good idea—after all, he can't live in a trailer with his dad forever—yet the concept of going from an insider to an outsider scares him. His quandary finds a focal point with the unapologetically flirty Dana, an artist visiting Dwyer to paint a mural. Wyatt's plot is as understated as her protagonist, but what it lacks in action it makes up for in nuance. Remy is a careful creation, a good old boy who's not entirely good, and who must come to terms with the nature of teen romance as well as the mountain-size chip on his shoulder. Wyatt also adds a sense of urgency with Remy's dad's plan to sell the family land. Readers will identify with Remy and his feeling of being torn between a comfortable past and uncertain future. —Daniel Kraus

Wynne-Jones, Tim. *A Thief in the House of Memory*. 2005. 224p. Farrar/Melanie Kroupa (9780374374785). Gr. 7–10.

Whenever 16-year-old Dec visits the house where his family lived before his mother's disappearance six years earlier, he slips into long-forgotten scenes that he had shared with her during his childhood. Drawn with a skilled hand, the protagonist is placed in a memorable eastern Ontario setting, where Dec's ancestral family home is preserved, museum-like, near his current house. The violent death of a man who breaks into the old house sets in motion a series of mysteries and revelations that drive Dec to remember things about his mother and try to learn the rest from her best friend and from his father, who guard their secrets well. Vividly written, the narrative conveys a strong sense of Dec's uneasiness, as past and present overlap in an unsettling way. The final revelations about his mother seem almost anticlimactic, as Dec has already developed a sure sense of who he is and where he is headed. An original coming-of-age story from the author of *The Maestro* (1996). —Carolyn Phelan

Zarr, Sara. *How to Save a Life*. 2011. 341p. Little, Brown (9780316036061). Gr. 8–12.

When high-school senior Jill MacSweeney learns that her widowed mother has agreed to an open adoption—no lawyers, no agencies, no background checks, no binding agreements—she is appalled and even more grief-stricken. Of course, her mom is lonely, but you can't just replace your husband—her dad—with a baby! To make matters worse, the baby's mother, Mandy, will live with Jill and her mother in the last month of her pregnancy. Told in the alternating voices of Jill and Mandy, this multilayered, complex story of life, death, and the meaning of family will simultaneously distress and gratify. The characters are achingly human. Jill, bewildered at the unexpected death of her father, has shut out her friends completely. Her mother, so ready to nurture and care for another, finds herself unable to cross the barrier of silence and grief Jill has constructed. Mandy needs a mother, not a baby, and cannot bear the thought of giving up this suddenly secure life that she has happened upon—a life her new baby will enjoy without her. Filled with so many frustrations, so many dilemmas needing reasonable solutions, and so much hope and faith in the midst of sadness, Zarr's novel is a rich tapestry of love and survival that will resonate with even the most cynical readers. —Frances Bradburn

Zarr, Sara. *The Lucy Variations*. 2013. 320p. Little, Brown (9780316205016). Gr. 9–12.

Pressure, expectation, the responsibility of "proving to the world and yourself that you weren't just taking up space." This has been privileged San Franciscan Lucy Beck-Moreau's childhood as a renowned concert pianist. But after a family betrayal eight months ago, the 16-year-old walked off the stage in Prague, and her controlling grandfather's words haunt her: "I take this as your final decision, Lucy." Now, though, Lucy's talented pianist brother, Gus, has a new teacher, Will, and he has taken a special interest in Lucy, asking her questions such as "What do you love?" and encouraging her to find the fun in music again. As she and Will grow closer, their relationship begins to cross lines, and she eventually wonders if Will has her best intentions at heart—a question that's perhaps not fleshed out enough in the novel's end. But Zarr (*Story of a Girl*, 2007) does what she does best. Writing in the third person, she really, truly gets inside her characters' minds and shows us what makes them complex human beings—their faults, fears, and hopes. The supporting characters, from best friend Reyna to English teacher Mr. Charles, are also deeply drawn, and each provides insight as Lucy searches for her own sense of self. The novel itself is structured like a musical composition with three movements of varying tempos and the occasional intermezzo. This is a mellifluous novel about rekindling joy—in music, in the everyday, and in the beauty around us. —Ann Kelley

Zarr, Sara. *Story of a Girl*. 2007. 192p. Little, Brown (9780316014533). Gr. 10–12.

Deanna was 13 when her father caught her and 17-year-old Tommy having sex. Three years later, she is still struggling with the repercussions: how Tommy jokingly made her into the school slut; how the story became legend in her small town; how her father looked at her then—and now doesn't look at her at all. Her brother, Darren, has mistakes to handle, too: he lives with his girlfriend and their baby in his parents' basement. And while Deanna's mother seems numb, her father is perpetually angry and depressed. Meanwhile, in a misguided search for love brought on by the confusion of seeing Tommy again, Deanna intentionally hurts her two closest friends. Although she's more aware than most how a single event can define a person, Deanna still struggles to gain insight into herself, her family, and her friends. When she finally does, she's able to create small but positive changes in her relationships with them all. Characters are well drawn, especially Deanna, whose complicated, deeply felt emotions turn the story. There are plenty of heartbreaking moments, too, including a poignant confrontation with Tommy. Though nothing is miraculously fixed by the close, everyone's perspective has changed for the better. This is a thoughtful, well-executed debut from an author who understands how to write for teens. —Krista Hutley

Zarr, Sara. *Sweethearts*. 2008. 224p. Little, Brown (9780316014557). Gr. 8–12.

Zarr's debut novel, *Story of a Girl* (2007), drew many teen readers with its heartbreaking depiction of a girl whose identity is defined by a mistake made when she was 13. Her second novel speaks to the deep friendships that grow among young people who have suffered trauma. At age nine, Jennifer Harris and Cameron Quick were school outcasts and each other's only friend. After Cameron's father verbally abused them and tried to force the children to engage in sexual activity with each other, Jennifer and Cameron escaped, but they never told anyone of the incident. Cameron and his family abruptly left town, and Jennifer was told that Cameron had died. Now 17, Jennifer has changed her name and her image: pretty, popular "Jenna" has an equally pretty and popular boyfriend and is a model of self-confidence and responsibility. Then new student Cameron arrives, and Jenna's world turns upside down. Her strong bond with Cameron is still there, and together they attempt to confront their shared past. Zarr's writing is remarkable. Through Jenna's matter-of-fact first-person narrative, she conveys great delicacy of feeling and shades of meaning, and the realistic, moving ending will inspire excellent discussion. —Debbie Carton

Zenatti, Valerie. *When I Was a Soldier*. 2005. 250p. Bloomsbury (9781582349787). Gr. 8–11.

For immigrant Valerie, 18, the required two-year Israeli army service is an exciting rite of passage. She gets to leave home, be considered equal to boys, and feel like a real citizen. The military training fascinates her, even if she misses her bitchy best friends ("friends and rivals forever"), and she is haunted by memories of the boyfriend who dumped her. Zenatti's fast, wry, present-tense memoir, translated from the French, begins like a contemporary YA novel: "What will I wear?" is the important question for Valerie's farewell party. But later, when Valerie confronts the politics and propaganda, she has a breakdown: "Who is the enemy?" she wonders. "Why am I fighting?" Zenatti's family immigrated to Israel from France when Valerie was 13 (she now lives in Paris), and much of the memoir's power is in the writer's dual perspective as newcomer and participant. Valerie is entranced by contemporary Israeli diversity and intellectual life, even as she sees Palestinian "poverty, sadness, hatred." There is no heavy message. Readers will be swept into Valerie's military experience only to realize she can't justify why she is there. The honest conflict about haunting issues in daily life is prime teen material, and readers on all sides of the war-peace continuum, here and there, will find much to talk about. —Hazel Rochman

Zevin, Gabrielle. *Memoirs of a Teenage Amnesiac*. 2007. 288p. Farrar (9780374349462). Gr. 6–10.

Contemporary realism, set askew, is the silver streak of Zevin, whose *Elsewhere* (2005) depicted a teen's experiences in the afterlife. This equally sensitive, joyful novel, her second for YAs, tackles the slippery nature of human identity, deceptively tucked within a plot familiar from TV soaps. After high-school junior Naomi conks her head, she can't remember anything that happened since sixth grade. She is by turns mystified and startled by evidence of her present life, from the birth-control pills in her bedside table to her parents' astonishing, rancorous split. Eventually, the memories return, leaving Naomi questioning the basis of a new, intense romance, and wondering which of her two lives, present or former, represents her most authentic self. The amnesia device could have been more convincingly played, but Zevin writes revealingly about emotions and relationships. Especially vivid is the Hepburn-Tracy bond Naomi shares with yearbook co-chief Will, whom she wounds with her lurching self-reinvention even as she discovers deeper feelings: "I had thought the way I felt about Will was just a room, but it had turned out to be a mansion." Pulled by the heart-bruising love story, readers will pause to contemplate irresistible questions: If the past were a blank slate, what would you become? Does the search for one's truest identity necessarily mean rejecting all that has gone before? —Jennifer Mattson

Graphic Novels

Abadzis, Nick. *Laika*. Illus. by Nick Abadzis. 2007. 208p. First Second (9781596431010). Gr. 8–12.

Classic dog-story themes such as loyalty serve as a backdrop for this fictionalized account of Laika, the first living creature launched into outer space. A charming and scruffy little dog, Laika survives an uncaring master and life as a stray before becoming part of the Russian space program circa 1956, just as the Soviet Union had achieved a huge victory over American competition. With a stilted romanticism that doesn't fit the story's tone, Laika is established as "a very special dog," but soon the focus of the complex tale turns away from the dog to Yelena Dubrovsky, the trainer responsible for preparing Laika and the other dogs for the rigors of testing. Through Dubrovsky, the progress of the program and the incredible pressure on the scientists are given effective form. The rough-hewn art, similar to Joann Sfar's Dungeon comics, makes the characters appear constantly nervous and uncertain, lending immediacy to the all-pervasive atmosphere of strict formality and enforced patriotism. An extensive bibliography of sources is appended. —Jesse Karp

Abel, Jessica, and Gabe Soria. *Life Sucks*. Illus. by Warren Pleece. 2008. 192p. First Second (9781596431072). Gr. 10–12.

Dave's life is full of the typical twentysomething frustrations. His job as night manager at the local Last Stop convenience store is retail hell. Rosa, the cute goth girl he has a crush on, doesn't even know he exists. And oh, yeah, his boss, Vlad, turned him into a vampire to make him a better employee. When Wes, his bully-of-a-vampire-older-brother, steps in as rival for Rosa's affections, his sucky life gets suckier. Dave, the vampire equivalent of a vegetarian (he only eats plasma from the blood-bank), has to find some way to outsmart Wes' evil plans. This hilarious tale strikes perilously close to the reality of the slacker twentysomething life. Abel and Soria hit their mark with plenty of attitude and just enough snark to let their characters come to life. Pleece's art marvelously captures the humor of the mundane that lends the book's crew of late-night wage-slave vamps believability and energy. A really fun read! —Tina Coleman

Abouet, Marguerite. *Aya*. Illus. by Clément Oubrerie. 2007. 112p. Drawn & Quarterly (9781894937900). Gr. 9–12.

Intelligent, practical, and kind older teen Aya has best girl friends besotted by romance and sex. She also seems to know a plethora of guys who are either intoxicated with their own studliness or a bit dim. Set in late-1970s Ivory Coast, this accessible, engaging story features a relatively simple plotline—smart girl frustrated by less-forward-thinking friends and family—and delightfully thorough characterizations that resound with emotional universality as they manifest the particulars of a time and a place American readers otherwise rarely glimpse. In perfect keeping with the narrator's youthful perspective, the young people's parents are visually exaggerated to go with stunted personalities. The locale is evoked handsomely in scenes set in Aya's working-class neighborhood, in her father's boss's chic mansion with its multiple living rooms, and during luminous nights some of the youngsters spend at the Thousand Star Hotel—that is, the nocturnally deserted market square. References to the period's worldwide hit TV show, *Dallas*; the aural backdrop of French pop music; and the cast's Ivorian traditional garments given a disco-twist vivify the rich cultural mixture of Western and newly independent African elements that *Aya* depicts. Abouet's storytelling is straightforward but gently nuanced, while Oubrerie's cartooning mixes sepia with bright hues that seem to reflect the ambient sunlight. —Francisca Goldsmith

Aristophane. *The Zabime Sisters*. Illus. by Aristophane. 2010. 96p. First Second (9781596436381). Gr. 7–10.

Aristophane was a French writer and artist who produced only a handful of comics works before his untimely death in 2007. The first of these to make it to the U.S. is the story of three sisters who live on the Caribbean Island of Guadeloupe. We follow them on the way to see a fight between two local boys, one a notorious bully, while they engage in universal childhood pursuits that Tom Sawyer himself would have recognized: exploring the dangerous parts of the forest, stealing mangoes from the wrong orchard, sneaking a taste of rum to their own detriment. The writer proves deft at revealing the politics of childhood—the negotiations, cruelties, and kindnesses that exist between friends and especially between sisters—and the white expanses and thick, inky lines of his art readily evoke not only the proper emotions but also the sun-drenched environment. Lyrical, even literary in its tone, *The Zabime Sisters* is for developed readers looking for something off the beaten path. Includes suggested discussion questions. —Jesse Karp

Bechdel, Alison. *Fun Home: A Family Tragicomic*. Illus. by Alison Bechdel. 2006. 240p. Houghton (9780618477944). Gr. 9–12.

This is a father-and-daughter story. Bechdel's mother and two brothers are in it, of course, but Bruce Bechdel had the biggest impact on his eldest child and so is naturally the other main character in her autobiographical graphic novel. Emotionally and physically reserved, to the point of brusqueness, he busied himself restoring—and then some—the Victorian-era house he bought for the family in the Pennsylvania town in which he was born and lived virtually all his 44 years. He enlisted the kids for never-ending interior and exterior modifications of the place in what obviously was his major creative outlet. For a living, he taught twelfth-grade English and ran the small undertaking business that occupied part of his parents' house and that the kids called the fun home. Bechdel doesn't even hint about how ironic she and her brothers meant to be, because she is a narrative artist, not a moralist or comedian, in this book and because she has a greater, real-life irony to consider. After disclosing her lesbianism in a letter home from college, her mother replied that her father was homosexual, too. Alison suddenly understood his legal trouble over buying a beer for a teenage boy, all the teen male "helpers" he had around the house, and his solo outings during family vacations to New York. Bechdel's long-running *Dykes to Watch Out For* is arguably the best comic strip going, and *Fun Home* is one of the very best graphic novels ever. —Ray Olson

Benjamin. *Orange*. Illus. by Benjamin. 2009. 144p. Tokyopop (9781427814630). Gr. 11–12.

Starting with the literal and figurative bang of a falling body smashing into a car, Orange—one in Tokyopop's new line of full-color graphic novels—tells its story in flashback through some of the most beautiful art rendered in modern manga. Orange is a girl who feels "pathetic and alone," troubled by empty friendships with people she feels are poseurs and boyfriends who treat her poorly and make unwanted sexual advances. But a chance meeting at a crucial moment with a mysterious man who makes the ultimate romantic sacrifice brings her story back to that inevitable bang in a surprising way. While Orange's inner narrative is drenched in nihilism, the pastel washes of the art encompass an extraordinary range and depth of emotion. The melancholy blue of her mood and the fluid and vibrating life of her city are counterpointed by sharp flares of color and faces real enough to reach out and touch. Featured in huge panels that often take advantage of splash and double-splash pages, the art plays to the format's strengths to stupendous effect. A sure winner for teen girls feeling the crush of angst or for art lovers who want to marvel at some terrific visuals. Features copious (and gorgeous) artwork extras. —Jesse Karp

Campbell, Ross. *Shadoweyes*. Illus. by Ross Campbell. 2010. 204p. SLG (9781593621896). Gr. 8–12.

It would be insufficient to say that *Shadoweyes* is the most realistic graphic novel ever produced about an African American teenage girl in a future dystopia who mutates into a manga-style creature, becomes a superhero, and ends up rescuing a young girl from a zombie. Far out on the surface, the plot touches on many teen-relevant issues, such as politics, friendship, adolescence, responsibility, and loneliness. It also features a predominantly female African American cast and, with surprisingly comfortable ease, a transsexual character as well. The significance of that would be empty, of course, without the weight and believability of the story's characters and relationships, and the heart-tugging emotions they sometimes produce. Most convincing is the sharp dialogue, which speaks with such familiar rhythms and sentiment that teens will swear it came out of their own mouths. The art, too, balances a sleek manga technique, credible future looks and grunge fashions, the grotesquerie of zombie flesh, and inventive page composition to sell a grimy future where crime and poverty have run rampant. Campbell (*Water Baby*, 2008) has combined many familiar elements into a unique whole, and though the ending satisfies, it promises a second volume that will be much anticipated. —Jesse Karp

Card, Orson Scott, and Mike Carey. *Ender's Shadow: Battle School*. Illus. by Sebastian Fiumara. 2009. 128p. Marvel (9780785135968). Gr. 10–12.

Marvel has surpassed the dandy *Ender's Game: Battle School* (2009) with this flawless, terrific graphic adaptation that expands the Ender Universe. The diminutive Bean grew up on the streets, where his keen, tactical intelligence help him survive and get him noticed by the insidious Hegemon, an organization charged with recruiting an army to combat the imminent invasion of insect-like aliens. Bean's story can easily stand alone, though it runs concurrently with and reflects Ender's rise through the rigors of Battle School and quest to escape the brutality of a vicious older-brother figure. While Ender was assailed by peer and psychological issues identifiable to childhood, Bean proves to be more of a fantasy figure; much of the enjoyment comes from the reaction his cold brilliance engenders in his peers and in adults, who begin to wonder who exactly is the puppet and who the masters. Fiumara contrasts the scruffiness of the streets and the cold technology of the school with sharp use of shadows and color, while Carey skillfully conveys sentiment and suspense in the search for Bean's heritage and brings the mystery to a breathless and surprisingly emotional close. The book ends on a cliffhanger that demands its forthcoming follow-up or, better yet, a look at Card's captivating source material. —Jesse Karp

Carey, Mike. *Re-Gifters*. Illus. by Sonny Liew and Marc Hempel. 2007. 128p. DC Comics/Minx (9781401203719). Gr. 7–9.

Well-developed characters, plot, and setting make this graphic novel a standout for both dedicated comics readers and those less eager to explore titles in the format. Korean American teenager Dixie and her best friend, Avril, practice hapkido, a martial art. There is a big hapkido tournament coming up in their South Central Los Angeles neighborhood, but Dixie, who has a fiery disposition, loses her focus when she develops a crush on another teen hapkido artist, Adam. She spends her contest entry fee on an exorbitant gift for him and then realizes that he has no romantic interest in her. When Dixie attempts to win a free spot in the tournament at a neighborhood (library-centered!) competition, the other contestants, who are rougher street kids, disparage her efforts. Plot twists, which are both credible and nicely paced, include a falling out between Dixie and Avril, an accident that provides Dixie with an entry ticket to the big event, vengeance on Adam, and a new flame for Dixie. The black-and-white artwork is bouncy and pops with expressive faces, postures, and martial arts moves. This story works visually and as a sound narrative where action, romance, and introspection combine in an enjoyable and realistically multiethnic whole. —Francisca Goldsmith

Castellucci, Cecil. *The Plain Janes*. Illus. by Jim Rugg. 2007. 176p. DC Comics/Minx (9781401211158). Gr. 9–12.

For the first book in a new series aimed at teenage girls, DC Comics recruited novelist Castellucci (*Boy*

Proof, 2004, and *The Queen of Cool*, 2005) to write this story about outsiders who come together, calling up themes from the author's popular YA novels. Relocated to suburbia after a brush with disaster in the big city (and fueled by an urge not to be terrified of the world as a result), Jane rallies a small group of outcasts into a team of "art terrorists," shaking the town from its conservative complacency by putting bubbles in the city fountain and wrapping objects on the street as Christmas packages. Their activities end up rallying the local teenagers to their cause and working the adults into a dither. The book has its share of stereotypes—the science geek, the psychotically overprotective mother, the irrepressible gay teen—but this is thought-provoking stuff. The art, inspired by Dan Clowes' work, is absolutely engaging. Packaged like manga, this is a fresh, exciting use of the graphic-novel format. —Jesse Karp

Cliff, Tony. *Delilah Dirk and the Turkish Lieutenant*. Illus. by Tony Cliff. 2013. 176p. First Second (9781596438132). Gr. 6–12.

Selim is used to being an overlooked and underpaid member of the Turkish Janissary Corps, but when the Agha's men capture a prisoner—the scandalous woman who calls herself Delilah Dirk—Selim finds out the hard way that maybe he needs a little excitement in his life. Delilah is a swashbuckling heroine who will have readers constantly wondering what will happen next. Selim, on the other hand, is more reserved—longing for some tea and quiet—but once he gets sucked into Delilah's orbit, he's unable to resist the taste of adrenaline. Anchoring the story is Cliff's lush artwork. Each panel brims with distinctive people and detailed settings without ever feeling overstuffed. His glowing, vibrant color palette changes smoothly, transitioning easily from warm candlelight to dusty fields to grassy farmland. One two-page spread in particular is a masterpiece of serenity, as Delilah and Selim enjoy a quiet, purple-hued night by a campfire before once more rushing into the fray, whisking readers eagerly along with them. A terrific action story for both older and younger teens and anyone else with an insatiable appetite for high adventure. —Snow Wildsmith

Dembicki, Matt, ed. *Trickster: Native American Tales*. 2010. 232p. illus. Fulcrum (9781555917241). Gr. 8–12.

This graphic-format collection of Native American tales featuring an old folk favorite—the trickster—hits an impressive trifecta of achievements. First, it's a wildly successful platform for indie-comic creators and an excellent showcase for their distinctive styles. From David Smith and Jerry Carr's heroic, animation-inspired "Trickster and the Great Chief" to the Looney Toons zaniness of "Rabbit's Chocktaw Tail Tale," by Tim Tingle and Pat Lewis, there's a bit of visual panache here for every taste. Second, this is one of the very infrequent graphic novels to focus on Native American themes and events, a surprising absence that this book—along with Shannon and Dean Hale's *Calamity Jack* (2010)—remedies with respect and imagination. Lastly, as Native American folklore is so directly tied to the culture's spirituality, this proves the rare graphic novel that handles such issues without specifically attaching them to standard religious practices. With stories that vary in emotional tone, matching the ever-shifting appearance and character of the trickster himself and the lessons he teaches and learns, this collection is an ideal choice for dipping into over and over. A dandy read for those interested in history, folklore, adventure, humor, or the arts, and a unique contribution to the form. —Jesse Karp

Dunning, John Harris. *Salem Brownstone: All along the Watchtowers*. Illus. by Nikhil Singh. 2010. 96p. Candlewick (9780763647353). Gr. 9–12.

Bound in purple cloth, with oversize pages filled with hallucinatory black-and-white visuals, this graphic novel immediately looks and feels unlike anything else out there. Astonishingly the work of two first-time creators, this is a book that both takes full advantage of its form and offers something unique in the current graphic-novel market: a deep strangeness that pervades every panel, every figure, and even every object within. Although Dunning's humorously dry writing and the bizarrely calm affect of an array of enjoyable characters help create the creepy tone, Singh's flowing, surreal perspectives and vaguely Ditko-esque landscapes of alternate planes are what will cast readers into an unfamiliar and occasionally uncomfortable world. Even amid the constant barrage of obtuse and off-kilter imaginings, there are indelible images that stand out: tortured smoke haunting the air over a mansion; intertwined souls trapped within the insectoid eye of a fly. What's it about? Well, the plot concerns Salem's inheritance of a magic orb from his deceased father, after which he is abetted by the freakish denizens of Dr. Kinoshita's Circus and opposed by the Seven Dark Elders of Midnight City. But what it's really about is the thrill of the genuinely weird. —Jesse Karp

Fleming, Ann Marie. *The Magical Life of Long Tack Sam*. Illus. by Ann Marie Fleming. 2007. 176p. Riverhead (9781594482649). Gr. 9–12.

Fleming's great-grandfather, Long Tack Sam, began life in a nineteenth-century Chinese village and died more than 70 years later in Austria. In between, he performed as a world-class magician and lived for significant portions of time on every continent except Africa and Antarctica. Fleming herself, born a year after his death, invested time, money, and travel in exploring her great-grandfather's story or, more accurately, the versions of his biography provided by far-flung relatives, fellow magicians, and former neighbors. Presenting both her search and what she found in a pastiche of succinctly written narrative (lots of it), cartoon drawings, old handbills, clippings, and photos, Fleming successfully shows how dramatic the role of international politics in a particular person's life can be. In the case of Long Tack Sam, both world wars, U.S. and Canadian laws written to bar Chinese immigrants, and the rise and fall of vaudeville as popular entertainment shaped, shifted, colored, and textured daily existence. Fleming makes that kaleidoscope of influences accessible and virtually tangible, not only as they formed Long Tack Sam but also on her own essence. Very appealing for biography readers, twentieth-century world-history buffs, and comics enthusiasts alike. —Francisca Goldsmith

Gipi. *Notes for a War Story*. Illus. by Gipi. 2007. 128p. First Second (9781596432611). Gr. 10–12.

Revisiting themes from his first American release, *Garage Band* (2007), Italian writer and artist Gipi tells a much darker story of disassociated youth and the bonds of friendship. Giuliano, Christian, and Little Killer wander aimlessly about an unidentified Balkan country, avoiding the militia and the shelling that a ubiquitous war has brought to their homeland. When they get into the good graces of Felix, a charming and dangerous war profiteer, they become embroiled in his crime operations and are sent to the big city, where their friendship and mettle are put to the test. As grim as could be, from the bleak narration to the intentionally gruesome, black-and-white art, *War Story* never loses track of the fact that these are children, swept up in a situation too difficult for most adults to grasp. Their youth—evidenced by their covetous enthusiasm for motorcycles and video games—exacerbates the class jealousies, which flare up repeatedly, and the braggadocio with which two of the trio head toward their disturbing and inevitable end. —Jesse Karp

Guibert, Emmanuel, Didier Lefèvre, and others. *The Photographer: Into War-Torn Afghanistan with Doctors Without Borders*. 2009. 288p. illus. First Second (9781596433755). Gr. 9–12.

In 1986, photographer Didier Lefèvre documented a seasoned Médecins Sans Frontières (Doctors Without Borders) team en route to a region in the way of the insurgents' war with the Soviet army supporting Afghanistan's then-Marxist government. This wedding of his photos and Guibert's European-realist comics records his arduous, frightening round trip from Normandy, where his mother lived. During the succeeding 20 years, Lefèvre lost the diary of his return trip but not his photographs. Scandalously few were published at the time, but they profit considerably by appearing in bulk and in this context; they put us near-palpably into their setting. What at first appears to be a very rough visual continuum, constantly jump-cutting from drawings to photos and back, quickly becomes suspenseful. Verbal development comes in the speech balloons and captions of the drawings; no printing invades the photos, which become the powerful payoffs of the verbiage, at least until Lefèvre's return trip, in which, his film and his health running out, he nearly perished. He took very few pictures then, and here Guibert rises to the challenge of maintaining the scary impetus of Lefèvre's adventure. Perhaps no medium other than this one could convey so tangibly what it is to deliver "human services" in a war zone in one of the least geographically hospitable, most beautiful places on earth. A magnificent achievement. —Ray Olson

Hernandez, Gilbert. *Sloth*. Illus. by Gilbert Hernandez. 2006. 128p. Vertigo (9781401203665). Gr. 9–12.

Love and Rockets co-creator Hernandez takes a break from chronicling the lives of the inhabitants of the Latin American village of Palomar and their stateside relatives to create a brand-new set of characters. The title of his book about them refers to troubled teen Miguel Serra, who reacts to his broken home and the vapidity of suburban life by willing himself into a coma. He emerges a year later, walking at a glacial pace that leads other kids to tauntingly call him Sloth—which happens to be the name of the rock band he had formed with girlfriend, Lita, and mutual friend Romeo. When the three conduct a *Blair Witch*–like investigation of a lemon orchard said to be haunted by an eerie Goatman who can inhabit the bodies of his victims, they stumble onto the truth behind the urban legend. Hernandez developed his Palomar cast over the course of two decades, but in *Sloth* he has created a trio of vivid, sympathetic characters and an equally convincing milieu right off the bat, as well as sequences, particularly the nocturnal scenes in the mysterious orchard, as pictorially gorgeous as anything he's ever drawn. Given his masterful visual chops, that's saying something. —Gordon Flagg

Heuvel, Eric. *A Family Secret*. Illus. by Eric Heuvel. 2009. 64p. Farrar (9780374322717). Gr. 7–12.

Published in conjunction with the Anne Frank House and the Resistance Museum of Friesland, this moving graphic novel translated from the Dutch tells of Holocaust perpetrators, rescuers, collaborators, and bystanders through the experience of one family under Nazi occupation in Amsterdam. It is in the tradition of Art Spiegelman's classic *Maus* (1986), not only in format and the historical facts of the millions who perished, but also in the unsentimental truth of the complex humanity: victims are far from saints, survivors are haunted by guilt. The art is in ink and watercolor, with very clear, highly detailed panels, eight or nine per page. The gripping story begins with a contemporary young teen, Jeroen, whose grandmother, Helena, tells him for the first time about her teenage years in Holland. Many panels show a tiny profile of Gran now as she remembers the Nazi-Resistance conflict right in her family's living room. Her policeman father went along with the Dutch Nazi Party to get a promotion, while her mother remained in furious opposition. One pro-Nazi brother can't wait to join the army, and the other brother secretly participates in the Resistance. Helena's friend Esther, a Jewish refugee from Germany, tells her about Krystallnacht and other atrocities. When the Dutch Nazis come for Esther's family, Helena's father refuses to rescue her friend. After the war, he is executed as a collaborator. But secrets are revealed right up to the present, and in all their complexity, they will stay with readers forever. With its companion, *The Search* (2009), this is a must for the Holocaust curriculum. —Hazel Rochman

Hinds, Gareth. *Beowulf*. Illus. by Gareth Hinds. 2007. 128p. Candlewick (9780763630225). Gr. 6–9.

Candlewick's first foray into the graphic-novel format proves an odd blend of ancient history and modern action. It's an epic poem seen as a video game. *Beowulf*, written circa 800 CE, is the story of a warrior-hero charged with dispatching the marauding monster Grendel and its terrible mother. An action epic in any form, this abridged translation is no exception, and it retains the original's dominant themes, including what warriors, and fathers, leave behind for future generations. The original's poetry has become prose narration, loaded with portent and melancholy even amid images of bloody (very bloody) battles between sword and claw. Hind's watercolor art is thick with atmosphere and grand in its conception of vast halls and shadowed caves, but the line work is somewhat amateurish. The book makes a gorgeous whole, though; the long, wordless battles reproduced on glossy, high-quality paper are particularly noteworthy. It all feels a bit like dressing a Lethal Weapon movie up like a Shakespearean drama, but this offering will have high appeal for many, particularly fans of video games and action movies. —Jesse Karp

Hinds, Gareth. *The Odyssey*. Illus. by Gareth Hinds. 2010. 256p. Candlewick (9780763642662). Gr. 7–12.

As the proliferation of recent *Odyssey* graphic novelizations approaches the record held by Shakespeare adaptations, it is perhaps appropriate that Hinds, the Bard's premiere sequential adapter, should produce the most lavish retelling of Homer yet. Showing great artistic evolution since his rough-and-tumble *Beowulf* (2007), Hinds lets the epic story take its time, with a slow build and pages that aren't afraid to alternate packed dialogue with titanic action. The sumptuous art, produced with grain, texture, and hue, evokes a time long past while detailing every line and drop of sweat on Odysseus' face and conveying the sheer grandeur of seeing a god rise out of the ocean. Teens may be baffled by the hero's commitment to the same pantheon of gods who heap trouble in his path, but they will not lose touch with the universal qualities of steadfastness that Odysseus still embodies. The mythic trials have seldom felt more grueling or genuine, and this makes a perfect pairing with Tim Mucci and Ben Caldwell's adaptation for a slightly younger audience from the All-Action Classics series, affording a chance to see how an archetypal story can function so powerfully at both the realistic and the stylized ends of the artistic spectrum. A grand example of Hinds' ability to combine historical adventure with human understanding. —Jesse Karp

Hine, David, and Fabrice Sapolsky. *Spider-Man Noir*. Illus. by Carmine Di Giandomenico. 2009. 112p. Marvel (9780785129233). Gr. 10–12.

Superheroes in re-imagined worlds don't necessarily have a proud tradition. For every smashing success (Frank Miller's *Dark Knight Returns*, 1986; Mark Waid's *Kingdom Come*, 1996), there are many silly, commercially driven failures. Hine, who has been in the business since 1980 with popular characters such as the X-Men and the Teen Titans, and his collaborator, Sapolsky, score a resounding success here. The first of Marvel's new Noir line, which places familiar heroes into pulp-inspired 1930s narratives, throws young Peter Parker into a world of gangster-run streets and crusading newspapermen, as the young man steps into the role of a fearsome vigilante in the tradition of the Shadow. Even as the story spins familiar characters and motivations in a slightly different direction and melds the pulp sensibility with an accurate and detailed historical depiction, Di Giandomenico's art displays a fluid depth and is drenched in shadow, creating an atmosphere entirely appropriate to noir. Along with a surprising complexity in supporting characters like Aunt May and Ben Urich (here a heroin addict) comes a moral shading that will offer older readers something to chew on, though rest assured that the heroic themes of integrity, courage, redemption, and idealism come through loud and clear. Features fun, illuminating bonus materials, too. —Jesse Karp

Hwa, Kim Dong. *The Color of Earth*. Illus. by Kim Dong Hwa. 2009. 320p. First Second (9781596434585). Gr. 10–12.

The first in a trilogy, this beautifully scripted and drawn Korean *manhwa* provides a truly intimate but respectful journey in the company of a young girl and her widowed mother. Spanning Ehwa's life from ages 7 to 16, each chapter shows the progress of her sexual awakening, much more as an emotional and social reality than a set of physical circumstances. As Ehwa moves from the open curiosity of childhood that fixates on body parts to the mysteries of attraction and her own heartbreak, she and her mother navigate common issues that range from defending one's feelings from bullies (little boys in Ehwa's life; gossipy men in her mother's) to mutual attraction (a young monk and a visiting boy from a more monied class for Ehwa; an itinerant painter/scholar for her mother). The mother and daughter share their stories with each other in a developmentally appropriate and credible fashion. The black-and-white art is presented in generous panels and several full-page spreads. While there is some nudity appropriate to the narrative, both the natural and social worlds are depicted to call attention to facial expressions rather than body parts. A variety of flowers adorns the pages, lending a palpable scent of perfume to this heady and gentle read. This is an exquisite and feminist-positive story, richly literate and imaginative. Readers will eagerly await the subsequent volumes. —Francisca Goldsmith

Igarashi, Daisuke. *Children of the Sea, v.1.* Illus. by Daisuke Igarashi. 2009. 320p. VIZ Media (9781421529141). Gr. 7–12.

When she was little, Ruka saw a ghost at the aquarium—a fish that disappeared in a wave of light—but no one would believe her. Now that she is a teen, fish are disappearing from aquariums all over the world and mysterious children are found living in the oceans. Together with two such children, Umi and Sora, Ruka begins to wonder how all of the clues are connected. Just what is the sea trying to tell them? This oversize manga mostly sets the scene for the series, but that doesn't make it any less striking. Ruka is a strong main character, caught between being a child and becoming a woman, and between a father who loves her but left her anyway and a mother who isn't cut out for parenthood. Igarashi's storytelling is quiet, thoughtful, and thought provoking, but it is his drawings that make this manga so amazing. Extremely detailed settings turn panels into mini-masterpieces, and the ocean scenes are so vivid that readers will feel that they are underwater themselves. VIZ's handsome packaging does justice to Igarashi's stunning work, making this a beautiful, must-have addition to any graphic-novel collection. —Snow Wildsmith

Iwaoka, Hisae. *Saturn Apartments, v.1.* Illus. by Hisae Iwaoka. 2010. 192p. VIZ Media (9781421533643). Gr. 9–12.

As fans of Japanese comics know, character development is king in manga, and *Saturn Apartments* is a series that proves the rule. Humans have moved to an immense apartment complex in the sky after earth was declared a nature preserve, with those able to afford better views living on the top floors. After his father plunges to his death, middle-school graduate Mitsu takes over his dad's job as a window washer, allowing him a view of all levels of both the structure and society. The detailed artwork, particularly the carefully rendered backgrounds, offers insight into the characters and their place in society that the narrative leaves out. There are no car chases, no high drama, and no explosions, yet the gentle stories are compelling, as are the characters and their palpable yearning for light, for love, and, most of all, for a glimpse of home. This story of a young teen struggling to live alone will appeal to YAs, and the introspective nature of the narrative will have plenty of crossover appeal for adult readers as well. —Eva Volin

Jablonski, Carla. *Resistance.* Illus. by Leland Purvis. 2010. 128p. First Second (9781596432918). Gr. 7–10.

The first of a trilogy, this stirring graphic novel set in 1940 in the French countryside authentically expresses the personal standoffs and immediate drama of children who are drawn into the Resistance when German soldiers occupy their village. Paul and his younger sister, Marie, fume at each other even as they help hide their Jewish friend, Henri, after his parents disappear. Their own father is being held by the Germans, and the confusion about who is on which side is always present—that is part of the wartime horror. Resistance fighters, brave as they are, can be petty and vindictive, and so can those they assist. "What took you so long?" a fugitive asks his rescuer, who snaps back, "Sorry for the inconvenience; I thought I should keep you alive." Along with the suspenseful rescues and spy-story elements (including a library book with marked words that deliver secret messages), readers will be held by the realistic characterizations and grim events, all fleshed out in Purvis' quavery artwork, which is especially adept at conveying the young characters' wrenching emotions. In the end, the villagers witness the deportations as packed trains pass by, and Henri realizes, "This is just the beginning." An excellent addition to the Holocaust curriculum, especially with the author's lengthy afterword, which offers additional context and also argues that history too often makes everything black and white. —Hazel Rochman

Jensen, Van. *Pinocchio, Vampire Slayer*. Illus. by Dusty Higgins. 2009. 128p. SLG (9781593621766). Gr. 9–12.

The premise for this graphic novel is really almost too good to be true. Basing their puppet on the darker original by Carlo Collodi rather than the sanitized Disney stiff, Jensen and Higgins' Pinocchio never becomes a real boy, and although there is a cricket, he is no Jiminy. Here, Pinocchio looks on in terror as Geppetto is killed by vampires. The puppet, who vows vengeance, is equipped with the world's finest vampire-slaying weapon: his regenerative wooden stake of a nose. Heavy shadows and thick lines dominate the panels and provide a midnight-black atmosphere for all the gory mayhem, but it's the humor that makes this so memorable. Zingers come fast and furious as Pinocchio peppers the combat sequences with lies, and the art can land a chortle with little more than a well-timed facial expression. There's also surprising heart at the story's center that plays with the core theme of fatherhood. There won't be many teen (or adult) graphic-novel readers who won't want this book for its concept alone, and the execution doesn't disappoint. —Ian Chipman

Kelly, Joe. *I Kill Giants*. Illus. by J. M. Ken Nimura. 2009. 184p. Image (9781607060925). Gr. 9–12.

Barbara Thorson, bullied and friendless, will not back down. She is smart and angry, won't follow the rules, won't let anyone close, and sees things no one else does. In short, she is a very disturbed girl, and the power of *I Kill Giants* is its ability to convey the reality of a frightened little girl's pain along with the wonder of her apparent fantasies. Kelly's portrayal of the material is nothing short of literary, echoing the similarly combined elements in Roald Dahl's *Mathilda* (1988), just as the giants that Barbara describes to her tentative new friend Sophia recall Quentin Blake's illustrations in *The BFG* (1982). Nimura's line work also retains the jittery quality of the British illustrator's style, creating a world of sharp tension. As Barbara begins to let people in, her insistence that the giants are coming threatens these intensely longed-for relationships. Whether or not they exist, the metaphor of giants to symbolize the vast terrors of a person's inner life has never been better realized. Along with Matt Phelan's *The Storm in the Barn* (the 2009 *Booklist* Top of the List winner for Youth Fiction), this is graphic storytelling at its zenith: employing fantasy to offer profound insight and take readers on a deeply emotional journey. —Jesse Karp

Kelso, Megan. *Artichoke Tales*. Illus. by Megan Kelso. 2010. 232p. Fantagraphics (9781606993446). Gr. 9–12.

In Kelso's first graphic novel, everyone's hair looks like an inverted artichoke. Though that seems to betoken a fantasy, the only magic here is the healing effected by the herbal prescriptions old Charlotte dispenses from the Quicksand family's apothecary. This is a family saga spanning three generations and embracing a civil war between North and South whose causes are similar to some of those that produced the U.S. Civil War. The book begins with the present, postwar generation, specifically with Brigitte, Charlotte's granddaughter, and Adam, a soldier in the North's "police" forces. They fall in love, of course, reprising a family pattern, for Charlotte met Brigitte's grandfather, Jimmy, while studying in the North. Though the Quicksand men have important scenes, Kelso concentrates on the Quicksand women to portray a society of greater gender equity than humanity has produced and includes scenes of birth and lovemaking. Kelso's striking visual conceits (e.g., singing expressed by two lines forming an opening funnel from the mouth), turquoise-on-white drawing, jump-cut transitions, and constantly shifting viewpoints conjure a richness of implication and feeling of which her light-seeming, cartoony style would seem prima facie incapable. But here, as in the contemporary nonfantasy stories of *The Squirrel Mother* (2006), she is a thorough and intelligent artist whose work is moving and invaluable. —Ray Olson

Kim, Derek Kirk. *Good as Lily*. Illus. by Jesse Hamm. 2007. 55p. DC Comics/Minx (9781401213817). Gr. 10–12.

On her eighteenth birthday, Korean American Grace suddenly finds herself surrounded by three very corporeal essences of herself: as a small child, as a

30-year-old woman, and as "a cranky old fart." Each of these incarnations is at an emotional precipice, which teenage Grace helps resolve, allowing the other self to quietly disappear. Kim and Hamm take on a huge task here, mingling snatches of teenage Grace's everyday life of parents and peers with the troubles caused by her other selves. But they pull it off nicely. Kim's pacing and plotting are excellent, and Hamm's black, white, and gray artwork is lively, witty, and full of appropriate comedy and melodrama. The interplay between the selves is complex but easy to follow: very young Grace and very old Grace don't have the same taste in television programs; 30-year-old Grace is a more appropriate love interest for drama teacher Mr. Levon than is teenage Grace (who has a crush on him). Both insightful and fun, the tale, part fantasy, part romance, part growing-up story, will hook a wide variety of readers (not only graphic-novel fans) as it tracks the course of a character's evolution at crucial junctures in her life. —Francisca Goldsmith

Kim, Susan, and Laurence Klavan. *Brain Camp.* Illus. by Faith Erin Hicks. 2010. 160p. First Second (9781596433663). Gr. 7–10.

From its shock opening right out of a horror movie, this graphic novel sets the scene for an old-fashioned scare story. A throwback to the sort of paranoia that *Rosemary's Baby* and *The Stepford Wives* capitalized on so well, the tale follows Lucas, a tough kid from the wrong side of the tracks, and Jenna, an Asian girl who isn't measuring up to her siblings' grade averages, as they are bundled off to Camp Fielding, where they're guaranteed to become high-performance go-getters. But something very strange is going on there: counselors sneak into the cabins at night with hypodermic needles, and kids start acting like supersmart zombies. Kim and Klavan, who balanced adventure and kids' social issues so well in *City of Spies* (2010), do the same in another well-rounded adventure here, as the far-out (and kind of gross) climax mixes with genuine insight into dealing with parents, fitting into a new crowd, and handling the pressures of performance. Hicks' line work is cool enough to assuage older readers who might be suspicious of the summer-camp setting. —Jesse Karp

Lagos, Alexander, and Joseph Lagos. *The Sons of Liberty, v.1.* Illus. by Steve Walker and Oren Kramek. 2010. 176p. Random (9780375856709). Gr. 8–12.

The superhero, once the embarrassing social outcast of American culture, has lately been recognized as a potent metaphor adaptable to an array of themes and, now, historical eras. Two young slaves on the run, pursued by a bounty hunter and his ferocious pack of dogs, are experimented on by Ben Franklin's heinous son William and wind up with electrically charged superpowers. Overseen by Ben himself as well as true-life abolitionist Benjamin Lay, the slaves bring some hurtin' back to their tormentors. History offers few villains as vile as slaveholders, but this graphic novel is far from being a simple revenge thriller. The use of historical figures and well-researched (but embellished) history, and a willingness to flesh out characters and set up situations to pay off in future installments, makes for an uncommonly complex, literate, and satisfying adventure. The slick art, with wiry figures reminiscent of Mark Bagley's *Ultimate Spider-Man* work, feels more modern than the story suggests and will be inviting to teen readers. In the style of Robert Morales and Kyle Baker's *Captain America: Truth* (2004), this first installment of a series respects history (with some dramatic liberties taken) and uses superpowers effectively as an empowerment allegory. —Jesse Karp

Langridge, Roger. *Thor: The Mighty Avenger, v.1.* Illus. by Chris Samnee. 2010. 128p. Marvel (9780785141211). Gr. 8–12.

In the torrential downpour of Thor titles raining down around the mythological superhero's cinematic debut, this reader-friendly delight is far and away the pick of the litter. Readers meet the mysterious blond-haired God of Thunder with no memory when historian Jane Foster watches him get tossed out of a Norse exhibition one day. After the gallant fellow helps her out and she takes him in, an utterly charming romance ensues, even as Thor participates in some Norse debauchery and hunts down the secrets of his past. Langridge deserves top marks for taking a character whose story possibilities might seem limited and imbuing him with a fresh and highly engaging life, and for dropping in some fun, non-marketing-driven guest appearances (Ant-Man? Captain Britain? Really?). Samnee's art grounds the vigorous superhero action with expressive faces, subtle lighting tones, and an individual style that makes the drama sing. The bad news: there's only four issues collected here (plus the Stan Lee and Jack Kirby origin story). The good news: the second volume, which concludes the story, is already available. —Jesse Karp

Larson, Hope. *Mercury*. Illus. by Hope Larson. 2010. 240p. Atheneum (9781416935858). Gr. 9–12.

Larson (*Chiggers*, 2008) won an Eisner Award for Special Recognition in 2007 and is establishing an oeuvre of thoughtful, girl-centric graphic novels that often feature touches of unobtrusive fantasy, lending a dreamy quality that helps characterize her distinctive storytelling style. Mercury tells two tales: one of Josey, who lives in a small Canadian town in 1859; and the other of her descendant, Tara, who has returned to the same town in 2009, a year after her house burned to the ground. Tenth-grader Tara's burgeoning relationships and her difficulty reacclimating to her old school will be more identifiable than Josey's forbidden courtship with itinerant prospector Asa, but the use of two time lines delineates the different eras' outlooks on family and romance, which brings some immutable human truths into high relief. The gentle dose of magic realism doesn't feel incongruous and underscores the powerful ways in which past touches present. The insights unfold leisurely, but patient readers will find themselves deeply invested. Comparisons to Craig Thompson's *Blankets* (2003) wouldn't be inappropriate, but Larson continues to perfect her own unique style and offers something the graphic format is sadly short on: a coming-of-age story for girls. —Jesse Karp

Lasko-Gross, Miss. *A Mess of Everything*. Illus. by Miss Lasko-Gross. 2009. 232p. Fantagraphics (9781560979562). Gr. 9–12.

The stellar follow-up to *Escape from "Special"* (2008) picks up the semi-autobiographical narrative right where *Escape* left it. Melissa is in high school, dealing with the problems and pressures of being a teenager as well as with an anorexic best friend, slipping grades, and experiments with drugs, not to mention attempts at romance, the class trip gone wrong, and trying to figure out how to be cool. With her own mixture of insecure angst and sarcastic smarts, Melissa manages to keep pushing forward. Given the burgeoning maturity of the main character, *Mess* is suitably more intense than *Escape*, reflecting a sort of ratcheting up of the emotional level, as it were. Heightened narrative intensity conjures a perfect atmosphere for Melissa's adventures in growing up. The art, washed and faded and varying wildly from almost abstract to more traditional comics style, also reflects the moodiness of adolescence wonderfully. The writing comes across as so genuine and true a teen's voice that the book feels more like an illustrated journal, capturing Melissa's awkward emergence from her unique personal perspective. Spot-on about the late-teen experience while avoiding overly nostalgic feelings. —Tina Coleman

Lat. *Kampung Boy*. Illus. by Lat. 2006. 144p. First Second (9781596431218). Gr. 8–11.

Malaysian cartoonist Lat uses the graphic-novel format to share the story of his childhood in a small village, or *kampung*. From his birth and adventures as a toddler to the enlargement of his world as he attends classes in the village, makes friends, and, finally, departs for a prestigious city boarding school, this autobiography is warm, authentic, and wholly engaging. Lat depicts small children—including himself—as mostly mop-topped, toothy, bare-bottomed, or sarong-draped—while the important adults in his life often appear in billowing trousers or dramatic spectacles. Everything is wonderfully detailed in his scribbly black-and-white sketches; each page is crammed with heavily inked action scenes, which are explained in simple but eloquent prose. Some passages recall past behavior; others focus on cultural events and surroundings—a wedding, a rubber plantation, Lat's circumcision ("It took place on a banana trunk. In two minutes it was over! . . . just like an ant bite!"). Filled with humor and affection, the book is a delight; readers will enjoy it not only as an introduction to a well-known Southeast Asian artist but also as a story of boyhood that encompasses both universals and the specifics of a time and place. —Francisca Goldsmith

Lat. *Town Boy*. Illus. by Lat. 2007. 192p. First Second (9781596433311). Gr. 9–12.

This sequel to *Kampung Boy* (2006) takes up the Malaysian cartoonist's memoir in the 1960s, at the point where he arrives in Ipoh to continue his education at a boarding school. Lat's family moves to town as well, but Lat focuses more on his social life than his studies or his parents. Ipoh is a multicultural place, and Lat's friends include Indians, Chinese, and other south Asians. His best friend, Frankie, is ethnic Chinese, and, with Frankie by his side, Lat learns about record players, cheating at PE, and how to ask a girl to the movies. Page layout is more varied than in *Kampung Boy*. There are still many full-page illustrations, and Lat continues to depict himself as a mop-topped, bandy-legged kid, but there are also intervening passages laid out in panels and some wondrously detailed crowd scenes that consume entire spreads. Occasionally, characters speak in their native languages, which remain untranslated, but this won't get in the way of the reader's enjoyment; it simply adds another dimension to Lat's impressive world building. —Francisca Goldsmith

Love, Jeremy. *Bayou, v.1*. Illus. by Jeremy Love and Patrick Morgan. 2009. 160p. DC Comics/Zuda (9781401223823). Gr. 9–12.

Lee Wagstaff warns, "The Bayou is a bad place. Ain't nuthin' good ever happened around here." At the outset of this powerhouse historical fantasy comic, Lee's white friend, Lily, is snatched and swallowed whole by a dim-witted giant from the bog, and Lee's father is accused of kidnapping the girl. Lee returns to the Bayou, determined to follow the creature, rescue Lily, and prove her father's innocence. What ensues is a journey that honors the tenacious spirit of African Americans living in the Depression-ravaged Jim Crow era of the deep South. Originally a webcomic and beautifully translated to the printed page, in many ways *Bayou* is to *Alice in Wonderland* what *O Brother, Where Art Thou?* is to *The Odyssey*, as Love combines southern lore and African folktales to create a dark, haunting otherworld that Lee ventures into. Some events are disturbing—the opening scene, in which Lee enters the Bayou to retrieve the body of a boy who met his demise in an Emmett Till–like manner, is particularly haunting, and his blank eyes will linger in the mind long past reading. Indeed, the fact-based atrocities depicted throughout are far more chilling than any of the fantastical horrors Lee encounters. Dauntless readers will be captivated by the grotesque beauty on display here. —Courtney Jones

Lutes, Jason, and Nick Bertozzi. *Houdini: The Handcuff King*. Illus. by Jason Lutes and Nick Bertozzi. 2007. 96p. Hyperion (9780786839025). Gr. 6–9.

Following Houdini on the morning of his leap (while handcuffed) into the frigid Boston River, readers gain a remarkably complete picture of his world. They will meet his wife, Bess; his strong-arm man, Beatty; reporters desperate to get a quote; and crowds hungry for a glimpse of him. Most of all, they get to know Houdini himself, who, as an extensive introduction notes, was probably the most famous man in the world at the time. Proud and obsessed—with his skill, his fame, and his wife—Houdini was a showman of the highest order who knew he represented hope to his adoring American public. He also knew that he had an unprecedented talent for self-hype. Avoiding overt, showy tricks themselves, Lutes and Bertozzi use clean, simple storytelling and crisp, clear black-and-white art to create not only a portrait of the man but also that sense of suspense and anticipation Houdini generated in his performances. Endnotes linked to specific pictures offer background on everything from anti-Semitism (Houdini was Jewish) to handcuffs. A bibliography of mostly older adult titles is appended. —Jesse Karp

McAdoo, David. *Red Moon*. Illus. by David McAdoo. 2010. Cossack Comics (9780615353241). Gr. 7–10.

A combination hero's journey and apocalyptic thriller, this graphic novel is told entirely from the point of view of a small dog. After Mox runs away from his family, he starts having visions of an ominous red moon heralding destruction and runs afoul of a pack of crows determined to bring a new world order where birds, not humans, reign supreme. McAdoo works environmental awareness and animals' ability to "predict" natural disasters into his story and ends with a sci-fi race against time. Mox is just the type of ordinary Joe who often stars in adventure quests—a sort of Frodo Baggins with more hair—and the other characters are carefully constructed, with clear, ringing voices that will linger in readers' minds. McAdoo's highly detailed style—stark black and white with color only for the sinister red moon—adds gripping tension to every panel. Although there is violence and intensity here, it is nothing beyond what middle-school audiences can handle. Teens who have aged out of Erin Hunter's Warriors or Brian Jacques' Redwall books will be taken by this action-packed, beautifully illustrated tale. This self-published graphic novel simply should not be missed. —Snow Wildsmith

Mechener, Jordan, and A. B. Sina. *Prince of Persia: The Graphic Novel*. Illus. by LeUyen Pham and Alex Puvilland. 2008. 190p. First Second (9781596432079). Gr. 9–12.

After enjoying various forms as a video-game character, the eponymous prince finally leaps from the screen to the page in this magnificent and complex graphic novel. The prince, according to each iteration of the game, which has spanned nearly two decades, has been everything from an "Aladdin-like street urchin" to a "battle-hardened fugitive." Here, he is manifested in two parallel stories that twine about and bleed together like twin wisps of smoke. One takes place in the ninth-century city of Marv and features a prince on the run from his destiny as his kingdom is assailed from within. The other takes place 400 years later, in the same city, as a princess discovers a young man in the ruins of the old palace, hiding from a doomful prophecy. The stories can be maddeningly complex to sort through, but that really only adds to the fascination, with distinct color palettes and visual clues to help sort matters out when the chronology becomes difficult. No mere video-game rip-off, the end result is a story defined by layers instead of linearity, with drama, adventure, and revelation all unfolding in equal measure, resulting in a book that's even better with repeat readings. A forthcoming movie about the prince will only increase interest. —Ian Chipman

Medley, Linda. *Castle Waiting*. Illus. by Linda Medley. 2006. 456p. Fantagraphics (9781560977476). Gr. 9–12.

A long time ago in the happy kingdom of Putney, a king and a queen accidentally snub the local wicked witch. The result is the standard curse: a 100-year sleep brought on, you guessed it, when the princess pricks her finger on a needle. But what happens after the princess awakes and goes off with her charming prince? There's nothing left for a castle full of characters to do except to wait. Thus the stage is set for a surprising, quite wonderful story. Lady Jain, a pregnant woman with a mysterious past, arrives at the castle seeking refuge. She's relieved to discover that the castle's inhabitants are warm, welcoming, and willing to let her leave her past behind. Medley's characters, including ladies-in-waiting Patience, Prudence, and Plenty, and Sister Peace, a bearded nun, are sweet yet surprisingly down to earth, and they make the lofty old keep into a home. The story feels both traditional and fresh, and Medley's art is clean and crisp, with strong linework that gives a real sense of fun and animation. A hefty tale that's well worth the time. —Tina Coleman

Myrick, Leland. *Missouri Boy*. Illus. by Leland Myrick. 2006. 112p. First Second (9781596431102). Gr. 9–12.

In this graphic novel, Myrick contributes a heartfelt glimpse of his youth, presenting vignettes that reflect life growing up in a small town. From marveling at the creation of a perfect paper airplane and swimming nude in a nearby lake with his friends to muffing an opportunity with a pretty girl and seeing death close up, the author shares memories of his boyhood and teen years. Even if Myrick's specific memories aren't ours, they touch and connect us as readers, encouraging us to remember our own youth. There are no terrible secrets or great revelations here. It's the tenderness and intimacy of the spare words and pictures that set the book apart. Myrick's art, from the rich colors to the panel layouts, works on a gut level. It seems so simple, yet it speaks independently of the words, providing a subtext and an emotional nuance that create a sense of the wistful hope of childhood. A fine example of the graphic novel. —Tina Coleman

Neri, G. *Yummy: The Last Days of a Southside Shorty*. Illus. by Randy DuBurke. 2010. 96p. Lee & Low (9781584302674). Gr. 8–12.

Robert Sandifer—called "Yummy" thanks to his sweet tooth—was born in 1984 on the South Side of Chicago. By age 11 he had become a hardened gang-banger, a killer, and, finally, a corpse. In 1994, he was a poster child for the hopeless existence of kids who grow up on urban streets, both victims and victimizers, shaped by the gang life that gives them a sense of power. Neri's graphic-novel account, taken from several sources and embellished with the narration of a fictional classmate of Yummy's, is a harrowing portrait that is no less effective given its tragic familiarity. The facts are laid out, the suppositions plausible, and Yummy will earn both the reader's livid rage and deep sympathy, even as the social structure that created him is cast, once again, as America's undeniable shame. Tightly researched and sharply written, if sometimes heavy-handed, the not-quite-reportage is brought to another level by DuBurke's stark black-and-white art, which possesses a realism that grounds the nightmare in uncompromising reality and an emotional expressiveness that strikes right to the heart. Like Joe Sacco's work (*Footnotes in Gaza*, 2010), this is a graphic novel that pushes an unsightly but hard to ignore sociopolitical truth out into the open. —Jesse Karp

Rucka, Greg. *Batwoman: Elegy*. Illus. by J. H. Williams. 2010. 192p. DC Comics (9781401226923). Gr. 9–12.

There are a number of reasons why this story arc, which appeared last year in *Detective Comics* following Batman's (for now anyway) death, is a departure from more traditional caped-crusader fare. For starters, Batwoman (aka Kate Kane) is the most prominent gay character in DC's universe, and she kicks ass with combat boots, not stilettos (though her suit is still painted on). This volume deftly blends the story of her origin as a superhero with a dark thriller that pits her against Gotham's newest resident crazy, the High Madame of the Religion of Crime. In flashbacks, Kane gets kicked out of the military for standing tall at the conflicting crossroads of "Don't ask, don't tell" and the West Point Honor Code that says "A cadet will not lie, cheat, steal, or tolerate those who do." In the present thread, she locks horns with the gothy villain Alice, who speaks entirely in quotations from Lewis Carroll. All this makes for a nuanced, literary, and culturally charged story, but the real knockout element is Williams' art nouveau–inspired compositions. The consistently arresting layouts and twirling line work cross the design sensibility of Alphonse Mucha with Gotham City's special blend of midnight grittiness. Rucka and Williams have crafted a superhero comic that is ambitious and unique in its approach, and it deserves to be read and then read again to appreciate the fullness of its smart storytelling and even more impressive artistry. —Ian Chipman

★ Satrapi, Marjane. *Persepolis: The Story of a Childhood*. Illus. by Marjane Satrapi. 2003. 160p. Pantheon (9780375422300). Gr. 9–12.

Satrapi's great-grandfather was Iran's last emperor, the one overthrown by the father of the shah overthrown in the 1979 Islamic revolution. Doubtless their pedigree of former greatness somewhat shielded her leftist family from the Ayatollah Khomeini's authoritarian regime, and her extraordinary autobiography in comics, which reflects her perspective from ages 10 to 14, probably understates the violence that swirled around her, cresting in the outbreak of the Iran-Iraq war. At first, the revolution freed an uncle who idolized her and some of her parents' friends from prison, but soon the tide turned, and the former prisoners had to flee (at least one was killed before he could). Her father and uncle explained modern Iran's past to her, all but dispelling her childish religiosity, and she joined her parents at political demonstrations. When an Iraqi missile destroyed Jewish neighbors, however, her parents determined to use their upper-middle-class means to get out. Satrapi's cursive, geometrical drawing style, reminiscent of the great children's author-artist Wanda Gag's, eloquently conveys her ingenuousness and fervor as a child. —Ray Olson

Satrapi, Marjane. *Persepolis 2: The Story of a Return*. Illus. by Marjane Satrapi. 2004. 192p. Pantheon (9780375422881). Gr. 9–12.

At the end of *Persepolis*, 14-year-old Satrapi stares aghast at the sight of her mother fainting over her departure from Islamic-revolutionary Iran for school in Vienna. It's an image that demanded this continuation of her memoir-in-comics, which many may find more congenial than its predecessor because of its initial setting in the areligious West. There Satrapi endured initiations into sex, drugs, and partying, and travails over peer and love relationships that mirrored those of her Western fellow students; she was an exile, however, essentially on her own emotionally (though her mother visited once, lifting her spirits as nothing else would) and even physically, especially after breaking up with her first love. Finally unable to cope, she became homeless for three months and, after hospitalization for exposure, returned to Tehran, where the second half of this book transpires, eventuating in an ill-starred marriage to a fellow art student. Satrapi's high-contrast, bold-lined, stencil-ish artwork remains very much at the service of one of the most compelling youth memoirs of recent years. —Ray Olson

Schrag, Ariel, ed. *Stuck in the Middle: Seventeen Comics from an Unpleasant Age*. 2007. 224p. illus. Viking (9780670062218). Gr. 7–10.

How bad was it in junior high? Comics artists visualize the anguish in this honest, acutely perceptive compendium of cartoon black humor. Editor Schrag, who relived her high-school years in several books, including *Potential* (2000), adds herself to an impressive roundup of artists, including Aaron Reiner (*Spiral-Bound*, 2004), Lauren Weinstein (*Girl Stories*, 2005), and Daniel Clowes, whose comics were adapted into an Oscar-nominated movie, *Ghost World*. Occasionally repetitious, the comics nevertheless hit the mark in terms of emotional content, whether the subject is making friends, embarrassing parents, or suffering through a first date. Wildly disparate in style, the black, white, and gray-tone artwork ranges from Eric Enright's minimalist contribution, with figures that look like toddler toys, and Jace Smith's freewheeling, bug-eyed monster-kid comic to Joe Matt's stark, crisply drawn contribution. Kids going through adolescence will relate; so will those who have come out on the other side. —Stephanie Zvirin

Shakespeare, William. *Julius Caesar*. Illus. by Mustashrik. 2008. 208p. Abrams/Amulet (9780810970724). Gr. 8–12.

Abrams' generally high-quality Manga Shakespeare line reaches its pinnacle thus far with *Julius Caesar*, the bard's tragedy of conspiracy, warfare, and bloody revenge. Abridged text is spread out to render it less intimidating, and the most dramatic scenes are given plenty of room to breathe. Rome itself is portrayed as a YA-friendly mixture of classical architecture and modern weapons of war, the citizens dressed in Flash Gordon fashion and Judge Dredd headgear. What truly shines in this work, though, is the superlative visualization by newcomer Mustashrik. Working in stark white and inky black, he has created a spare but intense landscape that mirrors the emotions of the characters, and combines a sense of dreamlike isolation with a minimal backdrop that suggests a stage on which the drama is normally enacted. Using shadow, he has managed to make the assassination simultaneously graphic yet subtle, and by alternating tight focus and long shots, and using a thick brush to exemplify expressions, he has fittingly crafted a visual tour de force of Mark Antony's speech. Especially for the more artistically minded, this is a raw, striking, and powerful introduction to Shakespeare. —Jesse Karp

Shakespeare, William. *The Tempest: The Graphic Novel; Original Text*. Illus. by Jon Haward. 2009. 144p. Classical Comics (9781906332693). Gr. 7–12.

In the Shakespearean graphic-novel crowd, if Gareth Hinds' adaptations are subtle and thoughtful artists, and the Manga Shakespeare series are wild, unpredictable rock stars, then the Classical Comics series might be the no-nonsense teachers of the group. With straightforward draftsmanship and three text versions (original, plain, and quick), Classical Comics titles are ready-made to lure intimidated students and aid in curricular comparisons that highlight the levels on which Shakespeare works. But with the publication of the original version of *The Tempest*, this solid, practical series has just added its first superstar. In vibrant color that far outmatches the standard, somber "historical" palette, the bitter and over-protective Prospero, looking like an extra-psychedelic Doctor Strange, maroons King Alonso and his men on his magical island. All the great strengths of the sequential art form are brought to bear, with creative panel shape and size, border textures, word balloon effects, dynamic motion, and magical figure work that makes the fairies sparkle and the harpy blaze like an inferno. It's such a resounding success that readers may actually forget they're learning something. Of the multitudinous Shakespeare graphic adaptations now available, this is the first to take total advantage of the medium's full potential, appropriately aligned to the Bard's most fantastical work. —Jesse Karp

Shiga, Jason. *Meanwhile*. Illus. by Jason Shiga. 2010. 80p. Abrams/Amulet (9780810984233). Gr. 6–9.

In this graphic-novel mind boggler, Shiga blows the choose-your-own-adventure concept out of the water. Readers play the role of little Jimmy and on the first page make the seemingly innocuous decision of ordering a vanilla or chocolate ice-cream cone. Tubes connect panels in all directions and veer off into tabs to other pages, creating a head-spinningly tangled web of a story (well, stories; the book claims to have 3,856 different possibilities). The crux is that Jimmy stumbles into the lab of an affable mad scientist and is allowed to tinker with three inventions: a mind reader, a time machine, and the Killitron, which obliterates all life on earth aside from the user's. Jimmy's carefree fiddling with the three devices isn't merely a way to lead readers through the subsequent head trip of an adventure; it's also just about the perfect kid-friendly initiation to the many-worlds interpretation of quantum mechanics (no, really), in which each decision and action split reality into distinct parallel universes. It's unfathomably, almost unreasonably complex. Given this book and a distraction-free hour or two, readers will either end up looking like Jimmy on the cover—clutching their skulls in googly-eyed exasperation—or will arrive at a nifty new way of looking at reality. It's maddening and challenging, all right, but that's precisely what makes it so crazy fun. —Ian Chipman

Siddell, Thomas. *Gunnerkrigg Court: Orientation*. Illus. by Thomas Siddell. 2009. 296p. Archaia (9781932386349). Gr. 6–12.

The first 14 chapters of Siddell's popular webcomic are collected here in an alluring hardcover. The premise, best described as science-fantasy, involves a young girl named Antimony plopped into a strange boarding-school/industrial-complex, which, like the reader, she knows nothing about. Discrete chapters (some of which fast-forward the general story arc while others flit off on whimsical digressions) all feature varying levels of jaw-dropping peculiarity, devilish bursts of humor, and sublime creativity that lurk at the ends of the school's myriad corridors. The darkly hued artwork is deceptively simplistic and displays a flair for the crucial details of setting and atmosphere; Siddell's knack for setting enigmatic scenes that take pages to become clear lifts the experience from merely intriguing to simply spellbinding. Yes, there are dull echoes of most boarding-school fantasy (including that Potter one), plumbing the depths of abandonment, burgeoning friendship, and ultimate belonging, and dedicated readers can follow along online for free; but Siddell's one-man show of weirdly inventive one-upmanship is too good to pass up. That it's both appropriate and appealing for a wide age range, boys and girls, seals the deal. Oh, and Neil Gaiman's a huge fan. There's no reason to think his massive audience wouldn't also be. —Ian Chipman

Sievert, Tim. *That Salty Air*. Illus. by Tim Sievert. 2008. 112p. Top Shelf (9781603090056). Gr. 11–12.

No, this isn't a Classics Illustrated edition of *Moby-Dick*, but it is a terrific graphic novel about an obsessive man battling large creatures from the sea. Dirt poor, Maryanne and Hugh live in a shack by the sea. Their only source of income is the fish Hugh catches each morning, a chore that seems to bring him much enjoyment. The news that Hugh's mother has drowned destroys his love of "that salty air," and he turns to the bottle, leaving pregnant Maryanne pretty much alone. Sievert uses a monstrous squid to represent the bad news that storms into the couple's lives, and in the end the couple's battle with the creature symbolizes both humankind's struggle with the elements and Hugh's struggle within himself. Words are few and carefully placed. The crisp, black-and-white illustrations on slick paper do most of the work, taking readers right into the eye of the metaphorical and physical storm and giving them a taste of the intense emotions nature can elicit in those who interact with it. An amazing, strong, well-paced graphic novel about relationships and what we must be do to keep them on course while we are submerged in the complexities of life. This is as much for adults as it is for teens. —Kevin King

Small, David. ***Stitches*****. Illus. by David Small. 2009. 344p. illus. Norton (9780393068573). Gr. 9–12.**

Prolific, Caldecott Medal–winning Small makes the leap to the graphic novel with a spare and unflinching memoir. Set on a black page, the haunting words "I was six" preface a scene of 1950s, soot-stained Detroit. Successive panels dolly slowly in on a boy sprawled out on the floor, drawing. "Mama had her little cough" breaks the reverie, and we're off into the nightmare of Small's upbringing, dominated by his mother's hateful silences and his physician father's pipe-smoking impassivity. At 14, the boy goes in for minor throat surgery (which was secretly for the cancer his father gave him by subjecting him, as a baby, to X-rays) and wakes up maimed and effectively muted with a severed vocal cord—an outcome made all the more devastating because it is so potently metaphoric of his family life. The suffocating silences of the household swell in grays and blacks with more nuance than lesser artists achieve with full rainbows of color, and Small's stark lines and intricacies of facial expression obliterate the divide between simplicity and sophistication. Like other "important" graphic works it seems destined to sit beside—think no less than *Maus*—this is a frequently disturbing, pitch-black funny, ultimately cathartic story whose full impact can only be delivered in the comics medium, which keeps it palatable as it reinforces its appalling aspects. If there's any fight left in the argument that comics aren't legitimate literature, this is just the thing to enlighten the naysayers. —Ian Chipman

Smith, Jeff. ***Bone: One Volume Edition*****. Illus. by Jeff Smith. 1,344p. Cartoon (9781888963144). Gr. 6–12.**

Mere months after publishing the final installment of the long-running fantasy saga *Bone*, Smith collects all 13 years' worth of it in a single, massive volume. As many comics fans know, the series chronicles the adventures of the Bone cousins—plucky Fone Bone, scheming Phony Bone, and easygoing Smiley Bone—who leave their home of Boneville and are swept up in a Tolkienesque epic of royalty, dragons, and unspeakable evil forces out to conquer humankind. The compilation makes it evident how fully formed Smith's vision was from the very beginning—although the early chapters emphasized comedy, as do the final pages, the tale quickly found its dramatic bearings. His remarkably accomplished drawing style, in the manner of such comics masters as Walt Kelly and Carl Barks, was fully formed from the start, too. Libraries that have missed out on individual Bone series titles should seize this opportunity to make up for the fact, and those who have collected the series all along will do well to acquire the collected edition to supplement or supplant those doubtless well-worn volumes. But be prepared for overdues: even the most voracious readers will be hard-pressed to get through this hefty, phone book–like tome before they're supposed to return it. —Gordon Flagg

Spiegelman, Art. ***Little Lit: Folklore & Fairy Tale Funnies*****. 2000. 64p. HarperCollins/Joanna Cotler (9780060286248). Gr. 4–12.**

The 1992 presentation of a special Pulitzer Prize to Spiegelman for *Maus* signaled the arrival of a new art form: the graphic novel. What Spiegelman did has now taken firm root in the field of books for young readers, growing some of the most visually exciting books in ages. In this book Spiegelman and his wife, Francoise Mouly, art editor of the *New Yorker*, invited 15 stellar talents to create original graphic stories that poke often ironic fun at tales from that Mother Goose woman and other traditional sources. Some of the contributing artists will be familiar to lovers of children's lit: William Joyce, for example, has some fun with a cracked version of "Humpty Dumpty," and David Macaulay struts his creative stuff in "Jack and His Mom and the Beanstalk," perhaps the funniest and most aesthetically agreeable tale in the collection. Others—Daniel Clowes and Chris Ware, among them—will be more familiar to fans of graphic novels for adults. Still other talents and tales reflect the original inspiration for this art form: the Sunday funnies and "all in color for a dime" comic books. Regardless of their sources, though, all that's old is arrestingly new again in this delightfully eye- and imagination-stimulating collection. It's an extravagant treat for readers of all ages. —Michael Cart

Stassen, Jean-Philippe. *Deogratias: A Tale of Rwanda*. Illus. by Jean-Philippe Stassen. 2006. 96p. First Second (9781596431034). Gr. 11–12.

The tragedy and international shame of the Rwandan genocide that took place in the 1990s is realized in this fictional and symbolism-studded parable. The title character, a dehumanized Hutu man, crawls through many of these clear-line, full-color pages, often hallucinating and in need of drink in a fruitless effort to drown his memories of the rapes, pillages, and massacres visited upon the Tutsi minority. European responsibility for the ethnic war is presented cogently and without reluctance through the actions and dialogue of several Belgian characters. Stassen, a Belgian who lives in Rwanda, depicts the horror and violence (including brutal rape and the starvation of children) in small, compact panels and uses moody colorings and expressive characterizations to convey much of the human tragedy. Several pages of background on the genocide will help ease readers unfamiliar with the history into the story. For the same mature teen audience that reads Joe Sacco's *Safe Area Gorazde: The War in Eastern Bosnia, 1992–1995* (2002), this book vividly shows the power of fiction to introduce fact. —Francisca Goldsmith

Steinberger, Aimee Major. *Japan Ai: A Tall Girl's Adventures in Japan*. Illus. by Aimee Major Steinberger. 2008. 183p. Go! Comi (9781933617831). Gr. 9–12.

Accompanied by two friends, Steinberger, a professional animator and devotee of that special brand of cuteness that hails from contemporary Japan (think Sanrio's Hello Kitty and similar artistic and commercial ventures), provides a charming recapitulation of their visit there. Steinberger's height (she's six feet tall), along with such things as the language barrier, immediately marked the trio as tourists, but their devotion to such Japanese-inspired pastimes as cosplay (dressing up as manga, anime, and fantasy characters) and Steinberger's interest in Japanese Volks dolls gave them several avenues into popular culture, where they found considerable enjoyment. Steinberger tells their story largely in black-and-white, manga-style line drawings, with the occasional application of bright colors. Manga and anime fans will appreciate the gentle travelogue, and even readers unfamiliar with Japanese culture today will like Steinberger and her pals and be intrigued by their observations on what it can be like to be a tourist. —Francisca Goldsmith

Sturm, James. *Satchel Paige: Striking Out Jim Crow*. Illus. by Rich Tommaso. 2007. 96p. Hyperion (9780786839001). Gr. 6–12.

Sturm, a 2004 Eisner Award winner (with Guy Davis) for *Fantastic Four: Unstable Molecules* and the author of *The Golem's Mighty Swing* (2001), returns to baseball in this graphic novel about fictional Emmet Wilson, a black farmer whose moment of glory as a player in the Negro Leagues came when he scored a run off the great pitcher Satchel Paige. Shortly after that, an injury ends Wilson's career and forces him to return to the life of a farmer. Strum focuses on Wilson's plight in the racist South of the 1940s, but also shows how his brief encounter with the legendary Paige—an iconic force against Jim Crow laws—provided lifelong inspiration. Tommaso's black-and-white artwork brings out the stark times and emotions with strong, powerful lines, but also grandly evokes Paige's quiet patience and his electrifying dynamism on the mound. This visually powerful, suspenseful, even profound story makes an excellent choice for readers interested in baseball or in the history of race relations. An appended section fills in more about the times and provides a springboard for discussion. —Jesse Karp

Tamaki, Mariko. *Skim*. Illus. by Jillian Tamaki. 2008. 144p. Groundwood (9780888997531). Gr. 11–12.

Canadian essayist and adult-books author Tamaki and her cousin, an artist, dive into the graphic format by using high school as a fertile setting for pungent commentary on racial, cultural, and sexual issues. Pudgy Asian American Skim suffers the contempt of the popular crowd at her all-girl school and ponders the repercussions of the recent suicide of a local boy. The source of her greatest anguish, however, is her intense love for her drama teacher, Ms. Archer, an affection only briefly requited before the teacher leaves without explanation. The narrative, mainly in diary form, feels accurate and realistic, drenched in a sense of confusion and nihilism, and the art, influenced by Craig Thompson's *Blankets* (2003), reflects the spare, gloomy emotional landscape in which Skim exists. This story will appeal to many female comics fans, though readers may, in the end, be slightly turned off by a resolution that awkwardly introduces some odd sunlight into the otherwise dark world. —Jesse Karp

★ Tan, Shaun. *The Arrival*. Illus. by Shaun Tan. 2007. 128p. Scholastic/Arthur A. Levine (9780439895293). Gr. 6–12.

Recipient of numerous awards and nominations in Australia, *The Arrival* proves a beautiful, compelling piece of art, in both content and form. Tan (*The Lost Thing*, 2004) has previously produced a small body of off-kilter, frequently haunting stories of children trapped in surreal industrial landscapes. Here, he has distilled his themes and aesthetic into a silent, fantastical masterpiece. A lone immigrant leaves his family and journeys to a new world, both bizarre and awesome, finding struggle and dehumanizing industry but also friendship and a new life. Tan infuses this simple, universal narrative with vibrant, resonating life through confident mastery of sequential art forms and conventions. Strong visual metaphors convey personal longing, political suppression, and totalitarian control; imaginative use of panel size and shape powerfully depicts sensations and ideas as diverse as interminable waiting, awe-inspiring majesty, and forlorn memories; delicate alterations in light and color saturate the pages with a sense of time and place. Soft brushstrokes and grand Art Deco–style architecture evoke a time long ago, but the story's immediacy and fantasy elements will appeal even to readers younger than the target audience, though they may miss many of the complexities. Filled with subtlety and grandeur, the book is a unique work that not only fulfills but also expands the potential of its form. —Jesse Karp

Tan, Shaun. *Tales from Outer Suburbia*. Illus. by Shaun Tan. 2009. 96p. Scholastic/Arthur A. Levine (9780545055871). Gr. 7–12.

After teaching the graphic format a thing or two about its own potential for elegance with *The Arrival* (2007), Tan follows up with this array of 15 extraordinary illustrated tales. But here is an achievement in diametric opposition to his silent masterpiece, as Tan combines spare words and weirdly dazzling images—in styles ranging from painting to doodles to collage—to create a unity that holds complexities of emotion seldom found in even the most mature works. The story of a water buffalo who sits in a vacant lot mysteriously pointing children "in the right direction" is whimsical but also ominous. The centerpiece, "Grandpa's Story," recalling a ceremonial marriage journey and the unnameable perils faced therein, captures a tone of aching melancholy and longing, but also, ultimately, a sense of deep, deep happiness. And the eerie "Stick Figures" is both a poignant and rather disturbing narrative that plays out in the washed-out daylight of suburban streets where curious, tortured creatures wait at the ends of pathways and behind bus stops. The thoughtful and engaged reader will take from these stories an experience as deep and profound as with anything he or she has ever read. —Jesse Karp

Telgemeier, Raina. *Smile*. Illus. by Raina Telgemeier. 2010. 224p. Scholastic/Graphix (9780545132053). Gr. 6–9.

The dental case that Telgemeier documents in this graphic memoir was extreme: a random accident led to front tooth loss when she was 12, and over the next several years, she suffered through surgery, implants, headgear, false teeth, and a rearrangement of her remaining incisors. Accompanying the physical treatment came social rough spots with friends, while puberty delivered another set of curveballs with crushes, maturing bodies, and changing family expectations and judgments. Both adults and kids—including various dental professionals and younger siblings—are vividly and rapidly portrayed, giving quick access to the memoirist's world. Telgemeier's storytelling and full-color cartoony images form a story that will cheer and inspire any middle-schooler dealing with orthodontia. At the same time, she shows how her early career choice as an animator took root during this difficult period—offering yet another gentle reminder that things have turned out fine for the author and can for her reader as well. —Francisca Goldsmith

TenNapel, Doug. *Ghostopolis*. Illus. by Doug TenNapel. 2010. 288p. Scholastic/Graphix (9780545210270). Gr. 6–9.

Frank Gallows, a weary officer from the Supernatural Immigration Task Force, and Garth Hale, a young boy with an unspecified incurable disease, are the dual heroes in this ghost-driven graphic novel. When Frank sends a troublesome horse skeleton back over to the afterlife, he accidentally zaps the boy along as well. The sinister ruler of Ghostopolis feels threatened by the boy (who, naturally, has all sorts of off-the-charts latent powers) and sends his buggy minions after him. Frank enlists the help of an ex-flame (who's also a ghost) to cross over to the other side and rescue the boy. Sure, there's a lot of characters with not a lot of characterization and a few too many good-for-you messages poking out from all the madcap antics, juvenile jokes, and overblown dramatics, but all in all, the story is a good blend of creepy, grotesque, and wacky. He's got a few lumps to work out as a storyteller, but TenNapel—best known as the creator of the cross-platform character Earthworm Jim—is a terrific cartoonist and in fine form here. —Ian Chipman

★ Thompson, Craig. *Blankets*. Illus. by Craig Thomson. 2003. 592p. Top Shelf (9781891830433). Gr. 10–12.

Thompson's graphic-novel debut, *Goodbye Chunky Rice* (1999), was a delicate parable of loss that garnered deserved acclaim. The eagerly awaited, autobiographical follow-up to it is more ambitious, more accomplished, and more accessible. Thompson recalls growing up in a religious family in rural Wisconsin, particularly his affectionate tussles with his younger brother, with whom he shared a bed and the titular blankets. A few years later, he experiences the painful intensity of first love with Raina, a girl from Michigan he meets at a regional church camp. When the pair are separated, his loss of faith in his love for Raina presages his later loss of religious faith. The blanket motif reappears throughout the work, forthrightly as the handmade quilt Raina gives him, and more subtly as the blank sheets of paper he confronts as a budding artist. Eschewing the usual alt-comics cynicism, Thompson's evocation of high-school romance manages to be both romanticized and clear-eyed. His visual mastery shows in fluid line work, assured compositions, and powerful use of solid black areas and negative space. Weighing in at nearly 600 pages, this is a genuine graphic novel, with a universal appeal that suits it for any collection. —Gordon Flagg

Thoreau, Henry David. *Thoreau at Walden*. Illus. by John Porcellino. 2008. 112p. Hyperion (9781423100386). Gr. 8–12.

The latest high-quality graphic-format book from folks associated with the Center for Cartoon Studies introduces another significant historical personage, Henry David Thoreau. Although the life and work of the nineteenth-century transcendental philosopher and protoenvironmentalist might seem an odd choice for adaptation into sequential art, Porcellino, alternative comics writer/artist and master of the minicomic, has found a way to translate Thoreau's thinking into an involving read that exudes lightness and tranquility. Marrying his minimalist line work to Thoreau's minimalist philosophy, Porcellino manages a striking unity of words and art that works as an effective ode to simplicity. Thoreau's writings, excerpted out of chronological order, are recast into a narrative that moves from the philosopher's self-ostracism from society and his time at Walden and into the feeling of calm reverie he took from his experiences. This will be a difficult sell to casual readers, but budding philosophers and readers looking for an unusual work will be delighted. Extensive endnotes include explanations and attributions for the excerpts and a short bibliography. —Jesse Karp

Urasawa, Naoki, and Osamu Tezuka. *Pluto, v.1.* Illus. by Naoki Urasawa. 2009. 192p. VIZ Media (9781421519180). Gr. 10–12.

Europol Detective Gesicht begins to suspect a terrible relationship between several ritualistic murders. Soon he is on a desperate quest to find an unknown force that is systematically trying to wipe out the seven most powerful robots in the world—including Gesicht himself. In a tribute to Osamu Tezuka's (the "God of Manga") classic *Astro Boy*, Urasawa takes one of Tezuka's story arcs and reimagines it as a noir detective story. Along the way, he brings in themes of racism, war, and what it means to be human. The story subtly ramps up the danger, occasionally veering off into side stories to flesh out the world of Detective Gesicht and the other robots. Nothing is overdone, and readers will discover new elements to the story with each reading. Urasawa's darkly realistic, gritty style of art imbues each character and setting with a weighty vitality, and his careful pacing and deft use of panels show that he is truly a master of his craft. It's no wonder that Pulitzer Prize winner Junot Díaz has called Urasawa a "national treasure."—Snow Wildsmith

Van Meter, Jen. *Hopeless Savages: Greatest Hits, 2000–2010.* Illus. by Christine Norrie et al. 2010. 360p. Oni (9781934964484). Gr. 8–12.

After their career as punk rockers, Dirk Hopeless and his wife, Nikki Savage, attempted something truly edgy—raising kids in the suburbs. As their youngest daughter, Zero, navigates the dangerous waters of high school, readers are taken into the home of a family that is all too ordinary, despite reality-TV crews, kidnappings, and international espionage. Together with her older brothers Rat and Twitch and big sister Arsenal, Zero discovers that family—like a band—is strongest when it sticks together. Van Meter's rocking graphic-novel trilogy is collected here into one omnibus edition. Humor, drama, and over-the-top action are combined in just the right amounts, with the action used to highlight the thoughtful subplots, which explore themes of relationship building, parental expectations, and rebellion against societal norms. Illustrated by a host of hip and talented artists—including Bryan Lee O'Malley, Ross Campbell, Andi Watson, and Chynna Clugston Flores—and with only comic violence, mild swearing, and no sex, *Hopeless Savages* is a terrific choice for both adult and teen graphic-novel collections. —Snow Wildsmith

Varon, Sara. *Robot Dreams.* Illus. by Sara Varon. 2007. 208p. First Second (9781596431089). Gr. 6–12.

In this nearly wordless graphic novel, Dog's desire for a companion is satisfied the day Robot arrives by mail. Dog assembles Robot, and their adventure begins. After visiting the library, watching movies, and eating popcorn, the companions end up at the dog beach. Robot is hesitant to frolic in the waves at first, but after a short pause, he dives right in. The result is unfortunate—a rusty, immobile Robot. Unsure of what to do for his friend, remorseful Dog abandons Robot on the sand to dream of what might have been (depicted first in brown tonal artwork as opposed to the color used to designate actions in real time) had things turned out differently. While Robot is used and abused, and eventually disposed of in a scrap yard, Dog agonizes over his companion, then begins searching for a new one with mixed, sometimes comic results. Varon's drawing style is uncomplicated, and her colors are clean and refreshing. Although her story line seems equally simple, it is invested with true emotion. Her masterful depiction of Dog's struggles with guilt and Robot's dreams of freedom effectively pulls readers into this journey of friendship, loss, self-discovery, and moving forward. Use this as Exhibit A to prove that graphic novels can pack an emotional punch equal to some of the best youth fiction. —Kevin King

Vollmar, Rob. *The Castaways*. Illus. by Pablo G. Callejo. 2007. 64p. NBM (9781561634927). Gr. 6–9.

Nominated for comicdom's most prestigious award, the Eisner, back in 2002, *The Castaways* is back, in a gorgeous hardcover edition. The art, filled with cartoon realism (think Robert Crumb without the crass humor), was originally in black and white. Here it has been washed in greenish-gray hues that highlight the resounding melancholy of the story. Drawn from our collective American mythology, this is the swiftly paced story of 13-year-old Tucker, forced to leave home during the Great Depression. Hopping a train, he meets an aging black tramp named Elijah, who illuminates for him the romance and danger of the hobo's life and also the wrenching need for a home. Details, such as the contents of Tucker's backpack, are effortlessly integrated into the story. Only the newly added epilogue, superfluous and overly sentimental, detracts from this beautiful, powerful vision of a different era. Even readers reluctant to pick up a book about American history will be pulled into this adventure of deep longing and honor. —Jesse Karp

Wang, Jen. *Koko Be Good*. Illus. by Jen Wang. 2010. 304p. First Second (9781596435551). Gr. 9–12.

A richly woven story of three misfits, each of whose intersecting lives threatens to crash and burn, but who survive and even thrive emotionally, unfolds in gorgeous watercolor-hued panels and tight, credible dialogue. Koko is a twentysomething who really wants to be "good," although she has a tendency to do just the wrong thing so often that others have difficulty trusting her motives. Slightly older Jon wants to join his older girlfriend in do-good work in Latin America, but she drops him. Faron, a teenager somewhat younger and less independent than Koko, works in a Vietnamese restaurant, where he is the scapegoat. All three characters are fully developed, delightfully drawn, and actively portrayed in contemporary San Francisco, whose neighborhoods also come to life on the large pages. This is stellar storytelling and art, opening a complex but accessible window onto real-life situations and self-discoveries. It should be most appealing to literary graphic-novel readers, other readers willing to cross over for the sake of a high-quality bildungsroman, and anyone else looking for beautiful and subtle art. Much more than a boy-meets-, or -loses-, -girl affair, the story of Koko, Jon, and Faron is a multicultural fable in which universal truths are made fresh and inspiring. —Francisca Goldsmith

Way, Gerard. *The Umbrella Academy, v.1: Apocalypse Suite*. Illus. by Gabriel Bá. 2008. 192p. Dark Horse (9781593079789). Gr. 9–12.

The newest superhero kids on the block are just that—kids. At least they start out kids in the first Umbrella Academy collection, written by the lead singer of My Chemical Romance (Way) and superbly illustrated by Brazilian graphic artist Bá. When the diminutive orphans turned masked crime fighters first appear in the public arena, with their wealthy patron, Sir Reginald Hargreeves, keeping watch, their nemesis is a mobile, death-ray-zapping Eiffel Tower. Twenty years later, it takes Hargreeves' death to bring the gang members, now grown and separated by their own idiosyncratic ambitions, back together to face a new enemy: estranged sister Vanya, the only one of them presumed to be powerless. Newly gifted with destructive powers by a race of robotic aliens, Vanya will stop at nothing to destroy the world unless her siblings stop her. Way and Bá provide all the ingredients of a superhero team to rival the X-Men and make its colorful adventures a hit. —Carl Hays

Way, Gerard. *The Umbrella Academy, v.2: Dallas*. Illus. by Gabriel Bá. 2009. 192p. Dark Horse (9781595823458). Gr. 9–12.

Apocalypse Suite (2008), written by the front man of the emo-punk outfit My Chemical Romance and drawn by Eisner winner Bá, provided a dizzying refreshment of the superhero group, adding here a dash of severely dysfunctional dynamics and there a glug of gleeful peculiarity. The story line of this follow-up swarms like an electron cloud around a plan to avert the Kennedy assassination—or are they trying to avert the plan to avert the plan? Way has a special affinity for enigmatic plotlines, in which minor details and major occurrences are left unexplained for ages, and he isn't afraid to literally end the world, which has happened at least twice in Umbrella Academy history. Information gets doled out in morsels and roundhouse kicks as the squabbling squad of super-stepsiblings zips back and forth in time and works to save the world from, well, themselves and their beyond-clever powers. Rumor's ability to tell a lie and have it come true offs an Abraham Lincoln monument run amok, mirroring the the first book's opening, in which zombie-robot Gustave Eiffel terrorizes Paris with his tower. Such stuff makes spectacular fodder for Bá's chunky, irresistibly hooky art, bursting with constellations of weird, exciting, and funny touches. Fresh, bitter, ultraviolent, oddly touching, *The Umbrella Academy* may be the shrewdest, wildest superhero thing going in mainstream comics. It's certainly among the finest. —Ian Chipman

Wilson, G. Willow. *Cairo*. Illus. by M. K. Perker. 2007. 160p. Vertigo (9781401211400). Gr. 9–12.

A drug-smuggling Egyptian in possession of a djinn-friendly hookah (djinn = genie), an Israeli soldier caught out in Cairo and endangered by her allegiance and her gender, an overeager female journalism student from America, an even younger American Lebanese youth, and a far more experienced male journalist who has never traveled beyond Cairo are brought together in a story that moves with grace and vigor. The opening pages depict each character's travails until they are brought together under duress by strong-arm robbers and mischievous underworld spirits. Panels of varying sizes differently aligned vividly portray chases through modern Cairo's streets, alleys, and coffeehouses and in an underworld in which gravity sometimes fails, leaving the characters walking on the ceiling. Each main character is near-tragically flawed yet worthy of sympathy, so that the sweet ending suits the ensemble drama. Scripting and art complement each other well in an adventure with lots of appeal for readers willing to try a literary graphic novel and for those simply looking for the next good one. —Francisca Goldsmith

Wood, Brian. *Demo*. Illus. by Becky Cloonan. 2005. 288p. AiT/Planet Lar (9781932051421). Gr. 9–12.

After only a few glances, you grok why indie-comics mavens rave about the 12-issue comic *Demo*. Cloonan's artwork progresses from strength to strength, beginning as an Americanized take on grunge manga (big eyes, blank faces, bristling or moppy or no hair, lots of little-line detail) in stark black and white, proceeding through reduced lineation and varying amounts of shading to selectively mounting wholly drawn figures on manipulated photo imagery in the last three stories. Also employing a huge range of angles-of-vision and perspective points, it looks like a billion bucks. The story lines aren't bad, either. They're about late-teens-to-early-thirties crises of separation from home, lover, or way of life. Early on, protagonists have scary psychokinetic powers, such as killing with a spoken word or concentrated rage and shape-shifting according to others' expectations. Writer Wood soon modified and eventually dropped that conceit. The hapless young father in the story excerpted for the inaugural *Year's Best Graphic Novels, Comics & Manga* (2006) is just a never-miss rifle shot, and the three twentysomethings in the especially effective "Midnight to Six" are unusual only in having stuck to "The Slacker Pledge" they signed in eighth grade. Lacking recurring characters, *Demo* altogether is less reminiscent of other comics series than of a thematic rather than continuous-narrative novel, such as John Horne Burns' *The Gallery* (1947). High praise, maybe, but deserving. —Ray Olson

★ Yang, Gene Luen. *American Born Chinese*. Illus. by Gene Luen Yang. 2006. 240p. First Second (9781596431522). Gr. 10–12.

With vibrant colors and visual panache, indie writer-illustrator Yang (*The Rosary Comic Book*, 2003) focuses on three characters in tales that touch on facets of Chinese American life. Jin is a boy faced with the casual racism of fellow students and the pressure of his crush on a Caucasian girl; the Monkey King, a character from Chinese folklore, has attained great power but feels he is being held back because of what the gods perceive as his lowly status; and Danny, a popular high-school student, suffers through an annual visit from his cousin Chin-Kee, a walking, talking compendium of exaggerated Chinese stereotypes. Each of the characters is flawed but familiar, and, in a clever postmodern twist, all share a deep, unforeseen connection. Yang helps the humor shine by using his art to exaggerate or contradict the words, creating a synthesis that marks an accomplished graphic storyteller. The stories have a simple, engaging sweep to them, but their weighty subjects—shame, racism, and friendship—receive thoughtful, powerful examination. —Jesse Karp

Yang, Gene Luen. *Boxers*. Illus. by Gene Luen Yang. 2013. 336p. First Second (9781596433595). Gr. 7–11.

Yang, Gene Luen. *Saints*. Illus. by Gene Luen Yang. 2013. 176p. First Second (9781596436893). Gr. 7–11.

In *American Born Chinese* (2006), Yang spoke to the culture clash of Chinese American teen life. In *Boxers*—the first volume in a two-book set, concluding with *Saints* (2013)—about the Boxer Rebellion at the end of the nineteenth century in China, he looses twin voices in harmony and dissonance from opposite sides of the bloody conflict. *Boxers* follows a young man nicknamed Little Bao, who reacts to religious and cultural oppression by leading the uprising from the provinces to Peking, slaughtering "foreign devils" and soldiers along the way. Between the two books, Yang ties tangled knots of empathy where the heroes of one become the monsters of the other. Little Bao and his foil from *Saints*, Four-Girl, are drawn by the same fundamental impulses—for community, family, faith, tradition, purpose—and their stories reflect the inner torture that comes when those things are threatened. Yang is in superb form here, arranging numerous touch points of ideological complexity and deeply plumbing his characters' points of view. And in an homage to the driving power of stories themselves, Bao is captivated by visions sprung from lore: the spirits he believes possess him and his fighters. Much blood is spilled as Little Bao marches toward his grim fate, which is even more unsettling given that Yang hasn't fundamentally altered his squeaky clean, cartoonishly approachable visual style. A poignant, powerhouse work of historical fiction from one of our finest graphic storytellers. —Ian Chipman

Yang, Gene Luen. *The Eternal Smile*. Illus. by Derek Kirk Kim. 2009. 176p. First Second (9781596431560). Gr. 9–12.

This dream-team matchup of Yang (*American Born Chinese*, 2006) and Kim (*Same Difference and Other Stories*, 2004) brings together three strikingly different graphic short stories. Which is accurate to a point, because in reality (or fantasy, depending on how you want to look at it) there are six stories, as each tale wends its way into a world-shifting denouement that reveals a mirror narrative. In the first, a comic-fantasy adventure, a plucky young knight vanquishes monsters to win the princess's love. In the second, a wacky cartoon spoof on Uncle Scrooge, a tycoon frog's latest wealth-grabbing scheme leads him to create an entire religion around a mysterious smile in the sky. In the last, a lonely peon trapped in a humdrum working world falls prey to e-mail fraud. Revealing what each of the stories is really about would kill the fun, but suffice it to say that what unites them all is escapism, and not as a negative connotation. You can escape into creativity, flee the limiting confines foisted on you by others, or dream of a sunnier world to inhabit. Visually, each story is a world unto itself, drastically different from the others but defined by a well-polished sensibility that works wonders in concert with the multilayered themes being explored. Absolutely not to be missed by anyone who welcomes the leaps available solely to graphic storytelling. —Ian Chipman

Yoshinaga, Fumi. *Ôoku: The Inner Chambers, v.1*. Illus. by Fumi Yoshinaga. 2009. 216p. VIZ Media (9781421527475). Gr. 10–12.

Drawing on themes found in such diverse works as Margaret Atwood's *Handmaid's Tale* (1985), Brian K. Vaughan's *Y: The Last Man* comics, and James Clavell's *Shogun* (1975), *Ôoku* envisions an alternate history in which a plague decimates the male population of eighteenth-century Japan. Mizuno is a healthy young man who grants his seed to the poor women of his village, who would never be able to afford the courtesans that provide such a favor. But he must leave his good deeds and his true love behind when he is inducted into the Inner Chamber, the female shogun's private "stash" of healthy men. Fending off the aggressive advances of the other concubines and proving his intelligence and fencing skills, Mizuno is maneuvered into the position of the secret swain, whose duty to the new and contemptuous shogun is both a sacred and deadly one. Opting for slow-building intrigue and character development, *Ôoku* explores themes of commoditization and gender with intelligence, and the graceful, uncluttered art creates an elegant world of privilege and duty. An exceptionally strong beginning to a very intriguing manga series. —Jesse Karp

Historical Fiction

Alvarez, Julia. *Before We Were Free*. 2002. 160p. Knopf (9780375815447). Gr. 7–10.

What is it like for a 12-year-old girl living under a ruthless dictatorship in the Dominican Republic in 1960? Alvarez draws on her own cousins' and friends' experiences to tell the political story through the eyes of Anita, whose father is involved in a plot to assassinate the dictator and bring democracy to the island. This doesn't have the passionate lyricism of Alvarez's great adult novels. The pace, at least for the first half of the book, is very slow, perhaps because the first-person, present-tense narrative stays true to Anita's bewildered viewpoint and is weighed down with daily detail and explanation of the political issues ("I feel just awful that my father has to kill someone for us to be free"). Yet it is Anita's innocence, her focus on the ordinary, that young readers will recognize. She's busy with school, friends, getting her period, falling in love, even as the secrets and spies come closer and, finally, the terror destroys her home. Her father is arrested; she and her mother are in hiding. There's no sensationalism, but Anita knows the horrific facts of how prisoners are tortured and killed. Trying to block out the truth, she loses her voice, even forgets the words for things, until she starts to write in a secret diary. Readers interested in the history will grab this. Like Lyll Becerra de Jenkins' *The Honorable Prison* (1988), about a young girl whose father resists a Latin American dictatorship, and Beverley Naidoo's *The Other Side of Truth* (*Booklist*'s 2001 Top of the List winner for youth fiction), Alvarez's story will also spark intense discussion about politics and family. —Hazel Rochman

Anderson, Laurie Halse. *Chains*. 2008. 320p. Simon & Schuster (9781416905851). Gr. 7–10.

In the spring of 1776, Isabel, a teenage slave, and her sister, Ruth, are sold to ruthless, wealthy loyalists in Manhattan. While running errands, Isabel is approached by rebels, who promise her freedom (and help finding Ruth, who has been sent away) if she agrees to spy. Using the invisibility her slave status brings, Isabel lurks and listens as Master Lockton and his fellow Tories plot to crush the rebel uprisings, but the incendiary proof that she carries to the rebel camp doesn't bring the desired rewards. Like the central character in M. T. Anderson's Octavian Nothing duet, Isabel finds that both patriots and loyalists support slavery. The specifics of Isabel's daily drudgery may slow some readers, but the catalogue of chores communicates the brutal rhythms of unrelenting toil, helping readers to imagine vividly the realities of Isabel's life. The story's perspective creates effective contrasts. Overwhelmed with domestic concerns, Isabel and indeed all the women in the household learn about the war from their marginalized position: they listen at doors to rooms where they are excluded, and they collect gossip from the streets. Anderson explores elemental themes of power ("She can do anything. I can do nothing," Isabel realizes about her sadistic owner), freedom, and the sources of human strength in this searing, fascinating story. The extensive back matter includes a documented section that addresses many questions about history that readers will want to discuss. —Gillian Engberg

★ Anderson, M. T. *The Astonishing Life of Octavian Nothing, Traitor to the Nation; v. 1: The Pox Party*. 2006. 368p. Candlewick (9780763624026). Gr. 10–12.

M. T. Anderson's first volume in the Octavian Nothing duet is an episodic, highly ambitious story, deeply rooted in eighteenth-century literary traditions, which examines, among many other things, pre-Revolutionary slavery in New England. The plot focuses on Octavian, a young black boy who recounts his youth in a Boston household of scientists and philosophers (The Novanglian College of Lucidity). Octavian soon learns that he and his mother are objects of one of the Collegians' experiments to learn whether Africans are "a separate and distinct species." Octavian receives an education "equal to any of the princes in Europe," until financial strains shatter Octavian's sheltered life of intellectual pursuits and the illusion that he is a free member of a utopian society. As political unrest in the colonies grows, Octavian experiences the increasing horrors of what it means to be a slave. The story's scope is immense, in both its technical challenges and underlying intellectual and moral questions, and Anderson employs multiple viewpoints and formats. Once acclimated to the novel's style, readers will marvel at Anderson's ability to maintain this high-wire act of elegant, archaic language and shifting voices, and they will appreciate the satiric scenes that gleefully lampoon the Collegians' more buffoonish experiments. Anderson's impressive historical research fixes the imagined College firmly within the facts of our country's own troubled history. The fluctuations between satire and somber realism, gothic fantasy and factual history will jar and disturb readers, creating a mood that echoes Octavian's unsettled time as well as our own. Anderson's book is both chaotic and highly accomplished, and, like Aidan Chambers' recent *This Is All* (2006), it demands rereading. Teens need not understand all the historical and literary allusions to connect with Octavian's torment or to debate the novel's questions, present in our country's founding documents, which move into today's urgent arguments about intellectual life; individual action; the influence of power and money, racism and privilege; and what patriotism, freedom, and citizenship mean. —Gillian Engberg

Anderson, M. T. *The Astonishing Life of Octavian Nothing, Traitor to the Nation; v.2: The Kingdom on the Waves*. 2008. 592p. Candlewick (9780763629502). Gr. 10–12.

The story begun in *The Astonishing Life of Octavian Nothing, Traitor to the Nation; v.1: The Pox Party* (2006), a National Book Award winner and a Printz Honor Book, continues in this volume, which offers more awe-inspiring reinterpretations of America's birth. After escaping the members of an Enlightenment college, Octavian, a teenage black slave, flees with his sympathetic tutor to the imperiled city of Boston, where the pair poses as loyalists to the Crown. As the war escalates, Octavian joins a Loyalist navy regiment that promises freedom to African Americans and enters into battle against the Patriots. Aside from a few essential interjections from others, Octavian narrates in the same graphic, challenging language used in the previous book, which Anderson has described as an "unintelligible eighteenth-century Johnsonian Augustan prose." But readers need not grasp every reference in the rich, elegant tangle of dialects to appreciate this piercing exposé of our country's founding hypocrisies. Even more present in this volume are passionate questions, directly relevant to teens' lives, about basic human struggles for independence, identity, freedom, love, and the need to reconcile the past. Viewed through historical hindsight, Octavian's final, wounded optimism ("No other human generation hath done other than despoil, perhaps we shall be the first") will resonate strongly with contemporary teens. —Gillian Engberg

Arrington, Frances. *Prairie Whispers*. 2003. 176p. Philomel (9780399239755). Gr. 7–12.

"Oh what a tangled web we weave, when first we practice to deceive" might be the slogan of this taut story set on the South Dakota prairie. Colleen's sister is stillborn, but her mother is too ill to know. Colleen seeks help, and, ironically, the woman in the nearby covered wagon has also given birth. That infant is well, but Mrs. O'Brien knows that she is dying. She tells Colleen that she doesn't trust her husband and begs her to take the baby. One baby without a mother; one mother without a baby. Colleen makes the switch, and though she promises herself that she will tell the truth, the baby brings so much happiness that she keeps the secret. When the baby's suspicious father returns, one lie spins into another. Arrington masterfully tightens the noose in each short chapter as Colleen desperately tries to keep the pledge she made to Mrs. O'Brien, knowing that she brings danger closer as Mr. O'Brien figures out what has transpired. There are a few manipulations, but readers will be caught up in Colleen's story. The book ends as Colleen is about to tell her parents the truth. What will she say? How will her family react? Such questions will make an excellent writing exercise for teachers who use this book in the classroom. —Ilene Cooper

Auch, Mary Jane. ***Ashes of Roses*****. 2002. 249p. Holt (9780805066869). Gr. 7–12.**

The harsh side of the Irish American immigration story is dramatized in this first-person narrative of Rose Nolan, 16, who is filled with hope when she comes with her family to New York City in 1911, but faces so much hardship and disappointment that she almost returns to the misery she left back in Limerick. Her parents do go back, and Auch shows clearly why, even as Rose and her younger sister, Maureen, insist on staying, despite the wrenching family parting and the girls' daily struggle for survival. This is, unfortunately, very much a step-by-step docunovel, and the research sometimes shows. But the facts are riveting, whether it's the inspection on Ellis Island (Rose's baby brother has trachoma, so the officials won't let him in); the prejudice as well as the support the sisters get from other immigrants; or the unspeakable working conditions in the sweatshops. Rose finally gets a job at the Triangle Shirtwaist Factory, and the unforgettable climax of the story is her account of the tragic fire: her friends are among the 146 people who perish in the flames. They leave her with the drive to work for fair, safe working conditions, and she finds her courage and her place. Excellent supplementary reading for social studies classes. —Hazel Rochman

Avi. ***Sophia's War: A Tale of Revolution*****. 2012. 320p. Simon & Schuster/Beach Lane (9781442414419). Gr. 6–8.**

In 1776, 12-year-old Sophia and her parents live in British-occupied New York City. When John André, a charming English officer, is quartered in their home, Sophia idealizes him. But after he refuses to help her brother, a captured American soldier who later dies on a squalid prison ship, her opinion changes. Sophia becomes a spy in 1780 and discovers André's plot to capture West Point with the help of the traitorous American general Benedict Arnold. Unable to pass along the information through the usual channels, she travels northward on her own, hoping to alert the American forces to Arnold's treachery. The book's riveting opening scene, in which Sophia watches as Nathan Hale is hanged as a spy, foreshadows the danger she knowingly accepts by engaging in espionage. Few historical novels are as closely shaped by actual events as this one during the last 100 pages. Working within the bounds of credibility, Avi manages to keep the fictional narrator on the scene for a good deal of the action and uses real moments to bring the imagined story to its dramatic heights. A glossary of eighteenth-century terms and an author's note are appended. Pair this intriguing historical novel with Steve Sheinkin's *The Notorious Benedict Arnold* (2010). —Carolyn Phelan

Bagdasarian, Adam. ***Forgotten Fire*****. 2000. 288p. DK Ink/Melanie Kroupa (9780789426277). Gr. 8–12.**

Other than Kerop Bedoukian's childhood memoir *Some of Us Survived* (1978) and David Kherdian's story of his mother, *The Road from Home* (1979), very little has been written for young people about the Turkish genocide of the Armenians, which left about one and a half million dead. Based on a true story, this powerful historical novel tells about the tragedy through the personal experience of Vahan Kenderian, child of one of the richest and most respected Armenians in Turkey. He's 12 years old when his home is invaded and his protected life is torn apart. The child who was never even allowed on the streets after dark sees his father led away by police and many of his family and friends butchered before his eyes. His sister poisons herself to avoid being raped. His mother begs him and his brother to run away; they do, and even now he asks himself if he should have left her to die. He runs the wrong way. His brother dies. The first-person narrative is quiet, without sensationalism, but the stark horror of the first few chapters is almost unbearable. Then just as you feel the horror can't go on, the story becomes a kind of episodic survival adventure. For the next three years, the boy is on the run, hiding in homes and stores and stables, disguised as a girl, a person unable to speak or hear, a beggar—until, finally, he finds a safe place. The writing is simple, almost monosyllabic at times, with a haunting, rhythmic voice that's like a drumbeat. As he leaves the country at last, Vahan feels the return of all he's had to suppress, especially his longing for his mother's face and voice, "for the brown hair she had, for her bones and rags." A significant addition to Holocaust literature. —Hazel Rochman

Bartoletti, Susan Campbell. ***The Boy Who Dared.*** **2008. 192p. Scholastic (9780439680134). Gr. 6–12.**

In *Hitler Youth: Growing Up in Hitler's Shadow, Booklist*'s 2005 Top of the List for youth nonfiction, Bartoletti included a portrait of Helmuth Hübener, a German teenager executed for his resistance to the Nazis. In this fictionalized biography, she imagines his story as he sits in prison awaiting execution in 1942 and remembers his childhood in Hamburg during Hitler's rise to power. Beaten and tortured to name his friends, he remembers how he started off an ardent Nazi follower and then began to question his patriotism, secretly listened to BBC radio broadcasts, and finally dared to write and distribute pamphlets calling for resistance. The teen's perspective makes this a particularly gripping way to personalize the history, and even those unfamiliar with the background Bartoletti weaves in—the German bitterness after WWI, the burning of the books, the raging anti-Semitism––will be enthralled by the story of one boy's heroic resistance in the worst of times. A lengthy author's note distinguishes fact from fiction, and Bartoletti provides a detailed chronology, a bibliography, and many black-and-white photos of Helmuth with friends, family, and members of his Mormon church. This is an important title for the Holocaust curriculum. —Hazel Rochman

Bennett, Veronica. ***Cassandra's Sister.*** **2007. 240p. Candlewick (9780763634643). Gr. 9–12.**

On the heels of the film *Becoming Jane,* this timely novel, inspired by Jane Austen's life and work, blends romance and tart courtship commentary successfully enough to create new Austen fans, gratify existing ones, and send both back to the stacks for more. Bennett, who previously meshed literary biography and fiction in *Angelmonster* (2006), about Mary Shelley, achieves even greater success here. Beginning when 18-year-old Austen wrote *Sense and Sensibility,* and ending nearly a decade later as its publication glimmered on the horizon, the plot focuses on the close bond between Jenny (Jane's childhood nickname) and elder sister Cass as they bide their time before marriage. The more emotional Jenny, swept along by the prospect of euphoric true love, simultaneously questions her patience for the marital drudgery of "childbearing and preserve making." The siblings' romantic quandaries will be enough to engage many teens, even some unacquainted with Austen, but affection for the celebrated author will enhance readers' appreciation for this homage, which gracefully mimics Austen's style and unobtrusively refers to beloved plots and characters. True to biographical record, this does not end in a treacly happily-ever-after; the thought-provoking conclusion frames spinsterhood as a prerequisite for the author's success. Examples of the scholarship that guided Bennett aren't provided in the author's note, but motivated readers will easily find the abundantly available materials on their own. —Jennifer Mattson

Bradley, Kimberly Brubaker. ***For Freedom: The Story of a French Spy.*** **2003. 192p. Delacorte (9780385729611). Gr. 6–12.**

Teenage Suzanne David is so focused on her dreams of becoming an opera star that she barely notices the growing Nazi presence in her French hometown of Cherbourg, until an air raid in 1940 literally puts the death and devastation at her feet. Her innocent appearance, iron will, and schedule as a singer-performer attract the attention of a local Resistance leader, who recruits her to become a spy and entrusts her to transport encoded Allied messages. Based on interviews with the real Suzanne David (who married an American soldier in 1945 and moved to Tennessee), this taut, engrossing WWII novel instantly immerses readers in the horrors faced by everyday citizens during the Nazi occupation. The real focus, however, is the skin-crawling suspense story about one of France's youngest spies. Each chapter brings new intrigue and often shocking revelations, made all the more intense by the facts about codes and disguises and the fast-paced, first-person narration. There aren't many accounts for young readers about the French Resistance, and from setup to conclusion, this one resonates with authenticity, excitement, and heart. The teenage hero who must keep her spying a secret, even from her parents, will thrill historical fiction fans. —Roger Leslie

Breslin, Theresa. *Remembrance*. **2002. 304p. Delacorte (9780385730150). Gr. 7–12.**

Through the personal experience of five teenagers, Breslin captures the reality of WWI on the battlefront and at home in Britain. The story is long, and the historical facts and issues are spelled out. The drama is in the detail, not only about the battlefield slaughter but also about the revolutionary changes the war brought for women, whatever their class. The characters are beautifully drawn. Freed from the restrictions of her genteel upper-crust family, Charlotte volunteers as a nurse in France. Her brother, Francis, is against the war, and his letters home express his deep conflict about why he is fighting. Charlotte becomes friends with working-class Maggie, who grabs her new opportunities for education. Francis and Maggie are in love. Maggie's older brother can't wait to get to the front, and he's killed there. Her younger brother lies about his age to enlist and avenge his brother's death, but ends up helping a wounded enemy soldier. This is a sure bet for history classes. —Hazel Rochman

Bruchac, Joseph. *Code Talker*. **2005. 240p. Dial (9780803729216). Gr. 6–9.**

Six-year-old Ned Begay leaves his Navajo home for boarding school, where he learns the English language and American ways. At 16, he enlists in the U.S. Marines during WWII and is trained as a code talker, using his native language to radio battlefield information and commands in a code that was kept secret until 1969. Rooted in his Navajo consciousness and traditions even in dealing with fear, loneliness, and the horrors of the battlefield, Ned tells of his experiences in Hawaii, Guadalcanal, Bougainville, Guam, Iwo Jima, and Okinawa. The book, addressed to Ned's grandchildren, ends with an author's note about the code talkers as well as lengthy acknowledgments and a bibliography. The narrative pulls no punches about war's brutality and never adopts an avuncular tone. Not every section of the book is riveting, but slowly the succession of scenes, impressions, and remarks build to create a solid, memorable portrayal of Ned Begay. Even when facing complex negative forces within his own country, he is able to reach into his traditional culture to find answers that work for him in a modern context. Readers who choose the book for the attraction of Navajo code talking and the heat of battle will come away with more than they ever expected to find. —Carolyn Phelan

Burg, Ann. *All the Broken Pieces*. **2009. 224p. Scholastic (9780545080927). Gr. 6–10.**

Airlifted from Vietnam at the end of the war and adopted by a loving American family, Matt Pin, 12, is haunted by what he left behind, even as he bonds with his new little brother and becomes a star pitcher on the school baseball team. In rapid, simple free verse, the first-person narrative gradually reveals his secrets: his memories of mines, flames, screams, helicopters, bombs, and guns, as well as what the war did to his little brother ("He followed me / everywhere, / he follows me still"). But this stirring debut novel is about much more than therapy and survivor guilt. When his parents take Matt to a veterans' meeting, he hears the soldiers' stories of injury and rejection and begins to understand why the school bully calls him "frog-face" ("My brother died / Because of you"). There is occasional contrivance as Matt eavesdrops on adults. But the haunting metaphors are never forced, and the intensity of the simple words, on the baseball field and in the war zone, will make readers want to rush to the end and then return to the beginning again to make connections between past and present, friends and enemies. —Hazel Rochman

Cadnum, Michael. *Blood Gold*. **2004. 224p. Viking (9780670058846). Gr. 7–12.**

Cadnum's latest foray into historical fiction offers readers a gripping adventure set during the 1849 California gold rush. The story opens in the steamy, danger-filled jungles of the Isthmus of Panama. Eighteen-year-old William Dwinelle and Ben Pomeroy, his friend and traveling companion, are the odd men out among the party of fortune seekers traveling through the risky, little-used jungle route. William's quest is not gold; instead, he hopes to find the man who abandoned his friend Elizabeth. Surviving bandits, a cholera epidemic, and a harrowing ocean voyage to San

Francisco, William encounters greed, murder, and revenge in gold rush–era California. Cadnum's painstaking attention to historical detail brings the setting vividly to life and skillfully captures both the obvious and obscure nuances of life in the era. Complementing the historical insight is an expertly crafted, fast-paced, engrossing adventure story full of fascinating characters. This is historical fiction that boys in particular will find irresistible. —Ed Sullivan

Carvell, Marlene. *Sweetgrass Basket*. 2005. 160p. Dutton (9780525475477). Gr. 10–12.

Mattie and Sarah try to be good when their father, a Mohawk, sends them to Pennsylvania's Carlisle Indian Boarding School at the turn of the twentieth century. He believes it's best, but the children suffer abuse. Mattie, falsely accused of stealing, is beaten and publicly shamed, and things only get worse. The sisters tell their story in alternating first-person, free-verse narratives, which reveal their close bond, their longing for home, and the vicious pressure to assimilate (Mrs. Dwyer says that "if we work hard, we will be as good as white people"). A few adults are kind, and the sisters make new friends, but the school director encourages bullying and betrayal. The girls' voices sometimes sound similar, but different typefaces make it easy to tell who is speaking, and readers will be deeply moved by the sisters' loving connection in a world of cruel authority. Carvell based the story on the experiences of the members of her husband's Mohawk family, four of whom attended Carlisle. A gripping drama of displacement and forced assimilation. —Hazel Rochman

★ Chambers, Aidan. *Postcards from No Man's Land*. 2002. 320p. Dutton (9780525468639). Gr. 9–12.

Winner of the British Carnegie Medal, this very long novel is part thrilling WWII love story and part edgy, contemporary, coming-of-age fiction. In Holland in 1944, Dutch teenager Geertrui fell passionately in love with a wounded young British soldier, and she hid him from the enemy. That soldier's grandson, Jacob, a British teenager, is now in Amsterdam to visit the grave of the grandfather he never knew, and he falls in love with a beautiful young woman, even as he's attracted to an openly gay young man. The length of the story and the tortuous connections between past and present may turn off some readers, but the individual stories are riveting as past secrets are revealed and linked with what Jacob discovers about himself. Chambers weaves together past and present with enough plot, characters, and ideas for several YA books, but he does it with such mastery that all the pieces finally come together, with compelling discoveries about love, courage, family, and sexual identity. Common to all the stories is the heroism of ordinary people. Jacob finds no neat answers, just a sense of the rich and painful confusion of what it means to be human. —Hazel Rochman

Chan, Gillian. *A Foreign Field*. 2002. 192p. Kids Can (9781553373490). Gr. 7–10.

Fourteen-year-old Ellen, who lives near a Canadian air base that the Royal Air Force is using for training during WWII, has what she considers a tedious job as her war work: looking after her disobedient, airplane-mad younger brother, Colin. Colin introduces her to Stephen, a very young RAF trainee from the base, who begins to visit their family regularly, but Ellen finds him more of an embarrassment than a kindred spirit or potential boyfriend. Slowly over the next year, however, they find common ground and their friendship grows and deepens into love. Simultaneously, the horrors of war gradually become more real to them both. Chan beautifully captures the particular tensions and intensity of wartime relationships in this quiet, absorbing novel. Though the third-person story is told from Ellen's point of view, many well-written letters and a few vivid nightmares interspersed with the narrative text give readers insight into Stephen's thoughts, feelings, and relationships as well. The occasional use of strong language is true to the characters and events of the novel. In one instance, Stephen, sobbing after a fatal accident during a training mission, tells of "the faces we could see through the canopy, their mouths stretched in screams as the plane fell—the faces of our friends—and there was fuck all we could do." An affecting novel with a strong cast of believable characters and a well-realized historical setting. —Carolyn Phelan

Chapman, Fern Schumer. ***Is It Night or Day?*** **2010. 192p. Farrar (9780374177447). Gr. 6–10.**

Chapman based this spare historical novel on her mother's experience of coming to America to escape Nazi persecution. At age 12, Edith is sent by her German Jewish parents to relatives on Chicago's South Side in 1937. Oppressed by her aunt, who makes Edith work as a maid, and teased at school, where she starts off in first grade until she learns English, Edith suffers prejudice, including anti-Semitism in the girls' locker room ("Dirty Jew!"); and after the U.S. declares war, other children view her as an "enemy alien" and call her "Dirty Kraut." Even worse, she receives almost no word from her parents, until the final shocking news about the camps comes in 1945. In Edith's bewildered, sad, angry voice, the words are eloquent and powerful. Did her parents want to get rid of her? Why does her older sister, also in Chicago, not call? Just as heartbreaking is an early letter from her mother: "I open the door and no one is there." On a lighter note, baseball helps Edith, and her hero, Hank Greenberg, inspires her to take pride in her Jewish heritage. As with the best writing, the specifics about life as a young immigrant are universal, including the book's title, which is drawn from a quote by a Sudanese immigrant "Lost Boy" who arrived in the U.S. in 2001. —Hazel Rochman

Chotjewitz, David. ***Daniel Half Human: And the Good Nazi.*** **2004. 304p. Atheneum (9780689857478). Gr. 7–12.**

In Hamburg, Germany, in the 1930s, Daniel enjoys being part of the Hitler Youth until he discovers his mother is Jewish and he is thrown out of his elite school. He still has fun with his best friend, Armin, who falls in love with Daniel's Jewish cousin; but tension mounts, racism is rampant, and Armin begins to stay away, though he takes risks and warns his friend to hide. Daniel's return to Hamburg in 1945 as interpreter for the Allies frames the novel, which switches among the viewpoints of too many characters, including Daniel's parents, who fight about whether to leave the country. But the detailed history woven into the fiction (including the effect of Germany's defeat in WWI, Hitler's rise, and the violence of Kristallnacht) helps make this clearly translated novel an important title for the Holocaust curriculum, especially given the friendship drama that keeps raising ethical questions to the very last page. —Hazel Rochman

Clinton, Cathryn. ***A Stone in My Hand.*** **2002. 208p. Candlewick (9780763613884). Gr. 6–12.**

Set in Gaza City in 1988, this story of a Palestinian girl and her family living under Israeli military occupation will bring readers very close to the daily news images of children at war. Malaak, 11, tells it with powerful immediacy in spare first-person present-tense chapters that capture her terror and dislocation. She is traumatized when her father is killed (a Palestinian terrorist bomb blows up the bus when he is crossing the border to seek work in Israel). In Gaza, her friend Tariq saw his father shot by Israeli soldiers. Now her anguish is that her older brother, Hamid, wants to join the Islamic Jihad. The young girl's narrative captures the experience of the occupation and the never-ending cycle of anger and retaliation. Yet, Clinton gets beyond any simplistic political message. The Palestinians are diverse in class, religion, and politics. Even within Malaak's family, her older sister watches Egyptian soap opera, while her furious brother is drawn to violence. Malaak finds courage and risks her life, but there's no sweet solution. This is bound to spark debate wherever there is passionate concern about the Middle East. But one book can't do it all. Recommend this with Danielle Carmi's *Samir and Yonatan* (2000), translated from the Hebrew, and with other books about what it is like to be young there now. —Hazel Rochman

Compestine, Ying Chang. ***Revolution Is Not a Dinner Party.*** **2007. 256p. Holt (9780805082074). Gr. 6–9.**

Known for her picture books, Compestine grew up in China, during the Cultural Revolution, and her autobiographical novel tells the history from the viewpoint of the young, protected, privileged child who loses her innocence when political brutality invades her home. For nine-year-old Ling, things always seem clear. She's close to her loving father, who teaches her English and about freedom in America, but she feels distant from her tense, angry mother. During the course of four years, repression increases, and eventually the Red Guards arrest Dad as a class enemy. Ling feels the repression in other ways, too; she stands up to class bullies who try to cut off her "bourgeois" hair. Always she is sustained by memories of her brave father and his dream of freedom. In clipped lyrical sentences, Compestine's first-person narrative sets a naive child's struggle to survive against betrayal and courage in one neighborhood and also the political panorama of spies and slogans. —Hazel Rochman

Cooper, Michelle. *A Brief History of Montmaray*. 2009. 304p. Knopf (9780375858642). Gr. 7–10.

The kingdom of Montmaray, on a tiny island in the Bay of Biscay, consists of the castle that the FitzOsbornes have called home for hundreds of years, and a small village that, by 1936, is populated by a last loyal family. In the opening entries in her new diary, 16-year-old Sophie FitzOsborne, niece to the rather mad king, dwells upon such all-consuming matters as her upcoming introduction to English society and how much of a ninny she becomes in the presence of the handsomely aloof Simon. At first, the rumors of strife from the mainland involving Fascists and Communists are nothing but distasteful conversation traps for Sophie, but soon they become frighteningly close. Pitting a dying monarchy against the rush of the modern world, Cooper has crafted a sort of updated Gothic romance where sweeping adventure plays equal with fluttering hearts; and without ever leaving the confines of the tiny island or landing a single kiss, Sophie finds no shortage of both. It takes some time for the plot to gain momentum and for the characters to fully cohere, but inviting historical details that situate the story in the social and political world of pre-WWII Europe lend traction to the slower parts before readers are dashed into a breathless finale. A smart and stirring choice to usher fans of the Brontës into the twentieth century. —Ian Chipman

Couloumbis, Audry. *Summer's End*. 2005. 192p. Putnam (9780399235559). Gr. 7–10.

The day before her thirteenth birthday, Grace's older brother, Collin, burns his draft card at a local sit-in. At first, Grace is concerned that her brother has upstaged her, once again. But her worries widen when her enraged father, a Korean War veteran, turns Collin out of the house. While Collin stays with sympathetic friends and her parents battle over ideological differences, Grace escapes to her grandmother's farm, where her large, boisterous extended family enfolds her and eventually her parents, helping everyone find new understanding and forgiveness. Grace's colloquial voice, filled with colorful southern phrasing, occasionally sounds too mature. But as in her Newbery Honor Book, *Getting Near to Baby* (1999), Couloumbis creates a vivid, affecting cast of characters, and sifts through a family's complex sorrow, anger, and love with incisive clarity and honesty: "I purely hated them all," says Grace of her feuding family. In addition, the questions that Grace and her young cousins ask about the Vietnam War may help contemporary readers articulate their own concerns about war, patriotism, and personal morality. —Gillian Engberg

Crowe, Chris. *Mississippi Trial, 1955*. 2002. 231p. Penguin (9780803727458). Gr. 7–12.

The 1955 murder of 14-year-old Emmett Till in Mississippi and the trial of his racist killers are at the center of this strong first novel. Crowe tells the story through the eyes of a white teenager, Hiram, 16, who is spending the summer with his beloved grandpa. The boy meets young Emmett, a lively African American visitor from Chicago, who refuses to go along with the submissive ways expected of a good black boy in the segregated community. When Emmett is tortured and killed, Hiram believes he knows one of the perpetrators, and he attends the trial. The facts are horrifying, and Crowe stays true to the newspaper accounts. What moves this beyond docudrama is Hiram's relationship with Grandpa, which has always been strong, unlike that with his father. At times Hiram's relationship with Dad (mainly offstage) seems added on to the story, and there's just too much about the cute, small-town "characters." But Crowe shows violent racism in daily life as well as in the drama of the trial, and he adds an edgy whodunit mystery element that will hold readers to the end. Teens will recognize how easy it is for Hiram to be a bystander to bigotry and will feel the horror of his sudden awakening to the evil that is part of "normal" life. —Hazel Rochman

Crowley, Suzanne. ***The Stolen One*****. 2009. 416p. Greenwillow (9780061232008). Gr. 8–12.**

Set in Elizabethan England, this novel tells of 16-year-old Kat, who has grown up in a country cottage under the care of a foster mother. After her death, Kat goes to London in hopes of learning her parents' identities. There she is taken under the wing of Queen Elizabeth I, and soon a rumor swirls through court that Kat's mother is the queen herself. The mystery of Kat's past is intertwined with the always-involving question of whether her heart lies with one of the handsome rogues at court or with a young farmer back home. Interspersed with Kat's first-person narration are passages from a secret journal, written years before. Though readers unfamiliar with Tudor history may find themselves lost at times, particularly in the journal entries, all becomes clear in the concluding chapters. An author's note identifies historical details that inspired the novel. Historical fiction fans will find Kat a strong, engaging heroine and her story a compelling one. —Carolyn Phelan

Cushman, Karen. ***The Loud Silence of Francine Green*****. 2006. 228p. Clarion (9780618504558). Gr. 6–9.**

Set in Los Angeles in 1949, Cushman's latest historical novel captures the terrors and confusions of the McCarthy era. Eighth-grader Francine admires her outspoken, precocious friend Sophie, who was kicked out of public school for painting "There is no free speech here" on the gymnasium floor. Francine feels muzzled at home and at her rigid Catholic school, "the land of 'Sit down, Francine' and 'Be quiet, Francine.'" Her worries escalate as Communist scares in Hollywood grow, and Sophie and her playwright father fall under suspicion. Cushman adroitly transforms what could have been a didactic story about intellectual freedom into an integrated, affecting novel about friendship and growing up. Described in Francine's authentic voice, which is filled with period slang, the smoothly inserted historical details, from Montgomery Clift to backyard bomb shelters, personalize Francine's adolescent struggles rather than simply marking a place and a time. Readers will skip over unknown cultural references ("My heart pounded like a Gene Krupa drum solo") and savor the story of friends and family tensions, the sly humor, and the questions about patriotism, activism, and freedom, which bring the novel right into today's most polarizing controversies. Sure to provoke lively class discussion, this will easily absorb independent readers in search of a rich, satisfying story about early adolescence. For another young person's view of the McCarthy hunts, suggest Ellen Levine's *Catch a Tiger by the Toe* (2005). —Gillian Engberg

Davies, Jacqueline. ***Lost*****. 2009. 256p. Marshall Cavendish (9780761455356). Gr. 7–10.**

Essie lives a hardscrabble life with her widowed mother and younger siblings on the Lower East Side of Manhattan in the early 1900s. The grim specter of poverty always hovers, yet Essie's spirit, her talent for creating beautiful hats, and her bountiful love for her little sister Zelda help to imbue their lives with joy and positive energy. As chapters alternate between earlier and later settings, we follow Essie to work at the Triangle Shirtwaist Factory. The plot builds—and so does a gradual awareness of cracks in Essie's grasp of reality. She is in denial about an accident that has taken Zelda's life, and she pursues a friendship with the mysterious Harriet Abbott, who shows up to work at the Triangle but does not seem at all like a typical working girl. Davies weaves two historic events—the disappearance of a wealthy heiress escaping family scandal and the catastrophic Triangle Shirtwaist fire of 1911, graphically depicted—into a lively tale of striving, unspeakable loss, and an eventual life-affirming resolution. —Anne O'Malley

Davis, Tanita S. ***Mare's War*****. 2009. 343p. Knopf (9780375857140). Gr. 6–9.**

Octavia and Tali don't have a grandma; they have Mare, a sports-car-driving, chain-smoking anti-grandma. And she's forcing them into a cross-country road trip for one long summer. Told in postcards, letters, and chapters alternating between "then" and "now," the girls' minor tiffs and insecurities literally take a backseat to Mare's experiences in the 6888th, the only battalion of African American women to serve overseas during WWII. Mare left home at age 17 and lied about her age to pursue a better life in the Women's Army Corps. She ended up first in Birmingham, England, then France. At times the story becomes a bit self-conscious, with a constant refrain of "How come we've never learned about this in school?" But where this title excels is in depicting the women of the 6888th at the cusp of adulthood, discovering their inner strengths while achieving things far beyond their expectations. Those interested in learning more about this slice of history should check out Brenda Moore's adult title *To Serve My Country, to Serve My Race* (1996). —Courtney Jones

Disher, Garry. ***The Divine Wind: A Love Story*****. 2002. 176p. Scholastic/Arthur A. Levine (9780439369152). Gr. 9–12.**

Set in a small northwest Australian coastal town, this WWII story is about friends and enemies close to home. It's also about love and family heartaches and discovering personal courage and betrayal. After the war, Hartley Penrose tells his story, looking back to 1938 when he was 16, and he and his sister, Alice, were best friends with Mitsi Sennosuke, who was born of Japanese parents and raised in Australia. With a big cast and an action-filled plot, Disher creates a vital, physical sense of the place as well as the secrets of the community. Even before the war, the official and personal racism is clear, toward "Japs" and also toward Aborigines, who are looked on as black "impurities" in the way of the white immigrant settlers. The characters are drawn without sentimentality. Mitsi is angry as well as loving; submissive at home, raucous with her friends. For a brief, rapturous period, Hartley and Mitsi are lovers, but then he's torn between loyalties. Readers will recognize the political parallels with the U.S., as well as the personal truth of how feelings can change from friendship and love to hate and indifference—and maybe back again. —Hazel Rochman

★ Donnelly, Jennifer. ***A Northern Light*****. 2003. 396p. Harcourt (9780152167059). Gr. 7–12.**

Donnelly's first YA novel begins with high drama drawn straight from history: Grace Brown's body is discovered, and her murder, which also inspired Theodore Dreiser's *An American Tragedy*, is the framework for this ambitious, beautifully written coming-of-age story set in upstate New York in 1906. Sixteen-year-old Mattie Gokey is a waitress at the Glenmore Hotel when Brown is murdered. As she learns Brown's story, her narrative shifts between the goings-on at the hotel and her previous year at home: her toil at the farm; her relationship with her harsh, remote father; her pain at being forbidden to accept a college scholarship. "Plain and bookish," Mattie is thrilled about, but wary of, a handsome neighbor's attentions, and she wonders if she must give up her dream of writing if she marries. In an intelligent, colloquial voice that speaks with a writer's love of language and an observant eye, Mattie details the physical particulars of people's lives as well as deeper issues of race, class, and gender as she strains against family and societal limitations. Donnelly adds a crowd of intriguing, well-drawn secondary characters who help Mattie define her own desires and sense of self. Many teens will connect with Mattie's deep yearning for independence and for stories, like her own, that are frank, messy, complicated, and inspiring. —Gillian Engberg

Dowd, Siobhan. ***Bog Child*****. 2008. 336p. Random/David Fickling (9780385751698). Gr. 8–11.**

While cutting peat in the Irish hills, Fergus McCann and his uncle discover a body preserved by the bog. Archaeologists and politicians fight over the find, while Fergus starts to dream about the past of the bog child he names "Mel." Dowd slowly reveals the story of Mel's mysterious death, an apparent murder, amid the 1980s troubles of Northern Ireland and the hunger strike of the Long Kesh political prisoners. Fergus' imprisoned older brother joins the strike as Fergus is blackmailed into delivering packages that may contain bomb-making supplies. The history, which will likely be as unfamiliar to American teen readers as the story's dialect, may need fleshing out with additional sources, but the intriguing characters and their motivations and sacrifices will translate directly to contemporary readers. The plotlines are braided together into a strong story that is rich in language, setting, and theme. Fans of David Almond's work will savor the similar religious influences and the elements of magical realism. A budding romance with the archaeologist's daughter, exuberant Cora, will delight readers, who will wonder, as Fergus does after his first kisses, "Why wasn't the whole world doing this all the time?" —Cindy Dobrez

Dowd, Siobhan. *A Swift Pure Cry*. 2007. 320p. Random/David Fickling (9780385751087). Gr. 10–12.

Everything's been wrong since 15-year-old Shell's Mam died. Her father forces his kids to say the rosary and then gets drunk. They live from money he skims off donations he collects for the church. Shell is left to take care of her younger brother and sister in their Irish village; her only joy comes in stolen moments with a local lad. Then her guy goes off to America, and though Shell pretends otherwise, she is pregnant. In a scene both graphic and horrific, Shell delivers a stillborn baby girl. The novel could have gone several ways, but perhaps because it is based on a true story, its path is unexpected. A dead baby is found, and the authorities, thinking it is Shell's, accuse her of murder. Moreover, the authorities suspect her own dad is the baby's father. Or perhaps the baby's father is the new priest. The words *pure* and *cry* in the title are apt, for this novel has a lyrical purity to it, and its cry is from the heart. Dowd evokes her setting impressively, and she realizes her characters with a sensitivity that is, at times, breathtaking. Not always easy to read, but well worth it. —Ilene Cooper

Draper, Sharon. *Copper Sun*. 2006. 320p. Atheneum (9780689821813). Gr. 9–12.

Best known for her contemporary African American characters, Draper's latest novel is a searing work of historical fiction that imagines a 15-year-old African girl's journey through American slavery. The story begins in Amari's Ashanti village, but the idyllic scene explodes in bloodshed when slavers arrive and murder her family. Amari and her beloved, Besa, are shackled, and so begins the account of impossible horrors from the slave fort, the Middle Passage, and auction on American shores, where a rice plantation owner buys Amari for his 16-year-old son's sexual enjoyment. In brutal specifics, Draper shows the inhumanity: Amari is systematically raped on the slave ship and on the plantation, and a slave child is used as alligator bait by white teenagers. She adds to the complex history in alternating chapters that flip between Amari and Polly, an indentured white servant on Amari's plantation. A few plot elements, such as Amari's chance meeting with Besa, are contrived. But Draper builds the explosive tension to the last chapter, and the sheer power of the story, balanced between the overwhelmingly brutal facts of slavery and Amari's ferocious survivor's spirit, will leave readers breathless, even as they consider the story's larger questions about the infinite costs of slavery and how to reconcile history. A moving author's note discusses the real places and events on which the story is based. Give this to teens who have read Julius Lester's *Day of Tears* (2005). —Gillian Engberg

Duble, Kathleen Benner. *The Sacrifice*. 2005. 224p. Simon & Schuster/Margaret K. McElderry (9780689876509). Gr. 6–9.

What was it like to be accused during the Salem witch hunts in 1692? Duble brings the history close through the viewpoint of Abigail, 10, who is accused of working with the devil, imprisoned, and tried along with her older sister. The social history is intensely dramatic: the spread of fear and hatred; the horrific conditions in the packed jail; the public meetings, with the accusers "moaning and groaning and screaming for the accused to stop tormenting them." But it is the story of one young girl and her family that will grab readers. Abigail is always in trouble for not knowing her place as a woman, and the book opens with her in the stocks for daring to run and raise her skirt above her knees. Her strong mother supports her irrepressible nature, unlike weak Father, who is mentally ill and whose "fits" frighten people (is he in the devil's thrall?). The surprising climax of family sacrifice is heartrending. The author's note adds another surprise:

some of Duble's own Puritan ancestors were accused of witchcraft, and this novel imagines their story. Arthur Miller's *The Crucible* and Ellen Levine's *Catch a Tiger by the Toe* (2005) are excellent fiction connections; suggest Marc Aronson's *Witch-Hunt* (2003) for factual perspective. —Hazel Rochman

Dubosarsky, Ursula. ***The Golden Day.*** **2013. 160p. Candlewick (9780763663995). Gr. 7–12.**

The classic Australian film *Picnic at Hanging Rock* finds its literary equivalent in fellow Aussie Dubosarsky's dark, languid look into the inscrutable wells of secrecy to be found in little girls. In the shadow of the Vietnam War, 11 bored school girls are taken on a short field trip to the local gardens by their idealistic teacher. Together with the teacher's apparent paramour, the girls are led to a seaside cave wherein the two adults vanish forever. When the girls are repeatedly questioned about the disappearance, their own self-interest compels them to stay silent and senselessly guard the truth, until the keeping of the secret, not the secret itself, becomes the most important thing. In a stunning feat of perspective, Dubosarsky inhabits all 11 girls at once, snaking through a thousand small joys and triumphs and fears and petty grudges as they absorb life's bleakest truths as well as their own complicity in them: "Their eyes were clear but their hearts were dishonest." Reminiscent of Janne Teller's *Nothing* (2010), this is a masterful look at children's numb surprise to the most unsavory of adult developments. Though it's not really a surprise, is it? They knew all along that the world was full of terrible things.
—Daniel Kraus

Elliott, Patricia. ***The Pale Assassin.*** **2009. 335p. Holiday (9780823422500). Gr. 7–10.**

Aristocrat Eugénie lives in a Parisian bubble. Preoccupied with fashion and shopping, she is thrilled to be out promenading with her governess and nearly oblivious to the roiling despair of Paris as it begins its descent into revolution in 1789. Innocence has its limits, however, and Eugénie slams into reality when her guardian sends her off to an austere convent for safekeeping. Her beloved older brother, Armand, becomes aloof as he enters into political involvement with the constitutional cause. Step by step, Eugénie's world disintegrates and terrorism threatens from every corner. Elliott moves from fantasy (*Murkmere*, 2006, and *Ambergate*, 2007) into historical fiction and skillfully weaves the story of the French Revolution into the plot, illuminating the grim reality of class warfare while neither oversimplifying events nor overwhelming the narrative with information. Adding to the intrigue, a secretive and villainous political operative stalks Eugénie, having persuaded her guardian to hand her over in marriage when she turns 16. The best aspect of this excellent work of historical fiction is Eugénie herself. Her gradual coming-of-age and growing political awareness provide resonant depth to what becomes a highly suspenseful survival tale.
—Anne O'Malley

Engle, Margarita. ***Hurricane Dancers.*** **2011. 160p. Holt (9780805092400). Gr. 6–10.**

Engle, whose award-winning titles include the Newbery Honor Book, *The Surrender Tree* (2008), offers another accomplished historical novel in verse set in the Caribbean. Young Quebrado's name means "the broken one," a child "of two shattered worlds." The son of a Taíno Indian mother and a Spanish father, he is taken in 1510 from his village on the island that is present-day Cuba and enslaved on a pirate's ship, where a brutal conquistador, responsible for thousands of deaths throughout the Americas, is held captive for ransom. When a hurricane destroys the boat, Quebrado is pulled from the water by a fisherman, Naridó, whose village welcomes him, but escape from the past proves nearly impossible. Once again, Engle fictionalizes historical fact in a powerful, original story. With the exception of Quebrado, all the characters are based on documented figures (discussed in a lengthy author's note), whose voices narrate many of the poems. While the shifting perspectives create a somewhat dreamlike, fractured story, Engle distills the emotion in each episode with potent rhythms, sounds, and original, unforgettable imagery. Linked together, the poems capture elemental identity questions and the infinite sorrows of slavery and dislocation, felt even by the pirate's ship, which "remembers / her true self,

/ her tree self, / rooted / and growing, / alive, / on shore." —Gillian Engberg

Fleischman, Sid. *The Entertainer and the Dybbuk*. 2007. 160p. Greenwillow (9780061344459). Gr. 6–9.

Motivated, as he explains in his afterword, to create a personal remembrance of the 1.5 million Jewish children killed in the Holocaust, Fleischman pairs Freddie, a struggling, ex-GI ventriloquist, with Avrom, the ghost of one such victim, in a short, provocative tale that leavens the tears with laughter. Freddie's career isn't exactly taking off as he wanders postwar Europe—until he opens a closet and discovers smart-mouthed Avrom, who offers to put a better line of patter into Freddie's mouth in exchange for help finding a certain murderous SS officer. Countering Freddie's understandable reluctance with both gags and gut-wrenching war stories, Avrom moves in, and Freddie begins to display stunning vocal tricks to ever-larger audiences. Avrom then cajoles his host into keeping kosher, and even undergoing an ersatz (or is it?) bar mitzvah. Ultimately, the search takes the two to America, where in a satisfying (if credulity-straining) climax, they find their quarry standing trial for a new crime, and Avrom exacts a triumphant revenge for the old ones. The narrative voice here sounds adult, but the talented Fleischman is still both entertaining and thoughtful. Avrom's wisecracking will counterbalance matter-of-fact accounts of Nazi cruelty for young readers, but it's likely to be older ones who will best appreciate the novel's eloquent "inner voice" of conscience, which takes on a definite symbolic cast, and the way in which Freddie's public and private identities shift as the story progresses. —John Peters

Fletcher, Christine. *Ten Cents a Dance*. 2008. 320p. Bloomsbury (9781599901640). Gr. 9–12.

When Ruby replaces her ailing mother in the tough, meatpacking "Yards" of 1940s Chicago, the feisty teen can't stand the job's grimness and poverty wages: "I spent eight hours a day stuffing hogs' feet in jars, and we still ate beans." When handsome bad-boy Paulie urges her to try the Starlight Dance Academy, and get paid to dance with men who show up each night, she can't resist this far more lucrative prospect. While her mom believes Ruby has changed jobs to become a nightshift telephone operator, Ruby sashays into the wee hours as a dance-hall girl looking for glamour and adventure. Readers will be riveted by Ruby's journey as she leaves one desperate existence for another and finds herself drawn deeper into a world that is hard-edged and even dangerous—especially when she begins to let Paulie lead her down a dubious path. Blatant racism, crime, and the swing-era music scene permeate the backdrop of Fletcher's absorbing wartime novel, which will have readers rooting for its spirited, soul-searching heroine. —Anne O'Malley

Fletcher, Susan. *Alphabet of Dreams*. 2006. 292p. Atheneum/Ginee Seo (9780689850424). Gr. 6–9.

In a richly imagined novel, Fletcher dovetails her own characters and plot with an utterly familiar New Testament story. Mitra comes from Persian royalty, but most of her family is dead. Now disguised as a boy, she steals food and shelters in burial caves with her younger brother, Babak. Political enemies of their father pursue them, as does the magus Melchior, who has heard of Babak's gift for dreaming others' dreams. The complications facing a pubescent girl living as a boy and the rhythms of desert life form one intriguing dimension to the novel; another is the journey set in motion when Babak dreams of a portentous star, and the siblings follow Melchior and his two magi companions as they seek the king it represents. Teens will recognize their own longings in proud, headstrong, and passionate Mitra; steer slightly older readers to Anne Provost's *In the Shadow of the Ark* (2004), another novel about a resilient young woman swept along by biblical events. —GraceAnne A. DeCandido

Fletcher, Susan. *Walk across the Sea*. 2001. 212p. Atheneum (9780689841330). Gr. 6–10.

Liza McCully defies the father she loves when she helps a boy, Wah Chung, escape the violent expulsion of the Chinese community from her coastal town in California in 1886. Her father is the lighthouse keeper, and the setting is a dramatic part of this fine historical novel, not only because Liza lives and works in the lighthouse and hides the fugitive there but also because the lighthouse is on a tiny island, cut off from the mainland except at ebb tide, when Liza can walk across the bottom of the sea. The stormy ocean is always there, both barrier and defense, a strong physical reality that makes Liza think about the big moral and religious issues. Though most of the local people, including Papa, want the "heathen" Chinese out because they threaten jobs, Liza feels confused and can't bear that she does nothing when the stricken families are driven away. She even quotes Jesus to Papa ("I was a stranger, and ye took me in"), but the biblical metaphors are not slick messages. One of the best things about the story is Liza's sympathy for Papa, who loses his lighthouse job because of the shelter his daughter gives the stranger. —Hazel Rochman

Flood, Nancy Bo. *Warriors in the Crossfire*. 2010. 144p. Front Street (9781590786611). Gr. 6–9.

The novel opens with friends Joseph and Kento fending off a shark attack while spearfishing in the middle of the night, a gripping scene that isn't even close to the book's most intense sequence. Set on the island of Saipan at the end of WWII, this is the story of natives who were caught between the ruthlessness of the Japanese and American armies. Joseph is the son of a chief, while Kento's father is one of the occupying Japanese. "Go ahead, Japanese and Americans, greedy bullies, battle it out and leave so we can have our island back," Joseph thinks, but when the fighting does finally arrive the consequences are well beyond anything he could have dreaded. Conflicted yet determined, Joseph is an ideal mix for a story of heroism—he wants to be a warrior like his ancestors, but in these horrific circumstances that means persevering through, not facing death and destruction head on. Saving his family comes down to finding a bit of fresh water while in hiding or being lucky enough not to catch a stray bullet. An afterword describes the real-life account of what happened on Saipan, where almost all of the Japanese soldiers were killed, and duty-bound Japanese civilians were rounded up to take their own lives by jumping off what is now known as Suicide Cliff. Intense and powerful reading that avoids bleakness by celebrating family, culture, and a longing for peace. —Ian Chipman

Foxlee, Karen. *The Anatomy of Wings*. 2009. 288p. Knopf (9780375856433). Gr. 8–12.

Set in a small Australian town in the early 1980s, this shining debut novel charts a young girl's grief after the death of her older sister. Months before Beth's fatal fall, 10-year-old Jennifer's beautiful singing voice disappears. When and why it "got stuck" forms a central mystery that unifies Jennifer's narrative, which loops fluidly between past and present. Each clue leads back to events from the tumultuous year before Beth died, and Jennifer's search for her voice becomes a larger search for how her beloved sister was lost and what it means to leave childhood behind. In this sensitive, original story, Foxlee explores familiar elements: the warmth and suffocation of living in "Nowheresville"; the chasm of misunderstanding between parents and adolescent children. Jennifer loves the comfort and solidity of facts, and she collects information like currency, but her observations are also poetic and washed with magic realism. Not all the plot's tangents are well integrated, but the story works as memory does, with skips, gaps, and sudden, piercing moments that are as illogical and illuminating as a dream. With heart-stopping accuracy and sly symbolism, Foxlee captures the small ways that humans reveal themselves, the mysterious intensity of female adolescence, and the surreal quiet of a grieving house, which slowly and with astonishing resilience fills again with sound and music. —Gillian Engberg

Frost, Helen. *The Braid*. 2006. 112p. Farrar/Frances Foster (9780374309626). Gr. 7–10.

When their family is evicted from the Western Isles of Scotland in 1850, teenage sisters Jeannie and Sarah are torn apart. Jeannie goes with her parents and younger siblings to Cape Breton, Canada. Her older sister, Sarah, hides so she can stay behind with Grandma. Before they separate, the sisters braid their hair together and cut it off, each taking half the braid ("You / me / sisters / always"). The tale unfolds in plain narrative poems, presented in the girls' alternating voices: Jeannie speaks of her brutal ocean crossing, during which her father and younger siblings perish, and of her struggle as a stranger in the new

country; Sarah talks about her loneliness, her love, and her illegitimate baby. The braid is both powerful fact and stirring metaphor in the girls' story of lasting connections, oceans apart, and it extends to encompass themes of home, shelter, and heritage, as well as the yearning for family wherever one lives. In concluding notes, Frost explains the poetic forms she used, which braid together the two immediate voices with echoing words and rhythms. As in Frost's *Keesha's House* (2003), the book will inspire both students and teachers to go back and study how the taut poetic lines manage to contain the powerful feelings.
—Hazel Rochman

Frost, Helen. *Crossing Stones*. 2009. 184p. Farrar/ Frances Foster (9780374316532). Gr. 7–12.

Two pairs of siblings, Muriel and Ollie Jorgensen and Emma and Frank Norman, have grown up together on adjacent Michigan farms. Hints of romance stir among the group just as WWI breaks out, but independent Muriel refuses Frank's kiss before he leaves for the front. Ollie follows Frank to war, and in letters blackened with censors' ink, he details the battlefield horrors and his sorrow at the news that Frank has been killed. At home, Muriel finds inspiration in her suffragist aunt's protests in Washington D.C., while the more traditional Emma observes, "Making sure everyone is fed / and clothed and cared for—that also takes a kind of pluck." Frost, whose titles include the Printz Honor Book *Keesha's House* (2003), once again offers a layered, moving verse novel. Each selection, alternately narrated by Muriel, Ollie, and Emma, is shaped to reflect the characters' personalities and relationships: Muriel's free-flowing entries indicate her restless curiosity; Emma and Ollie's sonnets follow complementary rhyming patterns, adding a structural link between the characters as they fall in love. The historical details (further discussed in an author's note) and feminist messages are purposeful, but Frost skillfully pulls her characters back from stereotype with their poignant, private, individual voices and nuanced questions, which will hit home with contemporary teens, about how to recover from loss and build a joyful, rewarding future in an unsettled world.
—Gillian Engberg

Gardner, Sally. *The Red Necklace*. 2008. 384p. Dial (9780803731004). Gr. 9–12.

A Gypsy boy, Yann, and the dwarf who has raised him are caught up in drama on and off the stage, where they work with a magician and his automaton. Outside their Parisian theater, revolution is beginning to boil. Inside, the magician is murdered by the villainous Count Kalliovski, who has Yann in his sights as well. So begins a finely crafted tale that crosses years and crisscrosses countries, as Yann becomes a young man with a mission: to save the lovely Sido from her heartless father, even as he struggles with the extraordinary gifts bestowed upon him by his Gypsy heritage. If the success of historical fiction depends on how well setting and story mesh, this is a very successful book, indeed. Gardner sweeps readers into a turbulent time, dissecting eighteenth-century French society and the evolution of the revolution, from a yearning for liberty to a chaotic bloodbath. The history becomes personal when seen through the eyes of an astoundingly rich, carefully drawn cast, whose lives are interwoven like pieces of string in an elaborate cat's cradle. Scores are waiting to be settled on every page; this is a heart-stopper.
—Ilene Cooper

Geras, Adele. *Troy*. 2001. 352p. Harcourt (9780152164928). Gr. 10–12.

Geras frames her latest ambitious novel around the *Iliad*, beginning a decade into the Trojan War. Instead of detailing the battles between gods or men, she imagines the stories of Troy's women, adding new characters to the archetypes in Homer's epic. Orphan sisters Xanthe and Marpessa live in Priam's palace as maids and surrogate daughters to Andromache and Helen, respectively. As the war escalates, pivotal moments from the *Iliad*'s plot serve as backdrop for Xanthe and Marpessa's coming-of-age: while the familiar men (Paris, Achilles, etc.) slay one another, the sisters fall in love with the same man and care for their grieving households. Readers, particularly those unfamiliar with the *Iliad*, may struggle initially with the novel's multiple plot threads. But Geras cleverly fills in gaps with the words of visiting Gods and Gossips, as she tells a sexy, sweeping tale, filled with drama, sassy humor, and vividly imagined domestic details that will be accessible to most older teens (and adults), particularly fans of historical romances. Readers may want to follow this with Clemence McLaren's *Inside the Walls of Troy* (1996) or *Waiting for Odysseus* (2000), both written in women's voices. —Gillian Engberg

Glass, Linzi Alex. *The Year the Gypsies Came*. 2006. 260p. Holt (9780805079999). Gr. 8–11.

Growing up in a wooded Johannesburg suburb 40 years ago, Emily, 12, takes her white privilege for granted. Her anguish is mostly about her parents' daily fights, and when they take in a family of wandering Australians, "Gypsies," she hopes tensions at home will ease. As it turns out, the Gypsy trailer holds unspeakable violence that spills over into Emily's family. Seen through Emily's viewpoint, the characters are one-dimensional: her perfect older sister ("pure and good"); adulterous, narcissistic Mother; cold, distracted Father. In contrast there's Buza, the wise, saintly Zulu night watchman, who teaches and comforts Emily with stories—from Zulu folklore to Mandela's speech in court. What will hold readers in this first novel are the powerful family story and the horror of the racist regime. Buza is Emily's true parent-caregiver, and only later does she confront the distress of his legally enforced, lifelong isolation from his real daughter and family. When Buza is arrested for not having appropriate papers, Emily finally sees the daily police brutality, and the war of apartheid enters her home. —Hazel Rochman

Grant, K. M. *Blue Flame*. 2008. 256p. Walker (9780802796943). Gr. 7–10.

Grant takes thirteenth-century Occitania and anchors its tangled religious and territorial conflicts with the story of two young lovers, Raimon, son of a Cathar weaver, and Yolanda, daughter to the Catholic Count Berenger. Under Berenger's permissive rule, Cathars and Catholics live peacefully, but that changes once signs of the legendary Blue Flame appear. This treasure, said to have been lit when Christ died, is to be returned to the Occitan to keep it "free in the paths of righteousness." As the French king works to conquer Occitania, the land is divided from within: an inquisitor arrives to cleanse away the heretic Cathars, and the atmosphere of fear he breeds causes horrific betrayals on both sides. Raimon and Yolanda must do what they think is right in a time when the true path of righteousness is hidden. Characters are as complex as the moral issues they face, and Grant's nuanced, thought-provoking look at the religious conflicts they face will resonate today. Though the themes are weighty, there is no lack of action, suspense, or romance here as Raimon and Yolanda struggle to save each other. A truly harrowing escape from a burning death and a heartbreaking separation will lead readers eagerly into the next book in the Perfect Fire trilogy. —Krista Hutley

Grant, K. M. *Blood Red Horse*. 2005. 288p. Walker (9780802789600). Gr. 6–9.

In the tradition of Kevin Crossley-Holland's Arthur trilogy and Catherine Jinks' Pagan novels, this epic of the Crusades offers a historical perspective on modern conflicts, and lays bare the gap between propaganda about the Crusades and the "dismal, stinking nightmare" of warfare's reality. Onlookers scoff when 13-year-old William de Granville chooses Hosanna, a charismatic red stallion with a puny, impractical build, for his first warhorse. But after what seems to be a miraculous recovery from a grave injury, Hosanna earns widespread respect and a celebrated place in the campaign for Jerusalem, which William and his elder brother, Gavin, have zealously joined. Left behind is Ellie, who is promised to Gavin but feels more connected to William. Awaiting the Crusaders is the noble strategist Saladin and his young ward, Kamil, who eventually lays claim to Hosanna—and is similarly inspired by the horse's soulful presence. The parallel coming-of-age stories are compelling, and Grant portrays both sides of the conflict without demonizing or idealizing either. The novel's only false note is the overdone mysticism surrounding Hosanna; in the end, perhaps the stallion's most amazing achievement is the way in which its story—the first in a planned trilogy—transcends boundaries of gender and genre, with something to offer fans of equestrian fare, historical fiction, and battlefield drama alike. —Jennifer Mattson

Gratz, Alan. ***Samurai Shortstop.*** **2006. 280p. Dial (9780803730755). Gr. 8–11.**

Growing up in Tokyo in the 1890s, after the emperor outlawed the samurai tradition of his ancestors, Toyo was not trained in the old disciplines. He must find his own path between the old ways and the new ones, which are symbolized for Toyo by the sport he loves: baseball. In the riveting opening scene, Toyo watches his father help Toyo's beloved uncle Koji perform seppuku, a samurai ritual involving disembowelment and decapitation. Soon after this disturbing event, Toyo becomes a boarder at the most esteemed high school in Tokyo. His high hopes are tempered by a brutal hazing inflicted on the entering class, and the ongoing cruelty of the students in power. Under his father's tutelage, Toyo's growing understanding of traditional samurai arts enables him to grow in skill and self-discipline both on and off the playing field. An engaging protagonist in a harsh, difficult situation, Toyo must work to earn the respect of his father and his teammates, but he will have readers' sympathies from the beginning. Unfolding through the convincing portrayals of individuals in turmoil, the story culminates as most baseball novels do—in the big game. An appended author's note discusses Gratz's research and lists his sources. A memorable chronicle of boys' inhumanity to boys, and a testament to enduring values in a time of social change. —Carolyn Phelan

Havill, Juanita. ***Eyes Like Willy's.*** **Illus. by David Johnson. 2004. 144p. HarperCollins (9780688136727). Gr. 6–9.**

In 1906, 10-year-old Guy's family leaves Paris to vacation in a small Austrian village, where he befriends a Viennese boy named Willy. Meeting every summer for several years, Guy and his sister, Sarah, grow closer to their friend, though over the years the boys' interests shift from sailing model boats to building a glider to flirting with the village girls. In 1914, war puts an end to the family's vacations, and in 1915, Guy joins the army, painfully aware that Willy may be in the opposite trenches. Havill's narrative flows through the years so quickly and records Guy's, Sarah's, and Willy's stories so matter-of-factly that readers may be taken unawares by the slowly building emotional power of this short novel. The story's extended time frame might hinder the book from finding its audience: a 10-year-old protagonist may put off older readers, and younger ones may not relate to Guy as a shell-shocked soldier in a sanitarium. Still, this spare, thoughtful story does a superb job of personalizing the pain of this brutal, futile war. One of the few novels for young people set during WWI, the book ends with an author's note providing background information as well as lists of books, films, and Internet sites. —Carolyn Phelan

Hemphill, Stephanie. ***Wicked Girls: A Novel of the Salem Witch Trials.*** **2010. 416p. HarperCollins/Balzer and Bray (9780061853289). Gr. 7–12.**

Hemphill follows her Printz Honor Book *Your Own, Sylvia* (2007) with another bold verse novel based on historical figures. Here, her voices belong to the "afflicted" girls of Salem, whose accusations of witchcraft led to the hangings of 19 townspeople in 1692. Once again, Hemphill's raw, intimate poetry probes behind the abstract facts and creates characters that pulse with complex emotion. According to an appended author's note, unresolved theories about the causes of the girls' behavior range from bread-mold-induced hallucinations to bird flu. In Hemphill's story, the girls fake their afflictions, and the book's great strength lies in its masterful unveiling of the girls' wholly believable motivations: romantic jealousy; boredom; a yearning for friendship, affection, and attention; and most of all, empowerment in a highly constricting and stratified society that left few opportunities for women. Layering the girls' voices in interspersed, lyrical poems that slowly build the psychological drama, Hemphill requires patience from her readers. What emerge are richly developed portraits of Puritanical mean girls, and teens will easily recognize the contemporary parallels in the authentic clique dynamics. An excellent supplementary choice for curricular studies of Arthur Miller's *The Crucible*, this will also find readers outside the classroom, who will savor the accessible, unsettling, piercing lines that connect past and present with timeless conflicts and truths. —Gillian Engberg

Hemphill, Stephanie. ***Your Own, Sylvia*****. 2007. 272p. Knopf (9780375837999). Gr. 9–12.**

As in Margarita Engle's *The Poet Slave of Cuba* (2006), this ambitious portrait uses poetry to illuminate the facts of a famous life, in this case, Sylvia Plath's. Although classified as fiction, the book draws from numerous nonfiction sources, including biographies and Plath's journals and letters, and each poem is accompanied by footnotes grounding Hemphill's imagined scenes within the facts. Rather than write in Plath's voice, Hemphill channels the voices of those who knew the poet in chronologically arranged poems, written from the perspective of family members, friends, colleagues, even Plath's doctor. Plath's own voice is evident in the poetic forms, though, with many of the poems written "in the style of" specific works. The result is an intimate, comprehensive, imaginative view of a life that also probes the relationships between poetry and creativity, mental fragility, love, marriage, and betrayal. Some readers may be slowed by the many poems that chronicle the bitter dissolution of Plath's marriage, and readers who know the Plath poems Hemphill references will have an advantage. But Plath's dramatic genius and personal struggles, particularly the difficulties of reconciling the writing life with the roles of wife and mother, have long attracted teen interest, and this accomplished, creative story may ignite new interest in Plath's original works. A bibliography of sources is appended. —Gillian Engberg

Hijuelos, Oscar. ***Dark Dude*****. 2008. 448p. Atheneum (9781416948049). Gr. 9–12.**

In his first novel for young adults, the Pulitzer Prize–winning author of *The Mambo Kings Play Songs of Love* (1987) proves himself to be a powerful, adept storyteller for teens. Rico, a Cuban American teen growing up in Harlem in the late 1960s, is tired—of working extra jobs to help his family; of the chaos and tragedy at school, where students are so inured to violence that, when classes close after a shooting, they behave "like it was suddenly a holiday"; of being hassled for his light skin and hair. When his parents threaten to send him to a military school in Florida, he runs away. Together with his best friend, Jimmy, who has just kicked a heroin habit, Rico hitchhikes to Wisconsin, where Gilberto, an older-brother figure from Harlem, has bought a farm that he shares with several hippie college students. In an unwavering, utterly believable voice, Rico details his Midwestern year, in which he adjusts to rural life, falls in love, and pursues his comic-book-writing aspirations. Most of all, though, he searches for a sense of self, ultimately realizing that "where you are doesn't change who you are." Frank, gritty, vibrant, and wholly absorbing, Rico's story will hold teens with its celebration of friendship and its fundamental questions about life purpose, family responsibility, and the profound ways that experience shapes identity. —Gillian Engberg

Hilmo, Tess. ***With a Name Like Love*****. 2011. 256p. Farrar/Margaret Ferguson (9780374384654). Gr. 6–9.**

It's 1957, and most people have refrigerators and flushing toilets. But 13-year-old Ollie and her four younger sisters travel with their mother and father, an itinerant preacher who brings his message of salvation and love all over the South. In fact, Ollie's father's name is Everlasting Love, and she knows there's no finer man, anywhere. When the family pulls into Blinder, Arkansas, the plan is, as always, to stay just three days preaching. Then Ollie meets a sad, dirty boy, whose mother is in jail for killing his father, and she knows they've got to stick around and right a wrong. Hilmo's first novel is a small gem of a book. The mystery of who killed Jimmy's father carries the action along, but this is really a family portrait that's suffused with the bickering, hopes, fears, and love found in big families. The supporting cast of Blinder citizens is also carefully drawn, flitting about but never landing on caricature, so the folks seem just a little larger than life. A warm and thoughtful look back. —Ilene Cooper

Hoffman, Alice. ***Incantation*****. 2006. 168p. Little, Brown (9780316010191). Gr. 9–12.**

Growing up in Spain around 1500 in the village where her family has lived for 500 years, Estrella, 16, knows that there are secrets in her home. As books are burned in the streets, and Jews from the nearby ghetto are murdered, she confronts the reality that she is a Marrano, part of a community of underground Jews who attend a special "church." The plot tangent involving Estrella's best friend, Catalina, jealous because Estrella has taken her boyfriend, seems too purposeful, but the historical fact is compelling, with the reason for the secrets spelled out in the horrifying persecution: Estrella is witness to her mother's burning and her brother's bones being broken by the police "one at a time." Acclaimed adult writer Hoffman, whose YA books include *Aquamarine* (2001), makes the history immediate in Estrella's spare, intense first-person narrative, in which tension builds as Estrella discovers her hidden identity. Suggest Deborah Siegel's *The Cross by Day, the Mezuzzah by Night* (1999) or June Weltman's *Mystery of the Missing Candlestick* (2004) to readers wanting other stories about Marranos. —Hazel Rochman

Houston, Julian. ***New Boy.*** **2005. 256p. Houghton (9780618432530). Gr. 8–11.**

As the first black student in an elite Connecticut boarding school in the late 1950s, Rob Garrett, 16, knows he is making history. He works hard not to fall off the honor roll, even as he misses his home in Virginia and feels like a stranger in the dorm and in class. When his friends in the South plan a sit-in against segregation, he knows he must be part of it. The author of this powerful debut novel, now a judge in Massachusetts, writes from the inside about the civil rights struggle, always clear about the blatant racism (the *n*-word is used throughout) and the differences within the African American community as they cut across class, region, and generations. There is almost too much fact woven into the fiction (for example, Rob's history essay about Reconstruction and his visit to Harlem, where he sees Malcolm X), and too much on the debates about integration and black power. But the honest first-person narrative makes stirring drama, touching on the fear and exhilaration of the group protests and the segregation in unexpected places, as well as Rob's personal discovery of failure and courage. A great addition to the history shelves, this brings up much for discussion about then and now. Suggest Viola Canales' *Tequila Worm* (2005) and Marlene Carvell's *Sweetgrass Basket* (2005), which also deal with prejudice at boarding school. —Hazel Rochman

Isaacs, Anne. ***Torn Thread.*** **2000. 192p. Scholastic (9780590603638). Gr. 6–12.**

The author of the uproarious tall tale *Swamp Angel* (1994) moves into a very different mode here in a grim Holocaust novel based on her mother-in-law's experience as a young teenage prisoner in a Nazi labor camp. The focus of Eva's story is always her bond with her fragile older sister, Rachel. They protect, even overprotect, each other, first in the Polish ghetto, and then for two years as prisoners in a Nazi labor camp in Czechoslovakia, where every day, every hour, is a struggle with hunger, disease, cold, and hard labor. Isaacs tells it without exploitation or sentimentality. She shows that there are Poles, and even some Jews, who help the Nazis and that many ordinary people are afraid to do anything or are just "uninterested." There is even one German camp officer who secretly does what he can to help the prisoners. The genocide horror is distanced because this is not a death camp, though Eva witnesses heartrending scenes of prisoners being marched to Auschwitz. Tension builds as the sisters, starving, sick, surrounded by filth, and checking each other's hair for lice, try to stay alive in the last months, one hour at time, until the Allies liberate the camp. As with the brother and sister in Anita Lobel's *No Pretty Pictures* (*Booklist*'s 1998 Top of the List winner for Youth Nonfiction) and in Schoschana Rabinovici's *Thanks to My Mother* (the 1998 Batchelder Award winner), family love is a fact of survival.
—Hazel Rochman

Jansen, Hanna. ***Over a Thousand Hills I Walk with You.*** **Tr. by Elizabeth Crawford. 2006. 344p. Carolrhoda (9781575059273). Gr. 7–10.**

Eight-year-old Jeanne was the only one of her family to survive the 1994 Rwanda genocide. Then a German family adopted her, and her adoptive mother now tells Jeanne's story in a compelling fictionalized biography that stays true to the traumatized child's bewildered viewpoint. Jeanne is witness to unspeakable horror, but the tragedy isn't exploited in her narrative. Nor is Jeanne sentimental about the world she loses: she feels jealous of her sister and distant from her father, and she takes her comfortable Tutsi Catholic home in Kibungo for granted. Readers unfamiliar with the history may be somewhat bewildered. Who are the Tutsis? Who are the Hutus? Why were almost a million people massacred? But that confusion is part of the story. An appended time line fills in some of the facts, but of course, there's no explanation. Woven into the child's story are brief, contemporary commentaries, set in italics, by Jeanne's German mother, who speaks to her child about loss, fury, survivor guilt, and healing. Occasionally, the narrative is too detailed, especially about daily life before the massacre, but Crawford's translation from the German is always clear and eloquent. An elemental account of perpetrators, victims, and bystanders ("And the world looked on. Or looked away"), this book is an important addition to the Holocaust curriculum. —Hazel Rochman

Jiménez, Francisco. *Breaking Through*. 2001. 208p. Houghton (9780618011735). Gr. 6–12.

Jiménez's autobiographical story *The Circuit* (1997) broke new ground with its drama of a Mexican American migrant child in southern California. It won many prizes and was a *Booklist* Editors' Choice selection. This moving sequel is a fictionalized memoir of Jiménez's teenage years in the late 1950s, when the family finally stayed in one place and Francisco and his brothers worked long hours before and after school to put food on the table. First, they picked strawberries in the fields. Later, the jobs got better: cleaning offices, washing windows and walls, waxing floors. The prose here is not as taut as in the first book, but Jiménez writes with simplicity about a harsh world seldom seen in children's books. He also writes about a scary, sad, furious, and broken father—like the father in An Na's *A Step from Heaven* (2001). He stays true to the viewpoint of a teenager growing up poor: the yearning (what would it be like to live in a house, rather than the crowded barracks?); the ignorance (college?); the hurt of prejudice. Yet he celebrates his Mexican roots even as he learns to be an American. The images are powerful, especially the one of the boy cleaning offices before dawn, with notes of English words to memorize in his shirt pocket. An excellent choice for ESL classes, this is a book for many readers, who may discover an America they didn't know was here. —Hazel Rochman

Jiménez, Francisco. *Reaching Out*. 2008. 208p. Houghton (9780618038510). Gr. 7–12.

Papa's raging depression intensifies young Jiménez's personal guilt and conflict in the 1960s: "So now you think you're better than us because you are going to college!" He is the first in his Mexican American migrant family to attend college in California. While at home, the family struggles with backbreaking work and lives without indoor plumbing; in college, Jiménez finds friends and mentors in class and at church, discovers the great literature in his native Spanish language, and joins César Chávez in the drive to unionize farm workers. Like his other fictionalized autobiographies, *The Circuit* (1997) and *Breaking Through* (2001), this sequel tells Jiménez's personal story in self-contained chapters that join together in a stirring narrative. As he works many jobs to send something home, he is haunted by memories of his childhood spent laboring in the fields, and in college, he tells no one that he was born in Mexico and is not an American citizen. Rooted in the past, Jiménez's story is also about the continuing struggle to make it in America, not only for immigrant kids but also for those in poor families. Never melodramatic or self-important, the spare episodes will draw readers with the quiet daily detail of work, anger, sorrow, and hope.
—Hazel Rochman

Jocelyn, Marthe. *Mable Riley: A Reliable Record of Humdrum, Peril, and Romance*. 2004. 288p. Candlewick (9780763621209). Gr. 5–10.

When 14-year-old Mable leaves home in 1901 with her older sister, who becomes a teacher in Stratford, Ontario, she keeps a diary of "humdrum" daily life; she also writes a wry, romantic adventure to entertain herself. Of course, the two works comment on each other, and some kids may end up skipping the made-up romance as Mable finds drama in "real life" not only in her first kiss but also in the exciting struggle of the suffragist movement. Mable makes friends with Mrs. Rattle, a neighbor who dares to wear bloomers, ride a bike, and live without a man. She invites Mable to a Readers' Club that is really a front for political action that climaxes when women in the local cheese factory strike against their appalling working conditions. The message is never strident because the funny, poignant diary entries show family and neighbors without reverence, especially the mentor-troublemaker, who refuses to know "her place" and teaches Mable to risk censure, even prison, rather than settle for something less than what she wants and what is right. —Hazel Rochman

Johnston, Tony. *Bone by Bone by Bone*. 2007. 192p. Roaring Brook/Deborah Brodie (9781596431133). Gr. 6–9.

In a small town in 1950s Tennessee, nine-year-old David, who is white, and Malcolm, who is black, are blood brothers. Although David's racist father has forbidden their friendship, the boys enjoy wild, free-spirited adventures, exploring caves and acting out their favorite stories (Br'er Rabbit). But as the boys grow older and David's father's threats escalate, David wonders if his dad is a member of the Klan. Is his best friend's life in danger? Like most of her characters, Johnston's novel is layered with disturbing contradictions that add depth and a vivid sense of the time and place. Nostalgic scenes of small-town comforts contrast with the horror in the searing accounts of racism, which are true to David's viewpoint, and Johnston's vocabulary reinforces the effect in bone-chilling shifts from gentle, folksy, poetic colloquialisms to brutal racial slurs, including rampant use of the *n*-word. The author, who grew up in the South, begins her book with a charged, personal note: "The raw language . . . is my father's language and reflects a way of thinking that has troubled me my whole life." Readers, too, will feel haunted by this powerful story of a child awakening to family secrets and violence, and the racially motivated terrorism enforced by the Jim Crow South. —Gillian Engberg

Kadohata, Cynthia. *Cracker! The Best Dog in Vietnam*. 2007. 320p. Atheneum (9781416906377). Gr. 6–9.

The author of *Kira-Kira* (2004) and *Weedflower* (2006) tells a stirring, realistic story of America's war in Vietnam, using the alternating viewpoints of an army dog named Cracker and her 17-year-old handler, Rick Hanski, who enlists to "whip the world" and avoid a routine job. From their training at a base in the U.S, complete with mean sergeant and close buddies, to their stalking the enemy, the heartfelt tale explores the close bond of the scout-dog team, relating how it detects booby traps and mines, finds the enemy, rescues POWs, and returns home to a heroes' welcome. Throughout the struggle, the dog and the teenager care for one another. There's no background on the conflict ("he didn't and couldn't understand what he was doing here in Vietnam"). Rather, the focus is on how Cracker uses her senses to help the team accomplish its goals, and on her physical bond with Rick, who understands Cracker's every movement. Give this to readers who liked Gary Paulsen's *Woodsong* (1990). —Hazel Rochman

Kadohata, Cynthia. *Kira-Kira*. 2004. 256p. Atheneum (9780689856396). Gr. 6–12.

Katie Takeshima worships her older sister, Lynn, who knows everything and takes care of Katie while their parents are working long hours in their small Georgia town in the late 1950s. It's Lynn who shows Katie the glittering beauty (*kira-kira*) of the stars and who prepares Katie for the prejudice she will encounter as one of the few Japanese American kids in their school. But when Katie is 10, Lynn, 14, falls ill, and everything changes. Slowly the roles are reversed: Katie becomes caregiver and does what Lynn has taught her. There's no surprise. It's clear that Lynn will die, and Katie goes through all the stages of grief. The real story is in the small details, never self-consciously "poetic" but tense with family drama. In her first novel for young people, Kadohata stays true to the child's viewpoint in plain, beautiful prose that can barely contain the passionate feelings. Just as heart wrenching as the sisters' story is what Katie knows of her father's struggle, whether it's his backbreaking work in the factory or his love for his

family. The quiet words will speak to readers who have lost someone they love—or fear that they could.
—Hazel Rochman

Karr, Kathleen. *The Boxer*. 2000. 144p. Farrar (9780374309213). Gr. 6–9.

This novel, set in New York City in 1885, concerns 15-year-old Johnny Woods, who works in a sweatshop to support his mother and his younger brothers and sisters until he is arrested for boxing at Brodie's Saloon. He's miserable as he begins his six-month prison sentence, but he turns his life around when a fellow inmate with money and influence takes him under his wing and trains him to become a professional boxer. After his release, Johnny works hard to get an education, improve his boxing skills, and get a home in Brooklyn for his family. Among the few historical fiction books for young people that focus on a lower-class character during peace time, this novel has a gritty setting and a clarity of purpose that some readers will find refreshing. The boxing scenes gain credibility through the author's training in the ring.
—Carolyn Phelan

Kent, Trilby. *Medina Hill*. 2009. 176p. Tundra (9780887768880). Gr. 6–9.

In 1935 in London's East End, 11-year-old Dominic has stopped speaking with anyone except his family. Is it because of his growing unease with his peers? "If I was really unlucky, I'd end up in the center of a circle of kids waiting to see me get beaten up." Or is it the tough times at home, with his mum's lungs growing weaker and his dad, a troubled Great War veteran, unable to find a job? Whatever the reason, the disability tortures him—the words are there, but he cannot get them out. When Uncle Roo steps in to take Dominic and his younger sister, Marlo, to his Cornwall village, Medina Hill, for the summer, Dominic is upset and reflects that "grown-up conspiracies are nothing new." What is new to him, though, are the village's eccentric characters; the captivating story of T. E. Lawrence that he discovers in a book; and an interesting new friend, Sancha, a fiercely independent Romany girl with a wooden leg who befriends the shy, speechless city boy. What had every promise of being a lazy, bucolic idyll turns into Dominic's coming-of-age summer. Maybe it's too much to expect this youngster to help turn the town's tide against expelling the Gypsy community from its borders, but Dominic does manage to gradually find his voice and his courage in Kent's highly original debut. —Anne O'Malley

Kerr, M. E. *Slap Your Sides*. 2001. 208p. HarperCollins (9780060294816). Gr. 7–10.

As a Quaker during WWII, teenager Jubal Shoemaker is a pacifist: "If a war comes, I will do everything to oppose it . . . So help me God." The more he prays about it, the surer he is. When it's time for him to be conscripted, he intends to follow his older brother Bud as a conscientious objector. But it's hard in their small Pennsylvania town to be against the war when patriotism is fervent. Jubal's growing relationship with a local young woman ends abruptly when her brother is killed at the front. The ideas are gripping, not only because Kerr is fair to all sides but also because the characters are complicated, arguing with themselves and each other: When it comes to killing civilians, aren't we as guilty as they are? Despite himself, Jubal cries when he hears the patriotic songs. His Quaker dad isn't nearly as strong a pacifist as his wife; the war breaks them both. And the fervent antiwar crusaders aren't particularly likable. The story's shocking ending says it all. —Hazel Rochman

Kerr, M. E. *Your Eyes in Stars*. 2006. 240p. HarperCollins (9780060756826). Gr. 9–12.

From the award-winning *Gentlehands* (1978), in which a teen discovers that his beloved grandfather was a Nazi, to *Slap Your Sides* (2001), about a teen struggling with his pacifist convictions, Kerr's historical fiction moves beyond simplistic divisions of friends and enemies. Her latest haunting novel, set in a small town in upstate New York during the Depression, is told from the perspective of teen characters and explores complex relationships—this time between Germans and Americans, Jews and gentiles. Fourteen-year-old Jessica, the daughter of the local prison's benevolent chief, becomes friends with new neighbor and classmate, Elisa, who is from Germany. While Jessica's mother is glad the newcomers are not Jews, who would bring down property values, Elisa's elitist mother won't even mix with the locals. Interwoven with Jessica's immediate, first-person narrative are stories of a young wrongfully convicted prisoner, a rich businessman bankrupted by the Depression, and an aristocratic, assimilated Jewish family that learns some shocking news. When Elisa returns to Germany, at first her letters are warm, but then they change. It's hard not to wonder if she has joined the Hitler Youth. Although there is a lot going on, secrets, intimate and political, drive the plot, expanding the warm friendship and coming-of-age story to reveal big issues of racism, class, and patriotism. —Hazel Rochman

Kindl, Patrice. *Keeping the Castle*. 2012. 224p. Viking (9780670014385). Gr. 7–11.

Seventeen-year-old Althea Crawley is facing a plight familiar to characters in Dodie Smith's *I Capture the Castle* (1949), Jane Austen's *Pride and Prejudice*, and PBS' *Downton Abbey*: "Perhaps one day women might be able to choose their husbands with no thought of money and position, but not in this day and age in Lesser Hoo, Yorkshire, England." Althea is on a quest to marry rich so that she may secure the family's only inheritance, a dilapidated castle on the edge of the North Sea. She also bears the burden of supporting her widowed mother, four-year-old brother, and two sour, wealthy stepsisters, who refuse to contribute financially to the household. Marriage prospects in tiny Lesser Hoo are slim, to say the least, until dashing and wealthy Lord Boring arrives on the scene. Matters are further complicated by a revolving cast of potential suitors, including Lord Boring's cousin, Mr. Fredericks, who is the Mr. Darcy to Althea's Elizabeth Bennet. As with any respectable story set in England in the nineteenth or early twentieth century, the ending is jam-packed with revelations, only some of which are surprising. In her first novel in a decade, Kindl (*Goose Chase*, 2001) writes with sharp, effervescent, period-specific language that is so spot-on readers may find themselves adopting a British accent. This witty take on classic Regency romances is frothy fun for YA Anglophiles. —Ann Kelley

Klass, Sheila Soloman. *Soldier's Secret: The Story of Deborah Sampson*. 2009. 224p. Holt/Christy Ottaviano (9780805082005). Gr. 6–9.

The author's note and chronology that close this novel give what little facts are known about the real Deborah Sampson: her penniless mother sold her into indentured servitude in 1768, during which time she educated herself, secretly learned to dress and act as a boy, and served in the Continental army for 17 months. Klass expertly fills in the gaps, drawing a portrait of a proud girl who, from her early fascination with Joan of Arc, becomes entranced with the idea of a real-life "heroine." Sampson, who fights under the pseudonym Robert Shurtliff, is strong, brave, and witty, yet as scared as any 22-year-old woman would be living among soldiers who might very well kill her for the offense of wearing britches. Klass doesn't shy away from the horrors of battle; she is also blunt regarding details young readers will wonder about, like how Sampson dealt with bathing, urination, and menstruation. What could have been a groan-worthy subplot—Sampson's romantic yearnings for a fellow soldier—is given just the right notes of restraint and realism. An admirable accomplishment, and a strong candidate to play alongside Anita Silvey's *I'll Pass for Your Comrade* (2008). —Daniel Kraus

Krinitz, Esther Nisenthal, and Bernice Steinhardt. *Memories of Survival*. Illus. by Bernice Steinhardt. 2005. 64p. Hyperion (9780786851263). Gr. 6–9.

During the many years before her death in 2000, Krinitz set down the story of her Holocaust survival in a series of 36 exquisite, hand-embroidered fabric collages and hand-stitched narrative captions. For this picture-book presentation, Steinhardt, Krinitz's daughter, reproduced those panels, adding eloquent commentary to fill in the facts and the history. The first panels show Esther, 10, with her loving family in a small Polish village in 1937 before the Nazis come. The soldiers arrive in 1939. When Esther is 15, they take her family away, and she never sees them again. She and her sister survive by hiding in the woods, and then, disguised as Polish Catholic farm girls, are taken in by a kind farmer. After the Russians come, Esther sees the death camps. The telling is quiet, and the hand-stitched pictures are incredibly detailed, with depth and color that will make readers look closely, whether at a scene of the communal baking before the war, a line of refugees and prisoners, or a picture of giant cabbages growing on human ashes in a corner of the death camps. Connect this to Jacqueline Woodson's *Show Way* (2005), about the quilts sewn by African American women from slavery times through today. —Hazel Rochman

Krisher, Trudy. *Uncommon Faith*. 2003. 263p. Holiday (9780823417919). Gr. 7–10.

In this novel by the author of *Spite Fences* (1994), multiple narratives offer a kaleidoscopic view of Millbrook, Massachusetts, in 1837–1838. Most of the 10 narrators, who often contribute no more than a page or two at a time, are young people in the community, but older citizens have their say—and their share of secrets. The frequent changes of narrator slow the story's pace in the beginning, when it is difficult to recognize voices and keep the large cast of characters straight. Readers will find themselves frequently turning back to the invaluable chart, "Families of Millbrook." Title character Faith Common is a quick-witted, brave young woman looking for her path in a family with rigid expectations and a society with limited roles for women. That issue, along with the dominance of religion and the issue of slavery, is among the themes developed in the book. The increasingly distinctive voices make this multilayered story richer and more compelling as it progresses. —Carolyn Phelan

Landman, Tanya. *The Goldsmith's Daughter*. 2009. 304p. Candlewick (9780763642198). Gr. 9–12.

For any author taking on the fall of the Aztec Empire, the danger is not being up to the event's inherent drama and tragedy. But Landman vanquishes such doubts with this pulse-pounding yet sensitive saga of a girl's struggle for true freedom. Itacate, ill-favored by the gods since birth, is 15 when her goldsmith father becomes aware of her artistic gifts. She is overjoyed to be welcomed into his workshop—anything to escape the drudgery of the kitchen and loom—but her happiness is snuffed by the jealousy of her twin brother, who retaliates by getting himself chosen as the holy sacrifice in next year's Tezcatlipoca festivities. Itacate privately rages against Tenochtitlán's bloodthirsty gods, but soon there are more immediate nemeses with their own unquenched thirsts: Spaniards. Using sturdy, almost old-fashioned prose, Landman constructs an immersive world that acknowledges both the Aztecs' brutality and sophistication. The romance that dominates the book's latter half does carry a few false notes, but it perfectly distills a culture clash that could only lead to doom. Though harrowing in spots, this has enough restraint to capture female, male, and adult readers alike. —Daniel Kraus

Larson, Kirby. *Hattie Big Sky*. 2006. 304p. Delacorte (9780385733137). Gr. 7–10.

In this engaging historical novel set in 1918, 16-year-old orphan Hattie Brooks leaves Iowa and travels to a Montana homestead inherited from her uncle. In the beautiful but harsh setting, she has less than a year to fence and cultivate the land in order to keep it. Neighbors who welcome Hattie help heal the hurt she has suffered from years of feeling unwanted. Chapters open with short articles that Hattie writes for an Iowa newspaper or her lively letters to a friend and possible beau who is in the military in France. The authentic first-person narrative, full of hope and anxiety, effectively portrays Hattie's struggles as a young woman with limited options, a homesteader facing terrible odds, and a loyal citizen confused about the war and the local anti-German bias that endangers her new friends. Larson, whose great-grandmother homesteaded alone in Montana, read dozens of homesteaders' journals and based scenes in the book on real events. Writing in figurative language that draws on nature and domestic detail to infuse her story with the sounds, smells, and sights of the prairie, she creates a richly textured novel full of memorable characters. —Kathleen Odean

Lasky, Kathryn. *Ashes*. 2010. 320p. Viking (9780670011575). Gr. 6–12.

In 1932 Berlin, blond 13-year-old Gabriella looks like the Aryan purists' ideal, but her strongly anti-Fascist

family members are derisively called "white Jews," and her astrophysicist father is friends with Einstein, whose theory of relativity is termed "Jewish physics" by the Nazis. From Gabriella's viewpoint, Lasky tells a gripping story about Hitler's early rise to power, including the Germans' bitterness about their suffering after WWI. Though the filling in of background history sometimes feels slightly contrived, the story is strengthened by the complex, individual characters, such as the pro-Hitler maid who is tired of being poor; the beloved teacher, who wants Gabriella to be a Hitler Youth leader; and Gabriella's sister, who becomes pregnant while dating an ardent Nazi. Like Anne Frank, Gabriella loves American movie stars. She is also a big reader, and at the start of each chapter, there is a quote from authors such as Hemingway, Heine, London, Remarque, and Twain, whose books are among those publicly destroyed in the wild, historic book burning that is the climax of this story. From the opening quote, by Heine—"Where they burn books, they will end by burning human beings"—the personal and the political history will haunt readers.
—Hazel Rochman

Lawrence, Iain. *Ghost Boy*. 2000. 326p. Delacorte (9780385327398). Gr. 7–10.

Painfully tall and thin and nearly blind, albino Harold Kline has been the focus of harassment in his small town since childhood. Now at 14, in a desperate escape from misery and loneliness, he runs away, joining a small circus en route to Oregon. Gradually, he wins acceptance from the other "freaks"—loving Princess Minikin; gruff, hairy Samuel the Fossil Man; and the omniscient Gypsy Magda. When he teaches the three lumbering circus elephants how to play baseball, the lovely Flip and Mr. Hunter, the circus owner, also accept him. Set shortly after WWII, this is a surprising book, full of pain and poignancy, with gratifying undercurrents of love and humor. The dark subject matter may make this book difficult to sell, even though the writing is good, and the bizarre characters are both sympathetic and believable. Still, teens that stick with Harold on his odyssey of discovery and self-acceptance will be rewarded by an intriguing novel that pushes the boundaries of reality.
—Frances Bradburn

Lawrence, Iain. *B for Buster*. 2004. 320p. Delacorte (9780385730860). Gr. 7–12.

Set during the spring of 1943, Lawrence's novel is a harrowing account of combat told from the perspective of 16-year-old Kak. Like Jack in Harry Mazer's *The Last Mission* (1979), Kak lies about his age in order to join the air force. But Jack, a Jewish American, wants to fight Hitler; Kak, nicknamed for his tiny Canadian hometown, just wants to flee his loveless, abusive parents and "like Captain Marvel . . . change [himself] from a boy to a hero." After his first "op," though, Kak is deeply shaken. Bert, who cares for the pigeons, finds a way to comfort the boy by putting a prize pigeon in his care. The dense mechanical specifics of planes and equipment may slow some readers, but the tender lessons of courage that Kak learns from Bert and his bird are captivating. In Kak's young, raw voice, Lawrence writes a gripping, affecting story about the thrill of flying, the terrifying realities of war, and the agony of reconciling personal fears and ideals with duty and bravery. —Gillian Engberg

Lester, Julius. *Day of Tears*. 2005. 176p. Disney/Jump at the Sun (9780786804900). Gr. 9–12.

From his first book, *To Be a Slave* (1968), Lester has told the history of slavery through personal accounts that relay the dehumanizing message of the perpetrators. Here he draws on historical sources to fictionalize a real event: the biggest slave auction in American history, which took place in Savannah, Georgia, in 1859. He imagines the individual voices of many who were there, adults and kids, including several slaves up for sale, the auctioneer, and the white masters and their families buying and selling the valuable merchandise. The huge cast speaks in the present tense and sometimes from the future looking back. A note fills in the facts. The horror of the auction and its aftermath is unforgettable; individuals whom the reader has come to know are handled like animals, wrenched from family, friends, and love. Then there's a sales list with names, ages, and the amount taken in for each person. Brave runaways speak; so does an abolitionist who helps them. Those who are not heroic are here, too, and the racism is virulent (there's widespread use of the *n*-word). The personal voices make this a stirring text for group discussion. —Hazel Rochman

Magoon, Kekla. ***Fire in the Streets*****. 2012. 336p. Aladdin (9781442422308). Gr. 6–10.**

In this powerful sequel to the multiple award winner *The Rock and the River* (2009), the viewpoint shifts from Sam to his former girlfriend, Maxie, 14. Her first-person, present-tense narrative sets her intense story against the political struggle in 1968 Chicago, where she joins her older brother, Raheem, in the militant Black Panther party and strives to fight a racist system. While white protestors are busy with antiwar demonstrations, Maxie's people are fighting an actual war. As she attends the Panthers' political-education classes and helps in their health clinic, she knows for herself what poverty means: "A high standard of living means always having food and shelter and a warm coat in the winter." She tries to get close again with Sam, who cannot get over the assassination of his Panther brother. Why is Sam meeting a white guy in a car outside the clinic? Close with her girlfriends, she loves Raheem, who struggles to support their family, including their unemployed single-parent mom, in a tiny apartment. Who is betraying the Panthers? What should Maxie do when she finds out the truth? Tension builds to the very end, and the shocking climax is unforgettable. The personal struggle moves the politics beyond rhetoric. —Hazel Rochman

Magoon, Kekla. ***The Rock and the River*****. 2009. 208p. Aladdin (9781416975823). Gr. 6–10.**

In Chicago in 1968, Sam, 14, obeys his father, an eloquent civil rights leader who is close with Dr. King and is passionately committed to nonviolent protest. But after King is assassinated and Sam witnesses police brutality toward a friend, Sam follows his rebellious older brother, Stephen ("Stick"), and joins the Black Panthers, whose revolutionary platform is the opposite of the nonviolent philosophy that Sam has been taught at home. Then Sam's father is stabbed. Will the brothers retaliate with violence? True to the young teen's viewpoint, this taut, eloquent first novel will make readers feel what it was like to be young, black, and militant 40 years ago, including the seething fury and desperation over the daily discrimination that drove the oppressed to fight back. Sam's middle-class family is loving and loyal, even when their quarrels are intense; and Magoon draws the characters without sentimentality. Along with the family drama, the politics will grab readers, especially the Panthers' political education classes and their call for "land, bread, housing, education, clothing, justice, and peace." A long author's note fills in background in this important title for YA American history classes. —Hazel Rochman

Mankell, Henning. ***A Bridge to the Stars*****. 2007. 176p. Delacorte (9780385734950). Gr. 6–9.**

It all started with the solitary dog, the one that 11-year-old Joel saw from the hall window that bitterly cold winter night in 1956. Where was it heading? To a star, perhaps? Joel vows to find out, and each night thereafter, he slips outside to search for the dog while his lumberjack father, blissfully unaware, snores away in the next bedroom. Then one night, Joel returns home to find his father is gone. He can't help wondering if Dad has abandoned him like his mother did years earlier. Joel is desperate until he discovers that his lonely father has spent the night with a local barmaid. Could she become Joel's new mother? Clearly things are changing in his family and in their small village in the far north of Sweden. "Something's got to happen," he thinks. And so it does in this quiet but deeply satisfying coming-of-age story by the internationally celebrated Swedish author of the adult mystery series featuring Inspector Kurt Wallander. Mankell's unhurried pace is not for every child-reader, but those who welcome character-driven fiction will treasure this beautifully realized novel. —Michael Cart

Manzano, Sonia. ***The Revolution of Evelyn Serrano*****. 2012. 224p. Scholastic (9780545325059). Gr. 6–9.**

Starting with the title, this wry, moving debut novel does a great job of blending the personal and the political without denigrating either. Growing up in the Puerto Rican East Harlem barrio in 1969, Rosa, 14, changes her name to Evelyn and tries to be more mainstream.

Then her activist *abuela* arrives from Puerto Rico and moves in, and Evelyn feels as if she's found "an older overdone version of me." Abuela inspires Evelyn to join the Young Lords, the political activists who are working closely with the Black Panthers and fighting for Puerto Rican rights. But Evelyn's mama does not approve, especially when the activists occupy the neighborhood church to demand food and shelter for the poor. Evelyn's first-person narrative is filled with irreverent one-liners, but it never denies the realism of daily struggle: the "heat and stink of our neighborhood." Rooted in the author's own experience, the teen's intense narrative is set against real-life political events (reports from the *New York Times* are documented in an appendix), while the family drama and revelations continue right up to the end. —Hazel Rochman

Mazer, Harry. ***A Boy at War: A Novel of Pearl Harbor*****. 2001. 105p. Simon & Schuster (9780689841613). Gr. 7–9.**

This is one of those stories that divides cleanly into before, during, and after. Adam lives with his military family in Honolulu and tries to make friends with the civilian kids at his high school. Tension builds over his father's implied order that Adam must not have friends whose parents are Japanese, and Adam's growing camaraderie with Davi Mori. Adam, Davi, and their Hawaiian compatriot, Martin, are fishing in Pearl Harbor when the Japanese planes begin to fire. The scenes that follow are not for the fainthearted: Adam's father's ship is bombed and sinking, Martin is wounded, and Davi is struck down by an American sailor. Then, Adam boards the West Virginia during a bloody battle. The chaos subsides, but the bitterness of prejudice and the numbness following his father's death remain with Adam. Written in the third person, a refreshing change of pace in historical fiction today, this economical story will grab readers from the beginning and draw them into Adam's point of view. Readers' ready identification with Adam, son of an authoritarian father and new boy at school, makes his electrifying experiences during the attack all the more riveting. With clearly drawn, sympathetic characters and a gripping story, this memorable novel lends itself to booktalks. —Carolyn Phelan

McCaughrean, Geraldine. ***Cyrano*****. 2006. 128p. Harcourt (9780152058050). Gr. 7–10.**

With a beautiful mix of swashbuckling action, witty insult, passionate love, and heartbreaking melancholy, British Carnegie Medalist McCaughrean retells the story of the classic French play about Cyrano de Bergerac. A champion swordsman and brilliant sardonic wit, he is a celebrity in Paris society and on the battlefield, the epitome of panache with his swagger and irreverence. But all his life he has loved his beautiful young cousin, Roxanne, and she cannot see beyond his ugly face with its huge nose. So Cyrano writes eloquent love letters to her, which he gives to Christian, a young, handsome soldier, and, of course, Roxanne falls in love with what she thinks is Christian's soul. Although Cyrano's brash invective is hilarious—not only about the society fops and his powerful, pompous enemies but also about his "sundial" face ("When you have a cold, monsieur, Belgium floods!")—his letters are heartbreaking. The timeless love story, tenderly told in plain poetry, will thrill teens, especially those who want a hero with flair and integrity. Great for readers' theater and for reading aloud. —Hazel Rochman

McCaughrean, Geraldine. ***The Kite Rider*****. 2002. 240p. HarperCollins (9780066238746). Gr. 6–9.**

Twelve-year-old Haoyou watches in horror as his father dies as a result of being sent aloft tied to the mast as a "wind tester" to predict the success of a ship's voyage. When Di Chou, the ship's brutal first mate, who ordered the wind test, plans to marry Haoyou's newly widowed mother, the boy, with the help of Mipeng, a distant cousin, takes action. To prevent the wedding, he signs a very drunk Di Chou aboard a different ship and volunteers himself as the new wind tester so the ship can leave before the first mate comes to his senses. Haoyou's exploit leads to his becoming a kite rider for a traveling circus. Mipeng, who is considered to be a medium, helps Haoyou by serving as his link to the sky spirits. The story is a genuine page-turner, with the tension increasing after the circus performs for the capricious Kublai Khan and when Di Chou comes back into the picture. McCaughrean fully immerses her memorable characters in the culture and lore of the ancient Chinese and Mongols, which makes this not only a solid adventure story but also a window to a fascinating time and place rarely used as a background in children's fiction. —Sally Estes

McCormick, Patricia. *Never Fall Down*. **2012. 224p. HarperCollins/Balzer and Bray (9780061730931). Gr. 9–12.**

McCormick, the acclaimed author of *Sold* (2006) and *Purple Heart* (2009), has now written a novel based on the life of Cambodian peace advocate Arn Chorn-Pond. The story begins with an 11-year-old Arn in 1975 in Battambang, Cambodia. The war between the government forces and the Khmer Rouge is remote until the day the Khmer Rouge arrive in his town and, taking all the children captive, march them into the countryside, where they become, essentially, slave laborers. Arn survives the killing fields through a combination of luck and musical ability. But his life changes again when Vietnamese forces invade Cambodia and, overnight, the boy is forced to become a Khmer Rouge soldier. He will eventually escape to Thailand and then to the U.S., but the four years of genocide in between are an unspeakable experience of suffering, torture, and death. This is not an easy book to read, as it unveils the truth about one of the most hideous examples of inhumanity in the twentieth or any other century. McCormick has done a remarkable job of creating an authentic first-person voice for Arn and using it to lay bare his almost unimaginable experiences of horror. The resulting book is powerfully, hauntingly unforgettable. —Michael Cart

Mead, Alice. *Girl of Kosovo*. **2001. 128p. Farrar (9780374326203). Gr. 5–10.**

Based on the experience of one Albanian family caught up in the ethnic wars in Kosovo, this moving novel tells the story through the eyes of a young girl, Zana Dugolli, 11, who sees her father and two of her brothers killed in an attack on her village. Her foot is smashed, and she spends months alone in the hospital, shocked and depressed. When she returns home, she sees killers round up people in her schoolyard. Her enraged older brother joins the terrorist underground, but Zana hears her father's voice in her head: "Don't let them fill your heart with hate." There's no exploitation of the brutality, but the facts are devastating. Mead provides a historical introduction about the conflict as well as an afterword about her own 1999 visits to refugee camps. But readers will see that Zana can't make out the politics—she doesn't care about Serbs or Albanians or NATO. She knows that in war everyone becomes an enemy. The power in the story is the personal drama, especially Zana's enduring bond with her Serbian best friend and neighbor. There's much to talk about. Add this to the Holocaust curriculum. —Hazel Rochman

Meyer, L. A. *Bloody Jack: Being an Account of the Curious Adventures of Mary "Jacky" Faber, Ship's Boy*. **2002. 288p. Harcourt (9780152167318). Gr. 6–9.**

At the age of 12 or so, Mary lives by her wits, begging and stealing on the streets of London, and sleeps under Blackfriars Bridge with a small gang of orphans. When her friend Charlie is murdered, she dons his clothes, calls herself Jacky Faber, and signs on as a ship's boy on the *Dolphin*, a Royal Navy frigate. In addition to dealing with the challenges of learning how to do her job and stay out of trouble, she must hide her gender while dealing with unexpected changes in her body and her emotions. When she falls in love with one of her shipmates and reveals her secret to him, the two of them have even more to hide. From shooting a pirate in battle to foiling a shipmate's sexual attack to surviving when stranded alone on a Caribbean island, the action in Jacky's tale will entertain readers with a taste for adventure. Phrases from old ballads echo through the text as well as some of the chapter headings, adding to the period feel of the telling. A first novel with a strong voice that is also a memorable piece of historical fiction. —Carolyn Phelan

Meyer, L. A. *Curse of the Blue Tattoo: Being an Account of the Misadventures of Jacky Faber, Midshipman and Fine Lady*. **2004. 384p. Harcourt (9780152051150). Gr. 6–9.**

Taking up where the original story of *Bloody Jack* (2002) left off, this early-nineteenth-century adventure story begins with Jacky Faber, no longer disguised as a ship's boy, leaving the *Dolphin* and going to her new home, the Lawson Peabody School for Young Girls. There Mistress Pimm takes on the formidable task of transforming the indomitable scamp into a young lady. Good-hearted but spirited and unconventional, Jacky tries to learn, but finds it impossible to conform to an ideal of womanhood that does not include "lewd" exhibitions of singing and dancing, dressing in men's clothing, consorting with drunkards and prostitutes, and using language as salty as any sailor's. Though her boldness puts her in situations dangerous to her safety and her virtue, Jacky manages to bring the complete downfall of a detestable preacher and good fortune to her many friends. The characterizations are undeniably broad, but one of the riches of this entertaining novel is the large, Dickensian cast of colorfully named figures—e.g., the enigmatic theatrical duo Mr. Fennel and Mr. Bean. Happily, the book's conclusion promises a sequel with Jacky at sea once more. —Carolyn Phelan

Miller, Sarah. *Miss Spitfire: Reaching Helen Keller*. 2007. 240p. Atheneum (9781416925422). Gr. 8–11.

Miller's accomplished debut imagines Annie Sullivan's first experiences with her famous pupil, Helen Keller, from the young teacher's train ride to Alabama, during which she anticipated teaching a charge who had "no words, only sensations," to the breakthrough at the water pump, where she taught Helen to use language. Miller bases her story on Sullivan's letters, excerpts of which begin each chapter, and in Sullivan's voice, Miller muses about the monumental questions and challenges that she faced: "It's up to me to show [Helen] that communication between people exists at all." Many lengthy passages detailing the wild, messy intimacy and the violent physical altercations between Sullivan and young Helen may tire some readers, but they amplify the visceral sense of Sullivan's exhausting struggle. In language that often reads like poetry, Miller creates a strong portrait of Sullivan's accomplishments, as well as her character—volatile, ferociously intelligent, and yearning for love and belonging, just like Helen. "Words bridge the gaps between two minds. Words are a miracle," Sullivan says. Miller's words reach beyond the historical facts here, encouraging readers to think about the small miracles of connection they can accomplish with language every day. Photos, a chronology, and an extensive bibliography conclude this stirring, fictionalized account. —Gillian Engberg

Miller-Lachmann, Lyn. *Gringolandia*. 2009. 290p. Curbstone (9781931896498). Gr. 9–12.

Imprisoned and brutally tortured for six years by the Pinochet military dictatorship in Chile, Daniel Aguilar's activist father, Marcelo, is finally released in 1986 and allowed to join his refugee family in Madison, Wisconsin. Papa is crippled, angry, and haunted by thoughts of those he left behind. The story is told in alternating first-person, present-tense narratives by Daniel, 17, and his activist girlfriend, Courtney, who writes letters to Pinochet urging Marcelo's release. Starting with the first chapter, the descriptions of torture are detailed. But this novel covers crucial historical events that have been too long ignored. Most compelling are the teens' nonreverential narratives about living with a survivor. Half-paralyzed, Papa stinks of vomit, stale alcohol, and cigarettes. He rages at his wife, and the damage spreads to Daniel and Courtney. The strength of this novel is the honesty of Daniel's mixed feelings about "my father, the freedom fighter."—Hazel Rochman

Morpurgo, Michael. *Private Peaceful*. 2004. 208p. Scholastic (9780439636483). Gr. 7–12.

In this WWI story, the terse and beautiful narrative of a young English soldier is as compelling about the world left behind as about the horrific daily details of trench warfare: the mud, rats, gas attacks, and slaughter. At 15, Thomas lied about his age in order to follow his beloved older brother, Charlie, to fight in France. Now, nearly two years later, as Thomas sits waiting in the dark for the horror he knows will come at dawn, he remembers it all. Growing up as a poor farm boy in a happy family, he was always close to Charlie and to their brain-injured brother, Joe, a character Morpurgo draws with rare tenderness and truth. Thomas and Charlie even loved the same girl;

Charley married her, but she writes to them both. Thomas also remembers British brutality, from the landlord who threatened the family with eviction if Charlie didn't enlist to the cruel army sergeant who tried to break Charlie's spirit. Charlie may be too perfect, almost a Christ figure, but it's Thomas' viewpoint of the brother he loves. Suspense builds right to the end, which is shocking, honest, and unforgettable. —Hazel Rochman

Myers, Anna. *Tulsa Burning*. 2002. 184p. Walker (9780802788290). Gr. 8–10.

When abusive, good-for-nothing Pa was alive, 15-year-old Noble was "just something to hit"—certainly not someone who would be allowed to pursue an education, let alone his friendship with the "coloreds" down the road. Far from being liberated by his father's death, however, he and his mother must still struggle when they move in with the corrupt, racist town sheriff and his ailing wife because "banks don't put no stock in half-growed boys and worn-out women." Noble's coming-of-age story—complete with "impure thoughts" about childhood friend Cinda, his raw hatred for the sheriff, and conflicted feelings about his late father—is set in rural Oklahoma in 1921, around the time that an actual race riot occurred in Tulsa. In this emotional page-turner, Myers expertly captures an era of poisonous racism while conveying the strong, true voice of a courageous young man who puts himself on the line twice for his black friend Isaac and gradually discovers the difference between fighting for justice and plain vengeance. Compassion and hope prevail in a powerful novel. —Karin Snelson

Myers, Walter Dean. *Riot*. 2009. 192p. Egmont (9781606840009). Gr. 7–12.

In this fast, dramatic novel told in screenplay format, Myers takes on a controversial historical conflict that is seldom written about: the New York Draft Riots of 1863, when struggling Irish immigrants protested being called up by Lincoln to "die for the darkies" in the Civil War. The story focuses on 15-year-old Claire, the biracial daughter of a black man and a white Irishwoman. The diverse voices, from all sides—black, white, and mixed race; soldier and policeman; racist, looter, and victim—will draw readers into the fiery debates. "The swells are looking to send us off to fight for the Colored," says an angry Irishman who has nothing. "Coloreds don't have nothing either," is one reply. There are no easy resolutions, idealized characters, or stereotypes, and the conflicts are unforgettable. A policeman does not want to shoot the looters. A weary soldier "clean forgot what this war was about." Maeve, a bigoted white teen, does change in the end, but only a little. Great for readers' theater, this is sure to spark discussion about race, class, conflict, and loyalty, then and now. —Hazel Rochman

Naidoo, Beverly. *Burn My Heart*. 2009. 224p. HarperCollins/Amistad (9780061432972). Gr. 7–12.

On a Kenyan farm in the early 1950s, Matthew, 11, and Mugo, 13, are friends but not equals. Long ago, Matthew's white grandfather had sailed from England and "acquired" 5,000 acres. Mugo's Kikuyu grandfather lost his ancestral land, and his family was forced to work as laborers for the white settlers. Now the Mau Mau rebels are determined to reclaim land from the whites in a violent uprising. Matthew's dad is sure his workers are loyal. But after a fire on the farm rages out of control, Mugo's family is falsely accused of arson, Mugo witnesses his father's torture in prison, and the family is detained without trial in a forced labor camp. As in Naidoo's previous historical novels, including the apartheid story *Journey to Jo'burg* (1986), the politics are sharply personalized through the daily lives of young people. Naidoo's afterword fills in more historical background. The dramatic plot is riveting (who started the fire?), and so is the setting, where wild animals and people live close to each other. Told from the alternating third-person viewpoints of Mugo and Matthew, the friendship story is haunting, and the terse narratives show the differences within each community. Mugo's older brother joins the Mau Mau. Matthew's white neighbors are rabid racists. Many readers will find parallels to contemporary questions about the differences between terrorists and freedom fighters. —Hazel Rochman

Naidoo, Beverley. ***Out of Bounds: Seven Stories of Conflict and Hope.*** **2003. 192p. HarperCollins (9780060507992). Gr. 6–10.**

Each of these short stories, set in a different decade in South Africa, from the 1950s onward, personalizes the political oppression and struggle from the viewpoint of a child. What was it like to be a "Coloured" (mixed-race) child under apartheid and be separated from your father when he was reclassified as black? To be a white boy shunned at school because your "Commie" parents have "native" friends? To hear your mother ordered around and called "girl" by her white employer? Or to be one of the first black students in an all-white school that doesn't want you? More docudrama than fiction, this book doesn't have the depth and complexity of Naidoo's *The Other Side of Truth* (2001), but Naidoo knows her country's history—the crude, ignorant racism, the suffering, the courage—and her diverse young viewpoints bring the politics of oppression and struggle into daily life. This will be an invaluable starting point for group discussion about contemporary South African history, especially when read with the introductory historical overview and the endnotes about each decade. Archbishop Tutu's moving foreword speaks of the incredible absence of revenge and retribution in the new South Africa, and many of these stories show that hope lies in personal connections. —Hazel Rochman

Napoli, Donna Jo. ***Alligator Bayou.*** **2009. 288p. Random/Wendy Lamb (9780385746540). Gr. 7–10.**

In 1899, five Sicilian immigrants were lynched in small Tallulah, Louisiana. The facts from this little-told chapter in American history frame Napoli's wrenching novel about a 14-year-old Sicilian, Calogero, who joins male relatives in Tallulah after his mother's death. Legally segregated from both whites and blacks, the Italians maintain an insular life, focused on their thriving produce business, until Calo's secret crush on African American Patricia begins to dissolve social barriers between the two communities, even as tensions with whites escalate into shocking violence. Through Calo's active questioning, Napoli integrates a great deal of background history that is further explored in an extensive author's note. Readers learn, right along with naive Calo, the draconian specifics of Jim Crow laws and the complex factors of fear and economics that fueled the South's entrenched bigotry. A few passages do have a purposeful feel, particularly those between Calo and his tutor, but Napoli's skillful pacing and fascinating detail combine in a gripping story that sheds cold, new light on Southern history and on the nature of racial prejudice. —Gillian Engberg

Napoli, Donna. ***Bound.*** **2004. 192p. Atheneum (9780689861758). Gr. 7–12.**

Drawing from traditional Chinese Cinderella stories, Napoli sets this tale in a small village during China's Ming period. Since her beloved father's death, Xing Xing has become "hardly more than a slave," serving her acrimonious stepmother and pitiable stepsister, Wei Ping, whose botched, bloody foot binding has left her perilously unwell. A dangerous trip in search of medicine for Wei Ping brings Xing Xing into the wider world, but she returns to find home more treacherous than before. Napoli creates strong, unforgettable characters—particularly talented, sympathetic Xing Xing—and her haunting, sometimes violent tale amplifies themes from well-known Western Cinderella stories, making them fascinating questions: Could ancestors serve as "fairy godmothers"? In a society that so grossly undervalues females, what does "happily ever after" really mean? Teens and teachers will want to discuss the layered themes of freedom, captivity, love, human rights, and creative endeavor within this powerful survival story, which, like the yin and yang forces Xing Xing thinks about, balances between terror and tenderness, and is both subversive and rooted in tradition. —Gillian Engberg

Newth, Mette. ***The Transformation.*** **2000. 208p. Farrar (9780374377526). Gr. 8–12.**

Set in fifteenth-century Greenland, this story brings together two very different people. Navarana is an Inuit girl who, along with her people, is suffering through desperately difficult climatic change: an endless winter. Brendan is a monk, sent to Greenland to convert the heathens. When Navarana first stumbles across Brendan, he is almost frozen and survives only with Navarana's mostly patient (sometimes impatient) care. The experience brings the two together physically, but there are resounding clashes as they try to forge a relationship spiritually and emotionally while remaining true to their own beliefs. Navarana, who is learning to be a shaman, is in many ways the more easily recognizable character: the brave, smart, female risk taker is a familiar icon to readers. But Brendan, though equally interesting, is more obscure: he is fully invested in his religion and secure in his own superiority, but he's still the fragile little boy who was kidnapped from his mother. Newth transcends mere characterization to paint the philosophical questions that separate these characters. Without sermonizing, she brilliantly shows two different life views that must somehow be reconciled so Brendan and Navarana can be together. The story is also a cracking good adventure, with danger around every ice floe. Only the ending, in which a pregnant Navarana must go on a vision quest to rescue the sun, and so end the winter, seems oddly anticlimactic. Ingwersen's translation from the Norwegian is a lyrical gem. This is beautifully crafted in many ways. —Ilene Cooper

Nuzum, K. A. *A Small White Scar*. 2006. 192p. HarperCollins/Joanna Cotler (9780060756390). Gr. 6–9.

Since his mother's death, Will's job has been to look after his twin brother, Denny, who has Down syndrome. Their father's word is law on the ranch, and 15-year-old Will knuckles under as the story begins. But he soon devises an escape plan that leads toward the rodeo, and beyond, to spending his days as a cowboy without the responsibility of watching his brother. When Denny follows Will across the plains, that plan takes an unexpected twist, leading Will to confront the people he loves and hates most and forcing changes in all their lives. Set in Colorado in 1940, the novel transports readers to a vividly realized setting as the boys move across the country on horseback and encounter hazards from a poisonous snake to a swollen river. But external dangers are not the engine driving the plot. Will's frustration, determination, and flashes of anger give the story its momentum as he struggles to emerge from his childhood and finds no clear path toward becoming an adult. Part family tale, part adventure, part journey narrative, this coming-of-age story has an emotional core that will touch even readers who never dreamed of competing in a rodeo. An unusually fine first novel. —Carolyn Phelan

O'Dell, Kathleen. *Bad Tickets*. 2007. 240p. Knopf (9780375838019). Gr. 9–12.

Mary Margaret Hallinan is a good Catholic girl until she meets Jane. Jane is a risk taker, someone who instructs Mary Margaret to say yes to life. In this case, yes means heading into Portland to partake of the hippie lifestyle, complete with plenty of marijuana. With insight and humor, O'Dell gives the good-girl–bad-girl story new depth. Everything is done well. The 1967 setting is freshly evoked, even as it shows that time hasn't changed the way friendships twist and turn. Equally interesting is O'Dell's take on romance. Mary Margaret finally turns her longtime crush, Mitch, into a boyfriend, though Jane thinks Mitch is a "bad ticket," someone who will lead Mary Margaret nowhere. Mary Margaret knows a lot about going nowhere. Her mother married her genial father when she became pregnant, and now, five children later, she fights with her daughter and tries to make the best of her diaper-filled life. Thanks in part to Jane's helping her see life differently, but mostly because of her own strength of character, Mary Margaret is able to shape her romance with Mitch into a relationship of equals. The schoolgirl in the mini skirt on the cover may attract readers, but the picture doesn't do justice to the strong female characters inside. —Ilene Cooper

Orlev, Uri. *Run, Boy, Run*. 2003. 192p. Houghton/Walter Lorraine (9780618164653). Gr. 7–12.

Orlev is a Holocaust survivor, and his award-winning novels about being a child in the Warsaw ghetto, including *The Man from the Other Side* (1991), are widely read. This new story is not based on his own experience, but it does come from real life—the experience of an illiterate ghetto survivor who escaped into the Polish countryside, stealing, foraging, begging, working. The boy is nurtured by some and hated by many. He hides his circumcision and invents a Catholic identity; he forgets his real name, his family, and the street where he lived. In one unforgettable incident, he loses his right arm because a Polish doctor refuses to operate on a Jew. He survives, immigrating to Israel, where Orlev hears him tell his story. The narrative is simple and spare, factual about everything from hunting with a slingshot to making a fire with a piece of glass, and it's always true to the viewpoint of a boy who thinks he is "about nine." —Hazel Rochman

Ostlere, Cathy. ***Karma.*** **2011. 519p. Penguin/Razorbill (9781595143389). Gr. 9–12.**

After her Hindu mother's suicide, 15-year-old Maya and her Sikh father travel from Canada to India for a traditional burial. The year is 1984, and on the night of their arrival in New Delhi, Prime Minister Indira Gandhi is assassinated by her Sikh guards. When the city erupts in chaos, both Maya and her father find themselves in great danger. Through a sequence of horrifying events, father and daughter are separated, and Maya is left alone in a violent foreign country where she must rely on the help of strangers to reach safety. In her YA debut, acclaimed adult author Ostlere offers a riveting, historically accurate coming-of-age tale of gutsy survival, self-sacrifice, and love. Set during a six-week period, the novel in verse makes the most of its lyrical form with lines of dialogue that bounce back and forth in columns across the page and singularly beautiful metaphors and similes that convey potent detail and emotion. With artful compassion, Ostlere reveals the infinitely complex clash of cultures within both India and Maya's family, and although the allusions to karma could have seemed awkward in less talented hands, here they lead into well-framed larger questions that will stay with readers. A fascinating, epic page-turner. —Frances Bradburn

Oughton, Jerrie. ***Perfect Family.*** **2000. 208p. Houghton (9780395986684). Gr. 6–9.**

The oddly named Welcome Marie O'Neal is the product of a 1950s eastern North Carolina small town, a gossip-hungry place where a teenager who becomes pregnant is sent away "to boarding school" or "to visit family." Oughton takes readers back to a time before legalized abortion, when young women visited grimy, back-street houses and often fled in fear, choosing to raise their babies when faced with the reality of their choices. This is Welcome's story, but it is also the story of a family that supports and loves—and forgives—its own, a family that works. It's about a young woman growing up who makes the ultimate sacrifice and atones for it. And though the story takes place years ago, it's still relevant to teens today: it deals with making choices, looking to the future, and realizing that, though no family is truly perfect, some families are just right for new babies and teens. —Frances Bradburn

Park, Linda Sue. ***A Long Walk to Water: Based on a True Story.*** **2010. 128p. Clarion (9780547251271). Gr. 6–9.**

After 11-year-old Salva's school in Sudan is attacked by brutal rebel soldiers in 1985, he describes several terrifying years on the run in visceral detail: "The rain, the mad current, the bullets, the crocodiles, the welter of arms and legs, the screams, the blood." Finally, he makes it to refugee camps in Ethiopia and then Kenya, where he is one of 3,000 young men chosen to go to America. After he is adopted by a family in Rochester, New York, he is reunited with the Sudanese family that he left behind. There have been several books about the Lost Boys of Sudan for adults, teens, and even elementary-school readers. But Newbery Award–winning Park's spare, immediate account, based on a true story, adds a stirring contemporary dimension. In chapters that alternate with Salva's story, Nya, a young Sudanese girl in 2008, talks about daily life, in which she walks eight hours to fetch water for her family. Then, a miracle happens: Salva returns home to help his people and builds a well, making fresh water available for the community and freeing Nya to go to school. The switching viewpoints may initially disorient some, but young readers will be stunned by the triumphant climax of the former refugee who makes a difference with the necessities that we all take for granted. Teachers may want to point out the allusion to Nelson Mandela's *A Long Walk to Freedom* (1995) echoed in this moving book's title. —Hazel Rochman

Park, Linda Sue. ***When My Name Was Keoko*****. 2003. 208p. Clarion (9780618133352). Gr. 5–9.**

Except for Sook Nyul Choi's *Year of Impossible Goodbyes* (1991), very little has been written for young people about the Japanese occupation of Korea. Park, who won the Newbery Medal for *A Single Shard* (2001), set in twelfth-century Korea, draws on her parents' experiences as well as extensive historical research for this story. The plot unfolds through the alternating first-person narratives of Sun-hee, who is 10 years old in 1940, and her older brother, Tae-yul. They lose their names and their language when they are forced to use Japanese at school and in public. The far-off war comes closer, and hardship increases with brutal neighborhood roundups. Always there are secrets: Who's a traitor? Who's pretending to be a traitor? Sun-hee tries to help her uncle in the resistance, and she's overcome with guilt when she puts him in terrible danger. Tae-yul becomes a kamikaze pilot for the Japanese: he loves learning to fly, but his secret aim is to help the Americans. There's also family conflict, especially about the submissive role of a young girl: Does she disobey her father for the good of her country? Why doesn't her father resist? The two young voices sound very much the same, and the historical background sometimes takes over the narrative. The drama is in the facts about the war, and Park does a fine job of showing how the politics of the occupation and resistance affect ordinary people. —Hazel Rochman

Pearsall, Shelley. ***Trouble Don't Last*****. 2002. 160p. Knopf (9780375814907). Gr. 5–10.**

Far from the romantic Underground Railroad stories about brave abolitionists and hide-and-seek adventure, this powerful historical novel is harsh and realistic, not only about the brutal effects of slavery that the runaways carry with them forever but also about the prejudice and hardship they encounter on their journey to freedom. First-novelist Pearsall is a museum historian in Ohio, and her astonishing story is based on fact. Her runaway heroes are brave and determined to save each other; they're also rough, mean, and frightened. The conductors aren't saints: some are scared runaways, and their help is often limited. The patrollers are always close. The story is told by Samuel, 11, who is forced to run with Harrison, an old slave, from the Kentucky plantation to Ohio in 1859, and finally to freedom in Canada. Harrison hates taking orders, even from the conductors, and Samuel rages at having to disguise himself as a girl. Yet when they find shelter with caring people, Samuel says with simple eloquence that his words of thanks are too small and what he wants to say is too big. This is a thrilling escape story, right until the very last chapter, but always there's the memory of daily life under slavery and the anguish of family separation. Samuel's mother was sold off when he was a baby: will he ever see her again? —Hazel Rochman

Peck, Richard. ***The River between Us*****. 2003. 176p. Dial (9780803727359). Gr. 7–12.**

At the start of the Civil War, two mysterious young women get off a boat in a small town in southern Illinois, and 15-year-old Tilly Pruitt's mother takes them in. Who are they? Is the darker-complexioned woman the other woman's slave? Tilly's twin brother, Noah, falls in love with one of them—rich, stylish, worldly Delphine, who shows Tilly a world of possibilities beyond her home. When Noah runs away to war, Tilly and Delphine go after him, find him in the horror of an army tent hospital, and bring him back; but their world is changed forever. Peck's spare writing has never been more eloquent than in this powerful mystery in which personal secrets drive the plot and reveal the history. True to Tilly's first-person narrative, each sentence is a scrappy, melancholy, wry evocation of character, time, and place, and only the character of Delphine's companion, Calinda, comes close to stereotype. A final historical note and a framing device—a grandson writing 50 years after the story takes place—make the reading even better, the revelations more astonishing. It's a riveting story that shows racism everywhere and young people facing war, not sure what side to be on or why. —Hazel Rochman

Peck, Richard. ***A Year Down Yonder*****. 2000. 144p. Dial (9780803725188). Gr. 6–10.**

With the same combination of wit, gentleness, and outrageous farce as Peck's Newbery Honor book, *Long Way from Chicago* (1998), this sequel tells the story of

Joey's younger sister, Mary Alice, 15, who spends the year of 1937 back with Grandma Dowdel in a small town in Illinois. It's still the Depression; Dad has lost his job, and Mary Alice has been sent from Chicago to live with Grandma and enroll in the "hick-town" 25-student high school. As in the first book, much of the fun comes from the larger-than-life characters, whether it's the snobbish DAR ladies or the visiting WPA artist, who paints a nude picture of the postmistress (nude, not naked; he studied in Paris). The wry one-liners and tall tales are usually Grandma's ("When I was a girl, we had to walk in our sleep to keep from freezing to death"), or Mary Alice's commentary as she looks back ("Everybody in this town knew everything about you. They knew things that hadn't even happened yet"). That adult perspective is occasionally intrusive, and Mary Alice sometimes seems younger than 15, though her awkward romance with a classmate is timeless. The heart of the book is Grandma—huge and overbearing, totally outside polite society. Just as powerful is what's hidden: Mary Alice discovers kindness and grace as well as snakes in the attic. Most moving is Mary Alice's own growth. During a tornado she leaves her shelter to make sure that Grandma is safe at home. In fact, as Mary Alice looks back, it's clear that Grandma has remained her role model, never more generous than when she helped her granddaughter leave. —Hazel Rochman

Peck, Robert Newton. *Horse Thief*. 2002. 192p. HarperCollins (9780066237916). Gr. 7–12.

Western fans are in for a treat with this fast-paced, satisfying Depression tale of a teenage orphan who rescues 13 horses from the slaughterhouse and finds a family in the process. Seventeen-year-old Tullis Yoder works in a shabby rodeo in Chicalookee, Florida ("We was only a bunch of boys. Yet with a biting ache to be men, as battered and bowlegged and brawly as the regular rodeo pokes that got bruised, got paid, got drunk. In that order"). Tullis can't wait to start bull riding, but in the action-packed opening chapter, his first ride results in his losing two fingers on his right hand. He gets patched up by the kindly local doctor, who sees in him her own long-dead son. When the rodeo falls apart, the livestock are sold to the slaughterhouse. But Tullis is determined to save his beloved horses, and so begins a convoluted and surprisingly funny odyssey, chock-full of engaging characters. Peck's dialect and comic timing are right on target. Even sophisticated urban teens may find themselves drawn by the rip-roaring story and gentle humor. —Debbie Carton

Peet, Mal. *Life: An Exploded Diagram*. 2011. 416p. Candlewick (9780763652272). Gr. 9–12.

Peet's arresting new novel begins in the destruction of WWII and ends in the explosive devastation of 9/11. In between, young Clem and his girlfriend, Frankie, find themselves de facto combatants in another conflict: England's class war. Frankie, a child of privilege, is the daughter of the wealthy landowner for whom Clem's father works. Peet breathes new life into this old story with the urgency of the two teens' attraction for each other and their terrible need for secrecy. In a separate plotline, the Cuban missile crisis is about to boil over, and in a bold move, Peet takes readers across the Atlantic and into the White House, making President Kennedy and his staff characters in the novel. Peet writes with a white hot fury at the idiocy of both America and Russia, and the political story is as beautifully written as that of Clem and Frankie. As he did in *Tamar* (2007), Peet again defies the rules of YA fiction. Many of his major characters are adults; in fact, the story is told in retrospect by an adult Clem. Without one iota of sentimentality, Peet creates an explosive world where love is frowned upon and "the past has bloody teeth and bad breath." It is a world that demands deep examination and thought, and Peet has done a splendid job of creating it. —Michael Cart

Peet, Mal. *Tamar*. 2007. 432p. Candlewick (9780763634889). Gr. 9–12.

It was her taciturn but beloved grandfather, William Hyde, who gave Tamar her strange name. But in 1995, when she was 15, he committed suicide, leaving her to wonder if she knew him at all. Later, when she opens the box of WWII memorabilia that he left her, she's struck by the need to find out what it means, who he really was, and where she fits in. Tension mounts incrementally in an intricate wrapping of wartime drama and secrecy, in which Tamar finds her namesake and herself. Forming the backbone of the novel are intense, sometimes brutal events in a small Dutch town in Nazi-occupied Holland and the relationship between the girl's namesake, a member of the Dutch Resistance; Dart, a code operator assigned to help him; and Marijke, the love of his life. Peet's plot is tightly constructed, and striking, descriptive language, full of metaphor, grounds the story. Most of the characters are adults here, and to some readers, the Dutch history, though deftly woven through the story, will seem remote. But Peet's sturdy, emotionally resonant characterizations and dramatic backdrop will pull readers forward, as will the secret that gradually unravels. Despite foreshadowing, the outcome is still a stunner. Winner of Britain's 2005 Carnegie Medal, this powerful story will grow richer with each reading. —Stephanie Zvirin

Pignat, Caroline. *Greener Grass*. 2009. 276p. Red Deer (9780889954021). Gr. 7–10.

In 1847, 15-year-old Kit is jailed for digging up potatoes on confiscated land to feed her starving family, and during the three weeks that she is incarcerated, she reflects on the past year in Ireland: the blight, famine, evictions, and deaths. Lord Fraser, an Englishman, wants to repossess the land where Kit's family lives for grazing, and his estate manager, Lynch, sets fires to drive people from their homes. Much as Kit hates working as a kitchen maid in the estate's Big House, her family needs the money. Then she loses her job, and as she watches her mother sell family treasures, including the Bible and the bed, her sorrow ("I never cried once for fear of never being able to stop") and raging hatred make her plot dire revenge. Complicating everything further is Kit's love for Lynch's son, who loves her back. But can he stand up to his brutal dad? True to Kit's voice, the plain, rhythmic language ("My home was gone. My heart was broken") is lyrical but never ornate. The tension in the story and in the well-developed characters is always rooted in daily detail, and it builds to the final question, which suggests a possible sequel: Will Kit make it onto the ship to Canada? —Hazel Rochman

Polak, Monique. *What World Is Left*. 2008. 224p. Orca (9781551438474). Gr. 7–12.

Growing up in a secular Jewish home in Holland, Anneke cares little about Judaism, so she has no faith to lose when, in 1943, her family is deported to Theresienstadt, the Nazi concentration camp. At 14, she suffers backbreaking labor and foul, unsanitary conditions along with more than 40,000 prisoners, who are all crowded into a town built for 7,000. Always there is the terror of being sent on the dreaded transports to the gas chambers. Based on the experiences of the author's mother, who survived two years in Theresienstadt but did not speak about it for more than 60 years, this novel is narrated in Anneke's first-person, present-tense voice. The details are unforgettable: Anneke's irritation with her pesky little brother; her friendship and romance with young people who are sent, later on, to the death camps; the hunger that drives her and her grandfather to eat the enamel in their cups; her shame and anger. The questions raised in the author's note will lead readers back to the parallel, heartbreaking issues in the fictional story. Why did the author's mother keep silent for so long? Was she ashamed that she survived because her father, a famous artist, helped the Nazis by prettying up the model camp for a Red Cross inspection? And why did the Red Cross fall for it? An important addition to the Holocaust curriculum. —Hazel Rochman

Pratchett, Terry. *Dodger*. 2012. 368p. Harper (9780062009494). Gr. 8–12.

On a stormy night in early Victorian London, an able young man named Dodger rises from the sewers in response to a scream, fights off two thugs, and rescues a damsel in distress. Dodger continues to rise throughout the novel, as his love for the mysterious lady motivates this tosher (scavenger for lost coins and other treasures in London's sewers) to elevate himself and leads him to a closer acquaintance with a string of historical figures, including Dickens, Disraeli, and ultimately, the queen and her consort. While most writers would be well advised not to include such characters in their books, Pratchett manages to humanize them without diminishing them or throwing the story off-kilter. However lowly Dodger's origins, he remains the most memorable character in the book. Living by his wits and unencumbered by conventional morality, this trickster hero expertly navigates the underbelly of his city as he carries out a bizarre scheme resulting in justice and mercy. The temptation to quote sentences, whole paragraphs, and possibly entire chapters is almost irresistible, because the pleasure of reading the novel is in the language as much as in the characters and well-researched period setting. Often amusing, this Victorian romp of a novel is lovingly crafted and completely enjoyable. —Carolyn Phelan

Preus, Margi. *Heart of a Samurai*. 2010. 320p. illus. Abrams/Amulet (9780810989818). Gr. 7–11.

Manjiro is 14 when a freak storm washes him and his four fishing companions onto a tiny island far from their Japanese homeland. Shortly before starving, they are rescued by an American whaling ship. But it's 1841 and distrust is rampant: the Japanese consider the whalers "barbarians," while the whalers think of the Japanese as "godless cannibals." Captain William Whitfield is different—childless, he forges a bond with the boy, and when it comes time for Manjiro to choose between staying with his countrymen or going to America as Whitfield's son, he picks the path of adventure. It's a classic fish-out-of-water story (although this fish goes into the water repeatedly), and it's precisely this classic structure that gives the novel the sturdy bones of a timeless tale. Bracketed by gritty seafaring episodes—salty and bloody enough to assure us that Preus has done her research—the book's heart is its middle section, in which Manjiro, allegedly the first Japanese to set foot in America, deals with the prejudice and promise of a new world. By Japanese tradition, Manjiro was destined to be no more than a humble fisherman, but when his 10-year saga ends, he has become so much more. Wonderful back matter helps flesh out this fictionalized version of the same story told in Rhoda Blumberg's *Shipwrecked! The True Adventures of a Japanese Boy* (2001). —Daniel Kraus

Reeve, Philip. *Here Lies Arthur*. 2008. 352p. Scholastic (9780545093347). Gr. 7–10.

Powerfully inventive, yet less romanticized than most stories set in the medieval Britain, this novel retells the story of King Arthur from a fresh perspective. Readers first glimpse Gwyna, the novel's disarming narrator, as "a snot-nosed girl" hiding in the brambles from a marauding band of brutes led by Arthur, "the King that Was and Will Be." Taken under the wing of the king's bard and advisor, Myddrin (the Merlin figure), who disguises her first as a lad and then as that fictional lad's half-sister, Gwyna takes part in or observes many significant scenes, from the day Arthur takes the sword offered by a lady beneath a lake until the day of his death. In Gwyna's telling, many traditionally esteemed characters are revealed as unworthy, and some reviled ones are shown as heroic. Seemingly supernatural elements of the storied events are shown to be mere conjuring tricks, while the most magical power that Myddrin wields is the creative storytelling that shapes history into legend and makes it immortal. Events rush headlong toward the inevitable ending, but Gwyna's observations illuminate them in a new way. Arthurian lore has inspired many novels for young people, but few as arresting or compelling as this one. —Carolyn Phelan

Rinaldi, Ann. *The Redheaded Princess*. 2008. 224p. HarperCollins (9780060733742). Gr. 6–9.

In Rinaldi's latest work of historical fiction, the popular author looks to the life of Elizabeth I leading up to her spectacular reign in Renaissance England. The stage is set by a helpful historical preface, which illuminates the circumstances of Elizabeth's traumatic childhood, fraught with brutal political treachery. (Her own father routinely had his wives murdered for suspected affairs and for not producing a son.) Rinaldi makes history come alive through her portrayal of the tough, precocious heroine—at the outset, Elizabeth muses that "it is never good when you hear a horse galloping up to your home in the middle of the day or night. Night is worse, of course." Religious and political tensions of the day emerge in the course of the story, and through it all, the princess comes into her own as a self-possessed young woman with the steely courage to face the chicanery and rivalries besetting the court. The rich scene-setting and believable, appealing heroine will satisfy Rinaldi's many fans, especially those captivated by the slice of the same history the author explored in her book about Lady Jane Gray, *Nine Days a Queen* (2005). And, for readers who may have first encountered Elizabeth I in Kathryn Lasky's Royal Diaries treatment, this more substantial portrait offers a natural next step. —Anne O'Malley

Salisbury, Graham. ***Eyes of the Emperor*. 2005. 240p. Random/Wendy Lamb (9780385729710). Gr. 7–10.**

Like Harry Mazer's *Heroes Don't Run* (2005), this novel is about a teen, this time from Honolulu, who lies about his age to enlist in the U.S Army during WWII. But Eddie Okubo, 16, is Japanese American, and the racism he encounters in the military is as terrifying to him as the fire of the enemy. Here Salisbury draws on his interviews with many Japanese American veterans who remember their experiences in powerful detail—their patriotism, courage, and anguish. Eddie's frank, first-person narrative weaves in the facts of how the "Japs" were segregated from the regular soldiers, assigned unskilled hard labor and marches to nowhere, and then, in a shocking (failed) experiment that was ordered by President Roosevelt, were directed to act as enemies and train attack dogs to pick up the so-called Japanese body odor. The cruel training, the vicious prejudice from many officers, the camaraderie among the soldiers, and the mixed-up news from family bring a view of American history seldom told and open up the meanings of homeland and patriotism. Salisbury's *Under the Blood-Red Sun* (1994), which was also set in Hawaii after Pearl Harbor, won the Scott O'Dell Award for Historical Fiction. —Hazel Rochman

Salisbury, Graham. ***Island Boyz: Short Stories*. 2002. 260p. Random (9780385729703). Gr. 7–12.**

In the first story of this memorable collection, 15-year-old Vinny weighs the risks of a dangerous jump and the pressure of his friends. His decision, quiet and irreversible, transforms him. The following stories, all set in Hawaii and many taking place in the mid-twentieth century, follow teenage boys through similarly pivotal moments—choices complicated by fear, shame, confusion, cultural identity, bullies, war, desire, and new ideas of masculinity. In "Mrs. Noonan," a boarding-school student turns his obsession with a faculty wife into unexpected revenge; in "Hat of Clouds," a boy tries to help his brother who has lost a leg in Vietnam. Salisbury's characters are fully formed, distinct but familiar, and he writes about the tropical setting with vivid, tangible details that electrify each boy's drama with constant reminders of wildness: a lava flow's scorching heat; the sudden violence of storms; the "cool earth smells of mud and iron." Many of these stories have appeared in previous anthologies. But collected together, they gain new life. Preceding and cementing them together is a nostalgic free-verse poem about what it meant to be one of the "boyz": "talking low / feeling tall / dreaming of girls / of love." —Gillian Engberg

Schmidt, C. A. ***Useful Fools*. 2007. 272p. Dutton (9780525478140). Gr. 9–12.**

As a journalist, Schmidt reported from Peru for many years. Her groundbreaking novel is disturbing and complex, not only because it is told from alternating viewpoints but also because the politics and savage brutality change its characters profoundly. Alonso, 15, is a poor cholo, a citified Indian who lives in a shantytown on the edge of Lima, far from the luxurious home of beautiful Rosa, who is white. His mother, Magda, organizes the community clinic where Rosa's father volunteers as a pediatrician. Rosa helps out there, and she and Alonso fall in love. Then Alonso's mother is killed when the Senderistas, the Shining Path revolutionary guerillas, bomb the clinic. They condemn Magda as a "useful fool," who is keeping the corrupt system going for the bourgeosie. The police are just as brutal as the guerillas; they are experts at murder, torture, and rape. After Alonso's drunken abusive father loses his job and the shattered family moves to a shack without electricity or water, Alonso is persuaded to join the guerillas in the mountains. Can he prove himself and kill? Should he? Will his love for Rosa survive? The Romeo-and-Juliet love story will grab some readers; others will be drawn to the haunting, intense issues of politics and justice and the character of a loving teen so desperate that he joins murderous rebels. At the heart of the tale is the question, "When is a terrorist a freedom fighter?" —Hazel Rochman

Schmidt, Gary D. ***Lizzie Bright and the Buckminster Boy*. 2004. 224p. Clarion (9780618439294). Gr. 7–12.**

Turner, the rigid minister's son, doesn't fit in when his family moves from Boston to the small town of Phippsburg on the coast of Maine in 1912. It's not only that Maine baseball is different from the game he knows; he's just plain miserable. Then he makes friends with a smart, lively young teen, Lizzie Griffin, living in a small, impoverished community founded by former slaves on nearby Malaga Island. When the town elders drive Lizzie's people off the island, Turner stands up for them, but he can do nothing. Lizzie eventually dies in an insane asylum. The novel may be too long and detailed for some readers, with every plot strand and character accounted for. But the removal of the Malaga community really happened, and Schmidt weaves that history into a powerful tale of friendship and coming-of-age, adding a lyrical sense of the coastal landscape. Characters are drawn without reverence in this haunting combination of fact and fiction that has a powerful and tragic climax. —Hazel Rochman

Schmidt, Gary D. *Okay for Now*. 2011. 368p. Clarion (9780547152608). Gr. 6–9.

In this stand-alone companion to *The Wednesday Wars* (2007), a Newbery Honor Book set in the late 1960s, Schmidt focuses on Holling Hoodhood's classmate Doug Swieteck, who is furious when his volatile father gets fired and moves the family to tiny Marysville, New York. Eighth grade gets off to a rocky start, particularly after Doug's brother is blamed for a series of local break-ins, and Doug, too, is viewed with suspicion. Life at home with his hard-drinking dad is rocky as well, especially after Doug's second brother returns from Vietnam without his legs. In addition to brief character references, this title shares much with *The Wednesday Wars*. Here, John James Audubon's portraits of birds, rather than Shakespeare's plays, provide a cultural awakening, and once again, Schmidt skillfully makes a reluctant boy's connection with the works a plausible and moving catalyst for strength and growth. Schmidt stretches credibility with another wish-fulfilling ending, but readers will likely forgive any plot contrivances as they enjoy Doug's distinctive, rhythmic narration, inventively peppered with "stats" about his life, which reveals hard, sometimes shocking truths about the time period and, most of all, Doug's family. Delivered in a wholly believable voice, Doug's euphemisms are heartbreaking and authentic, as when he describes his dad's violence: "He has quick hands." Reproductions of Audubon plates introduce each chapter in this stealthily powerful, unexpectedly affirming story of discovering and rescuing one's best self, despite family pressure to do otherwise. —Gillian Engberg

★ Schmidt, Gary D. *The Wednesday Wars*. 2007. 265p. Clarion (9780618724833). Gr. 6–9.

On Wednesday afternoons, while his Catholic and Jewish schoolmates attend religious instruction, Holling Hoodhood, the only Presbyterian in his seventh grade, is alone in the classroom with his teacher, Mrs. Baker, who Holling is convinced hates his guts. He feels more certain after Mrs. Baker assigns Shakespeare's plays for Holling to discuss during their shared afternoons. Each month in Holling's tumultuous seventh-grade year is a chapter in this quietly powerful coming-of-age novel set in suburban Long Island during the late '60s. The slow start may deter some readers, and Mrs. Baker is too good to be true: she arranges a meeting between Holling and the New York Yankees, brokers a deal to save a student's father's architectural firm, and, after revealing her past as an Olympic runner, coaches Holling to the varsity cross-country team. However, Schmidt, whose *Lizzie Bright and the Buckminster Boy* (2005) was named both a Printz and a Newbery Honor Book, makes the implausible believable and the everyday momentous. Seamlessly, he knits together the story's themes: the cultural uproar of the '60s, the internal uproar of early adolescence, and the timeless wisdom of Shakespeare's words. Holling's unwavering, distinctive voice offers a gentle, hopeful, moving story of a boy who, with the right help, learns to stretch beyond the limitations of his family, his violent times, and his fear, as he leaps into his future with his eyes and his heart wide open. —Gillian Engberg

Sedgwick, Marcus. *The Foreshadowing*. 2006. 288p. Random/Wendy Lamb (9780385746465). Gr. 8–11.

"I have seen the future again, and it is death. I can no longer pretend it is my imagination." As a young child, Alexandra (Sasha) saw that her friend would die. Now, at 17, her premonitions, always of death, have returned. It is 1915, and as WWI rages on, Sasha yearns to do something useful, like her father, a respected doctor in Brighton, England. Then her abstract terrors of war become immediate: one brother is killed; the other joins the army and disappears to France. In nightmares, Sasha sees his murder. Desperate to save him, she joins a volunteer nursing corps, hoping to find him on the battlefields. A few plot elements, such as Sasha's bond with a similarly clairvoyant soldier, feel contrived. But readers will be haunted by the unusually powerful, visceral view of war's horrors—the ruined landscapes of mud and wire, the gore and stench of mutilated bodies—in which the real and the supernatural are inextricably linked. In Sasha's compelling, urgent narrative, Sedgwick skillfully connects young peoples' struggles for power and self-determination with the deepest questions about fate, free will, and the meaning of patriotism. —Gillian Engberg

Sedgwick, Marcus. *Revolver*. 2010. 160p. Roaring Brook (9781596435926). Gr. 7–10.

Sedgwick's historical mystery, set in the Arctic Circle in 1899 and 1910, makes good use of the word *chilling*. Outside their remote Scandinavian village, Sig's father dies of exposure after trying to rush home across a frozen lake. The reason for his carelessness becomes apparent to Sig when a hulking beast of a man arrives at their tiny shack with a Colt revolver, demanding his share of a stolen wealth of gold. But Sig has his own Colt hidden in the storeroom, and some very pressing questions. Who is this brute at the door? Is there really a hidden treasure? And, most important, can he bring himself to use that revolver to save himself and his family? As the claustrophobic tension in the Arctic cabin mounts, Sedgwick doles out bits of backstory set a decade earlier in the Alaska gold rush, and the climax reveals that there hasn't been a single superfluous detail in the intricate, freezer-burn buildup. A carefully crafted story effectively rigidified by taut plotting and the crystalline atmospherics of its isolated setting. —Ian Chipman

Selvandurai, Shyam. *Swimming in the Monsoon Sea*. 2005. 224p. Tundra (9780887767357). Gr. 8–11.

As lush and languid as its Sri Lanka setting, this novel tells the story of 13-year-old Amrith, whose complicated life becomes even more so with the appearance of his Canadian cousin, Niresh. Amrith lives with his adoring godmother and her supportive family in 1980 Colombo. But although he lives in luxury, he is poverty-stricken when it comes to knowing his own family. There is mystery surrounding the death of his beloved mother and alcoholic father, and because of the circumstances of his parents' marriage, his extended family shuns him. So when Niresh turns up with his father, who has come to sell off family property, Amrith is anxious to make a connection. Eventually, he realizes his feelings for Niresh go beyond friendship, which finally makes him aware of his sexual identity. This is much closer stylistically to European novels such as Per Nilsson's *You & You & You* and Andreas Steinhofel's *Center of the World* (both 2005) than to our own plot-driven YA novels, with situations arising organically from the characters. What captures readers is the way the story rolls in waves, mimicking how Amrith looks at himself, then looks away. The luxuriant language, with details of architecture and verdant gardens, doesn't call attention to itself, but refreshes like a breeze. Selvadurai, who wrote so gracefully for adults in *Cinnamon Gardens* (1998), now does the same for teens. —Ilene Cooper

Sepetys, Ruta. *Between Shades of Gray*. 2011. 352p. Philomel (9780399254123). Gr. 7–12.

Sepetys' first novel offers a harrowing and horrifying account of the forcible relocation of countless Lithuanians in the wake of the Russian invasion of their country in 1939. In the case of 16-year-old Lina, her mother, and her younger brother, this means deportation to a forced-labor camp in Siberia, where conditions are all too painfully similar to those of Nazi concentration camps. Lina's great hope is that somehow her father, who has already been arrested by the Soviet secret police, might find and rescue them. A gifted artist, she begins secretly creating pictures that can—she hopes—be surreptitiously sent to him in his own prison camp. Whether or not this will be possible, it is her art that will be her salvation, helping her to retain her identity, her dignity, and her increasingly tenuous hold on hope for the future. Many others are not so fortunate. Sepetys, the daughter of a Lithuanian refugee, estimates that the Baltic States lost more than one-third of their populations during the Russian genocide. Though many continue to deny this happened, Sepetys' beautifully written and deeply felt novel proves the reality is otherwise. Hers is an important book that deserves the widest possible readership. —Michael Cart

Sheppard, Mary C. ***Seven for a Secret*****. 2001. 192p. Groundwood (9780888994370). Gr. 10–12.**

At first blush there seems little to interest American teens here, but the concerns of three Canadian girls are universal. The setting is a small fishing village on the coast of Newfoundland, 1960. Despite the year, indoor plumbing, electricity, even highways are things of the future. Nevertheless, 15-year-old Melinda, the story's narrator, loves Cook's Cove, especially during the summer when city cousin, Kate, joins her and her cousin Rebecca, daughter of the village doyenne. This summer turns out to be full of secrets. A hidden birth certificate shows that Rebecca is not who she thinks she is, and Melinda discovers that her memories of her father aren't accurate. Sheppard goes from strength to strength here. Her description of a place both comforting and oppressive is written with perfect pitch, and she doesn't compromise with the ending: Rebecca won't have a chance to explore her artistic talent; Melinda, who is bright enough for a scholarship, gets pregnant (the sex scene is short but vivid) and will probably end up like her mother, who works in the fish cannery. Yet even as Melinda accepts her fate, she feels the contentment born of the familiar and harbors the hope that her daughter may use the coming highway to travel to a more fulfilling life. —Ilene Cooper

Sheth, Kashmira. ***Keeping Corner*****. 2007. 288p. Hyperion (9780786838592). Gr. 7–12.**

Engaged at 2 and married at 9, 12-year-old Leela is awaiting her *anu* ceremony, after which she will move to her in-laws' home. But her husband is killed, and she suddenly becomes a widow. Her loving family follows the Brahman customs: Leela's head is shaved, her bright clothes are exchanged for plain ones, and most difficult of all, she must "keep corner," unable to leave her family's home for one year. She fears the saying that a widow's life "is like a living death," but India's fight for independence is escalating, and through discussions with her brother and her female tutor, both followers of Gandhi, Leela begins to question tradition: "Who started this? And why? Can anyone benefit from it?" Burying herself in news reports, literature, and her own writing, Leela determines to forgo the tradition of widows, who seem to "melt into darkness," and with the support of her brother and tutor, she begins to dream of a hopeful future as an educated, professional woman. Sheth (*Blue Jasmine*, 2004) sets up a thrilling premise in which politics become achingly personal as Leela's brave, tumultuous coming-of-age plays out in intimate detail against the backdrop of her nation's independence. Idealistic teens will be caught up in the human-rights issues, and the vivid cultural specifics, memorable characters, and the bold adolescent's challenge to tradition will attract a wide readership. —Gillian Engberg

Siegelson, Kim. ***Trembling Earth*****. 2004. 176p. Philomel (9780399240218). Gr. 7–12.**

Far from any romantic slave escape and rescue story, this Civil War novel is told from the viewpoint of Hamp, 12, a poor white kid in the Okefenokee Swamp area, who, with his dog, tracks down a runaway, Duff, for the bounty. But the two fight and bond, then Hamp helps Duff escape. Siegelson knows the swamp area, and she makes the place a dense presence on every page, including details about the particular birds, insects, other animals, and plants that may be too much for some readers. But the wilderness facts root the story in amazing moments of danger and protection, whether the boys are avoiding alligators or finding direction by watching the birds, the shadows, and the stars. This is one of the few Civil War stories to show the Confederate side in all its complexity. Hamp has never seen a "Negra," never mind had a slave. Papa didn't support slavery; in fact, he fought the Yankees, and he lost a leg. When Hamp tells Duff about Pa's loss, Duff's answer says it all: "Never met mine. Old Massa bought Mama when she was heavy with me, but he didn't want Daddy." Now Duff is searching for his sister who was sold away. The survival adventure will draw kids, many of whom will want to talk about how Hamp overcomes his prejudice and learns the hard truth. —Hazel Rochman

Smith, Andrew. *In the Path of Falling Objects*. 2009. 336p. Feiwel and Friends (9780312375584). Gr. 10–12.

Jonah and his younger brother, Simon, have it pretty tough, and it's about to get tougher. Their junkie dad's in prison, their mom's abandoned them, and their older brother is off fighting in Vietnam. The brothers hit the road and hitch a ride with Mitch, a sociopath, and his pregnant companion, Lilly. After an intense opening murder scene, the book only grows bloodier during the journey through the southwestern desert. The story unfolds from multiple viewpoints, including missives from the brother in Vietnam that become increasingly more unhinged. This counterpoint effectively mirrors the brothers' increasingly violent and desperate plight, unable to either stop or get away from the lunatic at the wheel. Like all great psychopathic characters, Mitch steals the show for much of the story, but Smith also deftly layers in sibling dynamics that are both supportive and combative. A relentless, bleak thriller that nails the claustrophobic sense of being totally out of control, and moving fast. —Ian Chipman

Smith, Sherri L. *Flygirl*. 2009. 288p. Putnam (9780399247095). Gr. 7–10.

This breakthrough title adds a new story to the shelves of WWII books. Here, the enemy is not just a foreign threat; it is also prejudice—of both race and gender—here at home. In 1941, black high-school graduate Ida Mae Jones, 18, worries about her soldier brother, who is on the front, and longs to fight for her country, too. Her late dad taught her to fly a crop-dusting plane, and when the U.S. starts the WASP (Women Airforce Service Program), she is determined to join up. The slights against women are constant, as is racial prejudice, including the *n*-word. Ida Mae is so light-skinned that she can pass as white, which means leaving her family and friends and creating a new identity. She goes through the rigorous training program, bonds with some fellow trainees, and flies for her country. The details about navigation are exciting, but tougher than any flight maneuver are Ida Mae's loneliness, shame, and fear that she will be thrown out of the military, feelings that culminate in an unforgettable climax. Always, there is the reality of living under Jim Crow. An afterword fills in the history of the WASP, which notes that while records do not show that there were any black female pilots at the time, those records do not tell the truth about pilots like Ida Mae. —Hazel Rochman

Spinelli, Jerry. *Milkweed*. 2003. 224p. Knopf (9780375813740). Gr. 7–12.

Spinelli's narrative is manic, fast, and scattered, authentically capturing the perspective of a young child during the Nazi occupation of Warsaw who doesn't know if he's a Jew or a Gypsy; he has never known family or community. He lives by stealing; his name may be Stopthief. This boy lives in the ghetto, where the daily atrocities he witnesses—hanging bodies, massacres, shootings, roundups, transports—are the only reality he knows. His matter-of-fact account distances the brutality without sensationalizing or lessening the truth. He first finds shelter with a gang of street kids, where one fierce older boy protects him, invents an identity for him, and teaches him survival skills. Later he lives with a Jewish family. The history is true, so although Spinelli's narrator is young, the brutal realism in the story makes this a book for older children. —Hazel Rochman

Stolz, Joëlle. *The Shadows of Ghadames*. 2004. 128p. Delacorte (9780385731041). Gr. 6–10.

In the Libyan city of Ghadames at the end of the nineteenth century, Malika is dreading her twelfth birthday. That is the time when, according to her family's Berber customs, she will be close to marriageable age and confined to the world of women. In Ghadames that means restriction to the rooftops, "a city above the city, an open sunny town for women only, where . . . they never talk to men." Malika longs to live beyond the segregated city and travel, like her father, a trader. But the wider world comes to Malika after her father's two wives agree to harbor, in secret, a wounded stranger. The story of an outsider who unsettles a household and helps a young person to grow is certainly nothing new, and some of the lessons here are purposeful. But Stolz invigorates her tale with elegant prose and a deft portrayal of a girl verging on adolescence. The vivid backdrop is intoxicating, but the story's universal concerns will touch readers most: sibling jealously, confusion about adult customs, and a growing interest in a world beyond family. —Gillian Engberg

Sturtevant, Katherine. *The Brothers Story*. 2009. 288p. Farrar (9780374309923). Gr. 9–12.

Kit longs to rise in the world, but to do so would mean leaving his Essex village for London Town and abandoning his twin brother, Christy, who is "simple" and cannot care for himself. Yet the terrible privations of the Great Frost of 1683–84, the coldest winter in England's history, may leave the increasingly desperate 15-year-old no choice. In giving us Kit's story, with its echoes of the Biblical tale of Joseph and his brothers, Sturtevant has done a breathtakingly good job of recreating not only the earthy sense of Restoration England—its sights, smells, sounds, lusts, and longings—but its ethos, as well. Her readers discover, dramatically, not only how Kit and his colorful contemporaries feel but also how they think—about themselves, their stations, their society, their moral behavior and responsibilities, and, yes, their God. There are no easy answers to the difficult questions that confront and sometimes torment Kit; nor is it an easy world, this character reflects: "At first it was nearly a satisfaction to me to be suffering again, as the poor are born to do." Sturtevant's book is not only a stunning story but a challenging and deeply satisfying work of social conscience. —Michael Cart

Sturtevant, Katherine. *A True and Faithful Narrative*. 2006. 256p. Farrar (9780374378097). Gr. 6–9.

In this sequel to *At the Sign of the Star* (2000), 16-year-old Meg, living in seventeenth-century London, struggles to sort out her conflicted feelings about two suitors. One, Edward, asks Meg what he can bring back for her from his sea voyage. Meg flippantly inquires if he can "manage to be captured by pirates and enslaved in North Africa," offering a new narrative for her father's bookstore to sell. Meg's silly reply haunts her when she learns that Edward has indeed been kidnapped and enslaved. Meanwhile, Will, her father's apprentice, helps her collect the money needed to secure Edward's release and hopes to win her heart. When Edward returns, Meg finds him changed by his brutal experiences in captivity and fascinated by Muslim society in Algiers, where a kind master treated him as a son. As he tells his promised story, Edward's description of his experiences challenges conventional English assumptions of Muslim culture and broadens Meg's worldview. Sturtevant once again offers readers a story depicted with great clarity and many vivid details of everyday life. Written in the first person, the narrative reveals Meg as a strong-willed yet vulnerable young woman who emerges as a well-rounded, convincing individual, able to see events from different viewpoints. —Carolyn Phelan

Tal, Eve. *Double Crossing: A Jewish Immigration Story*. 2005. 216p. Cinco Puntos (9780938317944). Gr. 7–10.

Based on the experience of the author's grandfather at the turn of the twentieth century, this novel starts off as the archetypal Jewish coming-to-America story. Raizel, 12, leaves the Ukraine with her father, a devout peddler who flees pogroms and conscription into the czar's army, intending to send for the rest of his family later. The separation, the trauma, the dream of golden America, the journey across Europe, the ocean voyage, the inspections and arrival at Ellis Island—the historical detail is dense. But Raizel's lively first-person narrative is anything but reverential. She misses her brother, but she is jealous because he gets to go to school, and she resents her father's keeping kosher, which means they stay hungry during the journey in the crowded ship. Her view of adults and kids, family and strangers, back home and on the perilous adventure, brings the people on the journey very close. Best of all is the shocking surprise that changes everything, even Papa—a haunting aspect of the immigrant story left too long untold. —Hazel Rochman

★ Taylor, Mildred D. *The Land*. 2001. 392p. Penguin/Phyllis Fogelman (9780803719507). Gr. 7–12.

Like Taylor's Newbery Medal book, *Roll of Thunder, Hear My Cry* (1976), this powerful historical novel, a prequel to *Roll of Thunder*, refuses to "whitewash" history. Drawing directly on her family history, Taylor goes back to the time of Reconstruction to tell a searing story of cruelty, racism, and betrayal. She also tells a thrilling coming-of-age story about friendship, hope, and family strength. Paul-Edward narrates it in his own voice, which combines a passionate immediacy with the distance of an adult looking back. Born of a part-Indian, part-African slave mother and a white plantation owner, he is raised in Georgia by both parents and treated "almost" as if he were white. He eats at his white father's table—except when there are guests. He learns to read, and his best friend is his white brother, Robert, who is the same age. His greatest enemy is Mitchell, the son of black sharecroppers, until Paul teaches Mitchell to read, and Mitchell teaches Paul to fight. Paul grows up and falls in love with a strong, independent woman, but his focus is on working the land, his own land. It's rare to find detail about work and business in books for children. The novel will make a great discussion title in American history classes, and it could easily be paired with any number of stories about immigrants' struggles to follow their dreams in America. Taylor's characters are drawn without sentimentality. Paul-Edward's granddaughter will be Cassie Logan, and readers who remember her from *Roll of Thunder* will grab this landmark book and be astonished by its powerful story. —Hazel Rochman

Thal, Lilli. *Mimus*. Tr. by John Brownjohn. 2005. 398p. Firefly/Annick (9781550379259). Gr. 8–11.

The medieval kingdoms of Moltovia and Vinland have been engaged in a bitter and destructive war for years, but an end may finally be in sight. Twelve-year-old Prince Florin of Moltovia is called from his childhood games to his father's side for a peace celebration hosted by King Theodo in Vinland. Upon his arrival, Florin finds it has all been a terrible ruse; the King of Moltovia and his guards are chained in the castle's dungeon, and Florin is forced to apprentice to Mimus, Theodo's seemingly cruel and certainly repellent court jester. If Florin, in a motley suit, bells, and donkey ears, fails to learn his new role and amuse King Theodo, his father will be killed. This outstanding translation from the German brings an author with rich, complex, and very clever storytelling skills to American teens. Readers will be both fascinated and horrified by the barbarity and grit of the times, and by young Florin's humiliating decline from powerful kingdom's rightful heir to soulless beast of entertainment housed in the castle's bestiary. Although the story wraps up a bit too neatly in the end, this is a sophisticated and engrossing historical tale by a writer who brings exceptional attention to detail, character development, and theme.
—Holly Koelling

Tingle, Rebecca. *The Edge on the Sword*. 2001. 288p. Putnam (9780399235801). Gr. 7–10.

In her exciting, poignant first novel set in the late 800s, Tingle imagines one year in the early life of the oldest daughter of King Alfred of West Saxony, Aethelflaed, who became known in Welsh and Irish records as the "most renowned queen of the Saxons." This is Flaed's fifteenth year, the year in which she reluctantly becomes betrothed to her father's friend and ally, Ethelred of Mercia, a man she doesn't know. She also acquires a personal guardian called Red, an envoy sent by Ethelred to protect her from enemies who might want to prevent the alliance. Resentful, she tests Red to the hilt, even giving him the slip once, only to end up in grave danger from which he rescues her. Then, with her father's approval, Red begins to train her how to fight like a man, with sword, knife, and shield, on horseback, and on foot. Tingle's research is obvious, and her graceful, tightly plotted narrative is steeped in a tangible sense of time and place—of the culture as well as the unrest, danger, and violence. Flaed is a spirited hero whose coming-of-age makes for an enthralling tale. She relishes the freedom her father allows her and the scholarship she achieves at his behest as she grows into a leader able to guide her people in peace and war. A first-rate example of historical fiction.
—Sally Estes

Tingle, Rebecca. ***Far Traveler*****. 2005. 240p. Putnam (9780399238901). Gr. 7–10.**

In *The Edge on the Sword* (2001), Tingle wrote about 15-year-old Aethelflaed, daughter of Alfred the Great, who became a powerful ruler in her own right. Little is known about her daughter Aelfwyn, who disappeared from historical record and literature following Aethelflaed's death in 919. Intrigued by the girl's disappearance, Tingle has created an immensely satisfying backstory for Aelfwyn (Wyn), which mixes fact and fiction as it vividly depicts the political turmoil of the time. Wyn's life is probably more romantic than that of the historic Aelfwyn. At 16, Wyn seems shy and scholarly, but when her uncle commands her to marry or enter a convent, she disguises herself as a traveling bard and flees. Wilfrid, a Northumbrian king beleaguered by Norse invaders, offers the bard protection, friendship, and trust—a trust that may be shattered by a plan that can endanger England and force Wyn to choose between her own people and heritage and her friend Wilfrid. An introductory note provides a few facts about the real Wyn. —Chris Sherman

Tocher, Timothy. ***Chief Sunrise, John McGraw, and Me*****. 2004. 160p. Cricket (9780812627114). Gr. 6–9.**

Fifteen-year-old Hank Cobb, tired of his transient ballplayer father's drinking and abuse, jumps at a chance to run away. Soon he meets mysterious Chief Sunrise, a great pitcher who claims to be a Seminole, who is trying to track down New York Giants manager John McGraw for a shot at the majors. While traveling north, the pair has a variety of experiences—from comical (playing on a girls' team) to dramatic (Chief faces prejudice). But perseverance pays off, bringing a surprising revelation about Chief's identity as well as a rewarding friendship and chance to shine on the diamond. The story is both entertaining and thought-provoking. In language appropriate to the book's 1919 setting, the likable protagonist relates the tale, incorporating abundant baseball detail as well as a growing personal awareness of civil rights issues, on and off the field. An author's note discusses McGraw, the struggles black players faced prior to the Negro Leagues, and Charlie Grant, who, like the fictional Chief, concealed his true identity to play. —Shelle Rosenfeld

Townley, Roderick. ***Sky*****. 2004. 272p. Simon & Schuster/Richard Jackson (9780689857126). Gr. 7–10.**

Fifteen-year-old Alec "Sky" Schuyler prefers to speak through his piano. His widower father, however, worries that Sky's passion for jazz will lead to a degenerate life. After sneaking into a rare performance by legendary jazz pianist Art Olmedo, Sky saves the blind musician's life on his way home. Angered by Sky's deceit, his father removes the piano from their apartment and later confronts and humiliates his son at a jazz session. In desperation, Sky runs away and turns to the old musician for help. Subplots involve Sky's school friendships, his budding sexuality, and a sexual harassment episode involving an English teacher with "more than pentameters on his mind." The 1959 Greenwich Village Beat scene is vividly recreated, with cameos by Allen Ginsberg and Gregory Corso. Sky's relationship with Olmedo is perhaps a bit too "copacetic," but his passion for jazz and struggle for self-determination will connect with contemporary teens. —Linda Perkins

Turnbull, Ann. ***No Shame, No Fear*****. 2004. 304p. Candlewick (9780763625054). Gr. 5–9.**

In 1662 the British Parliament passed the Quaker Act, making it treason to refuse to swear an oath of allegiance to the King and also making it illegal for the Friends of Truth, another name for the Quakers, to meet. It is during this time that 15-year-old Quaker Susanna and 17-year-old Anglican William meet and fall in love. To complicate matters, William, the son of the mayor, finds himself drawn to the Quaker faith, and Susanna's parents, friends, and mentor are imprisoned and persecuted. Susanna is also targeted for punishment after she continues to hold meetings with the children while the adults are in jail. This is a well-told historical tale, engaging and informative. The quality of the storytelling makes one wish for further resources or a historical note, but that doesn't detract from an enjoyable reading experience. —Cindy Welch

Venkatraman, Padma. *Climbing the Stairs*. 2008. 256p. Putnam (9780399247460). Gr. 6–9.

Growing up in a progressive family in Bombay during WWII, 15-year-old Vidya hopes that college is in her future, though her classmates are preparing for arranged marriages. After her father is severely injured in a riot, her life suddenly, irrevocably changes. Vidya, her older brother, and their parents move to Madras to join her grandfather's traditional household, where men and women live separately and Vidya's powerful aunt disdains the newcomers. When Vidya finds time after chores and schoolwork, she escapes upstairs to her grandfather's library, where she meets a young man who seems to understand her. In her first novel, Venkatraman paints an intricate and convincing backdrop of a conservative Brahmin home in a time of change. Vidya's first-person narrative conveys her pain, guilt, and hopes, as well as the strong sense of self that enables her to act with courage and occasionally with nobility in difficult circumstances. In an author's note, Venkatraman comments on several elements of the novel, including Gandhi's nonviolent revolution, Indian volunteers in the British army during WWII, and her family history. The striking cover art, which suggests Vidya's isolation, as well as the unusual setting, will draw readers to this vividly told story. —Carolyn Phelan

Voorhoeve, Anne C. *My Family for the War*. 2012. 400p. Dial (9780803733602). Gr. 7–12.

Franziska's wealthy Berlin family has converted from Judaism to Christianity, but when the Nazis come, her parents must send her at age 11 on the Kindertransport to safety in England. During the anguished parting, her father is arrested; her mother escapes over the border to Holland; and her best friend does not make it onto the transport. When the train arrives at the English station, there is no one to meet her, but she finds a home with a kind, Orthodox Jewish family in London. "What I had learned to hate, even to hide, was a source of joy in my host's family." Now called Frances, she bonds closely with her loving foster mother. Will she ever see her biological mother again? Does she want to? Originally published in Germany and translated in clear, direct prose, this novel, told from a young girl's perspective, is also a gripping history of how the war in Europe affected ordinary people. As London is bombed, Frances is temporarily evacuated to a cruel, rural family, and some of the locals hate her because she is Jewish and German. Then the news filters in about the transports and the death camps. When will the U.S. join the Allies? Will her mother survive Belsen? With the personal Kindertransport history, the intense drama about family, faith, guilt, love, and loyalty in wartime makes this an important addition to the Holocaust curriculum. —Hazel Rochman

Watkins, Steve. *Down Sand Mountain*. 2008. 336p. Candlewick (9780763638399). Gr. 7–12.

In 1966, a white kid discovers the cruelty in his small, segregated Florida mining town, where "everybody knew everybody else, unless they were colored," and racism is the norm, in himself, too. All Dewey, 12, wants is to fit in and have people like him, but that gets even harder after he stains his face with black shoe polish to dance in the local minstrel show, and the white bullies choose him as a target. Then his father, a miner, runs for city council again, even though he always loses because he wants to improve the blacks' neighborhood, where Dewey hates going. In his debut YA novel, award-winning adult author Watkins tells a classic loss-of-innocence story. The simple, beautiful prose remains totally true to the child's bewildered viewpoint, which is comic when Dewey does not get the big picture ("you never knew what was really going on"), anguished when he finally sees the truth. The plot includes Dewey's secret romance with his classmate and the sweet revenge on the bullies, and the daily detail about small things. Multiple local characters sometimes slow the story. Still, there is neither too much nostalgia nor message, and readers will be haunted by the disturbing drama of harsh secrets close to home. —Hazel Rochman

Weaver, Will. *Full Service*. 2005. 240p. Farrar (9780374324858). Gr. 7–10.

At his mother's suggestion, 15-year-old Wisconsin farm boy Paul Sutton takes a summer job "in town," pumping gas at the local Shell station. "You need to meet the public," his mother says, and for a boy from a conservative Christian background, what a revelation that public proves to be! There's Harry, a retired gangster (and murderer?); a family of hippies headed for San Francisco (it being 1965); a group of popular local kids (S. E. Hinton would have called them "Socs"); and more. It's enough to test one's faith. Of course it does, repeatedly, as Paul falls in love; discovers beer, marijuana, and rum-soaked cigars; and begins to question his most deeply held beliefs. There's a lot of familiar material in this coming-of-age novel that seems a sometimes uneasy mix of *A Prairie Home Companion* and *The Outsiders*, but Weaver is a wonderful stylist and his beautifully chosen words put such a shine on his deeply felt story that most teens will be able to find their own faces reflected in its pages. Chances are, they'll like what they see. —Michael Cart

★ Wein, Elizabeth. *Code Name Verity*. 2012. 352p. Hyperion (9781423152194). Gr. 9–12.

If you pick up this book, it will be some time before you put your dog-eared, tear-stained copy back down. Wein succeeds on three fronts: historical verisimilitude, gut-wrenching mystery, and a first-person voice of such confidence and flair that the protagonist might become a classic character—if only we knew what to call her. Alternately dubbed Queenie, Eva, Katharina, Verity, or Julie, depending on which double-agent operation she's involved in, she pens her tale as a confession while strapped to a chair and recovering from the latest round of Gestapo torture. The Nazis want the codes that Julie memorized as a wireless operator before crash-landing in France, and she supplies them, but along the way also tells of her fierce friendship with Maddie, a British pilot whose quiet gumption was every bit as impressive as Julie's brash fearlessness. Though delivered at knifepoint, Julie's narrative is peppered with dark humor and minor acts of defiance, and the tension that builds up between both past and present story lines is practically unbearable. A surprise change of perspective hammers home the devastating final third of the book, which reveals that Julie was even more courageous than we believed. Both crushingly sad and hugely inspirational, this plausible, unsentimental novel will thoroughly move even the most cynical of readers. —Daniel Kraus

Wells, Rosemary. *Red Moon at Sharpsburg*. 2007. 240p. Viking (9780670036387). Gr. 6–9.

Her school shuttered at the outbreak of the Civil War, India Moody, a 12-year-old Southerner, receives tutoring in natural sciences from progressive Emory Trimble, who encourages the smart, restless girl to aim for college. Soon enough, though, India must set aside her ambitions to shoulder the traditional burdens of women in wartime—nursing the wounded, comforting the grieving, stoically enduring even as her "heart tears down its middle seam." India's fierce hopes and restrained romance with Emory will hold readers, as will images etched by Wells' poetic, forceful writing, including unflinching scenes of the battlefield at Antietam, where bodies "blacken and bloat like sausages." An author's note and bibliographic note conclude, although neither address one unforgettable moment of magical realism in which green lights rise from the chests of dead soldiers: "Emerald stars . . . spill from the fallen men as far as a person can see." In a novel so clearly grounded in historical accuracy, readers will certainly wonder if this vivid scene has any factual basis. The overall impact of the novel is a potent call for peace and decency in any era, as well as a welcome representation of the Southern civilian experience for young adults. —Jennifer Mattson

Whelan, Gerard. *The Guns of Easter*. 2000. 167p. O'Brien (9780862784492). Gr. 6–10.

Growing up in the early twentieth century, 12-year-old Jimmy Conway feels removed from the direct consequences of war in Ireland even though his father is a soldier. For Jimmy, the conflict seems to be a complicated adult struggle that has little to do with his life in the slums of Dublin. However, when violence erupts literally down the street, his views about war are shaken, and he learns firsthand about treachery when he must risk his life to find food for his family. Whelan immerses readers in a harsh, yet poignant, journey that finds Jimmy learning much about the Irish people, his family, and most important, himself. The exciting plot moves effortlessly, enhanced by plenty of details to add character depth and historical context, and Whelan wisely avoids both extreme tragedy and overzealous triumph. The result is a fine adventure, with some realistic, genuinely heart-tugging twists. —Roger Leslie

Whelan, Gerard. ***A Winter of Spies*****. 2002. 191p. O'Brien (9780862785666). Gr. 6–10.**

Ireland, 1920, and the war that raged through *The Guns of Easter* (2000) comes closer to home for the Conway family. This time, the conflict is seen through the point of view of plucky, 11-year-old Sarah, who has secretly been smuggling guns to help the cause for independence. The previous novel's major conflicts took place in the streets of Dublin, but the action in this one is largely at the Conway house: when two suspicious men move in next door, Sarah witnesses some dubious goings on, which may be the work of spies or counterspies. Although Sarah's active participation in the story is limited to the beginning and end, her observations give a clear picture of her character, and she raises thoughtful questions about what drives people to create such destruction. Recent events, such as the situation in the Middle East, will make the novel's portrayal of everyday people caught up in war even more stirring. A sequel that is just as strong as its predecessor, which won several book awards in Ireland. —Roger Leslie

Whelan, Gloria. ***Listening for Lions*****. 2005. 208p. HarperCollins (9780060581749). Gr. 6–9.**

In 1919, in British East Africa, 13-year-old Rachel loses her missionary parents during an influenza epidemic. When she turns to her English neighbors for help, the Pritchards ensnare her in a shocking, ill-intentioned scheme. Disowned by their rich family, they had planned to send their daughter, Valerie, to her grandfather's estate in England, where they hoped she would help to reinstate them in his will. But after Valerie dies of flu, the Pritchards conspire to send Rachel, whose red hair matches their daughter's. Whelan creates deliciously odious villains in the Pritchard parents, who, with shameless cunning, manipulate Rachel into agreeing to the deceit. Once in England, Rachel and the perilously ill grandfather develop a surprisingly strong, affectionate bond, although she continues the ruse, believing that "one more disappointment would be the end of the old man." In a straightforward, sympathetic voice, Rachel tells an involving, episodic story that follows her across continents and through life stages as she grapples with her dishonesty, grief for her lost parents and life in Africa, and looming questions about how to prepare for grown-up life at a time when few choices were allowed to women. Gentle, nostalgic, and fueled with old-fashioned girl power, this involving orphan story will please fans of Frances Hodgson Burnett's classic *The Secret Garden* (1912) and Eva Ibbotson's *The Star of Kazan* (2004). —Gillian Engberg

White, Ruth. ***Memories of Summer*****. 2000. 144p. Farrar (9780374349455). Gr. 7–12.**

When 13-year-old Lyric, her older sister, Summer, and their father move to Flint, Michigan, from rural Virginia, Summer (who has always been a little odd) makes a swift and frightening slide into full-fledged schizophrenia. Her behavior changes from withdrawn to bizarre: she hears voices, speaks with invisible people, and becomes increasingly more paranoid. Lyric and her father must finally make the painful decision to commit Summer to the state hospital, and Lyric must steel herself to the fact that she has lost the motherly, beautiful sister of her childhood. As always, White excels at the music of hill-country speech, but here proves she has an ear for city voices as well. The 1955 setting is authentic but not distracting to the themes of loss, grief, and acceptance. Teens interested in the subject of mental illness or those who have read books such as Sonya Sones' *Stop Pretending* (1999) will find this an accurate, sympathetic portrait of one family's effort to support their sick child. —Debbie Carton

Williams, Susan. ***Wind Rider*****. 2006. 320p. HarperCollins/Laura Geringer (9780060872366). Gr. 6–9.**

Set on the steppes of Central Asia 6,000 years ago, Williams' stirring coming-of-age story begins with a *pour-*

quoi tale about how the wild horse became domesticated. After Fern discovers a wild foal trapped in a bog, she keeps her find a secret; horses are prized food among her hunting and gathering tribe. She names the foal Thunder, and in between chores, she steals time with the animal. Dreams lead her to try something unknown: "Who in all the world had ever sat upon a living horse?" Eventually her community discovers her secret, and when Thunder proves her usefulness by carrying loads, Fern is allowed to keep her. Still, she wonders if the rumors whispered by suspicious family and neighbors are true: "Maybe I was some strange animal-talker person! . . . Was I touched with darkness, as my mother said?" Williams' novel combines the exciting animal story with Fern's wrenching questions about growing up, which will resonate instantly with contemporary teens. Fern aggressively strains against her mother's expectations and her society's traditional gender roles, and it is these timeless struggles, narrated in Fern's poetic voice, that transform Williams' impressively researched details into a vividly imagined, wholly captivating world. Jean Craighead George and Louise Erdrich fans will particularly love the animal connections, but most teens will admire Fern's unbending courage and her search for a place in the world and a love to share. —Gillian Engberg

Wilson, Diane Lee. *Firehorse*. 2006. 336p. Simon & Schuster/Margaret K. McElderry (9781416915515). Gr. 7–10.

It's 1872, and 15-year-old Rachel often escapes the confines of corsets and social strictures by going for gallops on her beloved horse around her small-town Illinois home. When her father moves the family to Boston and the horse is sold, she has a difficult time adjusting to her father's demands of ladylike behavior and her mother's coaxing her toward womanly pursuits. The author of *Black Storm Comin'* (2005), Wilson paces the story well, with tension building: an arsonist is at work setting fires in Boston and the horses needed to pull fire equipment are falling ill at an alarming rate. At first only her grandmother seems to understand the importance of Rachel's dream of becoming a veterinarian, but soon she has other allies, and a path that appeared to be blocked begins to open before her. The love interest and the mystery that are integral to the story are secondary to Rachel's pursuit of her goal, which begins with helping one firehouse horse recover from burns. The novel's finest achievement, though, is the convincing depiction of family dynamics in an era when men ruled the household and women, who had few opportunities, folded their dreams and put them away with the linens they embroidered. —Carolyn Phelan

Wiseman, Eva. *Puppet*. 2009. 240p. Tundra (9780887768286). Gr. 7–12.

Times are hard in Julie Vamosi's Hungarian village in the late nineteenth century, and the townspeople, including her father, blame the Jews. After Julie's best friend, Esther, a young servant girl, disappears, the rumor spreads that the Jews cut her throat and drained her blood to drink with their Passover matzos. The townspeople even beat a terrified Jewish kid, Morris, and force him to lie and say that he witnessed the ritual murder in the synagogue and that his own father took part. "Kill the Jews" is the mob's subsequent cry. Then Esther's drowned body is found in a stream, and there is no sign of any violence. Is Julie brave enough to face the mob with the truth? Will the court listen? Based on the records of a trial in 1883, this searing novel dramatizes virulent anti-Semitism from the viewpoint of a Christian child. There is some contrivance as Julie eavesdrops on the townspeople's plots and sees Morris beaten to "confess." But her first-person narrative reveals good and bad people on all sides, including her own brutal dad, the kind Jewish doctor, and the sympathetic defense lawyer. The tension builds to the trial scenes, and the climax is electrifying with its public drama on the witness stand and the heartbreak between Morris and his dad. Adults will want this, too. —Hazel Rochman

Wolf, Allan. *The Watch That Ends the Night*. 2011. 472p. Candlewick (9780763637033). Gr. 9–12.

With the 100-year anniversary of the *Titanic* disaster approaching, expect a new flood of works addressing the infamous disaster, though it's difficult to believe any will surpass this masterpiece. Using free-form poems from the points of view of two dozen travelers, Wolf has composed a multi-octave chorus of voices that is alternately—sometimes simultaneously—spirited, angry, frightened, and mournful. There is the crew ("But my *Titanic*, she is a *graceful* whale," says Captain E. J. Smith), the first-class elite ("The only ice I knew of / was in the gin and tonic that I lifted," says businessman Bruce Ismay), the third-class rabble ("We waited for someone to show us to our boats," says hopeful immigrant Olaus Abelseth), and, in two brilliant, audacious moves, a ship rat that seems to represent the desperate will to live ("follow the food") and the iceberg itself, a godlike monolith that acts as omniscient narrator and Greek chorus ("I am the ice. / I see tides ebb and flow. / I've watched civilizations come and go."). Wolf leaves no emotion unplumbed, no area of research uninvestigated, and his voices are so authentic they hurt. Nothing recommends this to a YA audience in particular, but who cares? Everyone should read it. Outstanding, insightful back matter completes this landmark work. —Daniel Kraus

Yolen, Jane, and Robert J. Harris. ***Girl in a Cage.*** **2002. 240p. Philomel (9780399236273). Gr. 6–10.**

The team that brought readers the immediacy and impact of *The Queen's Own Fool* (2000) returns with another historical page-turner. In 1306, the English king Edward Longshanks captured Marjorie, the 11-year-old daughter and heir of Scotland's King Robert the Bruce, and kept her in a cage. From this shard of history, Yolen and Harris fashion a riveting first-person narrative. As Marjorie battles hunger, the elements, and stark terror, she remembers her father's quest to rally the Scots to his crown, her regal stepmother, and her beloved uncle Neil. The story doesn't understate the vicious fighting or the use of women as pawns, but it also shows the courage of those who, through just and kind acts, stood up for their country. What is particularly engrossing is how Marjorie works out in her own mind how a princess should behave, even when caged like an animal. Yolen and Harris allow readers to see that courage can take many forms and that honor knows neither age nor gender. —GraceAnne A. DeCandido

Yolen, Jane, and Robet J. Harris. ***Prince Across the Water.*** **2004. 320p. Philomel (9780399238970). Gr. 6–10.**

Yolen and Harris tell the story of a young highlander who fights for Bonnie Prince Charlie at Culloden. Just 13 and prone to seizures, Duncan is disappointed when he is not allowed to join his father and the other men of the village in answering their clan chief's call to war. But before the year is out, he has shouldered his father's work, suffered the loss of loved ones, fought in a bloody battle, and helped his prince in an unexpected way. The convincing depictions of people and relationships earlier in the story deepen the sense of despair during the battle, which is realistically depicted as cruel, violent, and gory. Structured in three sections, the novel creates a strong sense of life in the Scottish Highlands in 1745–1746, of the carnage at the battle of Culloden, and of Duncan's growing awareness of the world and his place in it. Combining a sensitive portrayal with dramatic tension, Trina Schart Hyman's sensitive jacket art promises exactly what this novel delivers: a spirited historical adventure and a sympathetic hero. —Carolyn Phelan

Yolen, Jane, and Robert J. Harris. ***Queen's Own Fool.*** **2000. 416p. Philomel (9780399233807). Gr. 7–12.**

The life of Mary Queen of Scots gets a fascinating new telling in this sweeping novel narrated in the voice of a female Jester—La Jardiniere. When orphan Nicola Ambruzzi performs for the French court with her troupe of players, the bold, smart-mouthed peasant girl wins the interest and affection of Mary, and Nicola joins the court as an entertainer and truth-telling companion to the new queen. A deep friendship develops as Nicola follows the queen through her dramatic life in France and Scotland, finally leaving Mary before the queen's flight to England. With an outsider's eye for vivid detail, Nicola makes the cultural and historical particulars of costume, food, houses, court personalities, and politics easily imaginable. Readers without previous knowledge of the period may have trouble keeping track of characters and become weighed down by the book's dialects and sprawling length. But the exciting story of conspiracies and power upheavals

offers a rich introduction to the tumultuous history, and readers will respond to the poignant experiences of alienation, romance, intrigue, betrayal, and justice as Nicola and the young queen come of age. A brief author's note helps separate fact from fiction.
—Gillian Engberg

Yolen, Jane, and Robert J. Harris. *The Rogues*. 2007. 320p. Philomel (9780399238987). Gr. 6–10.

With swift brutality, wealthy lords in the Scottish highlands have cleared their estates of tenant farmers to turn the land over to grazing sheep, whose wool could be sold to British textiles factories at a greater profit. In this fourth Scottish-tale collaboration by Yolen and Harris, Roddy Macallan's family is one of the victims. When their pleas meet deaf ears, the farmers embark on dramatic, often heartbreaking journeys to Glasgow or to distant American cities. Roddy turns back to search for a treasured jewel he is sure his mother, before her death, said lay hidden in their cottage. At least if he could get this "blessing," the family could sell it for desperately needed funds. The risky journey almost kills the intrepid lad. Not only must he face the heartless laird, or lord, but also the laird's vicious henchman, Rood. Then there is the mysterious rogue, Alan Dunbar, a highlander who is fighting the laird in his own way. Can Roddy trust him, or would Dunbar just as soon steal the valuable blessing for himself? Although Roddy finds the treasure a wee bit too easily at the outset, the suspense mounts and the plot races along flawlessly in this excellent historical adventure.
—Anne O'Malley

★ Zusak, Markus. *The Book Thief*. 2006. 512p. Knopf (9780375831003). Gr. 10–12.

Death is the narrator of this lengthy, powerful story of a town in Nazi Germany. He is a kindly, caring Death, overwhelmed by the souls he has to collect from people in the gas chambers, from soldiers on the battlefields, and from civilians killed in bombings. Death focuses on a young orphan, Liesl; her loving foster parents; the Jewish fugitive they are hiding; and a wild but gentle teen neighbor, Rudy, who defies the Hitler Youth and convinces Liesl to steal for fun. After Liesl learns to read, she steals books from everywhere. When she reads a book in the bomb shelter, even a Nazi woman is enthralled. Then the book thief writes her own story. Readers may be slowed by viewpoints that shift from past to present time, but as in Zusak's enthralling *I Am the Messenger* (2004), the astonishing characters, drawn without sentimentality, will grab readers. More than the overt message about the power of words, it's Liesl's confrontation with horrifying cruelty and her discovery of kindness in unexpected places that tell the heartbreaking truth.
—Hazel Rochman

Mystery and Suspense

Abrahams, Peter. *Behind the Curtain*. 2006. 352p. HarperCollins/Laura Geringer (9780060737047). Gr. 6–9.

The second entry in the Echo Falls Mystery series, as successful as its predecessor, starts with puzzling questions that spring right from Ingrid Levin-Hill's own life: Why is her football-mad older brother suddenly so much stronger, and why has her father been so tense lately? The plot unfolds slowly at first, but Abrahams' exceptional overlay of detail, especially descriptions of the particular stresses and the goofy occurrences that mark Ingrid's experiences as an eighth-grader, makes the story very convincing as the action builds. Ingrid discovers anabolic steroids are behind her brother's improved performance and new aggressiveness (and also behind some of the mysterious behavior of various people in her town), but just as she is about to do something with her knowledge, she is kidnapped. She escapes, but police don't believe her story, and she has to set up her own sting to prove she is telling the truth. A timely issue gives this mystery a "ripped from the headlines" flavor, but the real kick for readers comes from a believable eighth-grade heroine's investigation of a high-school scandal. —Connie Fletcher

Abrahams, Peter. *Bullet Point*. 2010. 304p. HarperTeen (9780061227691). Gr. 9–12.

It's common enough to call a book a page-turner, but here's one that should've been printed on a scroll—those pesky page turns take far too much time. With an engulfing plot, multifaceted characters, and a plausibility rare to the genre, Abrahams' latest beats you senseless and leaves you for dead. Great, huh? When a budget crunch squeezes out his school's baseball program, 16-year-old Wyatt moves across the state to take advantage of another school's team. It's there that he meets Greer—a few years older, beautiful, and equipped with wildly fluctuating mood swings. The frequent arguments between the two are the book's heart, skipping fluently and believably between impatience, attraction, desperation, and hope. Like almost all characters in the book, Greer's good/bad status is perpetually in doubt, especially when her incarcerated dad helps arrange a meeting between Wyatt and his biological father, who also resides in the local prison. When Wyatt begins to suspect his father's innocence, he gets curious—and in trouble. Edgier and sexier than most YA novels dare, Abrahams' thriller wrenches guts with a Richard Price–like facility. Readers will be as irretrievably drawn in as Wyatt. —Daniel Kraus

Beaudoin, Sean. *You Killed Wesley Payne*. 2011. 368p. Little, Brown (9780316077422). Gr. 9–12.

The cliques rule the rackets in Salt River High. The two top outfits, the Balls (football players, "wearers of no-irony crew cuts") and Pinker Casket (thrash rockers, "most appropriate for funerals or virgin sacrifices"), are hurtling toward a turf war, and all the assorted mid-level cliques (and even the crooked Fack Cult T) are constantly looking for an angle to ride to prominence. At the center of the maelstrom is a body, Wesley Payne, a former member of the Euclidians (nerds, "fingertip sniffers"), who was found wrapped in duct tape, hanging upside down from the goalposts. Teenage private dick Dalton Rev arrives to sort out the murder, locate a missing hundred grand, and if everything rolls his way, ride off into the sunset with the adorable Macy Payne, Wesley's sister. Beaudoin plays a Chandler hand with a Tarantino smirk in this ultra-clever high-school noir, dropping invented brand labels on everything from energy-drink ingredients (Flavor Flavah) to the Almighty ("Oh my Bob!"). Ever checking his moves against what his crime-novel hero, Lexington Cole, would do, Dalton himself is so straight hard-boiled, it's screwy: "Dalton played it cool. He played it frozen. He was in full Deano at the Copa mode." But in the end, none of the stylistic pastiche and slick patter would matter if they weren't hitched to such a propulsive mystery, with enough double-crosses and blindsiding reveals to give you vertigo. Moreover, the opening "Clique Chart" might just be the funniest four pages you'll read all year. —Ian Chipman

Bell, Hilari. ***The Last Knight.*** **2007. 368p. Eos (9780060825034). Gr. 7–10.**

This enjoyable novel from the Knight and Rogue series seamlessly combines fantasy, mystery, and adventure, but Bell's most notable accomplishment is the two main characters: the knight and the rogue. A young knight errant in a society where that occupation has not been viable (or anything but laughable) for a couple of centuries, Sir Michael approaches the world in an honest, straightforward manner. His page, Fisk, an admitted con artist who has learned through hard experience that a sideways approach often works best, looks upon his master's heroic exploits with terror, exasperation, irony, and grudging admiration for his courage. From chapter to chapter, the narration alternates between the two and makes their differences apparent from the start. Each has his secrets, some of which are revealed as they work to free an imprisoned lady, and later, having learned that she was accused of poisoning her husband, attempting to recapture her. With an undercurrent of wry humor and narration that leaves some things unsaid, this intelligently written novel will challenge and reward readers. —Carolyn Phelan

Blundell, Judy. ***What I Saw and How I Lied.*** **2008. 288p. Scholastic (9780439903462). Gr. 8–12.**

In this sophisticated thriller, 15-year-old Evie grows up quickly when she discovers her adored parents are not the people she thought they were. While on vacation in Palm Beach in 1947, Evie's parents, Joe and Bev, get involved in a shady business deal with the Graysons, another couple on holiday. Meanwhile, Evie begins a flirtation with Peter, a handsome ex-GI who served with Joe and just happens to be staying at their hotel. Evie soon learns that Peter's presence is no coincidence and that he threatens to uncover a terrible secret that Joe has kept since the war. Then Bev, Joe, and Peter go boating, but only two of them return. Evie must sort through secrets, lies, and her own grief to find the truth. Using pitch-perfect dialogue and short sentences filled with meaning, Blundell has crafted a suspenseful, historical mystery that not only subtly explores issues of post–WWII racism, sexism, and socioeconomic class, but also realistically captures the headiness of first love and the crushing realization that adults are not all-powerful. —Jennifer Hubert

Bradbury, Jennifer. ***Shift.*** **2008. 256p. Atheneum (9781416962199). Gr. 7–12.**

Before they start college, Chris and his best friend, Win, bike 3,000 miles across country from their home in West Virginia to California. On the way, they get into a big fight, and Win disappears. Now an FBI agent is at Chris' college dorm asking questions, and Chris is being followed. Along with the mystery and the mounting suspense come flashbacks to the friends' cross-country adventure. Some metaphors and messages are too heavily spelled out (including a character wrestling with an angel), and, of course, Chris' search for his friend is a search for himself. But Bradbury's keen details about the bike trip, the places, the weather, the food, the camping, and the locals add wonderful texture to this exciting first novel, as Chris remembers the trip and returns to find what really happened. Best of all is the friendship story; many teens will recognize how even between close buddies, there's rivalry, anger, and heartbreak. —Hazel Rochman

Brooks, Kevin. ***Lucas.*** **2003. 432p. Scholastic/Chicken House (9780439456982). Gr. 8–10.**

Brooks, author of *Martyn Pig* (2002), offers an-edge-of-the-seat story that has overtones of classics such as *The Ox Bow Incident* and *To Kill a Mockingbird*. Fifteen-year-old Cait lives on a small British island and knows from the moment she sees Lucas walking on the causeway that connects her home to the mainland that he will play a significant part in her life. A handsome, prescient young drifter, Lucas is tagged as a thief by the rougher elements on the island. Cait's college-age brother has begun hanging out with one of them—Oxford student Justin, who has a dark side. As Justin becomes a danger, and Lucas a blessing, both Cait and the reader feel the confluence of events building with an intensity that is almost painful. In a final scene, the extensive foreshadowing that has permeated the book builds to a terrible climax. It's not so much what Brooks writes about (sometimes the plotting is over the top), but the way he writes. There's a purity to his style that pervades the narrative, which is by turns sweet, taut, and terrifying. The relationship between Cait and her father has a reality and honesty that's affecting. Teens may pick this up for its sheer intensity, but once they put it down, they'll ponder its meanings. —Ilene Cooper

Clements, Andrew. *Things Hoped For*. 2006. 176p. Philomel (9780399243509). Gr. 8–11.

Since leaving West Virginia for New York City two years ago, Gwen has been living with her grandfather and studying violin at the Manhattan School of Music. Now a senior, she finds tensions rising as the conservatory auditions that will determine her future as a violinist approach. When Grampa disappears after leaving a reassuring, though cryptic, message on the answering machine, shy Gwen is unsettled but determined to carry on with her routine. Several days later, the manner of his reappearance is a shock, but by that time Gwen has an ally: Robert, a trumpet student who wants to help and seems uniquely qualified to do so. Robert will be better known to readers of Clements' *Things Not Seen* (2002) as Bobby, who woke up invisible one morning and struggled to become visible again. Gwen's story, which takes place two years later, is already disquieting when an unpredictable and dangerous character enters the story, drawn by Robert's experience with invisibility. That subplot recedes in importance, though, beside the realistic depiction of a young woman who is thrown off kilter by emotional turmoil and not just regains her balance but also gains a new level of confidence. This offers a riveting story line, engaging characters, and intriguing insights into the development of musical artistry.
—Carolyn Phelan

Cormier, Robert. *The Rag and Bone Shop*. 2001. 155p. Delacorte (9780385729628). Gr. 8–10.

Terse and terrifying, this final book from Cormier will leave a lasting impression. Jason, almost 13, is a shy, ineffectual child, who takes being bullied as a matter of course—but if he sees someone else being pushed around, he may strike back. When the seven-year-old girl who lives next door is murdered, Jason is horrified. He was the last one to see her alive. He wants to do everything he can to help find the killer, so when the police come calling, he tells them all he knows. What he doesn't know is that Trent, a detective adept at extracting confessions, has been called into the case—and Trent has Jason in his sights as the murderer. Cormier presents a cat-and-mouse game so tense that readers will feel they must escape the pages just as Jason wants to extricate himself from the stuffy, cell-like room where his interrogation is taking place. But this is not just Jason's story. Cormier delves into the psyche of Trent without much of a nod to the fact that this is a book for young people. Readers will get a glimpse into the adult world, and find it sad and ugly. The book's horrifying, surprising conclusion will engender discussion, and there may be disagreement about how well it works. Yet, it's hard to imagine any reader not coming away from this shaken. Cormier, who died in 2000, left at the top of his game.
—Ilene Cooper

Cummings, Priscilla. *Red Kayak*. 2004. 224p. Dutton (9780525473176). Gr. 6–9.

In this satisfying crime and coming-of-age drama, a toddler drowns in a kayak accident after friends of teenage Brady, the victim's neighbor, vent some anger against the child's dad by drilling holes in the bottom of his craft. It was a mean-spirited prank—but no one was supposed to die. What happens now? Revealing the terrible secret would implicate Brady's friends in the drowning, and it clouds his whole world with guilt and fear. Cummings works plot and characterizations skillfully, building suspense as the evidence unfolds and as Brady wrestles with his decision and tries to come to terms with his own responsibility. Brady's eastern-Maryland surroundings and heritage (his father, a waterman, struggles to make a living from crabbing) are also vividly evoked. Brady's ultimate decision is both anguished and well reasoned, making for a realistic conclusion. —Anne O'Malley

Deuker, Carl. *Payback Time*. 2010. 304p. Houghton (9780547279817). Gr. 7–10.

Deuker (*Gym Candy*, 2003) really cranks up the suspense in his newest page-turner, combining a Seattle high-school football team's march toward the state championship game with a school reporter's investigation of an apparent ringer that the coach has slipped in to bolster the defense. Mitch doesn't think much of his new assignment as sports reporter, but when he sees how Coach McNulty keeps Angel—a reclusive new student who shows star-quality abilities in practice—benched until late in each hard-fought game, his suspicions are aroused. Thrilled to think that he has caught wind of an actual cheating scandal, Mitch digs into Angel's past. What he discovers stirs up far more trouble than he has bargained for, and pitches him into a series of terrifying situations. The game action alone is riveting even for readers who don't know a naked bootleg from a hook-and-ladder play, but Deuker enriches the tale with several well-tuned subplots and a memorable narrator-protagonist who turns a corner on his own self-image while weathering brutal tests of his courage and determination. Definitely one for the top shelf. —John Peters

Ehrenhaft, Daniel. *Drawing a Blank: or, How I Tried to Solve a Mystery, End a Feud, and Land the Girl of My Dreams*. Illus. by Trevor Ristow. 2006. 336p. HarperCollins (9780060752521). Gr. 8–11.

Surprising in format as well as plot, Ehrenhaft's novel intersperses chapters of first-person narrative with episodes of Signy the Superbad, a superhero comic strip drawn by the narrator and inspired by his experiences. For Carlton, drawing comics is both a way of life and a retreat from it. Shipped off to a New England prep school by his distant father, who seems obsessed by an ancestral Scottish feud, Carlton copes by going through the motions at school and drawing his own alternate reality. A phone message from his father's kidnapper jolts him into action—and divides the novel into before, when Carlton's life features classmates barging into his room to conduct their annual "Who-Would-You-Bang Forum," and after, as Carlton and his enigmatic new friend Aileen roam the Scottish countryside attempting to find Carlton's father and recover an ancient dagger. For a self-described misanthrope, Carlton makes a very engaging character, caring but wary, vulnerable but game, and readers occasionally willing to suspend disbelief will find the narrative highly entertaining and sometimes enlightening. Intermittent footnotes supply information on various people (Dylan Thomas, Keith Richards, etc.) and facts and fictional details (prehistoric stone circles, a recipe for bannocks, Carlton's half-sister's imaginary friend). A fresh, effervescent combination of mystery, adventure, and teen angst. —Carolyn Phelan

Flinn, Alex. *Nothing to Lose*. 2004. 288p. HarperCollins (9780060517502). Gr. 7–12.

The author of *Breathing Underwater* (2001) and *Breaking Point* (2002) mines her legal background to good effect in this new novel. A year has passed since Michael fled his impossible home life to join a traveling carnival. Now the 17-year-old runaway has returned to Miami to find his mother going on trial for the murder of his savagely abusive stepfather. What really happened? Only Michael knows the whole truth, but will he come forward? In a narrative that—in brief, alternating chapters—moves backward and forward in time, Flinn expertly reveals how very complicated this question is. The result is a fast-paced, readable mystery that is rooted in the psychology of battered-spouse syndrome and its impact on an entire family. An inside look at carnival life and Michael's growing love for another carny named Kirstie add gritty texture and a layer of emotional richness to the already intriguing plot. —Michael Cart

Gantos, Jack. *The Love Curse of the Rumbaughs*. 2006. 192p. Farrar (9780374336905). Gr. 10–12.

"I expect you might think the story . . . is perversely gothic in some unhealthy way," begins narrator Ivy, and despite her protestations that what follows is a "plain and true small-town story," readers will quickly discover that Gantos adheres faithfully to the gothic novel's elements and utterly shatters the boundaries between the sacrosanct and the perverse. Identical albino twins Abner and Adolph Rumbaugh are an oddity in their small Pennsylvania town, but as a child, Ivy adores the elderly pair and spends free hours playing at their pharmacy. Then she discovers their family curse—a warped, overwhelming love for their deceased mother, which drives them to horrifying acts to preserve her memory. As Ivy grows older, the twins' terrifying secret begins to make sense, and her own ties to the curse become clear. The intimations of incest, the details of mutilated corpses, a bizarre sex scene, and the story's creepy plotline may raise plenty of eyebrows and limit the book's audience, and lengthy passages explaining the curse may slow some readers. Still, teens (and college students) who have studied the gothic novel tradition will find many familiar, skillfully re-created elements in the tale, along with provocative questions about free will and genetic engineering, while horror fans will admire the author's ability to ably—even gleefully—spin such a shocking, darkly comic tale. —Gillian Engberg

Giles, Gail. ***Shattering Glass*****. 2002. 224p. Roaring Brook (9780761315810). Gr. 8–10.**

"Simon Glass was easy to hate . . . we each hated him for a different reason, but we didn't realize it until the day we killed him." The tension-filled story's narrator is Young Steward, a member of the cool group run by Rob Haynes, a student who transferred in and immediately took over with a wide-reaching power. Rob manages to transform Simon, the class nerd—and transform his classmates' attitude toward Simon—with the finesse of Svengali. But Simon is not content with his newfound popularity. He begins collecting information about his benefactors, and the secrets he learns about them, especially Rob and his devastating past, come out in a horrifyingly realistic scene in which the boys beat Simon to death. This first novel has flaws. Some of the adults are caricatures, and if you look too closely at the plot, you'll find cracks in places. But the pacing is superb, and the story's twists are unexpected and disquieting. Heading the chapters are the comments of those involved, five years after the event. This conceit extends the story and will keep readers wondering. Fans of Nancy Werlin's books will appreciate this one; it's a page-turner. —Ilene Cooper

Golding, Julia. ***Cat among the Pigeons*****. 2008. 432p. Roaring Brook (9781596433526). Gr. 6–9.**

Cat is back for another dramatic adventure at London's Theatre Royal on Drury Lane. Coming quickly on the heels of *The Diamond of Drury Lane* (2008), this latest escapade features our heroine, Catherine Royal, desperately trying to protect Pedro Hawkins, a young former slave who happens to be an outstanding actor. Pedro's ex-master, the villainous Kingston Hawkins, will stop at nothing to try to capture his "property" and return to the West Indies with him. Cat engages the whole theater company, along with the theatergoing public, in rallying to Pedro's defense. After confronting some pro-slavery plotters, she needs to run for her own life and disguises herself as a schoolboy with the help of some allies at Westminster School. Golding weaves a fine historic tale about the antislavery battle in England in the 1790s by way of an ensemble of colorful characters, death-defying adventures, witty dialogue and narration, and lively action. Fans of the first book will not want to miss this sequel, but *Pigeons* also stands as an outstanding solo performance. —Anne O'Malley

Golding, Julia. ***The Diamond of Drury Lane*****. 2008. 432p. Roaring Brook (9781596433519). Gr. 7–10.**

The Drury Theater, where she was abandoned as a baby, is the only home Catherine Royal has ever known. When she learns the theater owner has a deposited a diamond somewhere on the premises, she vows to help keep it safe. The whereabouts of the diamond is a thread that runs through a story with as many cliff-hangers as there are chapters in the book. But real thrills also come from the varied, sharply drawn cast that populates the Covent Garden area of early-eighteenth-century London. Violin virtuoso Pedro, a young African who was once a slave, seems trustworthy—but is he? Roughneck Billy wants Cat's affection, and he'll take what he can't get. Jonathan, the theater prompter, may be involved in insurrection. Then there are the nobs, Lord Francis and Lady Elizabeth, who befriend Cat, a relationship that causes problems for all concerned. Golding, who won a 2006 Smarties Prize for this in Britian, is a talented scene setter. From the spectacles in the theater to the filth of the city streets, she offers a view of London that readers can grasp with all their senses. This first book in the Cat Royal Quartet ably sets the stage for what's to come. —Ilene Cooper

Haines, Kathryn Miller. *The Girl Is Murder*. **2011. 352p. Roaring Brook (9781596436091). Gr. 7–10.**

Iris Anderson used to be a private-school girl. She also used to have a mother and a father with two legs. But after her father was injured at Pearl Harbor, her mother became depressed and committed suicide. By the time Pop returns home to start a detective business, the family's fortunes have fallen, and 15-year-old Iris finds herself living on the Lower East Side and attending P.S. 110 with kids a lot tougher than she is. This is the premise of a smart offering that gives both mysteries and historical fiction a good name. Here the mystery surrounds Tom, a boy at school who disappears. Pop has been hired to solve the case, but Iris can see that doing the required legwork on only one leg can be pretty exhausting. So she takes it upon herself to become her father's assistant. That gets her to places she shouldn't be, like the Savoy in Harlem; hanging out with the wrong people; and lying to just about everybody. The mystery is solid, but what makes this such a standout is the cast. Sounding as though they're right out of the 1940s (well, a 1940s movie, anyway), the characters, young and old, leap off the pages. Iris, intriguing and infuriating, captures the tension inherent in the teenage years, no matter what the decade. This joint is jumping. —Ilene Cooper

Hoffman, Mary. *The Falconer's Knot*. **2007. 288p. Bloomsbury (9781599900568). Gr. 8–11.**

Hoffman set her acclaimed Stravaganza novels in an alternate world that resembled sixteenth-century Italy. In this suspenseful mystery, Hoffman leaves the alternate worlds behind and locates her story in the real-world history of fourteenth-century Umbria. Sixteen-year-old Silvano, a handsome nobleman, admires Angelica, a local merchant's wife, from afar. Then Angelica's husband is murdered, and Silvano becomes the prime suspect. Until his innocence is proven, Silvano takes refuge in a Franciscan friary, where he enjoys making pigments for local artists and finds himself attracted to a lovely novice at the adjoining abbey. But a series of mysterious deaths puts Silvano under greater suspicion, and he determines to find the murderer. The publisher has compared this novel to Umberto Eco's *Name of the Rose* (1983), and there are certainly similarities between the books' friary settings and central mysteries. Hoffman makes the story her own with an exciting tangle of murder suspects and romantic intrigues. The plot is crowded with characters, and the intricate details about pigment preparation and fourteenth-century art and life will slow some readers and fascinate others. Hoffman creates utterly engaging characters and vivid settings, and she skillfully turns up the suspense, wrapping her varied plot threads into a satisfying whole. Readers will race through to the satisfying fairy-tale conclusion, which includes some empowering twists for the female characters. —Gillian Engberg

Horowitz, Anthony. *Eagle Strike*. **2004. 272p. Philomel (9780399239793). Gr. 7–12.**

Alex Rider, reluctant teen MI6 operative, is back for another adventure, complete with a missile-loaded getaway bicycle and a man who wants to destroy not the whole world but just the parts of it that grow or manufacture illegal drugs, such as heroin and cocaine. The action begins after Alex recognizes a Russian assassin very much out of place in the sleepy French town where Alex is vacationing, and the ensuing chase takes the dynamic hero through a life-size video game before ending with an airport-runway save involving American nuclear weapons and *Air Force One*. Once again, Horowitz tells a tight story, and his knack for descriptive action drives readers through the very accessible plot. Teens need not have read previous Rider adventures to enjoy this one. —Cindy Welch

Jinks, Catherine. *Evil Genius*. **2007. 496p. Harcourt (9780152059880). Gr. 7–10.**

Is it possible to cultivate readers' affection for a character who has been trained from his tenderest years to dismiss evil as a "loaded word"? Australian writer

Jinks, author of the Crusades-era Pagan series, successfully meets the challenge in this very different novel. She devises gradations of wrongdoing so steep that her antihero's adversaries leave him (almost) smelling like a rose. At age seven, child prodigy Cadel Piggott lands in a shrink's office for illegal computer hacking, where psychologist Thaddeus Roth delivers startling counsel: "Next time, don't get caught." Thaddeus is an agent of Cadel's real father, a brilliant crook who, from behind bars, manages to place Cadel at the secretive Axis Institute for World Domination. By 13, Cadel is earnestly studying "Infiltration, Misinformation, and Embezzlement," but as he increasingly relies on an outside friendship, he privately plots to extricate himself from the paterfamilias. Comic-book fans will enjoy the school's aspiring villains (including one who floors foes with deadly B.O.), but this is more than a campy set-piece. Cadel's turnabout is convincingly hampered by his difficulty recognizing appropriate outlets for rage, and Jinks' whiplash-inducing suspense writing will gratify fans of Anthony Horowitz's high-tech spy scenarios. Although some of the technical concerns of evil geniuses (firewalls, tax shelters, nanotechnology) may stymie less-patient readers, most will press on, riveted by the chilling aspects of a child trapped in adult agendas that, iceberglike, hide beneath the surface. —Jennifer Mattson

Key, Watt. ***Alabama Moon*****. 2006. 240p. Farrar (9780374301842). Gr. 6–9.**

This excellent novel of survival and adventure begins with the death of young Moon's father, an antigovernment radical who has been living off the land in rural Alabama with Moon for years. Moon has never known any truth but his dad's, and so he tries to continue his father's lifestyle. Unfortunately, Moon quickly finds himself in the claws of civilization, as personified by a sadistic cop. After a brief stint in jail (a lifetime of hunting and gathering leaves Moon hilariously pleased with the prison food), Moon again lights out for the territories, only to be recaptured and end up in reform school. Of course, no reform school is gonna keep Moon in check. Key's first novel is populated with memorable characters—such as Moon's reform-school buddy's dad, whose life is devoted to drinking and shooting machine guns—and studded with utterly authentic details about rural Alabama and survivalism. Stylistically, the book is perfectly paced, and Moon's narration is thoroughly believable. A terrific choice for reluctant readers and also for fans of Gary Paulsen's Brian novels. —John Green

Larbalestier, Justine. ***Liar*****. 2009. 388p. Bloomsbury (9781599903057). Gr. 9–12.**

Micah Wilkins is a senior at a New York City private school, an extraordinarily talented runner, and a compulsive liar. She's masqueraded as a boy, invented family members, and hidden her relationship with handsome fellow student Zach Rubin. When Zach dies under mysterious and horrific circumstances, Micah's history of lying brings her under suspicion. Larbalestier creates and sustains a marvelous tension, as readers ponder what part of Micah's narrative is true. "Before" and "After" entries call to mind John Green's *Looking for Alaska* (2005), and like that titular character, Micah is wonderfully complex, both irritating and immensely likable. A supernatural element is well supported by Micah's obsession with genetics; she frequently cites facts learned in school to try to understand what is going on inside her. Larbalestier effortlessly and realistically shows the ethnic and socioeconomic diversity of Micah's world (she is African American), something teens of color will appreciate. The unresolved ending will certainly provoke discussion, sending readers back to the text for a closer rereading. —Debbie Carton

Lisle, Janet Taylor. ***Black Duck*****. 2006. 240p. Philomel/Sleuth (9780399239632). Gr. 7–10.**

David, a 14-year-old aspiring journalist, suspects that his elderly neighbor, Ruben, has a story to tell about Prohibition in their Rhode Island town, and he wonders "how to pry it out of the geezer." Surprisingly, Ruben opens up, and his chapter-length recollections of "rumrunners and highjackers, fast boats and dark nights," form the bulk of this gripping, layered mystery, which begins with young Ruben's discovery of a dead body. Questions about the corpse's identity draw Ruben into a dangerous local smuggling war. Transitions between then and now are sometimes jarring, and David is more narrative device than defined character: he poses the questions that the reader wants answered. Still, the setting's cinematic detail brings the exhilarating action close, and readers will easily see themselves in young Ruben, whose boiling frustration with family and convention lead him deeper into adventure. The ethical questions will also fascinate teens: Were the locals less guilty than the big-city crime bosses? How do you piece together a story when "there's no way of getting back there for a clear view"? —Gillian Engberg

Lynch, Chris. *Freewill*. 2001. 160p. HarperCollins (9780060281762). Gr. 9–12.

It won't take long for readers to realize that Lynch's book is written in second person. It may take them a bit longer to grasp that the speaker, 17-year-old Will, is actually talking to himself. Lynch ably carries off this complicated construct, giving the story the immediacy of experience but also the restricted perspective of a disturbed young man. Will, who usually expresses himself through wood carving, is so accustomed to loneliness that he's startled when he begins to make friends with Angela, a girl in his woodworking class. But just when he's taking tentative steps to open up, his sculptures begin turning up near the dead bodies of teenagers from his small community. Will is terrified that he has become "the carrier pigeon of death." This is a dark, rich young adult novel that offers something to think about as well as an intriguing story, and Lynch captures Will's confusion and unfolding understanding with sensitivity and tenderness. —Susan Dove Lempke

Mazer, Norma Fox. *The Missing Girl*. 2008. 288p. HarperTeen (9780066237770). Gr. 9–12.

Like Robert Cormier's *Tenderness* (1997), this novel peeks into the mind of a villain with ominous effectiveness. The story unfolds through several viewpoints—including that of an obsessive predator, who might have been plucked right out of adult crime fiction. The five Herbert sisters don't know he's watching them. They're too preoccupied by their own needs: Beauty, the oldest (who is actually quite plain), counts the days until she can leave home; Fancy, learning-disabled, talks and talks and drives everybody crazy with her chatter; and Autumn, the youngest, feels ignored within her noisy, busy family. Because money is tight, 14-year-old Stevie, the angry and emotional sister, is chosen to move in with an aunt. On the day of her departure, while the family is in sad confusion, 11-year-old Autumn disappears. Her confinement in the kidnapper's home is horrific, and though Mazer isn't overly graphic, she does include some chilling sequences. Autumn's escape (if very like a made-for-TV movie scene) is both gripping and satisfying, yet there's substance here, too. Mazer's strong characterizations and her portrayal of family relationships stand out. Quiet Mim, the second oldest, does fade into the background (that she turns out to be gay seems an awkward attempt at differentiation), but the others—angry, selfish, and loving by turns—become distinct within the first several chapters, and their bonds as sisters emerge as authentic and as strong as steel. —Stephanie Zvirin

McCaughrean, Geraldine. *The White Darkness*. 2007. 384p. HarperCollins (9780060890353). Gr. 7–10.

Fourteen-year-old Symone's only friend is an imaginary incarnation of Captain Laurence "Titus" Oates, an explorer who accompanied Robert Scott on his failed expedition to the South Pole. Sym is passionate about the Antarctic, and her infatuation is fed by Uncle Victor, an eccentric family friend who has cared for Sym and her mother since Sym's father's death. When Victor surprises Sym with a trip to "the Ice," she has some doubts, especially when she discovers that her mother can't come. But her excitement overshadows her initial misgivings—until she realizes that Uncle Victor has an obsession of his own that runs deeper than the glaciers and threatens her life. It's not always clear whether Titus' voice is imagined or if it's meant to be shy, bookish Sym's only link to the outside world, but McCaughrean's lyrical language actively engages the senses, plunging readers into a captivating landscape that challenges the boundaries of reality. Best suited to older, better readers despite the age of the protagonist, this imaginative, intellectually demanding novel offers plenty of action. —Jennifer Hubert

McNamee, Graham. *Acceleration*. 2003. Random/ Wendy Lamb (9780385901444). Gr. 9–12.

"Acceleration: escalation of increasingly destructive aberrant behavior," the stuff that serial killers are made of. That's what teenage Duncan finds out after he begins investigating a shocking journal that turns up in the Toronto subway lost-and-found where he works. When the police refuse to take it seriously, Duncan enlists the aid of two very different friends to help him find out the identity of the diary's author, who has apparently graduated from eviscerating animals and setting fires to tracking human prey. McNamee smoothly integrates snapshots from Duncan's escapades with a new buddy and his wild best friend, who lives teetering on the edge of the law, with information plucked from the diary. He never overexploits the sensational potential of the subject and builds suspense layer upon layer, while injecting some surprising comedy relief that springs from the boys' friendship. Less convincing is Duncan's guilt for a death not of his making, which is presented as the raison d'être for his need to find the sick killer. Characters are more than stereotypes here, though it's the mystery and the boys' repartee that give the novel its page-turning punch. —Stephanie Zvirin

McNamee, Graham. *Bonechiller*. 2008. 304p. Random/Wendy Lamb (9780385746588). Gr. 7–10.

Something is out there, in the cold nothing of the Canadian winter, making teenagers disappear. McNamee's follow-up to *Acceleration* (2003) is another page-turning thriller, this time with an eerie supernatural edge that will appeal to fans of psychological horror. Newcomer Danny and his brainy friend Howie have been chased down and stung by a Windigo, a massive cannibalistic beast. Now they are infected, racing against time before being compelled to give in to the beast in the frozen tundra. Ash, whose boxing wows Danny before her kisses do, and Pike, Howie's pyromaniac brother, also join the hunt. The book starts out with a bang as Pike sets fire to a convenience store, followed by a night race through the icy wilderness. The cold atmosphere pervades the book, and readers will shudder as Danny grows colder himself. Enough backstory is presented to give the characters dimension, but most of the focus is on the danger at hand. The book climaxes in an ammo-laden action sequence that will keep readers perched on the edges of their seats. —Heather Booth

Morgenroth, Kate. *Jude*. 2004. 288p. Simon & Schuster (9780689864797). Gr. 9–12.

In her YA debut, adult thriller writer Morgenroth tells the compelling story of Jude, 15, who is caught in a world of murder, drugs, and cover-ups that reaches into his Connecticut home and high school. The action is fast as Jude confronts the worst and best in himself, and the story reveals surprising secrets about people Jude thinks he can trust. Sworn to silence by the killer of his violent, drug-dealing dad, Jude moves into the wealthy home of the mother he has never known, and he switches to an elite private school. His mother is up for reelection as district attorney, and to save her reputation, he pleads guilty to a drug crime he didn't commit. He spends the next five years in prison, where he suffers constant abuse. Always he struggles to avoid being like his dad, and he longs for recognition from the mother who treats him like a stranger. There's a minimum of cursing and obscenity, but the dialogue still sounds pitch-perfect, and the intricacies of betrayal and discovery continue to the end of the novel. Readers will be caught by the thrilling mystery as well as Jude's fear, shame, anger, and search for home. —Hazel Rochman

Northrop, Michael. *Gentlemen*. 2009. 256p. Scholastic (9780545097499). Gr. 10–12.

This is a rare sort of book that may work just as well for reluctant readers as it will avid ones. Mike (the narrator), Tommy, Mixer, and Bones form the core of the remedial set at their small-town high school. When Tommy goes missing and their reviled English teacher, Mr. Haberman (who's trying to get them to read *Crime and Punishment*), starts acting awfully strange, the three remaining friends jump to some alarming conclusions. Despite the teacher's Raskolnikov act, this is not a reworking of Dostoevsky's classic in a modern high-school setting; rather, the book works as an amplifier of both the boys' suspicions and the plot's intrigue, and while readers familiar with it will certainly glean more, it is by no means a prerequisite to get caught up in the mystery. The guessing game of what happened to Tommy, how guilty Haberman is, and what are the boys going to do about it propels the action, and the well-rounded characters and their plausible obsessions provide buoyancy to the story. Laced throughout is a steely and intricate look at the permutations of adolescent friendship and the various roles that teens adopt or are assigned in both their social and academic worlds. A riveting thriller? Yep. A nuanced examination of morality? Yep again. What's amazing is that they never get in each other's way. —Ian Chipman

Peacock, Shane. *Eye of the Crow*. 2007. 260p. Tundra (9780887768507). Gr. 7–10.

In the first intriguing volume in an ambitious new series, Peacock imagines Sherlock Holmes' youth and his entrée into crime solving. In 1867 London, 13-year-old loner Sherlock lives in poverty, more interested in watching people and reading crime blotters than attending school. His curiosity is piqued when an Arab youth insists he has been wrongly arrested for a vicious murder. Sherlock's search for the truth leads him into a shadowy, vividly described London, where he encounters both allies and enemies, and brings unforeseen tragedy to those he holds dear. Creative references to Doyle's characters abound—Sherlock's brave, new friend, Irene, is the daughter of one Andrew C. Doyle—and Sherlock himself is cleverly interpreted. Peacock casts him as a half-Jewish victim of prejudice, whose struggles between head and heart and justice and vengeance make him both fascinating and complex, at the same time providing a credible rationale for the skill, ego, stoicism, and penchant for disguises so familiar in Doyle's iconic adult detective. Information about Doyle's creation would have enriched this story, and young people familiar with Holmes canon will best appreciate Peacock's riffs; but plenty of readers will like the smart, young detective they find here, and find themselves irresistibly drawn into his thrilling adventures. —Shelle Rosenfeld

Plum-Ucci, Carol. *The She*. 2003. 288p. Harcourt (9780152168193). Gr. 8–12.

When Evan Barrett was six, he listened as his parents died at the helm of their freighter, but he didn't need ship-to-shore communication to know they were in trouble; he heard the unholy shrieking of the She, a monstrous presence that devours ships off the New Jersey coast. Now Evan is a senior in high school, and circumstances bring those long-blocked memories to the forefront of his consciousness, forcing him, along with his older brother and Grey, a tough, troubled girl, to ride the water and face the She. Demonstrating the same ability to craft a mystery that she used in her Printz Honor Book, *The Body of Christopher Creed* (2000), Plum-Ucci carefully combines many plot elements, including the story of unstable Grey, who hears the She, but is fighting her own demons. A fantastic twist reveals that the Barretts' death may have had more to do with drug running than the supernatural. Or did it? The serpentine story, which does contain some strong language, will grip readers—even those who may not be interested in the well-researched seafaring details that add color and depth. Only Grey's story line is over the top; but that's fine, given the rest of this exciting adventure, which hardly allows readers a moment to take a breath. —Ilene Cooper

Runholt, Susan. *The Mystery of the Third Lucretia*. 2008. 244p. Viking (9780670062522). Gr. 7–10.

While visiting a Minneapolis art museum, 14-year-old best friends Kari and Lucas (both girls) are reprimanded by an artist copying a Rembrandt painting. Then, while visiting London with Kari's journalist mother, the kids see the same man, recognizable despite a disguise, copying another Rembrandt. When international reports herald the discovery of a previously unknown Rembrandt painting, Kari and Lucas, both talented artists themselves, recognize the work of the "Gallery Guy." Their suspicions lead them to Amsterdam, where, along with Kari's mother, they uncover an international forgery scam that implicates a top Dutch curator. Like Blue Balliett's *Chasing Vermeer* (2004), Runholt's debut is a clever, well-structured mystery that seamlessly folds art history into its exciting premise. The forged painting tells the ancient Roman story of Lucretia, signaling a theme of women's rights that Runholt carries throughout the book, from the girl's innocent questions about Amsterdam's red-light district to the strong female characters who drive the story. The pacing occasionally lags, but by the story's end, Runholt skillfully pulls in what could have become peripheral narrative tangents. Kari's authentic narration, her strong realistic friendship with Lucas, the cosmopolitan settings, and the carefully plotted mystery combine in a winning read that ends with the suggestion of continued adventures. —Gillian Engberg

Smith, Roland. *Peak*. 2007. 256p. Harcourt (9780152024178). Gr. 8–11.

Fourteen-year-old New Yorker Peak ("It could have been worse. My parents could have named me Glacier, or Abyss, or Crampon.") Marcello hones his climbing skills by scaling skyscrapers. After Peak is caught climbing the Woolworth Building, an angry judge gives him probation, with an understanding that Peak will leave New York and live with his famous mountaineer father in Thailand. Peak soon learns, however, that his father has other plans for him; he hopes that Peak will become the youngest person to climb Mt. Everest. Peak is whisked off to Tibet and finds himself in the complex world of an Everest base camp, where large amounts of money are at stake and climbing operations offer people an often-deadly shot at the summit. This is a thrilling, multifaceted adventure story. Smith includes plenty of mountaineering facts told in vivid detail (particularly creepy is his description of the frozen corpses that litter the mountain). But he also explores other issues, such as the selfishness that nearly always accompanies the intensely single-minded. A winner at every level. For more mountaineering adventures, suggest Edward Meyers' *Climb or Die* (1994) and Michael Dahl's *The Viking Claw* (2001), both for a slightly younger audience. —Todd Morning

Springer, Nancy. *The Case of the Gypsy Good-bye*. 2010. 176p. Philomel (9780399252365). Gr. 6–9.

The series that features Enola Holmes, the (much) younger sister of Sherlock, continues to be flat-out among the best mysteries being written for young people today. Not only are the mysteries sharp attention holders but the conclusions are well thought out, with i's dotted and t's crossed in true Holmesian fashion. But now it appears readers will have to say adieu to Enola in what looks to be the final book. Here Enola, about to turn 15, takes on two mysteries. She must discover the whereabouts of a lovely duchess who disappeared down the Baker Street Subway station. But, more important, Enola receives a curious message from her mother, who deserted her a year ago. Now Enola learns her fate. Springer has always neatly inserted social messages into this series. They come to the forefront once again, set against evocative details of Victorian London. Solid adventure meshes with the personal longings of a girl estranged from her brothers and longing for her mum. Flap copy says this is the last book, but Sherlock ends it by telling his sister, "I cannot wait to see what on Earth you will do next." Us too. —Ilene Cooper

Updale, Eleanor. *Montmorency: Thief, Liar, Gentleman?* 2004. 240p. Scholastic/Orchard (9780439580359). Gr. 6–9.

"Sewage stinks, but rich people, on the whole, don't." This truism forms the core of Updale's Dr. Jekyl and Mr. Hyde–style crime story. When thief Montmorency isn't living the high life as a respectable gentleman, he plays the role of his own servant, Scarper, who skulks through sewage tunnels to steal from London's wealthiest neighborhoods. Instead of greeting Montmorency/Scarper's misdeeds with a karmic comeuppance, Updale openly admires the ingenuity of a con artist who is able to maneuver within rigidly stratified Victorian society. Many readers will find the absence of a moral slant refreshing, and Montmorency's heart-pounding brushes with discovery add a palpable layer of suspense. It's tough to pinpoint the target audience, though—some readers will react negatively to the absence of characters their own age, and find the abundant period details overly fussy (in one scene, Montmorency lingers over the subtle flavors of whisky). This will appeal the most to older kids who enjoy immersing themselves in historical atmosphere, including some adult devotees of Victorian detective fiction. —Jennifer Mattson

Valentine, Jenny. *Me, the Missing, and the Dead*. 2008. 208p. HarperTeen (9780060850685). Gr. 9–12.

Lucas feels surrounded by the missing: his sister avoids home, his mother is absorbed in a midlife crisis, his grandfather has dementia, and his journalist father went missing years ago. With so many ghost-like family members, it's not surprising that Lucas begins to sense a connection with the dead. While waiting in a London office lobby, a funeral urn draws his attention, and he feels an overpowering urge to know the person inside. A string of ensuing coincidences tie him—and his father—to the deceased, Violet, a famous pianist. Is she trying to communicate with him? Lucas embarks on an investigation into her life, and his spine-tingling discoveries allow him to powerfully and finally lay the memory of his father to rest. Lucas's pitch-perfect voice, the authentic family relationships, the mild psychic element, and the poignant, coming-of-age mystery will stay with the reader long after the book ends. An award winner in the UK, Valentine's debut novel shines richly like the polished wood of Violet's urn. —Heather Booth

Van Draanen, Wendelin. *Sammy Keyes and the Cold Hard Cash*. 2008. 304p. Knopf (9780375835261). Gr. 6–9.

No matter who asks Sammy Keyes the question "What are you up to?" the answer's always the same: trouble. While sneaking up the fire escape to Gram's apartment in a seniors-only complex, where Sammy illicitly resides, she surprises an old man sneaking down. The encounter is apparently too much for the gent, as he suffers a heart attack and (after demanding that Sammy empty his pockets of greenbacks) kicks the bucket. To avoid jeopardizing her living arrangement, Sammy calls 911 from the apartment next door to Gram's, which is occupied by elderly Mrs. Wedegwood. Then all hell breaks loose, and what seems to be a delicious monetary windfall for Sammy gives rise to both a mystery and a moral quandary. Adding zest and teen interest to the quirky puzzle, whose geriatric backdrop initially seems an odd venue for young readers, are generous helpings of raucous comedy (most involving rotund Mrs. W.'s inability to stay upright on her toilet), a wonderfully cheeky first-person narrative, and smoothly integrated interactions between Sammy and her age mates. The result is an exceptionally good entry in an already remarkable series. —Stephanie Zvirin

Werlin, Nancy. *Double Helix*. 2004. 256p. Dial (9780803726062). Gr. 9–12.

With *Killer's Cousin* (1998), *Black Mirror* (2001), and now this exciting book to her credit, Werlin has proved herself to be one of the best youth thriller writers working today. Her plotting here is a little creaky, as it has been in past books, but she is a master at building suspense and creating the sort of clever manipulations that keep readers eagerly turning the pages. This time, Werlin delivers more than just a solid thriller-cum-growing-up story. She offers a thoughtful consideration of genetic engineering and takes a stand, but not at the expense of an intriguing mystery. Eli Samuels, 18, can't get close—not to his caring but preoccupied dad; not to his smart, generous girlfriend, Viv; and certainly not to his mother, who has been institutionalized for years with a devastating midlife degenerative disease, the gene for which Eli may carry. Confused, heartsick, unable to get the answers he seeks from Dad, and needing time to think about his life, Eli decides to forgo college and, despite his father's unexpectedly vehement disapproval, takes a job at Wyatt Transgenetics, where he receives a surprisingly warm welcome from world-renowned geneticist Dr. Quincy Wyatt. What's all that about? Readers will be as intrigued as Eli, who discovers more than he ever bargained for. A solidly crafted, thoughtful novel featuring a clever, obsessed kid who finds truths, small and large, about life, family, and, of course, himself. —Stephanie Zvirin

Werlin, Nancy. *The Rules of Survival*. 2006. 272p. Dial (9780803730014). Gr. 7–10.

Living with an unpredictable, psychotic mother has taught Matthew how to survive. Constantly on alert, he and his sister, Callie, devotedly shelter their younger stepsister, Emmy, from their mother's abuse and worry about staying safe. Matt insists that "fear isn't actually a bad thing . . . It warns you to pay attention, because you're in danger. It tells you to do something, to act, to save yourself," but his terror is palpable in this haunting, powerful portrayal of domestic dysfunction, which is written in retrospect as a letter from Matt to Emmy. Unfortunately, the adults in the children's life, a distant father and an apathetic aunt, don't help, though Matt sees a spark of hope in Murdoch, who dates his mother, Nikki, and then leaves when he becomes another target for her escalating rage. It is Murdoch, with a violent past of his own, who is willing to risk getting involved and eventually becomes the change agent that the children so desperately need. The author of *Double Helix* (2004), Werlin reinforces her reputation as a master of the YA thriller, pulling off a brilliant departure in this dark but hopeful tale, with pacing and suspense guaranteed to leave readers breathlessly turning the pages. —Cindy Dobrez

Westerfeld, Scott. *So Yesterday*. 2004. 256p. Penguin/Razorbill (9781595140005). Gr. 7–12.

Like M. T. Anderson's *Feed* (2002), this hip, fascinating thriller aggressively questions consumer culture. Seventeen-year-old Hunter lives up to his name. A "cool hunter," he's paid by corporations to comb his native Manhattan in search of street style that could become the next new trend. Hunter meets and falls for his fellow teen culture-watcher Jen, just before Hunter's boss mysteriously disappears. Jen and Hunter hold the most clues, and their wild, increasingly dangerous search uncovers a plot to subvert a consumer system that dictates what is cool. Readers may have trouble sorting through some of the plot's connections and anticonsumerist messages. But Hunter tells a captivating, suspenseful story about how product desire is created, using a first-person voice that is cynical ("magazines are just wrapping for ads") and precociously wise (he riffs on the origins of everything from the Internet to neckties) while remaining believably naive and vulnerable when it comes to girls. Teens will inhale this wholly entertaining, thought-provoking look at a system fueled by their purchasing power. —Gillian Engberg

Wynne-Jones, Tim. *The Uninvited*. 2009. 352p. Candlewick (9780763639846). Gr. 9–12.

After a stormy affair with a professor, NYU student Mimi Shapiro heads to a remote Canadian farmhouse owned by her father, Marc, a famous painter. On arrival in the idyllic riverside setting, though, she finds Jay, a 22-year-old musician, already ensconced in the house. Jay, she discovers, is her half-brother, and he welcomes her into his comfortable life with his mother and her lesbian partner. Readers learn long before the newfound siblings, however, that Marc fathered another child: Cramer, a twentysomething loner who supports his mentally unstable mother. Is he the sole intruder who stalks and then breaks into the river house? The distance between what readers and characters know creates the story's central coil of tension, and Wynne-Jones adds extra measures of creepiness in teen-movie scenes of vulnerable Mimi, alone and threatened in the house, and in the flashes of sexual attraction that the half-siblings share. The mystery's violent conclusion will shock many, but it's Wynne-Jones' atmospheric prose and sophisticated exploration of elemental coming-of-age themes that will involve readers most. —Gillian Engberg

Zusak, Markus. *I Am the Messenger*. 2005. 368p. Knopf (9780375830990). Gr. 9–12.

Ed is a 19-year-old loser only marginally connected to the world; he's the son that not even his mother loves. But his life begins to change after he acts heroically during a robbery. Perhaps it's the notoriety he receives that leads to his receiving playing cards in the mail. Ed instinctively understands that the scrawled words on the aces are clues to be followed, which lead him to people he will help (including some he'll have to hurt first). But as much as he changes those who come into his life, he changes himself more. Two particular elements will keep readers enthralled: the panoply of characters who stream in and out of the story, and the mystery of the person sending Ed on the life-altering missions. Concerning the former, Zusak succeeds brilliantly. Ed's voice is assured and unmistakeable, and other characters, although seen through Ed's eyes, are realistically and memorably evoked (readers will almost smell Ed's odoriferous dog when it ambles across the pages). As for the ending, however, Zusak is too clever by half. He offers too few nuts-and-bolts details before wrapping things up with an unexpected, somewhat unsatisfying recasting of the narrative. Happily, that doesn't diminish the life-affirming intricacies that come before. —Ilene Cooper

Speculative Fiction

Adlington, L. J. *Cherry Heaven*. 2008. 464p. Greenwillow (9780061431807). Gr. 8–11.

A companion novel to Adlington's *The Diary of Pelly D* (2005), this dystopian fantasy follows two streams of narrative in alternating chapters. Though separate in the beginning, the stories eventually cross and converge. Seventeen-year-old Luka tells of brutal, dehumanizing conditions in the water-bottling facility where she works as a slave laborer. After escaping, she makes her way back to her childhood home, Cherry Heaven, where 10 years ago she watched a man gun down her mother and sisters. Told in third person, the other story involves Kat, her sister Tanka, and their adoptive parents, who move from their old home in City Five to Cherry Heaven in the idyllic New Frontier, where the benevolent-sounding Overseas Humanitarian Agency has made it socially unacceptable to disrespect groups considered genetically inferior. This tale combines sisterly bickering, an unexpected love interest, and Kat's intellectual curiosity about puzzling elements in her new surroundings. Each narrative adds to the slowly emerging portrayal of a troubled society and to the gradual unfolding of the story's central mystery. In this complex, absorbing, and sometimes disquieting novel, Adlington creates a world that is distinctly different from our own, yet chillingly familiar. Pair it with M. T. Anderson's *Feed* (2002) for a thought-provoking discussion. —Carolyn Phelan

Adlington, L. J. *The Diary of Pelly D*. 2005. 288p. Greenwillow (9780060766153). Gr. 8–12.

A young driller breaking up rubble in war-devastated City Five unearths an old water can with a diary inside and then breaks Rules and Regulations by keeping it, rather than surrendering it to the authorities. So begins Toni V's relationship with the diarist, Pelly D, a teen who, before the war, had it all. Toni V enters the everyday thoughts and experiences of a privileged girl who, despite her societal status, may not be protected when the most powerful of the planet's three genetic clans demands all citizens be identified and sorted by genetic type. Although inspired by the buried diaries found in the Warsaw Ghetto, Adlington has crafted an original and disturbing dystopian fantasy told in a smart and sympathetic teen voice. Particularly skillful is the author's use of setting and detail to build slowly toward a full revelation of the unique physical, psychological, and political worlds Pelly D and Toni V inhabit. This provocative addition to the growing body of dystopian literature for teens is a disturbing book that shouldn't be missed. —Holly Koelling

Almond, David. *Clay*. 2006. 224p. Delacorte (9780385731713). Gr. 6–9.

In Almond's beautiful novel *Skellig* (1999), a boy finds a fragile angel-like creature in his garden shed, but in this book the magical realism goes much further. The author sets a Frankenstein monster story in a small, contemporary English town. Mischievous altar boy Davie explains how a strange new kid, Stephen, convinces him to steal the body and blood of Christ from church, which the boys use to create a huge clay monster that obeys their wishes. Should the boys send Clay to kill Mouldy, the vicious local bully? When Mouldy falls to his death in the local quarry, Davie wonders if Clay is responsible. Is the monster reading his thoughts? How much of Davie is in the monster? The scary monster-come-to-town story raises big issues about God, creativity, and evil, but Davie's first-person narrative is never preachy. Discussions about art ("our passion to create goes with our passion to destroy") and religion (Has God abandoned us because we created nuclear bombs and gas chambers?) are beautifully handled, as is the portrait of Davie's happy family. Rooted in the ordinariness of a community and in one boy's chance to play God, this story will grab readers with its gripping action and its important ideas.
—Hazel Rochman

★ Almond, David. *Kit's Wilderness*. 2000. 240p. Delacorte (9780385326650). Gr. 6–9.

Almond, whose *Skellig* is the *Booklist* 1999 Top of the List winner for youth fiction, creates a heartbreakingly real world fused with magic realism in this story, set in an English coal-mining town. Thirteen-year-old Kit Watson and his family have returned to Stonygate to care for Kit's recently widowed grandfather. Almost immediately, Kit is enticed by John Askew, also of an old mining family, into a game called Death. Like the other members of Askew's gang, Kit is left alone in an abandoned mine until he sees ghosts of ancestors who died there as boys. Kit's friend Allie tells him that the other kids pretend to see these apparitions, but Kit really does see—and Askew knows it. The boys share a bond. Both are artistic: Kit is a writer; Askew is an artist. And both are sensitive enough to perceive what may not be there. But Kit comes from a strong, loving family, and Askew is the child of an ineffectual mother and a father who's a vicious drunk. Slowly, as Kit hears stories from his grandfather and writes his own, he realizes he has a mission—to save John Askew, body and soul. Almond has set an enormous task for himself. He juggles several plot elements—the grandfather's fading mental capacities, Allie's acting aspirations, one of Kit's stories—along with the boys' struggle for redemption. But he succeeds beautifully, knitting dark and light together and suffusing the multilayered plot with an otherworldly glow. This is a long book, and a complex one, but Almond's language is a pleasure to read; and, as with *Skellig* the story's ruminations about death and the healing power of love will strike children in unsuspected ways. —Ilene Cooper

Almond, David. *The Savage*. Illus. by Dave McKean. 2008. 80p. Candlewick (9780763639327). Gr. 6–9.

A story-within-the-story that explores the means of handling grief forms the thrust of this compact book. After Blue Baker's father dies, his school counselor tries to get him to write down and explore his feelings. "I did it for a while, but it just seemed stupid." Instead, he secretly starts writing and drawing a story about a feral boy living alone in the woods. Blue's story—which slashes into the narrative, the moody and ragged artwork a mirror for Blue's inner turmoil—is interspersed with his struggle to cope with the loss of his father, run-ins with a bully, and difficulty reaching out to his mother and younger sister. The savage in his story is a violent, languageless creature who chases down, kills, and eats people who get too close. The line separating Blue and his imaginary savage becomes increasingly blurred, each bleeding into the other's world, leading to an inevitable, though earned, catharsis. Avoiding sentiment, this illuminating book captures the staggering power of raw emotions on young minds, and demonstrates the ways expression can help transform and temper them. —Ian Chipman

Almond, David. *Secret Heart*. 2002. 208p. Delacorte (9780385729475). Gr. 5–12.

The tiger that becomes Joe Maloney's alter ego first appears to him in a dream, and when he wakes, he discovers that a circus has come to Helmouth, the dreary village where he lives with his mother. Joe feels inextricably drawn to the great tent, but he cannot explain why. Words are difficult for the stammering boy, who finds it hard to separate what exists in his head from what exists in the world, a blurriness that continues when he meets Corrina at the big top, a girl who seems strangely familiar to him. What special bond draws these two together? What surprising destiny does Joe discover beneath the tent's blue ceiling, with its remnants of an ancient, golden sun; a silver moon; and stars? The answers are an exquisite demonstration that, as Corinna tells Joe, "The most important things are the most mysterious." The border between the numinous and the real is familiar territory for the British author, but this time he limns the landscape as seldom before—with heartbreaking yearning and richly powerful symbols that evoke both heaven and hell. With echoes of Ray Bradbury and William Blake, *Secret Heart* is filled with scenes of breathtaking beauty, wonder, and astonishment. It is an unforgettable achievement. —Michael Cart

★ Anderson, M. T. *Feed*. 2002. 240p. Candlewick (9780763617264). Gr. 9–12.

In this strange, disturbing future world, teens travel to the moon for spring break, live in stacked-up neighborhoods with artificial blue sky, and are bombarded by a constant advertising and media blitz through their feeds. They live with a barrage of greed and superficiality, which only one teen, Violet, tries to fight. Intrigued by Violet's uniqueness, Titus begins a relationship with her in spite of his peers' objections. Yet even he cannot sustain the friendship as her feed malfunctions and she begins to shut down. "They" refuse to repair her feed because she is too perceptive and rebellious. This didactic, also very disturbing book plays on every negative teen stereotype. The young people are bored unthinking pawns of commercialism, speaking only in obnoxious slang, ignoring or disrespecting the few adults around. The future is vapid and without direction. Yet many teens will feel a haunting familiarity about this future universe. —Frances Bradburn

Armstrong, Jennifer. *The Kindling*. 2002. 224p. HarperCollins (9780060080488). Gr. 7–10.

The Fire-us trilogy gets off to a dynamic start in this first entry set in 2007, five years after a catastrophic virus has apparently killed all the adults and nearly everyone else. Seven children seem to be the only survivors. They live as a family in a run-down house in a small Florida town; none of them remembers much about the Before Time. Teenage Teacher is the oldest and the keeper of The Book, a carefully constructed scrapbook in which she finds inspiration for the group. Mommy and Hunter are also teens; Action Figure, Teddy Bear, Baby, and Doll are younger children. Then teenage Anchorman (dubbed Angerman by the little ones) shows up and convinces the family to join him on a long trek to Washington, D.C., to find a Grown-up called President. The story is surprisingly realistic in its depiction of both the paranoia brought about by isolation and fear and the courage and mutual caring exhibited by the kids. There's plenty of adventure, too, which makes this not only a poignant foray into a frightening future but also an exciting survival tale that will mesmerize readers and leave them anxious for the next installment. —Sally Estes

Bacigalupi, Paolo. *Ship Breaker*. 2010. 336p. Little, Brown (9780316056212). Gr. 8–12.

This YA debut by Bacigalupi, a rising star in adult science fiction, presents a dystopian future like so many YA sf novels. What is uncommon, though, is that although Bacigalupi's future earth is brilliantly imagined and its genesis anchored in contemporary issues, it is secondary to the memorable characters. In a world in which society has stratified, fossil fuels have been consumed, and the seas have risen and drowned coastal cities, Nailer, 17, scavenges beached tankers for scrap metals on the Gulf Coast. Every day, he tries to "make quota" and avoid his violent, drug-addicted father. After he discovers a modern clipper ship washed up on the beach, Nailer thinks his fortune is made, but then he discovers a survivor trapped in the wreckage—the "swank" daughter of a shipping-company owner. Should he slit the girl's throat and sell her for parts or take a chance and help her? Clearly respecting his audience, Bacigalupi skillfully integrates his world building into the compelling narrative, threading the backstory into the pulsing action. The characters are layered and complex, and their almost unthinkable actions and choices seem totally credible. Vivid, brutal, and thematically rich, this captivating title is sure to win teen fans for the award-winning Bacigalupi. —Lynn Rutan

Barker, Clive. *Abarat*. 2002. 432p. HarperCollins (9780060280925). Gr. 7–12.

In the first of a planned four-book series, Barker imbues the traditional conventions of fantasy with a whimsical Wonderland quality, providing a host of bizarre characters, a fabulous landscape, and a coherent underlying mythology. Teenage Candy Quackenbush of Chickentown, Minnesota, begins (unbeknownst to her) a prophesied journey toward her destiny when she dives into a mysterious sea that appears outside the town. She is carried to Abarat, an unusual archipelago of 25 islands. Happy to get away from her abusive father, resigned mother, and boring town, Candy eagerly enters a series of zany adventures, making friends and eluding enemies as she finds herself caught in the struggle for power between the Lord of Midnight and the architect of the high-tech Commexo City. The multilayered adventure story not only embraces the lands of Oz, Wonderland, and Narnia but also offers a wink and a nod to Aldous Huxley's *Brave New World*. More than 100 full-color paintings by Barker are appropriately quirky, grotesque, and campy, effectively capturing and expanding on the nuances of the tale. —Sally Estes

Bell, Hilari. *Flame*. 2003. 352p. Simon & Schuster (9780689854132). Gr. 6–10.

Here's a rousing start to a new series, The Book of Sorahb, from the author of *A Matter of Profit* (2001) and *The Goblin Wood* (2003). Steeped in Persian mythology, the story is set in Farsala, a peaceful land now targeted for invasion by the Hrum, who have already conquered 28 other countries. As the enemy advances, routing the overconfident Farsalan army, three young people caught up in the fray move inexorably toward new futures in which they will play leading roles in the outcome and aftermath of the war. They are Soraya, the spoiled daughter of the Farsalan army's high commander; Jiaan, the high commander's peasant-born bastard son; and Kavi, an itinerant peddler and sometime con artist. Intrigue builds upon intrigue, with a history of Farsala woven into the story's main events. Once again Bell proves a master at crafting distinctive societies and characters, and readers will eagerly await the promised future installments. —Sally Estes

Bell, Hilari. *The Goblin Wood*. 2003. 304p. HarperCollins/Eos (9780060513719). Gr. 6–10.

After her mother is drowned as a sorceress, young hedgewitch Makenna flees into the woodlands. While there, she accidentally antagonizes some goblins, who plague her until she captures one, Cogswhallop, and inadvertently puts him in her debt. As she travels with Cogswhallop, she learns goblin rules about repaying a favor, and she soon finds herself united with goblins in a battle against the ruling Hierarchy, bent on eradicating all magical creatures. Five years later, a young knight comes to Goblin Wood to trap a powerful human sorceress who is thought to lead an army of enslaved goblins. By this time, Makenna has become a strategist par excellence and the Hierarchy's greatest threat. Leavened by humor and a dollop of romance, this well-crafted fantasy adventure demonstrates Bell's talent for creating enduring characters and worlds. It also has a cliffhanger ending that begs a sequel. The author of *A Matter of Profit* (2001) comes through again. —Sally Estes

Bell, Hilari. *A Matter of Profit*. 2001. 288p. HarperCollins (9780060295134). Gr. 6–10.

From the author of *Songs of Power* (2000) comes a dynamic combination of sf, thriller, and mystery that will draw readers in from the start. The T'Chin Empire, a confederation of 40 planets, each inhabited by a different sentient species, has surrendered to invading Vivitare forces without a fight, allowing Emperor Lessar to set up his court on T'Chin. Ahvren, the son of Saiden, who serves the emperor, plans to tell his father he no longer wants to be a warrior. When he arrives on T'Chin to confront his father, he learns there's a rumor that rebels are plotting to kill the emperor. Saiden offers Ahvren a deal: if Ahvren can find the rebels or prove they don't exist, Ahvren will be given a year to find another career. In so doing, Avhren also hopes to save his sister from being forced to marry the emperor's despicable son. So begins a tense, dangerous foray into another culture, with Ahvren enlisting help from the best scholar in the city, a member of the one intelligent race indigenous to the planet. By the end Ahvren learns a great deal about himself and about the larger picture of the T'Chins. Bell shows a strong ability to build a distinctive world and create convincing alien life forms and cultures, making this one of the best youth sf tales to come along in many years. —Sally Estes

Bell, Hilari. *Rise of a Hero*. 2005. 480p. Simon & Schuster (9780689854156). Gr. 7–10.

The dynamic follow-up to *Fall of a Kingdom* (entitled *Flame* in its 2003 original hardcover edition) is a strong middle book in the Farsala trilogy. Separated after Farsala falls to the invading Hrum, the three young protagonists work to defeat and expel the enemy: Soraya, daughter of the slain high commander of the Farsalan army, gets a lowly kitchen job in the Hrum army camp, where she searches for information about her mother and younger brother; Jiaan, bastard son of the high commander, reluctantly becomes high commander of what little is left of the Farsalan army and begins recruiting and training peasants and farmers; itinerant peddler Kavi, a double agent, works for both the Hrum and the Farsalans, though his heart is with the Farsalans. Despite the brave endeavors of the young people, what Farsala needs is a champion. According to legend, the hero Sorahb, slain centuries before, will return when Farsala most needs a leader; it seems the time is now. The characters maintain their distinctive identities here, class differences in the societies are indelibly rendered, and the importance of preserving values and making good choices comes across clearly. With a palpable sense of danger and an ending that promises much to be revealed, this is a sequel that will fly off the shelf. —Sally Estes

Bertagna, Julie. *Exodus*. 2008. 352p. Walker (9780802797452). Gr. 6–10.

Already a critical and popular success in the UK, where it was printed in 2002, this sweeping, futuristic fantasy envisions a ravaged earth, submerged almost entirely in water after a century of global warming–induced ice melt and storms. After her tiny island is consumed by the sea, 15-year-old Mara, aided by an antique Web-surfing device, guides her community to a towering city across the ocean. Her family is killed during the dangerous passage, and on arrival in glittering New Mungo, Mara and the islanders join a floating camp of desperate refugees who are barred from the heavily walled civilization. Realizing that survival for herself and the others depends on finding help behind the wall, Mara begins a monumental, nightmarish quest through layers of increasingly affluent, developed societies. Bertagna creates wholly imagined, extraordinarily vivid worlds, whether she's depicting the rich, earthy subsistence of the Treenesters or the eerily glossy, empty glamour of high-tech Noospace, where Mara delves into an exciting 3-D Internet and, despite the artificial environment, finds true friendship, help, and love. Astonishing in its scope and exhilarating in both its action and its philosophical inquiry, this accomplished first novel in a proposed trilogy will, like the works of Philip Pullman and J. K. Rowling, attract a wide age range of readers. —Gillian Engberg

Billingsley, Franny. *Chime*. 2011. 320p. Dial (9780803735521). Gr. 8–12.

Since her stepmother's recent death, 17-year-old Briony Larkin knows that if she can keep two secrets—that she is a witch and that she is responsible for the accident that left Rose, her identical twin, mentally compromised—and remember to hate herself always, no other harm will befall her family in their Swampsea parsonage at the beginning of the twentieth century. The arrival of Mr. Clayborne, a city engineer, and his university-dropout son, Eldric, makes Briony's task difficult. Clayborne's plan to drain the swamp has made the Old Ones unhappy, particularly the Boggy Mun, who has plagued the village's children with swamp cough in retaliation. When Rose's lingering illness turns into a cough, Briony knows that she must do whatever it takes, even revealing her secrets, to save her sister. While thwarting the advances of an arsenic-addicted suitor, Briony must also deny her feelings for Eldric, even as he helps her solve the puzzle that has become her life. Exploring the powers of guilt and redemption, Billingsley (*The Folk Keeper*, 1999) has crafted a dark, chilling yet stunning world. Briony's many mysteries and occasional sardonic wit make her a force to be reckoned with. Exquisite to the final word. —Angela Leeper

Black, Holly. *Tithe: A Modern Faerie Tale*. 2002. 320p. Simon & Schuster (9780689849244). Gr. 8–12.

With a hard-drinking rock singer for a mother and a band of faeries as childhood friends, 16-year-old Kaye's life has always been unconventional. But when she rescues a gorgeous knight, Roiben, from mysterious attackers, Kaye is thrown into a terrifying, otherworldly war between two faerie kingdoms. In this wildly imagined debut, Black tells a gothic fantasy that contrasts the faeire world's seductive horror against the gritty world of contemporary, industrial New Jersey. Black includes plenty of mysteries and some mature, sexy innuendo to keep the plot flying along: Is Kaye human? Which court is really in power? Who can be trusted? Does Roiben love Kaye, or is he under another's spell? What's become of Corny, Kaye's gay friend who has fallen for an abusive knight? But it's the riveting descriptions of the faerie world—a bacchanalian hell described in remarkable detail—that will most capture readers. Dark, edgy, beautifully written, and compulsively readable, this is sure to be a word-of-mouth hit with teens, even a few usually unmoved by magic and monsters.
—Gillian Engberg

Black, Holly. *Valiant: A Modern Tale of Faerie*. **2005. 320p. Simon & Schuster (9780689868221). Gr. 8–11.**

An exile from the Seelie court, the hunky, sensitive troll Ravus resides in a secret laboratory inside the Manhattan Bridge, ministers to other city-dwelling faeries with healing potions, and has exotic golden eyes and jutting fangs. Runaway Val meets the troll through a trio of homeless teens, runners in Ravus' potion-distribution network. They introduce Val to subway squatting, Dumpster diving, and "Never"—the drug faeries use to protect themselves from iron, but which affects humans like heroin. A twisted Agatha Christie–style plot unfolds as faerie partakers of Never begin to expire, and Ravus is accused of murder; Val's feelings for the troll prompt her to clean up her act and investigate the true poisoner. As in Black's companion novel *Tithe* (2002), the plot matters far less than the exotic, sexy undercurrents (including a scene where Val overhears teens having sex), the deliciously overripe writing, and the intoxicating, urban-gothic setting, where "everything was strange and beautiful and swollen with possibilities." —Jennifer Mattson

Blackman, Malorie. *Naughts and Crosses*. **2005. 400p. Simon & Schuster (9781416900160). Gr. 8–11.**

An alternative England is divided between the Naughts and the Crosses. Callum is a looked-down-upon naught, and, as readers slowly realize, he's white. His best friend, Sephy, a black Cross, comes from a privileged family for whom Callum's mother works. A misunderstanding leads to her firing, but Callum and Sephy maintain deep affection for one another. After Callum gets into Sephy's previously all-black high school, the world begins to close in on them. The premise—what would happen if societal roles were reversed—is not unfamiliar, but the way Blackman personalizes it makes for a thrilling, heartbreaking story. The tale unfolds in 117 short chapters, alternately narrated by Sephy and Callum, and readers will watch with something akin to horror as the teenagers try to sustain what has become love through serpentine wrong turns and events beyond their control: Sephy's do-gooder efforts, the suicide of Callum's sister, and Callum's family's turn to violence. Both fate and family conspire to keep the teens apart as the story winds to its inexorable conclusion. Gripping and deeply layered, this book will make readers question everything: race relations, government, friendship. But it is Callum and Sephy's love, tinged with a *Wuthering Heights*–like relentlessness, that wins in the end. —Ilene Cooper

Blackwood, Gary. *The Year of the Hangman*. **2002. 196p. Dutton (9780525469216). Gr. 6–9.**

Blackwood, the author of *The Shakespeare Stealer* (1998) and *Wild Timothy* (1987), creates a novel of alternate history set in 1777, after British forces have trounced the Continental Army and captured General Washington. Fifteen-year-old Creighton, wastrel son of a once-wealthy English family, finds himself bundled off to America for the good of his character. When his uncle's ship is attacked by a remnant of the American forces led by their stalwart general Benedict Arnold, Creighton is taken to New Orleans. There he befriends Benjamin Franklin and others still plotting against the British. Well imagined and well plotted, the story turns on questions of honor and of loyalty to one's country, one's family, and oneself. Readers will occasionally find themselves doing a mental double-take when discovering some new non-historical fact, but having the cage of preconceived notions rattled is a pleasure of alternate history novels, of which perhaps the best children's literature example is Joan Aiken's Dido Twite series. In the appended author's note, Blackwood separates fact from fiction and points interested readers to a website on "uchronia," or alternate history. —Carolyn Phelan

Block, Francesca Lia. *Pretty Dead*. **2009. 208p. HarperTeen (9780061547850). Gr. 9–12.**

The deluge of interchangeable vampire novels has grown to such proportions that it's genuinely startling when a true original emerges. Seventeen-year-old (in appearance, anyway) Charlotte is what she calls a "V word," yet lives a seemingly perfect life: gorgeous, brilliant, and wrapped in the finest of clothes and jewelry. What she lacks is a companion. But when her human friend Emily kills herself, she finds herself drawn to Emily's boyfriend, Jared, who reminds her of her beloved twin brother who died nearly a century ago. In the book's most powerful sequence, Charlotte describes to Jared her transformation at the hands of the vampire William in 1925, and how the two murderous lovers were present for everything from the bombing of Hiroshima and the dawn of the AIDS crisis to Kurt Cobain's suicide and the 9/11 attacks—almost as if their very proximity drew evil. Now, as Charlotte begins experiencing human-like symptoms (a broken nail, a zit, her period), William returns, and he brings with him an awful secret. Block is less concerned about mythology than she is with the malaise brought on by a vampire's eternity of sorrow. With mournful prose, she has created something psychologically complex, erotically charged, and unusually poignant. —Daniel Kraus

Bondoux, Anne-Laure. *The Killer's Tears*. 2006. 224p. Delacorte (9780385732932). Gr. 9–12.

Bondoux's latest novel is a haunting, provocative blend of allegory, gritty social commentary, and magic realism that, like David Almond's work, defies definition. The shocking contradictions begin with the first scene: a thief and murderer named Angel kills a farmer and his wife and settles into their home on the desolate tip of Chile. He spares the family's small son, Paolo, and surprises himself with the intense devotion he develops for the boy. Then a young, wealthy traveler arrives, and at Paolo's insistence, the stranger settles into the improbable household at the end of the earth. Eventually, the trio is pulled back into the wider world, and its fragile connections are threatened and torn. The symbolism occasionally feels too purposeful, the characters more representational than real. But Bondoux asks the largest questions about crime, punishment, and how souls can change in language that is both visceral and poetic, and with unsparing, emotional truth, she describes a world in which the morality of the heart doesn't always match the morality of civilized society. "Poets know how to transform things," says one character. "They look at the world and they absorb it like a drink. And then when they start talking, nothing is the same." Winner of France's prestigious Prix Sorcieres, this novel is filled with challenging ideas and potent language that will pull readers in new directions. —Gillian Engberg

Bray, Libby. *The Diviners*. 2012. 578p. Little, Brown (9780316126113). Gr. 9–12.

Here's your headline, boss: "Small-Town Dame Lands in Big Apple, Goes Wild, Tries to Stop Resurrection of Antichrist." It'll sell bundles! Indeed it will, as Bray continues her winning streak with this heedlessly sprawling series starter set in Prohibition-era New York. Slang-slinging flapper Evie, 17, is "pos-i-tute-ly" thrilled to be under the wing of her uncle, who runs the Museum of American Folklore, Superstition, and the Occult. Business is slow (i.e., plenty of time for Evie to swill gin at speakeasies!) until the grisly arrival of what the papers dub the Pentacle Killer, who might be the reincarnation of a religious zealot named Naughty John. Even Evie's new pals—hoofers, numbers runners, and activists, but all swell kids—are drawn into the investigation. It's *Marjorie Morningstar* meets *Silence of the Lambs*, and Bray dives into it with the brio of the era, alternating rat-a-tat flirting with cold-blooded killings. Seemingly each teen has a secret ability (one can read an object's history; another can heal), and yet the narrative maintains the flavor of historical fiction rather than fantasy. The rest of the plot—well, how much time do you have? The book is big and wants to be the kind of thing you can lose yourself in. Does it succeed? It's jake, baby. —Daniel Kraus

★ Bray, Libba. *Going Bovine*. 2009. 496p. Delacorte (9780385733977). Gr. 8–12.

In a giant departure from her Gemma Doyle trilogy, Bray's latest offering is an unforgettable, nearly indefinable fantasy adventure, as immense and sprawling as Cervantes' *Don Quixote*, on which it's based. Here the hero is Cameron, a 16-year-old C-plus-average slacker who likens himself to "driftwood," but he suddenly becomes the center of attention after he is diagnosed with Creutzfeldt-Jakob disease, the human variant of mad cow disease. In the hospital, he meets Dulcie, an alluring angel clad in fishnet stockings and combat boots, who presents him with a heroic quest to rescue the planet from an otherworldly, evil force. Guided by random signs and accompanied by a teen dwarf named Gonzo, Cameron sets off on a wild road trip across the U.S. to save the world, and perhaps his own life. Talking yard gnomes, quantum physics, cults of happiness, mythology, religion, time travel, the blues, Disney World, the vacuous machine behind reality TV shows, and spring break's beer-and-bikini culture all figure prominently in the plot, and readers may not feel equally engaged in each of the novel's lengthy episodes. But Bray's wildly imagined novel, narrated in Cameron's sardonic, believable voice, is wholly unique, ambitious, tender, thought-provoking, and often fall-off-the-chair funny, even as she writes with powerful lyricism about the nature of existence, love, and death. Familiarity with *Don Quixote* certainly isn't necessary, but those who know the basic plot will want to start over from the beginning and pick up on each sly allusion to the classic story. —Gillian Engberg

Bray, Libba. ***A Great and Terrible Beauty*****. 2003. 416p. Delacorte (9780385901611). Gr. 8–12.**

Gemma Doyle is no ordinary nineteenth-century British teenager; she has disturbing visions. Upon finding the diary of a young student who was also a visionary of sorts, Gemma and three classmates, each of whom, like Gemma, has a personal demon to overcome, follow the diarist's lead and travel into the Realms, a place of both joy and danger. The jacket, a photo of a young woman in a tightly laced corset and lacy camisole, bespeaks a steamy love story (Gemma does have some sexy dreams about a young gypsy), but the costume is really a metaphor for the strictures against women of the period, which Bray limns extremely well in her debut novel. The Realms and the mystery surrounding the diary are less well handled, yet there's no doubt the mystical elements, along with a touch of forbidden romance, will draw a large, enthusiastic audience, who will come away wanting more about stubborn, willful Gemma and the strange world whose doors she can open at will. —Stephanie Zvirin

Bray, Libba. ***Rebel Angels*****. 2005. 560p. Delacorte (9780385730297). Gr. 9–12.**

Once again, Gemma Doyle slips into the realm beyond her Victorian world, this time to find the fabled Temple and rebind the magic loosed in *A Great and Terrible Beauty* (2003). To accomplish her task, she journeys to London, where she sifts through terrifying visions and clues from a young madwoman, weeds out friend from foe, and defends herself and her friends from those, including the clever, evil Circe, who want the magic for themselves. Bray reprises previous events as the story moves along, but readers familiar with the first book will feel most at home here. They will find the same rich social commentary, romance, and adventure, even more sumptuously created. Gemma's relationship with her friends Anne and Felicity is one of the strengths of the book: the girls fight, support one another, and change as the story progresses—in both the real and magical worlds. Bray occasionally relies on magic to cover up bumps in the plot, but readers will sink into her compelling, well-paced story anyway, and relish the combination of historical novel and imaginative fantasy world building. Teens will long for another sequel. —Stephanie Zvirin

Brooks, Kevin. ***The Road of the Dead*****. 2006. 352p. Scholastic/Chicken House (9780439786232). Gr. 9–12.**

Fourteen-year-old Ruben Ford is sitting in his father's junkyard when he knows—knows—that his older sister, Rachel, has been raped and murdered. Perhaps it is his Gypsy blood that gives him second sight; Ruben can see and feel things others can't. He knows, for instance, that his ice-cold brother, Cole, is going to get into—and cause—trouble when he decides to go to desolate Dartmoor, where Rachel met her end. Brooks' great strength is his talent for intense description; he makes readers see, feel, and smell all that Ruben does—most of it coarse, disgusting, and ugly. The author uses an interesting technique to heighten that effect. Psychic Ruben can see things happening miles away, so Cole's battles with those responsible for Rachel's death are literally seen through Ruben's eyes. However, as in *Kissing the Rain* (2004), Brooks has trouble tying up loose ends. Thus, the question of how Cole comes upon a key piece of evidence is brushed away with Ruben's comment, "Does it matter?" Readers have sat through a lot of brutality (albeit strikingly written brutality) to get that information, so the answer is, well, yeah, it does. —Ilene Cooper

Bruchac, Joseph. *Skeleton Man*. 2001. 128p. HarperCollins (9780060290757). Gr. 5–9.

What will Molly do now that her parents have vanished? The answer may rest with the elderly stranger who claims to be her great-uncle. Credulous local authorities hope he is, and they're glad to send the sixth-grader to live with him. But is he who he claims to be? And why does he appear in Molly's increasingly vivid dreams as the skeleton monster she heard about in her Mohawk father's stories? Will Molly ever see her parents again? Will her dreams and reality merge with disastrous results? Although it's steeped in Mohawk lore and tradition, Bruchac's story is contemporary both in its setting and its celebration of the enduring strength and courage of Native American women. The plot occasionally seems as skeletal as the monster that stalks the pages, but Molly's plight will still engage readers' sympathy as she struggles to prove herself worthy of her namesake, Molly Brant, a dauntless eighteenth-century Mohawk warrior. —Michael Cart

Bunce, Elizabeth C. *A Curse Dark as Gold*. 2008. 414p. Scholastic/Arthur A. Levine (9780439895767). Gr. 7–10.

After her father's death, Charlotte and her younger sister, Rosie, take over the family business, a mill shadowed by a curse that goes back generations. Charlotte gives little credence to superstition, but when they can't pay the mortgage on the mill, Rosie conjures up Jack Spinner, an odd little man who promises them that he will spin a roomful of straw into gold—for a price. Despite an uncle who apparently wants to help the girls and a suitor who will do anything he can for Charlotte, her secret agreement with Spinner creates a vortex that threatens to destroy everything she holds dear. Set in England during the early days of the Industrial Revolution, the novel combines elements of fantasy and historical fiction with a love story between two strong-minded individuals. An appended author's note comments on the setting and the Rumpelstiltskin motif. With an appealing title and eye-catching jacket art, this first novel will surely find its audience. —Carolyn Phelan

Burgess, Melvin. *Bloodsong*. 2007. 384p. Simon & Schuster/Simon Pulse (9781416936169). Gr. 10–12.

Told from a number of different viewpoints, this stand-alone sequel to Burgess' unforgettable *Bloodtide* (2001) pushes the boundaries of YA literature with its masterful melding of sf and violent Viking myth. Based on a thirteenth-century Icelandic epic, the story focuses on 15-year-old Sigurd, son of *Bloodtide*'s Sigmund. In a futuristic war-torn England where organic machines with both flesh and circuitry live alongside human-animal hybrids, it's Sigurd's destiny to reclaim his royal lineage and unite the country. To this end, he accomplishes a series of impossible tasks, including slaying the genetically enhanced "dragon" Fafnir, rising from the dead three times, and ending war between the Niberlin and Portland families. But when Sigurd aligns himself with the Niberlin family, his fortunes turn, and his godlike capabilities are crushed beneath the iron wills of three very different women, each of whom wants to possess him. Burgess pulls no punches in his dark dystopian vision; classic themes of heroism, love, and betrayal are illustrated with violent imagery that is as shocking as it is utterly captivating. But readers who can manage the body count will discover that Burgess has breathed new life into an ancient tale, making it relevant and accessible to teens coming of age in a post-9/11 world. Although the first book was originally published for adults, this one is being marketed as YA. —Jennifer Hubert

Burgess, Melvin. *Lady: My Life as a Bitch*. 2002. 240p. Holt (9780805071481). Gr. 9–12.

Don't be fooled by the canine on the jacket of this unusual novel. She's not what she appears. Seventeen-year-old Sandra is taking a walk on the wild side—trading safe boyfriend Simon for riskier Wayne, staying out all night, and blowing off the national school examination. "Who wants to be good anyway?" she challenges her friend Annie with spirited abandon. Life is spinning waywardly along when suddenly what should happen but an alcoholic street person with whom she has an altercation changes her into a dog! Burgess' wild tale, set in Manchester, England, really takes off now as readers travel with Lady (formerly Sandra) on her adventures, relayed through the perspective of a sassy yet tenderhearted teen whose behaviors are distinctively, graphically canine. Is life as a human too restrained, too stressful, too unrewarding? Now Sandra has a chance to compare the exhilaration and novelty of a dog's life with her former existence, filled with routine, parents, and responsibility. Is being higher on the chain of evolution worth the price? Burgess, the author of the award-winning *Smack* (1998), has great fun with the construct and maintains it beautifully. At the same time, he gives teens much to think about in this bawdy, sophisticated, and occasionally sexually explicit adventure, with a host of well-drawn, unusual characters. —Anne O'Malley

Calhoun, Dia. *White Midnight*. 2003. 304p. Farrar (9780374383893). Gr. 9–12.

Fifteen-year-old Rose loves the Greengarden orchards and worries that the Dalriadas, barbarians from the Red Mountain, will destroy the Valley's agrarian civilization. Rose also fears the monstrous "Thing" locked in the attic of the Bighouse, home of Mr. Brae, master of Greengarden. Brae's only child, Amberly, died giving birth to the monster no one has seen. Nearly everyone, however, has heard his furious ranting. After her parents make a deal with Master Brae, Rose finds herself betrothed to the monster and expected to produce an heir. Visiting the attic only in the dark of night, Rose comes to know Raymont, who is not a monster, and becomes pregnant with his child. Threatened by Brae and haunted by Amberly, Rose discovers a family secret that has an impact on the fate of her baby and the future of the Valley. Brooding and atmospheric, sensual but not sexually graphic, this gripping fantasy questions the nature of such cultural components as family, race, and war, without sacrificing the story. Fans of *Firegold* (1999) will not be disappointed in this companion novel. —Linda Perkins

Card, Orson Scott. *Pathfinder*. 2010. 672p. Simon & Schuster/Simon Pulse (9781416991762). Gr. 8–12.

The first in a series, Card's latest title has much in common with his Ender Wiggins books: precocious teens with complementary special talents, callously manipulative government authorities, endlessly creative worlds, and Card's refusal to dumb down a plot for a young audience. Here he takes the notions of folding space and time, embracing paradox, "adopting a rule set in which . . . causality . . . controls reality, regardless of where it occurs on the timeline." Thirteen-year-old Rigg is a Pathfinder, one who sees the paths of others' pasts. Rigorously trained and thoroughly educated by his demanding father, Rigg is horrified when Father dies unexpectedly after a final order to find the sister he never knew he had. Rigg is accompanied on this journey by a small group of friends who have powers of bending and manipulating the flow of time. Card also skillfully twines a separate story line into the plot, featuring Earth's colonization of distant planets, led by the idealistic young pilot Ram Odin. Fast paced and thoroughly engrossing, the 650-plus pages fly by, challenging readers to care about and grasp sophisticated, confusing, and captivating ideas. As in L'Engle's Time Quartet, science is secondary to the human need to connect with others, but Card does not shy away from full and compelling discussions of the paradoxical worlds he has created. —Debbie Carton

Card, Orson Scott. *Ruins*. 2012. 544p. Simon & Schuster/Simon Pulse (9781416991779). Gr. 9–12.

At the end of *Pathfinder* (2010), Card left readers' minds sugar rushing from some of the tastiest brain candy in recent memory. The head trip continues here and dives even deeper into deliciously paradoxical logic traps. The story is nearly impossible to describe without revealing spoilers. But the central crisis that faces Rigg and his time-manipulating companions is the impending destruction of life on Garden (a planet colonized by humans more than 11 millennia ago).

Card doesn't craft the most artful of stories here, as the loads of explanatory passages can get a bit top-heavy. But the ideas he has his characters confront as they square off against hyperdeceitful machines, alternate versions of themselves, parasitic species, and dissension in their own ranks are so enthralling and tricky that it's easy to forgive him. This is philosophically challenging, mind-pretzeling stuff about time travel, engineered evolution, gene splicing, artificial intelligence, xenocide, and the very nature of what it means to be human and have a soul. Whatever sacrifices Card makes in craft are more than made up for in pure fascination. —Ian Chipman

Carey, Janet Lee. *Dragon's Keep*. 2007. 320p. Harcourt (9780152059262). Gr. 7–10.

In stunning, lyrical prose, Carey tells the story of Rosalind, a twelfth-century princess destined for greatness by a prophecy from Merlin: the twenty-first queen of Wilde Island, which is plagued by dragons, will do three great things. Rosalind is to be that queen, but because she was born with a finger that looks exactly like a dragon's claw, she always wears gloves of gold. If exposed, her deformity will mark her as a witch and spell her doom, so anyone who finds out about it has died. Her life takes a strange turn during the summer Rosalind is 16; she is plucked from the ground by a dragon and flown to its keep high in the mountains on another island to serve as nursemaid to its four motherless pips. Carey smoothly blends many traditional fantasy tropes here, but her telling is fresh as well as thoroughly compelling. Fantasy fans wanting a slightly different take on dragons might enjoy books by N. M. Brown and Jason Hightman. —Diana Tixier Herald

Cashore, Kristin. *Fire*. 2009. 480p. Dial (9780803734616). Gr. 8–12.

This prequel to *Graceling* (2008) introduces Fire, a monster-woman with the fundamental elements of her kind: a breathtaking beauty that inspires nearly irresistible sexual attraction and the dual powers of reading thoughts and bending another's will to her purposes. Though her father used his monster powers to control the kingdom for his own evil purposes, Fire struggles to use hers only for good. Her growing regard for the king, his brothers, and his sister leads to some uncomfortable dilemmas and decisions as well as, eventually, the revelation of old secrets. Drawn in to tip the delicate balance of forces struggling over the realm, she begins to trust herself to act on behalf of the royal family, though in doing so she violates a long-held principle that has held her considerable powers in check. Like its predecessor, this novel focuses on a young woman who thinks for herself, wields considerable powers, and acts courageously. While the two stories take place in adjoining lands and one character appears in both books, readers can enjoy this novel without having read *Graceling*. And enjoy it they will, with its vivid storytelling, strongly realized alternate world, well-drawn characters, convincing fantasy elements, gripping adventure scenes, and memorable love story. —Carolyn Phelan

★ Cashore, Kristin. *Graceling*. 2008. 480p. Harcourt (9780152063962). Gr. 9–12.

Feared as a killer since her childhood, Lady Katsa uses her unusual Grace (superhuman gift) in the service of her uncle, King Randa. She is beginning to rebel against his orders to kill or maim his more disloyal subjects when her path crosses that of Po. A young foreign prince with a mysterious Grace as well as wisdom beyond his years, Po convinces Katsa that she can stand up to the brutal king and put her gift to better uses. When Katsa joins Po on a quest, she throws herself headlong into a rescue mission and finds romance, self-knowledge, and justice along the way. Although many fantasy writers create intriguing alternate worlds and worthy adventures, as Cashore does in this well-imagined novel, she also offers believable characters with enough depth, subtlety, and experience to satisfy older readers. Katsa is a heroine who can physically overpower most men she meets, yet her strength is not achieved by becoming manlike. She may care little for fine clothes, but from her first kill to her first experience of lovemaking, Katsa's womanhood is integral to her character. An impressive first novel, this well-crafted and rewarding fantasy will leave readers hoping for more. —Carolyn Phelan

Clarke, Judith. *Kalpana's Dream*. 2005. 164p. Front Street (9781932425222). Gr. 6–9.

Who Am I? That's the question Miss Dallimore wants answered in an essay that will be due in six weeks. The assignment animates and alarms several of the young people in the freshman class and forms the underpinnings of this heartfelt novel that lightly wraps the realistic story lines in a flimsy gauze of magic realism. Neema, half Indian, half Australian, is one of the students. She is also dealing with a visit from her great-grandmother, who speaks only Hindi, and her unsettling feelings for a skateboarder named Gull Owens, with whom grandmother Nani has her own relationship. As Nani watches Gull fly by on his skateboard each night, she wishes that she might soar as he does. Clarke is brilliant at making gossamer connections between her characters. The interweavings can be common or unexpected, but they are always meticulously rendered. Unlike many young adult authors, Clarke takes special care with the adult characters, especially Nani, who is exquisitely drawn and shows that when hope and love are near the surface, age is of no consequence. Only Miss Dallimore and her boyfriend, who may or may not be a vampire, dent the story's magical circle. —Ilene Cooper

Clements, Andrew. *Things Not Seen*. 2002. 176p. Putnam (9780399236266). Gr. 7–10.

The first page is electrifying. Bobby, 15, looks at himself in the bathroom mirror and there's nobody there. No, he isn't blind. He can see. He can feel his body. But he's invisible. This is sf just on the edge of reality. Everything else is normal, and Bobby's first-person narrative takes readers through his experiences of telling his frantic parents but otherwise trying to keep it a secret. He walks outside in his Chicago neighborhood (swathed in clothes, he looks like a person). He hangs out in the university library, naked and unseen. He acts as spy in Sears corporate offices when he needs to. Of course, he can't go to school, but he's always felt pretty invisible there anyway, especially with the popular crowd. The plot details don't bear scrutiny, but Clements has lots of fun with the invisibility stuff in story and metaphor. Are there other invisible people like Bobby? Who would know? Can he find out what caused his condition and reverse it? But with all the play, there's an underlying realistic theme that's heartbreaking: Bobby meets a blind girl, Alicia, who lost her sight suddenly one day. Her condition can never be reversed. To her, Bobby will always be—no matter what—invisible. He confides in her; they laugh, quarrel, help each other, and fall in love. Clements isn't heavy-handed, but readers will easily be able to imagine what it must be like to have the world disappear. —Hazel Rochman

Colfer, Eoin. *Airman*. 2008. 416p. Hyperion (9781423107507). Gr. 10–12.

Author of the popular Artemis Fowl series, Colfer ventures into slightly different territory in this fantasy, which has the heft of historical fiction; a subset of characters whose physical attributes reflect their evil natures; dry humor; visceral horror; and swashbuckling action that keeps the story from becoming overly dark. Born in the basket of an air balloon, Conor Broekhart is sure he is destined to fly. But at 14, he accidentally witnesses the murder of his tutor and the sovereign of the tiny Saltee Islands where he lives, and everything changes. Villainous Marshall Bonvilain throws him into prison, convincing him that his family believes him guilty of the crime. Thus begins his new life as inmate Conor "Finn," who devotes his considerable abilities to breaking out of prison. Colfer grapples somewhat awkwardly with a few literary issues here: should he, for example, allow his hero to commit murder? There are also huge time gaps that are distracting and occasionally stall momentum. Readers may not notice, however, with so much else going for the book. —Stephanie Zvirin

Collins, B. R. *The Traitor Game*. 2008. 256p. Bloomsbury (9781599902616). Gr. 9–12.

Collins' debut novel is a compelling psychological drama about friendship and betrayal. The insecure and frightened Michael, horribly bullied in the past, makes a new friend in Francis. Michael shares his most important secret with Francis—Evgard, the fantasy world he created—and together they develop the world in remarkable detail. But when Michael receives a note proving that someone else knows about Evgard, he fears that Francis has betrayed him. Rather than confronting Francis, he decides to play the cruel game he believes Francis is playing, but Michael's wounded paranoia blinds him to the truth. Reality is echoed in Evgard by the tentative friendship between Argent, a young rebel turned slave, and Columen, the son of the twisted Duke. The Evgard story line stands on its own, as engrossing as the high-school story, with a heart-breaking conclusion that is well earned. Meanwhile, the misunderstanding that almost destroys Michael and Francis' relationship is portrayed with honesty and sensitivity—Francis is keeping a secret, but it's not the secret Michael thinks, making Michael's actions all the more agonizing. Although painful at times, their story has a hopeful conclusion, with each boy better understanding the other and becoming stronger. —Krista Hutley

Collins, Suzanne. ***Catching Fire*****. 2009. 400p. Scholastic (9780439023498). Gr. 9–12.**

At the end of *The Hunger Games* (2008), breathless readers were left in the lurch with any number of questions. Will Katniss lead an uprising against the Capitol? Does she fancy Peeta or Gale? Both? Neither? And perhaps most important, how in the world is Collins going to live up to the (well-deserved) hype? Without divulging too much, don't sweat it. The book opens with Katniss and Peeta reluctantly embarking on their victory tour through the 12 oppressed districts of Panem, where they witness more than a few surprising things. And right when it seems as if the plot might be going into a holding pattern between the first and third acts of the trilogy, a blindsiding development hurtles the story along and matches, if not exceeds, the unfiltered adrenaline rush of the first book. Again, Collins' crystalline, unadorned prose provides an open window to perfect pacing and electrifying world building, but what's even more remarkable is that aside from being tremendously action-packed science-fiction thrillers, these books are also brimming with potent themes of morality, obedience, sacrifice, redemption, love, law, and, above all, survival. Honestly, this book only needs to be good enough to satisfy its legions of fans. Fortunately, it's great. And if you were dying to find out what happens after the last book, get ready for pure torture awaiting the next. —Ian Chipman

★ Collins, Suzanne. ***The Hunger Games*****. 2008. 420p. Scholastic (9780439023481). Gr. 9–12.**

This is a grand-opening salvo in a new series by the author of the Underland Chronicles. Sixteen-year-old Katniss poaches food for her widowed mother and little sister from the forest outside the legal perimeter of District 12, the poorest of the dozen districts constituting Panem, the North American dystopian state that has replaced the U.S. in the not-too-distant future. Her hunting and tracking skills serve her well when she is then cast into the nation's annual Hunger Games, a fight to the death where contestants must battle harsh terrain, artificially concocted weather conditions, and two teenaged contestants from each of Panem's districts. District 12's second "tribute" is Peeta, the baker's son, who has been in love with Katniss since he was five. Each new plot twist ratchets up the tension, moving the story forward and keeping the reader on edge. Although Katniss may be skilled with a bow and arrow and adept at analyzing her opponents' next moves, she has much to learn about personal sentiments, especially her own. Populated by three-dimensional characters, this is a superb tale of physical adventure, political suspense, and romance. —Francisca Goldsmith

Collins, Suzanne. ***Mockingjay*****. 2010. 400p. Scholastic (9780439023511). Gr. 6–12.**

The highly anticipated conclusion to the Hunger Games trilogy does not disappoint. If anything, it may give readers more than they bargained for: in action, in love, and in grief. When the book opens, Katniss has survived her ordeal at the Quarter Quell, and she and her family are safe in District 13. Gale is there as well, but Peeta is being held at the Capitol as President Snow's very special prisoner. Events move quickly, but realization unfolds slowly as Katniss learns that she has been a pawn in more ways than she ever supposed and that her role as the face of the revolution is one with unanticipated consequences, including a climbing death toll for which she holds herself personally responsible. Collins does several things brilliantly, not the least of which is to provide heart-stopping chapter endings that turn events on their heads and then twist them once more. But more ambitious is the way she brings readers to questions and conclusions about war throughout the story. There's nothing didactic here, and the rush of the narrative sometimes obscures what message there is. Yet readers will instinctively understand what Katniss knows in her soul, that war mixes all the slogans and justifications, the deceptions and plans, the causes and ideals into an unsavory stew whose taste brings madness. That there is still a human spirit yearning for good is the book's primrose of hope. —Ilene Cooper

Cornish, D. M. *Lamplighter*. Illus. by D. M. Cornish. 2008. 736p. Putnam (9780399246395). Gr. 7–10.

In the second book of the Monster Blood Tattoo trilogy, young Rossamünd Bookchild, a lamplighter prentice in the Emperor's service, has trouble fitting in with the lamplighters, who think he is too small and timid to travel the highways lighting and dousing the lights or to aid travelers facing danger. However, his skills with potives and restoratives earn him a role as dispenser of healing draughts and repellents. Then Threnody, an arrogant young member of a feared society of female monster hunters and a burgeoning wit, is foisted on the lamplighters for training, and she joins Rossamünd as another outsider in the service. The pair face not only bizarre monsters but also treachery on the part of the power-hungry Master-of-Clerks, who usurps the position of the Lamplighter-Marshall and transfers Rossamünd and Threnody to the most dangerous post in the Half-Continent. The setting, characterizations, and relationships are as well limned as in *Foundling* (2006), and the suspense is palpable as the two young people find themselves facing incredible survival odds. Once again, Cornish's black-and-white drawings and the Explicarium, a glossary more than 100 pages long, add to the whole, and once again, the conclusion is a cliffhanger. A most fitting sequel that will leave readers eagerly waiting for the third book. —Sally Estes

Cornish, D. M. *Foundling*. Illus. by D. M. Cornish. 2006. 434p. Putnam (9780399246388). Gr. 7–10.

"Night, they used to say, was when monsters grew bold, when the knickers roamed and the bogles haunted." Rossamünd Bookchild, a boy saddled with a girl's name, journeys from Madam Opera's Estimable Marine Society for Foundling Boys and Girls, assigned to wander the dark roads at dawn and dusk as a lamplighter. In the first book in the Monster Blood Tattoo series, first-time author Cornish gives the Dickensian orphan story an original spin as Rossamünd faces a world at war with creatures such as the Grinnlings with their wicked, grinning mouths. The world building of the Half-Continent is expertly envisioned and peopled with intriguing characters: the evil Poundinch (who tricks Rossamünd onto the wrong boat early in his travels) and the beguiling Europe, an experienced monster killer (and slayer of men's hearts), who prefers tiny x-shaped tattoos to mark her kills instead of the usual monster-faced blood ones. Readers wanting to immerse themselves further into Cornish's fantastic world can wander for hours through more than 100 pages of glossary ("Explicarium"), detailed maps, and drawings of uniforms and ships. Cornish has added his own impressive black-and-white portraits to give the characters additional substance. At the close, the protagonist is poised for his next adventure, with enough secrets, promises, and mystery to create impatient demand. —Cindy Dobrez

Datlow, Ellen, and Terri Windling, eds. *The Green Man: Tales from the Mythic Forest*. 2002. 368p. Viking (9780670035267). Gr. 7–12.

There are some genuine gems in this enticing collection of 15 stories and 3 poems, all written specifically for this anthology, all featuring diverse takes on mythical beings associated with the protection of the natural world, and most involving a teen's coming-of-age. Delia Sherman takes readers into New York City's Central Park, where a teenager wins the favor of the park's Green Queen. Michael Cadnum contributes a dynamic retelling of the Daphne story. Charles de Lint offers an eerie, heartwarming story in which a teenager resists the lure of the world of faerie. Tanith Lee roots her turnabout tale in the myth of Dionysus, a god of the Wild Wood. Patricia McKillip steeps hers in the legend of Herne, guardian of the forest. Magic realism flavors Katherine Vaz's haunting story. Gregory Maguire takes on Jack and the Beanstalk, and Emma Bull looks to an unusual Green Man—a Joshua tree in the desert. All in all, this is a tasty treat for fantasy fans. —Sally Estes

De la Cruz, Melissa. *Blue Bloods*. 2006. 298p. Hyperion (9780786838929). Gr. 9–12.

Like the power brokers that are their parents and ancestors, members of the popular clique at New York's Duchesne School are Blue Bloods, continually reincarnated vampires endowed with preternatural beauty, charisma, and strength. The plot revolves around several teens, unaware of their heritage, who begin to manifest their true natures during a terrifying spate of vampire-to-vampire violence. At book's end, nonconformist Schuyler has emerged as heroine, having discovered a rift in Blue Blood history that lays the groundwork for forthcoming books. Grafting the chick-lit sensibility of her Au Pairs books onto horror themes, de la Cruz introduces a conception of vampires far different from traditional stake-fleeing demons, coupling sly humor ("What, the Committee was just a front for a bunch of blood-sucking B-movie monsters?") with the gauzier trappings of being fanged and fabulous—as well as abundant references to the taboo-laden "taking" of human familiars, a procedure with overtly sexual overtones. Although the novel isn't sure quite what it wants to be (satire? beach read? gothic saga?), many teens will savor the thrilling sense of being initiated into an exclusive secret society. —Jennifer Mattson

Delaney, Joseph. *Curse of the Bane*. Illus. by Patrick Arrasmith. 2006. 480p. Greenwillow (9780060766214). Gr. 6–9.

When readers met Tom Ward in *The Revenge of the Witch* (2005), the first entry in the Last Apprentice series, he was a callow lad, apprehensively apprenticed to the Spook, who routs the Dark from the County. The malevolent forces that came into play last time seem almost mundane compared to the challenges Tom and the Spook face now: a violent, deadly bane growing in strength and power to become the embodiment of evil. Despite the blood and gore, this tale is more than a well-crafted horror story. Delaney infuses his characters with depth and emotion, but equally important, he grows his world by contributing significantly to the back story. Readers learn the reason the Spook has strong feelings about women in general and witches in particular, and Tom discovers something unexpected about his mother and her wisdom. Delaney also does an exceptional job of interweaving stories, with one plot point leading insistently to the next; at the book's conclusion, readers can go over all Tom has learned by leafing through his journal. Kids will breathlessly await Tom's next adventure. —Ilene Cooper

Delaney, Joseph. *Revenge of the Witch*. Illus. by Patrick Arrasmith. 2005. 336p. Greenwillow (9780060766184). Gr. 6–9.

Delaney grabs readers by the throat and gives them a good shake in a smartly crafted story in which the horror is set within the parameters of a boy's new job. In an unspecified England some centuries ago, Thomas, the 12-year-old seventh son of a seventh son, is taken on as an apprentice by the local Spook. It's the Spook's job to keep the surrounding area free from witches, bogarts, and the creepy things that cause shivers in the night. Tom is not sure he's cut out for the solitary, scary life, and he soon finds himself in trouble, inadvertently freeing a terrifying witch, Mother Malkin, at the behest of a girl named Alice because he's desperate for a friend. Like Anthony Horowitz's *Raven's Gate* (2005), this is a gristly thriller; Delaney's descriptions of moldering bodies hoisting themselves from the earth and hairy pigs tearing into a witch's heart will have readers' eyes opening wide. Yet the twisted horror is amply buffered by an exquisitely normal young hero, matter-of-fact prose, and a workaday normalcy. Still, like Mother Malkin popping out of her earthy pit, bad things are always there to catch readers off guard. As the warning label on the cover notes, this is "Not to be read after dark." —Ilene Cooper

de Lint, Charles. *The Blue Girl*. 2004. 368p. Viking (9780670059249). Gr. 8–11.

Fifteen-year-old Imogene is new at Redding High School, and she's determined not to repeat the mistakes she made at her old school, especially after she meets Maxine, the good-girl friend she's always wanted—and needed. Then Imogene and Maxine encounter Ghost, the school's resident lost soul, and the girls embark on an adventure that moves back and forth between the dangers of the unforgiving high-school environment and a terrifyingly evil netherworld of fairies, supernatural creatures, and anamithim—soul-eaters who are attracted to Imogene's strong personality and who threaten her safety. De Lint's strong characters and riveting plotlines will work for even the most skeptical reader, and Imogene and Maxine are wonderful examples of strong young women faced with a variety of problems that appear to defy solutions—that is, until the girls realize that the simplest, yet most difficult, answer is within their control: bravery in the face of a friend's danger. —Frances Bradburn

Del Vecchio, Gene. *The Pearl of Anton*. 2004. 256p. Pelican (9781589801721). Gr. 7–10.

His brother having died years earlier, 15-year-old Jason inherits by default the Wizard's Stone, which has been passed down from father to eldest son for generations. Part coming-of-age story, part creation tale, and part struggle between various evils and Good, this is a complex tale of a desperate quest. Jason, accompanied by the village Teacher (a member of the Etha race) and a Manwarrior, travels the country in search of the Pearl of Anton, which must be united with the Wizard's Stone so that the boy can engage in a predestined battle against Pure Evil and Less Evil. Along the way, Jason must overcome his fears and insecurities and learn how to use his powers. The action is intense and the violence level high as the ghastly creatures of Pure Evil and Less Evil try to kill Jason before the final battle. Del Vecchio has created a richly detailed world, complete with a compelling history and wonderfully developed races, including elves and dwarfs as well as the Etha. The climactic battle is catastrophic and convincing, and the suspense leading up to it is almost overwhelming. Del Vecchio's first YA fantasy, this is sure to make a big splash among genre fans. —Sally Estes

Dickinson, Peter. *Angel Isle*. 2007. 512p. Random/ Wendy Lamb (9780385746908). Gr. 7–10.

In this sequel to Printz Honor Book *The Ropemaker* (2001), Dickinson returns to his beautifully created, four-dimensional universe for another perilous adventure. The Ropemaker has been gone for 200 years, and once again his secluded valley is in dire straits, its crumbling defenses vulnerable to forces from the Empire and marauding horsemen from the north. This time, a team of diverse characters set out on an arduous trek to find the Ropemaker in hopes that he can restore the ancient magic that protects the valley. Among their number, there is one who can listen to the words of the rivers and ocean; a horse with the wings of a roc; a powerful young magician; and an intelligent being from an alternate, seven-dimensional universe. Perhaps most compelling of all, however, is 12-year-old Maja, whose tribulations as she matures and learns to use her sensitivity to magic are thoroughly believable. The characters are as well developed as those in the first book, and the complex, multilayered story includes more heady explorations of time and magic, joined here by thoughts on the meaning of true love. This is sure to be a hit with fans of the earlier book. —Sally Estes

Dickinson, Peter. *The Ropemaker*. 2001. 376p. Delacorte (9780385729215). Gr. 7–12.

Dickinson works his own wonders in a thoroughly compelling tale that delves into the nature of both magic and time. According to legend, a powerful magician has isolated the Valley for 18 years to protect it from the armies of the Empire in the south and the fierce, marauding horsemen of the north. But now something is terribly wrong. Young Tilja sets out with her grandmother Meena, the boy Tahl, Tahl's grandfather, and an ill-spirited horse on a daunting quest to find the magician in hopes of his renewing the magic that protects the Valley. Their trek through the tightly controlled Empire is fraught with danger, which leads to some exciting scenes. And along the way, Tilja discovers her extraordinary power, a power that connects her to the Ropemaker, a mysterious being who appears along the route in many guises. It's left to Tilja and the Ropemaker to make things right in both the Valley and the Empire. Dickinson's world is vividly realized, his play with time and magic is totally credible, and his characterizations are fully developed—particularly that of Tilja, whose coming-of-age is beautifully portrayed. —Sally Estes

Doctorow, Cory. *For the Win*. 2010. 480p. Tor (9780765322166). Gr. 10–12.

Doctorow is indispensable. It's hard to imagine any other author taking on youth and technology with such passion, intelligence, and understanding. Although perhaps less urgent than *Little Brother* (2008), this effort is superior in every other aspect: scope, plot, character, and style. Set in the near future and in locations across the globe (though primarily China and India), the story involves a sweeping cast of characters making a living—if you want to call brutal conditions and pitiful wages a "living"—in such virtual-game worlds as Svartalfheim Warriors and Zombie Mecha. Many of them, like 15-year-old Mala (known by her troops as "General Robotwalla"), endure physical threats from their bosses to farm virtual gold, which is then sold to rich First World gamers. Then these brilliant teens are brought together by the mysterious Big Sister Nor, who has a plan to unionize and bring these virtual worlds—and real-world sweatshops, too—to a screeching halt. Once again Doctorow has taken denigrated youth behavior (this time, gaming) and recast it into something heroic. He can't resist the occasional lecture—sometimes breaking away from the plot to do so—but thankfully his lessons are riveting. With its eye-opening humanity and revolutionary zeal, this ambitious epic is well worth the considerable challenge. —Daniel Kraus

★ Doctorow, Cory. *Little Brother*. 2008. 384p. Tor (9780765319852). Gr. 8–12.

Seventeen-year-old techno-geek "w1n5t0n" (aka Marcus) bypasses the school's gait-recognition system by placing pebbles in his shoes, chats secretly with friends on his IMParanoid messaging program, and routinely evades school security with his laptop, cell, WiFinder, and ingenuity. While skipping school, Marcus is caught near the site of a terrorist attack on San Francisco and held by the Department of Homeland Security for six days of intensive interrogation. After his release, he vows to use his skills to fight back against an increasingly frightening system of surveillance. Set in the near future, Doctorow's novel blurs the lines between current and potential technologies, and readers will delight in the details of how Marcus attempts to stage a techno-revolution. Obvious parallels to Orwellian warnings and post-9/11 policies, such as the Patriot Act, will provide opportunity for classroom discussion and raise questions about our enthusiasm for technology, who monitors our school library collections, and how we contribute to our own lack of privacy. An extensive web and print bibliography will build knowledge and make adults nervous. Buy multiple copies; this book will be h4wt (that's "hot," for the nonhackers). —Cindy Dobrez

Dolamore, Jaclyn. *Magic under Glass*. 2010. 240p. Bloomsbury (9781599904306). Gr. 7–10.

Nimira is a "trouser girl," a performer from Tassim looking to make her way in a wealthier locale. But things have not been going well, so when a handsome young sorcerer, Hollin Parry, offers her a job, she is interested. Parry owns a life-size automaton that plays the piano and would like Nimira to sing in accompaniment. Yet once Nimira moves into Parry's home, she finds that things are not what they seem. Warned that the automaton is haunted, Nimira is shocked to find that under his metal exterior, he is actually a captive fairy prince named Erris. Soon Nimira is caught in a triangle between a persistent Parry and the tortured Erris, whom she longs to help. Dolamore successfully juggles several elements that might have stymied even a more experienced writer: intriguing plot elements, sophisticated characterizations, and a subtle boost of girl power; it's the women of the tale who have ingenuity, courage, and the power to turn events. Few fantasies end in one volume these days. Alas, this one could have had a perfect finale, but if not that, at least readers will have more of this strong heroine to look forward to. —Ilene Cooper

Doyle, Marissa. *Bewitching Season*. 2008. 352p. Holt (9780805082517). Gr. 7–10.

Twins Persephone and Penelope are of two minds about their coming-out season. Pen is excited about the social whirl. Persephone would rather be home studying magic with their beloved governess, Ally. But when Ally disappears somewhere in Kensington Palace, the girls must harness their magical skills amidst the swirl of balls and presentations to find her. This wonderfully crafted debut novel braids several very different story lines into an utterly satisfying whole. The mystery of Ally's whereabouts mingles with a plot to control the throne of the soon-to-be Queen Victoria. Persephone's strong attraction to her handsome neighbor, Lochinver, provides a romantic element that makes for twists and turns, some of which are obvious ploys, but fun nonetheless. All of this is spread with a patina of magic, which somehow never overwhelms, leaving the story in the world of reality rather than in the realm of fantasy. In the midst of all this plotting, characters might have been lost, but Doyle takes as much care with characters (even minor ones) as with story details. This delightful mélange of genres makes for a great alternative to the depressing overload of chick lit. —Ilene Cooper

Edwards, Janet. *Earth Girl*. 2013. 276p. Pyr (9781616147655). Gr. 9–12.

Tired of bitter, angst-ridden heroines and their associated dark dystopias? Look no further than Edwards' refreshing debut, set in the darn-near-utopian universe of 2788 and starring a confident, motormouthed, giggly 18-year-old named Jarra. She's Handicapped (an "ape" if you're rude), the one-in-a-thousand born with a condition that doesn't allow her to portal outside of Earth. And who wants to hang around boring old Earth? Nobody, unless you're studying "prehistory." So Jarra conspires to join a first-year college archaeology course of off-world teens to prove that an "ape" can sift through the ruins of New York City just as well as, or better than, any privileged Betan or Deltan or Gamman. Make no mistake, this is hard sf (though not *painfully* hard) that largely forgoes heart-pounding drama in favor of fascinating technicalities and flawless world logic. Yes, there is a romance, but it's far from the swooning sort: Jarra comes to respect the other-world "norms" she has set out to shock and soon is considering "boy and girling" with Fian, or even entering with him into a "Twoing contract." If these patient, intelligent particulars are making your eyes glaze over, that's because they're all too rarely found on Planet YA. As Jarra would (loudly) say, this book is "totally zan!" —Daniel Kraus

★ Farmer, Nancy. *The House of the Scorpion*. 2002. 400p. Simon & Schuster/Richard Jackson (9780689852220). Gr. 7–10.

Young Matteo (Matt) Alacrán is a clone of the original Matteo Alacrán, known as El Patrón, the 142-year-old absolute ruler of Opium, a country separating the U.S. and Aztlan, once known as Mexico. In Opium, mind-controlled slaves care for fields of poppies, and clones are universally despised. Matt, on El Patrón's orders, is the only clone whose intelligence has not been blunted. While still quite young, Matt is taken from the loving care of El Patrón's cook and placed into the abusive hands of a maid, who treats him like an animal. At 7, brought to El Patron's attention, he begins an indulged life, getting an education and musical training, though he is never allowed to forget that he is not considered human. Matt doesn't learn until he is 14 that El Patrón has had other clones, who have provided hearts and other organs so El Patrón can go on living. This is a powerful, ultimately hopeful, story that builds on today's sociopolitical, ethical, and scientific issues and prognosticates a compelling picture of what the future could bring. All of these serious issues are held together by a remarkable coming-of-age story, in which a boy's self-image and right to life are at stake. —Sally Estes

Farmer, Nancy. *The Islands of the Blessed*. 2009. 496p. Atheneum (9781416907374). Gr. 6–9.

The third volume of the fantasy series that began with *The Sea of Trolls* (2004) opens when a tornado (or perhaps Odin's Wild Hunt) destroys the village where Jack, now a young teen, lives. Then a revenge-seeking draugr appears, and Jack joins the town Bard and the mercurial shield maiden, Thorgil, to set things right. Their quest frames this exciting story, which contains a cast of lively, multifaceted characters: finfolks, berserkers, a terrifying hogboon, an albatross blown off course, and hobgoblins who fish with their toes. Farmer's richly imagined saga is filled with danger, action, delightful comedy, and sly jabs at contemporary issues, and she builds upon the series' strong foundation while exploring new themes and questions. Jack, a humble and appealing Everyman, continues his struggle to reconcile the colliding beliefs of the Druids, Norsemen, and Christians of his world, and he wonders about the fate of heroes: "Aren't there any tales about heroes who go home after slaying the monster and live happily ever after?" It is Jack, with his grounded humanity and his search for a moral path, who forms the heart of this memorable tale, but the entirety of Farmer's sweeping story will linger long after the intriguing conclusion. —Lynn Rutan

Farmer, Nancy. *The Land of the Silver Apples*. 2007. 496p. Atheneum (9781416907350). Gr. 6–9.

Safely returned from his perilous stint among Northmen, 12-year-old Jack reflects, "That's the nature of adventures. . . . They're nasty while they're happening and only fun later." For readers, though, there's satisfaction in both the nasty and the fun, and this sequel to *The Sea of Trolls* (2004) offers full measures of both. After Jack learns that his often-bratty little sis is a changeling (and that his real sister likely dwells with hobgoblins), a misguided exorcism results in Lucy's disappearance. Then the young bard must descend into the out-of-time Land of the Silver Apples to retrieve both of his lost siblings. In that richly imagined realm, surprises include a reunion with shield maiden Thorgil as well as creatures whose appearances deceive—shape-shifting knuckers; hideous yet likable hobgoblins; and lovely, soulless elves, whose inability to grow or age tinges their existence with tragedy. Occasionally, one wishes for a greater range of emotional tone to the predicaments, which plunge Jack into deep despair perhaps too consistently, but Farmer beautifully balances pell-mell action and quieter thematic points, especially the drawbacks of immortality and the wild tangle of Christian and pagan traditions in eighth-century Britain. Like the druidic life force Jack taps, this hearty adventure, as personal as it is epic, will cradle readers in the "hollow of its hand." —Jennifer Mattson

Farmer, Nancy. *The Lord of Opium*. 2013. 432p. Atheneum/Richard Jackson (9781442482548). Gr. 7–10.

Matteo Alacrán was created to be an organ donor for El Patrón, but he is spared this fate thanks to El Patrón's death and his assisted escape from Opium, a country between the U.S. and what was once Mexico. Matt has now returned to his nation and taken the reins of power as the new Lord of Opium. With its borders closed, the country's drug supply is piling up and imported resources are running low. Global nations are growing aggressive waiting for their drugs, while others want the natural resources only Opium can supply them—flora, fungi, animals, and other denizens of the preserved ecosystem that thrive there but are destroyed elsewhere. Matt is also trying to achieve his personal goals of stopping the drug trade, growing crops for food, and returning the eejits, Opium's preserved labor force, from their current state as microchipped mindless robots to fully functioning humans, all while making Opium self-sustaining. Most young readers who loved *The House of the Scorpion* (2002) when it was first released are now adults, and today's teen audience will need to read the first title in order to fully understand Farmer's brilliantly realized world. The satisfying ending is left open enough to allow for further stories, and Farmer includes an appendix that links real people and places to the book. A stellar sequel worth the wait. —Suanne Roush

Farmer, Nancy. *The Sea of Trolls*. 2004. 480p. Atheneum (9780689867446). Gr. 6–9.

In Farmer's latest, a battle-ax-size fantasy-adventure, rampaging Northmen (the polite term for Vikings) pass through a Saxon village and enslave two of its residents: an 11-year-old apprentice mage and his 5-year-old sister. When Jack offends the Northmen's touchy queen, she threatens to kill his sister unless he reverses a misfired spell—a task that requires a journey deep into icy troll country. The subsequent bouts with troll-bears, giant spiders, and dragons are thrilling, and boys in particular will delight in Farmer's portrayal of the initially terrifying Northmen as tellers of fart jokes and singers of rowdy songs. Lighthearted moments notwithstanding, Jack's archetypal quest is a dense one, heavily draped in Norse mythology, Old English lore, and ponderings about the differences between Christian and pagan cosmologies. In addition, many readers may find it difficult to accept Jack's deepening affection for his frequently barbaric kidnappers, not to mention the oft-repeated message, "All beautiful things attract destruction"—a worldview that comes to Jack straight from the bloody saga of Beowulf. Readers captivated by slash-'em-up Viking culture will happily plunge into this celebrated author's sixth novel, but many members of Farmer's traditional audience will emerge from the experience feeling alternately dazzled and dazed. —Jennifer Mattson

Fisher, Catherine. *Incarceron*. 2010. 448p. Dial (9780803733961). Gr. 9–12.

The vast prison Incarceron, made of metal and cutting-edge technology, was designed as a grand experiment: all undesirables would be sealed inside and given everything for a model utopia. But the experiment failed as Incarceron grew self-aware and tyrannical, resources dwindled, and prisoners divided into factions. Centuries later, prisoners exist under Incarceron's watchful eyes with one belief: no one from Outside enters, no one from Inside escapes. Finn, however, believes he's from Outside, and after he finds a crystal key that opens any door, he embarks on a journey to escape. Outside Incarceron, Claudia, the warden's daughter, is also looking for escape, from an arranged marriage and from her role in a plot to end Protocol, which forces inhabitants to live according to seventeenth-century norms. When she too finds a crystal key, she comes into communication with Finn, who she believes is the true prince of the Realm. This gripping futuristic fantasy has breathless pacing, an intelligent story line, and superb detail in rendering both of the stagnating environments. Fisher's characters are emotionally resonant, flawed, determined, and plagued by metaphysical questions. With some well-timed shocking twists and a killer ending, this is a must-have. —Krista Hutley

Fisher, Catherine. *Sapphique*. 2010. 464p. Dial (9780803733978). Gr. 9–12.

Fisher concludes her high-intensity, mind-bending duology in this sequel to *Incarceron* (2010). In the two months since Finn has escaped Incarceron and assumed his role as Prince Giles, he has failed to adapt to courtly life. Finn is wracked with guilt over leaving Kiero and Attia behind, and his brooding, unpolished demeanor makes him an easy target for the conniving queen. With their attempts to change the Realm stalled, even Claudia has doubts about Finn's real identity, which are worsened when another boy appears, claiming to be the true heir. In Incarceron, Kiero and Attia search for another way out, and when they run across the mad magician Rix, who may own the fabled Glove of Sapphique, they believe they've found it. Meanwhile, Incarceron is maneuvering behind the scenes, and sapient Jared may factor into its all-seeing design. Fisher further explores themes of reality, illusion, and freedom without losing her intensely original world building and authentic characters. The bittersweet conclusion may frustrate readers expecting a traditional happy ending (or even just a more conclusive one), but it fits perfectly—although a glimmer of hope may be all the characters receive, it's a real hope, and like the stars, it endures. —Krista Hutley

Funke, Cornelia. *Inkspell*. 2005. 672p. Scholastic/Chicken House (9780439554008). Gr. 6–9.

Readers who enjoyed Funke's *Inkheart* (2003) are in for a treat with this sequel, a stronger book than its predecessor. In the first volume of the trilogy, a few characters have the ability to "read" a character out of a book and into today's world. In this book the process is reversed, and most of the earlier characters are transported to the magical yet perilous and sometimes brutally violent land of the fictional book, also called *Inkheart*. Young Meggie has longed to visit that world, but once she travels there she realizes the consequences of her choice and the seeming impossibility of putting things right in either place. With the help of Fenoglio, the book's author, who now lives in the secondary world, she connives to turn events toward a good outcome. Though some readers will simply enjoy the adventure story, others will be intrigued by Fenoglio's reflections on the impossibility of controlling what he has created. As before, the book's focus shifts from one group of characters to another as the plot moves swiftly. An indispensable key to the numerous characters precedes the story. Readers will enjoy the many quotes at chapter headings from writers as diverse as Margaret Atwood, David Almond, Kate DiCamillo, Harper Lee, Pablo Neruda, Philip Pullman, J. K. Rowling, and T. H. White. In short, a booklover's book. —Carolyn Phelan

Gaiman, Neil. *The Graveyard Book*. Illus. by Dave McKean. 2008. 368p. HarperCollins (9780060530921). Gr. 6–10.

While a highly motivated killer murders his family, a baby, ignorant of the horrific goings-on but bent on independence, pulls himself out of his crib and toddles out of the house and into the night. This is most unfortunate for the killer, since the baby was his prime target. Finding his way through the barred fence of an ancient graveyard, the baby is discovered by Mr. and Mrs. Owens, a stable and caring couple with no children of their own—and who just happen to be dead. After much debate with the graveyard's rather opinionated denizens, it is decided that the Owenses will take in the child. Under their care and the sponsorship of the mysterious Silas, the baby is named "Nobody" and raised among the dead to protect him from the killer, who relentlessly pursues him. This is an utterly captivating tale that is cleverly told through an entertaining cast of ghostly characters. There is plenty of darkness, but the novel's ultimate message is strong and life affirming. Although marketed to the younger YA set, this is a rich story with broad appeal and is highly recommended for teens of all ages. —Holly Koelling

Galloway, Gregory. *The 39 Deaths of Adam Strand*. 2013. 272p. Dutton (9780525425656). Gr. 10–12.

At 16, Adam Strand has committed suicide 39 times and each time has returned to life whole and unscathed, no matter how violent his death. He is, Adam thinks, genetically hardwired to kill himself, and his condition is exacerbated by his rejection of a world where, he thinks, "we're all horrible." Better to find oblivion in death, for "the dead are perfect." Profoundly pessimistic and solipsistic, Adam begins to look beyond himself for the first time when a young girl whom he is fond of becomes perhaps ill, and he is called on to help her. Will his acts of charity be enough to temper his addiction to death? Galloway, the author of the Alex Award–winning *As Simple as Snow* (2005), offers a riveting second novel that explores the issue of suicide with a philosophical, never sensational, approach, inviting considerations of existentialism and nihilism. Adam is tragically out of tune with what he regards as a meaningless world in which fishing and drinking are the only ways to spend the summer he turns 17. Is his disaffection universal or is it an anomaly confined to his own troubled self? As it addresses these questions, Galloway's book requires careful reading, but the effort is well worth it. —Michael Cart

Gardner, Sally. *Maggot Moon*. 2013. 288p. Candlewick (9780763665531). Gr. 7–12.

The year is 1956. In an unnamed country of obvious allegorical weight, the totalitarian government of "the Motherland" keeps the "impure" in ghettos where they live off scraps and hope not to be dragged away to camps. Standish, 15, lives in Zone 7, a nasty place from which school is no respite—there, cruel teachers beat students and, on this particular day, kill one. Standish is expelled in the aftermath, and the next step for him may be the camps. Standish, however, knows a secret. The Motherland is hyping a moon landing that will prove to the world that they reign supreme with interstellar weaponry. But it's a fake: just across the park, accessible via a hidden tunnel, is a building that houses an artificial moon set. And one of the so-called astronauts has shown up in Standish's cellar missing his tongue. Gardner snatches elements from across history to create something uniquely her own: a bleak, violent landscape of oppression, as well as the seeds of hope that sprout there, revealed in Standish's tenacious, idiosyncratic voice over 100 short chapters. Crouch's frequent sketches of flies, rats, and maggots seem unrelated at first, but they emerge as further metaphor for the taking. This is alt-history second; first, it is an eerie, commanding drama. —Daniel Kraus

George, Jessica Day. *Princess of the Midnight Ball*. 2009. 300p. Bloomsbury (9781599903224). Gr. 6–10.

The Brothers Grimm tale "The Twelve Dancing Princesses" is vibrantly retold and set in a fictionalized nineteenth-century Europe. Galen, a soldier (and knitter) returning home from war, encounters an old woman who gives him an invisibility cloak and yarn possessing magical powers. While working as a gardener at the palace, he encounters the princess, Rose, and her 11 younger sisters. Because of a secret bargain their mother made with the evil King Under Stone, the princesses are cursed to dance each night till their shoes are worn ragged. Aided by the good magic held in his yarn, Galen solves the puzzle that has stumped many a prince and earns Rose's love and hand in marriage. Though cursed and in need of rescue, the sisters are feisty and cunning—not passive victims of their fate. Galen's magical knitting patterns will appeal to teens fond of this trendy hobby. This is a well-realized and fast-paced fantasy-romance that will find favor among fans of fairy tales, feisty heroines, and dashing young men with strength, cunning, and sensitivity. —Heather Booth

George, Jessica Day. *Sun and Moon, Ice and Snow*. 2008. 336p. Bloomsbury (9781599901091). Gr. 7–10.

Unnamed and rejected by her mother, a girl (known as the lass) jumps at the chance to leave her meager home after a great white bear offers her a deal: if she accompanies him to his ice palace for a year and a day, he will reward her and her family with wealth. At the palace, she is waited on by an odd assortment of creatures, including salamanders and a selkie, but there are sinister undercurrents beneath the luxury, leading to a series of horrifying deaths. George has adapted Norse myths and fairy tales to create this eerily beautiful, often terrifying world in which animals talk, trolls marry humans only to destroy them, and weather forces are actual characters. Mystery, adventure, the supernatural, and a touch of love are woven together to create a vivid, well-crafted, poetic fantasy for readers who have enjoyed works by Robin McKinley and Esther Friesner or who are ready to move from Gail Carson Levine's fairy-tale adaptations to more sophisticated fare. —Frances Bradburn

Gill, David Macinnis. *Black Hole Sun*. 2010. 352p. Greenwillow (9780061673047). Gr. 8–11.

Durango is the 16-year-old chief of a team of mercenaries who eke out a living on Mars by earning meager commissions for their dangerous work. Their current job, and the main thrust of this high-energy, action-filled, science-fiction romp, is to protect South Pole miners from the Dræu, a cannibalistic group who are after the miners' treasure. Two feisty women help Durango lead. Second-in-command Vienne and Durango care more for each other than either wants to admit, although there is little time for romance amid all the flying bullets and detonating bombs. Mimi, the other central woman and Durango's former chief, is now implanted in his brain as an artificial intelligence. The repartee between Durango and Mimi is particularly brilliant, but throughout the novel, the dialogue crackles with expertly delivered sarcastic wit and venom. If intelligent sophomoric humor exists, Gill is the master at creating it. The intriguing dystopian setting is a Mars purposely polluted by immigrants from Earth. Readers will have a hard time turning the pages fast enough as the body count rises to the climactic, satisfying ending, which will leave new fans hopeful for more adventures. —Cindy Dobrez

Goodman, Alison. *Eon: Dragoneye Reborn*. 2008. 544p. Viking (9780670062270). Gr. 7–10.

This mesmerizing story begins where most novels end: in a tension-filled climactic event, in which the fate of the protagonist and a nation hang in the balance. Goodman catapults the reader headfirst into a pivotal moment in the Empire of the Celestial Dragons, a world so richly imagined that it feels real. No detail is overlooked, from the smallest sensory description to the fascinating mythos of the elemental dragons. It is a new year, and 12 boys vie to become an apprentice to the ascendant Rat Dragon. Eon has trained for this moment for four years, but she and her master hide a dangerous secret. Eon is actually Eona, a 16-year-old girl with a singular talent. Females are forbidden to take part in dragon magic, and Eona faces disembowelment if discovered. As the story races forward, Eona becomes the fulcrum of a seesaw struggle for control of the Empire. Entangled politics and fierce battle scenes provide a pulse-quickening pace, while the intriguing characters add interest and depth. Eona's pivotal acceptance of her femininity, so ruthlessly repressed by both herself and her culture, gives this intricate fantasy particular weight. Readers will clamor for the sequel. —Lynn Rutan

Goodman, Alison. *Singing the Dogstar Blues*. 2003. 208p. Viking (9780670036103). Gr. 7–12.

Daughter of a sperm donor and a mother who is a famous newscaster, Joss is a wild, fun-loving girl who plays the harmonica. She's also a student of time travel at the Centre for Neo-Historical Studies. Her life turns upside down when Mavkel, the first Chorian to visit Earth, comes to study time travel and selects Joss to be his roommate and study partner. The partnership puts a crimp in Joss' usual freewheeling lifestyle, but she finds plenty of excitement and danger with Mavkel, including meeting an assassin and a confrontation with an anti-alien lobby group. In addition, she's fascinated with Mavkel's heritage, especially with the fact that the Chorians are a harmonizing species of twins who communicate through song. When Mavkel becomes ill and ends up on the brink of death, Joss has to break the center's strictest rule and go back in time to save her alien friend. This wildly entertaining novel successfully mixes adventure, humor, mystery, and sf into a fast-paced, thrilling story that will appeal to a wide audience. —Ed Sullivan

Gordon, Roderick, and Brian Williams. *Tunnels: Book 1*. 2008. 480p. Scholastic/Chicken House (9780439871778). Gr. 6–9.

Positing not just one secret civilization beneath London's streets but many, this compelling doorstopper debut in a new series (apparently to be called Tunnels) pits two teens digging into the disappearance of one's father against a subterranean colony kept in Victorian squalor by the advanced science and ominous preaching of a mysterious semireligious body called The Styx. Though a tad slow off the mark, the plot quickly picks up speed as Will and Chester discover chains of inhabited or once-inhabited caverns down below, while enduring both physical and psychological torture in the course of multiple chases, captures, separations, and escapes. After learning the shocking truth about Will's supposed sister, Rebecca (who may play a larger role in future episodes), the pair, plus a local ally, are last seen hiding aboard a train chugging its way into even deeper unknown realms. The authors add distinctive, vivid touches to the somewhat trendy "towns down below" premise (frequent references to digging, disturbing odors, and dirty clothing), and the murderous, refreshingly competent Styx makes an uncommonly challenging adversary. By all accounts, this appears to be a very promising series kickoff. —John Peters

Grant, Michael. *Gone*. 2008. 576p. HarperTeen (9780061448768). Gr. 6–9.

It's a scenario that every kid has dreamed about: adults suddenly disappear, and kids have free reign. In this case, though, it's everyone 14 and older who disappears, and the harsh reality of such unreal circumstances isn't a joyride after all. A girl driving with her grandfather plunges into a horrific car wreck; gas burners left on ignite a home with a young child trapped inside; food and medical supplies dwindle; and malicious youths take over as the remaining children attempt to set up some form of workable society. Even stranger than the disappearance of much of humanity, though, are the bizarre, sometimes terrifying powers that some of the kids are developing, not to mention the rapidly mutating animals or the impenetrable wall

20 miles in diameter that encircles them. This intense, marvelously plotted, paced, and characterized story will immediately garner comparisons to *Lord of the Flies*, or even the long-playing world shifts of Stephen King, with just a dash of X-Men for good measure. A potent mix of action and thoughtfulness—centered around good and evil, courage and cowardice—renders this a tour-de-force that will leave readers dazed, disturbed, and utterly breathless. Grant's novel is presumably the first in a series, and while many will want to scream when they find out the end is not the end, they'll be glad there's more in store. —Ian Chipman

Gruber, Michael. *The Witch's Boy*. 2005. 384p. HarperCollins (9780060761646). Gr. 6–9.

From the hypnotic mask on the cover to its perfect fairy-tale ending, this astonishing fantasy compels readers onward. Gruber, the author of several adult thrillers, has done much more than offer a well-structured adventure, full of mystery and magic—though he certainly does all that. He also plumbs the depths of the human heart and lays bare its emotions in a way that causes readers to respond instinctively. The story begins when a witch finds a baby so ugly that the note with it reads, "The devil's child for the devil's wife." The witch has no business with a child, but she fancies it, so she gets a bear to be its nanny and a hideous djinni to tutor it. Then she continues her life in service to her goddess. The more the witch underestimates parental responsibilities, the more hurt and angry the boy, Lump, becomes. Gruber cleverly weaves elements from familiar fairy tales into a saga that moves across forest, earth, and sea. But even more astute is his portrayal of the characters, especially Lump and his mother, who, locked in their own selfishness, must fight through disappointment, hatred, and anger to find forgiving love. This can be read at several levels, but those who plumb the deepest will reap the greatest reward. —Ilene Cooper

Hale, Shannon. *Book of a Thousand Days*. Illus. by James Noel Smith. 2007. 320p. Bloomsbury (9781410405821). Gr. 7–10.

The author of the Newbery Honor Book *Princess Academy* (2005) offers another captivating fantasy filled with romance, magic, and strong female characters. The story, based on a little-known fairy tale from the Brothers Grimm, takes place in an imagined ancient Central Asia. Orphaned Dashti is a hardworking, pragmatic girl, who grew up in the open, windswept steppes. She finds work in the city with a young noblewoman, Lady Saren. Then Lady Saren refuses an advantageous marriage, and as punishment, she and Dashti are sentenced to seven years in a sealed tower. A tiny window is the tower's only connection to the outside world, and it's there that Saren's two suitors, the terrifying Khasar and the handsome Tegus, come calling. Written in diary form in Dashti's voice, the gripping tale follows the two young women through their imprisonment and their escape into a grim world of warring societies. Readers will quickly embrace Dashti, an invincible storybook heroine with a healer's touch, who accomplishes battlefield heroics while nurturing a powerful, secret love for a lord. Fans of Gail Carson Levine's *Fairest* (2006) will embrace this similar mix of exotic, fully realized setting; thrilling, enchanted adventure; and heart-melting romance. —Gillian Engberg

Hale, Shannon. *River Secrets*. 2006. 304p. Bloomsbury (9781582349015). Gr. 7–10.

Hale, whose most recent novel, *The Princess Academy* (2005), was named a Newbery Honor Book, continues the story begun in *Goose Girl* (2003) and *Enna Burning* (2004) in this stirring, stand-alone adventure. The kingdoms of Bayern and Tira have just completed a war, and Bayern teenager Rizzo is astonished when he is chosen to join a company of the castle's best soldiers on a diplomatic mission to Tira. A poor swordsman with a reputation as "a brave fool," he knows that his most noteworthy talent may be "cramming two cherries into a single nostril." Once the company arrives in Tira, though, he learns why he was selected: he sees and remembers everything, without "seeming to pay attention to anything beyond dinner," making him an excellent spy. Tension between the kingdoms heightens with a series of recurring, pyrotechnic murders, just as Rizzo falls for an intrepid young Tiran. The story's pace is leisurely, but Hale's accomplished writing will easily pull readers into her vividly realized world. The expertly chosen, often poetic details set and pace the story, and the fully drawn characters, whose dialogue crackles with wit, will point readers to the underlying themes of cultural prejudice and the corruption of power that touch on contemporary political debates. Suspenseful, magical, and heartfelt, this is a story that will wholly envelop its readers. —Gillian Engberg

Hand, Elizabeth. *Illyria*. 2010. 144p. Viking (9780670012121). Gr. 10–12.

Growing up in 1970s Yonkers, Maddy and Rogan were called the "kissing cousins" of the Tierney clan. In a secret attic space, they find a toy theater, complete with lighting and stage effects that appear like magic, but no actors or audience. As their discovery stirs within them the desire to create, Aunt Kate, mysterious and unnaturally beautiful, brings their abilities to a boil. Determined to restore the family's long-abandoned theatrical heritage, Kate pushes Maddy and Rogan to nurture their gifts in the school's production of *Twelfth Night*. However, Rogan's wild nature is ever at odds with his haunting, melodious singing voice, and Maddy's glamour, no doubt the gift of their great-grandmother, an ingénue of the stage, shines dimly in the brilliance of Rogan's fey charms. Winner of the World Fantasy Award, Hand's slim novella is sublime and daring; she makes no mystery about the nature of the 15-year-old cousins' relationship. It's as sweet, sexual, obsessive, and devastating as any other first love. YA readers are entrusted with a narrative of burgeoning and squandered talent, unapologetic incest, familial decline on par with that of Faulkner's Compson family, and a hard-won ending that's, at best, tenuously hopeful. The subtlety and raw ache of the prose, and the realistic portrayal of artistic lives, triumphantly herald Hand's arrival into youth fiction. —Courtney Jones

Hardinge, Frances. *The Lost Conspiracy*. 2009. 576p. HarperCollins (9780060880415). Gr. 6–10.

Gullstruck is home to the Lace, an outcast tribe known for their perpetual smiles and decorated teeth, who fear and worship their three volcanoes while the rest of the island follows the traditions of the Cavalcaste invaders. In a Lace coastal village, Hathin cares for her sister Arilou, who may be a Lost, a people revered for their ability to travel independently of their bodies. Loathe to relinquish their new status, the villagers have hidden signs that Arilou may be only an imbecile, with Hathin bearing the brunt of responsibility. After a Lost Inspector visits the village and mysteriously dies, the terrified villagers cover that up as well, unaware that all the Lost on the island have died simultaneously; then the lies are discovered, and Arilou and the Lace are blamed for the deaths. When her village is massacred, Hathin escapes with Arilou and goes in search of revenge. This is only the beginning of a deeply imaginative story, with nuanced characters, intricate plotting, and an amazingly original setting. Though the narrative bogs down in world building, there is no shortage of tension or suspense as Hathin slowly uncovers the dangerous conspiracy threatening the island. A perfectly pitched, hopeful ending caps off this standout adventure. —Krista Hutley

Hartman, Rachel. *Seraphina*. 2012. 480p. Random (9780375866562). Gr. 9–12.

Hartman proves dragons are still fascinating in this impressive high fantasy. After 40 years of peace between human and dragon kingdoms, their much-maligned treaty is on the verge of collapse. Tensions are already high with an influx of dragons, reluctantly shifted to human forms, arriving for their ruler Ardmagar Comonot's anniversary. But when Prince Rufus is found murdered in the fashion of dragons—that is, his head has been bitten off—things reach a fever pitch. Seraphina, a gifted court musician, wants only to go unnoticed as the investigation draws close: she is the unthinkable, a human-dragon half-breed, and her secret must be protected. But when Prince Lucian Kiggs asks for her help with the murder investigation, she has no choice but to become involved, even if Kiggs' acute perceptiveness is a danger to her. Equal parts political thriller, murder mystery, bittersweet romance, and coming-of-age story, this is an uncommonly good fantasy centered upon an odd but lovable heroine who narrates in a well-educated diction with an understated, flippant tone. Fantasy readers young and old who appreciate immersion into a rich new culture will not mind the novel's slow build, especially as it takes wing and hurtles toward the stratosphere. This is an exciting new series to watch. —Krista Hutley

Haydon, Elizabeth. ***The Floating Island.*** **Illus. by Brett Helquist. 2006. 368p. Tor/Starscape (9780765308672). Gr. 6–9.**

Ven, the thirteenth Polypheme child, has grown up in his family's ship-building business and tried his hand in every department. On his fiftieth birthday (the equivalent of a human's twelfth), he draws the short straw and is sent out to inspect his family's new ship. When the ship is attacked by Fire Pirates, who are known for leaving no survivors, and the youth is ordered to scuttle the ship, he figures out a way to do in the pirates as well. After surviving, he is helped by a mermaid and by a kindly captain, who sends him to an inn run by his wife. It turns out that the captain's wife has peculiar rules intended to keep people safe from evil, and the inn is filled with interesting boarders—among them, a talking cat and a ghost. In her first book for young people, Haydon, a popular author of numerous fantasies for older readers, uses journal entries interspersed throughout a fast-paced narrative to help bring Ven to life. Her world building is as successful as her characters, with Helquist's occasional loose sketches providing some visual distraction and additional atmosphere. A delightful epic fantasy that will attract a readership both older and younger than the target audience. —Diana Tixier Herald

Heneghan, James. ***The Grave.*** **2000. 256p. Farrar/Frances Foster (9780374327651). Gr. 7–10.**

Thirteen-year-old Tom Mullen, shuffled from foster home to foster home since birth, is tough and independent, and thinks he doesn't need anybody. All that changes when he falls back in time through a hole at a construction site, beginning a vivid, emotionally charged journey to nineteenth-century Ireland that illuminates a tragic part of Ireland's past, and forever changes the present. The engrossing novel, which begins in 1974 Liverpool, is equal parts adventure, fantasy, and historical fiction. It is also a compelling story of a teen who learns the rewards of love and family, particularly in times of adversity. Tom's expressive, first-person narrative, reminiscent of an edgier Holden Caulfield and filled with period detail, vividly portrays the impact of Ireland's Potato Famine on individuals and families, while revealing the vulnerability beneath Tom's tough facade. Tom is a likable, three-dimensional character, whose dilemmas are compassionately and realistically revealed. Although some readers may find the book's resolution too fairy tale–like, it opens a door of possibilities for change, hope, and redemption. An author's note briefly describes the real-life events that inspired the book. An engaging, beautifully written story with a complex, appealing narrator. —Shelle Rosenfeld

Hoeye, Michael. ***Time Stops for No Mouse.*** **2002. 279p. Putnam (9780399238789). Gr. 6–9.**

Originally self-published in 2000, this is a fur-raising mystery that will delight fantasy lovers. The watchmaker Hermux Tantamoq, a wonderfully pompous older mouse, becomes totally infatuated with Linka Perflinger, a noted "adventuress, daredevil, and aviatrix," when she brings her watch into his shop for repair. But then she doesn't return to pick up the valuable timepiece, and Hermux is certain that she has met with foul play. After a fruitless trip to the police station to report her missing, Hermux decides to search for Ms. Perflinger himself. His adventures introduce readers to a memorable group of animal characters: Pup Schoonagliffen, mole reporter; Mirrin, Hermux's blind mouse friend; Tucka Mertslin, cosmetics tycoon mouse about to launch the Millennium Line of eternal youth products; Dr. Hiril Mennus, mole researcher and the villain of the story; and a large cast of chipmunks, beavers, squirrels, and evil rats. Hermux's underground universe works on several levels. Strongly attached to the human, it alludes effectively and humorously to all things rodent, and yet it is a charming, alternate world unto itself. The book is structured as tongue-in-cheek Dickens, and its short chapters with suspenseful endings make it a natural for reading aloud, especially to fans of such classics as *Stuart Little* and Brian Jacques' Redwall series. —Frances Bradburn

Hoffman, Mary. ***Stravaganza: City of Masks.*** **2002. 256p. Bloomsbury (9781582347912). Gr. 7–12.**

Belleza, a city that exists in a parallel dimension to sixteenth-century Venice, boils with political espionage, danger, and deception in Hoffman's vivid, suspenseful time-travel novel. Lucien, a twenty-first-century English boy, is being treated for cancer. When his father brings him an old Italian notebook to write in, his world changes as he falls asleep each night clutching his journal. At first he thinks he's dreaming of Venice, "a city floating on the water, laced with canals, and full of domes and spires." But soon it becomes clear that his dreams aren't dreams at all and that he has somehow entered Belleza as Luciano, one of the Stravaganti, a brotherhood of time travelers. Before long he meets the lovely, strong-willed, 15-year-old Arianna; becomes an apprentice for the powerful magician-scientist Rodolfo; and foils an assassination attempt on the violet-eyed Duchessa. As he learns to stravagate back and forth between time and worlds, his split life becomes increasingly complicated—and dangerous. Utterly fascinating, this rich, rip-roaring adventure—the first in a series—will no doubt whet readers' appetites for Italian history and culture as well as the next installment. —Karin Snelson

Hoffman, Mary. *Stravaganza: City of Stars*. 2003. 454p. Bloomsbury (9781582348391). Gr. 6–10.

Cruelly teased and tormented by her older stepbrother, Georgia feels trapped in an impossible family situation, with horseback riding as her only escape. After she buys a small statue of a winged horse, she discovers that it is a talisman with the power to transport her through space and time from modern London to Talia, a sixteenth-century, alternative Italy. Georgia first appears to Cesare, son of a horse master in Remora (Sienna), where he has recently witnessed the miraculous birth of a flying horse, a good omen. Still, there's trouble ahead for Cesare in Remora and for Georgia in both worlds, now that she has become one of the Stravaganti, time travelers between London and Talia. Readers of the *Stravanganza: City of Masks* (2002) will be pleased that several of the main characters reappear, which develops their stories a bit further while introducing a vivid new setting and an involving narrative focused on Georgia. The lovingly created, richly detailed locales are one of the distinctive pleasures of the series, along with the subtle portrayals of both major and minor characters. In other novels, shifts in point of view and setting often confuse the reader and impede the narrative, but here they propel the story, carrying readers along for an adventurous ride. This leaves readers with the hope of more to come. —Carolyn Phelan

Jacobs, John Hornor. *The Twelve-Fingered Boy*. 2013. 280p. Carolrhoda/Lab (9780761390077). Gr. 9–12.

At long last, here is a superhero story for the rest of us. Streetwise Shreve, 15, is serving a two-year stint in juvie, but at least his sideline—dealing candy—keeps things interesting. Enter new roommate Jack, a haunted 13-year-old (a "titty-baby" in juvie terms) rumored to have killed his parents and put five kids into the hospital. Jack has 12 fingers. That's weird. Even weirder? When angered, he can "go explodey"—psychically hurl people across the room. No wonder other parties are, shall we say, interested. Mr. Quincrux, an ominously bland fellow in a black suit, arrives to mentally invade the minds of Jack and Shreve and in the process accidentally lends Shreve a similar ability. What follows is miles away from the superhero battles you're expecting. After the two boys bust out, they live the desperate existence of itinerate thieves as they struggle to control superpowers fueled by pain. Jacobs' storytelling has the effortless velocity of early Dean Koontz, and his prose is textured with hard-boiled grit: each kid's supernatural flexing causes nosebleeds and vomiting, not to mention the realistic mangling of innocent people. An expertly spiced stew of attitude, humor, horror, and grief—and with a movie-ready plot to boot. Sequels? Probably. Let's make that *hopefully*. —Daniel Kraus

Johnson, Kathleen Jeffrie. *A Fast and Brutal Wing*. 2004. 192p. Roaring Brook (9781596430136). Gr. 8–11.

This clever, beautifully written tale stretches the boundaries of the imagination. Disparate perspectives describe the aftermath of a Halloween night in which a famous author goes missing after reportedly attacking local teens. Letters and a teenager's writing assignments are among the devices that reveal the magical element (characters can transform into animal form) as well as deep, realistic hurts: a family haunted by the disappearance of a father. The characters' increasingly frequent need to alter themselves and the thrill of their animal transformations are compellingly described. The subtle feline and birdlike qualities central to the human characters make the transformations believable and serve as a demonstration of Johnson's talent. Although the story's conclusion is a bit too swift and neat, this is a novel that readers will remember long after turning the final page. —Frances Bradburn

Jones, Diana Wynne. *Enchanted Glass*. 2010. 304p. Greenwillow (9780061866845). Gr. 6–9.

Fantasy is a field crowded with gifted newcomers. What happens when a veteran strides to the plate and takes another swing? If the veteran is Diana Wynne Jones, get your scorecards ready. She hits this irresistible new book out of the ballpark. Magician Jocelyn Brandon had always intended to pass his strange home, Melton House, and his trade secrets on to his grandson, Andrew. Unfortunately, Brandon died before he could complete his careful instructions, and Andrew, now grown, has forgotten much of what his grandfather tried to teach him as a child. The arrival of 12-year-old Aiden, who is seeking protection from dangerous magical beings, reawakens Andrew's memories. Surrounded by a fabulous cast of eccentric allies, including a parsnip-loving giant, Andrew finds himself in the middle of a mystery surrounding an enchanted glass. With a gleeful nod to *A Midsummer Night's Dream*, Jones hits all the bases, combining fluid storytelling, sly humor, and exquisitely drawn characters. The magical chaos culminates in a hilarious summer fete and a delightfully tidy resolution. This enthralling book proves that Jones is still at the top of her game. —Lynn Rutan

Jones, Diana Wynne. *House of Many Ways*. 2008. 416p. Greenwillow (9780061477959). Gr. 6–9.

It's been a long time coming, but Jones has finally returned to the madcap world of *Howl's Moving Castle* (1986) and *Castle in the Air* (1991) with an equally rollicking, enchantment-filled tale. Although the Wizard Howl (this time in the guise of an irritating, lisping little boy); his feisty wife, Sophie; and Calcifer the fire demon play important roles, the story centers on Charmain, a bookish teen. When Charmain's great-uncle William, the king's Royal Wizard, falls deathly ill and is taken in by elves for a cure, Charmain is sent to look after William's house, which is, indeed, a house of many ways and rooms and magic within. She begins reading William's books and discovers that she has inherited some of his gifts. Enriching this elaborate and satisfying comic fantasy are some delicious characters, including a little dog named Waif, who seems to be guarding Charmain; young Peter, who arrives to become the wizard's apprentice; the elderly king and his mysteriously vanishing treasury; the evil heir-apparent; and a fearsome creature called a lubbock. Long-standing devotees of this richly textured world, as well as new fans (who may have first encountered it through the 2005 animated film of *Howl's Moving Castle*), will find that their third visit fulfills every expectation. —Sally Estes

Jones, Diana Wynne. *Year of the Griffin*. 2000. 272p. Greenwillow (9780688178987). Gr. 7–10.

The sequel to *Dark Lord of Derkholm* (1998) retains the goofiness of its predecessor, continuing Jones' spoof of traditional fantasy conventions. Set at the poorly managed Wizard's University, the story follows the exploits of a select set of students, who manage to create enough havoc with the magic to ensure that the problems at the school are eventually on the way to being straightened out. The main characters are the griffin Elda, daughter of the great human wizard Derk; Lukin, crown prince of Luteria; Claudia, half-sister of the Emperor of the South; Olga, daughter of a former pirate-turned-gangster; Felim, brother of the Emir; and Ruskin, a dwarf revolutionary. Throw in, among other things, assassins hunting Felim, rogue griffins, magic jinxes, dwarf forgemasters, and senators of the Empire determined to execute Claudia, and there's mayhem and mirth aplenty. References to *Dark Lord* may entice readers to seek out that book, but the detailed characters and situations allow this novel to stand on its own. —Sally Estes

Jordan, Sherryl. *The Hunting of the Last Dragon*. 2002. 128p. HarperCollins (9780060289027). Gr. 6–10.

In this story within a story, Jude, a young, illiterate peasant at a monastery in 1356 England, unsparingly dictates to Brother Benedict the events that occurred

during a journey taken with a young Chinese noblewoman, Jing-wei. Having rescued Jing-wei from a band of traveling performers who were showing her as a heathen freak, Jude and the woman elude their pursuers, only to be driven off by superstitious villagers. It is Lan, a wise old Chinese woman (reputed to be a witch) who straightens Jing-wei's bound feet and reveals Jude's destiny: he must kill the last dragon, which has been terrorizing the people of St. Alfric's Cove, with Jing-wei's help and with Lan's knowledge, for the battle involves things known in China but not in England. As the journey progresses, the growing relationship between Jude and Jin-wei is beautifully realized in all its thorniness and mutual concern, as is Jude's being forced to fight his internal dragon, fear. Appropriate to the telling, the writing is mannered yet lyrical as the rich tale spins out into a lovely combination of fantasy, historical fiction, and romance.
—Sally Estes

Jordan, Sherryl. ***Secret Sacrament*****. 2001. 352p. HarperCollins (9780060289041). Gr. 8–12.**

Set in an ancient civilization, this New Zealand import is a riveting exploration into the impact childhood guilt has upon decisions made throughout life. Gabriel is only seven when he witnesses the brutal rape and slow death of a Shinali slave. From this point forward, he vows to become a healer, and he's eventually apprenticed to the men of the Citadel, healer-priests who work "in the regions of the human mind and spirit, as well as in surgery and medicine." Always aware of his early inability to help a woman in agony, his life is a restless struggle against pain, suffering, and evil, until he falls in love with Ashila, a beautiful Shinali woman who welcomes him into her family and into her life. His love for Ashila, coupled with his need to atone for his youthful failing, force Gabriel into exile from his beloved Citadel. Now begins fulfillment of the Time of the Eagle prophecy, when slave nation and conquering nation become equals. *Secret Sacrament* is a surprising book: violent, yet ultimately peaceful; bitter and despairing, yet ultimately hopeful. Although it appears reflective of the Christian tradition, with allusions to the coming savior and the sacrifice of a life to save a people, it is not overtly religious. Rather, it is a powerful story of the influence of good over evil, love over hate, and the potential impact of one person on a nation's history. —Frances Bradburn

Kindl, Patrice. ***Goose Chase*****. 2001. 214p. Houghton (9780618033775). Gr. 6–9.**

Trapped in a tower until she chooses between two equally ghastly suitors—an evil king and an insipid prince—Goose Girl needs a quick miracle. Enter her faithful, magical geese, which transport her away from the wedding dilemma and set in motion a classic adventure-chase that turns into a delightful, witty fairy-tale spoof. It seems Goose Girl's kindness to a shriveled old woman resulted in a reward: Goose Girl can form gold dust in her hair, cry tears of diamonds, and become a ravishing beauty—talents that have brought about her marriage predicament: "In the future I shall know precisely what to do if another old beggar woman comes pestering me while I'm herding my geese in the high meadow." Not easily discouraged, the dull prince pursues his darling and nearly becomes a meal for a hilariously disgusting trio of ogresses, who just happen to have captured his ladylove. After more escapes and perilous flights, Goose Girl falls into the clutches of the evil king. Just as the wedding is about to take place, the beggar woman arrives on the scene and works her magic. It seems the bold heroine was a princess all along, and the geese, when restored to their real form, are her older sisters. Kindl's humor, the strong characterizations, and vibrant action give the story wings. A happy ending is, of course, understood.
—Anne O'Malley

Klause, Annette. ***Freaks: Alive on the Inside!*****. 2006. 336p. Simon & Schuster/Margaret K. McElderry (9780689870378). Gr. 10–12.**

Seventeen-year-old Abel has spent most of his life at Faeryland, a resort offering "displays of oddities," featuring performers with unusual physical characteristics. Both of his parents are missing limbs, and his first girlfriend is Phoebe the Dog-Faced Girl, whose cheek fur is ever-present when they kiss. Abel feels "useless" and "handicapped" by his normality. Longing to find a sense of purpose (and eager to escape Phoebe's affection), he runs away. He soon discovers that Phoebe's fur-faced younger brother has followed him, and together the boys journey through the seedy, terrifying world of traveling sideshows, led in part by the mysterious dark-haired girl who appears to Abel urgently in dreams and begs to be rescued. Klause's wild historical fantasy enfolds numerous stories and characters, and readers may get bogged down in the wandering subplots that knit the story together. The characters often speak coarsely, occasionally dipping into broad sexual innuendos, and Abel's romantic interludes read with the steaminess of a bodice-ripper. But teens will be easily drawn in by the cliffhanger chapter endings; the vibrant, affectionately drawn cast of characters (including a seductive mummy); and the exuberant, often bawdy language, in which even emotions are visceral creatures: "A worm of anger squiggled in my gut," Abel says. Klause's suspenseful twist on the outsider's story, the grim horror of human exploitation, and the questions about belonging will fascinate readers. —Gillian Engberg

Knox, Elizabeth. *Dreamhunter*. 2006. 384p. Farrar (9780374318536). Gr. 9–12.

Readers pining for a fantasist to rival Philip Pullman or Garth Nix may have finally found what they seek in New Zealander Knox, the author of numerous novels for adults. Knox sets her first YA novel in a fictional nation called Southland, where turn-of-the-century society is coming to terms with a geographical marvel called "the Place," a harvesting ground for dreams that can be caught and sold to sleeping customers. Fifteen-year-old cousins Rose and Laura belong to a first family of dream hunting: Laura's father discovered the Place 20 years before, and Rose's celebrity mother is a sought-after dream-palace performer. When a test reveals that only reluctant Laura, not pert, confident Rose, has inherited the gift, Laura must contend not only with her shaken relationship with her cousin but also with the disappearance of her father, who has left behind puzzling messages about the true nature of dreams. Although Laura's transformation from wilting violet to intrepid avenger seems too abrupt, Knox's wide-angle narrative convincingly explores the nuances of the charismatic extended family and the personal and political implications of the dreamhunting phenomenon. Questions are not so much answered as deepened in anticipation of book 2 in the highly promising Dreamhunter Duet. —Jennifer Mattson

Knox, Elizabeth. *Dreamquake*. 2007. 464p. Farrar/Frances Foster (9780374318543). Gr. 9–12.

Knox's *Dreamhunter* (2006) deserved the widespread notice it received. This companion is just as good, making the resulting Dreamhunter Duet an organic whole that will be considered among youth fantasy's most significant recent works. Returning readers will quickly recall the complexities of Southland's turn-of-the-century reality, as Knox eases background into opening scenes describing 15-year-old Laura Hame's "act of spectral terror"—the novice dreamhunter's misguided protest against governmental exploitation of dreams. Her methods may have been crude, but her close-knit extended family rallies to investigate the questions at the heart of her action: Are the dreams harvested in the unearthly Place actually communicable memories? Are they "drug[s] of idleness," tools for mind control, or harmless, even healing entertainments? Underlying the mystery are larger coming-of-age themes: cousin Rose's participation in a debutante ball plays with notions of decorative femininity, while Laura's consuming attachment to magical "sandman" Nown seems a safe projection of her sexual desire (eventually satisfied, though not graphically depicted) for her human suitor, Sandy. The logic supporting the book's most metaphysical twists isn't always transparent, but like a poem whose images signal potent untapped meanings, Knox's haunting, invigorating storytelling will leave readers eager to return to its puzzles—and to reap its rewards. —Jennifer Mattson

Kostick, Conor. *Epic*. 2007. 384p. Viking (9780670061792). Gr. 7–10.

Kostick was a designer for the world's first live fantasy role-playing game in England, and his expertise is evident in this gripping first novel, set on New Earth, where violence has been banned for generations and conflicts are settled in the fantasy computer game Epic. Getting ahead in the real world means winning in the gaming world—and everyone plays. The unjust treatment of his parents by the Central Allocations committee, which ruthlessly rules the planet, sets teenager Erik and his friends on a perilous mission to challenge the committee and put an end to Epic. Erik's fantasy persona has been killed in a battle with a dragon, and he must prepare a new gaming identity. This time, he is a beautiful female swashbuckler named Cindella the sailor, and as he undertakes a dangerous struggle against the committee, he is threatened by death in both the fantasy world and hardscrabble reality. The action is nonstop, it's easy to keep track of who's who, and the story flows seamlessly as characters move between worlds, maintaining their individuality in both. A surefire winner with a sequel in the works and a third planned. —Sally Estes

Lanagan, Margo. *Black Juice*. 2005. 208p. HarperCollins (9780060743901). Gr. 9–12.

Lanagan's 10 fantasy short stories are set in cultures both familiar and unknown and are peopled with empathetic characters who battle nature, individuals, and events. The stories begin slowly, in part because readers must acclimate themselves to new worlds and situations, but Lanagan gradually draws readers into each brief, fresh reality. Perhaps the most memorable story is the first, "Singing My Sister Down," about a family that lovingly crafts a celebration of grief as one of their own sinks deeper and deeper into tar pits. Other moving stories include "The Wooden Bride," about a bride who is late for her own wedding, and "Youlinin," a strange story of unrequited love. Each selection is carefully shaped and uses both familiar and inventive language to such intriguing effect that English teachers may want to incorporate the stories into classroom writing exercises. —Frances Bradburn

Lanagan, Margo. *The Brides of Rollrock Island*. 2012. 320p. Knopf (9780375869198). Gr. 9–12.

After putting her phantasmagorical stamp on "Snow-White and Rose-Red" in the Printz Honor Book *Tender Morsels* (2008), Lanagan's second novel finds inspiration in selkie legends—seals who shed their skins to become human for a time—with this tale of elementary wrongs leading to elemental retribution. Shunned for her ugliness by most everyone in her tiny fishing village on Rollrock Island, Misskaela Prout becomes a sort of witch, gleaning the forgotten art of magicking human forms out of the seals lounging on the beach. Enchanted by lust, the Rollrock men soon forsake their wives and pay Misskaela to conjure their mates. Told in a variety of voices across several generations in what is essentially a series of linked novellas, the book spins out the ramifications of men keeping women hostage through love and cherished children, despite the women's innate desire to return to the sea. Though this is a more reflective affair than some of Lanagan's feistier works, her writing is as sumptuous as ever: a fine mist of lyrical elegance and sharp anguish that offers vast spaces to get lost in. The passage in which a boy joins his mother in seal form is pure poetry, expressing the inexpressible: "The best I can do is overlay a skin of man-words on the grunt and urge and song and flight and slump of seal-being." A haunting, masterfully crafted novel that, as one should by now expect from Lanagan, isn't a bit like anything else. —Ian Chipman

Lanagan, Margo. *Red Spikes*. 2007. 176p. Knopf (9780375843204). Gr. 10–12.

With Lanagan having published two acclaimed short story collections in close succession (*Black Juice* was selected as a Printz Honor Book in 2006), it wouldn't be surprising if the Australian fantasist's third outing—also comprising short stories—showed signs of exhausted reserves. Far from it, this razor-sharp assemblage thrusts readers just as exhilaratingly into alien, hermetic environments and uncompromisingly idiomatic points of view. Fans will anticipate some disconcerting, even horrific stuff. In one story, female monkeys in a haremlike group endure the rivalries of alpha males; in another, characters in purgatory witness a soul's descent into a howling, Hieronymous Bosch–like hell. While the stories always startle, they also often murmur about humanity's higher inclinations, including honor, compassion, and different kinds of love. Along with the patience required to acclimate to each story's fresh setup, the sophisticated slant of the collection makes the book most appropriate for the broadest, most mature readers—the monkey drama, for instance, includes upsetting scenes of animal-world rape, and several stories deal with childbirth and motherhood in a way rarely seen in books for teen readers. Such indifference to usual genre boundaries will only increase the admiration of Lanagan's fans and may serve to broaden her audience into the adult literary world. Young writers will relish the insights into each story's genesis provided in the closing notes. —Jennifer Mattson

★ Lanagan, Margo. *Tender Morsels*. 2008. 448p. Knopf (9780375848117). Gr. 10–12.

After a horrific upbringing, 15-year-old Liga and her two daughters are magicked away into another world, which differs in one crucial aspect: it is utterly safe and free from surprise. In time, though, the old world intrudes upon their quiet heaven, and Liga and her daughters must face a painful reunion with reality. At its essence, this is a story about good and evil, not at all unusual for a fantasy, but there isn't a single usual thing in the way that Lanagan (who won a 2006 Printz Honor for *Black Juice*) goes about it. As in *Red Spikes* (2007), Lanagan touches on nightmarish adult themes, including multiple rape scenarios and borderline human-animal sexual interactions, which reserve this for the most mature readers. She employs a preternatural command of language, twisting it into archaic and convoluted styles that release into passages of absolute, startling clarity. Drawing alternate worlds that blur the line between wonder and horror, and characters who traverse the nature of human and beast, this challenging, unforgettable work explores the ramifications of denying the most essential and often savage aspects of life. It isn't easy, but this book is nevertheless a marvel to read and will only further solidify Lanagan's place at the very razor's edge of YA speculative fiction. —Ian Chipman

Lanagan, Margo. *White Time*. 2006. 224p. HarperCollins/Eos (9780060743932). Gr. 8–11.

Although this is the second story collection by Australian author Lanagan to reach American readers, it was actually published abroad several years before her 2006 Printz Honor Book, *Black Juice*. Fans of Lanagan's fantastical, often surreal sensibility will regard its arrival as long overdue. Further showcasing her mastery of the craft, each story underscores Lanagan's talent for inspiring curiosity, disturbing sensibilities, and provoking thought. The collection comprises 10 stories of varying lengths that together demonstrate great versatility and highlight the author's talent for inventing entirely new realities and subtly shifting our own. The futuristic title story features a girl whose career exploration project finds her floating in a reservoir of "time out of time," where she is mentored by a troubled man who redirects stuck entities from other parts of the universe. "The Queen's Notice," set in an antlike hive, follows a befuddled warrior-creature whose valor requires him to assume a new role. In "Tell and Kiss," physical weight is accumulated by the unhealthy storage of thought and feeling, creating a problem for a boy secretly falling for his best female friend. The singular perspectives, environments, goals, and challenges of Lanagan's distinctive characters will both intrigue and stimulate teen minds. —Holly Koelling

Lancaster, Mike A. *The Future We Left Behind*. 2012. 384p. Egmont (9781606844106). Gr. 7–10.

The events of Lancaster's *Human.4* (2011) are thousands of years in the past, so distant now that Kyle Straker's account of humanity being "upgraded" by alien forces is considered superstition except by true believers known as Strakerites. But now it's time for a teen named Peter to upload his story into the worldwide shared space of the Link—and with a "<DUMP MEMORY>," we're off. Peter is a skeptic, too, until he meets cute Strakerite Alpha, who has uncovered a clue that links both of their fathers to a long-disbanded scientific committee charged with debunking the Straker Tapes. Secretly, though, the committee concluded the opposite: humankind arrogantly believes they are the creators of their own evolutionary destiny when really it is alien forces periodically upgrading our abilities for their own purposes. Lancaster effortlessly incorporates big ideas of science versus religion into his whiz-bang plot, along the way borrowing from the sf masters: the large-canvas orchestrations of Asimov; the yearning nostalgia of Bradbury; the who-stole-my-memories paranoia of Dick; the pro-gaming, prohacking bent of Doctorow; and the spirituality of Clarke.

Fans of *Human.4* didn't see this giant leap forward coming—and that more than anything is the hallmark of great sf. —Daniel Kraus

Lancaster, Mike A. *Human.4*. 2011. 240p. Egmont (9781606840993). Gr. 7–10.

From the first page, Lancaster has got you: "Warning: This data storage unit, or 'book,' has been designed to reprogram the human brain." Then Lancaster himself steps in as "editor," introducing the audiotape transcripts that are to follow, in which 15-year-old Kyle Straker relates a story of great historic value to the beings of the future. What kind of beings? Well, that's the story. Kyle was living a regular life until he was one of four volunteers to undergo hypnosis during a small-town talent show. By chance, while the four were under, the rest of humanity received an upgrade. When the four wake up, the entire town is frozen in place. Soon after, the townspeople come back to life, but they can no longer see or hear Kyle and his three companions, who have become little more than ghosts, fragments of old code that the new programs simply ignore. Wringing his Stephen King–like premise for all it is worth, Lancaster fashions a fast-paced, upsetting little thriller punctuated by ominous editorial notes that translate Kyle's details for the futuristic audience (example: explaining what "lips" were). The characters are somewhat thin, but few plots race along with this kind of speed and purpose. —Daniel Kraus

Langrish, Katherine. *The Shadow Hunt*. 2010. 336p. Harper (9780061116766). Gr. 6–9.

Thirteen-year-old Wolf is running away from the abbey where he was raised when he unexpectedly meets renowned knight Sir Hugo. Together, they capture a mysterious elf-child and return to Hugo's castle, where Wolf will be allowed to stay—if he gets the elf-child to speak. There, Wolf meets Nest, Hugo's 13-year-old daughter, who is dreading her arranged marriage and has her own reasons for helping the outcast elf-child. As Wolf and Nest grow more attached to the elfin youngster, whom they name Elfgift, Hugo's motivations for prompting Elfgift's speech become increasingly clear and unsettling. The arrival of a strange traveling jester to the castle ultimately leads to consequences for all in a darkly dramatic, intense denouement above and below the shadowy, mystical moors of Devil's Edge. In this medieval fantasy, Langrish, author of the Troll Trilogy books, provides a vividly rendered, engrossing tale. Epic themes—good and evil, faith and doubt, sin and redemption—are made personal and poignant through the losses and longings of the notably well-drawn, dimensional main characters, who seek meaning in a chaotic world where all is not what it seems. The diverse supporting characters, both human and supernatural, as well as the richly descriptive prose and imagined settings further enhance this sometimes provocative, beautifully wrought British import that illustrates the power of compassion and storytelling, for characters and readers alike. —Shelle Rosenfeld

Larbalestier, Justine. *Magic or Madness*. 2005. 288p. Penguin/Razorbill (9781595140227). Gr. 8–11.

In this fierce, hypnotic novel, character, story, and the thrumming forces of magic strike a rare, memorable balance. Reason is both the name of its 15-year-old Australian protagonist and a badge of defiance: Reason's mother champions rationality and deplores witchcraft, especially the "smoke and mirrors" practiced by her own mother, Esmeralda. When Reason's mom plunges into insanity and Reason must go to stay with Esmeralda, the wary teen, armed with only her survival instincts and a lucky ammonite fossil, attempts to stave off her grandmother's witchy influences. Then she steps through a door in Esmeralda's kitchen and emerges in New York City. There, as she grapples with the undeniable evidence that "magic is real," she is drawn into a terrifying entanglement with a cruel older witch. Reason's prickly first-person voice alternates with that of Esmeralda's gentle apprentice, Tom, and Reason's tough New York friend, the magically gifted Jay-Tee. The teens' distinct, frequently contradictory narratives intensify readers' concern for Reason and their desire to understand her circumstances. Readers looking for layered, understated fantasy will follow the looping paths of Larbalestier's fine writing, as graceful and logical as the coiled chambers of Reason's ammonite, with gratitude and awe.
—Jennifer Mattson

Lawrence, Michael. ***A Crack in the Line*. 2004. 336p. Greenwillow (9780060724771). Gr. 8–12.**

On the second anniversary of his mother's death, Alaric Underwood still grieves, but by placing his hands on his mother's small, beautiful handcrafted replica of their home, he can transport himself to the alternate reality his mother now inhabits, where he meets Naia, a girl who could be his twin. As similar as the teens' worlds are, chance has forced change. Naia's house is warm, orderly, and cared for; Alaric's is cold, chaotic, and unkempt. Alaric has a batty Aunt Liney who is missing from Naia's life, and he works an M. C. Escher jigsaw puzzle, one of the author's references to the artist's work, which includes chapter numbering that both descends and climbs. The first in a trilogy, this complex story of choices, fate, and acceptance is demanding. Teens will want to reread it to piece together the clues and connections. Sequels will likely clear up some of the mysteries, such as that of the teens' ancestor Aldous, but rich sensory details and acerbic secondary characters bring the multiplying realities to life in spite of the unsolved puzzles. Give this to older readers who enjoyed Jane Yolen's *The Wild Hunt* (1995) or Neil Gaiman's *Coraline* (2002); the book's conclusion, with its shocking metamorphosis, is sure to spark passionate discussion. —Cindy Dobrez

Leavitt, Martine. ***Keturah and Lord Death*. 2006. 196p. Front Street (9781932425291). Gr. 8–11.**

The romance is intense, the writing is startling, and the story is spellbinding—and it is as difficult to turn away from as the tales beautiful Keturah tells to the people of her village, Tide-by-Rood. But one day Keturah must use her storytelling skills with quite a different audience. Lost and hungry after following a stately hart through the forest, Keturah encounters Lord Death, who is ready to take her. Like Scheherazade, Keturah spins a story that she leaves unfinished and extracts from Lord Death a promise that if she finds her true love in a day, she can go free. But Lord Death is falling in love with her, and as the villagers begin to sense her alliance with this horrifying figure, her life twists and turns on itself. This novel gets so many things just right. Leavitt brings together a large cast of characters, but she personalizes them and weaves their stories into Keturah's, making it richer, denser, and more intricate. The plotting moves in and out of the everyday and the supernatural, but it's so finely tuned that the worlds seem one. Readers will be carried away on the wind of Leavitt's words, and few will be able to guess how she finally ends her story. —Ilene Cooper

LaFevers, Robin. ***Dark Triumph*. 2013. 400p. Houghton (9780547628387). Gr. 9–12.**

The riveting historical adventure that began with *Grave Mercy* (2012) here follows the story of another of Death's handmaidens, Sybella. Backtracking just a bit, the story starts with the climactic event of the previous book: Sybella warns Ismae, her dear friend and fellow killer from the convent of St. Mortrain, that troops protecting Brittany's young duchess are riding into a trap to be sprung by Sybella's despotic father. The story's parameters are the same as in the previous book (the struggle between various forces to decide Brittany's fate, the relationship between the young women trained in the deathly arts and the saint who directs them); and once again the tale is filled with vicious battles, heart-stopping escapes, and intricately devised scenarios. However, in this book the wounds are deeper as Sybella must come to terms with her past and how her secrets tie and untie her to a knight who is the bane of her existence and her hope for the future. LaFevers is that wonderful sort of storyteller who so completely meshes events, descriptions, and characters that readers get lost in the world she has concocted. It's a place where history mingles with mystery, and love is never expected. With one more daughter of Death seeking her fate, readers can expect a sequel. But how will they stand the wait?—Ilene Cooper

LaFevers, Robin. ***Grave Mercy*. 2012. 528p. Houghton (9780547628349). Gr. 9–12.**

In the late fifteenth century, Mortain, the god of death, has sired Ismae to be his handmaiden. She will carry out his wishes by working through the Convent, where she has found refuge from a brutal father and husband. After learning the Convent's wily warfare and womanly arts, and being apprenticed to Sister Serafina (poisons mistress and Convent healer), 17-year-old Ismae is sent to the high court of Brittany, ostensibly as the cousin (aka mistress) of the Breton noble Duval—but, in truth, she is there as a spy. Her tacit assignment is to protect the young duchess by assassinating Duval if he proves to be a traitor, a charge made more difficult because of the couple's attraction to each other. LaFevers has written a dark, sophisticated novel true to the fairy-tale conventions of castles, high courts, and good versus evil, and spiced with poison potions; violent (and sometimes merciful) assassinations; subtle seductions; and gentle, perfect love. With characters that will inspire the imagination, a plot that nods to history while defying accuracy, and a love story that promises more in the second book, this is sure to attract feminist readers and romantics alike. —Frances Bradburn

Le Guin, Ursula K. *Gifts*. 2004. 288p. Harcourt (9780152051235). Gr. 6–10.

Gifts, in the context of Le Guin's newest novel, inspire fear more often than gratitude. But this book is a gift in the purest sense, as the renowned fantasist's admirers have waited 14 years since the release of *Tehanu* (1990) for another full-length young adult novel. Providing an intriguing counterpoint to the epic third-person voice of Le Guin's Earthsea novels, this quieter, more intimate tale is narrated by its central character, Orrec. Born into a feud-riven community where the balance of power depends on inherited, extrasensory "gifts," Orrec's gift of Unmaking (which is wielded at a glance and is as fearsome as it sounds) manifests late and strangely, forcing him to don a blindfold to protect those he loves from his dire abilities. The blindfold becomes a source of escalating tension between Orrec and his stern father, and its eventual removal serves as a powerful metaphor for the transition from dependent youngster to self-possessed, questioning young adult. Although intriguing as a coming-of-age allegory, Orrec's story is also rich in the earthy magic and intelligent plot twists that made the Earthsea novels classics. One would expect nothing less from the author whose contributions to literature have earned her a World Fantasy Award, a Nebula Award, and, in 2004, a Margaret Edwards Award for lifetime achievement. —Jennifer Mattson

Le Guin, Ursula K. *Powers*. 2007. 502p. Harcourt (9780152057701). Gr. 8–12.

With compelling themes about the soul-crushing effects of slavery, and a journey plotline that showcases Le Guin's gift for creating a convincing array of cultures, this follow-up to *Gifts* (2004) and *Voices* (2006) may be the series' best installment. Like M. T. Anderson's Octavian Nothing, young slave Gavir, stolen as a baby from the Marsh tribes, has been educated by his masters. Gav responds with deep loyalty, but after a horrific betrayal, he flees, repudiating every aspect of his past and seeking to reconnect with his native people. Tension provided by a slavecatcher's pursuit cinches to thriller intensity, but Le Guin's storytelling mastery shows clearest in the ways Gav's perambulations express human relationships, and push the unformed teen to carve a future that doesn't deny his past—especially the poems and tales that once gave him joy. Told with shimmering lyricism, this coming-of-age saga will leave readers as transformed by the power of words as is Gav himself, who ultimately finds a lifeline that tugs him toward a spiritual homecoming. Based on the strength of the first three books in the Annals of the Western Shore, Le Guin's fans have ample reason to hope that the author may be building toward a fantasy cycle as ambitious in scope as her beloved chronicles of Earthsea. —Jennifer Mattson

Le Guin, Ursula K. *Voices*. 2006. 352p. Harcourt (9780152056780). Gr. 7–10.

Le Guin's new book pairs organically with its companion novel *Gifts* (2004), echoing themes of revenge, family legacies, personal morality, and a humanistic magic redolent more of earthy mysteries than flashy sorcery. Seventeen-year-old Memer, a "siege brat" resentful of the invaders who raped her mother and left her hometown "a broken city of ruins, hunger, and fear," dreams of one day delivering vengeance. Then Orrec and Gry arrive—the same teens who fled the Uplands in *Gifts*, now worldly, grown up, and, in Orrec's case, renowned as a Maker of stories. Orrec's tale spinning begins to erode the boundaries between the conquered and the conquerors, confronting Memer with decisions that temper her childhood dogmatism and press her to a deeper understanding of her mystical birthright. Readers who look to fantasy for traditional epic quests may consider this novel too contained, but the relevance of the slowly festering conflict between occupying and occupied cultures cannot be missed, and the author's understated writing flows as unstintingly as ever. One final note: the photo-collage jacket portrait of a dark-skinned girl is to be applauded, celebrating the diversity long present in Le Guin's fantasy but too infrequently evident on the covers of her books. —Jennifer Mattson

Levine, Gail Carson. *Fairest*. 2006. 336p. HarperCollins (9780060734084). Gr. 7–10.

Larger than most humans in Ayortha, 15-year-old Aza feels like "an ugly ox . . . a blemish." But in a kingdom devoted to song, Aza's voice is more beautiful and powerful than most; she can mimic any voice and throw the sound. At the king's wedding, Aza is blackmailed by the new queen, a poor singer, into a Cyrano de Bergerac arrangement: when the queen sings in public, Aza secretly provides the sound. As the queen's treachery deepens, Aza is astonished when the handsome prince initiates a friendship. In subtle details, Levine slowly reveals that the roots of the richly imagined story are cleverly tangled in the fairy tale "Snow White." The telling, in Aza's voice, is sophisticated, and readers may initially feel like foreign travelers who lack cultural context. But once connections become clear, they'll sink into the fairy-tale romance, the remarkable characters, and the wild, magical adventures. They will also recognize the questions about self-image and moral choices and experience the vicarious, heart-pounding thrill when Aza discovers love and confidence: "I strode away, feeling a thousand feet tall, and glad to be for the first time in my life. Kisses were better than potions." For a slightly older audience than Levine's *Ella Enchanted* (1997), this book makes a natural partner to Donna Jo Napoli's fractured fairy-tale novels, such as *Beast* (2000). —Gillian Engberg

Levithan, David. *Every Day*. 2012. 336p. Knopf (9780307931887). Gr. 9–12.

A (his only name) has a secret. Each morning he wakes up in a different body and life. Sometimes he is a boy, sometimes a girl; sometimes he is gay, sometimes straight; sometimes he is ill, more often well. The only unchanging facts are that he is always 16, and it is a different persona he "borrows" each day. It has always been this way for him, though he doesn't know why it should be. He does know that it is imperative that he do nothing to change his host's life, until he meets Rhiannon and, for the first time, falls in love. And then all bets are off. Levithan has created an irresistible premise that is sure to captivate readers. While the story requires a willing suspension of disbelief, the plot is so compelling that readers will be quick to comply. Aside from his premise, Levithan has done an extraordinary job of creating more than 30 characters, each one a distinct individual and each one offering fresh insights into A's character. Those familiar with Levithan's earlier work will not be a bit surprised to learn that his latest is beautifully written (lips are "gates of desire"; "sadness turns our features to clay, not porcelain"). All these elements work together to make a book that is a study in style, an exercise in imagination, and an opportunity for readers themselves to occupy another life, that of A himself. —Michael Cart

Link, Kelly. *Pretty Monsters*. Illus. by Shaun Tan. 2008. 400p. Viking (9780670010905). Gr. 9–12.

Link, who has two breathlessly received books of strange, surrealistic tales for adults under her belt, makes the leap into the YA fold with this collection of short stories (most previously published in separate anthologies) that tug at the seams of reality, sometimes gently, sometimes violently. In nearly every one of these startlingly, sometimes confoundingly original stories, Link defies expectations with such terrific turnarounds that you are left precipitously wondering not only "What's going to happen now?" but also "Wait, what just happened?" Her conception of fantasy is so unique that when she uses words like *ghost* or *magic*, they mean something very different than they do anywhere else. Perhaps most surprisingly—and memorably—is Link's dedicated deadpan delivery that drives home how funny she can be, no matter how dark the material gets. After gobbling up a group of campers, a monster with a self-proclaimed sense of humor bargains with the terrified lone survivor, "How about if I only eat you if you say the number that I'm thinking of? I promise I won't cheat. I probably won't cheat." Shaun Tan contributes a handful of small illustrations that are, of course, just plain delightful. —Ian Chipman

Lisle, Holly. ***The Ruby Key*****. 2008. 360p. Scholastic/Orchard (9780545000123). Gr. 6–10.**

In this strong opener to the Moon & Sun series, which is also a welcome first children's novel from seasoned fantasist Lisle, 14-year-old Genna and her brother are swept into a tricky bargain with an otherwordly lord. Humans in the village of Hillrush and nightlings in the forest have held an uneasy truce for centuries. But when Genna and Dan meet a nightling slave, they learn the truce is meaningless: Banris, the village head, has struck a deal with the nightling lord, Letrin, to trade his people's lives for immortality. The siblings and rebel nightlings concoct a plan to defeat their corrupt rulers, and Genna brokers a deal with Letrin that involves locating a nightling in hiding. The world Lisle creates is as distinctive and intriguing as any real place, with a complex history, well-developed societies, and a strong sense of magic. Many readers will find Lisle's creative embellishments of fairy lore especially arresting. Binding it all together is Genna's forthright, first-person narrative of the risky adventure, through which she remains steadfast even as her duties expand beyond her personal desires. Though one plot is resolved, hints of a possible romance for Genna and the promise of a larger catastrophe will leave readers clamoring for the next installment. —Krista Hutley

Lloyd, Saci. ***The Carbon Diaries: 2015*****. 2009. 336p. Holiday (9780823421909). Gr. 9–12.**

In the way that Cory Doctorow's *Little Brother* (2008) was a tale of national security run amok, this is a similar cautionary look at global warming. Laura Brown, a 16-year-old Londoner and punk rocker, documents a year in the very near future, 2015, in diary form. She refers to recent massive storms brought on by climate change that have ravaged the planet and led Britain to be the first country to try "carbon rationing." Each person is allotted a prohibitively small measure of carbon points to be used each month, essentially obsoleting such luxuries as air travel or even heating one's home. Laura navigates the increasingly punishing circumstances with a perfectly intoned half-bitter, half-astonished teenager's voice, complete with strains of near-future slang, and punctuates her diary with newspaper clippings and other taped-in bits of cultural detritus. As she weathers staggering uncertainty, kill-me-now family crises, and a timelessly confusing dating scene, she finds a release valve in music and her mates. Lloyd's immersive first novel, if a bit overlong, is transformative without ever being didactic and teases out information with remarkable restraint that never feels like withholding. While the book ends without a clean resolution, that only adds to a realism that, while certainly alarmist, could well be prophetic. Deeply compulsive and urgently compulsory reading. —Ian Chipman

Lowry, Lois. ***Messenger*****. 2004. 176p. Houghton/Walter Lorraine (9780618404414). Gr. 6–10.**

Like Lowry's hugely popular Newbery winner, *The Giver* (1993), this story dramatizes ideas of utopia gone wrong and focuses on a young person who must save his world. Teenage Matty lives with his caregiver in the Village, a place of refuge, where those fleeing poverty and persecution are welcomed with kindness and find a home. But the Village people are changing, and many have voted to build a wall to keep the newcomers out. The metaphor of the wall and the rage against immigrants ("They can't even speak right") will certainly reach out to today's news images for many readers. But Lowry moves far beyond message, writing with a beautiful simplicity rooted in political fable, in warm domestic detail, and in a wild natural world, just on the edge of realism. Matty lives with his blind caregiver, Seer. Both of them were driven from home and nearly perished. The drama is in their affection; in the small details of how they cook, care for their puppy, and tease one another. Matty teases Seer about his blindness, even though they both know Seer sees more than most. In contrast is the terror of Matty's secret powers and the perilous journey he must undertake to save the Village. The physical immediacy of his quest through a dark forest turned hostile brings the myth very close and builds suspense to the last heart-wrenching page. —Hazel Rochman

Lowry, Lois. *Son*. 2012. 400p. Houghton (9780547887203). Gr. 7–10.

Fans of *The Giver* (1993)—and they are legion—will find themselves immediately pulled back into the sterile, ordered world where conformity is the only virtue. The focus here is on 14-year-old Claire, and when readers first see her, she is strapped onto a table, masked, about to give birth. As a Birthmother, Claire's job is finished once her baby is born, until the next pregnancy. But unusual circumstances, including a cesarean, get Claire moved from the birthing center to the fish hatchery, and someone forgets to give Claire the pills everyone in the community takes—the ones that suppress feelings and individuality. Without that wall, Claire begins to long for her son and finds opportunities to see him. Slowly, readers of the previous titles in the quartet will come to understand that Claire's baby is not unfamiliar to them. When the boy disappears, Claire decides, against all odds, that she must find him. That brings her to a seaside community where she strengthens body, mind, and spirit to continue her search. One of *The Giver*'s strengths was the unvarnished writing style that reflected the book's ordered community. Lowry captures that same feeling again and turns it inside out as Claire moves through two more distinct settings, both haunting in their own right. Though her time at the seaside village may seem long to some readers (and it is—more than 10 years), the vividness of the descriptions—from the hardness of the rock to the roiling of the water—makes up for the length. Lowry is one of those rare writers who can craft stories as meaningful as they are enticing. Once again she provides plenty of weighty matters for readers to think about: What is important in life? What are you willing to trade for your desires? And the conflict that has been going on since stories began: Who is able to conquer evil?—Ilene Cooper

Lu, Marie. *Legend*. 2011. 320p. Putnam (9780399256752). Gr. 7–12.

All right, it has a plague. And, yes, it's set in some semblance of America in the not-so-distant future. Yet even with all the hordes of dystopian novels out there, this one still manages to keep readers on the edge of their seats. But even the nonstop action would mean little without Lu's well-toned ability to write characters to care about. One is June, a daughter of the Republic. Her perfect scores at the Trial have insured a great future for her. Then there is Day. A hero to the street people, he fights injustice and keeps an eye on his brothers and mother as they try to survive. Their narratives, told in alternating and distinctively voiced chapters, describe how circumstances bring them together. Day kills June's beloved soldier brother as he tries to get medicine for his own. With cold precision, June makes it her mission to exact revenge. What happens next, in macro terms, probably won't surprise, yet the delicious details keep pages turning to learn how it's all going to play out. Combine star-crossed lovers with the need to take down the Republic, and you've got the makings for a potent sequel. —Ilene Cooper

Madigan, L. K. *The Mermaid's Mirror*. 2010. 320p. Houghton (9780547194912). Gr. 8–10.

Lena, almost 16 and living in a northern California surfing community, has been forbidden by her father, a former surfer who suffered a terrible accident in the water years ago, from learning her peers' favorite sport. She is an excellent swimmer, though, and while spending time at the local beach, she begins to think she might be seeing a mermaid out in the waves. Being a practical girl, this of course strikes her as unlikely, but a host of subtle clues that include the discovery of her mother's true identity and fate lead her to an undersea world of mer-folk. Lena distances herself from her life on land as she takes up residence in her mother's community below the ocean, but eventually she must choose between her diverging destinies. Madigan does a stellar job of bringing readers inexorably from what at first seems like a realistic problem-novel plot of family issues to an enjoyable fantasy of a girl who finds that she is only half human. The characters, whether teen, child, or adult, are well-rounded and integrated into the plot. In addition to her parents, Lena must also consider the sensibilities of her younger brother and her best friend and figure out how she feels about her two boyfriends, one human and one mer. With highly imagistic descriptions and savvy dialogue, Madigan offers a rewarding and credible story that uses fantasy elements to bare truths about family ties. —Francisca Goldsmith

Madison, Bennett. ***September Girls.*** **June 2013. 352p. Harper (9780061255632). Gr. 9–12.**

Last winter, Sam's mother ran away into "something called Women's Land," leaving his father first catatonic, then weirdly proactive and involved in Sam's life. When Sam's brother returns from college, their father takes them to a beach town that appears to be run by beautiful blonde young women, whose accents are unplaceable and exotic. These Girls (with a capital *G*) seem bound by unknowable rules. Out of all these mysterious women, Sam finds DeeDee, who, like him, understands betrayal and parental abandonment but on a level that even he can't fathom. Split between Sam's observations of the events and passages from the Girls' collective attempts to explain their dramatic and confused origin ("First we are alone. We're not sure how we find one another, but we do. Then we are still alone, but in the way sardines are alone."), Madison's novel offers up a feast of mythology and human nature. The author nimbly exercises Sam's running-monologue narration; raunchy, sarcastic sentences and oddly vulnerable bro-speak weave with ethereal, spellbinding descriptions of love, scenery, or epiphany. This command of language, both informal and beautiful, lifts the work from a basic boy-meets-fantastical creature tale to something both familiar and tragically moving. This isn't just a supernatural beach read; it's a rare and lovely novel, deserving of attention from discriminating readers. —Courtney Jones

Marchetta, Melina. ***Finnikin of the Rock.*** **2010. 416p. Candlewick (9780763643614). Gr. 6–10.**

In her latest title, Marchetta, author of the 2009 Michael L. Printz Award winner, *Jellicoe Road*, steps deftly into the fantasy genre. Ten years before the story's start, assassins crept into the kingdom of Lumatere and murdered the royal family, with the possible exception of Balthazar, heir to the throne. As rumors circulated that Balthazar survived, a mystic cast a curse that created a magical barrier around the kingdom and prevented thousands who had fled from returning. Marchetta focuses her tale on 19-year-old Finnikin, the son of a former royal guard, who is serving in exile as an apprentice to Sir Topher, a former advisor to the murdered king. While aiding refugees, they meet a young novice who can enter others' dreams and claims that Balthazar has chosen Finnikin to "take his people home." As Finnikin gathers forces to return to the kingdom, intrigue and double-dealing ensue. The skillful world building includes just enough detail to create a vivid sense of place, and Marchetta maintains suspense with unexpected story arcs. It is the achingly real characters, though, and the relationships that emerge through the captivating dialogue that drive the story. Filled with questions about the impact of exile and the human need to belong, this standout fantasy quickly reveals that its real magic lies in its accomplished writing. —Lynn Rutan

Marchetta, Melina. ***Froi of the Exiles.*** **2012. 400p. Candlewick (9780763647599). Gr. 9–12.**

Printz Award–winning Marchetta returns to the world of *Finnikin of the Rock* (2010) for this second book in the Lumatere Chronicles. A member of the Lumateran Guard, young Froi is sent on a deadly mission into the neighboring kingdom of Charyn, where he discovers family connections and a tangled web of sexual abuse, love, and deception at the highest levels of the Charynite government. Rather than kill those who might endanger his beloved adopted country, Froi fights to save an emotionally damaged young queen and a kingdom that has been without children for 18 years. Though this sequel stands on its own as a complete story, those who have digested *Finnikin* will find it easier to grasp the tensions and intricacies that drive the plot. Marchetta's close attention to detail slows the pace initially, as she lays out the boundaries and topography of her imagined world. But dedicated readers will be richly rewarded, as soon enough the tale is transformed into a lush tapestry in which each stitch is a nugget of history and each splash of color a rounded character that engages readers' emotions. The expertly crafted ending is designed to leave fans old and new waiting with keen anticipation for the next entry. Fill the intervening time by suggesting Kristin Cashore's *Graceling* (2008) and *Fire* (2009), Lena Coakley's *Witchlanders* (2011), or Cassandra Clare's Mortal Instruments trilogy. —Cindy Welch

Marchetta, Melina. *Quintana of Charyn*. 2013. 528p. Candlewick (9780763658359). Gr. 9–12.

With previous installments of her mesmerizing Lumatere Chronicles, Marchetta allowed readers the satisfaction of piecing together parts of the puzzle that is the saga of the lands and peoples of Skuldenore, but the entire picture remained tantalizingly incomplete. Now, with this brilliant final volume, the remaining pieces snap perfectly into place. Froi sets out to find and protect pregnant Quintana, his strange and savage love; raise an army against the usurper; and prevent war. As in the previous volumes, the narrative is complex, alternating between Froi's journey and the concurrent events in Lumatere, but here the plot is more straightforward, while the previous volumes' excellent features—world building, plotting, and characterization—continue to shine. Marchetta builds on the reader's knowledge of this world, adding rich sensory details to help create the vivid setting. She skillfully expands our understanding of the large cast of characters, most from the earlier books, through her masterful depictions of relationships. Of special interest is the portrayal of the often unlikable Quintana, whose very existence is the catalyst that offers the promise of peace and hope. As Froi gains understanding of the disparate pieces that make up Quintana, readers put together the intricately plotted pieces that make this vivid and wholly satisfying story complete. A standout fantasy series. —Lynn Rutan

Marillier, Juliet. *Cybele's Secret*. 2008. 400p. Knopf (9780375833656). Gr. 7–10.

Adult-market fantasist Marillier enlarged her teen following with her first YA novel, *Wildwood Dancing* (2007), about five Transylvanian sisters with ties to the mercurial Other Kingdom. In this honeyed draught of a companion novel, bookish, 17-year-old Paula travels to Istanbul to assist her father in delicate negotiations for Cybele's Gift, a pagan totem raising a hue and cry among the city's Muslim clerics. Every bidder risks danger, so Paula and her father hire a bodyguard, Stoyan, who gradually becomes an active partner in Paula's efforts to decipher portents from the Other Kingdom—a plotline predicated on the first book's fairy world building but readily accessible to newcomers. Marillier embroiders Ottoman Empire cultural details into every fold and drape of her story, which also interweaves pirates, eunuchs, hidden currents of feminine power, and turbulent journeys across sea and land. Not every thread is neatly knotted; slow-burning questions about Stoyan's long-lost brother and Paula's exiled sister are too hastily dispatched. Of greater importance to teens, though, will be Paula's determination to be more than merely "curves and smiles, blushes and modest speech," and her incremental, often-muddled acknowledgment of her deepening feelings for earthy, solid Stoyan. Teens who didn't know Marillier when they started this sandalwood-scented adventure will rapidly place her alongside the likes of romantic-fantasy idols Shannon Hale and Sharon Shinn. —Jennifer Mattson

Marillier, Juliet. *Wildwood Dancing*. 2007. 416p. Knopf (9780375833649). Gr. 8–11.

On the night of each full moon, the five Transylvanian sisters who reside in the castle Piscul Dracului don their finest gowns. They raise their hands to create shadows against the wall, opening a portal to the Other Kingdom, where they will dance the night away with all manner of fantastical creatures. After nine years of full moons spent in delightful revelry, dark forces, both human and otherworldly, arise to encroach upon the sisters' happiness. Told by Jena, the second oldest sister, this detailed and mood-rich story covers much territory, both mundane and magical. Adult fantasy writer Marillier has uniquely reimagined and blended an assortment of well-known tales and characters—including fairies, dwarfs, witches, vampires, and a frog who is more than he seems—into a compelling whole in her first book for teens. By the end, all are cleverly bound together, and a mystery is solved. With much to say about human nature and choice, not unlike the moral in fairy tales of old, this will be a hit with older teen readers, especially girls. —Holly Koelling

McBride, Lish. *Hold Me Closer, Necromancer*. 2010. 352p. Holt (9780805090987). Gr. 9–12.

Sam has dropped out of college and is stalled in a fast-food job in Seattle. Interrupting the boredom of days waiting on Plumpy customers and evenings watching old movies with his friends, a scary guy named Douglas enters Sam's world. After a few pithy verbal threats, Douglas has Sam beaten and mauled by a sidekick—and later delivers teen Brooke's pretty blond head to Sam's door. The good news is that Brooke seems to be in no pain and is as sassy as ever. The bad news, as Sam finds out in short order, is that Douglas is a necromancer and has identified Sam, who hasn't a clue what his strengths are, as a rival. Before the week is out, Sam finds himself in a cellar, caged with another pretty girl, who is part werewolf, part fairy. And then there's Ashley, the parochial-school-uniformed 10-year-old who can orchestrate salvation for Sam by using her Blackberry and brains. With fine writing, tight plotting, a unique and uniquely odd cast of teens, adults, and children, and a pace that smashes through any curtain of disbelief, this sardonic and outrageous story's only problem is that it must, like all good things, come to an end. —Francisca Goldsmith

McKinley, Robin. *Spindle's End*. 2000. 432p. Putnam (9780399234668). Gr. 7–12.

More a retelling and expansion than a fracturing of a fairy tale, McKinley's spin on "Sleeping Beauty" takes readers into a credibly developed world, where professional fairies try to keep the rampant, unpredictable magic at bay. As in the original, a wicked fairy (here named Pernicia) curses the infant princess Rosie at her name-day ceremony: when she turns 21, Rosie will prick her finger on a spindle's needle and fall into a poisoned sleep. Orphan Katriona, 16, is not much of a fairy yet, but she kneels by Rosie's cradle, snatches up the crying baby, bestows on the princess her own power of speaking to animals, and takes the baby to raise as if she were Katriona's own. Years pass, and Rosie, who doesn't know she is the princess, grows into a stalwart, strong-minded girl, whose affinity with animals leads to her working as an apprentice to Narl, the village blacksmith. As the princess's twenty-first birthday nears, more and more disturbances occur throughout the land, and Rosie's whereabouts become known to the royal family—and to Pernicia. Rosie's close friendship with an orphan girl, Peony, plays a major role in the frenetic denouement. Posing as the princess, Peony pricks her finger and is carried off by Pernicia. Then Rosie, with Narl and an assortment of animals, sets out to confront Pernicia at her dark castle. Full of humor and romance as well as magic and adventure, and with an ending that has a decided twist, this spellbinding novel is bound to attract McKinley's fans and those who relish the genre. —Sally Estes

McKinley, Robin, and Peter Dickinson. *Fire: Tales of Elemental Spirits*. 2009. 304p. Putnam (9780399252891). Gr. 6–10.

McKinley and Dickinson follow up their previous collaborative work, *Water: Tales of Elemental Spirits* (2002), with this collection of five fiery tales. In "Phoenix," Dickinson's opening story, a boy living in a wooded conservation area tells Ellie the history of the Phoenix and how, at the age of 100, he found the god in a fire and has been living backward ever since. Dickinson's other stories follow young men discovering their destinies: in "Fireworm," Tandin must save his people from their ancient enemy, the fireworm; in "Salamander Man," Tib is chosen to free 27 salamanders from corrupt magicians. In McKinley's "Hellhound," Miri adopts an unusual dog from the pound with burning red eyes, and he proves to be a blessing. McKinley's stand-out concluding novella, "First Flight," follows a humble boy and his pet foogit as they make his brother's first dragon flight a success, shocking the Dragon Academy in the process. Dickinson's stories are told with a storyteller's cadence while McKinley's are modern and humorous, but all five are masterful in character, setting, and plot.
—Krista Hutley

McKinley, Robin, and Peter Dickinson. *Water: Tales of the Elemental Spirits*. 2002. 272p. Putnam (9780399237966). Gr. 7–12.

McKinley and Dickinson's first collaborative work offers six mesmerizing stories, three from each writer, steeped in the lore of merfolk and creatures of the sea. The writing is lyrical, and the characterizations are remarkably well developed. Themes resonate with clear-cut meaning, and emotions run the gamut—from fear and courage to love and joy. In the first story, Pitiable Nasmith's dismal life takes a turn for happiness when she learns her heritage and rescues a stranded sea-girl; in another, Jenny finds true love with the sea king's son; in a third, a ferryman tilts the contest between the Earth-mother and the Father-god by outwitting a sea serpent. Then there's the tale of Tamia, apprentice of the Guardian of Western Mouth, who finds herself facing the destructive Water Horse, which the Guardians have been unable to curb; and the story of the mer-king's daughter, who inadvertently awakens the deadly Kraken. In the final piece, Hetta's dreams of a desert land turn to reality with the help of a golden eye in a pool that stretches from Homeland to Damar, McKinley's well-known land. It's a bountiful collection for fantasy lovers. Despite the differences in themes and characters, the stories fit so nicely together that the collection will be very hard to put down. —Sally Estes

McNaughton, Janet. *An Earthly Knight*. 2004. 272p. HarperCollins (9780060089924). Gr. 7–10.

Sixteen-year-old Jenny, a high-born lass in medieval Scotland, "loves the dark and wild heart of the forest." In her wanderings she meets Tam Lin, an enchanted young lord with whom she forges a love pure enough to shatter a powerful curse. This is ancient, elemental stuff, culled from the ballad of a Scottish knight whose mortal lover rescues him from an evil fairy queen. McNaughton hits the tale's main points, including Jenny's pregnancy (the result of a euphemistically described night of passion), but invented conflicts give the story its forward momentum. Jenny finds herself earmarked for an advantageous betrothal and, in a subplot inspired by a different ballad, helps her sister recover from a traumatic encounter with an unscrupulous knight. In fact, McNaughton evokes the social and political landscape so vividly that readers may find the periodic swerves into high fantasy somewhat jarring. Even so, fans of historical fiction will find much to admire in this story of a spirited heroine and ecstatic young love. —Jennifer Mattson

McNeal, Tom. *Far Far Away*. 2013. 384p. Knopf (9780375849725). Gr. 7–10.

So it begins: "What follows is the strange and fateful tale of a boy, a girl, and a ghost." Ghostly Jacob Grimm, of the famous Brothers, narrates this tale of Jeremy and Ginger and their near-tragic encounter with town baker Sten Blix, whose long-held grudges figure in the disappearance of several village children. Unappreciated as a youngster, Blix has elevated revenge to a sweet art, and he holds Jeremy, Ginger, and an additional victim, Frank Bailey, in a hidden dungeon under the bakery, while Jacob desperately tries to tell parents and friends of the predicament. If he fails, the three may become grist in the baker's next batch of Prince Cakes. Reminiscent of "Hansel and Gretel" and rife with allusions to the Grimm Brothers' tales, this is a masterful story of outcasts, the power of faith, and the triumph of good over evil. McNeal's deft touch extends to the characterizations, where the ritual speech of traditional tales ("Listen, if you will") establishes Jacob's phantasmagoric presence amid the modernist American West. There are moments of horror (as there were in the Grimm Brothers' original tales), but they are accomplished through the power of suggestion. Details aplenty about Jacob and his famous sibling make this a fiction connector to both fairy tales and Grimm biographies, too. —*Cindy Welch*

McNish, Cliff. *Angel*. 2008. 312p. Carolrhoda (9780822589006). Gr. 7–10.

Heaven and earth mix in this arresting story. Freya has always wanted to be an angel. When she is eight, an angel visits her—which becomes the first of several long steps to hospitalization for delusions. Freya fights her way back, enters high school, and even finds a way into one of the cool crowds. Then Stephanie, who believes in angels, comes to the school, and the girls recognize each other. But while Stephanie wants to cleave to Freya, Freya can't quite come to terms with Stephanie, fearful of the reaction of her new, pressuring peer group. There's another reason as well. Freya has made a profound discovery: the angels she sees are real. On one level, this is a British school story, with cliques and bullies, but McNish goes further; his real accomplishment is melding the gritty ordinariness of everyday happenings with the magnificence of angels. For this, he needed the skills of a conductor, knowing when to play up the angelic choir and when to let it be heavenly background music. His descriptions of Freya's two angels—one light and one dark—dazzle, and as the story moves into higher realms, readers are given much to ponder. Vampires and werewolves have been given their due in fiction of late; the mystery of angels takes center stage here. —Ilene Cooper

Meldrum, Christina. *Madapple*. 2008. 416p. Knopf (9780375851766). Gr. 9–12.

Aslaug lives in isolation; the flowers and plants that her mother, Maren, uses to make their lives possible are more real to her than the outside world. Then Maren dies, and Aslaug makes her way to the nearby Maine town, where she finds her aunt Sara and teenage cousins Susanne and Rune. Aslaug hopes they will have a clue to her father's identity; she learns, as readers already have, that Maren proclaimed Aslaug a virgin birth. Aunt Sara, a charismatic preacher, wants none of this. But Susanne, enthralled with the writings of esoteric religionists and pagans, believes this is a possibility, while Rune is just enthralled with Aslaug herself. Then Aslaug finds herself pregnant, and divine intervention is once more a possibility. Plot summary does little justice to this haunting book, which is as much mysticism as it is story. Meldrum plunges deeply into the nature of reality. She uses language in a particularly arresting way, with the leaves and petals of the plants that are so much a part of Aslaug's life shimmering over the pages. If all this weren't satisfaction enough, Meldrum, a litigator, mixes faith and science with a solid mystery, told in the transcripts of a trial in which Aslaug is the defendant. There is much to ponder in this enthralling achievement from a debut author. —Ilene Cooper

Melling, O. R. *The Hunter's Moon*. 2005. 260p. Abrams (9780810958579). Gr. 8–11.

Melling's fantasy series, the Chronicles of Faerie, is popular in Canada. For its U.S. debut, the author has expanded this title, which is the series' first installment. Gwen, an American, and her Irish cousin, Findabhair, hope to spend Gwen's visit to Ireland seeking "the Faraway World." Both 16-year-olds are enamored with fantasy and Irish lore, but neither is prepared when, on the first night of their trip, the King of the Faeries whisks Findabhair away. Gwen's race around Ireland in pursuit of her cousin escalates into a mortal battle against archetypal, spiritual forces. Melling is an Irish history scholar, and she layers her fantasy with ancient battles, royalty, and Irish phrases (translated in an appended glossary) that, while sometimes purposefully inserted, add great depth to the thrilling action. Fans of Holly Black's *Tithe* (2002) will recognize a similarly dexterous juxtaposition of shifting worlds—opulent and mystical, realistic and contemporary—and they'll easily connect with both the story's timeless legends and modern teen emotions. Readers will cheer for timid Gwen, who, by the end of her quest, has become "a braveheart and a trueheart," and teen girls will swoon over the dashing love interests who round out the appealing supporting characters. Shimmering with magic, myth, and romance, this is a lyrically told, richly satisfying adventure that will leave fantasy fans, like Gwen, feeling "lost and glad, caught up in the flow of forever." —Gillian Engberg

Meyer, Stephenie. *Twilight*. 2005. 499p. Little, Brown/Megan Tingley (9780316160179). Gr. 9–12.

In the tradition of Anne Rice and YA titles such as Annette Curtis Klause's *The Silver Kiss* (1999) comes this heady romance that intertwines Bella Swan's life with that of Edward, an alluring and tormented vampire. Bella's life changes when she moves to perpetually rain-soaked Forks, Washington. She is instantly drawn to a fellow student, Edward Cullen, beautiful beyond belief and angrily aloof. Bella senses there is more behind Edward's hostility, and in a plot that slowly and frighteningly unfolds, she learns that Edward and his family are vampires—though they do not hunt humans. Yet Edward cannot promise that his powerful attraction to Bella won't put her in danger, or worse. Recklessly in love, Bella wants only to be with Edward, but when a vicious, blood-lusting predator complicates her world, Bella's peril is brutally revealed. This is a book of the senses: Edward is first attracted by Bella's scent; ironically, Bella is repelled when she sees blood. Their love is palpable, heightened by their touches, and teens will respond viscerally. There are some flaws here—a plot that could have been tightened, an overreliance on adjectives and adverbs to bolster dialogue—but this dark romance seeps into the soul. —Ilene Cooper

Michaelis, Antonia, and Anthea Bell. *Dragons of Darkness*. 2010. 568p. Abrams (9780810940741). Gr. 9–12.

Growing up, Christopher, a 14-year-old German, has always felt invisible next to his much-admired, daring older brother, Arne. After Arne vanishes during a trip to Nepal, though, Christopher is mysteriously transported there and begins a wild adventure of his own. In Nepal, he meets Jumar, a prince who is literally invisible, and Niya, a young Maoist rebel. Each character is looking for something different: Christopher seeks clues to Arne's disappearance; Jumar seeks revenge for a beloved friend's death; and Niya seeks ways to better his country. The threesome's quests soon intertwine, as do their questions about their place and purpose in the world, and together, they face warring factions of soldiers and Maoists along with color-eating dragons that have devastated the land. As in *Tiger Moon* (2008), Michaelis deftly interweaves magic and realism in an intricate, provocative story that explores the connections between people and events, the allure and dangers of an uncompromising idealism, and the power of love. Skillfully translated, the vivid, descriptive prose portrays unique settings and cultures, while the diverse characters' alternating stories build suspense and intimacy in scenes that are alternately droll and poignant, sorrowful and inspiring. The plotting is dense, but readers will be richly rewarded with this absorbing story about courage, compassion, personal growth, and the power of fairy tales to guide and illuminate human lives. —Shelle Rosenfeld

Michaelis, Antonia, and Anthea Bell. *Tiger Moon*. 2008. 464p. Abrams (9780810994812). Gr. 9–12.

Deftly interweaving Indian history, culture, and mythology, this richly layered tale, set in India at the beginning of the twentieth century, beautifully illustrates the power of storytelling. Having failed to escape a forced betrothal to brutish merchant Ahmed Mudhi, Safia is now a captive in his palace. While awaiting her wedding night, she is befriended by a palace servant, Lagan, and begins to tell him the story of a young thief, Farhad; his talking, sacred tiger companion; and their quest to retrieve the fabled Bloodstone in order to rescue a princess from the Demon King. Safia and Farhad's intersecting stories illuminate themes of destiny and free will; immortality and rebirth; compassion and humanity; and the power of stories to entertain, inspire, and transform. Originally published in Germany, Michaelis's novel is an absorbing epic with diverse characters, written in lyrical prose that combines vivid imagery with droll, sometimes pointed commentary and some mature plot elements: Safia is sentenced to death, for example, after Ahmed discovers that she is not a virgin. Michaelis proves a highly accomplished storyteller in this sweeping, beguiling tale where things and people are not always as they seem and where characters (and readers) discover that "stories are an excellent way of escape."
—Shelle Rosenfeld

Miéville, China. *Railsea*. 2012. 448p. Del Rey (9780345524522). Gr. 9–12.

Miéville, who last dabbled in the YA world with *Un Lun Dun* (2007), has done something very odd here indeed. While it's tempting to call this a steampunk spin on *Moby-Dick*, that would be as reductive and limiting as calling *Moby-Dick* itself a sea shanty. Instead of chasing whales on the sea, the crew of the diesel train *Medes* hunt moldywarpes—enormous, man-eating, molelike creatures who are only one of the countless menacing species who burrow in the perilous earth beneath a tangled ocean of train tracks. And it is one moldywarpe in particular, the great Mocker-Jack, that Captain Naphi is after—it's trendy for any captain worth her iron to have such a defining obsession, and she is fully aware that they hunt metaphor in beast form. Aboard for the grand adventure is your hero, young Sham (don't call him Ishmael). The world building is both dazzling and baffling, but the real show here are the stylistic whorls and eddies as Miéville pushes his prose into some very neat places. Hardly a sentence goes by without some invented word or feat of tricky phrasing that echoes the thorny prose of Melville's original. Both the world and the halting, chugging syntax take some time to get acclimated to, but when it all takes off, does it ever move. Though it is informed by both the themes and kaleidoscopic storytelling of Melville's great American novel, this is easily one of the most inventive and original YA fantasies in some time. —Ian Chipman

Moriarty, Chris. *The Watcher in the Shadows*. 2013. 336p. Harcourt (9780547466323). Gr. 6–10.

The second book in the Inquisitor's Apprentice series picks up where the first left off. And where's that? New York City—mostly the Lower East Side—at the turn of the last century. Ah, but this New York is overflowing with magic. Spells are cast, kabbalists reign, and dybbuks roam. Thirteen-year-old Sacha lives in a tenement with his parents; his rabbi grandfather, a mage of some repute; and his sister Bekah, a seamstress at the Pentacle Shirtwaist Factory, owned by the treacherous J. P. Morgaunt. Sacha may be only a young teen, but he is apprenticed to Inspector Wolf of the Inquisitor's unit of the NYPD—those tasked with investigating magical crime. The rather convoluted plot involves the murder of the Klezmer King (fried in his electric tuxedo) and a strike at the shirtwaist factory. Oh, and the dybbuk Sacha set free last time out reappears with dire consequences. But although this is full of story, what captivates is the world that Moriarty has created, one where magic is woven into its very fabric. That its many practitioners all have their own ways of casting spells is part of what makes these characters so memorable. But from crime lords to rebbes, it is their own particular wisdom that deepens the nonstop action. A touch of Chabon, a hiss of steampunk, and a blast of originality. —Ilene Cooper

Moskowitz, Hannah. *Teeth*. 2013. 288p. Simon & Schuster/Simon Pulse (9781442465329). Gr. 9–12.

Moskowitz's best novel since *Break* (2009) is actually reminiscent of that (literally) smashing debut: both books feature a teen struggling to protect his sick brother, and both deal with the extreme limits of noble self-harm. Rudy, 16, and his family have moved to "a place for last resorts," a remote island that is the home of the rare silver Enki fish, purported to have unsurpassed restorative powers—just what Rudy's 5-year-old brother, Dylan, needs to stave off death from cystic fibrosis. It is within the frigid ocean waves that Rudy encounters Teeth, an ugly, foul-mouthed half boy, half fish who is perpetually bruised and bloody from violent late-night encounters with cruel fishermen. The two become friends, maybe even more, but Teeth considers the fish his siblings, and Rudy needs the fish to feed his brother. Therein lies the conflict: how much is one of them willing to give up for the other? Despite the fantastical elements, this reads as realistic, even gritty, drama, fueled by Moskowitz's brand of stream-of-consciousness wonder, tumbling emotion, and dark undertones. Her handling of each characters' sexuality is particularly impressive in its refusal to generalize or simplify. Moskowitz's prose has always had charm; pair it with a great plot and this is what happens. —Daniel Kraus

Mourlevat, Jean-Claude, and Anthea Bell. *Winter's End*. 2009. 432p. Candlewick (9780763644505). Gr. 9–12.

In this timeless, dystopian tale of hope in dark times, four teenagers seek freedom from an oppressive society as well as the truth about their parents' mysterious deaths. Helen, Milena, Milos, and Bartolomeo are all students at gender-segregated boarding schools established by the repressive Phalange government. After Milena and Bart secretly escape, Helen and Milos set out to find them, a search that they hope will bring them in contact with the still-active underground resistance movement. The teens' dangerous journeys bring terrifying enemies, unexpected allies, heartbreaking tragedy, and a discovery of both the elemental strength of the human voice and the resiliency of the human spirit.

In his first novel for adolescents, French children's book author Mourlevat deftly blends fantasy, realism, and moments of violence as he explores broad themes of freedom, repression, and redemption. Translator Bell's visually evocative prose alternates third-person viewpoints among the diverse cast of engaging, sometimes fantastical characters, whose compelling personal stories skillfully build to a dramatic conclusion. An award winner in France, where it was first published, this absorbing, fablelike story celebrates the infinite power of love and courage to inspire others, build a community, and make a difference. —Shelle Rosenfeld

Murdock, Catherine Gilbert. ***Princess Ben*****. 2008. 352p. Houghton (9780618959716). Gr. 8–11.**

In this new offering, the author of *Dairy Queen* (2006) and *The Off-Season* (2007) shifts from a contemporary Wisconsin setting to a magical, snowbound kingdom. Once again, though, Murdock's protagonist is a winning, iconoclastic teen female. Princess Benevolence's life is upended during a single afternoon's tragedy: while visiting an ancestor's grave, her uncle and her mother are killed, and her father disappears. Ben, now the kingdom's heir, begins grueling lessons with her aunt Sophia, learning "myriad responsibilities and arts of royalty." Just as her tutelage becomes unbearable, she discovers a hidden wizard's room in the castle and begins teaching herself, using the enchanted spell books she finds there. Then tense negotiations to marry Ben to the sullen heir of a neighboring kingdom commence. Gathering her newfound magical knowledge, the princess flees the castle only to find grave dangers outside its walls. In delicious language that is both elevated and earthy, Murdock spins a rip-roaring yarn that borrows fairy-tale conventions (particularly from "Sleeping Beauty") and reverses them to suit her strong, resourceful heroine. The wild adventure, intricately imagined setting, memorable characters, and romance will charm readers, especially fans of Gail Carson Levine's *Fairest* (2006). —Gillian Engberg

Myracle, Lauren. ***Bliss*****. 2008. 304p. Abrams (9780810970717). Gr. 9–12.**

It's the summer of 1969, and Bliss has been unceremoniously dumped by her hippie parents into the custody of her grandmother. Soon Bliss finds herself adjusting to life as a freshman at a fancy Atlanta school—and it's a lot different from life on the commune. Although she quickly finds "normal" friends, she is drawn to Sandy, a gruff and unpopular girl with a long-standing grudge against Sarah Lynn, the icy beauty of the freshman class. The push and pull of the school drama is engaging enough, but there's another element pressurizing the situation: an unsettling voice calling to Bliss from inside one of the school buildings, a voice somehow related to strange blood rituals and a long-ago suicide. Myracle is running on all cylinders here, exercising an agile teenage drama, a Stephen King–like yarn of high-school horror, a cautionary tale of '60s race relations, and some affecting social commentary: each chapter begins with a period media quote, and the startling mix of Andy Griffith and Charles Manson perfectly distills the nation's teetering into terror. The conclusion is a bit awkward, but the lead up is unbearably tense and will have readers buzzing about the audacious plot twist that none of them saw coming. Bonus: the sequel, *Rhymes with Witches* (2005), has already been published. —Daniel Kraus

Ness, Patrick. ***The Ask and the Answer*****. 2009. 528p. Candlewick (9780763644901). Gr. 9–12.**

Ness brings the frantic chase of *The Knife of Never Letting Go* (2008) to a screeching halt at the beginning of this second book in the Chaos Walking trilogy. Todd and Viola have finally arrived in the town of Haven, only to find that their pursuers, an army led by the zealot Mayor Prentiss, have beat them there and set up a harsh new regime. Alternating chapters from both Todd's and Viola's points of view follow the two as they are separated and implicated into the schemes of both the oppressors and the resistance, both sides defined by the atrocities they perpetrate to achieve their goals. What results is an amalgamation of society's most brutal facets—fascism, terrorism, torture, ethnic cleansing—with all kinds of relevance to our world, even if the story is set on a made-up planet warring for identity as it awaits an influx of new settlers. While this book suffers from some of the same frustrating plot holes found in the first, Ness more than makes up for it with a relentless flurry of heavy-hitting issues, hinging on appeasement, complicity, and maintaining one's morality in the face of impossible choices. And the concept of Noise, so brilliantly conceived and executed in the first novel, is given even more depth as it becomes both a tool and a weapon. A notch less exhilarating than the first, this book is far weightier and no less stunning to read. If *Knife* provided the cut, this follow-up provides the fester. —Ian Chipman

Ness, Patrick. *The Knife of Never Letting Go*. 2008. 496p. Candlewick (9780763639310). Gr. 8–12.

Chased by a madman preacher and possibly the rest of his townsfolk as well, young Todd Hewitt flees his settlement on a planet where war with the natives has killed all the women and infected the men with a germ that broadcasts their thoughts aloud for all to hear. This cacophonous thought-cloud is known as Noise and is rendered with startling effectiveness on the page. The first of many secrets is revealed when Todd discovers an unsettling hole in the Noise, and quickly realizes that he lives in a much different world than the one he thought he did. Some of the central conceits of the drama can be hard to swallow, but the pure inventiveness and excitement of the telling more than make up for it. Narrated in a sort of pidgin English with crack dramatic and comic timing by Todd and featuring one of the finest talking-dog characters anywhere, this troubling, unforgettable opener to the Chaos Walking trilogy is a penetrating look at the ways in which we reveal ourselves to one another, and what it takes to be a man in a society gone horribly wrong. The cliffhanger ending is as effective as a shot to the gut. —Ian Chipman

★ Ness, Patrick. *A Monster Calls*. 2011. 224p. Candlewick (9780763655594). Gr. 7–10.

After the stylistic feats and dumbfounding originality of Ness' Chaos Walking trilogy, this follow-up effort comes as something of a surprise—an earthbound story concocted from a premise left behind by the late Siobhan Dowd. As Conor watches his mother succumb to cancer, he is pummeled by grief, anger, isolation, helplessness, and something even darker. At night, when he isn't trapped in a recurring nightmare too terrible to think about, he is visited by a very real monster in the form of a giant yew tree. The monster tells Conor three ambiguous, confusing stories, then demands a final one from the boy, one that "will tell me your truth." Meanwhile, Conor's mom tears through ineffective treatments, and Conor simmers with rage: "Everybody always wants to *have a talk* lately." But all that really happens is a lot of pussyfooting around the central, horrible fact that his mother is dying, and what does the monster mean about "the truth" anyway? A story with such moribund inevitability could easily become a one-note affair—or, worse, forgettable—but small, surgically precise cuts of humor and eeriness provide a crucial magnifying effect. Moreover, Ness twists out a resolution that is revelatory in its obviousness, beautiful in its execution, and fearless in its honesty. Kay's artwork keeps the pace, gnawing at the edges of the pages with thundercloud shadows and keeping the monster just barely, terribly seeable. Sidestepping any trace of emotional blackmail, Ness shines Dowd's glimmer into the deepest, most hidden darkness of doubt, and finds a path through. —Ian Chipman

Ness, Patrick. *Monsters of Men*. 2010. 608p. Candlewick (9780763647513). Gr. 9–12.

Ness, a forceful writer who chews through ideas at a blistering clip, takes on war, the heftiest of human follies, in the conclusion to his Chaos Walking trilogy. The genocidal tyrant Mayor Prentiss leads an army on one side, the terrorist healer Mistress Coyle heads a band of revolutionaries on another, and a massive legion of native Spackle threatens from a third. All three sides see only the complete annihilation of the others as the sole option for victory and survival, and they might be right, no matter how Todd and Viola use their formidable wills to advance peace as an influx of new colonists nears. It's a thick book, approaching Russian-novel territory, but it rarely feels bloated; and readers invested in the story will likely concede that Ness has earned the space. His rapid-fire litany of impossible choices makes for captivating thought fodder, and what has already been a potent display of the power of voice to drive, amplify, and transform a story gets a third, unexpected soloist. And in so doing he shows just how deep and complex, as well as how versatile, a symbolic narrative device like Noise can be.

For all the huge themes mauling at each other, though, it's the characters that ultimately stand out in this final act—the connections that bind them and change them and ruin them and redeem them. This is science fiction at its best, and is a singular fusion of brutality and idealism that is, at last, perfectly human. —Ian Chipman

Nix, Garth. *Lirael*. 2001. 496p. HarperCollins (9780060278236). Gr. 7–12.

Years have passed since the events in *Sabriel* (1996). The Old Kingdom is again under threat, this time from a sinister necromancer bent on freeing an ancient, incredibly evil being. Lirael, a daughter of the Clayr, despairs of ever gaining the gift of Sight that will mark her as an adult. Even so, she finds the fate of the kingdom in her hands and in those of Sameth, teenage son of the Abhorsen Sabriel and King Touchstone. With the help of the Disreputable Dog and Mogget, an elemental bound in the body of a cat that serves the Abhorsen, Lirael and Sameth wage a deadly war to stop the evil forces. There is some contrivance in the story, but the characterizations are appealing, and Nix not only maintains the intricate world he created for the earlier book but also continues the frenetic pace of the action and the level of violence. The cliffhanger ending sets readers up for a third book, to be called *Abhorsen*. —Sally Estes

November, Sharyn, ed. *Firebirds: An Anthology of Original Fantasy and Science Fiction*. 2003. 440p. Putnam/Firebird (9780142501429). Gr. 7–12.

The only theme in this gorgeous tapestry of a collection is that all the authors are part of the Firebird imprint. The 16 stories are richly romantic in the broadest sense, and they effortlessly transport readers. Delia Sherman's opening "Cotillion" evokes the spell of lute music and New York City in 1969; Garth Nix's creepy "Hope Chest" is a western stand-alone with a very unusual sheriff; Michael Cadnum and Meredith Ann Pierce turn old stories inside out. There's a cat tale (Diana Wynne Jones), and an odd changeling tale (Nancy Farmer), and a graphic novel by Emma Bull and Charles Vess. Nancy Springer takes a bemused and ironic look at what might happen when a girl wants her soul back. So many beguiling tales in one package make this a real find. —GraceAnne A. DeCandido

November, Sharyn, ed. *Firebirds Rising: An Anthology of Original Science Fiction and Fantasy*. 2006. 512p. Penguin/Firebird (9780142405499). Gr. 7–10.

Editor November follows *Firebirds* (2003) with an equally captivating collection of 16 original stories offering a rich variety of selections. "Huntress," by Tamora Pierce, which grew from news stories about teens "wilding" in New York City's Central Park, proves a strong jumping-off place. In Charles de Lint's "Little (Grrl) Lost," a human teenage girl and a Little teenage girl meet when the Little girl runs away from her home behind the bedroom baseboard. Patricia A. McKillip, Carol Emshwiller, and Emma Bull are also among the contributors. This volume contains more sf than its predecessor; November includes tales about genetic engineering and human-alien interactions, as well stories such as "Hives," by Kara Dalkey, a chilling, high-tech piece that takes teen girls beyond cell phones to "constant, voice-in-head-close contact"; and Tanith Lee's "The House on the Planet," a richly depicted, three-part tale about establishing a human colony on a distant planet. —Sally Estes

Noyes, Deborah. *The Ghosts of Kerfol*. 2008. 176p. Candlewick (9780763630003). Gr. 8–11.

Noyes' talent as an editor of creepy ghost stories is evident in her anthologies, *Gothic!* (2004) and *The Restless Dead* (2007). This brilliant collection is comprised of her own original tales, which are all based on Edith Wharton's 1916 story, "Kerfol." The first entry, set in 1613 in a French château, stays close to Wharton's original plot about a young woman on trial for the mysterious murder of her jealous husband, but Noyes employs a different narrative perspective—that of a serving girl. The four following, interconnected stories are set between 1802 and 2006. Noyes sometimes incorporates Wharton's phrases and dialogue from "Kerfol," but she cleverly adds her own style and twists to the original's gothic elements and themes of betrayal and vengeance. The story set in 1926 relates the tragedy of a gin-drinking party girl and brings Prohibition to life; the 1982 story features a young, thrill-seeking couple who visits a French château after dark. The ghost dogs of the original story feature in each of these unique, mesmerizing tales, as does the dark sensuality of the women. Although curious teens will be motivated to seek out the original Wharton story, Noyes supplies enough back matter to make that effort purely optional. —Cindy Dobrez

Noyes, Deborah, ed. *Gothic! Ten Original Dark Tales*. 2004. 256p. Candlewick (9780763622435). Gr. 7–10.

The slightly generic cover design and forthrightly generic title of this collection may lead many readers to expect shrieking heroines, dreary castles, lurking vampires, and other tropes of the gothic tradition. They wouldn't be wrong, but they wouldn't be exactly right, either. Sure, many of these original tales, by the likes of Joan Aiken, Neil Gaiman, Gregory Maguire, and Vivian Vande Velde, ape the vocabulary of the genre ("necromancer," "escritoire") and play with its abundant clichés (a house has as many "curses as it has spiders and silverfish"). But the maidens in peril still have to do their homework; twisted events are as likely to transpire in American suburbs as in dreary castles (in M. T. Anderson's exceptional "The Dead Watch," shape-shifting witches eat Triscuits and use ATMs); vampires whine about the garlic in the spaghetti sauce and then attack their babysitters. Ideal for high-school literature classes studying Shelley or Stoker (Gaiman's smirking contribution, which toys with genre definitions, would work particularly well in the classroom), this collection also provides an excellent opportunity to introduce fans of Koontz, Rice, and King to some of the most imaginative exponents of YA dark fantasy. —Jennifer Mattson

Noyes, Deborah, ed. *The Restless Dead: Ten Original Stories of the Supernatural*. 2007. 272p. Candlewick (9780763629069). Gr. 8–12.

"Whether motivated by shock, sorrow, self-preservation, or more subtle ambitions . . . the dead in this anthology are all restless, all awake when they shouldn't be, all conspiring to keep you up at night," writes Noyes in her introduction to this collection of terrifying stories from some of the most well-known authors writing for teens, including M. T. Anderson, Holly Black, Libba Bray, and Annette Curtis Klause. From vampires to vindictive ghosts, this diverse anthology has it all, and then some. In Kelly Link's wryly humorous entry, "The Wrong Grave," a young man digs up his dead girlfriend's corpse, only to find another girl in her grave. In Klause's poignant "Kissing Dead Boys," nearly every reaction to death is explored, sometimes lyrically, sometimes with deliciously gruesome detail. Many readers who may typically avoid short story collections will grab this one, provided that they are horror fans. The creepy cover, depicting a black-and-white photo of hands crawling out of the earth, and the evocative title aptly describe the contents and will deter the faint of heart, who probably aren't the best audience for many of these seriously scary tales. Highly recommended, and not just for reluctant readers. —Debbie Carton

★ Oppel, Kenneth. *Airborn*. 2004. 368p. HarperCollins/Eos (9780060531805). Gr. 6–9.

Matt Cruse is a cabin boy aboard the luxury passenger airship *Aurora* when the ship encounters a battered hot air balloon with an unconscious man aboard. Before dying, the man claims to have seen beautiful creatures swarming in the air over an uncharted island. Not until a year later, when Matt meets the man's granddaughter, Kate de Vries, who boards the *Aurora*, does he learn that the man wasn't hallucinating. Pirates board, rob, and kill, and a fierce storm grounds the *Aurora* on the very island that Kate's grandfather spoke about—which proves to be the pirates' secret hideaway. Though readers will need to suspend disbelief of the mysterious flying creatures, which Matt and Kate call "cloud cats," details of life and work aboard the ship as well as the dramatic escapade itself make this a captivating read. —Sally Estes

Oppel, Kenneth. *Darkwing*. 2007. 432p. HarperCollins/Eos (9780060850548). Gr. 6–9.

In his Silverwing series Oppel spun a contemporary fantasy about the world of bats. In this ambitious new stand-alone fantasy, he turns the clock back 65 million years to imagine the world of the bats' earliest ancestors, which he calls "chiropters." These tree-dwelling creatures are flightless, using their wings (which they call "sails") to glide through the air, from tree to tree. Only Dusk, youngest son of the colony's leader, has made an evolutionary leap; not only can he fly, he can also see at night, using echo vision. Predictably, the others regard him as a mutant to be shunned—all but his father, who wisely considers his son's differences as gifts. Dusk's real nemesis, however, is a beast (a "felid") called Carnassial, who is the first of his kind to be carnivorous and, like Dusk, is shunned by his own. Clearly the world is poised on the brink of remarkable change, and the future belongs to these two. Oppel writes with keen insight and empathy about the condition of being "other" in the context of a richly plotted, fast-paced story that—though sometimes too heavily anthropomorphized—is captivating reading from beginning to end. —Michael Cart

Oppel, Kenneth. *Skybreaker*. 2005. 384p. HarperCollins/Eos (9780060532277). Gr. 6–9.

In this anticipated sequel to Oppel's steampunk sky opera, *Airborn* (2004), selected as a 2005 Printz Honor Book, adventure calls when officer trainee Matt Cruse obtains navigational coordinates to a ghost ship stranded at dangerous heights. Realizing the ship's loot could help him vault class-related social obstacles, he warily joins a salvage expedition aboard a high-altitude skybreaker. Headstrong heiress Kate deVries participates, but many new characters are introduced, most significantly an intriguing Romany girl and a brash captain whose respective presences threaten the romance between Matt and Kate. The plot cleaves closely to that of *Airborn*, confronting the protagonists with a mystery left behind by an eccentric genius, a new airborn species, and adrenalin-pumping clashes with pirates. As in the first book, Oppel's loving evocations of his airtight alternate reality are more successful than his characterizations, a weakness that is troubling in exoticized descriptions of sandalwood-and-spice-scented gypsy Nadera. There's nothing new here, but Oppel fans and newcomers alike will happily stay aboard to the tinglingly good conclusion. —Jennifer Mattson

Paolini, Christopher. *Eragon*. 2003. 528p. Knopf (9780375826689). Gr. 7–12.

Was the mysterious blue stone that appears out of nowhere sent by accident or is teenage Eragon meant to have it? When a dragon, Saphira, hatches from it, beast and boy connect (in much the same way dragons and riders do in Anne McCaffrey's popular Pern series) and face danger together. In this story, Eragon is thrust into a new role as the first Dragon Rider in more than 100 years who is not under the evil king's control. After the king's ghastly minions kill Eragon's uncle as they search for the teen, Eragon and Saphira, mentored by the village's aged "storyteller," hunt for the killers and, in turn, find themselves being hunted. This unusual, powerful tale, begun when Paolini was 15 (he's now 19) and self-published in 2002 before being picked up by Knopf, is the first book in the planned Inheritance trilogy. It's obvious that Paolini knows the genre well—his lush tale is full of recognizable fantasy elements and conventions. But the telling remains constantly fresh and fluid, and he has done a fine job of creating an appealing and convincing relationship between the youth and the dragon. It's an impressive start to a writing career that's sure to flourish. —Sally Estes

Pattou, Edith. *East*. 2003. 480p. Harcourt (9780152045630). Gr. 6–10.

The author of *Hero's Song* (1991) and *Fire Arrow* (1998) weaves the essentials of the children's fairy tale "East o' the Sun and West o' the Moon" into a rich tapestry that will resonate with readers of books such as Robin McKinley's renderings of "Beauty and the Beast." The story, which gently unfolds in several distinct voices, focuses on Rose, the youngest of seven children. When Rose is almost 15, a white bear appears at the door, asking Father to turn over his youngest daughter. The animal carries Rose to a distant castle, where she lives contentedly. Every night, a mysterious visitor climbs into her bed and hides under the covers. Is it the bear? Is it the scaly monster she sees in her dreams? She feels she must know. Unfortunately, her willfulness seals the fate of her nighttime visitor, who falls into the hands of the patient Troll Queen and is whisked away to "an unreachable place."

Guilt sets in, and Rose begins a long, arduous journey to right the wrong she has done. What ensues is the stuff of epic tale telling, replete with high drama and compelling characterizations. —Sally Estes

Pearson, Mary E. ***The Adoration of Jenna Fox*****. 2008. 272p. Holt (9780805076684). Gr. 8–12.**

The ethics of bioengineering in the not-so-distant future drives this story. Jenna, 17, severely injured in a car crash, is saved by her heartbroken father, a scientist who illegally uses the latest medical technology to help her. Only 10 percent of her original brain is saved, but Dad has programmed her by uploading the high-school curriculum. She could live 2 years, or 200. Is she a monster or a miracle? Why have her parents hidden her away? The science (including allusions to the dangerous overuse of antibiotics) and the science fiction are fascinating, but what will hold readers most are the moral issues of betrayal, loyalty, sacrifice, and survival. Jenna realizes it is her parents' love that makes them break the law to save her at any cost. The teen's first-person, present-tense narrative is fast and immediate as Jenna makes new friends and confronts the complicated choices she must make now. —Hazel Rochman

Pfeffer, Susan Beth. ***The Dead and the Gone*****. 2008. 320p. Harcourt (9780152063115). Gr. 8–12.**

In *Life as We Knew It* (2006), veteran writer Pfeffer painted a terrifying picture of what happened in a rural Pennsylvania town after an asteroid hit the moon and cataclysmic changes on land and sea caused familiar life to grind to a halt. For readers who wondered if things were any better in a bustling city, here is the horrifying answer. On the night the moon tilts, 17-year-old Alex and his younger sisters are alone; their mother is at work, and their father is visiting Puerto Rico. No matter how the kids wish, hope, and pray, their parents don't return. It's up to Alex to do what's best. At first that means bartering for food and batteries and avoiding fighting with the rambunctious Julie—especially after sickly Bri is sent to live at a rural convent. Later it means rescuing Julie from rapists and steering her away from the corpses that litter the street, providing food for rats. Religion is one of the strong threads running through the novel. It would have been interesting to see Alex wrestle more with his staunch Catholicism, but in many ways, the Church anchors the plot. The story's power, as in the companion book, comes from readers' ability to picture themselves in a similar situation; everything Pfeffer writes about seems wrenchingly plausible. —Ilene Cooper

Pfeffer, Susan Beth. ***Life as We Knew It*****. 2006. 352p. Harcourt (9780152058265). Gr. 7–10.**

A meteor is going to hit the moon, and 16-year-old Miranda, like the rest of her family and neighbors in rural Pennsylvania, intends to watch it from the comfort of a lawn chair in her yard. But the event is not the benign impact predicted. The moon is knocked closer to Earth, setting off a chain of horrific occurrences: tsunamis, earthquakes, and, later, volcanic eruptions that disrupt life across the planet. Written in the form of Miranda's diary, this disquieting and involving story depicts one family's struggle to survive in a world where food, warmth, and well-being disappear in the blink of an eye. As life goes from bad to worse, Miranda struggles to find a way to survive both mentally and physically, discovering strength in her family members and herself. This novel will inevitably be compared to Meg Rosoff's Printz Award Book, *How I Live Now* (2004). Pfeffer doesn't write with Rosoff's startling eloquence, and her setup is not as smooth (why don't scientists predict the possibility of this outcome?). But Miranda and her family are much more familiar than Rosoff's characters, and readers will respond to the authenticity and immediacy of their plight. Each page is filled with events both wearying and terrifying and infused with honest emotions. Pfeffer brings cataclysmic tragedy very close. —Ilene Cooper

Pierce, Meredith Ann. ***Treasure at the Heart of the Tanglewood*****. 2001. 256p. Viking (9780670892471). Gr. 6–10.**

Pierce's latest is a mesmerizing tale is steeped in legends about Earth Mother. Brown Hannah, clad in brown leaves and with sprigs and buds growing in her hair, is a young healer who lives at the verge of

Tanglewood. She has no memory of how she came there, and her only companions are Magpie, Badger, three mischievous fox pups, and a mysterious wizard who forbids her to leave the wood. Legend has it that within the wood lies a fabulous treasure, sought by knights from Faraway Isle and guarded by Golden Boar. One knight survives the vicious boar, and as Brown Hannah nurses him back to health, she learns the joys of human companionship. But the wizard mutes the knight and turns him into a fox. Enraged, Hannah flees with the fox and her companions, determined to restore the fox to human form. During her journey, she changes into Green Hannah, then Golden Hannah. When she reaches the place from which she first came, she becomes Russet Hannah, the season turns to autumn, and she discovers not only who she is but also what the future will bring. The telling is lyrical and magical, elegant in imagery, and memorable in characterization. It's a glorious return for Pierce. —Sally Estes

Pierce, Tamora. *Terrier*. 2006. 592p. Random (9780375814686). Gr. 7–10.

Having followed her signature heroine into the next generation with her Trickster duet, Pierce now looks back into the history of Tortall and finds another fierce, lovable gal who won't take any guff. Sixteen-year-old Beka Cooper, born hundreds of years before Alanna drew her first sword, has just signed on as a Puppy (trainee) with her city's crime fighters, unofficially known as the Dogs. Beka's extrasensory gifts and a firsthand understanding of her tough beat help her to "scent" two heinous criminals, whom she delivers to justice—despite the limitations of her apprentice role—by rallying a lively network of informants, mentors, and allies. Pierce deftly handles the novel's journal structure, and her clear homage to the police-procedural genre applies a welcome twist to the girl-legend-in-the-making story line. Leisurely infusions of detail frequently slow things down, but homely, often comic pauses interspersing epic deeds have become touchstones of Pierce's storytelling, and not even the strained surprise ending will prevent fans from begging for more about the avenging pup known as a "Terrier among Dogs." —Jennifer Mattson

Pierce, Tamora. *Trickster's Choice*. 2003. 446p. Random (9780375814662). Gr. 7–12.

Readers who have delighted in the tales of Alanna the Lioness will be equally thrilled by this rich and complex tale of Alanna's teenage daughter, Aly. Aly longs to be a spy, like her father, and is prickly with her often-absent mother. When the 16-year-old dashes off, she is instantly captured by pirates and sold into slavery to a noble family, the Balitangs of the Copper Isles. There, the trickster god Kyprioth binds Aly to him: she is to keep her charges, the Balitang children, safe for the summer, and then she can go home. Aly hides her skills in magic and weaponry and her fierce intelligence in plain sight; watching her mind work is a wonder. She learns the language of crows and teaches them hers, and a crow of great power and sweetness makes himself into human form for her sake. A marvelous cast of characters, human, mage, and animal; a tangled web of political and racial tensions; and the promise of other Aly stories to come will engage Pierce's legions of fans and win over even more. —GraceAnne A. DeCandido

Pike, Aprilynne. *Spells*. 2010. 368p. Harper (9780061668067). Gr. 7–10.

In this second installment of a series that started with the best-selling *Wings* (2009), Laurel, who recently discovered she is a faerie, finds herself completely immersed in her new world when she begins studies at the Academy at Avalon. There she can spend more time with Tam, the faerie who is hopelessly in love with her, and also learn about the benefits and burdens her heritage entails. But the action really begins when she returns home. The trolls that stalked her in the previous book are more dangerous than ever, and this time Laurel is not the only one being targeted. Pike astutely mixes these breathtaking events with the real meat of the story: the angst and uncertainty Laurel feels as she tries to combine—and sometimes keep separate—her two lives. At the heart of that conundrum is the affection she feels for both her earthly love, David, and the deliciously different Tam. Mixing a little bit of Harry Potter and a lot of Twilight (Team David! Team Tam!), Pike has hit on a winning combination. Yet it is her own graceful take on life inside

Avalon that adds a shimmering patina sure to enthrall readers. This book leaves them wanting more. —Ilene Cooper

Pon, Cindy. *Silver Phoenix: Beyond the Kingdom of Xia*. 2009. 352p. Greenwillow (9780061730214). Gr. 9–12.

If the cover image of a fearless Chinese heroine reminds readers of such films as *Crouching Tiger, Hidden Dragon*, that's intentional; the story inside will, too. First-time novelist Pon has a screenwriter's talent for producing a sweeping saga, and in this, the first of two books set in ancient China, 17-year-old Ai Ling faces demons, monsters, and gods as she tries to fulfill her destiny. Frightened after a local man tries to blackmail her into marriage, Ai Ling resolves to journey to the emperor's palace, where her missing father was last seen. Along the way, she meets the handsome Chen Yong, who is of mixed parentage and on a quest to find answers to questions about his family that have haunted him his whole life. (In the story's prologue, readers get hints about his origins.) As in most martial-arts movies, the story sometimes takes a backseat to the action, but Pon doesn't stint when it comes to her characters. Ai Ling is a clever and determined heroine, Chen's younger brother is a witty teen whose girl-crazy ways transcend the centuries, and even the monsters have dimension. Pon's writing, both fluid and exhilarating, shines whether she's describing a dinner delicacy or what it feels like to stab an evil spirit in the gut. There's a bit of sex here, including a near rape, but it's all integral to a saga that spins and slashes as its heroine tries to find her way home. —Ilene Cooper

Pratchett, Terry. *The Amazing Maurice and His Educated Rodents*. 2001. 256p. HarperCollins (9780060012335). Gr. 6–9.

The Amazing Maurice, an opportunistic cat, talks Keith, a "stupid-looking kid" who plays a flute, and a horde of rats (with names like Dangerous Beans, Darktan, Hamnpork, Big Savings, Peaches, and Nourishing) into working pied-piper scams on various towns. In Pratchett's first Discworld novel for young readers, the motley crew readies itself to take on the isolated hamlet of Bad Blintz. Unfortunately, it didn't count on running into the mayor's conniving daughter (to whom everything is part of a fairy tale) or a pair of rat catchers working an evil scheme in the tunnels and sewers beneath the town. What ensues is scary mayhem, leavened with a big dollop of comic relief as the scammers become heroes and, eventually, cut a deal with the townspeople. Kids who like Brian Jacques' Redwall series and Robin Jarvis' Deptford Mice trilogy will feel pretty comfortable with the fast-paced (sometimes gory) action here. —Sally Estes

Pratchett, Terry. *A Hat Full of Sky*. 2004. 288p. HarperCollins (9780060586607). Gr. 6–10.

Incipient witch Tiffany Aching, who confronted danger in *The Wee Free Men* (2003), faces even greater peril in this equally quirky sequel. She is taken on as an apprentice witch by Miss Level, who is one person with two bodies—an oddity to say the least. Also, Tiffany is stalked and taken over by a hiver, an invisible, brainless entity that commands and distorts the mind of its host, which eventually dies. Luckily Tiffany is strong enough to hide a section of her mind within herself, but she is otherwise completely under the control of the hiver. It's the cantankerous Wee Free Men (or the Nac Mac Feegle) to the rescue, with the help of Miss Level and the wisest, most respected witch of all. The chase is part slapstick, part terror, and in the end, Tiffany herself sets things straight. Pratchett maintains the momentum of the first book, and fans will relish the further adventures of the "big wee hag," as Tiffany is known to the Feegles. —Sally Estes

★ Pratchett, Terry. *Nation*. 2008. 336p. HarperCollins (9780061433016). Gr. 7–10.

"Somewhere in the South Pelagic Ocean," a tidal wave wipes out the population of a small island—except for Mau, who was paddling his dugout canoe home after a month spent alone, preparing to become a man. The wave also sweeps a sailing ship carrying Daphne, an English girl, up onto the island and deposits it in the rain forest, where Mau finds her. Over the months that follow, they learn to communicate while welcoming more people to their shores and building a community of survivors. Mau searches for the meaning behind his people's gods, while Daphne applies her nineteenth-century knowledge of science and history to the many puzzles she discovers in this unfamiliar place. Broad in its scope and concrete in its details, this unusual novel strips away the trappings of two very different nations to consider what it is people value and why. Certain scenes are indelible: Mau's nonverbal communication to Daphne that a pregnant woman has landed, and she must help with the birth; or the terrifying yet awesome descent into a cave. Quirky wit and broad vision make this a fascinating survival story on many levels. —Carolyn Phelan

Pratchett, Terry. *The Wee Free Men*. 2003. 272p. HarperCollins (9780060012366). Gr. 6–10.

Pratchett turns the bogeymen of fairy tales and nightmares into reality in the latest book in his popular, comedic Discworld series. Young Tiffany Aching, incipient witch armed with a large iron frying pan, goes after the Elf Queen, who has taken Tiffany's little brother into Fairyland and who plans to use humans' dreams to conquer their world. Tiffany's companions on her quest are a talking toad, who used to be a human, and a band of fierce Wee Free Men, who are six inches tall, talk with a Scottish brogue, and are famous for "stealin' an' drinkin' an' fightin'!" The action is both manic and a little scary as the queen confronts her pursuers with a headless horseman, dreams that trap dreamers inside them, and more. In the end, Tiffany must face the Queen alone while attempting to sort out reality from nightmare. Both the humor and the danger will appeal to fans of Discworld; they will also draw readers who like J. K. Rowling's Harry, Hermione, and Ron. —Sally Estes

Pratchett, Terry. *Wintersmith*. 2006. 336p. HarperTempest (9780060890315). Gr. 7–10.

Here's the third Discworld story for younger readers in a series that began with *The Wee Free Men* (2003) and continued in *A Hat Full of Sky* (2004). Despite a stern warning from Miss Treason, the eccentric witch from whom 13-year-old Tiffany Aching is learning her craft, the girl has gone and danced with the wrong men. Having inserted herself into a dark reverse Morris dance in which summer and winter achieve their seasonal balance, Tiffany has attracted the amorous attentions of the Wintersmith. To express his ardor, he brings his chilly powers to bear, replete with Tiffany-shaped snowflakes burying the world in the rising drifts of his infatuation. While Granny Weatherwax, Miss Perspicacia Tick, and sundry veteran witches work with Tiffany to restrain the Wintersmith's zeal, the Wee Free Men set off to fetch a Hero to assist Tiffany, along the way adopting a cantankerous blue cheese. Add an assortment of junior witches-in-training, and yet another rollicking, clever, and quite charming adventure is brought to readers, who will find themselves delighted again—or for the first time—by Pratchett's exuberant storytelling. —Holly Koelling

Pullman, Philip, and John Lawrence. *Once upon a Time in the North*. 2008. 112p. Knopf/David Fickling (9780375845109). Gr. 7–10.

As he did in *Lyra's Oxford* (2004), Pullman returns to the world of His Dark Materials trilogy in this story of how aeronaut Lee Scoresby meets and befriends bear Iorke Byrnison. Pullman is as fine a writer as there is for young people, and this book is a small gem—literally—it's 112 pages and the size of a paperback. The story begins as Lee's cargo balloon drifts into the Arctic, landing in the icy environs of Novy Odense. The town is about to elect a new mayor, Ivan Poliakov, who wants to rid the place of bears, and Lee (along with daemon rabbit Hester) finds himself embroiled in local controversies. When Lee learns one of Poliakov's allies is a vicious criminal with whom he once had a run-in, he knows he must choose sides. Beautifully crafted and spilling over with action, the novel has the feel of an old western (one can almost see Gary Cooper as Lee). Matching Pullman's carefully calibrated prose is the book's thoughtful design. Everything works together—from the sturdy, blue cloth cover to the back matter, which features a miniature board game. Lawrence's stamp-sized ink engravings set the tale somewhere between fantasy and history. —Ilene Cooper

Reeve, Philip. *Fever Crumb*. **2010. 336p. Scholastic (9780545207195). Gr. 6–9.**

Set some centuries before the Hungry City Chronicles, yet still well into the future, this prequel series opener stars young Fever Crumb, reared by the Order of Engineers in the massive head of an unfinished statue, to operate with a slavish devotion to logic. (In one delightful scene, a group of engineers pours out of the head's nostril door "like a highly educated sneeze"). Uncertain of her heritage, as well as the source of the memories invading her mind, Fever embarks on a rather typical quest of discovery with anything-but-typical trimmings. London is a nearly medieval backwater, where relics of ancient technology hint at a time thousands of years ago when people still understood how to make circuit boards and microchips. Reeve's captivating flights of imagination play as vital a role in the story as his endearing heroine, hissworthy villains, and nifty array of supporting characters. Although there's all manner of foundation work to gratify readers familiar with the world introduced in 2003's Mortal Engines (including the genesis of Municipal Darwinism and the origins of a very familiar figure), Reeve has crafted a swiftly paced story worthy of standing alone, both in terms of where Fever's adventure may lead her next as well as the connections to the Hungry City Chronicles. It may not be possible for Reeve to ever fully explore this world, but that shouldn't keep him from trying, hopefully in many books to come. —Ian Chipman

Reeve, Philip. *Mortal Engines*. **2003. 320p. HarperCollins/Eos (9780060082079). Gr. 7–10.**

As the story opens, the great Traction City of London is chasing a small town. When one city takes over another, it processes all reusable materials to create power to run the motorized wheels that enable the city to travel over the land. London's mayor has bigger plans than the domination of a small town, plans involving the use of the weapon that laid waste to Earth millennia earlier. Several young people endeavor to stop the carnage—among them, Tom, an apprentice at the London Museum; a young woman who tries to kill the museum's head historian; the historian's daughter, Katherine; and an apprentice in the Guild of Engineers. The pace of the violence-filled story is frenetic, the sense of helplessness is palpable, and not all the young people survive. A page-turner, this adventure in a city-eat-city world will have readers eagerly suspending disbelief to follow the twists and turns of the imaginative plot. —Sally Estes

Reeve, Philip. *Predator's Gold*. **2004. 336p. HarperCollins (9780060721930). Gr. 7–10.**

Reeve ratchets up the action and the violence in the sequel to *Mortal Engines* (2003) as Tom and Hester, now in possession of the airship *Jenny Haniver*, which once belonged to an agent of the Anti-Traction League, find themselves being pursued by League forces. Scrambling to escape, they head north and land on the city of Anchorage, a small, nonpredator city that traces its name back to old America. Anchorage's young ruler has decided that the wheeled city will make its way over the frozen wastes back to the Dead Continent, and the vicious predator city Arkangel is following along right behind. Add to that a gang of Lost Boys, recruited and trained to infiltrate and burgle cities while its leader, Uncle, foments more nefarious plans. Despite Reeve's frequent flipping back and forth to tell the stories of various characters, this vividly told novel, the second in the Hungry City Chronicles, is still easy to follow; it's also gripping enough to leave readers anxious to find out what's to come. —Sally Estes

Riordan, Rick. *The Lightning Thief*. **2005. 384p. Hyperion/Miramax (9780786856299). Gr. 6–9.**

The escapades of the Greek gods and heroes get a fresh spin in the first book in the Percy Jackson and the Olympians series, about a contemporary 12-year-old New Yorker who learns he's a demigod. Perseus, aka Percy Jackson, thinks he has big problems. His father left before he was born, he's been kicked out of six schools in six years, he's dyslexic, and he has ADHD. What a surprise when he finds out that that's only the tip of the iceberg: he vaporizes his pre-algebra teacher, learns his best friend is a satyr, and is almost killed by a minotaur before his mother manages to get him to the safety of Camp Half-Blood—where he discovers that Poseidon is his father. But that's a problem, too. Poseidon has been accused of stealing Zeus' lightning bolt, and unless Percy can return the bolt, humankind is doomed. Riordan's fast-paced adventure is fresh, dangerous, and funny. Percy is an appealing, but reluctant hero, the modernized gods are hilarious, and the parallels to Harry Potter are frequent and obvious. Because Riordan is faithful to the original myths, librarians should be prepared for a rush of readers wanting the classic stories. —Chris Sherman

Riordan, Rick. *The Titan's Curse*. 2007. 320p. Hyperion/Miramax (9781423101451). Gr. 6–9.

Just after finding Bianca and Nico, two newly discovered half-bloods, Percy, Grover, Annabeth, and Thalia end up trapped between a helicopter and a manticore. Artemis and her Hunters save the day, but Annabeth disappears over a cliff; then Artemis rushes off to hunt a dangerous monster. Back at Camp Half-Blood, the Oracle foretells that Artemis must be rescued and makes a prediction that bodes ill for one of their number—but which one? Percy, who is supposed to remain behind while others pursue the quest, follows in search of the missing Annabeth. Their adventures range widely across the U.S., taking them to locales that include Washington, D.C., and the deserts of the Southwest and pitting them against the usual assortment of colorful adversaries. The Percy Jackson & the Olympians series is built around a terrific idea—that the half-mortal offspring of Greek gods live among us, playing out struggles of mythic scale—and Riordan takes it from strength to strength with this exciting installment, adding even more depth to the characters and story arc while retaining its predecessors' nonstop laughs and action. —Diana Tixier Herald

★ Rosoff, Meg. *How I Live Now*. 2004. 160p. Random/Wendy Lamb (9780385746779). Gr. 8–11.

A 15-year-old, contemporary urbanite named Daisy, sent to England to summer with relatives, falls in love with her aunt's "oldy worldy" farm and her soulful cousins—especially Edmond, with whom she forms "the world's most inappropriate case of sexual obsession." Matters veer in a startling direction when terrorists strike while Daisy's aunt is out of the country, war erupts, and soldiers divide the cousins by gender between two guardians. Determined to rejoin Edmond, Daisy and her youngest cousin embark upon a dangerous journey that brings them face to face with horrific violence and undreamt-of deprivation. Just prior to the hopeful conclusion, Rosoff introduces a jolting leap forward in time accompanied by an evocative graphic device that will undoubtedly spark lively discussions. As for the incestuous romance, Daisy and Edmond's separation for most of the novel and the obvious emotional sustenance Daisy draws from their bond sensitively shift the focus away from the relationship's implicit (and potentially discomfiting) physical dimension. More central to the potency of Rosoff's debut, though, is the ominous prognostication of what a third world war might look like, and the opportunity it provides for teens to imagine themselves, like Daisy, exhibiting courage and resilience in roles traditionally occupied by earlier generations. —Jennifer Mattson

Rosoff, Meg. *There Is No Dog*. 2012. 256p. Putnam (9780399257643). Gr. 9–12.

Have you ever wondered why there are earthquakes and hurricanes? Why plans fail and lovers break up? How an omnipotent deity lets evil occur in the world? Would it help if I told you God is a teenage boy? That's the premise of Printz winner Rosoff's new novel. Long story short, Mona, the mother of Bob (aka God), wins Earth in a poker game. What mother doesn't want to see her son get ahead? So Bob gets the job In the Beginning, but like so many teenage boys, he often can't see past his nether regions. And besides, he's a bit thick and won't buckle down, so fortunately the overworked Mr. B. has been designated as Bob's companion/assistant. Think Arthur (Dudley Moore) and his butler (John Gielgud). Then Bob falls for Lucy, a beautiful zoo worker, and Mr. B. knows all hell is going to break loose. It happens every time Bob gets involved with a human. Wildly inventive and laugh-out-loud funny, the story is told from the points of view of various characters: long-suffering Mr. B., virginal Lucy, dingbat Mona, and, of course, petulant, powerful, pissant Bob. In many ways, the book's parts add up to more than its sum, but it is not often that a book comes along that is both arch and thoughtful, silly and smart. This one's not quite like anything else out there. —Ilene Cooper

Rosetti, Rinsai. *The Girl with Borrowed Wings*. 2012. 300p. Dial (9780803735668). Gr. 7–12.

Frenenqer—a name meaning restraint—was born inside her father's imagination and sculpted into his vision of the perfect daughter. She has felt his invisible finger between her shoulder blades her whole life, forcing her meek, obedient, and modest actions. To compound the oppression, Frenenqer lives in a blazingly hot oasis in a Middle Eastern desert, marked by dirty white buildings, an unforgiving landscape, and no place to go, save to school and back home again. In an act of defiance, Frenenqer saves a black cat from certain death at the animal souk and brings him home. The cat is a shape-shifter, a Free person whom Frenenqer names Sangris. He has no constraints, no family, no rules to follow. Sangris, often taking the form of a boy, sprouts wings, and Frenenqer flies with him at night to places both real and magical. It's this juxtaposition of subjugation and freedom that propels Rossetti's spellbinding debut, as a girl owned by her father begins to experience life outside of narrowly defined spaces. With taut, lush writing ("the wind shut my eyes for me and rioted in my hair"), a stunningly imagined setting, and a premise that's unique among the stacks of paranormal romances, this one—written when Rossetti was a teenager—feels like a breeze in the desert. —Ann Kelley

★ Rowling, J. K. *Harry Potter and the Deathly Hallows*. 2007. 756p. Scholastic/Arthur A. Levine (9780545010221). Gr. 4–12.

The cloak of inevitability hangs on the final installment of the Harry Potter series. One must die, one will live. Friends will be distinguished from foes. All will be revealed. To Rowling's great credit, she manages this finale with the flair and respect for her audience that have permeated the previous six novels, though the mood here is quite different. The story has a certain flatness that extends through much of the book. Rowling can no longer rely on diversions like Quidditch matches and trips to Hogsmead for relief; Harry has made the decision not to return to Hogwarts. Aided by Hermione and Ron, he will instead search for the remaining Horcruxes that hide pieces of Voldemorte's soul. Danger and death are in the air, but Rowling skillfully deals both out in tightly controlled bursts that are juxtaposed against periods of indecision, false leads, and even boredom as the trio try to divine their next moves. Most startling are the new elements, including the not-altogether-successful introduction of the Deathly Hallows. These magical artifacts unnecessarily up the total of things that Harry is looking for by three, and the ownership of one of the Hallows, a wand, may lead to confusion for readers at a climactic moment. More successful additions, adding depth and weight, are the multilayered revelation of Dumbledore's family history and the brilliantly handled answer to the question of Severus Snape's allegiance. Throughout, Rowling returns to and embellishes the hallmark themes of the series: the importance of parental influences, the redemptive power of sacrifice, and the strength found in love. These truths are the underpinnings of a finale that is worthy of fans' hopes and expectations.
—Ilene Cooper

Rowling, J. K. *Harry Potter and the Goblet of Fire*. 2000. 734p. Scholastic/Arthur A. Levine (9780439554909). Gr. 5–12.

Was it worth the long, agonizing wait and all the hype and hoopla? You bet! Harry's fourth challenging experience will more than live up to his myriad fans' expectations—though the 734 pages divided into 37 chapters may be a bit daunting to younger readers. The very length, however, allows an even richer tapestry of magical events and humorous escapades, even as the tale takes the long-predicted darker turn. The first chilling chapter introduces Voldemort's plans to regain the power lost in his ill-fated attempt to kill Harry: "Come, Wormtail, one more death and our path to Harry Potter is clear." Harry, now 14, has a crush on a classmate at Hogwarts, but his interactions with his friends Ron and Hermione take up far more of the story. The theme of prejudice is raised—Hermione tries to raise awareness that the house elves are virtual slaves. But the big excitement comes from the news that the intramural Quidditch matches are to give way to the first Triwizard Tournament in years, a series of three ordeals undertaken by students from three rival schools of magic, who are to be selected by a goblet of fire. Although not old enough to be a candidate, Harry is named a participant by the goblet. Someone must have entered his name—but who? The first ordeal involves dragons, the second water, and the third a maze, which is rigged to send Harry into the hands of his sworn enemy, Voldemort. Any inclination toward disbelief on the part of readers is swept away by the very brilliance of the writing. The carefully created world of magic becomes more embellished and layered, while the amazing plotting ties up loose ends, even as it sets in motion more entanglements. The long climax races relentlessly to a stunning denouement that leaves the way open for the next episode. Let the anticipation begin. —Sally Estes

Rowling, J. K. *Harry Potter and the Half-Blood Prince*. 2005. 672p. Scholastic/Arthur A. Levine (9780439784542). Gr. 5–12.

With the Harry Potter Express chugging closer to its final destination, the sixth book in the series gets down to business. No more diversions about the welfare of house elves or the intricacies of Quidditch. This penultimate offering is more about tying up loose ends and fleshing out the backstory. Harry and the gang are back at Hogwarts, but the mood is grim. The wizard community is now fully aware that evil has returned, and the citizenry is afraid. Harry has been left bereft by the death of Sirius Black, and there are more killings to come. In a powerful early scene, readers learn that a pivotal figure is seemingly not to be trusted, yet throughout there are hints that he or she is a double agent. Later Harry becomes entangled with a former student known as the Half-Blood Prince, having accidentally acquired the prince's Potions textbook, but this turns out to be a mixed blessing. Rowling also devotes time to a carefully crafted telling of the story of Lord Voldemort's early life, which Harry and Dumbledore piece together by plucking other people's memories. Rowling is at the top of her game here. For those able to reach just beyond the engrossing tale, there is commentary relevant to today: how governments offer false security about perilous situations and how being in a constant state of war affects people's behavior. Harry is almost 17 now, and this is a book for older readers, who will best understand the moral implications of his choices. —Ilene Cooper

Rowling, J. K. *Harry Potter and the Order of the Phoenix*. 2003. 768p. Scholastic/Arthur A. Levine (9780439358064). Gr. 5–12.

No, you can't put it down, but believe me, you'll wish you could. This is not an easy book to lug around. Its worldwide hype aside, the fifth installment in Harry Potter's saga should be judged on the usual factors: plot, characters, and the quality of the writing. So how does it fare? One thing emerges quickly: Rowling has not lost her flair as a storyteller or her ability to keep coming up with new gimcracks to astound her readers. But her true skills lie in the way she ages Harry, successfully evolving him from the once downtrodden yet hopeful young boy to this new, gangly teenager showing all the symptoms of adolescence—he is sullen, rude, and contemptuous of adult behavior, especially hypocrisy. This last symptom of the maturing Harry fits especially well into the plot, which finds almost all of the grown-ups in the young wizard's life saying one thing and doing another, especially those at the Ministry of Magic, who discredit Harry in the media to convince the citizenry that Voldemort is not alive. Rowling effectively uses this plot strand as a way of introducing a kind of subtext in which she takes on such issues as governmental lying and the politics of personal destruction, but she makes her points in ways that will be clearly understood by young readers. To fight for truth and justice—and to protect Harry—the Order of the Phoenix has been reconstituted, but young Potter finds squabbling and hypocrisy among even this august group. And in a stunning and bold move, Rowling also allows Harry (and readers) to view an incident from the life of a teenage James Potter that shows him to be an insensitive bully, smashing the iconic view Harry has always had of his father. Are there problems with the book? Sure. Even though

children, especially, won't protest, it could be shorter, particularly since Rowling is repetitious with descriptions (Harry is always "angry"; ultimate bureaucrat Doris Umbridge always looks like a toad). But these are quibbles about a rich, worthy effort that meets the very high expectations of a world of readers.
—Ilene Cooper

Ryan, Carrie. *The Forest of Hands and Teeth*. 2009. 320p. Delacorte (9780385736817). Gr. 9–12.

Mary lives in a small village in the middle of the forest governed by the religious Sisterhood and bordered with a fence to keep out the Unconsecrated—a horde of the undead unleashed many generations ago by a mysterious and cataclysmic event. Life is simple but preordained; Mary fears her betrothal to a man she doesn't love almost as much as the hungry jaws slavering at the fence links. Under the colonial trappings, this is a full-blooded zombie thriller, reminiscent of the paragon of the genre, George Romero's 1968 film *Night of the Living Dead*. Soon Mary and a small band of desperate survivors are thrown together to outwit the undead and work through their own weaknesses, suspicions, and jealousies. Ryan's vision is bleak but not overly gory; her entry in the zombie canon stands out for how well she integrates romance with flesh-eating. The plot loses a little wind near the conclusion, but Ryan's ability to write a nail-biting escape scene will keep most readers riveted. —Daniel Kraus

Sedgwick, Marcus. *The Book of Dead Days*. 2004. 288p. Random/Wendy Lamb (9780385730556). Gr. 6–9.

Set during the dead days between Christmas and New Year's in a crumbling, old, European-like city, this story is as dark as a winter's night, illuminated with flashes of shooting-star brilliance. Once an urchin, Boy now belongs to Valerian, a magician. Although the master treats the child poorly, Boy follows his orders dutifully; Valerian is all he has got. So when Valerian reveals that he has only a few days to live (a pact with the devil is coming due), Boy winds his way through the fetid stink of the city, following Valerian's mysterious and dangerous instructions in a race to save his master's life. Sedgwick's highly visual writing makes for a true movie of the mind. It is reminiscent of Philip Pullman's work, with each detail adding to the fullness of Sedgwick's alternative world. Also like Pullman, Sedgwick draws characters so magnetic that readers will find it hard to look away. The plot is convoluted in places and a few key points want explanation (about one, a character says, "We may never know"). Still, this is a haunting novel that will keep readers engaged.
—Ilene Cooper

Sedgwick, Marcus. *Midwinterblood*. 2013. 272p. Roaring Brook (9781596438002). Gr. 9–12.

In the year 2073, a reporter named Eric is sent to Blessed Island to research a rare flower called the Dragon Orchid. There he finds an insular community of mysterious villagers, a delicious tea that has him losing days at a time, and a beguiling girl named Merle. In just 50 pages, we reach a shattering conclusion—and then start anew in 2011. An archaeologist is digging on Blessed Island, where he meets a quiet boy named Eric and his mother, Merle. So begins this graceful, confounding, and stirring seven-part suite about two characters whose identities shift as they are reborn throughout the ages. Sedgwick tells the story in reverse, introducing us to a stranded WWII pilot, a painter trying to resurrect his career in 1901, two children being told a ghost story in 1848, and more, all the way back to a king and queen in a "Time Unknown." It is a wildly chancy gambit with little in the way of a solid throughline, but Sedgwick handles each story with such stylistic control that interest is not just renewed each time but intensified. Part love story, part mystery, part horror, this is as much about the twisting hand of fate as it is about the mutability of folktales. Its strange spell will capture you. —Daniel Kraus

Shinn, Sharon. *The Safe-Keeper's Secret*. 2004. 240p. Viking (9780670059102). Gr. 7–12.

When she grows up, Fiona plans to be her village's Safe-Keeper, just like her mother, Damiana, who listens to, but cannot repeat, her neighbors' most troubling stories. Fiona's own family has plenty of secrets: Fiona doesn't know her father's identity, and on the night of her birth, the king's messenger left a mysterious baby with Damiana, asking her to keep and protect the child. The boy, Reed, and Fiona grow up in a bucolic setting as best friends, surrounded by a loving, extended family of magical adults. When Damiana falls ill, Reed and Fiona leave their childhood behind as they care for their mother and make startling discoveries about their respective parents. Shinn, whose fantasy titles for adults have earned her a wide teen following, heavily foreshadows a romance between Reed and Fiona, an element that may disturb some readers, particularly those in blended families. The romance is only hinted at, however, and teens will connect with Shinn's vividly drawn fantasy world as well as her provocative questions about truth, justice, and individual destiny. —Gillian Engberg

Shinn, Sharon. *The Truth-Teller's Tale*. 2005. 288p. Viking (9780670060009). Gr. 7–10.

Eleda sees the world in "all sharp edges and simple lines": she is a Truth-Teller, and she cannot speak a lie or hear one spoken. Her twin, Adele, whose name is a palindrome of Eleda's, is a Safe-Keeper, a listener who never betrays a confidence. Two halves of a whole, the sisters occasionally infuriate each other but frequently find that their complementary gifts prove useful—particularly as they stumble through adolescence, experiencing love and heartache, and sharing everything with their high-spirited friend, Roellyn. The novel's first half follows the girls from early childhood to their teens; the second half focuses on their seventeenth summer, when the arrival of two handsome strangers occasions both swooning romance and enough wild confusion to rival Shakespeare's most outrageous comedies. The rules governing the Truth-Telling and Safe-Keeping gifts sometimes feel too conveniently flexible, and Eleda—a slightly rigid personality, as befitting her Truth-Telling role—may appeal to readers less than her sister and the vivacious Roellyn. But the comforting fairy-tale rhythms of the girls' stories exert an irresistible pull, and Shinn's numerous fans will welcome a second helping of the refreshing tale spinning and charmingly homespun, village-centered fantasy culture that marked *The Safe-Keeper's Secret* (2004). —Jennifer Mattson

Shusterman, Neal. *Unwind*. 2007. 352p. Simon & Schuster (9781416912040). Gr. 6–9.

Following in the footsteps of Jonathan Swift, Shusterman uncorks a Modest Proposal of his own to solve a Pro-Life/Pro-Choice dilemma. Set in a future in which abortions are outlawed but parents have the option of signing over their 13- to 17-year-olds to be used as organ donors, the tale focuses on 16-year-old Connor, who falls in with other prospective Unwinds and finds a temporary refuge (thanks to a clandestine organization with its own peculiar agenda) before being captured and sent to Happy Jack Harvest Camp. Though laced with intrigue, betrayals, and narrow squeaks, the story is propelled less by the plot (which is largely a series of long set pieces) than by an ingeniously developed cast and premise. But even readers who gravitate more to plot-driven fiction will find this present-tense page-turner thrilling, though it's guaranteed to leave some feeling decidedly queasy—despite the (improbable) happy ending. —John Peters

Smith, Andrew. *The Marbury Lens*. 2010. 368p. Feiwel and Friends (9780312613426). Gr. 10–12.

Smith follows his last excavation of darkness, *In the Path of Falling Objects* (2009), with a read that is as disorienting as it is daring. Jack is abducted, drugged, and tied by an ankle to the bed of a sexual predator named Freddie for days before escaping. He tells only his best friend, Connor, but shared secrets can come laced with poison. During a summer trip to London, a stranger hands Jack a pair of glasses that peer into a corpse-strewn wasteland called Marbury, where Jack is on the run from a horde of men turned beasts led by Connor. As Jack flips between worlds, the sickening draw of Marbury becomes like a drug, hollowing him out as an inner voice screams: "Freddie Horvath did something to your brain and you better get help, Jack." A love interest tries to help Jack weather the onslaught of guilt and loathing, and yet another narrative layer comes from the story of a boy who was hung more than a century ago and whose ghost is now either haunting or helping Jack in both worlds. Mixing a trauma reckoning with dark, apocalyptic fantasy and notes of psychological horror, this commandeering novel's multiplicity is elusively complex yet never complicated: although the many gut-quivering story elements are not clearly defined, they always speak to each other, and Smith wisely leaves much up to the reader. People will talk about this book and try to figure it out and maybe try to shake it off. But they won't be able to. —Ian Chipman

Soto, Gary. *The Afterlife*. 2003. 176p. Harcourt (9780152047740). Gr. 7–10.

Combing his hair in the dirty bathroom of a club where a dance is being held, 17-year-old Chuy makes the mistake of telling the rodent-faced guy next to him that he likes his shoes. The young man returns the compliment by stabbing Chuy to death. Where any other story would end, Soto's begins. It follows Chuy for several days after his death, as the teenager recounts what he sees and experiences. His parents grieve, and his mother asks a cousin to kill Chuy's assailant; then he goes to his high school's basketball game and sees the effect his death has had on his friends, realizing their sadness will be fleeting. He saves the life of a homeless man, albeit only temporarily, and improbably, he finds his first girlfriend, Crystal, a specter who died from an overdose. Crystal's character is not as well developed as Chuy's, but their relationship is beautifully evoked, with Chuy grasping every thread of love he can as he slowly disappears. Soto has remade the setting of *Our Town* into Fresno, California, and he not only paints the scenery brilliantly but also captures the pain that follows an early death. In many ways, this is as much a story about a hardscrabble place as it is about a boy who is murdered. Both pulse with life and will stay in memory. —Ilene Cooper

Stiefvater, Maggie. *Lament: The Faerie Queen's Deception*. Illus. by Julia Jeffrey. 2008. 336p. Flux (9780738713700). Gr. 9–12.

Sixteen-year-old Deirdre Monaghan, a gifted harpist who regularly plays for weddings and other events, has the kind of stage fright that makes her physically ill before a performance, which is an inauspicious way to start a romance; but while vomiting before a competition, she meets a gorgeous boy who comes into the restroom to hold her hair. He is Luke Dillon, a flautist who proceeds to accompany her in a truly stellar performance. As four-leaf clovers start appearing everywhere, Deirdre develops telekinetic powers and encounters strange, unworldly people who seem to bear her ill will. Her best friend, James, also a talented musician; her beloved grandmother; and her mother all are in danger, as Deirdre is targeted by the queen of Faerie. Deirdre eventually discovers that she is a cloverhand, a person who can see the denizens of faerie, and Luke, not the only immortal who has her in his sights, is a gallowglass, an assassin assigned by the queen of Faerie to kill Deirdre but who falls in love with her instead. This beautiful and out-of-the-ordinary debut novel, with its authentic depiction of Celtic Faerie lore and dangerous forbidden love in a contemporary American setting, will appeal to readers of Nancy Werlin's *Impossible* (2008) and Stephenie Meyer's Twilight series. Illustrations by Jeffrey are fitting. —Diana Tixier Herald

Stiefvater, Maggie. *The Raven Boys*. 2012. 416p. Scholastic (9780545424929). Gr. 9–12.

The latest from Stiefvater, author of the Printz Honor Book *The Scorpio Races* (2011), defies easy synopsis. Consider that it is the story of 16-year-old Blue, from a family of psychics though she herself is not one. However, she does have the gift of amplifying others' psychic experiences. Oh, and she has been told that if she kisses her true love, he will die. Then there are wealthy, handsome Gansey and his three friends, Adam, Ronan, and Noah, all of whom are "Raven Boys," students at the prestigious Aglionby Academy. Gansey is obsessed with finding the body of the legendary sleeping king of Wales, Owen Glendower, using ley lines, invisible lines of energy that connect spiritual places. That a sinister someone else is also searching for the sleeping king adds chill-inducing danger to the complex and artful plot. Indeed, reading this novel is like walking through a tangled thicket and coming across one unexpected and wonderful surprise after another. In that respect, the book is marvelous, for not only is it filled with marvels, but it is also a marvel of imagination and, more prosaically, structure. Rich, too, in characterization, this fantasy-mystery rises to the level of serious literature, leaving readers hungering for more. And more there will be, for this is the first volume of a planned quartet. Waiting for the next book in the Raven Cycle will indeed be a test of readers' patience. —Michael Cart

Stiefvater, Maggie. *The Scorpio Races*. 2011. 416p. Scholastic (9780545224901). Gr. 8–12.

The island of Thisby, somewhere near Britain and replete with cars and electricity, is nevertheless fantastical, the home base of a fierce breed of water horses, the *capaill uisce*, man-eaters who rise from the autumn seas to terrorize the islanders. They can be captured and somewhat tamed, however, and once a year the island hosts a tourist draw, the Scorpio Races, a beachside contest often fatal to the riders. Sean Kendrick is one of the racers, a four-time champion on his trusty steed. Kate "Puck" Connolly is new to the races and the first woman rider. Due to a loophole in the rules, Kate's riding a regular horse, her beloved Dove, which she trusts to run true against the more frightening contestants. Both riders have deeper personal motives for wanting to win. Filling it with loving descriptions of wet, wind-tossed Thisby as well as exciting equine action, Stiefvater has created a thrilling backdrop for the love story that blooms between Sean and Puck. And in the water horses, based on mostly Celtic legends, she's created scary yet compelling forces of nature. A book appealing to lovers of fantasy, horse stories, romance, and action-adventure alike, this seems to have a shot at being a YA blockbuster.
—Karen Cruze

Stiefvater, Maggie. *Shiver*. 2009. 400p. Scholastic (9780545123266). Gr. 9–12.

Stiefvater would like to remind you that werewolves can be just as sexy as those headline-hogging vampires. Grace has always had a thing for the wolves in the woods behind her house, and when she finally meets the human form of a particularly enchanting wolf, Sam, the two cling to each other with the force of destiny. Time is running out, though, as these lycanthropes don't change with full moons but rather each year spend less time as humans and more as wolves, until the balance completely tips them into the animal world. While the two leads are almost entirely defined by how much they love each other, Stiefvater is able to take their romance seriously without turning it into an overly brooding affair, and defines their interactions with a fresh sense of humor and playful back-and-forths. A ticking clock provides plenty of dramatic tension throughout, while elegant writing that is especially intuitive about the animal world sets this apart from the bulk of paranormal romances.
—Ian Chipman

★ Stroud, Jonathan. *The Amulet of Samarkand*. 2003. 464p. Hyperion/Miramax (9780786818594). Gr. 6–12.

Picture an alternative London where the Parliament, composed of powerful magicians, rules the British empire. When five-year-old Nathaniel's parents sell him to the government to become a magician's apprentice, the boy is stripped of his past and is given over for training to a grim, mid-level magician from the Ministry of Internal Affairs. Over the next seven years, Nathaniel studies the lessons given by his cold master, but in secret he delves into advanced magic books, gaining skill beyond his years: he summons a djinn to steal the powerful amulet of Samarkand. Inspired by a desire for revenge, this bold act leads to danger and death. Nathaniel's third-person narrative alternates with the first-person telling of Bartimaeus the djinn, a memorable and highly entertaining character. Rude, flippant, and cocky, his voice reflects the injustice of his millennia of service to powerful magicians who have summoned him to do their capricious bidding. His informative and sometimes humorous asides appear in footnotes, an unusual device in fiction, but one that serves a useful purpose here. Stroud creates a convincingly detailed secondary world with echoes of actual history and folklore. The strong narrative thrust of the adventure will keep readers involved, but the trouble that is afoot in London extends beyond the exploits here. The unresolved mysteries will be more fully explored in the next two volumes of the trilogy. One of the liveliest and most inventive fantasies of recent years.
—Carolyn Phelan

Stroud, Jonathan. ***The Golem's Eye.*** **2004. 464p. Hyperion/Miramax (9780786818600). Gr. 7–12.**

This sequel to *The Amulet of Samarkand* (2003) takes up the story two years later, in 1868. According to Stroud's alternate history, London is governed by powerful magicians who keep the commoners in line through intimidation. Among the magicians maneuvering for power is the rather unlikable Nathaniel, now 14. When a golem destroys part of the British Museum, Nathaniel is sent to Prague to investigate the creature's origin. Once again, he calls on the powerful djinn Bartimaeus, one of the more memorable characters in fantasy literature, to help achieve his goals. Though bound by enchantments, Bartimaeus has a mind of his own and an ironic attitude that colors his witty commentary. Chapters narrated in first-person by Bartimaeus are interspersed with third-person narratives focused on Nathaniel or Kitty, a determined young commoner who appeared briefly in the first book. With a much larger role now, she emerges as a sympathetic young protagonist fighting against the injustices perpetrated by the ruling magicians. A dark, intriguing offering in a highly original fantasy series. —Carolyn Phelan

Stroud, Jonathan. ***Heroes of the Valley.*** **2009. 480p. Hyperion (9781423109662). Gr. 6–10.**

This refreshingly stand-alone adventure from the author of the Bartimaeus trilogy is a world apart from most contemporary fantasies, built akin to a double-layered Norse heroic epic. An unnamed valley is home to 12 houses descended from different heroes who long ago banded together to drive the monstrous Trows from their homeland. Now the valley is mostly peaceful, and the residents' sole affiliation with adventure is in retelling and arguing over the finer points of their namesake heroes' exploits. Young Halli Sveinsson (a likable prankster whose dominant characteristic is stubby-leggedness) of the House of Svein embarks on what he dreams will be a quest for vengeance and glory equal to those of his ancestor, but he quickly comes to realize that legend and lore have little relation to reality. Alongside the leisurely yet assured pacing and lively touches of humor, Stroud has crafted a credible and absorbing cultural construct—folkloric hero worship—with masterful prose that evokes two very different epochs in the valley, each with a distinct flavor of high adventure. The chasm that separates Halli from Svein becomes manifestly evident when Halli's moment of heroism arrives, and Stroud earns each and every gasp and cheer he'll garner from this very different sort of fantasy. Funny, exciting, thoughtful, and, most of all, timeless in the way of all tales worth spinning again and again. —Ian Chipman

Stroud, Jonathan. ***Ptolemy's Gate. 1v.*** **2006. 512p. Hyperion/Miramax (9780786818617). Gr. 6–9.**

The final volume in the Bartimaeus trilogy reveals more backstory and exposes greater complexity in the characters, even as the plot thunders along toward its colossal climax. The narrative alternates between first-person chapters from the djinni Bartimaeus' point of view to third-person chapters focused on Nathaniel, the magician, and Kitty, the commoner. Although Bartimaeus has lost none of his caustic wit, another side of his character is revealed through scenes in ancient Egypt and in the spirit world. A cabinet minister, Nathaniel sees the traditional power structure crumble around him, feels his own moral compass grow stronger, and takes actions that once would have been impossible for him. Now they seem inevitable. Kitty, after secretly studying magic, takes a challenge that few magicians would have dared: entering the spirit world and returning. Stroud's picture of this alternate world is one of the most remarkable scenes in recent fantasies. It leads readers' imaginations outside the realm of physical reality and offers an awareness of that reality as seen from the outside. For fans of Bartimaeus, Nathaniel, and Kitty, this will be the most satisfying volume of the three, as questions are answered and hidden depths are revealed. For readers who loved the earlier volumes for the sheer adventure, this, with its battles, magic, and great crashing conclusion, will not disappoint. A worthy ending to an exceptional saga. —Carolyn Phelan

Stroud, Jonathan. ***The Ring of Solomon.*** **2010. 416p. Hyperion (9781423123729). Gr. 6–9.**

Called a Bartimaeus Novel, Stroud's latest opens in a time and place (950 BCE Jerusalem) so far removed from the nineteenth-century British setting of the self-contained Bartimaeus trilogy that even the word *prequel* overstates the connection. Still, one unforgettable character from the trilogy energizes the current book as well. After outwitting and slaying his master in the opening chapters here, the mouthy, sardonic djinni named Bartimaeus is summoned to the service of yet another magician from King Solomon's court. Meanwhile, across the desert in Sheba, a young royal guard called Asmira embarks on a dangerous quest, hoping to save the queen and their land by stealing King Solomon's ring. Although Stroud's writing is never less than inventive and entertaining, the first 100-page section feels like a prelude to the rest of the novel, which takes off when idealistic Asmira encounters jaded Bartimaeus and they begin to make their way toward Solomon and his ring of power. The climactic scenes hold surprises for the reader as well as the characters. As in the trilogy, some chapters are related in third person, while others are narrated by Bartimaeus, and the latter chapters often include informative and amusing footnotes in his distinctive voice. A riveting adventure for Bartimaeus fans, old and new. —Carolyn Phelan

Taylor, Laini. Illus. by Jim Di Bartolo. *Lips Touch: Three Times*. 2009. 272p. Scholastic/Arthur A. Levine (9780545055857). Gr. 8–12.

Look beyond the title and cover art: Taylor's three novellas form a triptych of beautiful fantasy writing reminiscent of Charles de Lint and Neil Gaiman. Kisses are the unifying theme, with each story offering a different sort of locking lips, from giddy seduction to harsh power play. In "Goblin Fruit," misfit Kizzy meets a fascinating new student, an unbelievably gorgeous young man who ignores the popular girls to seek her out. Taylor tantalizingly foreshadows the ambiguous ending, teasing and enticing the reader much as Jack Husk entices Kizzy. "Spicy Little Curses Such as These" is set in India and offers intriguing and culturally respectful glimpses of both Indian religion and British colonialism. "Hatchling" reveals a fully realized world of sometimes malevolent immortals who steal and raise human babies as their pets. Present-day teen sensibilities blend with artful allusions to mythology and magic, pulling the reader into rich fantasy realms. The cover's close-up of a lovely woman's red lips, with red-orange flames licking at the superimposed title, lacks the powerful, delicately structured, and subtle poetry of Taylor's stories. But Di Bartolo, Taylor's husband, provides skillfully detailed pen-and-ink illustrations that are a fine match for the lyrical, romantic text. —Debbie Carton

Thompson, Kate. *The New Policeman*. 2007. 448p. Greenwillow (9780061174278). Gr. 7–10.

Heart-pounding Irish music is the common ground between material and magical worlds in this ambitious fantasy, which begins in western Ireland. When J. J. Liddy is 15, his mother jokingly asks for a birthday present of more time. From an eccentric neighbor, J. J. learns to his astonishment that his mother's request may not be impossible to fill. Bravely venturing into an alternate fairy world, J. J. takes on a thrilling, epic quest in which he confronts dark family rumors and tries to repair a cosmic time leak between his world and "the land of eternal youth." Thompson packs her mesmerizing, chaotic novel with Irish culture (including phrases defined in a glossary), interconnected mysteries, and sly questions about the stresses of contemporary life and the age-old frictions between religion and folklore. Readers will quickly overlook any creaky plot connections and fall eagerly into the rich, comic language and the captivating characters and scenes, particularly those that feature musicians (including talented J. J.), who play the "wild, anarchic music" that bridges worlds. Musical scores for Irish tunes (some written by Thompson) close each chapter in this soulful, wildly imagined tale that has already won several British awards, including the Guardian Children's Book Prize and the Whitbread Children's Book Award. Suggest it to fans of O. R. Melling's *The Hunter's Moon* (2005) and Eoin Colfer's Artemis Fowl books. —Gillian Engberg

Thomas, Lex. *Quarantine: The Loners*. 2012. 406p. Egmont (9781606843291). Gr. 10–12.

Take Michael Grant's *Gone* (2008) and Veronica Roth's *Divergent* (2011), rattle them in a cage until they're ready to fight to the death, and you'll have something like this nightmarish debut. It's an apocalypse writ small: a sick teen infects a Colorado high school with a disease so deadly that half the building is blown up by the military and the rest is sealed inside a giant dome. Every two weeks the ceiling is split for an air drop of food and supplies, and it's during these drops that the 1,000 surviving kids—split into warring cliques with names like the Nerds, the Sluts, and the Freaks—fight, steal, and even kill to make good. Because of a precontagion feud with Sam, the leader of Varsity (the jocks' gang), David is forced to eke out a loner's existence. But while protecting his younger brother, Will, from the horrors of the darkened hallways, David becomes an underground hero—which begins to infuriate Will, who also longs for the spotlight. Though not totally implausible, this is for fans of gritty sf dystopia, and Thomas' whirlwind pace, painful details ("old socks in a zip-lock freezer bag" serve as one character's pillow), simmering sexual content, and moments of truly shocking ultraviolence thrust this movie-ready high-school thriller to the head of the class. —*Daniel Kraus*

Tiffany, Grace. *Ariel*. 2005. 240p. HarperCollins/ Laura Geringer (9780060753276). Gr. 9–12.

Born from the dreams of a shipwrecked sailor, Ariel, the spirit from Shakespeare's *The Tempest*, sparks this retelling, or, perhaps more accurately, pretelling. When the sailor dies, Ariel does not, and she spends the following centuries shifting from one fantastical form to another, amusing herself in solitude until a very practical and very pregnant woman named Sycorax lands on her island to give birth to Caliban. Sycorax's lack of imagination confounds, then diminishes Ariel until she is weak enough to be imprisoned in a tree for her unwillingness to offer Sycorax any practical assistance. It is there Ariel remains while Caliban grows from infant to child, there that she becomes increasingly enraged. Preying on the dreams of the child, Ariel seeks revenge. By the time Prospero and his daughter, Miranda, arrive on the island, Ariel has found a way to manipulate certain tendencies in the human mind to gain her freedom and increase her power. This lush, lyrical, and elegantly expressive work is a strong mix of solid narrative storytelling, sensitive characterization, and fantasy. A familiarity with *The Tempest* enriches the reading but is not required, especially as the author so thoroughly liberates the story. An outstanding addition to Shakespearean retellings for strong teen readers. —Holly Koelling

Tomlinson, Heather. *Aurelie: A Faerie Tale*. 2008. 192p. Holt (9780805082760). Gr. 7–10.

This intriguing fantasy is set in a well-developed, vaguely northern European land where humans coexist with supernatural beings largely indifferent to their concerns. From their childhood friend Loic, a shape-shifting river drac, humans Netta, Aurelie, and Garin are gifted with the ability to see the Fae—fairy creatures who inhabit a mesmerizing world. As they grow older, though, the devoted friends grow apart: Netta is blinded, Aurelie becomes heir to her father's kingdom, and handsome Garin returns to his own country. Graceful prose leads the reader through a complex chronological narrative and a Shakespearean tangle of love stories. Aurelie's struggle to unite her friends and her world provides the novel's anchor, but her coming-of-age story, told in third-person accounts, alternates with first-person reports from other characters, who are all well developed. Tomlinson paces her tale well, building suspense both in the political arena, through increasing hostilities between families, and in personal relationships; Loic courts Aurelie, for example, even though each prefers another. It is the power of childhood friendship that overcomes the barriers of nationality and species to unite the characters. A stirring read. —Kathleen Isaacs

Tomlinson, Heather. *The Swan Maiden*. 2007. 304p. Holt (9780805082753). Gr. 6–10.

Sixteen-year-old Doucette is the third daughter of the comte and comtesse of Aigleron. Unlike her two older sisters, who are magical swan maidens with the freedom to fly and control their own lives, Doucette is being trained to be a noblewoman fit for a financially beneficial arranged marriage. Imagine Doucette's surprise when she finds that she, too, is a swan maiden;

her parents have lied about her identity and hidden her own dove-gray cloak of feathers. Defying her mother, she flies into the world, eager to claim her magical birthright and her own true love, Jaume the sheperd's son. In her debut novel, Tomlinson has melded several French fairy tales into a beautiful fantasy. Her descriptions of the swan maidens' transformations are so vivid that readers will imagine their own abrupt change from human to bird. The three trials that Jaume must complete to win Doucette's hand in marriage are far too realistic to be read without dismay and discomfort, and Doucette's and Jaume's love for each other is so tender that it will bring a smile to even the most cynical readers. Tomlinson is also able to convey the difficult choices freedom brings, especially for women contemplating love and marriage. Layered, elegantly written, and filled with unexpected twists and turns, *The Swan Maiden* soars with grace and power. —Frances Bradburn

Tomlinson, Heather. *Toads and Diamonds*. 2010. 288p. Holt (9780805089684). Gr. 8–12.

Set in the fictional Indian land of Hundred Kingdom, Tomlinson's memorable novel employs magic realism to explore a universal truth: an individual's gifts and talents are not always as they might seem. Stepsisters Diribani and Tana are blessed by the goddess Naghaliji in very different ways. When Diribani speaks, flowers and gemstones fall from her mouth. Tana's talent seems to be more of a curse: she produces frogs and snakes when she talks. While Diribani is held at the opulent court of the Believers, where her every jewel is collected and tallied for the kingdom's profit, Tana is chased from her village by its snake-fearing residents. Taking on the disguise of a mute stable hand, she returns, and with her unusual abilities, she saves the land. Tomlinson is a master craftsman, and as in her highly regarded *The Swan Maiden* (2007), she creates a vivid setting. Lavish details starkly contrast the two girls' lives and personalities while emphasizing their strength, purpose, and enduring love for each other, despite their predicaments. The complexities of the cultural backstory pose a challenge to readers, but this beautifully embroidered adventure is well worth the effort. —Frances Bradburn

Turner, Megan Whalen. *A Conspiracy of Kings*. 2010. 336p. Greenwillow (9780061870934). Gr. 7–10.

Following *The Thief*, a 1997 Newbery Honor Book, and *The King of Attolia*, a 2007 Best Book for Young Adults, Turner continues her exquisite series with another rich story that examines peace, power, leadership, and loyalty. After initial, tense prison scenes focused on Eugenides, the king of Attolia, the novel's viewpoint switches from third to first person, and Sophos, the reluctant king of Sounis who prefers poetry to politics, relates the adventures that precipitated his rise to questionable power. Tutors have drilled Sophos in imaginary attacks, but after he loses his family in a real invasion, he is bereft and goes into hiding as a slave on a nobleman's estate in order to avoid his sovereign responsibilities. Even though Eugenides' fans will miss his presence, he continues to pull strings from the sidelines as he joins leaders in high-priced alliances and prepares for an invasion. Turner's plotting remains deft, and the subtlety with which she balances her characters' inner and outer worlds will delight both series newcomers and fans, who will be waiting to grab this stand-out, stand-alone adventure, filled with all the expected intrigue and political machinations, from the shelves.
—Cindy Dobrez

★ Turner, Megan Whalen. *The King of Attolia*. 2006. 400p. Greenwillow (9780060835774). Gr. 8–11.

Fans of the irascible Thief of Eddis will recall that Gen and his frosty nemesis, Attolia, exchanged vows of love in *The Queen of Attolia* (2000). This second follow-up to Turner's 1997 Newbery Honor Book, *The Thief*, follows the turbulent months just after their union, primarily from the perspective of Gen's reluctant personal assistant, Costis, who despises the "goat-footed throne-stealing interloper" as much as the rest of Attolia's insubordinate court. Gradually, though, Costis gleans that there is more to King Gen than his oafish, irascible behavior would suggest. Turner's wide-ranging, third-person narrative tantalizingly limits readers' access to Gen, leaving readers to sift truth from Gen-masterminded subterfuge and to weigh his detractors' prejudices undiluted. The challenge of internalizing so many new characters may halt some readers, and many will mourn the replacement of concrete, action-oriented exploits with this situation's more subtle courtly and diplomatic stratagems. Staunch fans of Turner's roguish hero, particularly those who enjoyed the middle-grade-friendly *Thief* several years ago and whose reading capabilities have ripened, will reap the greatest rewards here. —Jennifer Mattson

Turner, Megan Whalen. *The Queen of Attolia*. 2000. 288p. Greenwillow (9780688174231). Gr. 6–9.

Gen, the likable, slippery rogue of *The Thief* (1997), is back, gliding easily through the secret passages and back rooms of the queen of Attolia's palace. This time, to his amazement and dismay, he is caught because Attolia's guards seem to know his escape route as well as he does. Badly beaten and flung into a dank dungeon, he awaits his fate. Meanwhile, the queen of Eddis cuts off the flow of water to Attolia, demanding the safe return of her thief. When Gen is returned alive but minus his right hand, the queen of Eddis releases the water but orders her border troops to confiscate the goods of the next 10 Attolian traders. Thus, war escalates between the two kingdoms, egged on by the unctuous, manipulative Mede ambassador to the Attolian court, whose nation covets both Attolia and Eddis. There's a great deal of political maneuvering and battling as well as individual angst on the part of the two queens and Gen, until Gen finally emerges from his self-imposed isolation to take part in resolving the conflict—by stealing the queen of Attolia herself. Turner maintains her well-created world and believable characterizations in a tale that once again includes a touch of magic. —Sally Estes

Vande Velde, Vivian. *Heir Apparent*. 2002. 336p. Harcourt (9780152045609). Gr. 6–9.

The terrifying implications of virtual reality gone awry get a lighthearted spin in Velde's latest novel, which is set in a technologically advanced future. Smart, alienated Giannine decides to celebrate her fourteenth birthday at a computer gaming center, where she chooses an elaborate, virtual-reality role-playing game. Set in medieval times, the game turns Giannine into an exiled princess who must stay alive until she can return to court and assume the throne. As Giannine plays, a group of censorship advocates break into the computer system, and Giannine suddenly discovers that she must complete the game in the allotted time or die. The evocative details, the plausible technology, and Giannine's sharp-witted narration will completely immerse readers in Giannine's world as she makes life-threatening decisions and evades danger. The thrilling sf drama and intricate game details will capture the Dungeons and Dragons set, and the slapstick humor, tough girl protagonist, and fairy-tale plot will widen the audience. A great title to spark discussion about censorship issues. —Gillian Engberg

Werlin, Nancy. *Impossible*. 2008. 384p. Dial (9780803730021). Gr. 7–11.

Date rape, a pregnant teen, and a shotgun wedding (of sorts)—must be a YA problem novel circa 1985, right? Not really. From a hidden letter, 17-year-old Lucy Scarborough learns "all sorts of melodramatic, ridiculous, but true things" about the circumstances surrounding her rape on prom night, her subsequent pregnancy, and why therapy and her signature pragmatism won't be much help against an ancient fairy's curse. By the Edgar Award–winning novelist whose thrillers include *The Rules of Survival* (2006), this tale, inspired by the song "Scarborough Fair," showcases the author's finesse at melding genres. Although it's perhaps overly rosy that Lucy's devoted foster parents take the curse in stride, Werlin earns high marks for the tale's graceful interplay between wild magic and contemporary reality—from the evil fairy lord disguised as a charismatic social worker to the main players' skepticism as they attempt to solve the curse's three archaic puzzles ("We've formed the Fellowship of the Ring when really we should've all just gone on medication"). Meantime, Lucy's marriage to childhood pal Zach, a development unusual in YA fiction but convincing in context, underlies the catapulting suspense with a notion that will be deeply gratifying to many teens: no destiny is unalterable, especially not when faced with tender love magic, "weird and hilarious and sweeter than [Lucy] ever dreamed," worked by truly mated souls. —Jennifer Mattson

Westerfeld, Scott. *Leviathan*. Illus. by Keith Thompson. 2009. 448p. Simon & Schuster/Simon Pulse (9781416971733). Gr. 7–10.

Instead of the Victorian era most often found in the steampunk genre, Westerfeld sets his new series in a Europe hovering on the edge of WW I. The ingenious premise is that Europe is divided not only into traditional historical camps, but also into Darwinists, who genetically manipulate animal "life-strands" into beasts and even whole self-contained ecosystems with wondrous capabilities, and Clankers, whose imposing constructions of metal and gears are a marvel of technological wizardry. Deryn Sharp, from Darwinist England, disguises herself as a boy to enlist on the *Leviathan*, a flying whale-ship, while Prince Alek, recently orphaned son of Archduke Ferdinand, finds himself on the run in a sort of walking Clanker tank. The plot is boosted almost entirely by exciting and sometimes violent fight sequences, but reading about (and seeing, thanks to Thompson's ample, lavish, and essential illustrations) the wildly imaginative creatures and machines provides nearly as much drive. Fans of Philip Reeve's *Mortal Engines* (2003) or Kenneth Oppel's *Airborn* (2004) will be right at home in Westerfeld's alternate reality. —Ian Chipman

Westerfeld, Scott. *Uglies*. 2005. 448p. Simon & Schuster/Simon Pulse (9780689865381). Gr. 7–10.

Fifteen-year-old Tally's eerily harmonious, postapocalyptic society gives extreme makeovers to teens on their sixteenth birthdays, supposedly conferring equivalent evolutionary advantages to all. When a top-secret agency threatens to leave Tally ugly forever unless she spies on runaway teens, she agrees to infiltrate the Smoke, a shadowy colony of refugees from the "tyranny of physical perfection." At first baffled and revolted by the rebels' choices, Tally eventually bonds with one of their leaders and begins to question the validity of institutionalized mutilation—especially as it becomes clear that the government's surgeons may be doing more than cosmetic nipping and tucking. Although the narrative's brisk pace is more successful in scenes of hover-boarding action than in convincingly developing Tally's key relationships, teens will sink their teeth into the provocative questions about invasive technology, image-obsessed society, and the ethical quandaries of a mole-turned-ally. These elements, along with the obvious connections to reality programs such as Miami Slice, will surely cause this ingenious series debut to cement Westerfeld's reputation for high-concept YA fiction that has wide appeal. Suggest M. T. Anderson's *Feed* (2002) and Westerfeld's own *So Yesterday* (2004) to readers antsy for the next installment.
—Jennifer Mattson

Whitcomb, Laura. *A Certain Slant of Light*. 2005. 288p. Houghton/Graphia (9780618585328). Gr. 9–12.

In sensuous prose, Helen, who has been dead for 130 years, describes what it's like to live as Light, clinging to a human host, then reentering an empty human body and becoming physically and emotionally attuned to the world. Helen is startled when she realizes that a student in her host's English class can see her. James, too, is Light, but he has taken over the body of Billy, who almost overdosed on drugs. Their joy at finding one another turns quickly to love, and James helps Helen locate an empty body that she can inhabit. Fellow student Jennifer seems the perfect choice, but the unhappiness in her fundamentalist family, as well as the chaos of Billy's household, mix uneasily with the pleasures the spirits are rekindling. Whitcomb writes beautifully, especially when she is describing the physical delights of sexual love and the horror the spirits endure as they fight through their personal hells to reach the other side. Her stereotypical portrayal of a Christian family jars when juxtaposed with the rest of the writing. Still, in many ways this will be irresistible to teens. —Ilene Cooper

Wooding, Chris. *The Haunting of Alaizabel Cray*. 2004. 304p. Scholastic/Orchard (9780439546560). Gr. 9–12.

In Wooding's alternative, Victorian London, a new plague is under way: an infestation of demonic creatures known as wych-kin. Thaniel Fox, a 17-year-old wych-hunter who calls forth both Buffy the Vampire Slayer and Indiana Jones, spends his time reducing wych-kin populations with methods that combine magic, superstition, and good old-fashioned gunslinging. After stumbling upon an obviously traumatized young woman on one of his expeditions, he swiftly discovers that she has escaped from the clutches of a powerful cult called the Fraternity. The connections between Alaizabel's plight, rising numbers of wychkin, and the Fraternity's plans are revealed by tantalizing degrees, as Thaniel; Alaizabel; Thaniel's guardian, Cathaline; and several colorful allies join forces to combat evil on a terrifying scale. This is dark fare, often graphically violent (a Jack-the-Ripper-type serial killer plays a role), but not gratuitously so. Wooding delivers characters to care about, including strong-willed and capable young women, deliciously scary bogeys drawn from world legend and lore, and philosophical underpinnings suggesting an imagination heavily steeped in Tolkien and Pullman. Though the action bogs down a bit in the middle as Wooding assembles his cast of good guys, the atmospheric scene setting and attention to chilling detail ensure his hold on fantasy enthusiasts. —Jennifer Mattson

Wooding, Chris. ***Storm Thief.*** **2006. 306p. Scholastic (9780439865135). Gr. 6–9.**

This novel from the author of *The Haunting of Alaizabel Cray* (2004) and *Poison* (2005) is a postapocalyptic fantasy with trappings reminiscent of the 1995 film *Waterworld*. The citizens of Orokos, a crumbling city surrounded by an endless ocean, live at the mercy of probability storms that "might steal a baby's eyes and replace them with buttons, or turn a house into sugar paper." Together with the chaotic conditions, the city's totalitarian government makes life miserable for marginalized "ghetto-folk" like teen thieves Moa and Rail. After the companions stumble upon a valuable artifact, they must flee pursuers who covet their find. Their journey brings them into contact with a half-mechanical homunculus and a group of rebels preparing to escape the city permanently. A familiarity with *Frankenstein and Rime of the Ancient Mariner*, clear sources of inspiration, will enrich appreciation of the novel, although most will simply like the inventive premise and the protagonists' tender relationship, never overtly romantic but replete with unspoken yearnings. —Jennifer Mattson

Woodson, Jacqueline. ***Behind You.*** **2004. 128p. Putnam (9780399239885). Gr. 7–12.**

"Even if you turn your back on the world you left, you're still pulled toward it, you're still turning around—always—to look behind you. To make sure everyone's o.k.," says teenage Jeremiah, who first appeared in Woodson's *If You Come Softly* (1998). In this moving sequel, Jeremiah is dead, killed by New York City police bullets. Like the main character in Gary Soto's *Afterlife* (2003), Jeremiah watches over the people he has left behind—his girlfriend, Ellie; his friends; his divorced parents—as each struggles through grief and tries to "keep doing what the living do," ultimately finding new connections with one another and themselves. *Softly* alternates between Jeremiah and Ellie's voices. Here Woodson includes the first-person perspectives of several other characters, and with so many different voices, the narrative becomes crowded, diluting each character's story. Still, Woodson writes with impressive poetry about race, love, death, and what grief feels like—the things that "snap the heart"—and her characters' open strength and wary optimism will resonate with many teens.
—Gillian Engberg

Yancey, Rick. ***The Curse of the Wendigo.*** **2010. 448p. Simon & Schuster (9781416984504). Gr. 9–12.**

Examples of literary horror don't come much finer than *The Monstrumologist* (2009), and Yancey's second volume sustains that high bar with lush prose, devilish characterizations, and more honest emotion than any book involving copious de-facings (yes, you read that right) ought to have. The new case: lepto luranis, aka the Wendigo, a vampiric creature whose mythic origins have monstrumologists divided. If they accept the existence of mystic shape-shifters, is not their "science" balderdash? Dr. Pellinore Warthrop has no interest until his former true love appears and begs him to find her husband—once Warthrop's best friend—who has gone missing in search of the creature. Yes, female characters have arrived to the series and smashingly so, none better than Lilly, the talkative 13-year-old scientist who gives Warthrop's faithful assistant, Will, his first kiss. *The Monstrumologist* was more propulsive, but the worthy trade-off here is the introduction of an alternate, monster-plagued 1888 New York, complete with irresistible historical cameos. So far, Yancey has written both books in the Monstrumologist series as if they were the last, going for broke and playing for keeps, no matter who or what ends up on the chopping block. This is Warthrop's *The Hound of the Baskervilles*; if we hold our breath, maybe part 3 will come faster. —Daniel Kraus

Yancey, Rick. *The 5th Wave*. 2013. 480p. Putnam (9780399162411). Gr. 9–12.

The Monstrumologist series set a bar for YA horror nearly impossible to match. Can Yancey do the same for sf? He makes a hell of an effort with this ambitious series starter set in the aftermath of a crushing alien invasion in which the aliens themselves never appeared. Seven billion humans have died in the months following the appearance of a giant mother ship. Wave 1: an electromagnetic pulse rendering all machines useless. Wave 2: tsunamis wiping out coastal cities. Wave 3: "the Red Death," a deadly plague carried by birds. Wave 4: "Silencers," humans who were implanted with alien intelligence as fetuses. We don't even want to know about Wave 5—do we? Monstrumologist fans will be surprised to discover that Yancey grounds his multiperspective survivalist thriller in two fairly conventional YA voices: Cassie, 16, whose grim solitary existence changes when she is rescued by hunky but mysterious Evan; and "Zombie," 17, ex–sports star thrown into a brutal boot camp to train as an alien killer. Yancey's heartfelt, violent, paranoid epic, filled with big heroics and bigger surprises, is part *War of the Worlds*, part *Starship Troopers*, part *Invasion of the Body Snatchers*, and part *The Stand*, but just close enough to dystopic trends to make this a sure thing for reviewers and readers alike. —Daniel Kraus

Yancey, Rick. *The Isle of Blood*. 2011. 560p. Simon & Schuster (9781416984528). Gr. 9–12.

After fighting off headless hordes in *The Monstrumologist* (2009) and a face-eating specter in *Curse of the Wendigo* (2010), Dr. Pellinore Warthrop and his trusty 13-year-old assistant, Will Henry, are enjoying a rare moment of tranquility when they receive a most horrific package: a nest woven from human body parts and dripping with *pwdre ser*—"the rot of stars." It is the revolting work of the *typhoeus magnificum*, aka the Unseen One, aka the holy grail of monstrumology, a creature so ravenous it will eat itself. And it must be found! The relationship between Will and his master has never been more complex: Will, subservient for so long, finds his rebellious streak when Warthrop takes on a new, more qualified assistant, while Warthrop's mountainous ego threatens to destroy them all. The middle section, a good 300 pages steeped in British and Russian espionage, lumbers on occasion. But once a human finger falls from the sky on a mysterious island off of Egypt, the horror comes roaring back. This is more ponderous and unwieldy than its predecessors, but Yancey's skill as a stylist cannot be denied. Purportedly, this is the final entry in the Monstrumologist series; Pellinore Warthrop—that mad genius!—will be terribly missed. —Daniel Kraus

★ Yancey, Rick. *The Monstrumologist*. 2009. 448p. Simon & Schuster (9781416984481). Gr. 9–12.

With a roaring sense of adventure and enough viscera to gag the hardiest of gore hounds, Yancey's series starter might just be the best horror novel of the year. Will Henry is the 12-year-old apprentice to Pellinore Warthrop, a brilliant and self-absorbed monstrumologist—a scientist who studies (and when necessary, kills) monsters in late-1800s New England. The newest threat is the Anthropophagi, a pack of headless, shark-toothed bipeds, one of whom's corpse is delivered to Warthrop's lab courtesy of a grave robber. As the action moves from the dissecting table to the cemetery to an asylum to underground catacombs, Yancey keeps the shocks frequent and shrouded in a splattery miasma of blood, bone, pus, and maggots. The industrial-era setting is populated with leering, Dickensian characters, most notably the loathsome monster hunter hired by Warthrop to enact the highly effective "Maori Protocol" method of slaughter. Yancey's prose is stentorian and wordy, but it weaves a world that possesses a Lovecraftian logic and hints at its own deeply satisfying mythos. Most effective of all, however, is the weirdly tender relationship between the quiet, respectful boy and his strict, Darwinesque father figure. "Snap to!" is Warthrop's continued demand of Will, but readers will need no such needling. —Daniel Kraus

Yee, Paul. *Dead Man's Gold and Other Stories*. Illus. by Harvey Chan. 2002. 104p. Groundwood/Douglas & McIntyre (9780888994752). Gr. 6–12.

Drawing on ghost stories told among early Chinese immigrants in Canada and the U.S., Yee brings the supernatural right into daily life, setting the harsh facts on the edge of horror or redemption. His plain, beautiful words speak with brutal honesty in 10 short stories about the immigrant struggle: the backbreaking work in the gold mines, on the railroads, in the forests, laundries, kitchens; the anguish of leaving home, and of being left behind; the dreams of riches and reunion; the shock of prejudice and betrayal. The tales are arranged chronologically, beginning with the nineteenth-century migration from China to Gold Mountain in the Pacific Northwest, and ending in the 1950s in a city near the Atlantic. In one story a woman finally gets to join her husband in the New World, only to find that he has a "local" wife who speaks English and wears modern clothes. Young lovers imprisoned and separated by harsh immigration restrictions are united after death. A gold miner steals from his best friend; a farm worker pushes his brother into the river; then the past haunts the living and won't let go. An eerie full-page illustration by Chan at the start of each story captures the strange, unsettled world of those who leave home to find home. —Hazel Rochman

Yolen, Jane. *Sword of the Rightful King*. 2003. 368p. Harcourt (9780152025274). Gr. 6–9.

Yolen takes elements of Arthurian legend and makes them her own in this involving novel. The central image of the sword in the stone comes to prominence not as the way an unknown boy becomes king but as a means devised by Merlinnus the mage to bind the people's allegiance more firmly to the young King Arthur. Besides Arthur and Merlinnus, the narrative closely concerns Sir Gawaine, who is determined to stay loyal to Arthur despite his mother's traitorous plots against the king, and young Gawen, who arrives at court to train as a knight and becomes an assistant to Merlinnus instead. In Yolen's hands, many characters who have been colorful cardboard figures in other books come to life as sympathetic human beings. Even Sir Kay, for all his flaws, is somehow likable as portrayed here, and Arthur's affection for him is understandable. Yet all is not well in Arthur's realm, even at his court: evil is real, magic is dangerous, assassins are abroad, and power is the only language universally understood. The revelation of a secret creates a surprise ending that departs from traditional Arthurian legend, though many will find it a satisfying climax. Combining old and new, adventure and idealism, this will leave many readers hoping for a sequel that is just as well written and intriguingly crafted.
—Carolyn Phelan

Yovanoff, Brenna. *The Replacement*. 2010. 352p. Penguin/Razorbill (9781595143372). Gr. 9–12.

The light paranormals—think vampires, werewolves, angels, faeries, demons—that flood young adult lit often share a similar problem: by merely tweaking established archetypes, they feel largely interchangeable. No such pitfalls bedevil Yovanoff, whose first novel is not only startlingly conceived from the ground up but will still appeal to the legions craving doom, gloom, and, yes, romance. Mackie lives in Gentry, a small town that owes its history of good fortune to an uneasy relationship with the supernatural underground dwellers who protect them. Their price? Merely an annual human sacrifice, which they take in the form of a stolen baby, leaving behind a fragile nonhuman replacement. Mackie is such a replacement, and despite his allergies to iron and blood, he has somehow survived to be a teen—but now is about to meet his makers. The two separate menageries of monsters—housed in a slag heap and a dump hill—are almost Victorian in bearing and possess an apocalyptic Bradburian worldview: "'We are pandemonium and disaster. We are the dancing, gibbering horror of the world,'" says the baddest of them all, the Dirt Witch. The climax is not perhaps what it might be, but Yovanoff's unsettling villains and intriguing moral ambivalence make this effort shockingly original and frequently breathtaking. —Daniel Kraus

Zevin, Gabrielle. *All These Things I've Done*. 2011. 368p. Farrar (9780374302108). Gr. 9–12.

It's 2083, and New York is not what it used to be. But as things go, 16-year-old Anya Balanchine has it pretty good. She lives in an apartment overlooking Central Park (what's left of it) with her bedridden grandmother, her mentally challenged older brother, and her clever younger sister. Because Anya's family was involved in organized crime, importing illegal chocolate among other things, they're still protected. Or are they? As Anya becomes involved with Win, the son of the state's new district attorney, mob unrest is beginning to infringe upon her life. There are a number of details that could make readers say, "Really?" Seventy years from now, girls are still wearing uniforms to Catholic schools and eating in the cafeteria just like always, yet they don't remember the Statue of Liberty? But while some of the details are problematic, the sweep of the book is original and compelling. The talented Zevin writes Anya and Win's high-wire romance as jolting for both the participants and readers. She knows this is going nowhere good: he's a believer in love, and neither of them understands how outside influences are impacting their romance. The breathcatching ending will leave everyone looking forward to the next title in the Birthright series.
—Ilene Cooper

YOUNG ADULT NONFICTION, 2000–2013

One-Fifth of the Pie and Growing

Gillian Engberg

As in the world of adult nonfiction, the start of the twenty-first century was promising for nonfiction for young adults. The years between 2000 and the first half of 2013 saw many literary high-water marks, innovative genre benders, and bold new explorations into envelope-pushing subjects, all written specifically for a young adult audience. The numbers, however, told a more sobering story. As we tallied up our counts, we realized that nonfiction books still made up only a fifth, on average, of our best-of selections. Despite the obvious room for growth that these ratios suggest, the start of the twenty-first century still serves as a time line of exciting developments in YA nonfiction. In his foreword to this volume, Michael Cart spotlights some of those milestones, from nonfiction titles winning top honors—such as Elizabeth Partridge's *John Lennon: All I Want Is the Truth*, which was named a Printz Honor Book in 2006—to the establishment in 2009 of YALSA's Award for Excellence in Nonfiction for Young Adults, an award we hope will continue to spur authors and publishers to produce even more outstanding nonfiction titles written just for teens.

Our top selections represent many more milestone moments, including standout youth editions of adult titles on topics of vital interest to teens. For example, in *Chew on This: Everything You Don't Want to Know about Fast Food*, by Eric Schlosser and Charles Wilson (2006), and *The Omnivore's Dilemma: The Secrets behind What You Eat*, by Michael Pollan and Richie Chevat (2009), the authors accomplish far more than just superficial rewrites of the adult editions. With additional content and expertly distilled text, these volumes serve as terrific examples of how to present complex, urgent subjects to a young audience.

Potentially controversial subjects weren't reserved for YA fiction alone in recent years. Authors of YA nonfiction have written riveting books about teens facing death sentences (Susan Kuklin's *No Choirboy: Murder, Violence, and Teenagers on Death Row*, 2008), attempting suicide (Brent Runyon's autobiographical *The Burn Journals*, 2004), living with AIDS (Judd Winick's *Pedro and Me: Friendship, Loss, and What I Learned*, 2000), and serving time in prison (Jack Gantos' exceptional memoir, *Hole in My Life*, 2002). Without condescension, these books reflect the real world that teens inhabit, offering unforgettable personal stories in the context of the reliable facts behind the headlines.

As with our fiction lists, corralling all of these exceptional nonfiction selections into categories involved a great deal of deliberation, second-guessing, and re-sorting. Biographies were particularly challenging. Do we create a specific section to spotlight the many memorable accounts of famous lives, from Frida Kahlo to Bill Gates, written for teens? We finally settled on the broad categories of arts, history, poetry, science, and social studies, but even those groupings became complicated. Do we place Catherine Reef's *E. E. Cummings: A Poet's Life* (2006), which has a Dewey number of 811, in poetry or in arts, along with other biographies of writers? And what about all of the wonderful biographies in verse, such as Margarita Engle's powerful *The Poet Slave of Cuba: A Biography of Juan Francisco Manzano* (2006), Carole Boston Weatherford's *Becoming Billie Holiday* (2008), and Jeannine Atkins' *Borrowed Names: Poems about Laura Ingalls Wilder, Madam C. J. Walker, Marie Curie, and Their Daughters* (2010)?

We decided on what seemed to be obvious: prose biographies went into the categories that best suited their subjects, while verse biographies went into poetry, alongside the many noteworthy poetry collections and anthologies, including several notable collections written in teen voices, such as *You Hear Me? Poems and Writing by Teenage Boys* (2000) and *Things I Have to Tell You: Poems and Writing by Teenage Girls* (2001), both edited by Betsy Franco.

All of this wrangling and arguing and recategorizing created a wonderful opportunity to revisit and celebrate the best nonfiction books for young adults published between 2000 and the first half of 2013, and we invite you to join in the conversation—and the arguments. Our hope is that as you move through these pages, you find yourself agreeing or disagreeing with our selections, mentally moving titles into other categories, spotting omissions and rejecting our favorites, and gradually making up your own best-of lists. The more people who read and promote their favorites, the more teen readers—and the field of YA nonfiction—will benefit.

Arts

Angel, Ann. *Janis Joplin: Rise Up Singing*. **2010. 120p. illus. Abrams/Amulet (9780810983496). Gr. 9–12. 782.42166092.**

In an introduction to this long-overdue portrait of "the first queen of rock," Sam Andrew, Janis Joplin's former bandmate and best friend, says, "There was electricity in the air when Janis was around. . . . She was vulnerable, powerful, super wide open, talented, and interesting in a kind of terrifying way." Building from Andrew's full-hearted and contradictory description, Angel presents a nuanced account of the groundbreaking musician's life, beginning with her challenging adolescence in Port Arthur, Texas. After giving up on fitting in, she sang along to the blues on long drives with equally rebellious teen friends and learned that she had a powerful voice. Tracking back to Joplin's childhood, Angel then moves on to the singer's early years of studying and music-making before she finally grabbed attention with Andrew's band Big Brother and the Holding Company. Angel writes with both a reporter's forthright, detached tone and a fan's enthusiasm, and she includes numerous revealing quotes from friends and family members, all sourced in the appended notes and bibliography. Without sensationalizing, she also discusses Joplin's sex-drugs-and-rock-'n'-roll lifestyle, which ended with the singer's alcohol-and-heroin-induced death at the age of 27. A groovy page design, patterned in shades of purple and acid green; a lively annotated time line; and unforgettable archival images will pull even more attention to this captivating view of a musician rarely spotlighted in books for youth. —Gillian Engberg

Bernier-Grand, Carmen T. *Diego: Bigger Than Life*. **Illus. by David Diaz. 2009. 64p. Marshall Cavendish (9780761453833). Gr. 7–10. 759.972.**

In this well-written and beautifully illustrated volume, the life of Mexican artist Diego Rivera, best known for murals depicting working people, is introduced in free verse. Similar in format to Bernier-Grand's *César: Sí, se puede! Yes, We Can!* (2004) and *Frida: Viva la vida! Long Live Life!* (2007), the book offers a chronological sequence of poems, each appearing either on a single page accompanied by a small illustration or on a left-hand page with a full-page picture on the right. Almost all written in first person from the artist's point of view, the poems convey information succinctly within a context of colorful narrative and clearly expressed emotion. Each poem stands alone, yet some words, ideas, and images recur, creating an interconnected sequence. A three-page appended biography clarifies and amplifies the information in the verse. Also appended are a glossary, a chronology, a source bibliography, notes, and quotes from the artist. Apart from four reproductions of Rivera's paintings and one photo of the artist, the illustrations are mixed-media pictures by Diaz. Depicting Rivera and his world, these iconic images glow with warmth, light, and color. In the backgrounds, some scenes incorporate imagery from Aztec art, which Rivera collected. A lively verse portrait illuminated with incandescent illustrations. —Carolyn Phelan

Bolden, Tonya. *Wake Up Our Souls: A Celebration of Black American Artists*. **2004. 128p. illus. Abrams (9780810945272). Gr. 6–12. 704.03.**

In her introduction, Bolden writes that her book, published in conjunction with the Smithsonian American Art Museum, is "not meant to be a comprehensive history of the black American artistic legacy." Instead, she offers a beautifully illustrated introduction, in simple, graceful language, to a selection of African American artists, beginning with the nineteenth century and moving to the present. Accompanying each small biography is a box featuring a well-reproduced, representative work from each included artist and a discussion, in clear, succinct language, that will encourage readers to look closely at the images (and visual art in general) and form their own opinions of what they see. A time line placing the artists in historical context would also have been welcome, but Bolden's text does a fine job of describing the larger social and political climate in which the artists worked as well as the pervasive discrimination they suffered, and her coverage of early African American cultural organizations, such as the Harlem Artist's Guild, is particularly fascinating. Elegant and concise, this handsome volume joins a growing collection of exceptional youth titles about African American visual artists. —Gillian Engberg

Crutcher, Chris. *King of the Mild Frontier: An Ill-Advised Autobiography*. 2003. 272p. Greenwillow (9780060502492). Gr. 8–12. 813.

Like his novels, Crutcher's autobiography is full of heartbreak, poignancy, and hilarity. Candid and casual, Crutcher shares stories from his childhood and adolescence in Cascade, Idaho. Reminiscences of some of his youthful rites of passage are laugh-out-loud funny, such as his humiliating initiation into his high-school athletic club. On a more serious note, he discusses his occasionally rocky relationships with his parents and siblings. He talks openly about his struggles with a bad temper that constantly got him into trouble, how he came to terms with questions about God, how he confronted intolerance, and how he found his own place in the world. He also shares several painful glimpses into his work as a child and family therapist trying to help people heal some very broken lives. This honest, insightful, revealing autobiography is a joy to read. Crutcher's fans will relish this intimate glimpse of the author, and the book may win some new readers for his fiction. —Ed Sullivan

Fleischman, Paul. *Zap*. 2005. 96p. Candlewick (9780763627744). Gr. 9–12. 812.

In a natural extension of his works for readers' theater (*Joyful Noise*, 1988; *Seek*, 2001), Newbery Medalist Fleischman offers his first "bona fide play." Framed as a performance for an imaginary audience armed with remote-control "zappers," this is actually seven plays mashed into one: a turgid rendition of Shakespeare's *Richard III* alternating at the audience's whim among six spoofs of other dramaturgical biggies, among them, "The Russian Play," "The English Mystery," and "The Southern Play." Playgoers and actors alike, particularly those with some experience of the less-mainstream genres lampooned (for example, absurdist theater, in which a crossword player requests "a three-letter word for despair"), will relish the irreverent chaos as the boundaries between the plays gradually erode. Not every adult will agree that the way to invigorate students' interest in the stage is to reinforce the perception of tedium surrounding theater's greatest works. Still, it's easy to imagine student actors tackling this with verve. Mature references and on-stage consumption of "whiskey" limit this to high-school casts. —Jennifer Mattson

Fleischman, Sid. *Escape! The Story of the Great Houdini*. 2006. 160p. illus. Greenwillow (9780060850944). Gr. 6–9. 793.8.

Could there be anyone more qualified than Newbery Medalist Fleischman to profile the "monarch of manacles" for young audiences? After all, as described in his autobiography, *The Abracadabra Kid* (1998), Fleischman first earned his bread as a magician. This same background imposes an unexpected limitation: although the bibliography suggests publications to aid aspiring illusionists, Fleischman states upfront that an unspoken covenant among magicians prevents him from revealing Houdini's secrets. It's a tribute to Fleischman's zinging prose that, even without spoilers, his account remains terrifically engaging, delivered in a taut sideshow patter packed with delicious vocabulary (*prestidigitator, bunkum*) that may prompt even the most verbally indifferent to a new enthusiasm for their dictionaries. The showy language comes with real substance, too, as Fleischman explores his subject's tireless self-reinvention (born Ehrich Weiss in a Budapest ghetto, the ambitious lad's stage name was just one of many image-buffing ruses); his virulent egomania; and his forays into early aviation and cinema. The showbiz details are as fascinating as the transformation of an immigrant whose "biggest sleight-of-hand was himself," and, thanks to the widely spaced type and compelling visuals, this will draw even those readers without a biography assignment hovering overhead. That's some trick, indeed. —Jennifer Mattson

Fleischman, Sid. ***Sir Charlie: Chaplin, the Funniest Man in the World*****. 2010. 288p. illus. Greenwillow (9780061896408). Gr. 6–10. 791.43.**

Following well-received titles about Mark Twain and Harry Houdini, Fleischman's third biography is a bittersweet celebration: it is the last book the author published before his death in March 2010. With a straightforward chronology, the chapters follow the famous comedian from his impoverished childhood in London slums through Hollywood stardom and his final years, during which he was knighted by Queen Elizabeth II. As in his previous books about famous lives, Fleischman infuses the narrative with energetic charm, and although the book is thoroughly documented with exemplary source notes, playful metaphors lend an almost tall-tale tone that echoes the humor of Chaplin's work: "Custard pies were flying," Fleischman writes in a description of the tangled movie business. The author also deftly integrates details of early moviemaking into the colorful accounts of Chaplin's tumultuous personal and professional lives, and he writes with unabashed enthusiasm for Chaplin's work: of the chase scene in The Kid, he writes, "If one can watch the sequence without tear ducts overflowing and heart in throat, one needs jumper cables." Young people with a noncurricular interest in Chaplin may be few, but once led to this fascinating, well-shaped, and entertaining title, they may well discover a curiosity about and appreciation for the films that made the great comedian famous. Photos and a time line complete this standout portrait. —Gillian Engberg

★ Gantos, Jack. ***Hole in My Life*****. 2002. 208p. Farrar (9780374399887). Gr. 8–12. 813.54.**

Jack Gantos' riveting memoir of the 15 months he spent as a young man in federal prison for drug smuggling is more than a harrowing, scared-straight confession: it is a beautifully realized story about the making of a writer. As Gantos himself notes: "[prison] is where I went from thinking about becoming a writer, to writing." His examination of the process—including his unsparing portrayal of his fears, failings, and false starts—is brilliant and breathtaking in its candor and authenticity. Particularly fascinating is his generous use of literary allusions to everything from Baudelaire to Billy Budd, which subtly yet richly dramatize how he evolved from a reader who became a character in the books he was reading to a writer and a character in his own life story. Gantos' spare narrative style and straightforward revelation of the truth have, together, a cumulative power that will capture not only a reader's attention but also empathy and imagination. This is great for every aspiring writer and also a wonderful biography for teens struggling to discover their deepest, truest selves. —Michael Cart

Glover, Savion, and Bruce Weber. ***My Life in Tap*****. 2000. 80p. illus. Morrow (9780688156299). Gr. 6–10. 729.7.**

Writing in alternating segments, tap sensation Glover and journalist Weber tell of Glover's rise to fame in an affecting biography that reveals the link between Glover's spirit and talent. With his ability nurtured by his mother, a single parent, Glover quickly found himself in the public eye, first as a drummer and then as a dancer on Broadway stages and television. Along the way, Glover apprenticed himself to such improvisational tap legends as Honi Coles and Jimmy Slyde, who jokingly called him "the sponge" as they shared with him their knowledge of dance and insight into life. Certainly, Glover's accomplishments are remarkable, but what makes this more than a celebrity bio is the deep respect and reverence Glover shows for his "uncles" and their advice, which was as much about how to be a man as it was about footwork. Black-and-white photos and typography that ricochets across the page with the rhythm of Glover's feet catch the vibrance of Glover's preforming style. —Randy Meyer

Greenberg, Jan. ***Romare Bearden: Collage of Memories*****. 2003. 48p. illus. Abrams (9780810945890). Gr. 3–9. 709.**

Romare Bearden filled his collages with images of everyday life as he lived it, and this beautiful, large-size volume with exquisite reproductions of his art is both a biography and an exciting, accessible introduction to his amazing work. Greenberg, who coauthored *Runaway Girl: The Artist Louise Bourgeois* (2003) for older readers, and the Printz Honor Book *Heart to*

Heart (2001), shows how Bearden drew on his childhood memories of growing up in North Carolina as well as his exciting adult years in Harlem to compose pictures that celebrate African American life and his feelings about his people. Greenberg talks about technique with clear poetry that takes the viewer up close to the pictures on the page ("Painted paper scissored into shapes. Scraps of fabric. Hands cut from a photograph. Bits and pieces pasted on a board"), and she relates Bearden's life story by making his images emotional representations of his feelings. Without being obtrusive, the documentation is exemplary, with notes at the back for direct quotes as well as a detailed chronology, a bibliography, a glossary, and a list of places to view his work. With each picture, there are details about technique, date, size, and location. This is the very best kind of artistic biography. Adults will want to see it, too. —Hazel Rochman

Greenberg, Jan, and Sandra Jordan. *Andy Warhol: Prince of Pop*. 2004. 176p. illus. Delacorte (9780385730563). Gr. 8–12. 770.

As in the authors' previous titles about iconoclastic artists, such as *Runaway Girl* (2003), about sculptor Louise Bourgeois, Greenberg and Jordan offer a riveting biography that humanizes their controversial subject without judgments or sensationalizing. Chronological chapters follow Warhol from his Pittsburgh youth through his infamous decades in New York City, ending with a chapter that examines his profound influence on American art and culture. With honesty and tact, the authors frankly discuss Warhol's insecurities (his struggles with "fiery acne," his wavering self-image); his sometimes astonishing detachment; and the infamous Factory studio, with its wild, experimental sex-and-drugs culture. Their lucid insight into the art is also exceptional. In clear, evocative language they describe how Warhol made his art, the cultural context in which he worked, his originality, and the controversies he raised. With the exception of a few missing references, the source notes are exemplary, adding dimension to the story. A chronology, a glossary of art terms, and numerous quotes from family, friends, critics, and Warhol himself bolster this highly readable, balanced, and fascinating survey of an American icon. —Gillian Engberg

Greenberg, Jan, and Sandra Jordan. *Christo and Jeanne-Claude: Through the Gates and Beyond*. 2008. 48p. illus. Roaring Brook/Flash Point (9781596430716). Gr. 6–9. 709.2.

In 2005, the dull gray of a New York City winter was interrupted when two indomitable artists, Christo and his partner, Jeanne-Claude, brought Central Park brilliantly to life with their outdoor work *The Gates*. Bright streams of saffron fabric panels attached to gates covered in the same material followed 23 miles of walkways through the park, offering delighted viewers an astounding sight, or as the authors put it, "a painting with nature as its canvas." This book, chronicling both *The Gates* as well as the artists' other projects, is as thoughtful, eye-opening, and meticulous as the work it celebrates. Using original research, the authors begin with an overview of *The Gates*—its scope, yes, but just as important, its purpose. In fact, throughout, Greenberg and Jordan strive to explain why the two artists would spend millions of dollars and years of time on artistic explosions that only last a matter of weeks. That they can make understandable to a young audience the concept of public ownership of art, as well as the freedom that comes with releasing the idea of permanence, is a tribute to their writing. Working in tandem are beautifully reproduced photographs (including a fabulous foldout) that chronicles other grand projects, past and future. Solid back matter complements a stunningly designed book that can't help but excite readers about art. —Ilene Cooper

Greenberg, Jan, and Sandra Jordan. *Runaway Girl: The Artist Louise Bourgeois*. 2003. 80p. illus. Abrams (9780810942370). Gr. 8–12. 730.

As in *Frank O. Gehry, Outside In* (2000), the authors once again make challenging art accessible and exciting to teen readers. This time they focus on Louise Bourgeois, one of the best-known living sculptors, whose work deals with primal themes of jealousy, betrayal, and shifting sexual identities—which, according to Bourgeois, are inspired by her painful childhood and her adulterous father. In clear, elegant prose, bolstered with numerous quotes from the artist, the authors seamlessly juxtapose stories of Bourgeois' life with relevant artworks, which are often explained in the artist's own words. Beautifully reproduced photographs, printed on well-designed pages, offer an excellent mix of the artist's personal life and her art, though the authors remind readers that "we don't have to know her story to have our own strong reaction" to her work. By showing the relationship among shapes, colors, materials, and emotions, the authors invite readers to approach even the most bewildering art with confidence and think about it in their own words. The book concludes with a glossary, a bibliography, and notes. —Gillian Engberg

Greenberg, Jan, and Sandra Jordan. *Vincent Van Gogh: Portrait of an Artist*. 2001. 144p. illus. Delacorte (9780385328067). Gr. 7–12. 759.9492.

Greenberg and Jordan, authors of titles such as *Chuck Close Up Close* (1998) and *Frank O'Gehry: Outside In* (2000), offer yet another outstanding artist's biography. In elegant, captivating language, they debunk myths about Van Gogh as lunatic and loner. Following his life story from birth to death, they describe the artist as an irascible, stubborn, and erratic member of a family that supported him through aborted attempts to become an art dealer and a preacher, before he finally settled on painting, a career fully supported by his brother Theo, with whom he lived in Paris. Also detailed are Van Gogh's years of drinking and schmoozing among the greats of the Montmartre art scene, organizing exhibitions, enjoying great friendships with other artists, and finally moving to the south of France, where he hoped to start an artist's collective. The authors do a remarkable job of presenting Van Gogh's complex personality (described by his brother as "gifted, delicate, and tender" and "cruel and hard-hearted"); his periods of manic energy; and the ear incident, in a straightforward, even understated way, showing that he was not "crazy," but rather suffered from epilepsy. They also help readers look at the painter's work, and at art in general, discuss the artist's motivations and techniques, and bring readers upclose with immediate, moving scenes of Van Gogh at work in the fields as he strove to paint his "high yellow note." An exceptional biography that reveals the humanity behind the myth. Reproductions, a glossary, and other appended material will help this find cross-curricular support. —Gillian Engberg

Macaulay, David. *Building Big*. Illus. by David Macaulay. 2000. 192p. Houghton (9780395963319). Gr. 7–12. 720.

In a companion to the video series *Building Big* with David Macaulay, Macaulay narrows his focus to the "nuts and bolts" of each structure. In signature sketches and succinct, engaging text, he deconstructs the design and engineering features that make each of the domes, tunnels, skyscrapers, bridges, and dams so exemplary. As usual, Macaulay knows just which view is required—cross section, detail study, elevation—to present the material so that it's easy to understand and appealing to readers. He even includes some subtle humor, such as a pair of cartoon mice on the Chunnel's tracks that note that *cheese* will become *fromage* when they reach the end. The videos, produced by WGBH Boston, and the book can easily be used independently, but together they offer a highly entertaining, instructive glimpse at some of construction's greatest stories, giving young people and adults the skills to look more closely at the structures around them. —Gillian Engberg

Macaulay, David. *Mosque*. Illus. by David Macaulay. 2003. 96p. Houghton/Walter Lorraine (9780618240340). Gr. 6–12. 726.

Once again Macaulay uses clear words and exemplary drawings to explore a majestic structure's design and construction. This time the story takes place in sixteenth-century Istanbul, where a wealthy patron has hired an architect to create a mosque and its support buildings. The spreads follow the complex through its planning and building, using Macaulay's familiar combination of labeled architectural drawings, sketches showing artisans at work, and thorough descriptions that are, perhaps, more technical than in some of his previous titles. In his foreword, Macaulay explains that he has based his story on a composite of actual historical people and mosques, and his images and words are filled with accurate details that reveal the history and culture of the time. This isn't an introduction to Islam; readers will want some basic knowledge of the religion. But in his respectful, straightforward explanation of the mosque's design, Macaulay offers an unusual, inspiring perspective into Islamic society that's removed from the charged headlines, and, as in all his work, he conveys a contagious awe and wonder at the design and engineering feats that societies have accomplished. Those fascinated by the technical story may want to refer also to Macaulay's *Building Big* (2000), which includes an excellent section about the Hagia Sophia Mosque. —Gillian Engberg

Madden, Kerry. ***Harper Lee*****. 2009. 224p. illus. Viking (9780670010950). Gr. 7–12. 813.**

From the Up Close series, this informative biography spotlights writer Harper Lee, who grew up in Monroeville, Alabama, and studied law in college before deciding to become a writer. After working and writing in New York City for many years, she found a publisher for her first novel. Her life was transformed by the publication of *To Kill a Mockingbird* (1960), which quickly became a best-seller, a Pulitzer Prize winner, and the basis for an unusually successful movie adaptation. Though Lee appreciated the critical acclaim, she found the unrelenting demands for interviews, public appearances, and personal contact increasingly unwelcome and withdrew. Given the writer's refusal to grant access to any biographer and her closest friends' and relatives' reluctance to discuss her, Madden has done a fine job of researching the novelist's life and presenting it with respect for her point of view. The sensitive treatment of race relations during Lee's youth and the section on three trials that may have inspired parts of her novel will interest students researching *To Kill a Mockingbird*. A lengthy acknowledgments section, source notes for the many quotes, and an extensive bibliography conclude this unusually readable biography of an elusive figure in American letters. —Carolyn Phelan

Marcus, Leonard S., ed. ***The Wand in the Word: Conversations with Writers of Fantasy*****. 2006. 208p. Candlewick (9780763626259). Gr. 6–9. 813.009.**

Spotlighting a genre that has mushroomed in popularity, Marcus' latest may draw in even those young people who typically prefer to read, rather than read about, the books and authors they admire. Following the same format as his *Ways of Telling: Conversations on the Art of the Picture Book* (2000), Marcus presents interviews with 13 fantasy luminaries, including Lloyd Alexander, Susan Cooper, Nancy Farmer, Brian Jacques, Garth Nix, Tamora Pierce, and Philip Pullman. The writers' distinct personalities and career paths emerge, as do intriguing similarities; many authors, for instance, speak of the profound impact of WWII (Diane Wynne Jones recalls that wartime hazards convinced her that "the most appalling and peculiar things are liable to happen at any time"). Each profile includes a black-and-white author's photo, a reading list, and a bit of ephemera, often a handwritten manuscript page. Although the absence of J. K. Rowling is surprising, this remains a rich resource that will be consulted as frequently by children's literature professionals as by genre fans themselves, many of whom will particularly welcome each fantasist's advice to aspiring authors—from the simple, sage words of Ursula Le Guin, "Read. Write. Read. Write. Go on reading. Go on writing," to Jane Yolen's delightfully blunt "BIC: butt in chair!" —Jennifer Mattson

Myers, Walter Dean. ***Bad Boy: A Memoir*****. 2001. 224p. HarperCollins (9780060295233). Gr. 7–12. 813.54.**

"I didn't want to be defiant. I wanted to be in the system that I was walking away from, but I didn't know how to get in." Many teens will see themselves in Myers' account of his troubled coming-of-age, especially since he offers no pat solutions. He doesn't analyze or laugh at his youth from an adult perspective, and he doesn't overdramatize his childhood self. He remembers how he felt: detached, hurt, lonely, ashamed, a failure. He loved his Harlem neighborhood, but it was hard being black and poor and a reader, especially since moving into a world of books isolated him from those around him. He was big and physically aggressive, quick to get angry and punch kids who laughed at his speech defect. He was always in trouble at school and often truant. In fact, he dropped out of high school, read and wrote alone, and narrowly escaped jail. The narrative is sometimes rambling and repetitive, and sometimes abstract: for example, Myers just touches on his searing discovery that his stepfather couldn't read. The most beautiful writing is about Mama: how she taught him to read, sharing *True Romance* magazines. He still feels ashamed about how he hurt her: "Later when I had learned to use words better, I lost my ability to speak so freely with Mama." The aching truth is that although books saved him and helped him become a famous writer, they moved him away from the adoptive parents he loved. —Hazel Rochman

Neimark, Anne E. *Johnny Cash*. 2007. 203p. Viking (9780670062157). Gr. 6–9. 782.4.

The life of the deeply troubled and powerfully influential music legend is brought vividly to life in this richly detailed biography in the new Up Close series. Neimark chronicles the hardscrabble life Cash's family led in rural Arkansas and discusses the horrible death of his older brother, Jack, which haunted Johnny the rest of his life. Cash is portrayed as a tortured soul wrestling with his faith in God and a predilection for self-destructive behavior, yet emerging as a self-educated, deeply spiritual, and compassionate man, who used his fame and influence to advocate for humane prison conditions and the rights of Native Americans. Cash's genius as a songwriter and musician as well as his incalculable influence upon music are skillfully explored, and Neimark frequently uses excerpts from Cash's own songs to enrich his compelling life story. Her sharp, immediate writing, which combines passages of dramatic, storylike narrative with more traditional biographical accounts, will foster readers' appreciation of the singer-songwriter's fierce individualism and his outlaw spirit. Sources are provided for quotes, and a list of further resources (unfortunately, there's no discography) will point interested readers toward more about this musical legend. —Ed Sullivan

★ Partridge, Elizabeth. *John Lennon: All I Want Is the Truth*. 2005. 256p. Viking (9780670059546). Gr. 9–12. 782.42166.

John Lennon's Aunt Mimi disapproved of his guitar hobby because "you could never make a living at it." Such anecdotes surface with delightful regularity in Partridge's biography of the influential mid-twentieth-century musician. As in *This Land Was Made for You and Me: The Life and Songs of Woody Guthrie* (2002), her mission is to uncover the person behind the image. Partridge unflinchingly reports on the outlet from public attention that Lennon sought in a debauched lifestyle, in which "booze, pills, and joints were consumed in astonishing amounts," and this may cause some readers to think that the sensational aspects of Lennon's life have been overemphasized. But many YAs will find the nonjudgmental tone refreshing, and those drawn by the rock-music theme will admire Partridge's sensitive analysis of the Beatles' creative output. Dynamic design distinguishes the book inside and out, from the eye-catching size and shape that cleverly mimics an old vinyl album cover to the abundant archival photos within. A discography and an immense bibliography set readers on the right paths. Despite source notes limited to quotes, this has the markings of a YA biography staple, as hard-hitting as Jan Greenberg and Sandra Jordan's *Andy Warhol: Prince of Pop* (2004), and equally compelling in its perspective on the Swinging Sixties.
—Jennifer Mattson

Partridge, Elizabeth. *This Land Was Made for You and Me: The Life and Songs of Woody Guthrie*. 2002. 192p. illus. Viking (9780670035359). Gr. 6–12. 782.42162.

Like her *Restless Spirit: The Life and Work of Dorothea Lange* (1998), Partridge's latest is a tender, unflinching biography of a free-spirited American artist. Bolstered by lyrics, quotes, and sketches (including some by Guthrie), the text follows the musician from his tragic dust-bowl childhood to his death. Partridge is careful to show Guthrie's complexities—his talent, his drive, his restless wandering, his open heart, and his troubled relationships. The rambling narrative style, thick with detail, may frustrate some readers, especially those using the book for research, and Partridge sometimes dramatizes what characters thought and felt without offering proper documentation (source notes often apply to quotes but not to narrative text). Nonetheless, Partridge still creates a searching portrait that is both broad and intimate, strengthened by black-and-white photographs that greatly enhance the sense of the artist's personality and times. For a younger audience, suggest Kathy Jakobsen's illustrated version of

Guthrie's *This Land Is Your Land* (1998) and Bonnie Christensen's *Woody Guthrie: Poet of the People*.
—Gillian Engberg

Raven, Nicky. ***Beowulf: A Tale of Blood, Heat, and Ashes*****. Illus. by John Howe. 2007. 96p. Candlewick (9780763636470). Gr. 6–12. 398.2.**

Although this may be the fourth or fifth adaptation of *Beowulf* "just in time for the movie," this one is undeniably the best—a gripping rendition of the Anglo-Saxon epic with highly evocative artwork by Howe, most famous for his artistic role in the blockbuster Lord of the Rings movie trilogy. Raven takes a few liberties that add welcome nuance to the story, imbuing some wry personality to the title hero (who stands head and shoulders above the wooden protagonists of most of the other recent editions) and fleshing out the supporting cast, especially the surprisingly droll narrator, Wiglaf. Howe's artwork could have risen from the same sketchbooks as his art for Tolkien, but it is nontheless spectacular, easily capturing the heroic grandeur and horrific gruesomeness of the tale. The entire book is handsomely adorned with flourishes of Old English lettering that heavily recall the now-familiar Elven script that covered mounds of Rings ephemera. This is a high-quality effort on all fronts; if you only buy one *Beowulf* this season, make it this one.
—Ian Chipman

Reef, Catherine. ***E. E. Cummings: A Poet's Life*****. 2006. 142p. illus. Clarion (9780618568499). Gr. 8–11. 811.**

Many teens have studied and liked at least a few of Cummings' poems, so this thoroughly researched survey of Cummings' life is sure to generate interest in the classroom and beyond. Reef chooses revealing anecdotes from the poet's youth that will speak directly to teens. After Cummings passed from confident child to awkward teen, Reef notes that he "was so self-conscious about his acne that he hid his face behind a newspaper when riding on streetcars." Numerous direct quotes from Cummings, his family, and his friends, along with many photos personalize the story, and Reef's enthusiasm for poetry is clear in her well-chosen excerpts from Cummings' poems and those of his contemporaries. She also skillfully places the poet within a larger cultural context, showing connections between his poetry and interests and the artistic and political movements of his times. Unfortunately, source notes refer only to direct quotes, but an extensive bibliography, a list of Cummings' works, and a glossary will aid researchers. A clear, engaging portrait of a poet whose refusal to write and live according to convention will endear him to teens.
—Gillian Engberg

Reef, Catherine. ***Ernest Hemingway: A Writer's Life*****. 2009. 172p. illus. Clarion (9780618987054). Gr. 8–12. 813.**

Reef, whose *E. E. Cummings: A Poet's Life* (2006) was a Best Books for Young Adults selection, offers another perceptive, captivating biography of one of the twentieth century's most influential writers. Hemingway said that he aimed "to make a picture of the whole world—or as much of it as I have seen. Boiling it down always, rather than spreading it out thin." Reef skillfully takes on the challenge of "boiling down" Hemingway's dramatic, globe-trotting life into a clear, complex portrait. Seamlessly integrated throughout the text, the numerous direct quotes—cited in appended source notes and contributed by friends, colleagues, and Hemingway himself—both support and refute commonly held views of the writer. Readers will gain nuanced understanding from such excerpts as the cutting notes from Hemingway's mother when he failed to meet his family's expectations, as well as the heartbreaking, tender messages he sent his first wife as their marriage fell apart. Throughout, Reef writes with descriptive, even-handed prose that includes both praise and criticism that Hemingway's work has inspired and is particularly restrained in accounts of the writer's final, tragic months before his suicide. An extensive bibliography, a list of major works, and well-chosen black-and-white photos further support the text. Teens jaded by too much classroom analysis of *The Old Man and the Sea* and Hemingway's short stories will come away from Reef's thorough, skillfully constructed biography with fresh interest in and appreciation for this American legend. —Gillian Engberg

Rosen, Michael. ***Shakespeare: His Work & His World.*** **Illus. by Robert Ingpen. 2001. 104p. Candlewick (9780763615680). Gr. 5–9. 822.3.**

Demonstrating ways in which the Bard's plays reflect his "extraordinary and dangerous times" (and every other time as well), Rosen outdoes even Diane Stanley and Peter Vennema's *Bard of Avon* (1992) in giving fair answer to the perennial student whine, "Why Shakespeare?" After opening with a briskly dramatic account of the famous overnight removal of an entire London playhouse, Rosen looks at medieval theater, then leads a high-energy tour through Elizabethan culture and daily life, describes the new style of theater and Shakespeare's place in it, examines four plays briefly and one (*Romeo and Juliet*) closely, and closes with a tribute to Shakespeare's language. With an unerring eye for the most exciting angle of view, the peak moment of intensity, and the telling facial details, Ingpen illustrates all of this in rich, golden tones, with an array of panoramic views, schematics, and powerfully expressive figures, both on the stage and off. Even readers whose previous experience with Shakespeare has been rounded with sleep will be persuaded by this robust introduction to give it another try. A time line and a reasonably child-friendly bibliography are appended. —John Peters

Rubalcaba, Jill. ***I. M. Pei: Architect of Time, Place, and Purpose.*** **2011. 128p. illus. Marshall Cavendish (9780761459736). Gr. 7–10. 720.92.**

This handsome book introduces the life and work of architect I. M. Pei. Born in China, he came to the U.S. in 1935 to study architecture. Though he never returned to his homeland to live, his later work expressed cultural and artistic values absorbed during his childhood in addition to his education as an architect and the strong influence of Corbusier. After discussing Pei's early work in urban redevelopment, Rubalcaba focuses on seven later projects around the world: the National Center for Atmospheric Research, the John F. Kennedy Presidential Library, the East Building of the National Gallery of Art, the Fragrant Hill Hotel, the Bank of China, the redesigned Louvre, and the Miho Museum. Each chapter looks at Pei's approach to one project, the challenges he encountered, and how he achieved his vision for the building. Illustrations include sketches, site models, and photos. Back matter includes a time line, a bibliography, source notes for quotes, and lists of suggested books and websites. Like Pei's buildings, the book's design has a clean aesthetic that is spacious, functional, and inviting. Color is used sparingly but effectively. The wide, white pages carry well-spaced lines of type, with red chapter headings, page numbers, and linear borders for illustrations. A fascinating introduction to this significant architect. —Carolyn Phelan

Rubin, Susan Goldman. ***There Goes the Neighborhood: Ten Buildings People Loved to Hate.*** **2001. 96p. Holiday House (9780823414352). Gr. 7–12. 725.**

Like Jan Greenberg and Sandra Jordan's *Frank O. Gehry: Outside In* (2000), Rubin's latest is an intelligent, entertaining look at mostly twentieth-century architecture. Each of the 10 chapters focuses on a structure that caused an outcry of disapproval when it was built, including both the famous (the Eiffel Tower, the Flatiron Building, the Pompidou Center) and the lesser known (Minneapolis' underground Walker Community Library). Written in simple, engaging language that never condescends, the stories reveal how architects identified and solved aesthetic and engineering problems, and include fascinating tidbits about each structure's history and neighborhood, and the extreme personalities that drove some projects. There is also information on contemporary art movements, the history of skyscrapers, and more. Each chapter opens with a photo-collage of the building and samples of criticism ("What is it? A toilet bowl?" reads text overlaying a photo of New York City's Guggenheim Museum), followed by scattered photographs and drawings, printed entirely in blue and white. The collages are witty, but the highly visual subjects demand more sparkling images and design, such as the hip, colorful visuals in *Frank O. Gehry* or the crisp, engaging layouts of David Macaulay's *Building Big* (2000). Fortunately, the winning text makes up for the lackluster format: the stories, the controversy, and the insight will encourage readers to look at and learn more about the structures that surround them. A bibliography and a well-rounded list of resources conclude. —Gillian Engberg

Sills, Leslie. *In Real Life: Six Women Photographers*. 2000. 80p. illus. Holiday House (9780823414987). Gr. 7–12. 770.

The author of *Inspirations* (1989) and *Visions* (1993) offers another outstanding collected biography of female artists. The artists—Imogene Cunningham, Dorothea Lange, Lola Alvarez Bravo, Carrie Mae Weems, Elsa Dorfman, and Cindy Sherman—represent widely disparate backgrounds and nearly a century of photographic excellence. In plain, direct language, Sills focuses on the artists' work, weaving in biographical details as they relate to the women's careers and beautifully articulating the significance of each artist's body of work within her larger cultural context. In discussing individual works, all well reproduced, Sills guides readers through the basics of how to look at and interpret photographs by questioning the photographer's subject, composition, lighting, and processing choices: "Is she trying to educate her audience, show a particular side of humanity, portray beauty, or make us laugh? Would her work be considered documentary, portraiture, abstract, or fantasy? Most important, what is the feeling you have when viewing the photograph?" Much more than just a biographical resource, this outstanding volume will help give young people the confidence to approach not only photography but also all the visual arts. The book concludes with an overview of camera mechanics and suggested reading lists. For other recent biographies of women photographers, direct readers to Elizabeth Partridge's *Restless Spirit* (1998) and Susan Goldman Rubin's *Margaret Bourke White: Her Pictures Were Her Life* (1999). —Gillian Engberg

Sullivan, George. *Berenice Abbott, Photographer: An Independent Vision*. 2006. 128p. illus. Clarion (9780618440269). Gr. 6–9. 770.92.

Born in Ohio in 1898, Abbott made her way to Greenwich Village in 1918, and then to Paris, where she found her calling in photography, which she practiced with uncommon drive and an uncompromising sense of purpose for 60 years, primarily in New York City. In the 1930s she received financial support from the Federal Art Project for an ambitious project called Changing New York, traveling through Manhattan, photographing its streets, buildings, shops, and houses with the straightforward realism that characterized all her work. Later projects included science photography and teaching. Sullivan brings together an enormous amount of information about Abbott and presents it in a clear, thoughtful manner. Through discussions of Abbot's life and work, Sullivan reveals her personal strengths and shortcomings as well as establishing the scope and significance of her accomplishments. Large, clear reproductions of Abbott's photos appear throughout the book, and readers looking for more examples are referred to books as well as an online resource. Back matter includes source notes for the many quotes used and an extensive list of books and interviews. A fine portrait of a significant photographer that will partner well with *Restless Spirit* (1998), Elizabeth Partridge's biography of Dorothea Lange. —Carolyn Phelan

Wooldridge, Connie Nordhielm. *The Brave Escape of Edith Wharton*. 2010. 192p. illus. Clarion (9780547236308). Gr. 7–10. 813.

Born into the well-heeled family that inspired the phrase "keeping up with the Joneses," Wharton exposed the social mores of Gilded Age America's upper classes from the inside. In this thoroughly researched, humanizing biography, Wooldridge writes with lively specifics about both the author and her time, beginning with Wharton's childhood and adolescence, when she kept her writing life secret, bowing to the societal belief that intelligent girls repelled suitable husbands. Like her characters, Wharton tested convention, and Wooldridge's skillful integration of Wharton's literary and personal lives includes matter-of-fact, detailed accounts of her intense relationships with numerous "bachelor friends," pictured among the many archival photos. Wooldridge also places the author's life in vivid context, and the fascinating reports of war between "new money" and "old money" in turn-of-the-last-century New York will easily interest contemporary readers, who will spot twenty-first-century parallels. Frequent, well-woven quotes from Wharton's family and friends contribute to a strong sense of an energetic, groundbreaking, and ferociously intelligent writer, but it's the many quotes in Wharton's own voice that leave the most indelible impact. Chapter notes, a bibliography, and a full list of Wharton's works close this well-rounded, handsomely illustrated portrait, which will find an enduring place on classroom and library shelves. —Gillian Engberg

History

Adler, David A. ***Frederick Douglass: A Noble Life*****. 2010. 144p. illus. Holiday (9780823420568). Gr. 6–10. 973.7.**

Adler, the author of more than 200 books for young readers, has now written a thoroughly researched, lucidly written biography of the great Frederick Douglass. Born a slave in 1817 or 1818 (the date is uncertain), Douglass fled to freedom in 1838 and subsequently became one of America's most celebrated abolitionists, orators, and passionate champions of freedom for African Americans. His autobiography, *Narrative of the Life of Frederick Douglass, an American Slave*, published in 1845, became a best-seller and catapulted him to fame. Of course, any story of Douglass is also the story of slavery, and Adler does an excellent job of exploring the atrocities and dehumanizing indignities that America's "peculiar institution" visited on those who lived in slavery. As demonstrated by Adler's generous use of quotations from Douglass' own writings, many of the most dramatic of these abominations are the ones that Douglass himself suffered both before and after he became a free man. Though Adler may sometimes be too much an advocate for Douglass, giving too little attention to some of the many controversies that visited Douglass' life and career, he nevertheless clearly demonstrates that Douglass was, indeed, one of the great men of the nineteenth century. —Michael Cart

Allen, Thomas B., and Roger MacBride Allen. ***Mr. Lincoln's High-Tech War*****. 2008. 144p. illus. National Geographic (9781426303791). Gr. 6–10. 973.7.**

The prologue to this intriguing book points out that although Lincoln grew up using tools and farm implements that his great-great-great-great-grandfather would have recognized, his own generation saw their world irrevocably changed by technological innovations, and he was the only President ever to be granted a patent (for a device to lift boats over shoals). Well researched and clearly written, the book discusses the course of the Civil War in terms of the development of new technology, from the ironclad and the submarine to the rapid-fire, repeating rifle and the use of railroads to carry troops and supplies. When the telegraph carried news from the front and Lincoln's orders to his generals, the term "commander in chief" became more than an honorary title for the president. The many illustrations include captioned black-and-white reproductions of period prints, paintings, and photos as well as clearly labeled drawings. Sidebars comment on such topics as the mass production of armaments. A lengthy bibliography, a discussion of online resources, and source notes for quotes are appended. Readers whose knowledge of the Civil War comes from historical novels and battle-by-battle historical accounts will gain a fascinating perspective on why the war progressed as it did and how it was ultimately won. —Carolyn Phelan

Aronson, Marc, and Patty Campbell, eds. ***War Is . . . : Soldiers, Survivors, and Storytellers Talk about War*****. 2008. 208p. Candlewick (9780763636258). Gr. 10–12. 810.8.**

In his provocatively titled introduction, "People Like War," Aronson writes: "If we ask people to fight for us—as we always have and always will—we owe them the respect of listening to them." Though differing (passionately) about war's inevitability, his coeditor, Campbell, feels likewise, and joins him in presenting a gathering of reminiscences, interviews, letters, published articles, and literary works that brilliantly convey war's terrible appeal as well as its realities and lasting effects on those whose lives are personally touched by armed conflict. Contributions include Ernie Pyle's eloquent account of wreckage on a D-Day beach, a Vietnam vet's nightmarish memories of combat, jokey letters home by Campbell's naive doughboy father, scathing accounts of sexual harassment in Iraq and elsewhere from several female ex-GIs, and a disturbing indictment of recruiting practices in today's high schools. Anyone considering enlistment will find these pieces (not to mention the many titles provided in the ample but not indigestible lists of war fiction and nonfiction at the end) to be mesmerizing reading. With this collection, Aronson and Campbell have provided an uncommonly valuable source of hard information and perceptive insight. —John Peters

Bachrach, Susan. D. *The Nazi Olympics: Berlin 1936*. 2000. 132p. illus. Little, Brown (9780316070867). Gr. 6–12. 796.48.

The story most often told about the 1936 Olympics is that of Jesse Owens' triumphant performance, which served as a slap in the face to Hitler and his theory of Aryan supremacy. Bachrach looks deeper than this feel-good interpretation to trace the troubled path of the games both in the U.S. and Germany, examining the escalating oppression of Jews, the building of the concentration camps, and U.S. efforts to start a boycott. Bachrach ties those threads together into a comprehensive narrative that provides the right amount of political background to tell the complete story of the games and their athletes—those who competed, those banned from competition, those later murdered in concentration camps, and those who took part in the boycott. Enriched with biographical sidebars and illustrated with photographs from the U.S. Holocaust Memorial Museum, this is a welcome addition to any sports or WWII collection. Chronology; further readings. —Randy Meyer

Barakat, Ibtisam. *Tasting the Sky: A Palestinian Childhood*. 2007. 192p. Farrar/Melanie Kroupa (9780374357337). Gr. 7–10. 956.95.

In a spare, eloquent memoir, Barakat recalls life under military occupation. In 1981, the author, then in high school, boarded a bus bound for Ramallah. The bus was detained by Israeli soldiers at a checkpoint on the West Bank, and she was taken to a detention center before being released. The episode triggers sometimes heart-wrenching memories of herself as a young child, at the start of the 1967 Six Days' War, as Israeli soldiers conducted raids, their planes bombed her home, and she fled with her family across the border to Jordan. She also recalls living under occupation and the thrill of being able to attend the United Nations school for refugees. The political upheaval is always in the background, but for young Barakat, much of the drama was in incidents that took place in everyday life. What makes the memoir so compelling is the immediacy of the child's viewpoint, which depicts both conflict and daily life without exploitation or sentimentality. An annotated bibliography will help readers fill in the facts. —Hazel Rochman

Bartoletti, Susan Campbell. *Black Potatoes: The Story of the Great Irish Famine, 1845–1850*. 2001. 160p. illus. Houghton (9780618002719). Gr. 6–12. 941.5081.

Through the voices of the Irish people, Bartoletti tells the history of the Great Irish Famine of the late 1840s. Eyewitness accounts and memories combine with devastating facts: one million died from starvation and disease; two million emigrated; the famine could have been avoided; the legacy was a bitter resentment against the English, who owned most of Ireland. The year-by-year political history is occasionally heavy going; but, as she did in *Growing Up in Coal Country* (1996), a *Booklist* Editors' Choice, Bartoletti humanizes the big events by bringing the reader up close to the lives of ordinary people. There are heartbreaking accounts of evictions, of the Irish starving while food is exported to England, and of deaths in the coffin ships that took the desperate to North America. The text is broken up with many black-and-white drawings from newspapers of the time, and a long final essay includes information about books, primary sources, library collections, and websites that readers can turn to for school reports and for research into their own family histories. It's a wonder there are so few nonfiction books about this subject for young people. —Hazel Rochman

★ Bartoletti, Susan Campbell. *Hitler Youth: Growing Up in Hitler's Shadow*. 2005. 176p. illus. Scholastic (9780439353793). Gr. 7–10. 943.086.

What was it like to be a teenager in Germany under Hitler? Bartoletti draws on oral histories, diaries, letters, and her own extensive interviews with Holocaust survivors, Hitler Youth, resisters, and bystanders to tell the history from the viewpoints of people who were there. Most of the accounts and photos bring close the experiences of those who followed Hitler and fought for the Nazis, revealing why they joined, how Hitler used them, what it was like. Henry Mentelmann, for example, talks about Kristallnacht, when Hitler Youth and Storm Troopers wrecked Jewish homes and stores, and remembers thinking that the victims deserved what they got. The stirring photos tell more of the story. One particularly moving picture shows young Germans undergoing de-Nazification by watching images of people in the camps. The handsome book design, with black-and-white historical photos on every double-page spread, will draw in readers and help spark deep discussion, which will extend beyond the Holocaust curriculum. The extensive back matter is a part of the gripping narrative. —Hazel Rochman

★ Bartoletti, Susan Campbell. *They Called Themselves the K.K.K: The Birth of an American Terrorist Group*. 2010. 176p. illus. Houghton (9780618440337). Gr. 7–12. 322.4.

Bartoletti follows multi-award-winning titles such as *Hitler Youth* (2005) with another standout contribution to youth history shelves. Here, she examines how the Ku Klux Klan formed and grew out of the ashes of the Civil War. Bartoletti, who taught eighth-graders for 18 years, writes in admirably clear, accessible language about one of the most complex periods in U.S. history, and she deftly places the powerfully unsettling events into cultural and political context without oversimplifying. It's the numerous first-person quotes, though, that give the book its beating heart, and her searing, expertly selected stories of people on all sides of the violent conflicts will give readers a larger understanding of the conditions that incubated the Klan's terrorism; how profoundly the freed people and their sympathizers suffered; and how the legacy of that fear, racism, and brutality runs through our own time. In an author's note, Bartoletti describes visiting a contemporary Klan rally as part of her research, and that bold, immersive approach to her subject is evident in every chapter of this thoroughly researched volume. Like the individual stories, the powerful archival images on every page will leave an indelible impression on young readers, who will want to move on to the extensive annotated resources. The adjacent "Story behind the Story" feature fills in more details about this lucid, important title, which should be required reading for young people as well as the adults in their lives. —Gillian Engberg

Bausum, Ann. *Denied, Detained, Deported: Stories from the Dark Side of American Immigration*. 2009. 112p. illus. National Geographic (9781426303326). Gr. 6–12. 325.73.

Does our nation, built by immigrants, have room for more newcomers? Should individual rights be sacrificed for homeland security? With personal narratives and heartbreaking photographs, this beautifully designed photo-essay connects past immigration issues of economics, racism, national security, and patriotism with what is happening now. A photo of the Statue of Liberty appears on the first spread with Emma Lazarus' famous inscription ("Give me your tired, your poor, / Your huddled masses"); opposite is a contemporary poem by Naomi Shihab Nye ("But not too tired, not too poor / And we will give you . . . the stares / that say you are not where or what you should be"). Individual chapters look closely at instances of immigration gone wrong, including Chinese immigrant laborers refused citizenship; Holocaust refugees denied entry; Japanese Americans detained; and Mexican farmworkers hired, fired, and exploited. Following these moving profiles, Bausum discusses crucial contemporary problems, including the post-9/11 debate about monitoring Islamic extremists. Throughout, she is passionate about the respect due to illegal immigrants, even as she shows the unions' concern that illegals keep wages low. The comprehensive back matter includes a 12-page annotated time line and lists of resources to guide readers, including adults. A landmark title, sure to spark intense discussion. —Hazel Rochman

Bausum, Ann. *Unraveling Freedom: The Battle for Democracy on the Homefront during World War I*. 2010. 96p. illus. National Geographic (9781426307027). Gr. 8–11. 940.3.

Writer of the Sibert Honor Book *Freedom Riders* (2006), Bausum looks at America during the WWI period, when fear and intolerance led to the persecution of German Americans, socialists, and peace activists. Beginning with the sinking of the passenger ship *Lusitania* by a German submarine, she discusses government propaganda and the mounting public intolerance, outrage, and violence against all things German. New sedition and espionage acts enabled officials to intimidate or imprison those who might disagree with their positions. Without belaboring the point, Bausum connects the dots between responses to the 1915 sinking of the *Lusitania* and the 2001 bombing of the World Trade Center. Although much of the detail in Bausum's chapter on the *Lusitania*'s sinking seems irrelevant to the main theme, the book as a whole is well focused, well reasoned, and clearly written. Handsomely designed, it features color reproductions of period photos, drawings, paintings, and documents. Back matter includes citations, notes, a bibliography, lists of recommended resources, a detailed time line, and a useful "Guide to Wartime Presidents," which identifies eight wartime periods in America and, for each, discusses whether (and how) freedom was curtailed and provides a presidential quote. A fascinating, informative book on a topic of perennial concern. —Carolyn Phelan

Bausum, Ann. ***Freedom Riders: John Lewis and Jim Zwerg on the Front Lines of the Civil Rights Movement.*** **2005. 80p. illus. National Geographic (9780792241737). Gr. 6–9. 323.**

In another excellent work of nonfiction, the author of the acclaimed *With Courage and Cloth* (2004) covers a civil rights topic less frequently addressed than *Brown v. Board of Education* or the 1963 March on Washington. Eschewing a general overview of the 1961 Freedom Rides for specific, personal histories of real participants in the dangerous bus integration protests, Bausum focuses on two college students from strikingly different backgrounds: Jim Zwerg, a white Wisconsin native who became involved during an exchange visit to Nashville, and John Lewis, a black seminarian and student leader of the nonviolence movement. Zwerg became an inadvertent figurehead when he was branded "nigger-lover" and singled out for a particularly harsh beating, while Lewis parlayed leadership skills cultivated during the rides into political success as a Georgia congressman. Incisively illustrated with archival photos (one of which shows Zwerg and Lewis side-by-side in a jail cell, "bloodied together as brothers in a common cause"), this moving biographical diptych prompts careful thinking about race (Zwerg himself believed he received disproportionate fame because he was white), and delivers a galvanizing call to action, encapsulated in Lewis' stirring foreword: "You can change the world." Zwerg likewise contributes a foreword; exhaustive, useful end matter concludes, including resource listings, a bibliography, and citations for quotes. —Jennifer Mattson

Bausum, Ann. ***With Courage and Cloth: Winning the Fight for a Woman's Right to Vote.*** **2004. 112p. illus. National Geographic (9780792276470). Gr. 6–12. 324.6.**

Though few readers will pick this up for browsing, students will be easily drawn by the details of the American women's suffrage movement. As a child, the author met Alice Paul, a famous suffragist, and was clearly inspired. This personal interest drives the detailed history, written in an objective but anecdotal fashion. The design is thoughtful and attractive: sepia-tone photographs are highlighted in purple and gold (purple, gold, and white were the signature colors of the movement), the dark purple text is clean, elegant, and very readable, and the general layout is artfully done. Detailed notes, a bibliography, thumbnail biographies, and a chronology make this an all-in-one text that provides a general background to a very specific time within the movement. The timely release of this title will make every woman more appreciative of the Nineteenth Amendment, as well as the tremendous sacrifices that made it happen. —Debbie Carton

Blumberg, Rhoda. ***Shipwrecked! The True Adventures of a Japanese Boy.*** **2001. 80p. illus. HarperCollins (9780688174842). Gr. 5–9. 952.**

Blumberg learned about Manjiro, the first Japanese person to live in the U.S., when she wrote the Newbery Honor Book *Commodore Perry in the Land of Shogun* (1985). Now she devotes an entire volume to his remarkable life, beginning with his childhood as a fatherless boy working as a fisherman to support his family. A shipwreck strands Manjiro on an island, where he is rescued by a passing whaling ship. He works with the crew, learning the particulars of whaling, and eventually becomes a surrogate son to the ship's captain, who takes Manjiro back to Massachusetts and to an education. After another stint at sea, Manjiro joins the gold rush and makes enough money to return to Japan. He avoids imprisonment and even death (the xenophobic era's sentence for Japanese who returned from foreign countries) by instructing the country's top officials about American customs and policies. He eventually becomes a samurai, helping broker the opening of Japanese ports to the rest of the world. Exemplary in both her research and writing, Blumberg hooks readers with anecdotes that astonish without sensationalizing, and she uses language that's elegant and challenging, yet always clear. Particularly notable is the well-chosen reproductions of original artwork, including some sketches by Manjiro himself, which help illustrate Japanese culture and viewpoints of the time, the whaling industry, and nineteenth-century America. An author's note, bibliography, and suggested websites conclude this outstanding biography. —Gillian Engberg

Bober, Natalie S. *Countdown to Independence: A Revolution of Ideas in England and Her American Colonies: 1760–1776*. 2001. 368p. illus. Atheneum (9780689813290). Gr. 7–12. 973.3.

According to John Adams, the American Revolution didn't begin with war; it began "in the minds of the people," in the 15 years leading up to battle. Bober's latest title presents a remarkably thorough, readable, and even-handed account of those critical pre-war years, examining events and personalities on both sides of the Atlantic that contributed to America's break from England—from the crowning of King George III to the writing of the Declaration of Independence. In previous books, such as *Thomas Jefferson: Man on a Mountain* (1988) and *Abigail Adams: Witness to a Revolution* (1995), Bober has distinguished herself by integrating meticulous research and compelling anecdotes to inspire readers to sympathize and connect with the history. She continues that tradition here. In clear, well-documented analysis, she shows the relationship between events and lends insight into major personalities—from Edmund Burke and George Grenville to Thomas Jefferson, John Adams, and Thomas Hutchinson—bringing them further to life through a fine selection of nicely reproduced portraits. She writes with an almost cinematic attention to physical detail, describing the rooms where revolutionary milestones took place and even the weather outside the windows. The result is a compelling, yet scholarly resource that places readers at the center of the action, encouraging them to learn about the historic events and people, care about them, and, perhaps, learn more by investigating the extensive bibliography. Even readers raised on political cynicism will come away feeling stirred by this powerful, exciting story of their government's birth. —Gillian Engberg

Bowers, Rick. *Spies of Mississippi: The True Story of the Spy Network That Tried to Destroy the Civil Rights Movement*. 2010. 128p. illus. National Geographic (9781426305955). Gr. 7–10. 323.1196.

With all the books on the civil rights movement for young people, it's hard to believe there's a topic that hasn't yet been touched. But Bowers, through impeccable research and personal investigation, seems to have come up with something chillingly new. In 1956, the state of Mississippi conceived a Sovereignty Commission that began as a propaganda outlet and morphed into a spy network, with a goal of stopping integration and crushing the civil rights movement in the state. Written with clarity and understated power, the book methodically shows how white politicians organized the network and willing blacks accepted payment to infiltrate groups like the NAACP, or in some cases rail against civil rights organizations in churches and African American newspapers. After the election of Governor Ross Barnett, the commission's tactics grew bolder, and violence became a part of the mix. Those with knowledge of the era will find this a vivid depiction of those turbulent days, but for them as well as students new to the history the extremes will be an eye-opener. The inset of photographs might have worked better spread throughout the text, but the story is so powerful it hardly needs visuals. Sources, an extensive bibliography, and copies of some of the commission documents (all were unsealed in 1998) are appended. —Ilene Cooper

Brimner, Larry. ***Black & White: The Confrontation between Reverend Fred L. Shuttlesworth and Eugene "Bull" Connor*****. 2011. 112p. illus. Boyds Mills/Calkins Creek (9781590787663). Gr. 7–12. 323.1196.**

Bombed, beaten, banned, and imprisoned, Reverend Fred. L. Shuttlesworth led the civil rights struggle for equality in Birmingham, Alabama, using nonviolent action to protest segregation in schools, stores, buses, and the hiring of police officers. He pressed his congregation to register to vote and to cast their ballots for civil rights supporters. Eugene "Bull" Connor, backed by the Ku Klux Klan, became a symbol of racist hatred and violence as he organized the southern segregationists to rally against Shuttlesworth. With a spacious design that includes archival pictures and primary source documents on almost every page, this accessible photo-essay recounts the events in three sections, which focus first on the preacher, then on the commissioner, and finally, on their confrontation. For readers new to the subject, the biographies will be a vivid, informative introduction, but even those who have some familiarity with the landmark events will learn much more here. Thorough source notes document the sometimes harrowing details and provide opportunities for further research, as does a list of suggested reading. Never simplistic in his depictions, Brimner shows the viewpoints from all sides: some middle-class blacks resented "Fred's" heavy-handed style—fiery, confrontational, dictatorial—even if they agreed with the goals; some whites in Birmingham did wish to see an end to segregation, though their voices were drowned out. A penetrating look at elemental national history. —Hazel Rochman

Colman, Penny. ***Where the Action Was: Women War Correspondents in World War II*****. 2002. 128p. illus. Crown (9780517800751). Gr. 6–9. 070.4.**

Colman, the author of several books on women's history, including *Rosie the Riveter* (2000), which chronicled the lives of women on the home front during WWII, now looks at women who spent the war years in the middle of the conflict as reporters and photographers. By using these journalists' words and pictures as well as her own authorial skills, Colman impressively recreates the backdrop of the war—the danger, confusion, even the stench—and introduces women whose skill at their jobs and bravery in the face of horror allowed them to report the news through their own unique perspectives. The book briefly looks at early women journalists, then follows pioneering reporters who were soon joined by other women, many of whom had to fight, and in some cases lie, to get credentials simply because of their sex. With more than 15 journalists followed through the text, it may not always be easy for children to distinguish between them, even though some, such as Martha Gellhorn and Margaret Bourke-White, stand out. However, the text is briskly readable, and the 70 black-and-white photos are impressive and well chosen. Source notes would have been appreciated, but this well-handled book profoundly captures both the times and the struggle of women who had the talent to do the job male reporters did, but had to fight harder to do it.
—Ilene Cooper

Crowe, Chris. ***Getting Away with Murder: The True Story of the Emmett Till Case*****. 2003. 128p. illus. Penguin/Phyllis Fogelman (9780803728042). Gr. 7–12. 364.15.**

Most American history books don't include Emmett Till, the black 14-year-old from Chicago who was brutally murdered while visiting relatives in the Mississippi Delta in 1954. But the gruesome, racially motivated crime and the court's failure to convict the white murderers was a powerful national catalyst for the civil rights movement. Crowe, the author of *Mississippi Trial* (2002), a YA novel about Till's story, begins this nonfiction account with the events that led to the murder: on a dare, Till allegedly flirted with a local white woman; several days later he was kidnapped by the woman's husband and other men. In accessible, succinct, and sometimes colloquial language, Crowe details what happened on the horrible night, the court proceedings, and how the nation responded-—the "aftershocks" of the unbelievable ruling. Crowe is particularly successful in placing the murder within its larger historical context, detailing life both in the segregated Jim Crow South and in Emmett's less volatile but still segregated Chicago, and he doesn't shy away from the horrifying details (there's a shocking black-and-white photo of Emmett's disfigured corpse among the illustrations). Crowe's occasional re-creations of events are vivid, but like the rest of the text, they would have been better served with more extensive source notes; only a few in-text references and a concluding bibliography are provided. But Crowe's powerful, terrifying account does justice to its subject in bold, direct telling, supported by numerous archival photos and quotes from those who remember, including Emmett's mother, who wrote on her son's gravestone: "A little nobody who shook up the world." A time line and a list of further resources conclude. —Gillian Engberg

Denenberg, Barry. *Shadow Life: A Portrait of Anne Frank and Her Family*. 2005. 240p. illus. Scholastic (9780439416788). Gr. 6–10. 940.53.

Readers of Anne Frank's diary may think they know her story, but this thoroughly researched volume offers much more, throwing light on the lives of Anne and her family before, during, and after the years in the secret annex. The first section discusses the Franks' life in Germany when Hitler came to power, their move to Amsterdam, and their lives during the next nine years. The second section, a fictional diary in the voice of Anne's older sister, Margot, offers a slightly different perspective on the time the family spent in hiding. Returning to nonfiction, the third and fourth sections recount what happened to the family members when they were discovered and sent to concentration camps, and describe Otto Frank's postwar efforts to find his daughters and the publication of Anne's diary. Inserting a fictional diary into a nonfiction work was an unusual choice, but the section effectively makes the people, their relationships, and their experiences more real. While Anne's diary is affecting in a way that no other version of her story could be, readers who hunger to know more will find this informative, involving book—with source notes, a detailed time line, a bibliographic essay, and lists of further resources—a great place to turn. Photos are included. —Carolyn Phelan

Ellis, Deborah. *Three Wishes: Palestinian and Israeli Children Speak*. 2004. 144p. Groundwood (9780888996084). Gr. 5–12. 956.04.

"They murdered my friend." Growing up separate and apart in a world of bombs, bullets, removals, checkpoints, and curfews, 20 Israeli and Palestinian young people talk about how the war has affected them. The author of *Parvana's Journey* (2002) and other novels about children in Afghanistan moves to nonfiction with 20 stirring first-person narratives by Jewish, Christian, and Muslim young people she interviewed in 2002. An accessible historical overview that is fair to all sides leads off, followed by brief individual profiles of the kids, which include a small photo, and the words of kids, who are traumatized, angry, hopeful, hateful, despairing, and brave. The wide range of voices shows the connections between warring neighbors despite the distances that separate them, and the personal details reveal the universals ("I just want to ride horses") in a moving way. Even the grimmest stories have a glimmer of hope, as in the account of a Palestinian girl whose Israeli and Palestinian friends return again and again to help rebuild her house, which is repeatedly bulldozed by soldiers. The specifics and the passionate immediacy of the voices will spark discussion on the Middle East and on civilians in war. —Hazel Rochman

Feldman, Ruth Tenzer. *Don't Whistle in School: The History of America's Public Schools*. 2001. 88p. illus. Lerner, lib. ed. (9780822517450). Gr. 6–10. 370.

Expertly encapsulating the major movements since colonial times, Feldman covers the history of public education without wasting a syllable. Information branches out in several directions, encompassing social and economic trends that affected education, support (or lack thereof) by key political figures, and landmark judicial rulings that caused national upheavals about everything from the study of evolution to integration to busing. Threaded through every chapter are details both nostalgic and dramatic. Descriptions of McGuffey Readers, the premiere of *Sesame Street*, and the global classroom depict education through several generations. Especially affecting are the text and pictures concerning duck-and-cover drills, the Little Rock Nine, and college protests about Vietnam. Feldman also addresses public education for Native Americans, African Americans, and immigrants of various cultures and nationalities. From dunce caps and Ichabod Crane to *The Blackboard Jungle* and Christa McAuliffe, this captivating history is a skeletal time line with plenty of muscle. Sepia-tone illustrations give readers a visual taste of yesteryear. —Roger Leslie

Fleming, Candace. *Ben Franklin's Almanac: Being a True Account of the Good Gentleman's Life*. 2003. 128p. illus. Atheneum (9780689835490). Gr. 6–9. 973.3.

There's no shortage of books on Franklin, but this biography, which springs from Fleming's lifelong fascination with the multitalented man, is unlike anything that has come before, and it bears no resemblance to Fleming's picture-book work. Designed more like a scrapbook than an almanac, it's a visually rich but densely packed amalgamation of anecdotal narrative, boxed insets, black-and-white reproductions of period documents and artwork, and material obtained from Franklin's personal papers—all organized into topical chapters on Franklin's family life, writings, scientific pursuits, and political involvement. The whole gives an excellent sense of the time in which Franklin lived, but the thematic organization here sacrifices continuity and leaves occasional gaps. The science section is perhaps the best as it falls neatly into invention-specific discussions. Lively anecdotes greatly expand the main text, and numerous quotes by and about Franklin give the man a truly human face, even as they raise questions that continue to puzzle historians. A fitting tribute to a "good gentleman" whose life was well and energetically lived. Websites and further readings are appended. —Stephanie Zvirin

Fleming, Candace. *The Lincolns: A Scrapbook Look at Abraham and Mary*. 2008. 192p. illus. Random/Schwartz & Wade (9780375836183). Gr. 7–12. 973.7092.

Using the same innovative scrapbook format employed in *Ben Franklin's Almanac* (2003) and *Our Eleanor* (2005), Fleming offers another standout biographical title, this time twining accounts of two lives—Abraham and Mary Todd Lincoln—into one fascinating whole. On spreads that combine well-chosen visuals with blocks of headlined text, Fleming gives a full, birth-to-death view of the "inextricably bound" Lincolns. Once again, Fleming humanizes her subjects and offers a broader perspective on their times with cleverly juxtaposed facts, anecdotes, and images. One page, for example, combines an 1861 map of the divided U.S. with detailed descriptions of what the new president and First Lady each tackled the day after Lincoln's inauguration (Fort Sumter and securing a dressmaker, respectively). Although the reproductions are often small and dark, the intriguing visual mix will easily draw readers and browsers alike. Included are paintings and etchings of heartrending historical events, church documents, handwritten notes, and political cartoons. Fleming's writing, filled with quotes and personal details, is just as lively as the assortment of images, and an extensive time line, suggested resources, and source notes round out the text. Starting with her personal introduction, this exemplary resource will prompt readers to consider how an individual's life story, and a country's history, are constructed. —Gillian Engberg

Fradin, Judith Bloom, and Dennis Brindell Fradin. *5,000 Miles to Freedom: Ellen and William Craft's Flight from Slavery*. 2005. 96p. illus. National Geographic (9780792278856). Gr. 6–9. 326.

Both exciting escape adventure and gripping history, this account of a husband and wife on the run from slavery traces their journey to freedom in the U.S. and across the world. Ellen is a light-skinned African American, daughter of the master who raped her mother. Disguised as a wealthy Southern gentleman, she escapes with her husband, William, disguised as her slave, and they travel by train and steamboat to freedom in Boston. When their astonishing story makes the fugitive couple famous, slave catchers come after them, so the Crafts leave for England, where they continue their abolitionist work, until their return home after the Civil War. The Fradins, whose many fine histories include *Ida B. Wells* (2000), draw heavily on the Crafts' personal accounts to add depth and

drama to the carefully documented narrative. The handsome design includes lots of photos, archival artwork, letters, and newspaper accounts.
—Hazel Rochman

Fradin, Judith Bloom, and Dennis Brindell Fradin. ***Fight On! Mary Church Terrell's Battle for Integration.*** **2003. 192p. illus. Clarion (9780618133499). Gr. 5–9. 323.**

As the Fradins point out in this well-researched biography, "A handful of people have received the bulk of the credit for the civil rights movement in the United States." Though most young people have never heard of Mary Church Terrell, her story is worth knowing. The book opens in 1950 with 86-year-old Terrell arranging to meet three friends at Thompson's Cafeteria in Washington, D.C. They knew that they would not be served, because three of them were black. But by documenting the restaurant's refusal, they laid the groundwork for a lawsuit that made its way to the Supreme Court and ended racial discrimination in the city's restaurants. The book's large format allows for plenty of illustrations, mainly period photographs that help readers visualize black neighborhoods in Memphis (where Terrell grew up) and Washington, D.C., as well as segregated venues like theaters and waiting rooms. Appendixes include source notes for the many quotations, a bibliography, and photo credits. Very readable and handsomely designed, this biography presents the life of an educated, energetic, and determined African American woman within the context of her times, which began in Lincoln's administration and ended in Eisenhower's. —Carolyn Phelan

Fradin, Judith Bloom, and Dennis Brindell Fradin. ***Jane Addams: Champion of Democracy.*** **2006. 200p. illus. Clarion (9780618504367). Gr. 6–9. 361.2.**

A fascinating and rich life is related in strong, unfussy prose by the Fradins. Known as Jennie as a child, the peace activist, founder of Hull House, and Nobel Prize winner felt like an ugly duckling. But college, Europe, and the discovery of good work that she could do in the city of Chicago transformed her. The settlement house she founded in 1889 provided a place for the poor to learn, to socialize, to share. She mobilized both workers and volunteers, wrote, spoke, studied, and raised funds. Most of the photographs are portraits; the text is enlivened when the images are those taken at Hull House or at marches. The narrative is smoothly written, and the opening anecdote, which describes how she became a garbage inspector of the Nineteenth Ward of Chicago in order to get the garbage picked up, is telling and draws readers into the story. Addams' bouts of depression and her deeply unpopular opposition to WWI are noted but do not unbalance the narrative. What shines is her everyday heroism, which changed lives. Excellent. —GraceAnne A. DeCandido

Freedman, Russell. ***Abraham Lincoln & Frederick Douglass: The Story behind an American Friendship.*** **2012. 128p. illus. Clarion (9780547385624). Gr. 5–9. 973.7092.**

This striking book opens in 1863 with a scene in the White House. Frederick Douglass, the well-known writer, editor, speaker, abolitionist, and former slave, is the only black man waiting in the crowded room outside Lincoln's office in hopes of meeting the president. After backtracking to tell the dramatic story of Douglass' rise from slave to free man to influential public figure, the discussion shifts to Lincoln, focusing first on his life and later on his conduct of the Civil War and the issue of slavery. Returning to the opening scene, the final chapters consider the men's different points of view and trace the respectful, increasingly warm relationship between Lincoln and Douglass through the remainder of the war. Freedman writes with clarity, intelligence, and a fine sense of vivid detail. He doesn't just point out that both these self-educated men had read and studied *The Columbian Orator*, he also includes the book's three-page "Dialogue between a Master and Slave" in the back matter. Also appended are source notes, a selected bibliography, a discussion of historical sites related to Lincoln and Douglass, and a list of credits for the well-chosen illustrations, which include period photos, prints, drawings, paintings, and documents. A well-researched, wonderfully readable book on "Lincoln's brief but telling friendship with Frederick Douglass."—Carolyn Phelan

Freedman, Russell. ***The Adventures of Marco Polo.*** **Illus. by Bagram Ibatoulline. 2006. 64p. Scholastic/ Arthur A. Levine (9780439523943). Gr. 7–10. 910.4.**

The name Marco Polo evokes images of faraway travels and exotic treasures: silks and spices, gold and jewels. Newbery Medal–winner Freedman takes readers along on Polo's journey in a book that is as beautiful as many of the sights the explorer observed. It begins at Polo's deathbed, his family begging him to confess his exaggerations. Even some contemporary scholars don't believe Polo went to China, but many observers think most of his tales were true. Using Polo's own descriptions (as told to a writer he met in prison), Freedman shepherds readers across deserts, down the Silk Road, and over mountains until the adventurer reaches the magnificent kingdom of Kublai Khan. Supporting Freedman's informative yet evocative prose are enchanting illustrations. Ibatoulline follows the historic journey with art inspired by different periods––for instance, he uses illuminated manuscripts as the basis for the European scenes. The original artwork is complemented by many historic illustrations, some from editions of Polo's *Description of the World*. The meticulous art notes call attention to the lack of text source notes, although Freedman does include an extensive, informative author's note about Polo's claims. With its thick, mottled pages and attractive design, this is a glorious piece of bookmaking; readers will find it a pleasure to explore. —Ilene Cooper

Freedman, Russell. ***Becoming Ben Franklin: How a Candle-Maker's Son Helped Light the Flame of Liberty.*** **2013. 96p. illus. Holiday (9780823423743). Gr. 6–9. 973.3092.**

If your image of Benjamin Franklin is a portly, balding old fellow carried through the streets of Philadelphia in a sedan chair, meet 17-year-old Ben. A runaway apprentice new to the city, he was strong, energetic, and ambitious, with intelligence and charm to spare. Freedman traces Franklin's life and work, showing how a mischievous boy became a rebellious apprentice, then a successful colonial printer, and finally an influential figure in the world and a pivotal figure in his nation's founding. Along the way, Franklin informs and amuses his countrymen with *Poor Richard's Almanack*, heats them with his stove design, enlightens them through his experiments on electricity, and protects them by inventing the lightning rod. Writing about a man whose long life included such varied interests and accomplishments must involve hard choices of what to leave out, but Freedman clearly enjoys the challenge. In chapters with titles such as "Dr. Fatsides in the Mother Country," he writes perceptively about every stage of Franklin's life, weaving in lively anecdotes as well as quotes from his *Autobiography* and other writings. The well-chosen color illustrations include period paintings, prints, and documents. Handsomely designed, solidly researched, and beautifully written, this is the go-to biography of Franklin for young people. —Carolyn Phelan

Freedman, Russell. ***In the Days of the Vaqueros: America's First True Cowboys.*** **2001. 70p. illus. Clarion (9780395967881). Gr. 5–12. 636.2.**

Talk about mixed-up historical myths. It turns out that the first cowboys were Indian cow herders who rode the range in Spanish Mexico nearly 500 years ago. They called themselves vaqueros (from *vaca*, the Spanish word for cow), and much later they taught the settlers of the American West their work and shared the tools of their trade. Freedman, who also wrote *Cowboys of the Wild West* (1983), tells the story with depth, clarity, and a vigor that conveys the thrilling excitement of the work and the macho swagger of the culture. The vaqueros' story is set against the sweep of history, from the time of Columbus (who brought cattle and horses) to the coming of the railroad, and, finally, the end of the open range. The book's design is beautiful, with spacious type on thick paper, and the dazzling illustrations—prints, paintings, and photos on almost every page, from Remington's "Stampede" paintings to Cisneros' drawings of vaqueros in action—will lure even reluctant history students and readers. Older readers will also be fascinated by Freedman's discussion of the U.S. romantic vision of the frontier cowboys, who were traditionally viewed by Spanish and Mexicans as just poor laborers on horseback. —Hazel Rochman

Freedman, Russell. *Lafayette and the American Revolution*. 2010. 96p. illus. Holiday (9780823421824). Gr. 6–9. 355.0092.

Inspired by an idealistic belief in the cause of liberty and a determination to prove himself worthy on the battlefield, Lafayette, a 19-year-old French nobleman, left his young wife and daughter, ignored a royal order, crossed the ocean to America, and took up a commission in the Continental army. Lafayette's courage and personal charm endeared him to Washington, who gradually gave him more difficult missions, culminating in the containment of Cornwallis' troops at Yorktown. Returning to France, Lafayette called for a constitutional monarchy but was accused of treason and imprisoned during the French Revolution. After his citizenship was restored, he continued speaking out for political freedom. In this solidly researched and smoothly written biography, Freedman creates a vivid portrait of Lafayette as he matures from an impetuous young man and inexperienced solider to a leader capable of wisdom as well as valor. Scenes on the battlefield are balanced with a nuanced portrayal of his filial relationship with Washington. A moving final scene takes place, surprisingly, in 1917. Masterfully designed with a spacious format and good use of color, the book includes many clearly reproduced paintings and prints. A time line, source notes, and a selected bibliography of sources are appended in this look at one of our Revolution's most intriguing heroes. —Carolyn Phelan

Freedman, Russell. *The War to End All Wars*. 2010. 192p. illus. Clarion (9780547026862). Gr. 6–10. 940.3.

In his signature lucid style, Freedman offers a photo-essay that examines WWI, the first global war in which modern weapons inflicted mass slaughter and an estimated 20 million people were killed. Interwoven into the big picture of the war's causes and consequences are unforgettable vignettes of German and Allied soldiers, drawn from reports, letters, and diaries, and the personal details are heartbreaking, as in the example of a Frenchman in the trenches who wrote "Humanity is mad" a minute before he was killed. Both the intimate accounts and the historical analysis are all carefully documented in appended chapter notes, and the book's open design, illustrated with maps and captioned photos on almost every page, will draw browsers into the passages of nonstop action and political discussion. Freedman contrasts the battle details of No Man's Land, trench warfare, machine guns, poison gas, tanks, and emerging aircraft technology with the military leaders' distance from the mass of soldiers and everyday people, and he shows the connections between this war and the causes of future conflict, including WWII and discord in the Middle East. An important addition to history curriculum.
—Hazel Rochman

Freedman, Russell. *Washington at Valley Forge*. 2008. 112p. illus. Holiday (9780823420698). Gr. 6–9. 973.3.

With most of the presidential-history attention this year directed at Abraham Lincoln, Freedman turns instead to the man whose remarkable display of leadership during the direst of times helped to found the Union that would eventually need preserving. The winter of 1777 was a bleak one for the Revolutionary army—though, as Freedman points out, even calling it an "army" is generous. A relatively inexperienced Washington made the decision to camp his ragtag bunch of irregulars at Valley Forge, a defensible location close to the British holed up comfortably in Philadelphia. With his usual clarity of focus and keen eye for telling quotations, Freedman documents how Washington struggled to maintain morale despite hunger, near-nakedness, and freezing conditions; as well, he managed to reconstruct failed supply lines, evade political maneuverings from within the Continental Congress, and train his troops to win a war. Throughout, high-quality reproductions depict Washington among the men, and with the numerous other influential people who played critical roles. While Washington is certainly the center of this book's cosmos, it is less a look at one venerable figure from history than it is a tale of the triumph of endurance. Lacing facts and history into a winning, if not always tremendously exciting, narrative, this solid book will dispel any fogginess children may have about why that winter in Valley Forge was such a pivotal time in our country's founding. —Ian Chipman

Freedman, Russell. ***Who Was First? Discovering the Americas.*** **2007. 88p. illus. Clarion (9780618663910). Gr. 6–9. 970.01.**

This well-designed, clearly written book looks at various ideas about the discovery of the Americas, including the famous voyages of Columbus in 1492, the claims that fifteenth-century Chinese explorer Zheng He may have sailed to the Americas, and the now-documented settlement of Vikings in Newfoundland around the year 1000. Next, the discussion turns to Native Americans, from ancient civilizations to the diverse societies that were here shortly before European contact. Freedman describes the long-accepted theory of the earliest inhabitants of North America crossing from Siberia over an ice bridge across the Bering Strait, dismissing it as "almost certainly wrong" in the light of more recent archaeological evidence. Beyond the very readable presentation of facts and theories, the book's main accomplishment is in showing that history is not a static body of knowledge, but an evolving process of logically interpreted evidence continually questioned, disputed, and revised in the light of new discoveries and theories put forth by "obsessed amateurs" as well as professional historians. Back matter includes chapter notes identifying the sources of quotes as well as a short discussion, chapter by chapter, of books, articles, and websites used in researching the book. The illustrations, many in color, include many excellent maps as well as reproductions of period drawings, paintings, engravings, and photos of people, artifacts, and sites. A well-researched, intelligent account of America's "discovery."
—Carolyn Phelan

Giblin, James Cross. ***Secrets of the Sphinx.*** **Illus. by Bagram Ibatoulline. 2004. 48p. Scholastic (9780590098472). Gr. 7–12. 932.**

The facts are amazing: the Great Sphinx of Egypt is nearly 4,500 years old; it is as long as a city block and as tall as a six-story building. Just as thrilling are the unsolved secrets. Who built the Sphinx and the three huge pyramids it appears to guard? Is the Sphinx a portrait of a particular pharaoh? In his signature plain style, the award-winning nonfiction author presents a wealth of scholarship, including perspectives on ancient Egypt's rich history and culture, the Rosetta Stone, and urgent contemporary issues of restoration and preservation. Giblin may spend too much time on crank theories about the Sphinx not being the work of the ancient Egyptians, but he vividly conveys the drama of recent discoveries, especially archaeological excavations that reveal startling new information about how the Sphinx was built and about the skilled men—and women—who labored to create it. The handsome book design helps make the complex text accessible. The picture-book-size layout is spacious, and the photorealistic gouache and watercolor illustrations are beautiful, including paintings of the desert, close-ups of the sculptured face, details of hieroglyphics, and portraits of famous figures through history. Giblin discusses how he used each of his sources in the combined "Source Notes and Bibliography," and many readers will want to follow his trail. —Hazel Rochman

Giblin, James Cross. ***The Life and Death of Adolf Hitler.*** **2002. 256p. illus. Clarion (9780395903711). Gr. 7–9. 943.086.**

Hitler's cold eyes stare out from the cover photograph of this excellent biography. Much of the book centers on Hitler's early years and rise to power after the First World War, with emphasis on the complicity or, in some cases, naivete of the German political leaders and industrialists. It also covers the failed appeasement efforts of the British and French in pre-WWII months. Giblin moves beyond political events and delves into the twisted realms of Hitler's strangely contradictory personality, with anecdotes about Hitler's love of dogs, his relationships with women, and his vegetarianism. Giblin wisely avoids cataloging all the battles and events of WWII and keeps the focus on Hitler's personal reaction to these events and his final, crazed days in his Berlin bunker. The last chapter deals with contemporary neo-Nazi movements throughout the world. Interspersed with the text are fascinating period photographs. Source notes are provided for each chapter, and the author includes a short informal essay, explaining why he wrote the book and which sources were particularly helpful. —Todd Morning

Greenfield, Howard. ***After the Holocaust.*** **2001. 160p. illus. Greenwillow (9780688177522). Gr. 6–12. 804.48.**

Greenfeld's *The Hidden Children* (1993) is a classic account of the children who survived in hiding from the Nazis in Europe. This book uses a similar approach to tell the story of what happened to young Holocaust survivors after the war. Greenfeld weaves the personal stories (based on his interviews with eight Jewish survivors now living in the U.S.) with his own commentary and a general history of the time. The readable, slightly oversize design features lots of black-and-white photographs, news photos, and family snapshots that capture what was lost. Occasional sidebars fill in the history, including one on U.S. immigration quotas in 1945 that denied entry to refugees. The truth of the individual voices gives the history immediacy. Many Jews faced anti-Semitism after the war, but what was it like for a teen to return home and knock on the door, only to be chased away by people who had grabbed the place when the young person's family was sent to the camps? What did young orphans do in the displaced-persons' camps, waiting for months for a country to take them in? Greenfeld has deliberately chosen a wide range of survivors who were young at the time of liberation, from several different countries and with a variety of war experiences. Several nearly died in the camps; a few had been in safe hiding places. Some were hungry for education after the war; some were wild for a good time. Some want to forget; some cannot. There's no sentimentality; one survivor is still haunted by the horrific revenge some ex-prisoners took on their guards. Greenfeld quotes Gabrielle Schiff, who talks about what she witnessed as a social worker in the DP camps: "At the risk of destroying a well-known cliche, I affirm that suffering does not make people any better; it often brings out the worst in them." There is no better book to answer the Holocaust deniers. As Greenfield writes, the post-Holocaust experiences are actually a continuation of the Holocaust itself, not a postscript. —Hazel Rochman

Haugen, Brenda. ***The Zodiac Killer: Terror and Mystery.*** **2010. 96p. illus. Compass Point, lib. ed. (9780756543570). Gr. 6–9. 364.152.**

The serial killer who terrorized California in the late 1960s and early '70s—he called himself Zodiac—is the subject of this heart-stopper of a book. In the beginning it seemed like an urban legend: two teens necking at a lover's lane are fired upon. After another similar killing, letters begin showing up at local newspapers, filled with inside information on the murders as well as uncrackable codes. Thus begins one of the episode's most infamous elements: the back-and-forth relationship between Zodiac and the newspapers reacting to his threats. Most of the chapters carry the grim inevitability of good true-crime writing: you know something bad is about to happen; you're just not sure what. Haugen goes briskly through the details with a curt efficiency well suited for teen readers: "She died less than 30 feet (9 m) from the station wagon. The killer got back in his car and left." Photographs are few, but the reproductions of Zodiac's letters pack a punch, and sidebars (*Dirty Harry* was based on the killings) add to the overall strong design. Zodiac was never captured, but Haugen's conclusions on his impact are savvy. It's a bit pricey, but smart writing and solid back matter make this gruesome package worth every penny. —Daniel Kraus

★ **Heiligman, Deborah.** ***Charles and Emma: The Darwins' Leap of Faith.*** **2009. 288p. illus. Holt (9780805087215). Gr. 8–12. 576.2.**

When the book opens, Charles Darwin is trying to make a decision, and he is doing so in time-honored fashion: drawing a line down a piece of paper and putting the pros of marriage on one side and the cons on the other. As much as Darwin is interested in wedded life, he is afraid that family life will take him away from the revolutionary work he is doing on the evolution of species. However, the pluses triumph, and he finds the perfect mate in his first cousin Emma, who becomes his comforter, editor, mother of his 10 children—and sparring partner. Although highly congenial, Charles and Emma were on opposite sides when it came to the role of God in creation. Heiligman uses the Darwin family letters and papers to craft a full-bodied look at the personal influences that shaped Charles' life as he worked mightily to shape his theories. This intersection between religion and science is where the book shines, but it is also an excellent portrait of what life was like during the Victorian era, a time when illness and death were ever present, and, in a way, a real-time example of the survival of the fittest. Occasionally hard to follow, in part because of the many characters (the family tree helps), this is well sourced and mostly fascinating, and may attract a wider audience than those interested in science. Austen fans will find a romance to like here, too. —Ilene Cooper

Helfer, Andrew. ***Malcolm X: A Graphic Biography.*** **Illus. by Randy DuBurke. 2006. 104p. Hill & Wang (9780809095049). Gr. 10–12. 320.54.**

This stirring graphic-novel-style biography weaves together black history with the personal story of the charismatic leader Malcolm X, whose confrontational approach to white racism was in marked contrast to Martin Luther King's policy of nonviolence. Helfer's text draws heavily on *The Autobiography* (1965), which Malcolm X wrote with Alex Haley, and DuBurke's realistic, black-and-white art, with an average of six frames per page, visualizes the political struggle as well as the inner anger and turmoil. Far from reverential, the account includes chapters on Malcolm X's life as a hustler and his own disturbing racism. Close-up images, all set against a backdrop of the civil rights movement, capture crucial events in Malcolm's life: the teacher who tells him that as a black man he can never be a lawyer, his passionate reading in the prison library, and his conversion to Islam. The book, which is part of the Novel Graphics line, evokes powerful visual drama and brings the big issues close in a way that is sure to interest YAs for biography assignments as well as discussion of the issues. —Hazel Rochman

Hillman, Laura. ***I Will Plant You a Lilac Tree: A Memoir of a Schindler's List Survivor.*** **2005. 256p. illus. Atheneum (9780689869808). Gr. 8–11.**

There are many YA Holocaust memoirs, but few of them deal with a teenager's survival in the concentration camps. That makes Hillman's affecting account particularly noteworthy. In 1942 Berlin, Hannelore, 16, bravely volunteers to be deported with her mother and two younger brothers to Poland. Of course, they are soon separated, and during the next three years Hannelore is moved through eight concentration camps. In clipped, first-person narrative, she remembers the worst: crammed cattle cars; backbreaking work from stone quarries to salt mines; beatings; hunger; her own rape; the smell of children's bodies in the crematoria. She tells it as she endured it, quietly relaying the facts without sensationalism or sentimentality. She remembers making friends, one of whom is beaten to death because of a relationship with a German soldier. Hannelore herself falls in love with a young prisoner, Dick. At the end of the book is a photo of the lovers reunited and married; no one else in the family photos survived. The author never fully explains how she and Dick get onto Schindler's list, which saves them from Auschwitz (an explanatory note about the list would have been helpful), but the arbitrariness of the list was as true to the Holocaust survival experience as the loss. —Hazel Rochman

Hinds, Kathryn. ***Everyday Life in the Roman Empire.*** **2010. 320p. illus. Marshall Cavendish/Benchmark (9780761444848). Gr. 7–10. 937.**

Among the many titles about the Roman Empire published for youth, this survey in Hinds' Everyday Life series stands out for its unusually detailed look at the daily lives of "all who contributed to the vitality and strength of ancient Rome," from emperors to slaves. Much of the colorful sense of the individuals' worlds comes from numerous excerpts from primary sources, including quotes from Homer and Ovid as well as anonymous poets. In fluid, approachable text, the chapters examine the varying customs, responsibilities, and domestic lives of patricians and citizens in both the city and countryside before moving on to a final, in-depth chapter about religion. It's the specifics that make this so engrossing, such as sample menus: roasted peacocks and flamingo tongues for the upper class, porridge and beans for humble rural dwellers. Also noteworthy are inclusive sections about women and children, even though, as Hinds points out, "Roman historians rarely wrote much about women; when they did, it was usually to criticize a woman for scandalous behavior." Frequent color images of ancient statues, friezes, and ruins contribute to the sense of immediacy; a mosaic of Roman women working out with weights in bikini-like clothing looks like a scene from *Self* magazine, for example. A glossary, extensive bibliography, and chapter notes conclude this title, a strong choice for students' research or personal interest. —Gillian Engberg

Hoose, Phillip. *Claudette Colvin: Twice toward Justice*. 2009. 144p. illus. Farrar/Melanie Kroupa (9780374313227). Gr. 7–12. 323.092.

Nine months before Rosa Parks' history-making protest on a city bus, Claudette Colvin, a 15-year-old Montgomery, Alabama, high-school student, was arrested and jailed for refusing to give up her seat to a white passenger. Hoose draws from numerous personal interviews with Colvin in this exceptional title that is part historical account, part memoir. Hoose's lucid explanations of background figures and events alternate with lengthy passages in Colvin's own words, and the mix of voices creates a comprehensive view of the Montgomery bus boycott and the landmark court case, *Browder v. Gayle*, that grew from it. At the center of the headline-grabbing turmoil is teenager Colvin, who became pregnant during the boycott; and her frank, candid words about both her personal and political experiences will galvanize young readers. On each attractively designed spread, text boxes and archival images, including photos and reproduced documents, extend the gripping story. As in Hoose's *We Were There, Too! Young People in U.S. History* (2001), this inspiring title shows the incredible difference that a single young person can make, even as it demonstrates the multitude of interconnected lives that create and sustain a political movement. Thorough chapter notes and suggestions for further reading close this title, which will find an avid readership beyond the classroom. —Gillian Engberg

Hopkinson, Deborah. *Shutting Out the Sky*. 2003. 144p. Scholastic/Orchard (9780439375900). Gr. 5–12. 307.76.

In the tradition of Russell Freedman's *Immigrant Kids* (1980), but much more detailed, this history of the 23 million immigrants who came to New York City from southern and eastern Europe at the end of the nineteenth century humanizes the statistics by weaving together the personal stories of five young people with the social conditions that caused them to emigrate, what they left behind, what they hoped for, what they found, and how they changed America. Amazing documentary photos by Jacob Riis and many others, as well as riveting quotes from archives and memoirs, add depth and drama to the accounts of young people, from street to school to sweatshop. At 16, Marcus Ravage convinces his parents to sell the family cow to pay for his journey from Romania. Lithuanian immigrant Pauline Newman becomes one of the first women labor organizers. Italian American Leonard Covello is ashamed to bring his friends home, even as he learns that he can become American without rejecting where he came from. Meticulous documentation, including full chapter notes, will help the many young people—and their parents and grandparents—who will want to know more and to research their own family roots. —Hazel Rochman

Kaufman, Michael T. *1968*. 2009. 160p. illus. Roaring Brook/Flash Point (9781596434288). Gr. 7–12. 909.82.

Kaufman, whose reporting career at the *New York Times* spans four decades, expertly draws young readers into the worldwide events of a single, watershed year: 1968. In this illuminating *New York Times* Book, each chapter focuses on a different hot spot around the globe, beginning with the Tet Offensive and the Vietnam War and moving through uprisings in New York, Paris, Prague, Chicago, and Mexico City, as well as the assassinations of Martin Luther King Jr. and Robert Kennedy. Reproductions of corresponding front-page articles from the *New York Times* open each chapter, while the full text of the articles appears in an appended section. The images, drawn from the *Times* archives, are riveting and will easily draw young people into the fascinating, often horrifying events of that "year like no other." An expanded introductory time line will help readers place the events in larger historical and cultural context. In a time in which newspapers seem to be losing ground among young people to online sources and *The Daily Show*, this insightful, clear-eyed, moving overview serves as a reminder of the fundamental importance of journalism—to gather accurate facts into the stories that become history. An essential volume for teens' understanding of the time period. —Gillian Engberg

King, Daniel. *Chess: From First Moves to Checkmate*. 2001. 64p. illus. Kingfisher (9780753453872). Gr. 4–12. 974.1.

International Grandmaster King's latest book on chess is a real gem. He begins with a brief look at chess history, from ancient India to the present. He then explains each chess piece, describes the algebraic notation of the board, explains special moves, and shows how to open the game and use effective strategies. Throughout, he offers training exercises, strategy quizzes, and trivia, all of which add depth and texture to his explanations. The computer-generated graphics are staggering. The colorful, multi-image illustrations are not only aesthetically appealing but also crystal clear and very effectively placed to enhance the text. They are certain to make this irresistible to browsers curious about the game as well as chess enthusiasts. Back matter includes information on the World Chess Championship competitions; a tribute to Garry Kasparov, the greatest chess champ of all time; the devious "gamesmanship" of psyching out an opponent; and the latest developments in computerized chess challenges. —Roger Leslie

Lanier, Shannon, and Jane Feldman. *Jefferson's Children: The Story of One American Family*. 2000. 144p. illus. Random (9780375805974). Gr. 6–9. 973.4.

"My name is Shannon Lanier. I am a twenty-year-old descendant of Thomas Jefferson and his slave Sally Hemings." In this unusual photo-essay, Lanier explores his family history and heritage, interviewing relatives he has known all his life and others he has only recently discovered, including some of Jefferson's descendants through his marriage to Martha Wayles Jefferson. The November 1998 announcement of DNA evidence of a connection between the Jefferson and Hemings families confirmed what many branches of the family had always known. Some of Sally's children had "passed" as white, resulting in a family with members who chose either a black or a white culture and others who did not know until recently that their background included both races. In this large, well-designed volume, each person or nuclear family is presented through a brief introduction and a few pages of reflections, accompanied by Jane Feldman's excellent black-and-white photos. The personal statements provide well-expressed points of view about how family members see themselves, their heritage, and racial issues in the U.S. today. Although some statements are more engaging than others (and the complexities of family lines and multigenerations can at times be confusing), they form a verbal mosaic that may challenge readers to think about the meaning of race in our society. This thought-provoking presentation of oral history encourages young people to talk with their elders, listen to their family stories, and get to know their extended families. Lanier holds out the hopeful vision that his family's story can extend to include all Americans, since "we are, through our common history and our common blood, truly one American family." —Carolyn Phelan

Lauber, Patricia. *Who Came First? New Clues to Prehistoric Americans*. 2003. 64p. illus. National Geographic (9780792282280). Gr. 5–10. 970.01.

Who were the first Americans? Where did they come from? How did they get here? When did they come? In a lively narrative that draws readers right into crucial research going on now, Lauber weaves together geology, archaeology, genetics, anthropology, and language, and shows how some recent archaeological findings challenge the classical theory that the first peoples came to Alaska from Siberia and settled first in the American Southwest. New evidence, including the recent discovery of an ancient skeleton in Washington, suggests that people might have arrived much earlier from Europe. Several Native American nations have claimed the skeleton and want to bury it as their religious beliefs demand; but scientists have sued the government to keep the bones for study. Especially compelling are the questions raised and the details about how experts work. How is carbon-14 dating done?

What does it prove? The inviting, spacious, magazine-style design, with lots of paintings, maps, photos, and screened insets, makes the complex information accessible. With so much to talk about, this will make a great cross-curricular classroom title, which will interest adults as well as the target readership. Includes a bibliography and websites. —Hazel Rochman

Li, Moying. *Snow Falling in Spring: Coming of Age in China during the Cultural Revolution*. 2008. 192p. illus. Farrar/Melanie Kroupa (9780374399221). Gr. 7–12. 951.05.

Before their house is ransacked and he's taken away by Red Guards during China's Cultural Revolution, Moying's father warns her, "Don't believe what you hear . . . and be very careful about what you say." Like Ji-li Jiang's *Red Scarf Girl* (1997), this stirring memoir makes the history personal by telling it from the perspective of a child who is shocked into confronting betrayal and violence close to home. Raised in a loving extended family, Moying is just 12 years old in 1966 when her world is suddenly transformed. Even some of her friends and mentors attack the purveyors of "Western ideology." Soldiers strip the bookshelves; students beat their teachers; the school principal hangs himself. The stirring detail, with occasional black-and-white photos, stays true to the young girl's viewpoint during the following 14 years, as Moying is sustained by her extraordinary grandmother, who includes friends, neighbors, and even some strangers in her "family." Moying's father smuggles out a reading list for her (from Mao's *Little Red Book* to Shakespeare is a big jump), and she and her friends secretly get novels by Jack London, Dickens, and more. The simple, direct narrative will grab readers with the eloquent account of daily trauma and hope. —Hazel Rochman

Marrin, Albert. *Flesh & Blood So Cheap: The Triangle Fire and Its Legacy*. 2011. 192p. illus. Knopf (9780375868894). Gr. 7–10. 974.7.

At the core of this landmark look at labor history is the detailed drama of the notorious 1911 Triangle Shirtwaist Factory fire, in which 146 workers died. Most of the victims were immigrant women between the ages of 14 and 23 who were burned or suffocated behind locked doors or who perished when they tried to escape the flames by jumping from windows. Their catastrophic deaths lead to changes in U.S. working conditions and fueled a campaign for union rights. This volume's excellent early chapters focus on the personal histories of the victims, many of whom were Russian Jews and Italian Catholics, and examine why their families left Europe, the passage to America, and life in New York City's tenements. Following chapters delve into the horrifying factory conditions that led to the fire. The highly readable book design features black-and-white photos on every double-page spread as well as newspaper accounts and biographical profiles, including those of leading protesters, such as Jacob Riis and Rose Schneiderman. Marrin further expands the discussion with disturbing contemporary parallels to underground sweatshops today. Sure to spark discussion, this standout title concludes with source notes and suggested-reading lists that will lead students to further resources for research and debate. —Hazel Rochman

Marrin, Albert. *George Washington and the Founding of a Nation*. 2001. 256p. illus. Fine Arts (9780525464815). Gr. 7–12. 973.4.

Marrin writes that in this book he has set himself a "double task," presenting an account of Washington's life and of the colonies' fight for independence. He's taken on a third task, too: that of revealing the work of the biographer. Throughout the book, he notes plainly what we know, what we can infer, and what we can never know about our first president. In the end, he succeeds admirably on all three fronts, melting the marble of the Washington legend into something very near flesh and blood. He conveys his subject's strengths, fears, and complexities in a portrait that asks readers to consider the icon as a man. We see Washington as a youth hungry for adventure and prestige, as a general who's better at inspiring his men than at planning battle strategies, and as an aging leader who would like to retire but cannot refuse a call to serve as president. The most revealing segments deal with Washington's attitude toward slavery. Marrin neither exploits nor excuses Washington's ownership of slaves, instead portraying him as a man of his time, one who could never reconcile his public philosophy of freedom with his private actions. Notes and a bibliography are appended. —Randy Meyer

Marrin, Albert. *The Great Adventure: Theodore Roosevelt and the Rise of Modern America*. 2007. 256p. illus. Dutton (9780525476597). Gr. 8–11. 973.91.

Along the lines of his *George Washington and the Founding of a Nation* (2001), Marrin offers a twin portrait of American society in a time of profound change and the life of a figure so dominant in the politics and self-image of the time that he has become an enduring symbol. A polymath who published some 18 million words and was the first American to receive a Nobel Prize, Roosevelt (no one who knew him well called him "Teddy") was also given to dancing exultantly around the big game he slaughtered, and to blasting (in print) the presidents who succeeded him. Marrin gives him "a place in the front rank of our country's heroes," particularly for his achievements in environmental conservation, but also shows him acting badly—for example, in the shameful Brownsville incident. Numerous endnotes and contemporary photos and prints add to this scholarly profile, which, like Betsy Harvey Kraft's *Theodore Roosevelt: Champion of the American Spirit* (2003), will give serious history students a solid grounding in the man's times, career, and forceful character. –John Peters

Maurer, Richard. *The Wright Sister*. 2003. 128p. illus. Roaring Brook (9780761315469). Gr. 5–9. 629.13.

Written for an older audience than the one for Jane Yolen's *My Brothers' Flying Machine* (2003), this handsome biography also spotlights the inventors' sister. Katharine Wright ran the household for her older brothers and their father during the years when Orville and Wilbur were developing and promoting their airplane. A graduate of Oberlin College, she gave up her career as a teacher to help them turn their airplane from a curiosity into a viable business. Clearly reflecting the societal rules and expectations of the time, the book portrays Katharine as an intelligent woman, valued for her role within the family, yet restricted by it. Even her brothers emerge as individuals here rather than the interchangeable "Wright brothers" found in many presentations. Quotations from diaries and letters bring the close-knit Wright family to life, making it all the more poignant when readers discover that Orville refused to see Katharine after her marriage at the age of 52, relenting only when she was on her deathbed. The layout is spacious, and the many well-chosen, black-and-white photos help visualize the Wrights and their times. An author's note and an extensive list of sources are appended.
—Carolyn Phelan

McClafferty, Carla Killough. *In Defiance of Hitler: The Secret Mission of Varian Fry*. 2008. 208p. illus. Farrar (9780374382049). Gr. 7–12. 940.53.

Rescue stories bring hope to the Holocaust darkness, and this stirring account of a young New York City journalist who secretly helped more than 2,000 refugees escape Nazi-occupied France blends exciting adventure with the grim history. Before the U.S. entered the war, Fry, 32, spent a year in Marseilles, using his relief organization as a cover for a hidden rescue operation which saved well-known artists, politicians, and scientists, including Marc Chagall and Heinrich Mann. In fact, part of the story is how Fry chose the few to save from all the desperate who lined up at his office. Along with the suspense of police raids and the gripping particulars about the brave rescuers on Fry's team comes the knowledge that victims faced with extermination were not welcome in the U.S. The author begins with a brief overview of Hitler's rise and the threat to the Jews, and then draws heavily on Fry's autobiography and his letters home, which detail his increasing stress. Some readers will skip the details, but many will want all the amazing information about the unassuming hero who saved so many. Photos are scattered throughout, and source notes and bibliography are appended. —Hazel Rochman

Metselaar, Menno, and Ruud van der Ro. *Anne Frank: Her Life in Words and Pictures*. 2009. 216p. illus. Roaring Brook (9781596435469). Gr. 6–12. 940.53.

Both authoritative and accessible, this small, square book, published in conjunction with the Anne Frank

House in Amsterdam and translated from the Dutch, offers the feel of an intense museum visit. Short quotes from Frank's *Diary of a Young Girl*, printed in bold type, are interspersed throughout the clear narrative, which covers both WWII history and the Frank family's personal story. The heavily illustrated pages feature news photos of Nazi train transports and concentration camps, including Auschwitz, where Anne died; pages from Frank's scrapbook, featuring pictures of herself, her family, and the movie stars she loved; excerpts from the *Diary*, in Frank's handwriting; and photos of the Secret Annex, including the movable bookcase that hid the entrance and the now-empty rooms, stripped of furnishings as the Nazi raid left them; still visible, though, are the lines scratched on the wall where Frank's parents marked her height as she grew up in hiding. Readers will be enthralled by the intimate details and by the ongoing mystery of who betrayed the family, and they will want to talk about the heartbreaking quote from Otto Frank, who, after reading the *Diary*, realized that he never knew his daughter. With the additions of a map, a bibliography, and historical notes, this is a must for *Diary* readers and for the Holocaust curriculum. —Hazel Rochman

Murphy, Jim. *An American Plague: The True and Terrifying Story of the Yellow Fever Epidemic of 1793*. 2003. 176p. illus. Clarion (9780395776087). Gr. 6–12. 614.5.

History, science, politics, and public health come together in this dramatic account of the disastrous yellow fever epidemic that hit the nation's capital more than 200 years ago. Drawing on firsthand accounts, medical and non-medical, Murphy re-creates the fear and panic in the infected city, the social conditions that caused the disease to spread, and the arguments about causes and cures. With archival prints, photos, contemporary newspaper facsimiles that include lists of the dead, and full, chatty source notes, he tells of those who fled and those who stayed—among them, the heroic group of free blacks who nursed the ill and were later vilified for their work. Some readers may skip the daily details of life in eighteenth-century Philadelphia; in fact, the most interesting chapters discuss what is now known of the tiny fever-carrying mosquito and the problems created by over-zealous use of pesticides. Recent real-life struggles, like those to contain the SARS epidemic, bring this "unshakeable unease" chillingly close. —Hazel Rochman

Murphy, Jim. *Blizzard! The Storm that Changed America*. 2000. 136p. illus. Scholastic (9780590673099). Gr. 5–9. 974.7.

On March 10, 1888, the weather on the eastern coast of the U.S. was so pleasant that families were picnicking. By Monday morning, however, a huge, destructive blizzard—actually two storms—stretched from Delaware north to Maine and as far west as the Mississippi River. New York City had 21 inches of drifting snow; Troy, New York, was blanketed under 55 inches. Supplies of fuel, food, and milk dwindled; power lines snapped; trains were trapped; nearly 200 ships were lost at sea; and an estimated 800 people died in New York City alone. No wonder some called the storm "The Great White Hurricane." Like Murphy's award-winning *The Great Fire* (1995), this is an example of stellar nonfiction. The haunting jacket illustration grabs attention, and the dramatic power of the splendid narrative, coupled with carefully selected anecdotes, newspaper accounts, and vintage and contemporary photos, will keep the pages turning. Murphy does a fine job describing the incredible storm, the reasons behind the tragic consequences, and the terrifying fates of victims. A splendid choice for booktalking. Notes are appended. —Jean Franklin

Murphy, Jim. *The Real Benedict Arnold*. 2007. 272p. illus. Clarion (9780395776094). Gr. 7–10. 973.3.

In his opening chapter, Murphy describes his difficult task: "to expose at least some of the rumors and folktales . . . so that we can see Benedict Arnold in as fair and objective a way as possible." This is no small feat since Arnold is one of the most vilified figures in American history, but Murphy found few primary sources to consult. Arnold kept no personal diary, and his wife burned his letters after his death. Using Arnold's surviving military journals and political documents, Murphy carefully contrasts popular myth with historical fact; one of the greatest strengths of the book is that Murphy never goes beyond his documentation to speculate. As far as possible, he meticulously traces Arnold's life, revealing a complex man who was actually as much admired as he was loathed. The opening chapters are slow, but the pace picks up quickly thereafter, and the accounts of Arnold's military campaigns are riveting. Especially fascinating is the description of a civil and military leadership—incompetent, ambitious, and greedy—that consistently undervalued and undermined Arnold. The chapters dealing with Arnold's treason are taut and suspenseful, and reveal much about how he is regarded today. Perhaps we can never know the real Arnold, but this splendid biography brings us close. The final section, "Notes, Sources and Related Asides," provides fascinating reading as well as additional resources. —Lynn Rutan

Murphy, Jim. *A Savage Thunder: Antietam and the Bloody Road to Freedom*. 2009. 112p. illus. Simon & Schuster/Margaret K. McElderry (9780689876332). Gr. 6–10. 973.7.

After a preface discusses why each side was fighting the Civil War, this informative volume opens with Lee's troops crossing the Potomac into Maryland and culminates in a detailed account of the battle at Antietam Creek. With 22,717 casualties, it was "the bloodiest single day of fighting in American history." The book's concluding chapters present the aftermath of the battle from the overwhelming task of burying the dead to the then-controversial Emancipation Proclamation, which Lincoln released a few months later. Throughout the book, many well-chosen quotes give voice to the observations, reactions, and reflections of common soldiers as well as those of their leaders, and bring the battle's horrors and poignancy into sharper focus. In a logical, accessible way, Murphy discusses the battle both in detail and in a broader context, making a good case that it changed the course of the Civil War. Reproduced in black-and-white, the many fine illustrations include period photos, drawings, engravings, and paintings, as well as several excellent battlefield maps indicating the movements of troops and positions of artillery for both sides. The presentation concludes with a highly readable section of "Notes and Sources" in paragraph form. A stirring, well-researched addition to Civil War shelves. —Carolyn Phelan

Myers, Walter Dean. *The Greatest: Muhammad Ali*. 2001. 156p. illus. Scholastic (9780590543422). Gr. 6–10. 796.83.

Myers tells the familiar story of Muhammad Ali's life and career in such a way as to inspire a new generation of readers, young people whose first glimpse of Ali may have come at the 1996 Olympics, when the Parkinson's-stricken former heavyweight champion lit the Olympic torch. Focusing on race, politics, religion, and boxing—"the arenas in which Ali's mark was indelible in . . . the national consciousness"—Myers vividly re-creates the life of the young Cassius Clay, from his childhood in segregated Louisville in the 1950s, through his Olympic triumph in 1960, to his rise as a professional fighter, culminating with the stunning victory over Sonny Liston in 1964. Then comes the dramatic second act of the Ali story—the transformation of young Clay into Muhammad Ali, a committed Black Muslim who would sacrifice his heavyweight title and face imprisonment by refusing to serve in the army during the Vietnam War. Myers succinctly summarizes the furor surrounding Ali's political activism, and he captures the excitement that Ali created in a generation of young African Americans (including Myers himself), who found in the brash, young boxer a new kind of hero. And, perhaps most vividly, Myers describes Ali the fighter, explaining his technique and offering a perceptive overview of the troubled business of boxing and the great physical risks the sport entails. This is finally a story about a black man of tremendous courage, the kind of universal story that needs a writer as talented as Myers to retell it for every generation. —Bill Ott

Nelson, Marilyn. *The Freedom Business: Including A Narrative of the Life & Adventures of Venture, a Native of Africa*. Illus. by Deborah Dancy. 2008. 72p. Boyds Mills/Wordsong (9781932425574). Gr. 9–12. 811.

In an extraordinary slave narrative recorded in 1798, Venture Smith remembers his capture in Guinea as a child; the horrific journey on the slave ship to Rhode Island; 30 years of hard labor; being sold and separated from his wife; and his years of work to buy his freedom and that of his family and to purchase his own land. Smith's original, first-person account, published in 1798, appears opposite Nelson's stirring poems, which are written in Smith's voice and both intensify and comment on his experiences. Some readers may decide to read Smith's whole continuous narrative before they begin again and read it with the poems. As in the book's title, the poems' elemental metaphor is the horror of people as "business commodities," investments to speculate on or convert to cash, a workforce bought and sold. But the triumphant climax reverses the business--"I own myself"--and then Smith earns enough to buy his pregnant wife, rejoicing that their child "will be born free." Never intrusive, Dancy's sepia background art in watercolor, acrylics, and collage includes ink lines that evoke chains and ropes and then broken bonds. It's surprising that this essential part of American biography and history isn't more widely known. Suggest this as a crossover title to adults. —Hazel Rochman

Nelson, Peter. *Left for Dead: A Young Man's Search for Justice for the USS Indianapolis*. 2002. 160p. illus. Delacorte (9780385729598). Gr. 6–12. 940.54.

Two history lessons run concurrently through this exciting, life-affirming book about war heroics and justice. While watching the classic bragging scene in the movie *Jaws*, 11-year-old Hunter Scott grew curious about one character's reference to the *U.S.S. Indianapolis*. Discovering that history usually glossed over or omitted the story, Scott began a six-year crusade, gathering information from the survivors and, eventually, ensuring that their mission and their unjustly maligned captain were appropriately honored. Narrative combines with interviews between Scott and the soldiers to give individualized synopses of the 1945 sinking and rescue, ensuing court-martial, crusade, and exoneration. Two insets of black-and-white photos add a personal touch by showing the soldiers then and now, and also Scott, ages 11 to 17. Even if the main text doesn't interest readers, they can't help but be awed by Scott's preface, which proves without question the impact one student can have on history. —Roger Leslie

Nelson, Scott Reynolds, and Marc Aronson. *Ain't Nothing But a Man: My Quest to Find the Real John Henry*. 2008. 64p. illus.National Geographic (9781426300004). Gr. 6–9. 973.

Not many history books are written in first person, but this is no ordinary history book. It traces a historian's quest for the man behind the legend of John Henry. Nelson's research involved listening to hundreds of variants of the song "John Henry," learning about post–Civil War railway construction projects, visiting possible sites for the legendary contest between man and steam drill, and in one groundbreaking moment, glancing at the 1910 postcard on his desktop, hearing the lyrics of a version of "John Henry" in his mind, and making a connection that no other modern historian had considered. Based on Nelson's *Steel Drivin' Man: John Henry, the Untold Story of an American Legend* (2006), this large-format volume retells the story for young people. Many period photos, paintings, and engravings, reproduced in shades of rust and sepia, are shown to good advantage in this handsomely designed book. Appendixes include suggestions for further reading and Nelson's notes on his sources and on the "John Henry" song variants, as well as the ongoing search for information about John Henry. Marc Aronson contributes a section on "How to Be a Historian," using Nelson's search as a model. A lively, insightful introduction to the active pursuit of history. —Carolyn Phelan

Oppenheim, Joanne. *Dear Miss Breed: True Stories of the Japanese American Incarceration during World War II and a Librarian Who Made a Difference*. 2006. 288p. illus. Scholastic (9780439569927). Gr. 7–10. 940.53.

Like Michael O. Tunnell's *The Children of Topaz* (1996), this passionately written history bears witness to the WWII injustices endured by Japanese Americans, from a vantage point of particular relevance to young people. In a poignant introduction,

seasoned children's writer Oppenheim explains how her hunt for a former classmate, a Japanese American, serendipitously led her to an Internet profile of San Diego children's librarian Clara Breed, and to a collection of letters written to Breed by her incarcerated Japanese patrons—grateful, illuminating responses to Breed's faithful missives and care packages containing books and other gifts. Although the letters (and interviews with their grown-up authors) form the narrative's bedrock, Oppenheim weaves them into a broader account, amplified by photos, archival materials (including a startlingly racist cartoon by Dr. Seuss), and moving quotations from the later reparation hearings: "I was just 10 years old when I became a 'squint-eyed yellow-bellied Jap.'" Along with the basic facts, Oppenheim urges readers to critically interpret primary sources and identify "governmental doublespeak"; the words "incarceration" or "concentration" are consciously employed here as correctives for softpedaling terminology like "internment" and "relocation." Unclear references in the children's letters are not always annotated, and the recurring discussion of professional concerns facing Breed (whose own letters to the camps have been lost) often seems to cater too obviously to Oppenheim's adult readers. But the aggregate deserves commendation for its sheer quantity of accessible, exhaustively researched information about a troubling period, more resonant now than ever, when American ideals were compromised by fear and unfortunate racial assumptions. Eight pages of unusually readable, wide-ranging endnotes and an exhaustive bibliography conclude, evidence of Oppenheim's all-consuming research process.
—Jennifer Mattson

Osborne, Linda Barrett. ***Miles to Go for Freedom: Segregation and Civil Rights in the Jim Crow Years.*** **2012. 128p. illus. Abrams (9781419700200). Gr. 6–10. 305.896.**

In this companion volume to *Traveling the Freedom Road* (2009), Osborne once again offers a handsome, highly readable overview of African American history, focusing here on both the South and the North during the late nineteenth century through the mid-twentieth century. Drawing on her work as a senior editor at the Library of Congress, Osborne bolsters her gripping account with many quotes from primary sources, including interviews with those who were young during the time period covered. The history and politics are brought home by the moving personal stories, which show that separate is not equal and demonstrate how the laws—written and unwritten—resulted in widespread discrimination, cruel prejudice, and humiliation. Period photos, including public events, such as a teen lynching; magazine illustrations; and prints fill every double-page spread. After the first section on the South, the following section about the North focuses on the Great Migration, exploring not only the reasons why African Americans left but also the often chilly reception they received when they arrived. The final short section about the nation as a whole ends with the triumph of *Brown v. Board of Education*, which opened the way for the civil rights movement. Spacious back matter includes a time line, extensive notes, and a bibliography. A must for classroom discussion and research. —Hazel Rochman

Osborne, Linda Barrett. ***Traveling the Freedom Road: From Slavery and the Civil War through Reconstruction.*** **2009. 128p. illus. Abrams (9780810983380). Gr. 6–9. 973.7.**

Published in association with the Library of Congress, where Osborne is a senior writer and editor, this fascinating, well-designed volume offers an essential introduction to the experiences of African Americans between 1800 and 1877. Osborne further narrows her topic by focusing on the lives of young people, beginning with the story of teenage sisters who escaped slavery in Washington, D.C., endured recapture, and, after winning their freedom, went on to become active abolitionists. Throughout, Osborne moves from similar, personal stories to broader historical milestones, and in highly accessible language, she provides basic background even as she challenges readers with philosophical questions: "Why did the Constitution, the basic rules that govern the

United States, allow slavery in the first place?" This fluid exchange between political events and intimate, human stories creates a highly absorbing whole that is made even stronger by the many young peoples' first-person recollections of the time period, culled from primary source materials. These voices create a sense of immediacy that's echoed in the exceptional selection of well-reproduced visuals, including photographs, magazine illustrations, and etchings. A concise time line, source notes, and a bibliography close the chapters. This unique, powerful, and clear overview contains valuable insights for readers of all ages and backgrounds. —Gillian Engberg

Partridge, Elizabeth. *Marching for Freedom: Walk Together, Children, and Don't You Grow Weary*. 2009. 80p. illus. Viking (9780670011896). Gr. 6–12. 323.1196.

The subtitle of this stirring photo-essay, drawn from an African American spiritual that was often quoted by Martin Luther King Jr., points to the book's focus: the essential role that young people played in the civil rights movement. Of course, the movement's adult leaders are represented, including Dr. King, John Lewis, Rosa Parks, and President Lyndon Johnson. Segregationist Governor George Wallace and his followers are also mentioned. But this overview, which zeros in on the Alabama protests in Selma and the March to Montgomery in 1965, emphasizes the essential impact that ordinary children and teens had on the movement. The vivid text is filled with quotes collected from Partridge's personal interviews with adults who remember their youthful experiences, including their terrifying confrontations with state troopers, during which marchers were attacked with whips, tear gas, and clubs. Filled with large black-and-white photos, every spread brings readers up close to the dramatic, often violent action. Recurring throughout the volume is the freedom fighters' credo that nonviolence did not mean passivity. Today's teen activists will want to talk about these gripping profiles of young people who made a difference; and for those who want to continue their research, the extensive back matter includes long notes and a bibliography of books, films, articles, and online sources. —Hazel Rochman

Philip, Neil. *The Great Circle: A History of the First Nations*. 2006. 148p. illus. Clarion (9780618159413). Gr. 6–9. 973.04.

Philip takes on a huge challenge here: to present a unified narrative that explains the complex and confrontational relationships between Native Americans and white settlers. This would be daunting enough had Philips just focused on several tribes or Indians from one part of the region, but he chooses to encompass the experiences of tribes across the country. He pulls it off, however, thanks to solid research, an engaging writing style, and a talent for making individual stories serve the whole. He begins by explaining the pitfalls that come with writing about First Nations. With such a vast history, he had to be selective in what he wrote about; in terminology alone, he faced numerous difficulties. Then, in fascinating chapter after chapter, he introduces particular tribes, focusing on their interactions with settlers. Underlying the strong narrative is Philip's explanation for white-Indian conflict: irreconcilable worldviews. Native Americans saw the world as a sacred circle, while whites thought of it in linear terms, with history gathering speed like a train running down a track. Top marks, too, for the volume's photographs and historical renderings, which so intensely illustrate the pages. A generous bibliography compensates for stylistically hard-to-follow source notes. —Ilene Cooper

Rappaport, Doreen. *Beyond Courage: The Untold Story of Jewish Resistance during the Holocaust*. 2012. 240p. illus. Candlewick (9780763629762). Gr. 7–12. 940.53.

With all the shelves of Holocaust books about the millions lost in the genocide, this is one of the few histories to focus in detail on Jewish resistance across Europe—those who fought back and saved others. The intricate deceptions are as compelling as the confrontations, and the underground escape stories make for thrilling adventure. The horror of what was left behind is always present: the ghettos, the camps, the transports, the Jews who did not support armed resistance, and those who did not get away, including some who fled to forests and starved to death or were murdered by their anti-Semitic neighbors. In addition to the chapters on the Warsaw Ghetto and Theresienstadt, there are also lots of lesser-known accounts of incredible resistance. In the Vilna Ghetto, arms were hidden in the library, the cemetery, in walls, and in wells. Always there are stories of the survivors' guilt, as with a man who left his mother to die alone. The uncluttered book design helps make the detailed history accessible, with spacious type on thick, high-quality paper and portraits, photos, and prints on every page, all meticulously documented in extensive chapter notes and a bibliography. That many young people played important roles in the resistance is a special draw for YAs. An important addition to the Holocaust curriculum. —Hazel Rochman

Reich, Susanna. *Painting the Wild Frontier: The Art and Adventures of George Catlin*. 2008. 160p. illus. Clarion (9780618714704). Gr. 7–12. 759.13.

Reich's own words ("As a white person writing about American Indians, I have tried to be respectful . . . but, like George, I cannot completely erase my cultural biases, no matter how hard I try,") reflect the dominant theme of her handsome biography of nineteenth-century painter George Catlin, famous for his portraits of Native American life. Underlying the lucid, detailed discussion of the artist, which is illustrated with beautiful archival prints and photographs of his work, are the whites' conflicting views of Indian peoples, then and now—especially the image of the "noble savage." Quoting extensively from Catlin's letters and notes, Reich shows how he was driven to paint authentic cultural rituals and individuals, to champion the Indians' cause, and to record their rich, vanishing way of life in all its diversity. At the same time, she never denies that Catlin exploited his subjects, exhibiting the "primitives," in the U.S. and abroad. There are long captions with the paintings, and the extensive back matter includes thorough chapter notes, a bibliography, and a time line. A great introduction to Catlin's work as well as an excellent title to use in social studies, history, and art classes. —Hazel Rochman

Rubin, Susan Goldman. *Fireflies in the Dark: The Story of Friedl Dicker-Brandeis and the Children of Terezin*. 2000. 48p. illus. Holiday (9780823414611). Gr. 5–10. 940.53.

"Of the 15,000 children who passed through Terezin, only 100 survived. But their artwork and writings live on as testimony to their lives and spirits." This heartbreaking picture book tells the children's story by focusing on their remarkable art teacher, Friedl Dicker-Brandeis, a Jewish artist from Czechoslovakia, who took art supplies and books with her to the concentration camp and ran secret classes for the children. She and nearly all her pupils perished at Auschwitz, but after the war, 5,000 of the children's drawings, paintings, and collages were discovered hidden in two suitcases. The pictures are now exhibited around the world, and many of them are beautifully reproduced on the pages of this book. Some of the work is naive in style; some is sophisticated. There are portraits, self-portraits, and pictures that show horrific camp conditions and dreams of home (for example, a family Passover supper). The facts, including the dates, in the brief captions make you return to the pictures ("Robert Bondy painted empty landscapes over and over again with his village in the distance"). Rubin interviewed several survivors, and she integrates their personal testimonies with the history of the camp. This is an excellent book to use across the curriculum in Holocaust studies, in art, history, and literature classes with middle-grade and older readers. Rubin's detailed references and sources include books, documentary films and videos, and websites to help students who want to know more. There's no sensationalism here. Everything is distanced, but the sense of loss is overwhelming. —Hazel Rochman

Ruggiero, Adriane. *American Voices from Reconstruction*. 2006. 103p. illus. Marshall Cavendish/Benchmark, lib. ed. (9780761421689). Gr. 8–11. 973.8.

Primary sources can be heavy reading, but this volume in the continuing American Voices series does an excellent job of bringing the history close by combining a wide selection of documents (including speeches, letters, diary entries, newspaper accounts, songs, and more) with clear commentary, stirring photos and paintings, and questions to think about and discuss. From Frederick Douglass' "What the Black Man Wants," in which he demands blacks be given the vote, to the Black Codes that restored white control over the newly freed slaves, Ruggiero connects each documented selection with the big issues. Former slaves and slave owners speak; so do President Lincoln, Booker T. Washington, Representative John R. Lynch ("I am treated not as an American citizen, but as a brute"), and many more. There are quotes from the Klan on "purity" and candid comments from abolitionists about the failures of Reconstruction in land reform. The spacious design, with thick paper, clear type, and lots of subheads and graphics, quotes, and questions, is very approachable, and the combination of voices and commentary will make readers think critically. Back matter includes a detailed time line, a glossary, and a bibliography. —Hazel Rochman

Sandler, Martin W. *Lincoln through the Lens*. 2008. 96p. illus. Walker (9780802796660). Gr. 7–9. 973.7092.

When Lincoln became president, photography was new, and he joined "the very first generation of human beings ever to be photographed." The medium became an invaluable source for historians to trace the life of one of America's most important presidents, and this extraordinary book is a tribute to the way contemporary and future generations came to view Lincoln. Beginning with a short biographical introduction and the first photograph of Lincoln after being elected to the Illinois House, Sandler goes on to cover a wide territory. Part biography, part history of the Civil War, the book touches on many interesting topics, including Matthew Brady (Lincoln's primary photographer), Lincoln's family, and several amazing finds, including a photo of Lincoln's second inauguration that shows the presence of several conspirators involved in the president's assassination, including John Wilkes Booth. The text skips around early on, but after that it moves steadily through Lincoln's presidency, emphasizing the war. Every step of the way there are fascinating photographs, full-page portraits often followed by battlefield scenes, even death-bed pictures of both Lincoln and Booth. Although it's the pictures that provide the "wow factor," Sandler's perceptive words have their own elegance. Well sourced and offering numerous ways to learn more (although, surprisingly, the fine Lincoln museum in Springfield is not cited), this will be an excellent tool for history classes; and browsers, too, will be caught up in Lincoln's story. —Ilene Cooper

Sheinkin, Steve. *Bomb: The Race to Build—and Steal—the World's Most Dangerous Weapon*. 2012. 272p. illus. Roaring Brook/Flash Point (9781596434875). Gr. 7–10. 623.4.

Using some of the same narrative techniques he used in the YALSA Award for Excellence in Nonfiction–winning *The Notorious Benedict Arnold* (2010), Sheinkin shapes the story of the Manhattan Project into a dense, complicated thriller that intercuts the action with the deftness of a Hollywood blockbuster. There are more characters than readers will be able to handle, but they'll follow the three main threads. The first is a tale of spy versus spy, as Soviet informants infiltrate America's Los Alamos laboratory. The second tracks the heroism of Knut Haukelid as he parachutes into Norway to destroy Germany's heavy water plant. Most amazing is Robert Oppenheimer's assemblage of the greatest scientific minds in the U.S. (aka "the world's largest collection of crackpots"), who under great duress design the most lethal weapon in history. Sheinkin's prose understandably favors plot machinations over character, and positioning photos in the back matter feels anticlimactic. Nonetheless, the painstakingly sourced narrative crackles and drives home the "strange mix of pride and horror" felt by the scientists who had just won the war—but lost something of equal worth. —Daniel Kraus

★ Sís, Peter. *The Wall: Growing Up behind the Iron Curtain*. Illus. by Peter Sís. 2007. 56p. Farrar/Frances Foster (9780374347017). Gr. 7–10. 943.7.

In an autobiographical picture book that will remind many readers of Marjane Satrapi's memoir *Persepolis*

(2003), Sís' latest, a powerful combination of graphic novel and picture book, is an account of his growing up in Czechoslovakia under Soviet rule. Written in several stands, the somewhat fragmented narrative never dilutes the impact of the boldly composed panels depicting scenes from Sís' infancy through young adulthood. Throughout, terrific design dramatizes the conflict between conformity and creative freedom, often through sparing use of color; in many cases, the dominant palette of black, white, and Communist red threatens to swallow up young Peter's freely doodled, riotously colored artwork. The panels heighten the emotional impact, as when Sís fleeing the secret police, emerges from one spread's claustrophobic, gridlike sequence into a borderless, double-page escape fantasy. Even as they side with Peter against fearsome forces beyond his control, younger readers may lose some interest as the story moves past his childhood, and most will lack crucial historical context. But this will certainly grab teens—who will grasp both the history and the passionate, youthful rebellions against authority—as well as adults, many of whom will respond to the Cold War setting. Though the term "picture book for older readers" has been bandied about quite a bit, this memorable title is a true example. —Jennifer Mattson

Sloan, Christopher. ***Bury the Dead: Tombs, Corpses, Mummies, Skeletons, & Rituals.*** **2002. 64p. illus. National Geographic (9780792271925). Gr. 5–9. 393.**

Kids will find it hard to resist picking up a book with words like *corpses* and *skeletons* in the title. And this one doesn't disappoint. Sloan, an editor at *National Geographic* magazine and the author of two previous books for children, does a terrific job of providing an intriguing, reader-friendly text that is not overshadowed by the fabulous color photographs from the National Geographic Society's archives. These pictures do not shirk from their subject: a full-page photo of a Peruvian mummy staring out from his burial cloth, his knees raised to his chest; a close-up of a "bog person" clearly showing, as the caption says, skin turned to leather by acidic conditions in the swamp. There are also many pictures of excavations, artifacts, and burial sites. Along with discussions of how and why people bury their dead are chapters on particular peoples and their traditions. There's material on the Egyptians, of course, but also on the Chinese, the terra-cotta soldiers of the Qin dynasty, and the Russian tombs of the Amazon women who lived between 800 and 100 B.C.E. Sloan had access to experts to vet his book, and it shows. This has the ring of authority and the look of quality. —Ilene Cooper

Stanley, Jerry. ***Cowboys and Longhorns: A Portrait of the Long Drive.*** **2003. 128p. illus. Crown (9780375815652). Gr. 5–12. 636.2.**

This fascinating portrait of a little-known part of American history confronts the popular mythologies of cattle drives and cowboys with gritty reality. Taking to task popular culture's image of the American cowboy, an image increasingly distorted over the years in books, motion pictures, and television, Stanley reveals that most American cowboys were vaqueros from Mexico and former African American slaves. Genuine cowboys were tough, hard-working individuals who had no time to think about shootouts, chasing villains, or wooing women. They spent their lives performing hazardous, unpredictable work for relatively little money. Stanley weaves together the history of the American cowboy with the story of the longhorns—the fierce, wild cattle that were hunted, rounded up, and driven by the thousands from Texas to Kansas along the dangerous Chisholm Trail. Using a variety of primary source materials, he constructs a riveting account of miserable, tedious, dangerous work, including graphic descriptions of cattle being beaten into submission, a gruesome practice positively barbaric by contemporary standards. Yet, Stanley also conveys an admiration for these gritty men, who came to epitomize the image of the American hero. Illustrated with maps and photographs, this fascinating, engrossing account of a piece of American history stripped of myths is a great choice for both informational and recreational reading. An excellent book to pair with Russell Freedman's *In the Days of the Vaqueros* (2001). —Ed Sullivan

Stone, Tanya Lee. ***The Good, the Bad, and the Barbie: A Doll's History and Her Impact on Us.*** **2010. 136p. illus. Viking (9780670011872). Gr. 7–10. 688.7.**

Everyone knows Barbie. And almost everyone has an opinion of her. Stone has done her homework and offers a particularly well-researched read. But she has also gotten many women (and men) to reminisce, comment, and argue about Barbie, and these voices add sparkle. Stone starts things off on a biographical note as she introduces Ruth Handler, Barbie's creator and a shrewd businesswoman who instinctively understood the Barbie concept would be a success even as detractors, mostly male, told her it wouldn't. The focus then moves to Barbie herself, in all her vast and varied incarnations. Much of Barbie's story is one of evolution, and readers will find it particularly fascinating to read that although Barbie was a leader in diversity, cloned into various roles and cultures, some customers still didn't find her ethnic enough, most often lamenting that no matter her color, Barbie usually had "good" hair. Near the end of the book, just when one wonders if Stone will mention what went on under Barbie's clothes, she goes there in a chapter called, "Banning, Bashing, and in the Buff." Closing on a higher plane, the book concludes with "Barbie as Art." Source notes, a bibliography, and lots of images, including an inset of color photos, add to an offering that pleases and intrigues. —Ilene Cooper

Taylor, Peter Lane, and Christos Nicola. ***The Secret of Priest's Grotto.*** **2007. 64p. illus. Kar-Ben (9781580132602). Gr. 7–10. 940.53.**

Part survival adventure, part searing history, and part discovery story, this amazing account describes how three Ukrainian Jewish families survived the Holocaust by hiding in a cave near their village for 344 days. Sixty years later, in 2003, Nicola explored the cave and found signs of human habitation. His Internet searches eventually connected him with some of the survivors, now living in Canada and the U.S., from whom he learned how 38 people, including toddlers and a 75-year-old grandmother, fled the Nazis and lived in four underground rooms, sealed off from the outside world. Color photos take readers to the site and show some of the people now, while black-and-white historical ones give an idea of the past. Particularly moving are the images of the relics found at the site—a shoe, a mug, a key to a house left forever. Readers will want more about the Ukrainian peasant who helped the families, but there's no denying the power of the story; when they came outside after nearly a year underground, some of the people had forgotten the sun. —Hazel Rochman

Taylor, Yuval, ed. ***Growing Up in Slavery: Stories of Young Slaves as Told by Themselves.*** **Illus. by Kathleen Judge. 2005. 240p. Lawrence Hill (9781556525483). Gr. 9–12. 306.3.**

Ten African Americans—among them Frederick Douglass and Harriet Jacobs, as well as less well-known individuals—tell what it was like to be a child and teenager under slavery. Taylor, who leads off with an excellent historical overview, has taken the long, stirring stories from his two-volume adult anthology *I Was Born a Slave* (1999), and he expands each smoothly and unobtrusively edited account with clear introductory notes and concluding commentary. The writers recall misery, cruelty, and horrific violence, but just as strong are their memories of courageous rebellion, both secret and open, including their shared triumph: once forbidden to read and write, they grew up to publish their life stories. The type is small, and the narratives are dense, but powerful full-page woodcuts help focus the drama. Invaluable for students in search of primary-source material, and many selections will make riveting read-alouds. A bibliography is appended. —Hazel Rochman

Turner, Glennette Tilley. ***Fort Mose and the Story of the Man Who Built the First Free Black Settlement in Colonial America.*** **2010. 48p. illus. Abrams (9780810940567). Gr. 7–10. 975.9.**

This well-researched book introduces Francisco Menendez, a strong, remarkable African man whose struggle for freedom in America predated the Civil War and even the American Revolution. Born in West Africa around 1700, Menendez was captured and sold as a slave in South Carolina. After fighting with the Indians of the southeast in the Yamasee War, in which they rose up against the English colonists, he went to St. Augustine seeking sanctuary and freedom but was enslaved by the Spanish. Eventually, he was granted unconditional freedom and named the leader of Fort Mose, Florida, the first "officially sanctioned free black town in what is now the United States." Though there are challenges in writing Menendez's life story when so little is known, particularly about his early life, Turner's graceful account clearly distinguishes between fact and supposition. The paragraphs discussing the transport of slaves and their treatment at the "pest" house on Sullivan's Island are particularly vivid and informative. Back matter includes a glossary, source notes for quotes, and an extensive source bibliography. Brightening every page of this large, handsome book are deep-green borders of tropical leaves. Illustrations include period paintings, drawings, maps, and documents. A significant addition to African American history collections for young people. —Carolyn Phelan

Walker, Sally M. ***Secrets of a Civil War Submarine: Solving the Mysteries of the H. L. Hunley*****. 2005. 64p. illus. Carolrhoda (9781575058306). Gr. 7–10. 973.7.**

The author of *Fossil Fish Found Alive* (2002) now discusses a different sort of discovery, the Confederate submarine *H. L. Hunley*. After sinking a Union sloop near Charleston, South Carolina, in 1864, the *Hunley* did not return to port. Although divers searched for more than 130 years, the sub was not found until 1995. Over the last 10 years, archaeologists have carefully raised the *Hunley* and painstakingly sifted through the 20,000 pounds of sediment it contained for artifacts and human remains and, ultimately, clues to why, when, and how the vessel sank. Walker begins with the history of the *Hunley*'s design and construction as well as its place in Civil War and naval history. She really hits her stride, though, in explaining the complex techniques and loving care used in raising the craft, recovering its contents, and even reconstructing models of the crew members' bodies. Back matter includes a detailed author's note, source notes, a bibliography, and recommended websites. Thoroughly researched, nicely designed, and well illustrated with clear, color photos, the book will serve as an informative guide to anyone interested in the *Hunley* or intrigued by archaeology. —Carolyn Phelan

Walker, Sally M. ***Written in Bone: Buried Lives of Jamestown and Colonial Maryland*****. 2009. 144p. illus. Carolrhoda (9780822571353). Gr. 7–11. 614.**

This unusual volume, suggested to Walker by a scientist at the Smithsonian Institution, dips into American history to introduce the work of forensic anthropologists. Focusing on colonial-era sites in the Chesapeake Bay region, the large-format book provides detailed discussions and intriguing close-up views of the grave excavations at Jamestown, Virginia, as well as in three Maryland locations: Providence, St. Mary's City, and Harleigh Knoll. With precision of her own,Walker describes the meticulous work of the archaeologists and other scientists who study skeletal remains, using physical clues as indicators of a skeleton's sex, age, birthplace, station in society, and length of time in the colonies. They combine trained observation, background knowledge, and scientific expertise with detective skills to illuminate facets of our history; the final chapter discusses how forensic anthropology has contributed to historians' understanding of colonial times. Nearly every page carries at least one illustration, usually a color photo but sometimes a helpful diagram, a map, or a period document or print. Back matter includes source notes, a source bibliography, a time line, and lists of recommended books and websites. The reading level is relatively high and the quantity of detailed information is not for everyone, but those intrigued by forensics and history will find this absolutely fascinating. —Carolyn Phelan

Warren, Andrea. ***Escape from Saigon: How a Vietnam War Orphan Became an American Boy*****. 2004. 128p. illus. Farrar/Melanie Kroupa (9780374322243). Gr. 5–12. 959.704.**

At the end of the Vietnam War, an eight-year-old Amerasian orphan named Long fled his country and found a loving home with his adoptive family in Ohio. With a new name, Matt Steiner, he grew up to be high-school valedictorian and athletic star, and now he is a doctor with his own happy family. But this stirring photo-essay is more than a rags-to-riches story. Always true to the child's viewpoint, Warren's clear narrative, with many documentary photos, begins as the boy struggles to survive in Vietnam, then describes the anguish of his abandonment by a loving grandmother no longer able to care for him; the kindness of rescuers at the orphanage, who arranged his adoption; and his terrifying evacuation on a plane under fire. The child-at-war story and the facts about the Operation Babylift rescue are tense and exciting. Just as gripping is the boy's personal conflict: his struggle to become American; his attempt to deny his sadness at what he left behind; and, finally, his pride in his roots ("I will never forget that my American heart is half Vietnamese"). Framing the biography is fascinating information, including Warren's account of the evacuation of her own adopted baby daughter on Operation Babylift; discussion about international adoption and Amerasian children; and a lengthy annotated list of sources. —Hazel Rochman

Weitzman, David. *Skywalkers: Mohawk Ironworkers Build the City*. 2010. 128p. illus. Roaring Brook/Flash Point (9781596431621). Gr. 7–10. 690.092.

How did Mohawk men come to build America's skyscrapers? The discussion begins with traditional Mohawk society as reported by colonial sources and fast-forwards to the 1800s, when the railways made wooden bridges obsolete and ushered in iron and steel technology. Hardworking and courageous, Mohawks learned ironwork on bridges. After a poorly designed steel bridge in Quebec collapsed during construction in 1907, killing many men from a single Mohawk community, those remaining began to work further afield on separate building projects. Many became ironworkers on skyscrapers in New York and other cities, a tradition that continues today. Quotes from primary sources are used very effectively throughout this well-written book, with an author's note, glossary, source notes, and bibliography appended. Creating a sense of impending disaster, the chapter on the Quebec bridge collapse illuminates how the designer dismissed alarming reports by workers and engineers and includes a dramatic narrative of the final days. Later chapters trace the history and traditions of Mohawk ironworkers throughout the last century and consider myths and realities of their portrayal in the media. The choice of period photos is excellent. Few writers make engineering and construction as fascinating as Weitzman, the author-illustrator of *Pharaoh's Boat* (2009). —Carolyn Phelan

Woelfle, Gretchen. *Jeannette Rankin: Political Pioneer*. 2007. 102p. illus. Boyds Mills/Calkins Creek (9781590784372). Gr. 6–9. 328.73.

By any measure, Jeannette Rankin was a woman ahead of her time. She was Montana's representative in Congress before women in other states even had the right to vote. Woelfle does a terrific job introducing Rankin, beginning with an attention-grabbing story in which an elderly Rankin, a lifelong pacifist, leads an antiwar protest during the 1970s. Woelfle then moves back in time, restarting the story with an anecdote about young Jeannette sewing up an injured horse on her father's ranch. Readers' interest level will stay high throughout as Rankin finds satisfaction in working as a social worker and then discovers her calling as a crusader for women's rights. Even during her two short tenures in Congress, Rankin never abandoned her core beliefs; she voted against both World War I and II declarations of war (in the case of the latter, standing alone). The high standard of writing is matched by the book's format. Informative sidebars are well integrated, and from the intense portrait on the cover to the well-chosen photos and historical material, the volume offers interesting things to look at on every page. A time line, a bibliography, and source notes bolster this robust introduction to a fascinating figure. Send younger readers to Trish Marx's *Jeannette Rankin: First Lady of Congress* (2006). —Ilene Cooper

Poetry

Alexander, Elizabeth, and Marilyn Nelson. ***Miss Crandall's School for Young Ladies & Little Misses of Color*****. Illus. by Floyd Cooper. 2007. 32p. Boyds Mills/ Wordsong (9781590784563). Gr. 6–10. 811.**

Twenty-four clear, beautiful poems in different voices tell the stirring history of white teacher Prudence Crandall, who defied bigotry in Canterbury, Connecticut, in 1833 by setting up a school for 20 young African American women, many of them freed slaves, who dared to attend. Alexander and Nelson, both Connecticut poets, use dramatic sonnets to tell how Crandall and her students braved resistance to "teach and learn." The pupils speak directly of the anguish of family parting (illiteracy "means silence when you leave home"); the wonder of learning ("I didn't know how much I didn't know"); the racism, including the "etymology" of invective ("no one in town will sell us anything"); and the horrifying climax of "Arson at Midnight," when 300 men attacked the school and closed it down. A long introduction details the historical facts, and in a final note the poets (Nelson is Connecticut's poet laureate) talk about how each has used the sonnet form. The images in their poems and in Cooper's quiet, dramatic pastel illustrations compellingly capture the haunting history. Pair this picture book for older readers with Suzanne Jurmain's *The Forbidden Schoolhouse* (2005) and books about the KKK. —Hazel Rochman

Atkins, Jeannine. ***Borrowed Names: Poems about Laura Ingalls Wilder, Madam C. J. Walker, Marie Curie, and Their Daughters*****. 2010. 224p. Holt (9780805089349). Gr. 6–9. 811.**

In 1867, three women who achieved great success were born: writer Laura Ingalls Wilder, entrepreneur Madam C. J. Walker, and scientist Marie Curie. All three had complicated relationships with their daughters, relationships that Atkins explores in this unusual volume of poetry. Each section follows one daughter from young childhood to adulthood, sketching out the facts of her life, but creating impressions of the emotional lives beyond the facts. Rose Wilder Lane grows up in rural poverty. Constricted by her mother's expectations, she leaves the Wilder farm to work, marry, and travel, but returns and helps to shape her mother's books. As a child, A'Lelia Walker watches her mother wash clothes for a meager living, but after her mother's hair products make them wealthy, A'Lelia grows up to become a patron of the Harlem Renaissance. Curie's elder daughter, Irène, knows early on that her mother's focus is on her work with radium. As an adult, Irène continues that work, earning her own Nobel Prize. In vivid scenes written with keen insight and subtle imagery, the poems offer a strong sense of each daughter's personality as well as the tensions and ties they shared with their notable mothers. Writing with understated drama and quiet power, Atkins enables readers to understand these six women and their mother-daughter relationships in a nuanced and memorable way. —Carolyn Phelan

Bernier-Grand, Carmen T. ***Frida: Viva la vida! Long Live Life!*** **Illus. by Frida Kahlo. 2007. 64p. Marshall Cavendish (9780761453369). Gr. 7–12. 811.**

As in her Pura Belpré Honor Book *César: Sí, se puede! Yes, We Can!* (2004), Bernier-Grand introduces a famous life with lyrical free-verse poems. Nearly every double-page spread pairs a well-reproduced painting by Frida Kahlo with an original poem that defines turning points in the artist's life. Bernier-Grand's words expertly extend the autobiographical imagery so evident in the art. A poem about Kahlo's family tensions appears opposite a painting of a very young Kahlo, standing naked and vulnerable beneath portraits of her family. Later pages focus on Kahlo's tumultuous marriage to Diego Rivera. The lines of poetry capture the images' themes of anguished love with the rhythm of an obsessive chant, alternating with a colder, more rational voice: "Diego my child Diego my lover Diego my husband. / (Diego has never been and never will be anyone's husband.) / Diego my mother Diego my father Diego my son." Readers who aren't familiar with Kahlo's life will want to begin with the appended quotes from Kahlo, the prose biography, and the chronology to glean more meaning from the poems' sometimes oblique references. As in Stephanie Hemphill's *Your Own, Sylvia* (2007) and Margarita Engle's *The Poet Slave of Cuba* (2006), the poems here artfully imagine a famous figure's heart and mind and push readers to wonder how words can capture the essence of a life. —Gillian Engberg

Carroll, Lewis. *Jabberwocky*. Illus. by Stephane Jorisch. 2004. 40p. Kids Can (9781553370796). Gr. 6–12. 821.

In *Through the Looking Glass*, Alice's response to "The Jabberwocky" is, "It seems very pretty, but it's rather hard to understand." Artist Jorisch's wild interpretation of Carroll's poem is both pretty and disturbing, and his puzzling visual narrative is wide open to interpretation. Jorisch sets the scene in a landscape that seems both futuristic and crumbling. Here, the personal story of a young man's struggle to heroically slaughter the Jabberwock and please his uniformed father plays out within a larger surreal world that's studded with surveillance cameras and television sets that seem to "burble" war rhetoric. Rendered in scribbly ink drawings and explosive watercolor washes, Jorisch's stylish, challenging scenes reference sophisticated themes—personal freedom, the pursuit of love and creativity in a bellicose society, the aftermath of war, the influence of the media—that high-school (and university) art and literature students will enjoy investigating. Teachers, too, may want this to liven up poetry units. Younger children, though, will probably find versions illustrated by Joel Stewart or Graeme Base much more accessible. —Gillian Engberg

Clinton, Catherine, ed. *A Poem of Her Own: Voices of American Women Yesterday and Today*. Illus. by Stephen Alcorn. 2003. 80p. Abrams (9780810942400). Gr. 6–9. 811.008.

"Poetry was born within American women, even before there was a nation known as the United States." So begins the stirring introduction to this handsome volume that captures the voices of 25 women poets, who talk about their own lives as they tell the story of America. Colonial woman Anne Bradstreet makes plain the woman's plight with images such as, "Who says my hand a needle better fits?" Phillis Wheatley tells about being a slave; Lydia Maria Child speaks about being an abolitionist. Poetry by Anne Sexton is here, as are works by Gwendolyn Brooks and Julia Alvarez. Some of the poems are well known, such as Emma Lazarus' "The New Colossus" and Julia Ward Howe's patriotic verse that became "The Battle Hymn of the Republic." The intelligent selection is matched by the fresh, open design, highlighted by Alcorn's exciting paintings, executed in casein paint. The pictures, which incorporate a dappled effect, are marvelously rich in both subject and style: the swaying torso pays "Homage to My Hips"; a hot dog falls from the sky into the waiting hands of a girl in "Good Hot Dogs." Short biographies of the poets are appended, along with notes from the author and illustrator. Inspiring on several levels. —Jennifer Mattson

Crisler, Curtis L. *Tough Boy Sonatas*. Illus. by Floyd Cooper. 2007. 88p. Boyds Mills/Wordsong (9781932425772). Gr. 10–12. 811.

In his debut offering for youth, Crisler presents a collection of potent, hard-hitting poems about growing up in Gary, Indiana. Written mostly in voices of young African American males, the poems evoke the grit and ash of crumbling, burned-out streets as well as the realities of hardscrabble life: "confrontation is all up yo' ass and in / yo' face at the same time." Many poems speak of terrifying violence; other selections talk about the struggles to claim a mature, male identity: "With faint / taint of milk breath and / small milk mustache / we want to be the alpha / male, with the balls / to take on those / out-there things." Written with skillful manipulation of sound, rhythm, and form, the poems are filled with sophisticated imagery and graphic words (including the *n*-word), and Cooper's illustrations extend, rather than distract from, the poems' impact. Created in sooty black and gray, the powerful drawings are mostly portraits of anguished young men. The speakers represent voices that are rare in books for youth, and their furious yearning for justice, love, safety, sex, and a good education is unforgettable, as is their hope in what Crisler calls hell: "I never felt poor like my poor / neighbors 'cause I had my crazy family." —Gillian Engberg

Engle, Margarita. ***The Poet Slave of Cuba: A Biography of Juan Francisco Manzano.*** **Illus. by Sean Qualls. 2006. 184p. Holt (9780805077063). Gr. 7–10. 811.**

In eloquent free verse, Engle dramatizes the boyhood of the nineteenth-century Cuban slave Juan Francisco Manzano, who secretly learned to read and wrote poetry about beauty and courage in his world of unspeakable brutality. His present-tense narrative begins when he is six, when his parents are set free. He remains behind with a mistress who treats him like a pet, making him perform for guests. When she dies, five years later, he is given to a cruel, crazy woman, who has him beaten and locked up at whim. He doesn't escape until he is nearly 16. Side-by-side with Juan's anguished voice are the narratives of other characters, including his mother, his demonic owners, and the white child who secretly tries to help. Qualls' occasional black-and-white sketches express Juan's suffering and strength, and a brief afterword fills in historical background. Related in fast-moving poetry, the cruelty is vivid, as is the boy's amazing inner power: tied, gagged, and beaten, Juan knows his owner "can't hear the stories I tell myself." Today's readers will hear the stories, though—and never forget them. —Hazel Rochman

Engle, Margarita. ***The Surrender Tree: Poems of Cuba's Struggle for Freedom.*** **2008. 192p. Holt (9780805086744). Gr. 6–12. 811.**

As in *The Poet Slave of Cuba* (2006), Engle's new book is written in clear, short lines of moving free verse. This time she draws on her own Cuban American roots, including stories from her grandmother, to describe those who fought in the nineteenth-century Cuban struggle for independence. At the center is Rosa, a traditional healer, who nurses runaway slaves and deserters in caves and other secret hideaways. Her husband, José, a freed slave, also speaks, and so does a refugee child, whom Rosa teaches to be a healer. Then there is the vicious slave hunter known as Lieutenant Death; his collection of ears is an unforgettable image of brutality ("shown as proof that the runaway slave / died fighting, resisting capture"). The switching perspectives personalize the dramatic political history, including the establishment of the world's first "reconcentration camps" to hold prisoners, as well as the role of slave owners who freed their slaves and joined the resistance against Spain. Many readers will be caught by the compelling narrative voices and want to pursue the historical accounts in Engle's bibliography. —Hazel Rochman

Franco, Betsy, ed. ***Things I Have to Tell You: Poems and Writing by Teenage Girls.*** **Illus. by Nina Nickles. 2001. 64p. Candlewick (9780763609054); paper (9780763610357). Gr. 7–12. 810.8.**

Franco's *You Hear Me? Poems and Writing by Teenage Boys* (2000) was frank and beautiful. Now she's collected the voices of a wide range of girls in poetry and immediate prose that speak with power and uncertainty about body image, seduction and betrayal, courage and failure, shame and pride. Nickles' black-and-white photos are a stunning addition. They are never literal views of the words but capture a diverse group of today's teenagers in all their various moods: as they cover up their secrets or celebrate being smart and strong or strut in the "Hallway between Lunch and English (Freud can kiss my sexually ambiguous arse"). There's not much sexual explicitness or cursing, but the talk is free—colloquial, ironic, sly, straightforward, sometimes angry or sad. Perhaps some of the messages are too articulate ("I break the stereotype of a girl as a dainty little thing who needs a man by her side in order to do anything"), but teens will listen and see themselves. —Hazel Rochman

Franco, Betsy, ed. ***You Hear Me? Poems and Writing by Teenage Boys.*** **2000. 128p. Candlewick (9780763611583). Gr. 7–12. 810.8.**

With more urgency than many YA novels, the poems and brief prose pieces in this fine anthology speak directly in teen voices about boys coming of age. They talk about love and anger ("I woke up pissed this morning"); about sex ("some good pussy") and jealousy ("You fell for gelboy and his hair"); about the "monster" drugs, family warmth, rejection, conformity, and bullying; about being gay ("queer is more than /

cocks and A.I.D.S.") and accepting that your father is gay. The poetry is rooted in a wide range of neighborhoods, families, and classrooms, and the language is direct and frank, with a rhythm ("I'm / not a / hip hop / Dred / retro / 4-pierced brother") and a physical immediacy in the imagery. Some voices are more private, about secrets, sadness, the weariness of the blues, and the loneliness when a girlfriend leaves ("the photograph torn in half"). In one of the best pieces, a boy thinks about his birth mother ("What if . . . ?"). There are no intrusive illustrations, just the images and music of the words, and lots of white space that makes it easy to browse. Many teens will recognize their search for themselves. —Hazel Rochman

★ Greenberg, Jan, ed. *Heart to Heart: New Poems Inspired by Twentieth-Century American Art*. 2001. 80p. Abrams (9780810943865). Gr. 5–12. 811.

Specially commissioned, original poems celebrate some of the finest twentieth-century American art in this beautiful, surprising volume. Such well-known writers as Nancy Willard, X. J. Kennedy, Lee Upton, and Angela Johnson wrote poems inspired by artworks created through the century, but the book's organization is thematic rather than chronological. The poems are grouped according to how the writer responded to the art: some tell a story about the whole painting; some speak from the perspective of an object within the artwork; some transform the visual elements into poetic metaphors; some talk about the artists and their techniques. From a tight diamante and pantoum to lyrical free verse, the range of poetic styles will speak to a wide age group. Younger children, for example, will love Deborah Pope's "On Lichtenstein's 'Bananas and Grapefruit,'" which melts quickly down the page to a delicious ending: "gulppulp / sweet part / eat / art." Teens (and adults) will enjoy the inquisitive depth of such selections as Ronald Wallace's "Mobile/ Stabile." Concluding with biographical notes on each poet and artist, this rich resource is an obvious choice for teachers, and the exciting interplay between art and the written word will encourage many readers to return again and again to the book. —Gillian Engberg

Greenberg, Jan, ed. *Side by Side: New Poems Inspired by Art from around the World*. 2008. 80p. illus. Abrams (9780810994713). Gr. 8–12. 811.

Following a similar format to her 2002 Printz Honor Book, *Heart to Heart* (2001), Greenberg offers another anthology of accomplished poems inspired by artworks. In this volume, Greenberg extends the book's geographical reach beyond the U.S., bringing together the work of poets and artists from around the globe. As in *Heart to Heart*, the poems are grouped loosely into categories, defined in Greenberg's inspirational introduction. Some tell stories; some speak in the voice of an object in the artwork; some explore the interaction between a viewer and an art object; and some focus on the elements of an artwork's composition. Each spread features a poem in its original language, the English translation, and an artwork, usually from the same country or culture as the poem. With a few exceptions, the reproductions of the art, which ranges from ancient to contemporary work, are sharp and clear, and the moving, often startling poems invite readers to savor the words and then look closely at each image. Teens will easily connect with the poems' universal themes, including identity, childhood memories, nature's mysterious power, and the powerful emotions and experiences that link us all. Biographical information about both the poets and the artists concludes this welcome title, which makes a natural partner to Naomi Shihab Nye's *This Same Sky* (1992). —Gillian Engberg

Janeczko, Paul B., ed. *Stone Bench in an Empty Park*. 2000. 40p. illus. Orchard (9780531302590). Gr. 5–12. 811.

Here is an iconoclastic haiku collection that breaks many traditional "rules," as compiler Janeczko admits in his introduction. The poems, written by Nikki Grimes, J. Patrick Lewis, Issa, and less familiar names, do not always follow the standard haiku pattern, yet all follow the spirit of the form. Instead of customary bucolic reflections, the selections reflect urban sights, sounds, and moments. Henri Silberman's black-and-white photographs are stunning. Some of them mirror the poetry so closely, they could have been the poet's inspiration. Wild geese soar above a chimney while the opposite page shows a roof top reflected in a puddle; the sharp angles of a car's tail fin contrast with the soft curves of a cat on an opposite page. This elegant verbal and visual gallery will provoke thought and stimulate creativity as it introduces urban charms to rural children and inspires city kids to recognize natural beauty in their neighborhoods. —Linda Perkins

Lewis, J. Patrick. *Black Cat Bone*. Illus. by Gary Kelley. 2006. 48p. Creative, lib. ed. (9781568461946). Gr. 7–12. 811.

The story of blues guitarist Robert Johnson—both the legend and the facts—hardly seems the stuff of a picture book. Johnson died young—in 1938, at 27, most likely poisoned in a dispute over a woman, or, as legend has it, the victim of a deal with the devil, who claimed Johnson's soul in exchange for mastery of the guitar. His influence on generations of blues, jazz, and rock musicians is unquestioned, however, and Lewis tells the story in evocative poems that use Johnson's lyrics to evoke the spirit of the blues and the hard times Johnson endured growing up in the Mississippi Delta. Like Wynton Marsalis' poems in *Jazz A B C* (2005), Lewis' imagery is probably too subtle for even middle-graders to grasp without help, but older readers with an interest in Johnson and the blues will feel the rhythm and understand the message of living for the moment and the music. Kelley's striking paintings, heavy with multiple shades of blue and brown, capture all the emotions that swirl around the Johnson myth: loneliness, obsession, and melancholy, of course, but also the up-tempo electricity generated by a bluesman in full cry. —Bill Ott

Lewis, J. Patrick. *Freedom like Sunlight: Praisesongs for Black Americans*. Illus. by John Thomson. 2000. 40p. Creative Editions (9781568461632). Gr. 5–12. 811.

Stunning illustrations by John Thompson take center stage in this attractively designed poetry collection that pays homage to legendary African Americans including Sojourner Truth, Arthur Ashe, and Rosa Parks. Using a range of styles and meter, the mostly rhyming poems are dramatic and reverential, but they evoke the spirit of their subjects and reference events in their remarkable lives without seeming overtly biographical or didactic. The simplest selections are often the best, their beautiful images not overwhelmed by the tribute: in "Baby Contralto," about Marian Anderson, "She brushed / her voice / Across the air / In colors / Not seen / Anywhere. / In colors / Beautiful / And strong. / She brushed / The air . . . / And painted song." But it's the radiant paintings, including a head-turning jacket portrait of the young Malcolm X, that will captivate a wide range of children and encourage repeated readings. Full-page, realistic images, elegantly balanced opposite poems on stark white backgrounds, powerfully capture the subjects in a mix of traditional portraiture, group scenes, and still life (the illustration for the poem about Langston Hughes, for example, shows only a sunlit desk with a typewriter, a coffee cup, an ashtray, and a smoking cigarette). Extensive biographical notes conclude a fine collection that can be used across the curriculum. —Gillian Engberg

Myers, Walter Dean. *Here in Harlem: Poems in Many Voices*. 2004. 88p. illus. Holiday (9780823418534). Gr. 7–10. 811.

In the introduction, Myers writes that he was inspired by Edgar Lee Masters' *Spoon River Anthology*, in which the people who live in a fictional town tell their stories in verse, and by his love of the Harlem community where he grew up. In each poem here, a resident of Harlem speaks in a distinctive voice, offering a story, a thought, a reflection, or a memory. The poetic forms are varied and well chosen. While some are formally expressed free-verse poems, others use the rhythm and rhyme of early blues songs or the graceful, informal cadences of conversational speech. Expressive period photos from Myers' collection accompany the text of this handsome book. Rather than illustrating specific poems, they help to create the look and feel of the time and place. Six vivid prose statements, called "Clara Brown's Testimony," appear throughout the volume and reflect different stages of her life. The rest of the pieces are poems revealing the experiences and personalities of 53 people, from student to retiree, from hairdresser to hustler, from live-in maid to street vendor-guitar player. Some of the individual poems are exceptionally strong and memorable. Collectively, they offer a colorful and warmly personal portrayal of Harlem. Whether used as a performance piece or read from cover to cover, this unusual book will be long remembered. —Carolyn Phelan

Nelson, Marilyn. ***Fortune's Bones: The Manumission Requiem.*** **2004. 32p. illus. Front Street (9781932425123). Gr. 7–12. 811.**

Fortune was a slave in eighteenth-century Connecticut, and when he died, his owner, a physician, rendered the bones to teach anatomy. In 1933 the physician's family donated the skeleton to the local Mattatuck Museum. Recently, the museum researched Fortune's story, and Connecticut Poet Laureate Marilyn Nelson, author of the award-winning *Carver: A Life in Poems* (2001), has written a series of six stirring poems to honor Fortune's life. Part funeral mass, part freedom celebration, her spare words are clear about the harshness of his servitude and what his remains tell about his backbreaking labor. In the climactic poem, "Not My Bones," Fortune himself speaks: "You can own someone's body, / the soul runs free." Nelson's small poems are framed by a wealth of facts as well as archival photos and images from the museum exhibit. Should Fortune's skeleton be kept on display, or should it be buried in consecrated ground? Moved by the poetry and the history, readers will want to join the debate. —Hazel Rochman

★ Nelson, Marilyn. ***A Wreath for Emmett Till.*** **Illus. by Philippe Lardy. 2005. 48p. Houghton (9780618397525). Gr. 9–12. 811.**

"I was nine years old when Emmett Till was lynched in 1955. His name and history have been a part of most of my life," writes the creator of award-winning *Carver* (2001) in the introduction to this offering—a searing poetry collection about Till's brutal, racially motivated murder. The poems form a heroic crown of sonnets—a sequence in which the last line of one poem becomes the first line of the next. "The strict form became a kind of insulation, a way of protecting myself from the intense pain of the subject matter," writes Nelson. The rigid form distills the words' overwhelming emotion into potent, heart-stopping lines that speak from changing perspectives, including that of a tree. Closing notes offer context to the sophisticated allusions to literature and history, but the raw power of many lines needs no translation. Nelson speaks of human history's deep contradictions: "My country, 'tis both / thy nightmare history and thy grand dream." But there's also the hope that comes from facing the past and moving forward: "In my house, there is still something called grace, / which melts ice shards of hate and makes hearts whole." When matched with Lardy's gripping, spare, symbolic paintings of tree trunks, blood-red roots, and wreaths of thorns, these poems are a powerful achievement that teens and adults will want to discuss together. —Gillian Engberg

Nye, Naomi Shihab. ***19 Varieties of Gazelle: Poems of the Middle East.*** **2002. 160p. Greenwillow (9780060097653). Gr. 5–10. 811.**

A Palestinian American raised in St. Louis and Jerusalem, Nye is a writer and anthologist whose poetry, fiction, and essays speak to a wide audience. This small, timely collection brings together her poems about the Middle East and about being Arab American. In her introduction she says that poetry cherishes the small details that big disasters erase, and her simple, concrete words show those details and their connections among soldiers, children, and "cousins" everywhere. Sometimes the details go on too long, and her quiet nature images carry too much message. It's the drama of the present war that will most move young readers, and the best poems bring big and small together, personalizing the disasters, showing the effects on one child, the loss inside a home, the fragile facts of daily life ("A brother and sister were playing with toys / when their room exploded"). There's no rhetoric, no sentimentality. Like Israeli writer Amos Oz, Nye takes no sides; her call for peace is to Arabs and Jews ("I'm not interested in / who suffered the most / I'm interested in / people getting over it"). The first poem is dated September 11, 2001, and this book will spark discussion and bring readers up close to what war and vengeance mean to people like themselves. —Hazel Rochman

Nye, Naomi Shihab. ***A Maze Me: Poems for Girls.*** **Illus. by Terre Maher. 2005. 128p. Greenwillow (9780060581893). Gr. 8–11. 811.**

In the thoughtful, inspiring introduction to her latest collection of original poems, Nye encourages young readers to write three lines in a notebook every day:

"You will find out what you notice. Uncanny connections will be made visible to you." The following poems draw from Nye's observations about nature, home, school, and neighborhood to make connections to a girl's inner world. The meaning in a few selections is oblique, particularly in spare lines that read like a zen koan. Most poems, though, speak with a powerful immediacy. When the speaker finds her mother's braid in an attic, there is the sharp, lonely realization that her parents will die: "I don't want to be / eighty years old / looking at the braid / all by myself." In other poems, she worries if a crush notices her, but there is a strong, contagious confidence in her voice: "Does he see me gleaming / in my chair?" In beautiful lines, the speaker's hopes extend to the wider world, and she wishes that, like tree frogs, humans had "something / we could / all sing / together, yes." A wide age range will respond to these deeply felt poems about everyday experiences that encourage readers to lean eagerly into their lives and delight in their passages. —Gillian Engberg

Nye, Naomi Shihab, ed. ***Is This Forever, or What? Poems and Paintings from Texas*****. 2004. 176p. illus. Greenwillow (9780060511784). Gr. 9–12. 811.008.**

The Texans in this anthology of art and poetry call their state "a deep breath"; a "landscape / lit like an overexposed photo"; a place where "cities and towns have wide margins around them." But don't expect swaggering, western stereotypes: "At least half the people in this book probably own no boots or cowboy hats," warns Nye in her funny, eloquent introduction. Organized somewhat arbitrarily, the poems include moving family tributes, furious self-revelations, and quiet, atmospheric vignettes that find grace and beauty in sun-baked neighborhoods, basic work, and everyday faces, such as the body-shop mechanic who "corrects the mistakes made by others . . . working the violence from warped / machines." Many poets, including Pat Mora, reference their Mexican heritage, and there are a few bilingual selections. The accompanying artworks are arresting without overpowering the words, and they echo the poems' wide range of styles with minimal abstractions, wildly colored Mexican imagery, and even a glistening, photo-realistic painting of donuts. Although Nye writes that she created this anthology to showcase "the beautiful diversity, the multiplicity of our state," this rich collection shows the universal currents and "the wide margins" that we all share. —Gillian Engberg

Okutoro, Lydia Omolola, ed. ***Quiet Storm: Voices of Young Black Poets*****. 2008. 128p. Disney/Jump at the Sun (9780786804610). Gr. 8–12. 811.008.**

This heartfelt collection features poems by young people, ages 13–21, from the U.S., Canada, England, Jamaica, Haiti, Barbados, Panama, St. Thomas, and several African countries. Okutoro (originally from Nigeria) has grouped the poems by theme and uses works by well-known poets such as Hughes, Angelou, and Clifton to introduce each section. Although the poems vary tremendously in style and sophistication, all resonate with the passionate sincerity that teen poets can communicate so well. The book jacket is splendid: elegant and lively, with a black-and-white photo of the head of a young African American (gender ambiguous) hanging upside down to let shiny deadlocks cascade next to a marvelous poem by a 16-year-old celebrating the diverse roots of African Americans. The brief biographical notes at the end personalize the poems and may encourage many readers to try their hand at poetry. Teachers can make good year-round use of this excellent curriculum support source, and it will have special meaning during African American history month.
—John Peters

Roessel, David, and Arnold Rampersad, eds. ***Langston Hughes*****. Illus. by Benny Andrews. 2006. 48p. Sterling (9781402718458). Gr. 7–10. 811.**

Hughes' poetry continues to have enormous appeal for young people. In this illustrated collection of 26 poems, Andrews' beautiful collage-and-watercolor illustrations extend the rhythm, exuberance, and longing of the words—not with literal images, but with tall, angular figures that express a strong sense of African American music, dreams, and daily life—while leaving lots of space for the words to "sing America." The picture-book format makes Hughes' work accessible to some grade-school children, especially for reading aloud and sharing, but the main audience will be older readers, who can appreciate the insightful, detailed introduction and biography, as well as the brief notes accompanying each poem, contributed by Hughes scholars Roessel and

Rampersad. Their comments, together with the quotes from the poet himself, will encourage readers to return to the book to see how Hughes made poetry of his personal life, black oral and musical traditions, urban experience, and the speech of ordinary people. Whether the focus is the Harlem Renaissance, the political struggle, Hughes' African heritage, or the weary blues, this book will find great use in many libraries. —Hazel Rochman

Turner, Ann. *Learning to Swim: A Memoir*. 2000. 128p. Scholastic (9780439153096). Gr. 6–12. 811.54.

"I didn't even know I could say no." In this courageous, poignant series of free-verse vignettes, Turner, the author of numerous books for young readers, recalls being sexually abused by a youth on a childhood summer vacation. Her learning to swim during that same summer provides the metaphorical framework: "sailing" along at first in happy innocence; "sinking" after neighbor Kevin takes her into her room, supposedly to read her a story, then "jams his hands / inside of me / and takes out his private parts / that I didn't ever know / could look so huge and strange. . . ." Cowed by his threats, she begins behaving in ways that worry her family. Eventually, she tells her mother and is able, at last, to go "swimming" ahead with her life. Turner addresses readers directly at the end—"Listen. / Telling is what matters"—and appends three hotline numbers for young people who may not have caring adults near them to listen and act. Her language and imagery are spare, direct, and, even with the passage of years, laced with strong, immediate feelings; it's a courageous, moving acknowledgment as well as a call to action for readers nursing secrets of their own.
—John Peters

Vecchione, Patrice, ed. *The Body Eclectic: An Anthology of Poems*. 2002. 208p. Holt (9780805069358). Gr. 8–12. 808.81.

Hand, hair, heel, elbow, blood, breast, skin, semen, vagina, bone, and more: this rich global anthology celebrates the human body with poetry (and a few pieces of prose) about love and beauty, laughter and tears, kissing and touching, body and mind. There's ugliness and suffering, too, including abuse, violence, and anorexia. But there are also lighter works, such as Shel Silverstein's "Unscratchable Itch." The physicalness of the words, images, and rhythm is always part of the meaning, whether it's the African American spiritual "Dem Dry Bones," Sherman Alexie's funny but searing "Giving Blood," or Stephen Dobyns' memory of a high-school dance. Most pieces are contemporary, but there are also classics by Byron, Shakespeare, Neruda, and others. An excerpt from Virginia Woolf's novel *Orlando* (1928) explores what editor Vecchione calls the "blurred lines" that gender can have. Excellent notes at the back introduce each writer and suggest more books to read. A great collection to show teens that literature is about their intimate selves and their connections with people everywhere. —Hazel Rochman

Weatherford, Carole Boston. *Becoming Billie Holiday*. Illus. by Floyd Cooper. 2008. 117p. Boyds Mills/ Wordsong (9781590785072). Gr. 6–9. 811.

In a series of free-verse poems and bluesy lyrics, headed by song titles, Weatherford retraces Holiday's childhood and early career in the renowned jazz singer's own voice. "At eleven, I had the body / of a grown woman, / the mouth of a sailor, and a temper / hot enough to fry an egg." Growing up in Baltimore, she moved to Harlem with her sometimes-absent mother after being molested by a neighbor, and quickly fell in love with late-night life. Dubbed "Lady Day," she earned money singing in clubs, was "discovered" by jazz enthusiast John Hammond, and battled racism on a groundbreaking tour with Artie Shaw's all-white band. Closing with Holiday's spectacular headline gig at the Café Society, where she sang "Strange Fruit"—"how could I not claim: / this is my song?"—Weatherford leaves the 25-year-old at a high spot in her career, before later troubles and drug addiction. After the whole story, readers will find a generous assortment of recommended reading and listening at the end of this proud, clear-voiced testimonial.
—John Peters

Science

Aronson, Marc. *Bill Gates*. 2008. 144p. illus. Viking (9780670063482). Gr. 6–10. 338.7.

For young people who wonder how Bill Gates became so wealthy so quickly, this biography opens chapters with (sometimes-wry) entrepreneurial principles, such as "Pick the Right Parents (or If You Can't, Learn to Be Intensely Competitive)." However, the book offers far more than business tips. It takes readers back in time, not just to Bill's childhood years in the Gates household, where intense competition was a way of life, but also to the period when personal computers were so new that a cocky teen who knew his stuff could bluff his way into important contracts as long as he had the know-how and determination to follow through. Though often critical of Gates' business practices, Aronson acknowledges that the man's most unsympathetic traits may have made his achievements possible. One of the most astute sections of the book analyzes Gates' recent turn toward philanthropy and compares him with nineteenth- and early-twentieth-century monopolists turned philanthropists. Black-and-white photos illustrate the text. An author's note, source notes, and lists of books, articles, and websites are appended. Well researched, thought-provoking, and up-to-date, this biography from the Up Close series offers insights into Gates' character as well as an engaging account of his life. —Carolyn Phelan

Blumenthal, Karen. *Steve Jobs: The Man Who Thought Different*. 2012. 256p. illus. Feiwel and Friends (9781250015570). Gr. 7–10. 621.390.

Walter Isaacson's best-selling biography, bolstered by 40 interviews with its subject, is the current gold standard for books about Steve Jobs, but Blumenthal's in-depth look at the innovator's life makes a close runner-up and a winner for younger audiences. Blumenthal, a former business reporter, uses a speech Jobs made to a graduating class at Stanford as an inviting hook to draw readers in. He told his audience stories about the most important incidents in his life, beginning with his adoption, and how the dots of his life connected in mysterious ways. His adoptive father was skilled with his hands and a perfectionist, a trait Jobs carried on, sometimes to extremes. The worst moments in Jobs' life, like being fired from Apple, the company he built, led him to bigger and better moments, and an eventual return to Apple, where he would give the world iPods, iPhones, and iPads. His final story was about his cancer, and his message was to "follow your heart and intuition." Through original interviews, a solid use of source material, and a wonderfully easy-going style, Blumenthal gives a full portrait of Jobs, with his many well-documented flaws (which here might be a tad underplayed), his original and far-sighted aesthetic, and his willingness to push himself and others to achieve the best—as he perceived it. One advantage this has over Isaacson's book is the well-placed sidebars that explain everything from how computer memory works to Jobs' distinctive wardrobe. This is a smart book about a smart subject by a smart writer. To be illustrated with photographs. Glossaries and sources are appended. —Ilene Cooper

Burns, Loree Griffin. *The Hive Detectives: Chronicle of a Honey Bee Catastrophe*. 2010. 80p. illus. Houghton (9780547152318). Gr. 6–10. 638.

The author of *Tracking Trash* (2007), Burns now spotlights a "dream team" of scientists as they work to determine what is threatening bee colonies and (by extension) agriculture, which depends on bees for pollination. After following hobbyist beekeeper Mary Duane as she inspects her hives, the discussion turns to a commercial beekeeper who reported in 2006 that 20 million bees had vanished in a mysterious and deadly phenomenon now known as colony collapse disorder (CCD). Fully illustrated with excellent color photos, the clearly written text introduces four scientists and follows them from the field to their labs as they investigate possible causes of CCD: pesticides, viruses, bacteria, and pests such as mites. The book demonstrates the urgent need for answers, the challenges of the scientists' ongoing research projects, and the importance of investigating a variety of possibilities. In the final pages, beekeeper Duane harvests honey from her healthy bees' hives. Throughout the presentation, readers learn about the anatomy, development, and social behavior of honey bees and observe the process of scientific investigation and its vital, real-world application. Appended are lists of recommended books, magazines, films, and websites as well as a glossary and a source bibliography. A fascinating book from the Scientists in the Field series. —Carolyn Phelan

Capuzzo, Michael. *Close to Shore: The Terrifying Shark Attacks of 1916*. 2003. 144p. illus. Crown (9780375822315). Gr. 7–12. 597.3.

The jacket photo, a gruesome close-up of an open-mouthed shark, sets the tone for this riveting adaptation of Capuzzo's similarly titled adult book about what occurred when, in 1916, a rogue shark traveled inland along a New Jersey creek, terrorizing residents of nearby towns. Extensive trimming has eliminated much about the individuals most involved in what happened, which occasionally makes for some confusion. But this book has a rich assortment of photos and news clippings not in the original, and the vividness and sheer physicality of Capuzzo's writing remains intact. In many ways this is a new book. Capuzzo reconstructs events with a novelist's flair and a scientist's attention to detail, and his pacing is relentless as the story moves from cultural history and shark physiology to close-ups of the crazed, disoriented beast slicing through the water. When the shark dies at the hands of two astounded fishermen, readers will experience relief as well as a sense of tragedy. As with the adult book, there are no notes—only a list of further readings that kids can use to find out more. —Stephanie Zvirin

Carson, Mary Kay. *The Bat Scientists*. Illus. by Tom Uhlman. 2010. 80p. Houghton (9780547199566). Gr. 7–10. 599.4.

With clear, informal prose and beautiful close-up color photos on every double-page spread, this exciting title in the Scientists in the Field series follows a team of dedicated bat specialists. Along the way, Carson dispels popular myths about the often maligned animals with solid information: bats are not blind, very few drink blood, and they are important pest controllers. The color photographs, including many full-page images, are spellbinding, from the image of a Texas cave filled with millions of adult bats to a close-up view of a single, walnut-sized baby. Many facts will be new to most readers—bats are the only mammals that fly; more than one-fifth of all the roughly 5,000 mammal species are bats—and young people will be easily drawn in by Carson's lucid, fascinating explanations of concepts and her vivid descriptions of scientists at work. The conservation message is urgent: bats' habitats are quickly disappearing because of overhunting, tourism, mining, and many other human-related causes. Whether describing the physics of echolocation or the present crisis of white-nose syndrome, Carson encourages readers to rethink stereotypes about creatures once scorned as flying vermin and shows how intricately their survival is tied to our own. Extensive back matter, including a glossary and a bibliography of books and websites, closes this standout resource. —Hazel Rochman

Farrell, Jeanette. *Invisible Allies: Microbes That Shape Our Lives*. 2005. 176p. illus. Farrar (9780374336080). Gr. 6–9. 579.

The author of *Invisible Enemies* (1998), Farrell now offers a fascinating, broad-ranging and imminently readable book on the beneficial roles of microbes. After stating some amazing facts about microbes and advising readers against "running, somewhat futilely, for a bar of soap," the introduction provides a vivid picture of Antony van Leeuwenhoek's discovery of microorganisms in 1676. The chapters that follow consider beneficial microbes in the production of bread, cheese, and chocolate as well as their vital role in the gut, where they break down certain foods, kill harmful microbes, and enable certain genes in the intestines to maximize digestion. Finally, Farrell explains the process by which microbes dispose of human waste in sewage treatment plants, noting that they are also used to clean up oil spills and toxins in the environments. Illustrations include photos as well as interesting archival material. Without talking down to her audience or hyping the grosser aspects of the subject, Farrell presents what is known about beneficial microbes and acknowledges the ongoing study of these amazing life-forms. —Carolyn Phelan

Fradin, Dennis Brindell. *With a Little Luck: Surprising Stories of Amazing Discovery*. 2006. 144p. illus. Dutton (9780525471967). Gr. 6–9. 509.

When Newton saw that apple fall, he was ready to make his monumental discovery. Yes, luck and accident played a role, but so did his focus on details. The same is true of the 11 thrilling breakthroughs described this collective biography. Each inventor-discoverer is concentrating on a problem when the unexpected leads to revelation: Alexander Fleming understood the importance of what happened after mold that grew in his messy lab landed on a dish of bacteria. The daily detail is almost as exciting as the sudden breakthrough. Whether Fradin is writing about the discovery of penicillin, Neptune, pulsars, or the Dead Sea Scrolls, he smoothly combines personal stories (including some about young people) with fascinating science, technology, and history. His style is open and chatty, and the book design is very attractive: thick paper, spacious type, occasional quotes in the margin, and black-and-white photos and prints. Some of the bibliographic notes for the biographies mention Fradin's contact with contemporary inventors. Caught by the thrilling science and the personal adventure, many readers will go on to find out more. —Hazel Rochman

Gore, Al, and Jane O'Connor. *An Inconvenient Truth*. 2007. 192p. illus. Viking (9780670062713). Gr. 6–12. 363.73874.

In this youth-focused adaptation of Gore's 2006 adult book and Oscar-winning documentary, Gore and O'Connor (credited as "adaptor") distill the material, creating an eye-opening story that targets kids' concerns. Gone are the political passages that begin with phrases such as "During the Clinton-Gore years . . ." The language is basic—*vector* in the adult book becomes "life forms that can carry"—and offers clear definitions of such terms as *greenhouse gases* and persuasive, accessible arguments for how the climate crisis has developed and what can be done to address it. The sturdy pages are filled with color photographs and charts, and the images are riveting. Like the pictures, the personal stories bring the facts close, and in addition to the urgent science, Gore's book shows how mentors can change lives. In his moving introduction, Gore speaks about how reading Rachel Carson's *Silent Spring* (1962) when he was 14 years old shocked him into environmental awareness, which developed further during his studies with pioneering scientist Dr. Roger Revelle at Harvard. Gore's research continues to raise controversy, but few, if any, books for youth offer such a dynamic look at the climate issues threatening our planet. —Gillian Engberg

Hakim, Joy. *Einstein Adds a New Dimension*. 2007. 468p. illus. Smithsonian (9781588341624). Gr. 7–12. 509.

After assuring readers that modern science is more astonishing than anything in science fiction, Hakim delivers as proof a typically brisk, intellectually challenging account of the development of quantum theory and modern cosmology. Writing largely in present tense, she introduces a teeming cast of deep thinkers who, despite some missteps (Ernest Rutherford's early claim that beta radiation was similar to X-rays is a "big goof"), delivered a series of brilliant experiments and insights to illuminate the decidedly weird goings-on, both inside the atomic nucleus and at the ends (if ends there be) of the universe. Hakim herself goofs occasionally (Teddy Roosevelt, not Albert Michelson, was the first American to receive a Nobel Prize) but nevertheless displays a real talent for lucidly explaining such difficult concepts as probability and quantum entanglement. Because her focus is on history, she only briefly considers the burgeoning subatomic particle zoo or the ins and outs of string theory. Supplemented by a digestible resource list and a generous assortment of illustrations, ranging from sharp color photos to editorial cartoons and science-inspired modern art, this third volume of a projected six makes another extraordinary cornerstone in the Story of Science series. Readers who enjoy having their intellects stretched will find this volume covers tough concepts in a very thorough and stimulating way. —John Peters

Hoose, Phillip. ***Moonbird: A Year on the Wind with the Great Survivor B95.*** **2012. 160p. illus. Farrar (9780374304683). Gr. 7–12. 598.072.**

Hoose, the author of *The Race to Save the Lord God Bird* (2004) and the heavily awarded *Claudette Colvin: Twice toward Justice* (2009), now turns his attention to another endangered bird, the rufa red knot. He focuses on one, B95 (dubbed Moonbird by researchers), which he calls "one of the world's premiere athletes," explaining that though "weighing a mere four ounces, he's flown more than 325,000 miles in his lifetime." Each year, red knots like Moonbird fly from their winter home in Tierra del Fuego, Argentina, to their breeding grounds in the Canadian Arctic, a journey of 9,000 miles. B95, now 20 years old, has made this remarkable flight 18 or more times. In this beautifully written and meticulously researched book, Hoose provides a complete account of the red knots' physiology, their flight patterns, feeding habits, habitats, and more. He also writes about those who study the birds and struggle to preserve the endangered species, which has dwindled in numbers from some 150,000 to less than 25,000. In addition to his attention to the birds, Hoose profiles those who study them and also provides a generous number of photographs, maps, and sidebar features that dole out background and ancillary material. His appendix includes elaborate source notes and an extensive bibliography. Sure to be one of the most well-received information books of the year, and deservedly so. —Michael Cart

Innes, Brian. ***DNA and Body Evidence.*** **2007. 96p. illus. M. E. Sharpe/Sharpe Focus, lib. ed. (9780765681157). Gr. 9–12. 614.**

Terms like *blood spatter, luminol,* and *DNA profiling* are now widely familiar from TV crime shows, mystery novels, and magazines. But what do the words really mean? Innes makes excellent use of his journalistic abilities as well as his familiarity with biochemistry and forensic science to provide answers in this entry in the Forensic Evidence series. A large part of the book is the science, and Innes never forgets that he's writing for lay readers. While he uses scientific terminology as he explains the history and evolution of DNA analysis, fingerprinting, and blood analysis, his easy-to-follow discussions are linked to real-world crimes, which elucidate as well as engage—the facts are disturbing, but Innes never sensationalizes. In "A DNA Casebook" he goes into cases that test the significance of DNA evidence (including the O. J. Simpson trial), discussing both limitations and successful applications of the technology. Particularly intriguing is the chapter "Questions of Law," which explores how changes in science have affected the legal system. The text is nicely spaced on the page, and the details never overwhelm, thanks to a generous assortment of color photos, diagrams, and insets. Even the page references in parentheses, which at first seem intrusive, work as helpful refreshers to the science. An altogether successful investigation of a high-interest topic. A brief bibliography and an index are appended. —Stephanie Zvirin

McClafferty, Carla Killough. ***Something Out of Nothing: Marie Curie and Radium.*** **2006. 144p. illus. Farrar (9780374380366). Gr. 7–10. 540.**

Like Nick Healy's overview, *Marie Curie* (2005), this readable biography examines Curie's life and work as a groundbreaking scientist and as an independent woman. Unlike Healy's, though, McClafferty's account is more detailed and includes extensive documentation with chapter source notes. The groundbreaking science is as thrilling as the personal story, which describes Curie's struggle to get to college, her happy marriage to Pierre Curie and their work together, and her recognition as the first woman to win a Nobel Prize, a prize she won again later for her work in chemistry. In addition to the triumph, though, McClafferty shows that Curie could be harsh and indifferent to her own family. The spacious design makes the text easy to read, and occasional photos, including one of the interior of the shed where she and Pierre began their research, bring the story closer. —Hazel Rochman

Murphy, Jim, and Alison Blank. ***Invincible Microbe: Tuberculosis and the Never-Ending Search for a Cure.*** **2012. 160p. illus. Clarion (9780618535743). Gr. 6–10. 616.9.**

Beginning with evidence of tuberculosis in a 500,000-year-old fossilized *Homo erectus* skull, this well-researched volume describes ineffective treatments for the illness in ancient Egypt and Greece before tracing the disease's course throughout European and American history. Although antibiotics once offered the hope of eradicating the disease, the emergence of drug-resistant TB has been a serious modern setback. In their broad discussion of tuberculosis, its effects, and the search for a cure, Murphy and Blank clearly present a broad range of historical periods and social issues. One noteworthy section tells how the romanticized, nineteenth-century view of consumption contrasted with the actual lives and deaths of those who suffered from the disease. Another describes the development of sanatoriums and the experiences of patients, including writer Betty MacDonald. With particular focus on the early twentieth century, the chapter "The Outsiders" discusses the difficulties encountered by African Americans and immigrants seeking care and treatment for TB. Illustrations, mainly archival photos, appear on nearly every double-page spread. The back matter is unusually rich and informative, with annotations in the source notes and bibliography. Wide ranging in breadth, yet always well focused on the topic at hand, this fascinating book offers a sharply detailed picture of tuberculosis throughout history. —Carolyn Phelan

Noyes, Deborah. *One Kingdom: Our Lives with Animals*. 2006. 144p. illus. Houghton (9780618499144). Gr. 7–10. 590.

In this insightful, provocative photo-essay, Noyes examines the ways in which human lives have overlapped with animals' and how our beliefs, culture, and science have been impacted throughout history by the essential but frequently paradoxical human-animal connection. Noyes, a former zookeeper, devotes significant discussion to conservation and the ethics of keeping animals in captivity, including a lengthy debate about zoos, noting that zoos provide an opportunity to bring humans and animals together but alter the natural behavior of the animals on exhibit. Readers will find the provocative questions Noyes raises compelling and challenging, and the lyrical, urgent prose, along with beautiful black-and-white photos of the animals up close, will draw serious readers and browsers alike. Suggest this for classroom debate fodder as well as personal reading for animal lovers. —Ed Sullivan

Schlosser, Eric, and Charles Wilson. *Chew on This: Everything You Don't Want to Know About Fast Food*. 2006. 304p. illus. Houghton/Graphia (9780618710317). Gr. 6–9. 394.1.

Including passages from Schlosser's best-selling adult book *Fast Food Nation* (2001) and other writings, the authors dish up a somewhat-less-stomach-churning look at the fast-food industry's growth, practices, and effects on public health. Folding in original interviews, recent statistics, and published research, along with such spicy taglines as "The Golden Arches are now more widely recognized than the Christian cross," they trace the hamburger's early years and the evolution of the McDonald's Corporation's revolutionary Speedee Service System. They follow with vivid tours through feedlots, abattoirs, and a chicken-processing plant to explore how fast food has achieved spectacular international success, particularly among an increasingly obese youth market, then round off with glimpses of Alice Waters' Edible Schoolyard initiative and other alternatives less likely to lead to gastric bypass surgery. Readers may not lose their appetites for McFood from this compelling study, but they will definitely come away less eager to get a McJob and more aware of the diet's attendant McMedical problems. Extensive endnotes, occasional photos. —John Peters

Treaster, Joseph B. *Hurricane Force: In the Path of America's Deadliest Storms*. 2007. 128p. illus. Kingfisher (9780753460863). Gr. 7–10. 551.55.

Journalist Treaster reported on Hurricane Katrina from New Orleans for the *New York Times*, and his gripping photo-essay blends particulars of the tragedy with an in-depth overview of America's hurricane history—including both the science of meteorology and the grim human drama. Treaster is not exploitative as he tells about the disaster and the heroic rescues, then confronts the facts about what technology can and cannot do: "for all the gadgetry and experience and devotion, scientists still don't know exactly where a hurricane will strike and with how much force." His warning is clear: there is a dire need for advanced planning and better methods for evacuation. Along with weather diagrams, there are lots of full-color photographs that bring close the high winds and surging seas of hurricanes, the shattered homes, and pictures of people rescued or lost. The extensive back matter is an integral part of the book, with detailed source notes, including subject references to *Times* articles, a Hurricane Katrina time line, and references to scientific articles, news reports, and books. The combination of headline news and high-tech detail makes the latest entry in the *New York Times* Book series a great science book for personal reading or classroom use. —Hazel Rochman

Turner, Pamela. *The Frog Scientist*. Illus. by Andy Comins. 2009. 64p. Houghton (9780618717163). Gr. 5–9. 597.8.

This lively volume from the Scientists in the Field series opens with biologist Tyrone Hayes and his team collecting frogs at a pond in Wyoming. After a short chapter on Hayes' background, the discussion returns to his work: he addresses the general question of why amphibian populations worldwide are declining by studying the effects of atrazine, an agricultural pesticide, on the reproductive organs of leopard frogs from a particular pond. Well organized and engagingly written, the text goes into detail about the process of analyzing the chemical's effects on the frogs, but pulls back from specifics to show how the experiment fits into the larger picture. A full-page diagram called "Tyrone's Experiment" lays out the hypothesis and procedures in a condensed, visual manner. Excellent color photos offer clear pictures of frogs and of this scientific team at work in the field and in the lab. Appendixes include a glossary and lists of books and websites. Throughout the book, Turner portrays Hayes as both a colorful personality and a dedicated scientist: the final chapter opens with a discussion of his four ear piercings and concludes with an overview of his research. A vivid, realistic view of one scientist at work. —Carolyn Phelan

Social Science

Alsenas, Linas. *Gay America: Struggle for Equality*. 2008. 160p. illus. Abrams/Amulet (9780810994874). Gr. 7–12. 306.76.

Alsenas' landmark history of American gay life focuses largely on public attitudes toward homosexuality and the seemingly endless struggle for gay rights. After a brief survey covering pre-twentieth-century America, Alsenas narrows his focus to offer a closer examination of more recent events. Thus, Chapter Two deals with the period 1910–39; Chapter Three, with 1940–59; and so on until the final chapter brings the reader to the present—and beyond. In an effort to humanize his material, the author begins each chapter with an individual story told from a "personalized" (i.e., lightly fictionalized) point of view. While this succeeds in dramatizing factual material, the effort may be unnecessary, since the epic story the author tells of the gradual emergence of gays and lesbians from the shadows is itself a compellingly human drama. Alsenas' often sprightly, always engaging style makes his history even more reader-friendly, as do the many archival photographs that enliven each page. This first-ever book to cover this material for young adults is essential reading for all young people—gay, lesbian, and straight. —Michael Cart

Bang, Molly. *Nobody Particular: One Woman's Fight to Save the Bays*. Illus. by Molly Bang. 2001. 32p. Holt (9780805053968). Gr. 6–12. 363.738.

Diane Wilson was a fourth-generation shrimper in Calhoun County, Texas, until June 20, 1989, when something happened that changed her life "in a flash." Reading the local newspaper, she discovered that she was living in one of the most polluted counties in America. It was the beginning of her transformation from "nobody particular—just a shrimper and momma" into a savvy environmental activist who courageously took on a giant corporation, her local community, and even the Environmental Protection Agency in her tireless quest to save the local bays and their ecology. In telling Wilson's story, Bang uses a format that is part picture book and part graphic novel. The story, in hand-lettered text and speech balloons, is in bordered squares containing panels of black-and-white cartoon art, which are printed over double-page spreads of beautifully executed full-color depictions of the bays' ecosystem, chemical pollution, and shrimp farming. The disparate elements work together well to offer an imperative wake-up call to readers who take the environment for granted, at the same time presenting a riveting, emotional story of how single individuals can make a difference in a world of bewildering complexity. —Michael Cart

Blumenthal, Karen. *Let Me Play: The Story of Title IX: The Law That Changed the Future of Girls in America*. 2005. 160p. illus. Atheneum (9780689859571). Gr. 6–9. 796.

As in *Six Days in October* (2002), a compelling overview of the 1929 stock market crash and a financial primer, *Wall Street Journal* editor Blumenthal uses specific facts and fascinating personal stories to give readers a wide view of history. Here, the author looks at American women's evolving rights by focusing on the history and future of Title IX, which bans sex discrimination in U.S. education. Profiles of groundbreaking female athletes and legislators deftly alternate with highlights of the women's movement, from the early twentieth century through today. The dull paper stock diminishes the many black-and-white photos, but the images are still gripping, and relevant political cartoons and fact boxes add further interest. Few books cover the last few decades of American women's history with such clarity and detail, and this comprehensive title draws attention to the hard-won battles, the struggles that remain, and the chilling possibility that rights, if not fiercely protected, can easily be lost. —Gillian Engberg

Ellis, Deborah. ***Children of War: Voices of Iraqi Refugees.*** **2009. 128p. illus. Groundwood (9780888999078). Gr. 7–12. 305.23086.**

As in *Three Wishes: Palestinian* and *Israeli Children Speak* (2004), Ellis gets behind the news images and lets the most vulnerable civilians bear witness to what today's wars are doing to their lives. With the help of interpreters, she interviews child refugees from Iraq, now living in Jordan, and a few who have made it to Canada. A brief general introduction talks about the contemporary politics and the ethnic and religious diversity, and Ellis is clear about the brutality of Saddam, his fall, the role of oil in the conflict, the U.S. invasion, and bombing. Accompanying each of the following interviews with young people is a brief introduction and a photo, although a few children didn't want to be identified. Some have strong opinions for and against Saddam and the U.S.; most do not. What is haunting are their graphic recent memories of what they witnessed, including school bombings, violence against their families, arrests, and displacement. One hates the invaders; another bonds with an American soldier who comes to search for weapons. Many live in a foreign country that does not want them. An important, current title that will have lasting significance. —Hazel Rochman

Ellis, Deborah. ***Our Stories, Our Songs: African Children Talk about AIDS.*** **2005. 156p. illus. Fitzhenry & Whiteside (9781550419139). Gr. 6–9. 362.1.**

The statistics about children orphaned by AIDS in sub-Saharan Africa are overwhelming: 11.5 million cases and rising. Ellis brings the numbers close, relating the facts of poverty, child labor, sexual exploitation, and the signs and symptoms of the disease. But more than that, she tells the personal stories of young people whom she interviewed and photographed in Malawi and Zambia. She spoke to them in their homes, at clinics, schools, hospitals, and counseling centers, and on the streets, in English and through interpreters. Many voices sound the same (perhaps because of translation), but the short, simple sentences and the small photographs capture a wide variety of individual experience. The authentic details speak of loss, fear, and grief; incredible kindness; and courage as well as hope for the future ("I would wear clean clothes every day and be paid every week"). The readable design includes informative boxed insets ("How not to catch AIDS," "Poverty,") and quotes, side-by-side with each child's immediate experience. Readers older than the target audience will want this, too, for both the basic information and the heart-rending stories. —Hazel Rochman

Freedman, Russell. ***In Defense of Liberty: The Story of America's Bill of Rights.*** **2003. 196p. illus. Holiday (9780823415854). Gr. 5–10. 342.73.**

Freedman is at his best in this compelling, timely discussion of the Constitution and civil liberties. In his signature clear, conversational prose, he talks about the history of the Bill of Rights, from the time it was first voted on two centuries ago through the ongoing struggle to keep people free. What does that word *people* mean? For a long time, the term didn't include African Americans, Native Americans, or women. Freedman devotes a chapter to each amendment, covering its origin, various interpretations, landmark Supreme Court cases, and, always, the contemporary scene, including the conflicts now raging about national security and individual freedom in the aftermath of 9/11. He cites many cases involving young people and he is careful to discuss many sides of controversial topics such as abortion and capital punishment. The book design is beautiful, with thick paper, lots of white space, historical prints (including an archival print of the Bill of Rights), and lots of photos. This is a must for classroom discussion and personal interest, and the source notes and annotated bibliography at the back, as spaciously laid out as the text, will help readers find out more. —Hazel Rochman

Graydon, Shari. ***Made You Look: How Advertising Works and Why You Should Know.*** **Illus. by Warren Clark. 2003. 120p. Firefly/Annick (9781550378153). Gr. 5–9. 659.1.**

Advertising, explains Graydon, is increasingly "the water in which we swim," a reference to a Ghanaian proverb, and some of the most sought-after fish in the pond are consumers in the 8–14 demographic. This lively analysis seeks to raise preteens' awareness of themselves as targets and vectors of advertising messages. Brimming with anecdotes, facts, and quotes ("In our factory, we make lipstick; in our advertising, we sell hope"), the text covers controversial programs that bring ads into the schools, and describes traditional marketing methods as well as "stealth" techniques: hiring "cool hunters" to hang around trendsetters, using movie product placements, drawing on the media resources of a conglomerate to tout entertainment products under the guise of objectivity. Graydon never simply holds forth. She often ends sections with a provocative question ("How many female mascots can you think of?"), and she helpfully includes addresses of watchdog organizations, tips for writing effective complaints, and an impressive set of endnotes. Young adults attracted by the hip jacket may cry "false advertising!" when they see the naive-looking cartoons inside, but once they start reading, they'll find themselves sucked in as readily as younger readers: "Made you look," indeed. —Jennifer Mattson

Herumin, Wendy. *Child Labor Today: A Human Rights Issue*. 2007. 112p. illus. Enslow, lib. ed. (9780766026827). Gr. 7–12. 331.3.

An estimated 218 millon children worldwide work in terrible conditions, and this powerful title in the Issues in Focus Today series combines up-to-date facts with moving portraits of individual children who, instead of going to school, are forced to toil in mines, factories, the sex trade; on farms; as domestics, soldiers, and more. Herumin draws on official reports and victims' personal narratives, including two obtained from her own phone interviews. The accessible design includes many full-color photos of contemporary young people trapped in harsh workplaces. Poverty, readers learn, is the main cause of child-labor violations, most of which occur in the Asian-Pacific region and in sub-Saharan Africa, but problems exist in the U.S., too, especially among migrant farm workers. This is bound to be a burning issue for young people, and many readers, inspired by stories such as that of Iqbal Masih, an escaped carpet weaver believed to have been killed for his activism, will welcome the closing call: "You can help. Your voice counts." Numerous chapter notes, a helpful bibliography, and websites will help potential activists to make a start. —Hazel Rochman

Howard, Helen. *Living as a Refugee in America: Mohammed's Story*. 2005. 48p. illus. World Almanac (9780836859584). Gr. 6–9. 073.0869.

In his own words, Mohammed, 15, now in high school in St. Louis, Missouri, tells how he fled the Taliban in Afghanistan and wandered in Iran and then Turkey before coming to the U.S. with his mother, brother, and sister. This excellent title in the Children in Crisis series weaves Mohammed's immediate, contemporary story together with facts about Afghanistan's recent history and about refugees driven by war and famine across the world. The readable, double-page spreads include Mohammed's first-person narrative, printed in italics; full-color, captioned photos of Mohammed, his family, and friends; and discussion about issues such as discrimination, cultural barriers, and maintaining dual identity. There is no sensationalizing; neither is there a happily-ever-after uplift. Mohammed's father is homeless somewhere in Greece; his mother suffers from depression; and the family shares one bedroom. A brave personal account such as this is the best way to draw readers to the plight of refugees today, and along with Mohammed's story, Howard lists ways kids can take action to help the displaced and provides an annotated list of international human rights organizations to contact. —Hazel Rochman

Kuklin, Susan. *No Choirboy: Murder, Violence, and Teenagers on Death Row*. 2008. 256p. illus. Holt (9780805079500). Gr. 10–12. 364.66092.

In previous books for youth, Kuklin has explored harrowing topics such as AIDS (*Fighting Back: What Some People Are Doing about AIDS*, 1988) and child slavery (*Iqbal Masih and the Crusaders against Child Slavery*, 1998). Her latest title, about individuals who received death-row sentences while they were teenagers, is another direct, compassionate, and eye-opening inquiry. The prisoners' words, drawn from Kuklin's interview transcripts, form the bulk of the narratives, but Kuklin's voice frequently cuts in with details about the events leading up to the alleged crime, legal issues, and the prisoners' backgrounds. Some chapters also include commentary from the prisoners' lawyers and the prisoners' own writing (one, Nanon Williams, is a published author). The mix of voices makes for a somewhat chaotic but riveting whole that combines powerfully with the occasional photos and hand-drawn portraits of the subjects. Kuklin presents, with signature frankness, the men's memories of their young lives; the murders, for which some claim innocence; and the brutal realities (including rape and other acts of extreme violence) of incarcerated life, first on death row and then in maximum-security prison, where most of the prisoners are now held. In unforgettable later chapters, families of prisoners and victims both speak about their grief and loss, and the closing section focuses on a world-renowned anti–death penalty attorney. This isn't a balanced overview of capital punishment. Instead, it is a searing and provocative account that will touch teens' most fundamental beliefs and questions about violence, punishment, our legal and prison systems, and human rights. An author's note and extensive resources conclude. —Gillian Engberg

Levithan, David, and Billy Merrell, eds. ***The Full Spectrum: A New Generation of Writing about Gay, Lesbian, Bisexual, Transgender, Questioning, and Other Identities.*** **2006. 288p. illus. Knopf (9780375832901). Gr. 8–11. 306.76.**

The 40 contributions to this invaluable collection about personal identity have two things in common: all are nonfiction and all are by writers under the age of 23. Beyond that, diversity is the order of the day, and the result is a vivid demonstration of how extraordinarily broad the spectrum of sexual identity is among today's gay, lesbian, bisexual, transgender, and questioning youth. That said, some of the topics addressed in these essays and poems are familiar (the agony of coming out, the heartbreak of religious opprobrium). What is new and encouraging, however, is that so many young people have felt free enough to share the truth about themselves in print and under their own names; as coeditor Levithan notes in his introduction, "One way to effect change is to share truths. To tell our stories." Insightful, extraordinarily well written, and emotionally mature, the selections offer compelling, dramatic evidence that what is important is not what we are but who we are. —Michael Cart

Macy, Sue. ***Swifter, Higher, Stronger: A Photographic History of the Summer Olympics.*** **2004. 96p. illus. National Geographic (9780792266679). Gr. 6–10. 796.48.**

The official length of a marathon is not the 24 miles run by an ancient Greek messenger but 26 miles, 385 yards. Why the discrepancy? The greater distance can be traced to the 1908 London Games, where Queen Alexandra dictated a route that would give her family a close-up view. Such fascinating tidbits abound in this photo-rich history of the Summer Olympics. Macy, a seasoned writer of sports history for children, opens with background on the Games, then turns to broader themes, such as controversies and sportsmanship. Though her approach isn't strictly chronological, one comes away with a strong sense of how defining Olympian moments can provide a springboard to world history—as in the 1956 water polo competition, when fury over the Soviet Union's bombing of Hungary resulted in an unusually violent match between the two nations. Macy concludes with almanac-like features, a general note on her research methods, and titles for further reading. This comprehensive resource will attract readers aplenty during the games, though there's much to entice sports-loving kids even after the torch has gone out. —Jennifer Mattson

Margulies, Phillip, and Maxine Rosaler. ***The Devil on Trial: Witches, Anarchists, Atheists, Communists, and Terrorists in America's Courtrooms.*** **2008. 224p. illus. Houghton (9780618717170). Gr. 8–12. 345.73.**

In this well-researched and affecting offering, Margulies and Rosaler tie some of the most important trials in American history to the country's frequent need to find a "devil: not just a threat to the community, but an incarnation of evil." Five cases are examined in depth: the Salem witch trials, in which the threat was literally the devil; the Haymarket bomb trial, which

put anarchists in the devil's suit; the Scopes "monkey trial," in which evolution locked horns with religion; the Alger Hiss case, which pitted Communism and democracy; and the trials of Zacarias Moussaoui, the face of evil for a new century. With an oversize format, a crisp typeface, and an illustration-filled design, this is an appealing-looking read. However, it is not light reading; the depth in which the authors examine these trials is both complete and sobering, especially when set against whatever public sentiment was raging at the time. Putting these trials into a historical context is something they do particularly well. Readers will learn as much about why religion and science were butting heads in the 1920s as they will about the Scopes trial (which was originally a test case encouraged by the ACLU). Impeccably sourced, with an extensive bibliography, this examination does sometimes drop a few threads (what *did* happen to Salem's Tituba?) and sometimes stretches the devil connection. Yet young people who spend time with this intriguing title will find themselves more deeply and thoughtfully informed about the U.S. and its legal system.
—Ilene Cooper

Pollan, Michael, and Richie Chevat. *The Omnivore's Dilemma: The Secrets behind What You Eat*. 2009. 352p. illus. Dial (9780803734159). Gr. 6–10. 338.10973.

Pollan's adult edition of *The Omnivore's Dilemma* (2006) was a watershed book. A *New York Times* best-seller, a James Beard Award winner, and a *Booklist* Editors' Choice selection, its personal, informed, adventurous exploration of the American food chain inspired thousands of readers to learn and care about what they eat. This exemplary young readers' edition offers much more than just a simplified, condensed version of the original. Adapted by Richie Chevat, it follows, in Pollan's accessible, funny, first-person voice, the same progression as the adult original. Four meals create the framework for Pollan's investigation into how food arrives on the table: an industrial dinner (from McDonald's), an industrial organic meal, a dinner made from local sustainable ingredients, and a dinner made mostly from foods that Pollan hunted and gathered. Expertly edited, the book retains the original's provocative anecdotes and questions, while presenting the background information in even more expanded and accessible terms. The open, attractive format includes visuals that are all new here, including diagrams, sidebars, and personal photos of the book's characters. Also new is an appended interview with Pollan, as well as a welcome closing chapter, "The Omnivore's Solution," with tips for conscious eating. Just as powerful as the adult edition but perfectly tuned to a young audience, this title is essential food for thought. —Gillian Engberg

Runyon, Brent. *The Burn Journals*. 2004. 384p. Knopf (9780375826214). Gr. 8–12. 362.28.

On the sixteenth page of this incisive memoir, eighth-grader Brent Runyon drenches his bathrobe with gasoline and ("Should I do it? Yes.") sets himself on fire. The burns cover 85 percent of his body and require six months of painful skin grafts and equally invasive mental-health rehabilitation. From the beginning, readers are immersed in the mind of 14-year-old Brent as he struggles to heal body and mind, his experiences given devastating immediacy in a first-person, present-tense voice that judders from uncensored teenage attitude and poignant anxiety (he worries about getting hard-ons during physical therapy) to little-boy sweetness. And throughout he is anguished over his suicide attempt and its impact on his family: "I have this guilt feeling all over me, like oil on one of those birds in Alaska." Runyon has, perhaps, written the defining book of a new genre, one that gazes as unflinchingly at boys on the emotional edge as Zibby O'Neal's *The Language of Goldfish* (1980) and Laurie Halse Anderson's *Speak* (1999) do at girls. Some excruciatingly painful moments notwithstanding, this can and should be read by young adults, as much for its literary merit as for its authentic perspective on what it means to attempt suicide, and, despite the resulting scars, be unable to remember why. —Jennifer Mattson

Siddiqui, Haroon. *Being Muslim*. 2006. 144p. Groundwood (9780888997852). Gr. 8–12. 297.

In the wake of 9/11, "Islam-bashing" bears all the symptoms of racism as it holds up the relatively few fanatics as representative of all 1.3 billion Muslims. That's the argument of award-winning Canadian journalist Siddiqui, past president of PEN Canada, a writers' group that is a leading advocate of free speech. His clear, passionate discussion confronts international issues that are in the news now, including recent controversies over cartoon representations of Prophet Muhammad, the debate surrounding the wearing of the hijab (traditional headscarf), and issues of faith and feminism, suicide bombing, and more. While clearly concerned about terrorism and other dangers, Siddiqui attacks the propaganda of collective guilt. Without preaching or political jargon and drawing on his travels and interviews in Muslim countries, he shows that the extremists are being challenged by a new generation of Muslims, and welcomes the current internal reformation. He also asks penetrating questions: for example, why does the U.S. turn a blind eye to suffocating restrictions on women in Saudi Arabia? Including documented chapter notes and an "Essential Reading" list, this timely volume in the Groundwork Guide series is sure to spark debate. Like Jane Springer's *Genocide* (2006), also part of the series, this is excellent for classroom discussion. —Hazel Rochman

Winick, Judd. ***Pedro and Me: Friendship, Loss, and What I Learned*****. 2000. 187p. illus. Holt (9780805064032). Gr. 8–12. 362.1.**

Winick, part of the 1993 television cast of MTV's *Real World, San Francisco,* uses his cartoonist skills to take readers back to the house where the show was set and tell the story of fellow cast mate Pedro Zamora, an AIDS educator who died in 1994 from complications related to HIV. Part lesson about AIDS, part biographical sketch, this book differs from the many graphic novels that rely on action drawings or high-octane plotting. It is facial expressions that count most here, and they are Winick's forte as he briefly recalls how he came to the show; his evolving friendship with Zamora, whose background he describes; and his growing understanding of AIDS, which broadened the boundaries of his world. More about the show would have been useful: Winick assumes familiarity with the setup and cast, which some teens may not have. And the resemblance between Winick and Zamora in the artwork (a photo on the jacket does show some likeness in real life) is occasionally disconcerting. Most memorable is Winick's heartfelt description of Zamora's final days (he died at the age of 22), which are described with great tenderness and a keen sense of the loss of a friend. —Stephanie Zvirin

Appendix: Top 50 YA Books, 2000–2013

The following titles were selected by *Booklist*'s Books for Youth editors as the top 50 titles published for young adults between the years 2000 and 2013. Throughout the volume, a star (★) appears next to each title's full review, indicating its placement on this list.

1. Alexie, Sherman. *The Absolutely True Diary of a Part-Time Indian*. 2007. 256p. Little, Brown (9780316013680). Gr. 7–10.
2. Almond, David. *Kit's Wilderness*. 2000. 240p. Delacorte (9780385326650). Gr. 6–9.
3. Anderson, M. T. *The Astonishing Life of Octavian Nothing, Traitor to the Nation; v.1: The Pox Party*. 2006. 368p. Candlewick (9780763624026). Gr. 10–12.
4. Anderson, M. T. *Feed*. 2002. 240p. Candlewick (9780763617264). Gr. 9–12.
5. Bartoletti, Susan Campbell. *Hitler Youth: Growing Up in Hitler's Shadow*. 2005. 176p. illus. Scholastic (9780439353793). Gr. 7–10. 943.086.
6. Bartoletti, Susan Campbell. *They Called Themselves the K.K.K: The Birth of an American Terrorist Group*. 2010. 176p. illus. Houghton (9780618440337). Gr. 7–12. 322.4.
7. Bray, Libba. *Going Bovine*. 2009. 496p. Delacorte (9780385733977). Gr. 8–12.
8. Cashore, Kristin. *Graceling*. 2008. 480p. Harcourt (9780152063962). Gr. 9–12.
9. Chambers, Aidan. *Postcards from No Man's Land*. 2002. 320p. Dutton (9780525468639). Gr. 9–12.
10. Collins, Suzanne. *The Hunger Games*. 2008. 420p. Scholastic (9780439023481). Gr. 9–12.
11. Doctorow, Cory. *Little Brother*. 2008. 384p. Tor (9780765319852). Gr. 8–12.
12. Donnelly, Jennifer. *A Northern Light*. 2003. 396p. Harcourt (9780152167059). Gr. 7–12.
13. Farmer, Nancy. *The House of the Scorpion*. 2002. 400p. Simon & Schuster/Richard Jackson (9780689852220). Gr. 7–10.
14. Freymann-Weyr, Garret. *My Heartbeat*. 2002. 160p. Houghton (9780618141814). Gr. 8–12.
15. Gantos, Jack. *Hole in My Life*. 2002. 208p. Farrar (9780374399887). Gr. 8–12. 813.54.
16. Going, K. L. *Fat Kid Rules the World*. 2003. 177p. Putnam (9780803729483). Gr. 8–12.
17. Green, John. *The Fault in Our Stars*. 2012. 336p. Dutton (9780525478812). Gr. 9–12.
18. Green, John. *Looking for Alaska*. 2005. 240p. Dutton (9780525475064). Gr. 9–12.
19. Greenberg, Jan, ed. *Heart to Heart: New Poems Inspired by Twentieth-Century American Art*. 2001. 80p. illus. Abrams (9780810943865). Gr. 5–12. 811.

20. Hartnett, Sonya. *Surrender*. 2006. 256p. Candlewick (9780763627683). Gr. 9–12.
21. Heiligman, Deborah. *Charles and Emma: The Darwins' Leap of Faith*. 2009. 288p. illus. Holt (9780805087215). Gr. 8–12. 576.2.
22. Johnson, Angela. *The First Part Last*. 2003. 144p. Simon & Schuster (9780689849220). Gr. 6–12.
23. Lanagan, Margo. *Tender Morsels*. 2008. 448p. Knopf (9780375848117). Gr. 10–12.
24. Koertge, Ron. *Stoner and Spaz*. 2002. 176p. Candlewick (9780763616083). Gr. 8–12.
25. Levithan, David. *Boy Meets Boy*. 2003. 208p. Knopf (9780375824005). Gr. 9–12.
26. Lockhart, E. *The Disreputable History of Frankie Landau-Banks*. 2008. 352p. Hyperion (9780786838189). Gr. 7–12.
27. Na, An. *A Step from Heaven*. 2001. 156p. Front Street (9781886910584). Gr. 9–12.
28. Nelson, Marilyn. *A Wreath for Emmett Till*. Illus. by Philippe Lardy. 2005. 48p. Houghton (9780618397525). Gr. 9–12. 811.
29. Ness, Patrick. *A Monster Calls*. 2011. 224p. illus. Candlewick (9780763655594). Gr. 7–10.
30. Oppel, Kenneth. *Airborn*. 2004. 368p. HarperCollins/Eos (9780060531805). Gr. 6–9.
31. Partridge, Elizabeth. *John Lennon: All I Want Is the Truth*. 2005. 256p. illus. Viking (9780670059546). Gr. 9–12. 782.42166.
32. Pratchett, Terry. *Nation*. 2008. 336p. HarperCollins (9780061433016). Gr. 7–10.
33. Rapp, Adam. *Punkzilla*. 2009. 256p. Candlewick (9780763630317). Gr. 10–12.
34. Rosoff, Meg. *How I Live Now*. 2004. 160p. Random/Wendy Lamb (9780385746779). Gr. 8–11.
35. Rowling, J. K. *Harry Potter and the Deathly Hallows*. 2007. 756p. Scholastic/Arthur A. Levine (9780545010221). Gr. 4–12.
36. Satrapi, Marjane. *Persepolis: The Story of a Childhood*. Illus. by Marjane Satrapi. 2003. 160p. Pantheon (9780375422300). Gr. 9–12.
37. Schmidt, Gary D. *The Wednesday Wars*. 2007. 265p. Clarion (9780618724833). Gr. 6–9.
38. Sís, Peter. *The Wall: Growing Up behind the Iron Curtain*. Illus. by Peter Sís. 2007. 56p. Farrar/Frances Foster (9780374347017). Gr. 7–10. 943.7.
39. Stork, Francisco X. *Marcelo in the Real World*. 2009. 320p. Scholastic/Arthur A. Levine (9780545054744). Gr. 9–12.
40. Stroud, Jonathan. *The Amulet of Samarkand*. 2003. 464p. Hyperion/Miramax (9780786818594). Gr. 6–12.
41. Tan, Shaun. *The Arrival*. Illus. by Shaun Tan. 2007. 128p. Scholastic/Arthur A. Levine (9780439895293). Gr. 6–12.
42. Taylor, Mildred D. *The Land*. 2001. 392p. Penguin/Phyllis Fogelman (9780803719507). Gr. 7–12.
43. Teller, Janne. *Nothing*. Tr. by Martin Aitken. 2010. 240p. Atheneum (9781416985792). Gr. 7–12.

44. Thompson, Craig. *Blankets*. Illus. by Craig Thomson. 2003. 592p. Top Shelf (9781891830433). Gr. 10–12.
45. Turner, Megan Whalen. *The King of Attolia*. 2006. 400p. Greenwillow (9780060835774). Gr. 8–11.
46. Wein, Elizabeth. *Code Name Verity*. 2012. 352p. Hyperion (9781423152194). Gr. 9–12.
47. Wolff, Virginia Euwer. *True Believer*. 2001. 272p. Atheneum (9780689828270). Gr. 7–12.
48. Yancey, Rick. *The Monstrumologist*. 2009. 448p. Simon & Schuster (9781416984481). Gr. 9–12.
49. Yang, Gene Luen. *American Born Chinese*. Illus. by Gene Luen Yang. 2006. 240p. First Second (9781596431522). Gr. 10–12.
50. Zusak, Markus. *The Book Thief*. 2006. 512p. Knopf (9780375831003). Gr. 10–12.

Index

A

H

Y

Z